# DOCTOR STRANGE

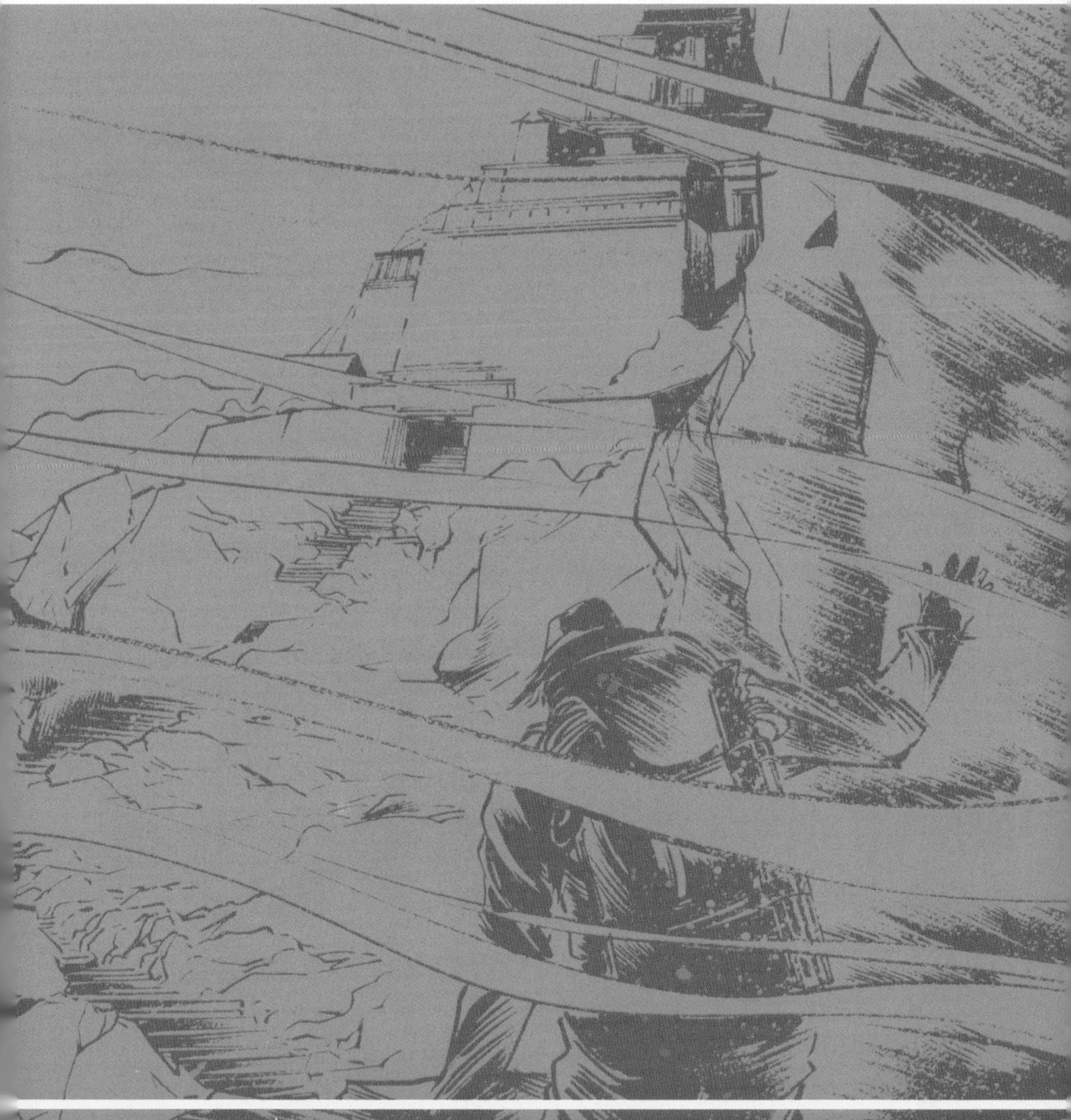

COLLECTION EDITOR: **JENNIFER GRÜNWALD**
ASSISTANT EDITORS: **ALEX STARBUCK & NELSON RIBEIRO**
EDITOR, SPECIAL PROJECTS: **MARK D. BEAZLEY**
SENIOR EDITOR, SPECIAL PROJECTS: **JEFF YOUNGQUIST**
SENIOR VICE PRESIDENT OF SALES: **DAVID GABRIEL**
SVP OF BRAND PLANNING & COMMUNICATIONS: **MICHAEL PASCIULLO**
COVER & BOOK DESIGN: **JEFF POWELL**

EDITOR IN CHIEF: **AXEL ALONSO**
CHIEF CREATIVE OFFICER: **JOE QUESADA**
PUBLISHER: **DAN BUCKLEY**
EXECUTIVE PRODUCER: **ALAN FINE**

**DR. STRANGE: SEASON ONE.** Contains material originally published in magazine form as DEFENDERS #1. First printing 2012. ISBN# 978-0-7851-6387-9. Published by MARVEL WORLDWIDE, INC., a subsidiary of MARV ENTERTAINMENT, LLC. OFFICE OF PUBLICATION: 135 West 50th Street, New York, NY 10020.  $24.99 per copy in the U.S. and $27.99 in Canada (G #R127032852); Canadian Agreement #40008537.  Printed in the U.S ALAN FINE, EVP - Office of the President, Marvel Worldwide, Inc. and EVP & CMO Marvel Characters B.V.; DAN BUCKLEY, Publisher & President - Print, Animation & Digital Divisions; JOE QUESADA, Chief Creative Officer, T BREVOORT, SVP of Publishing; DAVID BOGART, SVP of Operations & Procurement, Publishing; RUWAN JAYATILLEKE, SVP & Associate Publisher, Publishing; C.B. CEBULSKI, SVP of Creator & Content Development; DA GABRIEL, SVP of Publishing Sales & Circulation; MICHAEL PASCIULLO, SVP of Brand Planning & Communications; JIM O'KEEFE, VP of Operations & Logistics; DAN CARR, Executive Director of Publishing Technology; SUS CRESPI, Editorial Operations Manager; ALEX MORALES, Publishing Operations Manager; STAN LEE, Chairman Emeritus. For information regarding advertising in Marvel Comics or on Marvel.com, please contact Niza Di Director of Marvel Partnerships, at ndisla@marvel.com. For Marvel subscription inquiries, please call 800-217-9158. **Manufactured between 7/16/2012 and 8/27/2012 by R.R. DONNELLEY, INC., SALEM, VA, U**

10 9 8 7 6 5 4 3 2 1

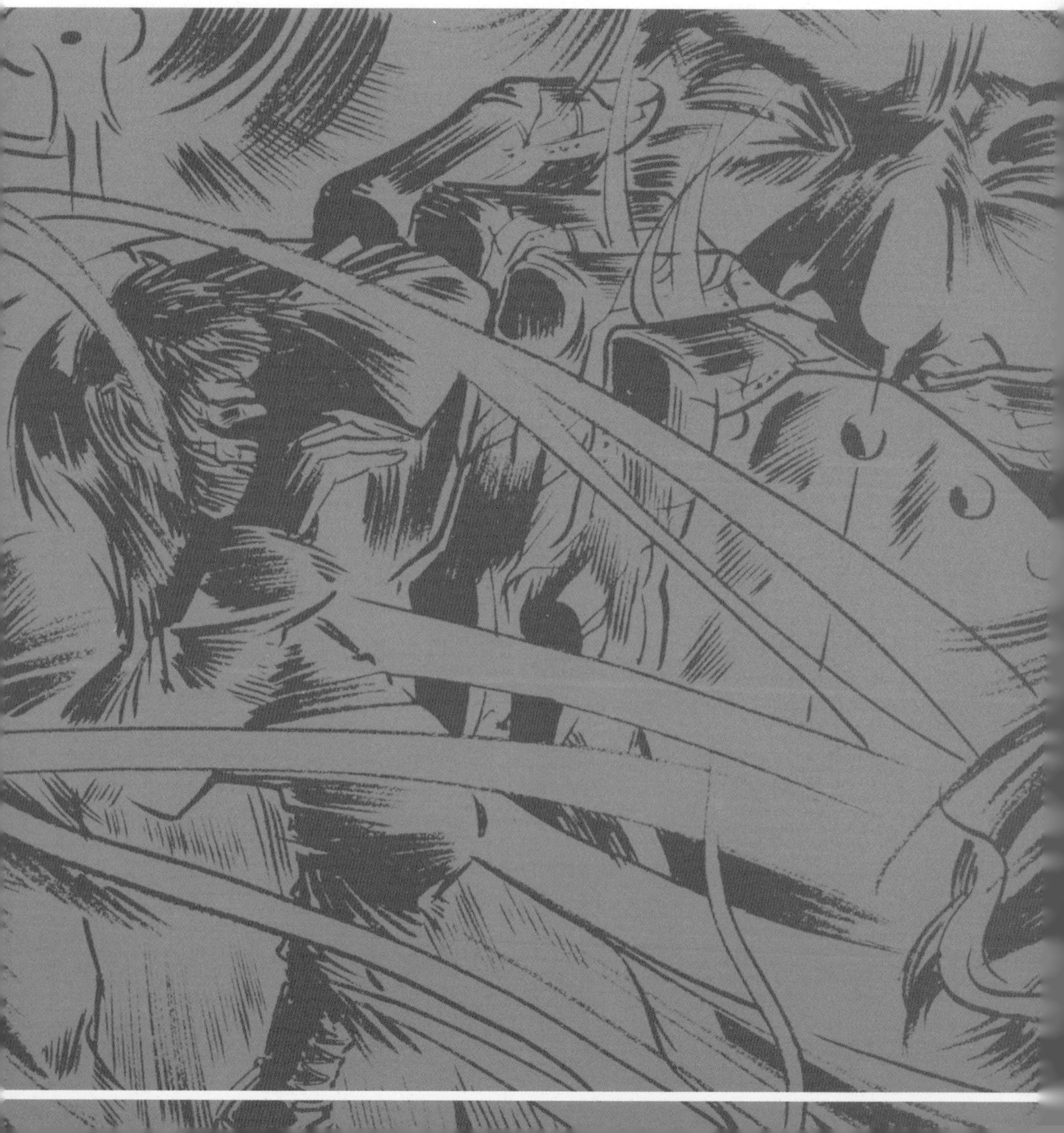

# DOCTOR STRANGE

WRITER
**GREG PAK**

ARTIST
**EMMA RIOS**

ADDITIONAL INKS
**ALVARO LOPEZ**

COLOR ARTIST
**JORDIE BELLAIRE**

LETTERER
**VC'S CLAYTON COWLES**

COVER ARTIST
**JULIAN TOTINO TEDESCO**

EDITOR
**ELLIE PYLE**

CONSULTING EDITORS
**ALEJANDRO ARBONA
& JOHN DENNING**

EXECUTIVE EDITOR
**TOM BREVOORT**

## SEASON ONE

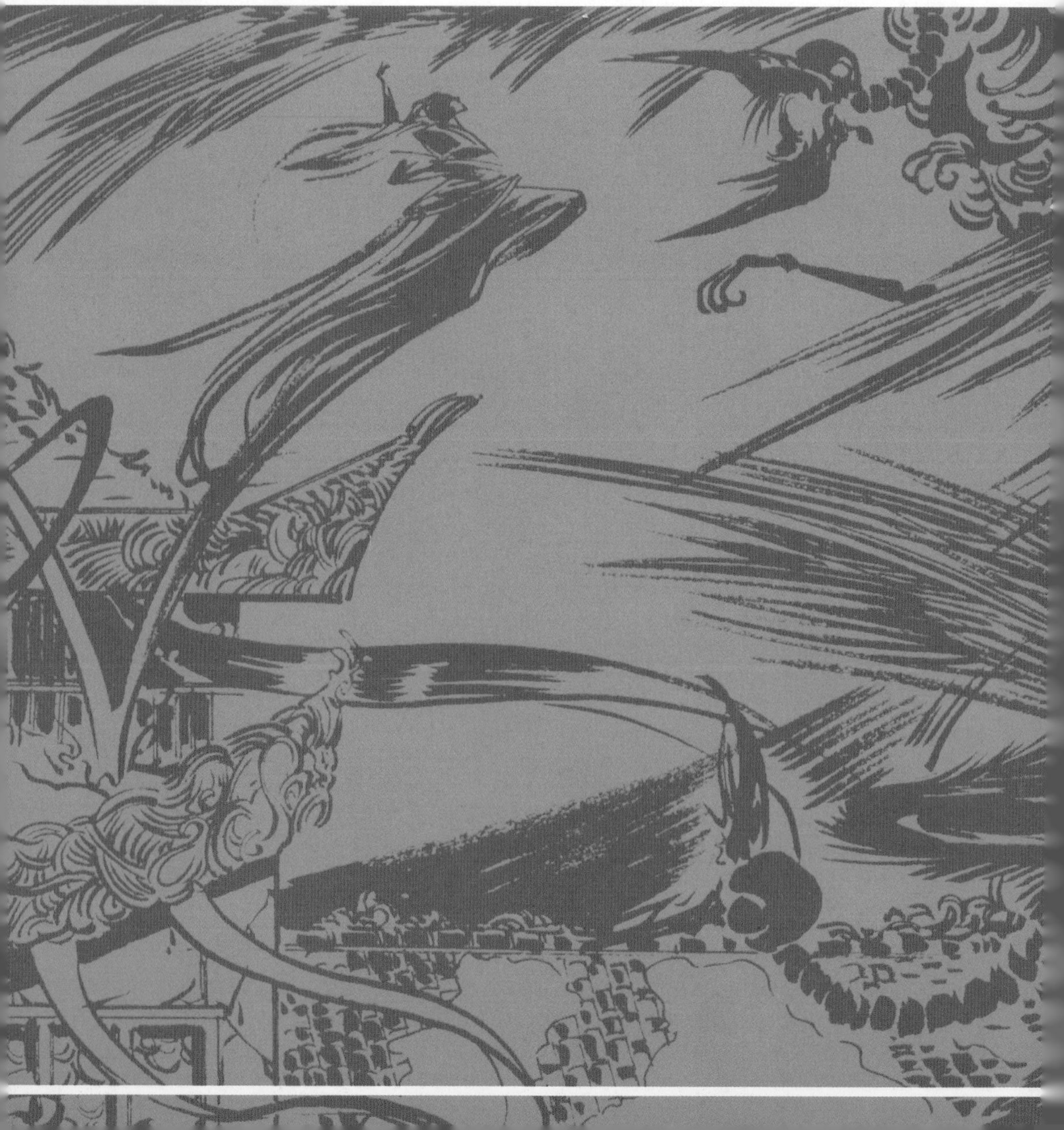

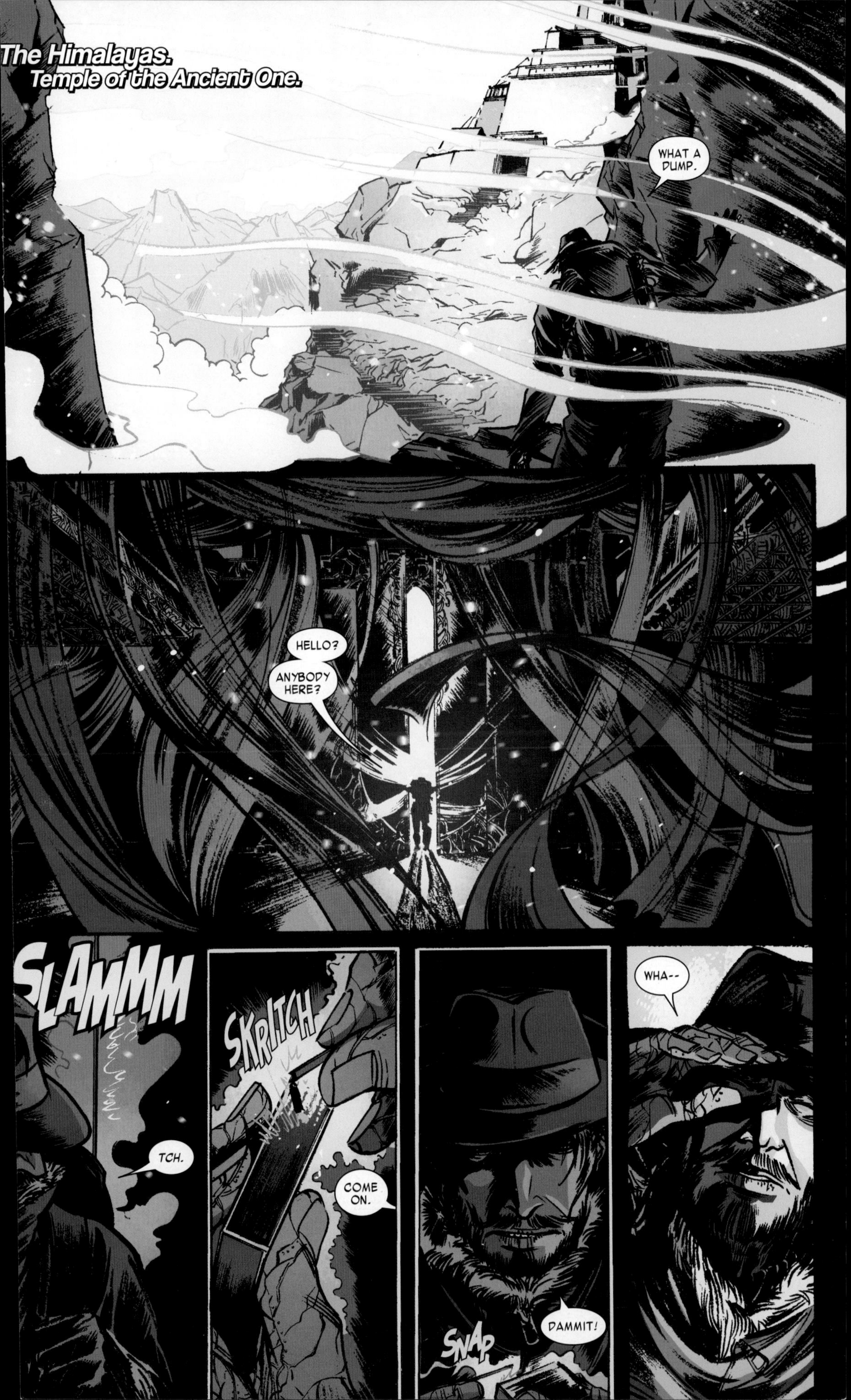
The Himalayas.
Temple of the Ancient One.
WHAT A DUMP.
HELLO?
ANYBODY HERE?
SLAMMMM
TCH.
SKRITCH
COME ON.
SNAP
DAMMIT!
WHA--

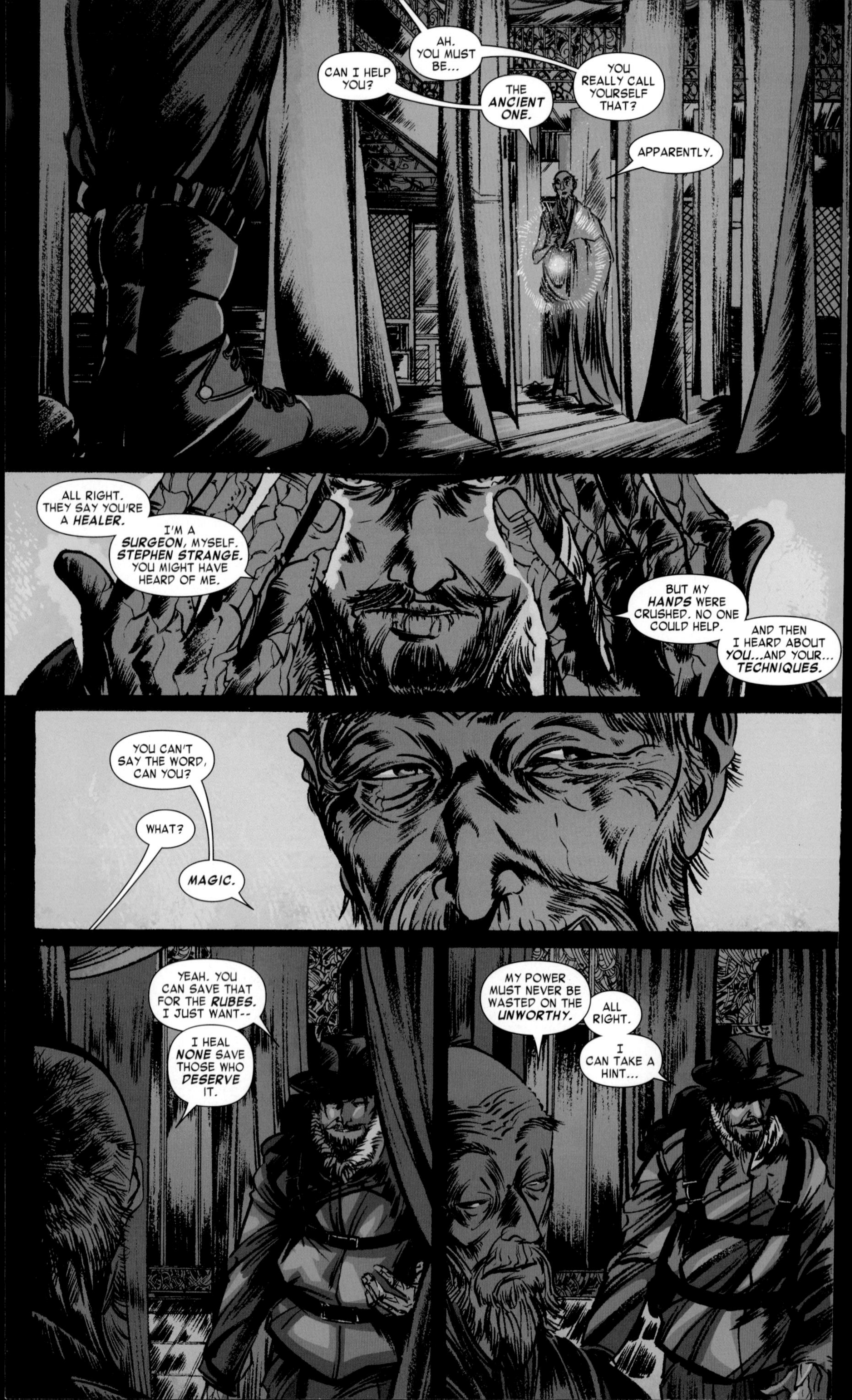

CAN I HELP YOU?
AH. YOU MUST BE...
THE ANCIENT ONE.
YOU REALLY CALL YOURSELF THAT?
APPARENTLY.
ALL RIGHT. THEY SAY YOU'RE A HEALER.
I'M A SURGEON, MYSELF. STEPHEN STRANGE. YOU MIGHT HAVE HEARD OF ME.
BUT MY HANDS WERE CRUSHED. NO ONE COULD HELP.
AND THEN I HEARD ABOUT YOU...AND YOUR... TECHNIQUES.
YOU CAN'T SAY THE WORD, CAN YOU?
WHAT?
MAGIC.
YEAH. YOU CAN SAVE THAT FOR THE RUBES. I JUST WANT--
I HEAL NONE SAVE THOSE WHO DESERVE IT.
MY POWER MUST NEVER BE WASTED ON THE UNWORTHY.
ALL RIGHT.
I CAN TAKE A HINT...

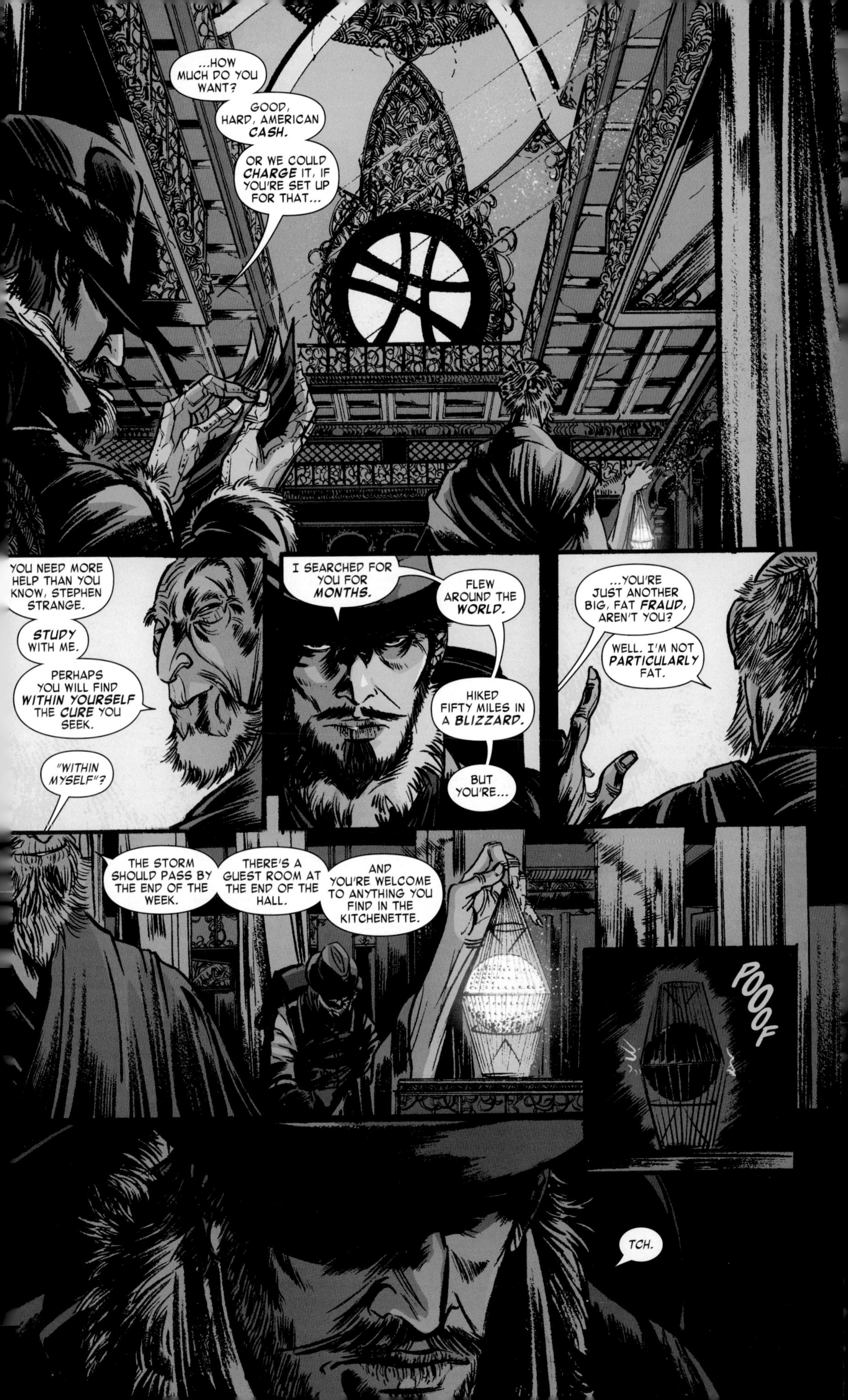
...HOW MUCH DO YOU WANT?
GOOD, HARD, AMERICAN CASH.
OR WE COULD CHARGE IT, IF YOU'RE SET UP FOR THAT...
YOU NEED MORE HELP THAN YOU KNOW, STEPHEN STRANGE.
STUDY WITH ME.
PERHAPS YOU WILL FIND WITHIN YOURSELF THE CURE YOU SEEK.
"WITHIN MYSELF"?
I SEARCHED FOR YOU FOR MONTHS.
FLEW AROUND THE WORLD.
HIKED FIFTY MILES IN A BLIZZARD.
BUT YOU'RE...
...YOU'RE JUST ANOTHER BIG, FAT FRAUD, AREN'T YOU?
WELL. I'M NOT PARTICULARLY FAT.
THE STORM SHOULD PASS BY THE END OF THE WEEK.
THERE'S A GUEST ROOM AT THE END OF THE HALL.
AND YOU'RE WELCOME TO ANYTHING YOU FIND IN THE KITCHENETTE.
POOOF
TCH.

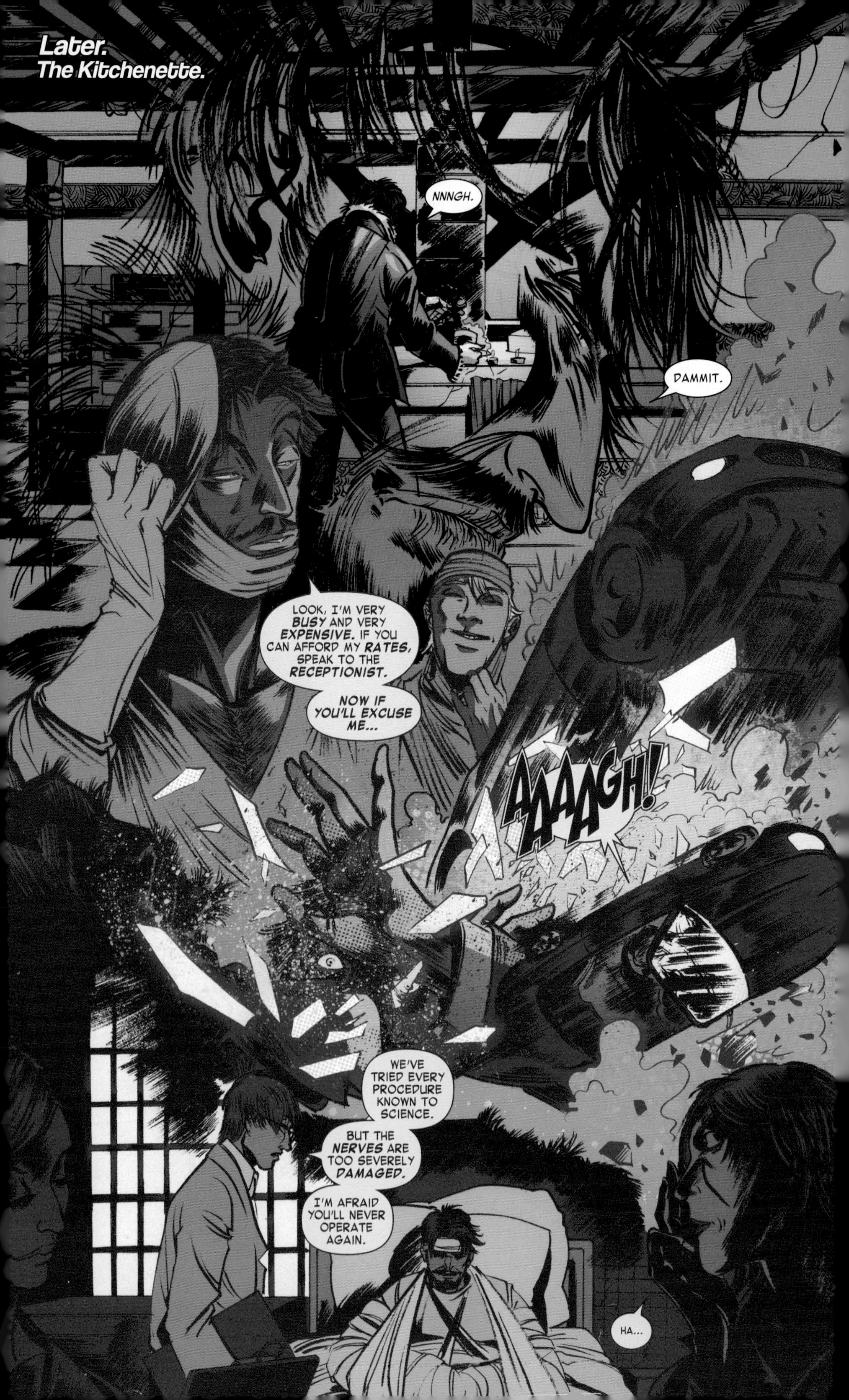
Later.
The Kitchenette.
NNNGH.
DAMMIT.
LOOK, I'M VERY BUSY AND VERY EXPENSIVE. IF YOU CAN AFFORD MY RATES, SPEAK TO THE RECEPTIONIST.
NOW IF YOU'LL EXCUSE ME...
AAAAGH!
WE'VE TRIED EVERY PROCEDURE KNOWN TO SCIENCE.
BUT THE NERVES ARE TOO SEVERELY DAMAGED.
I'M AFRAID YOU'LL NEVER OPERATE AGAIN.
HA...

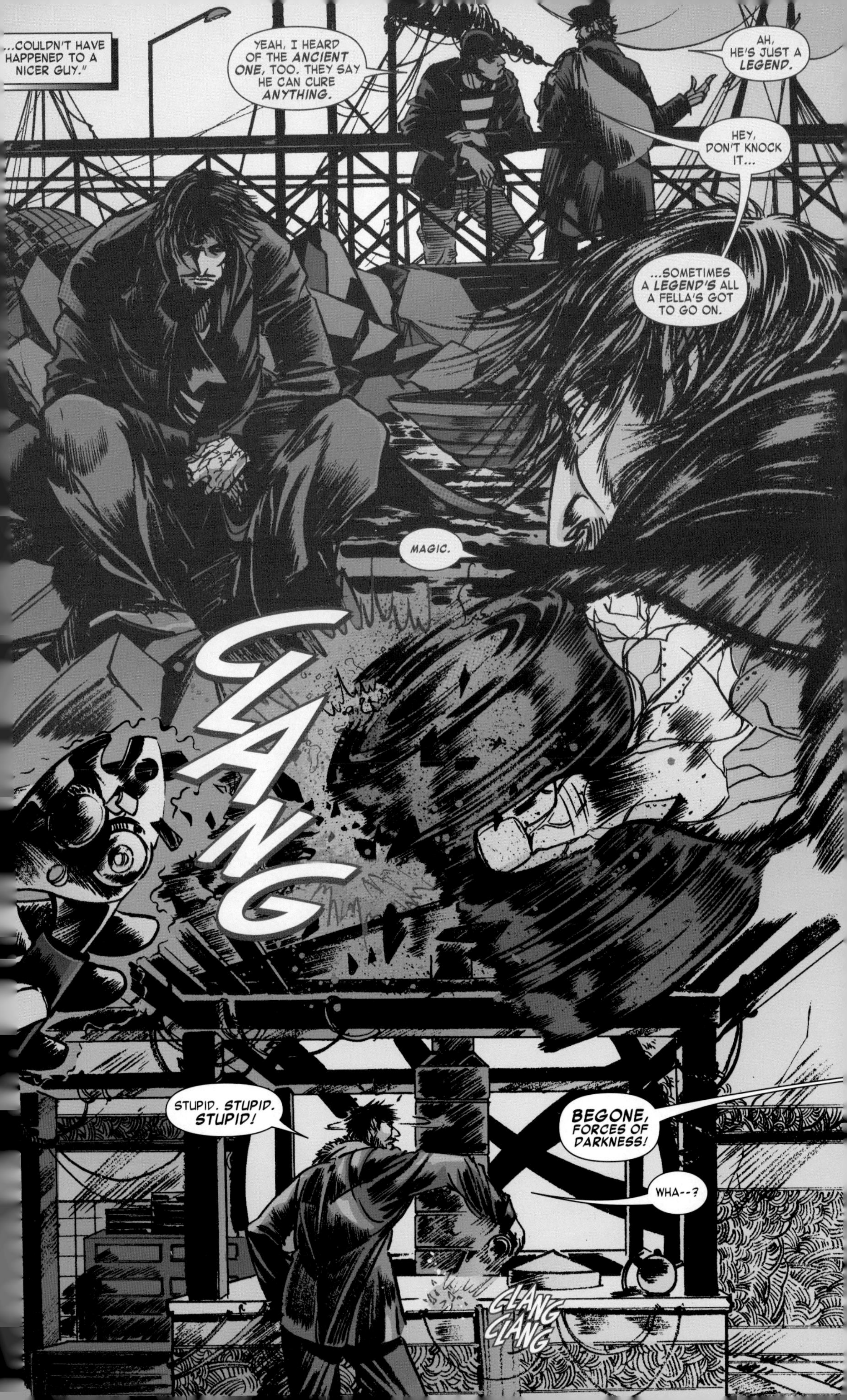
...COULDN'T HAVE HAPPENED TO A NICER GUY."
YEAH, I HEARD OF THE ANCIENT ONE, TOO. THEY SAY HE CAN CURE ANYTHING.
AH, HE'S JUST A LEGEND.
HEY, DON'T KNOCK IT...
...SOMETIMES A LEGEND'S ALL A FELLA'S GOT TO GO ON.
MAGIC.
CLANG
STUPID. STUPID. STUPID!
BEGONE, FORCES OF DARKNESS!
WHA--?
CLANG CLANG

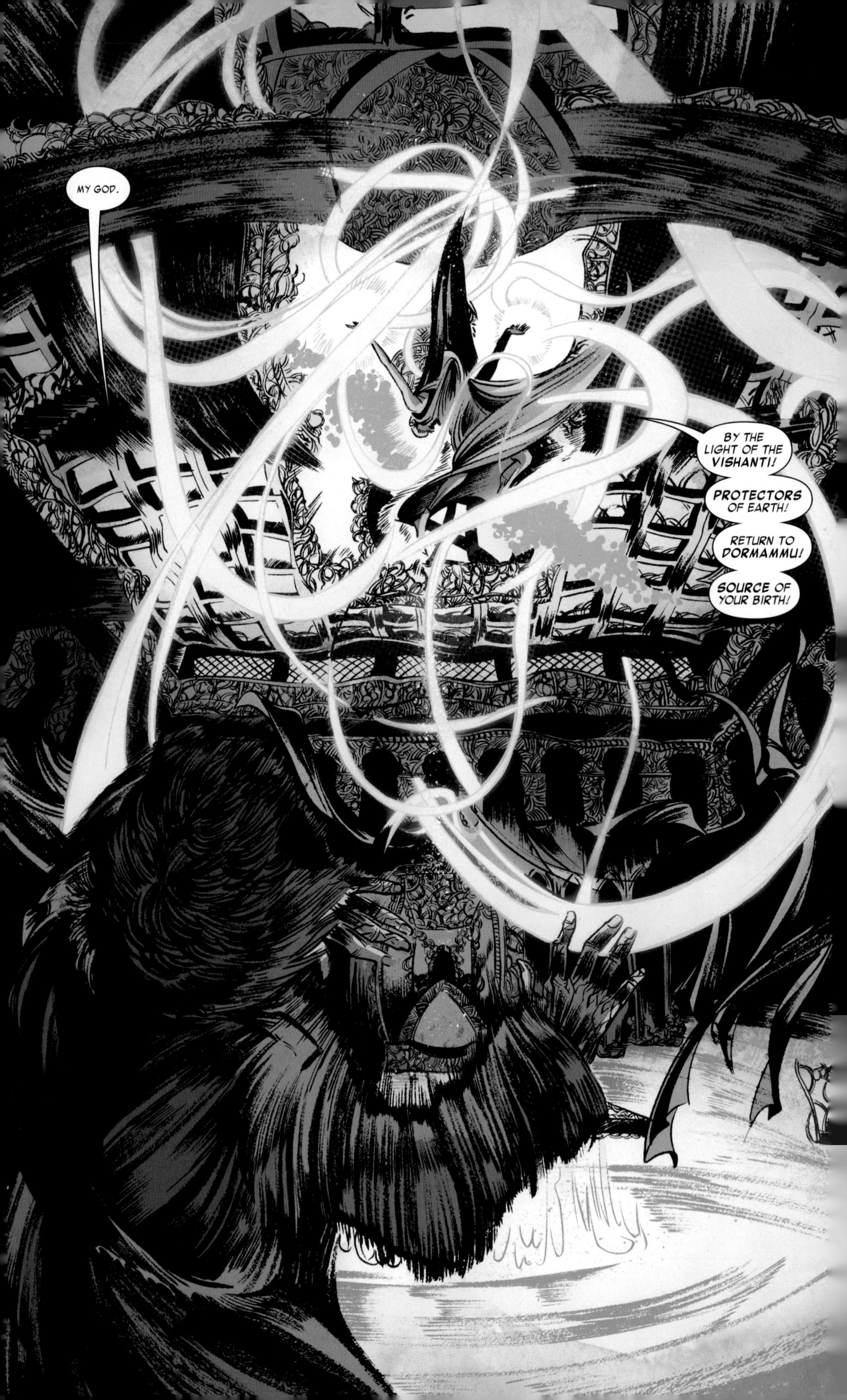
MY GOD.
BY THE LIGHT OF THE VISHANTI!
PROTECTORS OF EARTH!
RETURN TO DORMAMMU!
SOURCE OF YOUR BIRTH!

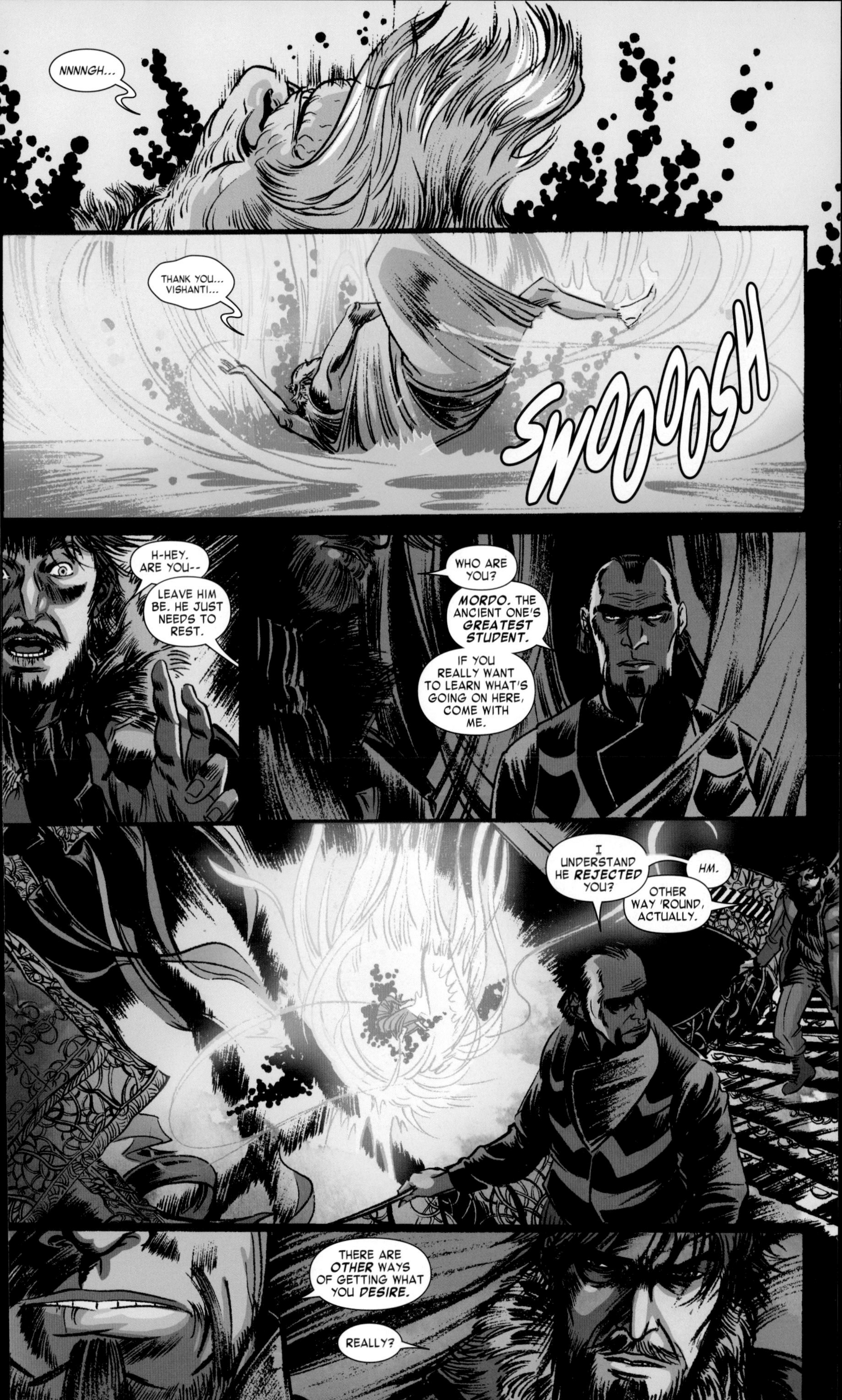
NNNNGH...
THANK YOU... VISHANTI...
SWOOOOSH
H-HEY. ARE YOU--
LEAVE HIM BE. HE JUST NEEDS TO REST.
WHO ARE YOU?
MORDO. THE ANCIENT ONE'S GREATEST STUDENT.
IF YOU REALLY WANT TO LEARN WHAT'S GOING ON HERE, COME WITH ME.
I UNDERSTAND HE REJECTED YOU?
HM.
OTHER WAY 'ROUND, ACTUALLY.
THERE ARE OTHER WAYS OF GETTING WHAT YOU DESIRE.
REALLY?

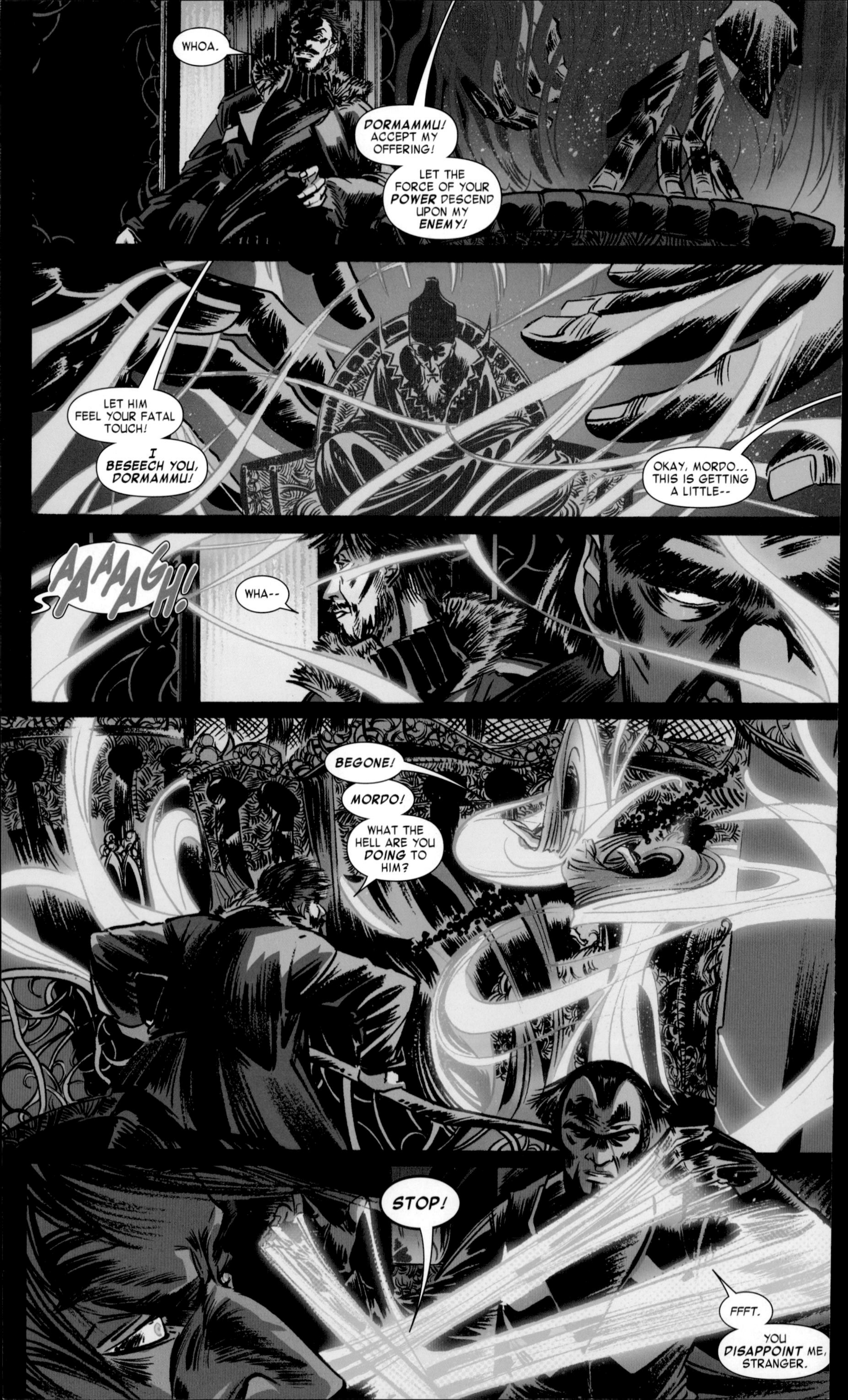
WHOA.
DORMAMMU! ACCEPT MY OFFERING!
LET THE FORCE OF YOUR POWER DESCEND UPON MY ENEMY!
LET HIM FEEL YOUR FATAL TOUCH!
I BESEECH YOU, DORMAMMU!
OKAY, MORDO... THIS IS GETTING A LITTLE--
AAAAAGH!
WHA--
BEGONE!
MORDO!
WHAT THE HELL ARE YOU DOING TO HIM?
STOP!
FFFT.
YOU DISAPPOINT ME, STRANGER.

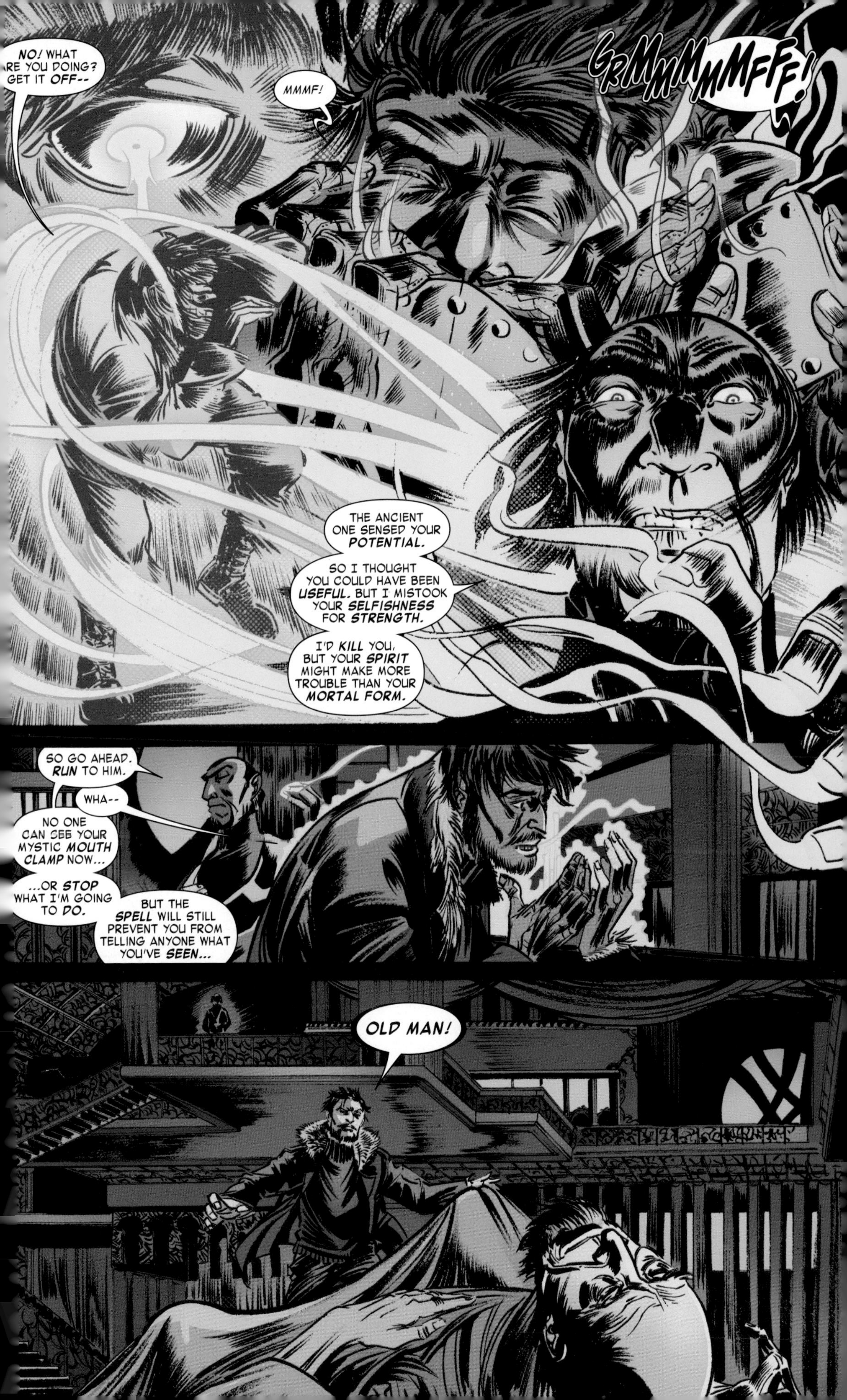
NO! WHAT ARE YOU DOING? GET IT OFF--
MMMF!
GRMMMMMMFFF!
THE ANCIENT ONE SENSED YOUR POTENTIAL.
SO I THOUGHT YOU COULD HAVE BEEN USEFUL. BUT I MISTOOK YOUR SELFISHNESS FOR STRENGTH.
I'D KILL YOU, BUT YOUR SPIRIT MIGHT MAKE MORE TROUBLE THAN YOUR MORTAL FORM.
SO GO AHEAD. RUN TO HIM.
WHA--
NO ONE CAN SEE YOUR MYSTIC MOUTH CLAMP NOW...
...OR STOP WHAT I'M GOING TO DO.
BUT THE SPELL WILL STILL PREVENT YOU FROM TELLING ANYONE WHAT YOU'VE SEEN...
OLD MAN!

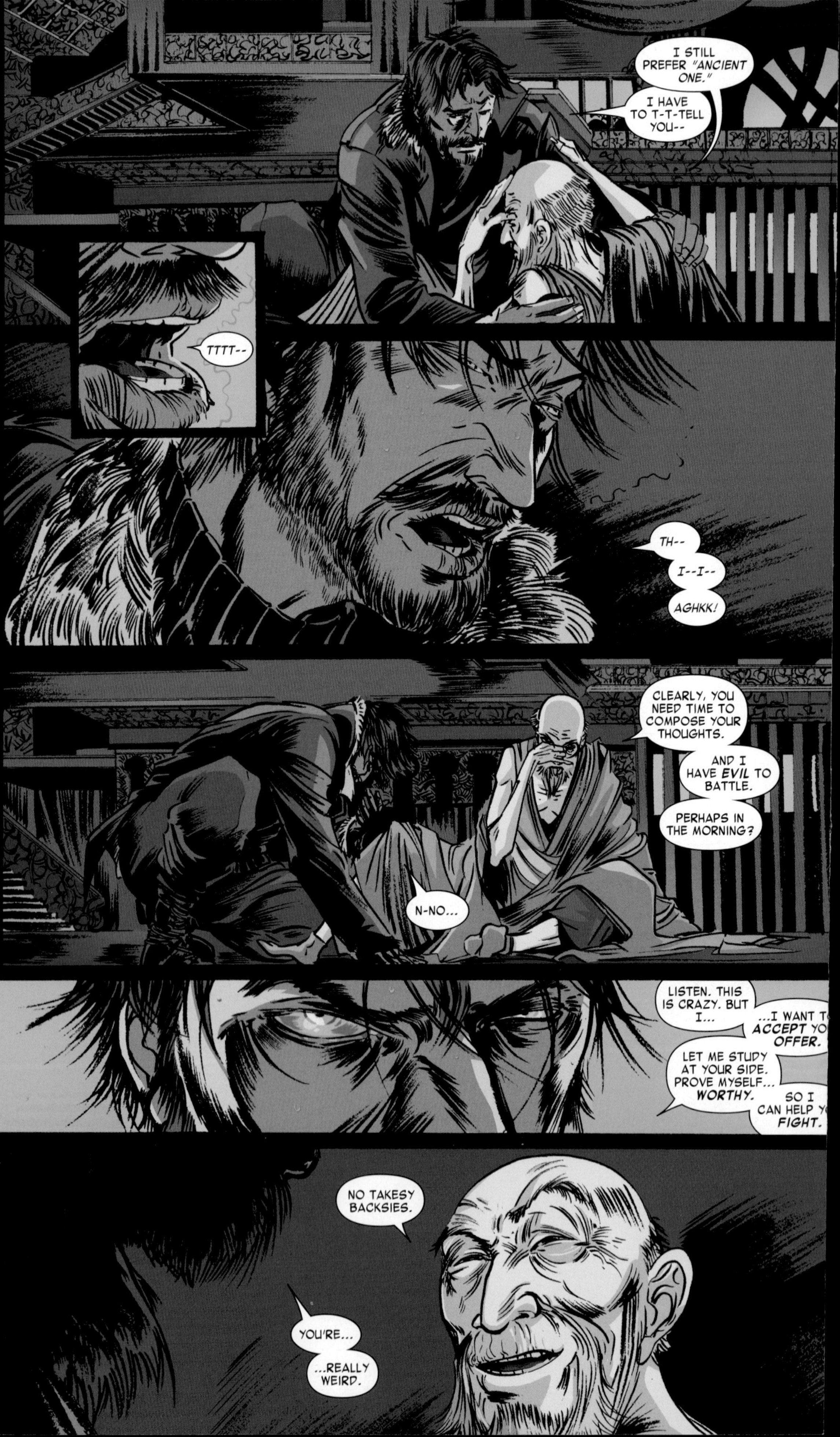

I STILL PREFER "ANCIENT ONE."
I HAVE TO T-T-TELL YOU--
TTTT--
TH--
I--I--
AGHKK!
CLEARLY, YOU NEED TIME TO COMPOSE YOUR THOUGHTS.
AND I HAVE EVIL TO BATTLE.
PERHAPS IN THE MORNING?
N-NO...
LISTEN. THIS IS CRAZY. BUT I...
...I WANT T
ACCEPT YO
OFFER.
LET ME STUDY AT YOUR SIDE. PROVE MYSELF... WORTHY.
SO I CAN HELP Y
FIGHT.
NO TAKESY BACKSIES.
YOU'RE...
...REALLY WEIRD.

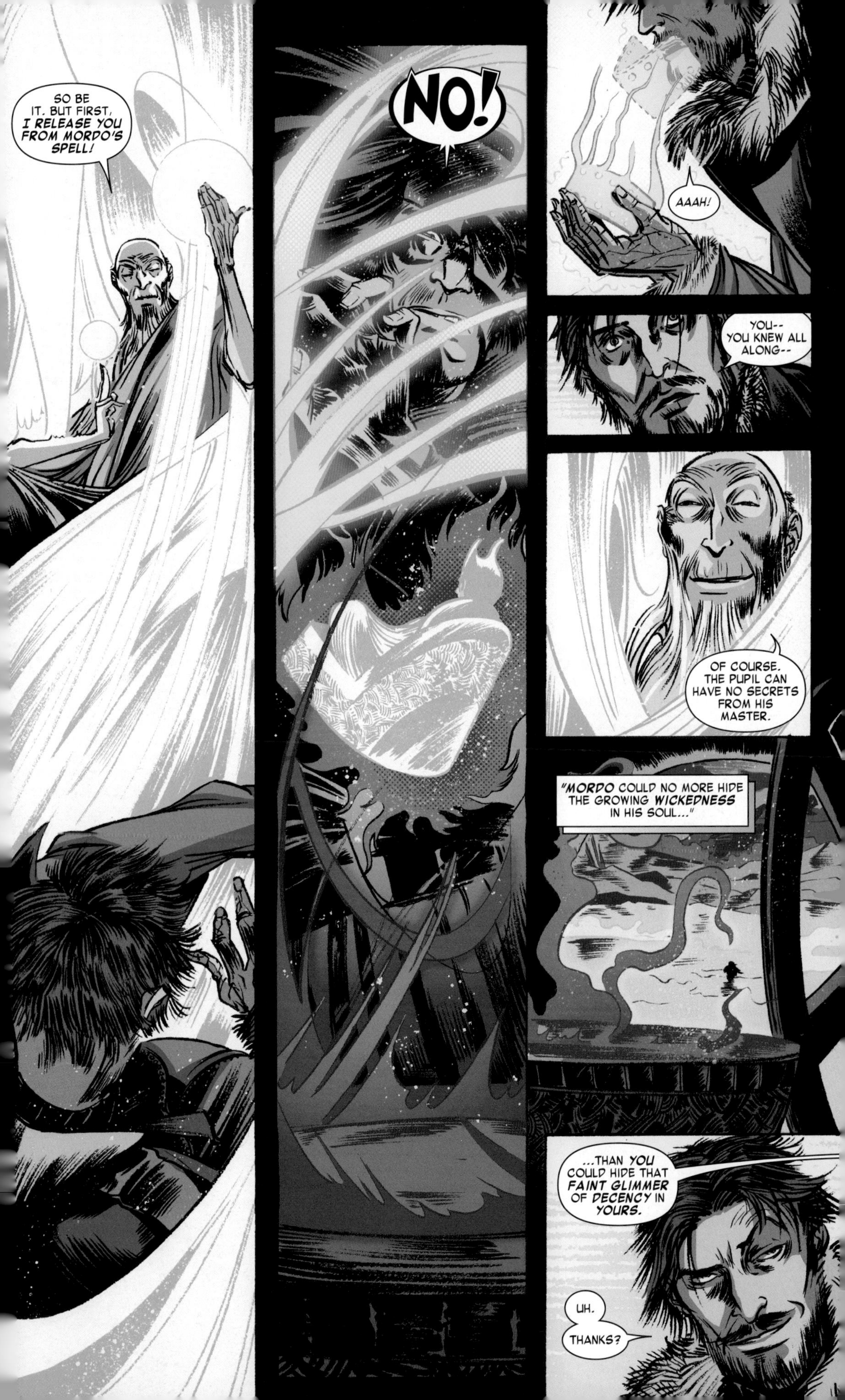
SO BE IT. BUT FIRST, I RELEASE YOU FROM MORDO'S SPELL!
NO!
AAAH!
YOU-- YOU KNEW ALL ALONG--
OF COURSE. THE PUPIL CAN HAVE NO SECRETS FROM HIS MASTER.
"MORDO COULD NO MORE HIDE THE GROWING WICKEDNESS IN HIS SOUL..."
...THAN YOU COULD HIDE THAT FAINT GLIMMER OF DECENCY IN YOURS.
UH.
THANKS?

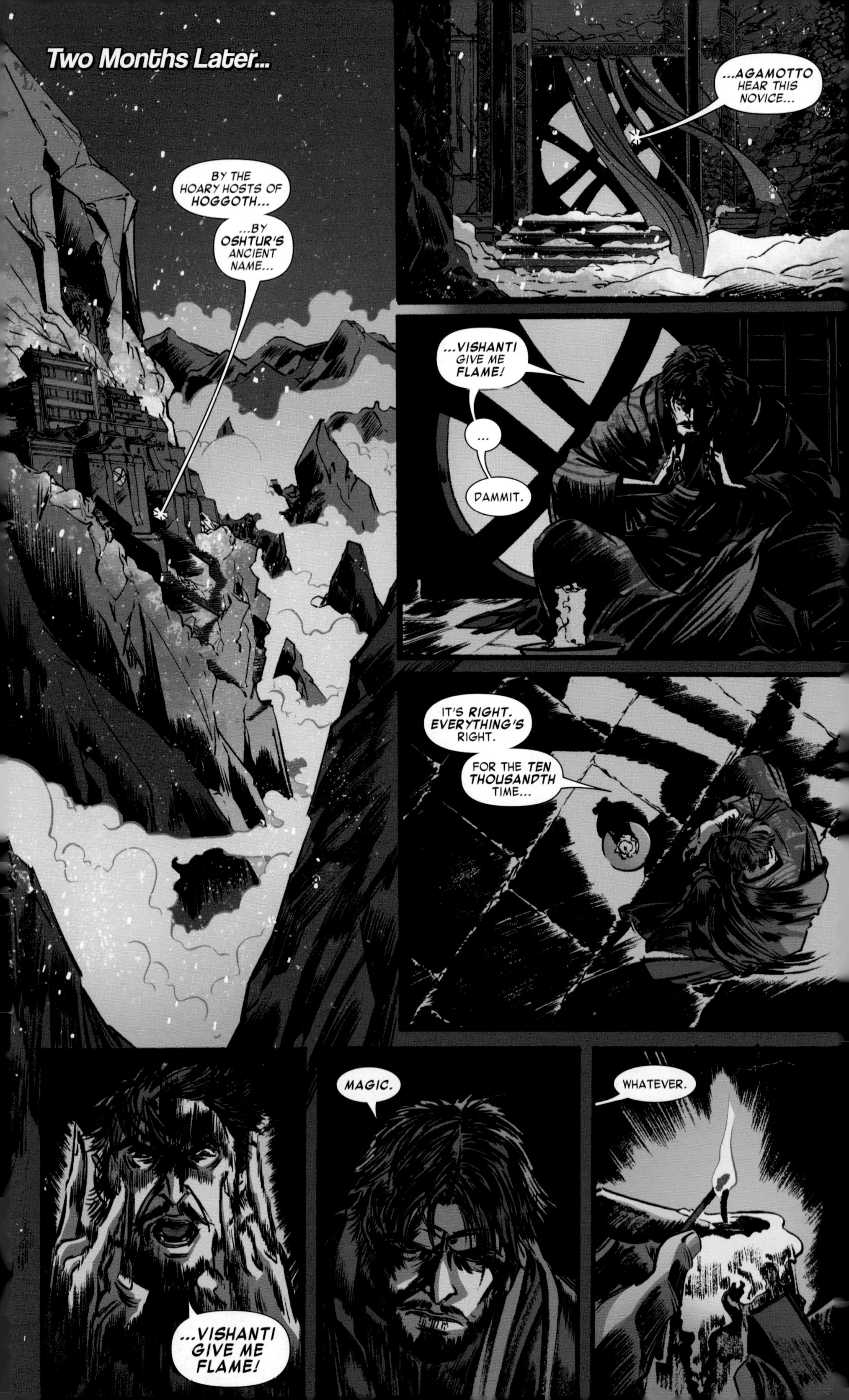
Two Months Later...
BY THE HOARY HOSTS OF HOGGOTH...
...BY OSHTUR'S ANCIENT NAME...
...AGAMOTTO HEAR THIS NOVICE...
...VISHANTI GIVE ME FLAME!
...
DAMMIT.
IT'S RIGHT. EVERYTHING'S RIGHT.
FOR THE TEN THOUSANDTH TIME...
...VISHANTI GIVE ME FLAME!
MAGIC.
WHATEVER.

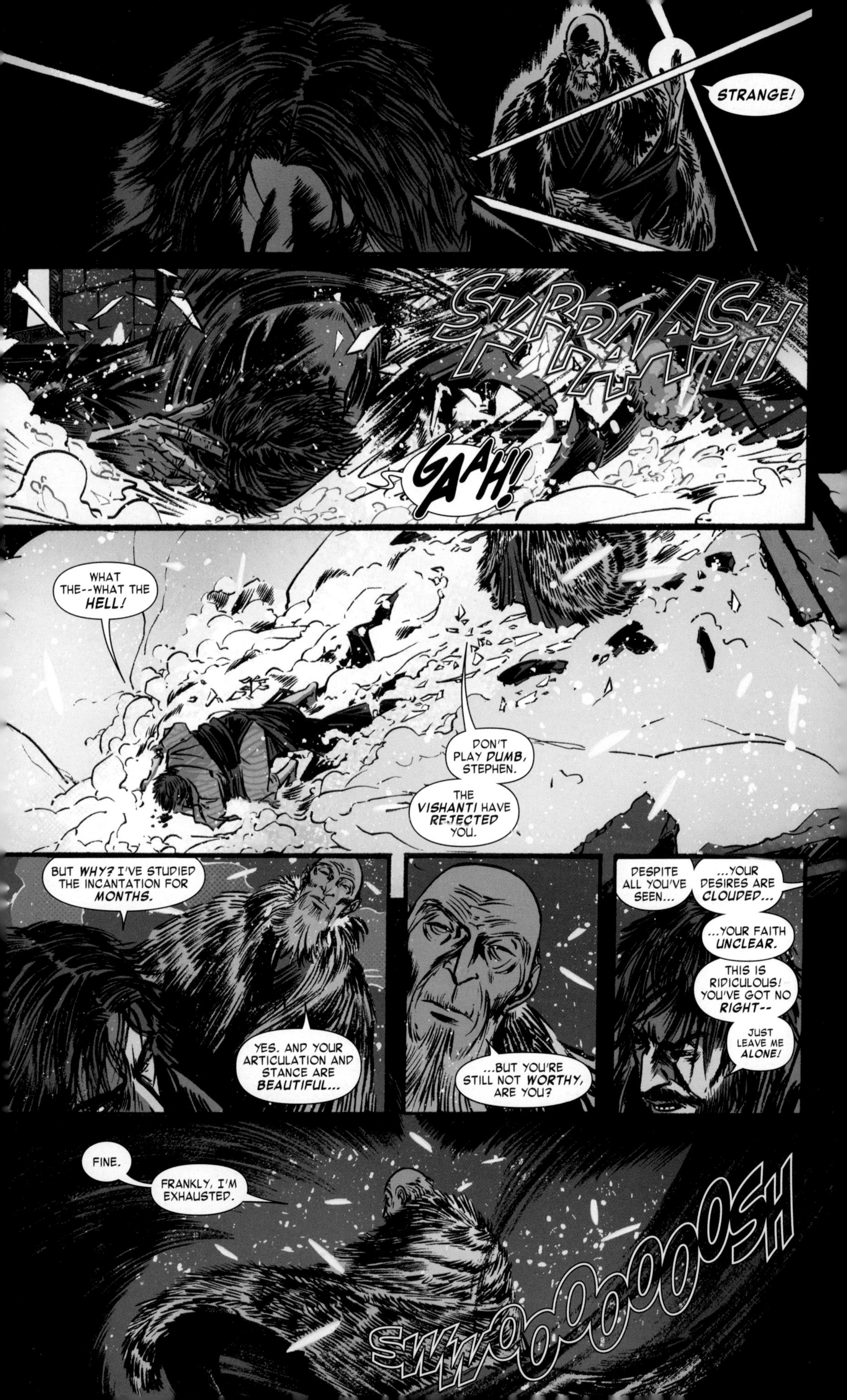
STRANGE!
GAAH!
WHAT THE--WHAT THE HELL!
DON'T PLAY DUMB, STEPHEN.
THE VISHANTI HAVE REJECTED YOU.
BUT WHY? I'VE STUDIED THE INCANTATION FOR MONTHS.
YES. AND YOUR ARTICULATION AND STANCE ARE BEAUTIFUL...
...BUT YOU'RE STILL NOT WORTHY, ARE YOU?
DESPITE ALL YOU'VE SEEN...
...YOUR DESIRES ARE CLOUDED...
...YOUR FAITH UNCLEAR.
THIS IS RIDICULOUS! YOU'VE GOT NO RIGHT--
JUST LEAVE ME ALONE!
FINE.
FRANKLY, I'M EXHAUSTED.
SWOOOOOOOOSH

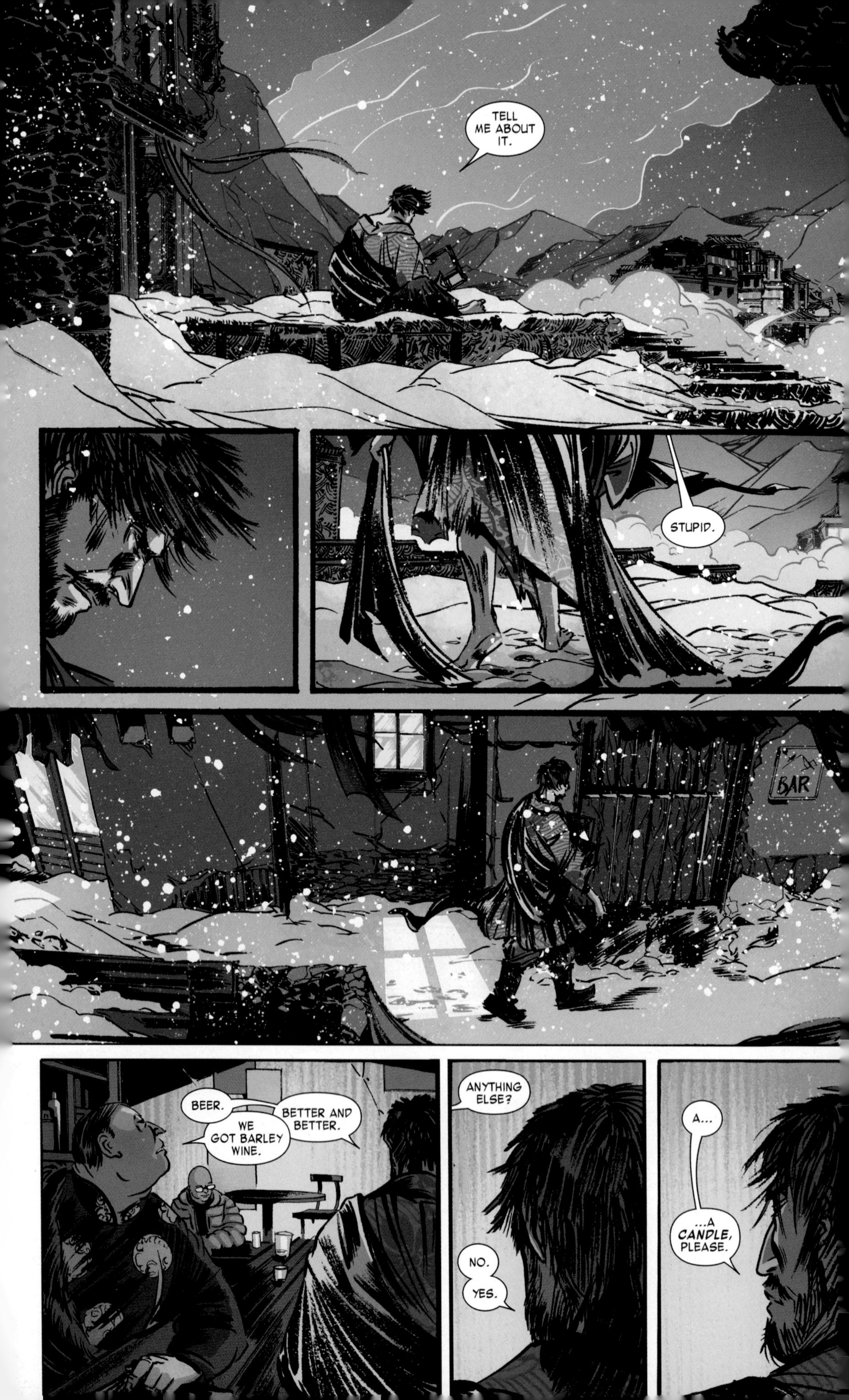
TELL ME ABOUT IT.
STUPID.
BAR
BEER.
WE GOT BARLEY WINE.
BETTER AND BETTER.
ANYTHING ELSE?
NO.
YES.
A...
...A CANDLE, PLEASE.

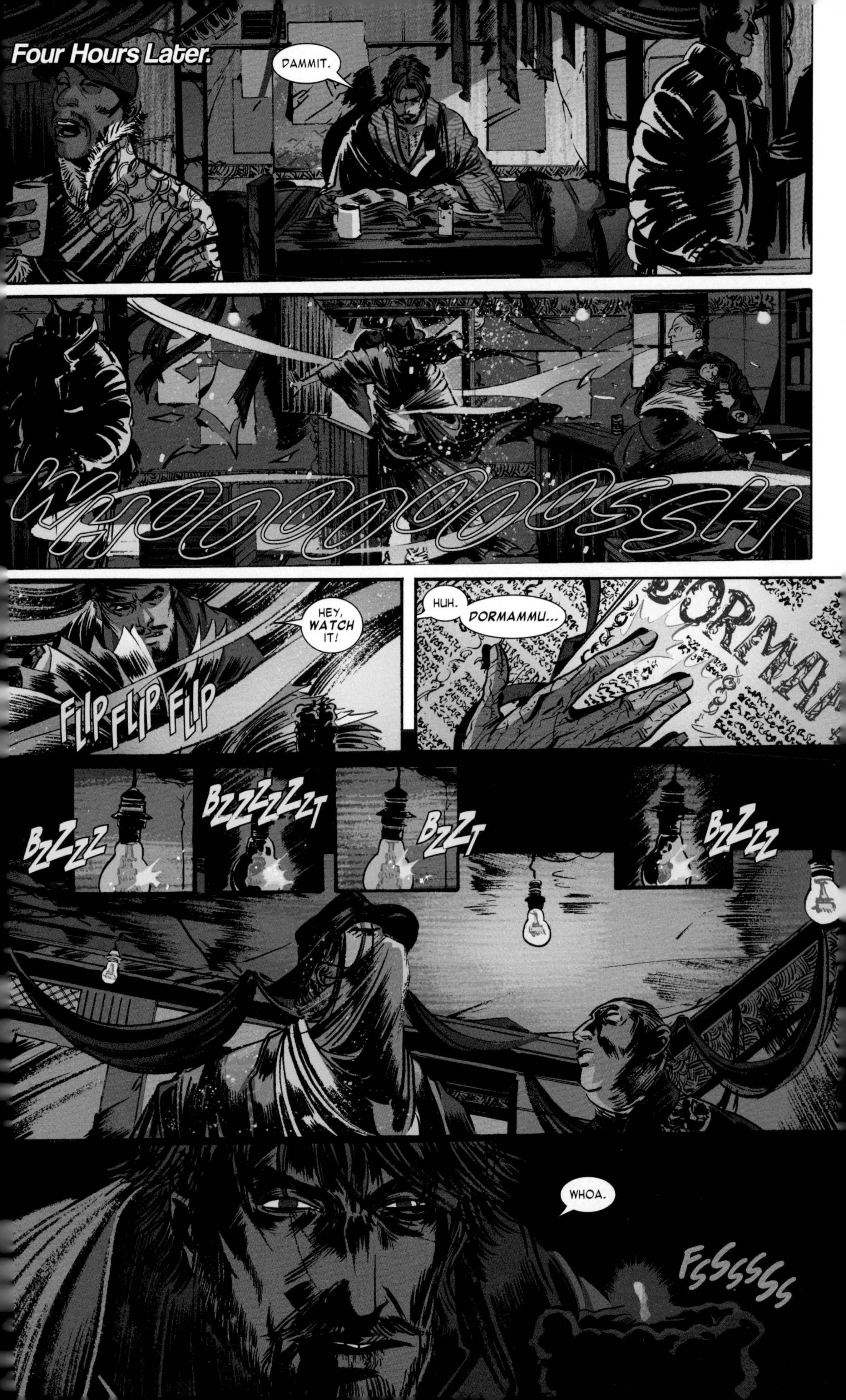

Four Hours Later.
DAMMIT.
WHOOOOOOOOOSSH
HEY, WATCH IT!
FLIP FLIP FLIP
HUH.
DORMAMMU...
BZZZZ
BZZZZZZZT
BZZT
BZZZZ
WHOA.
FSSSSSS

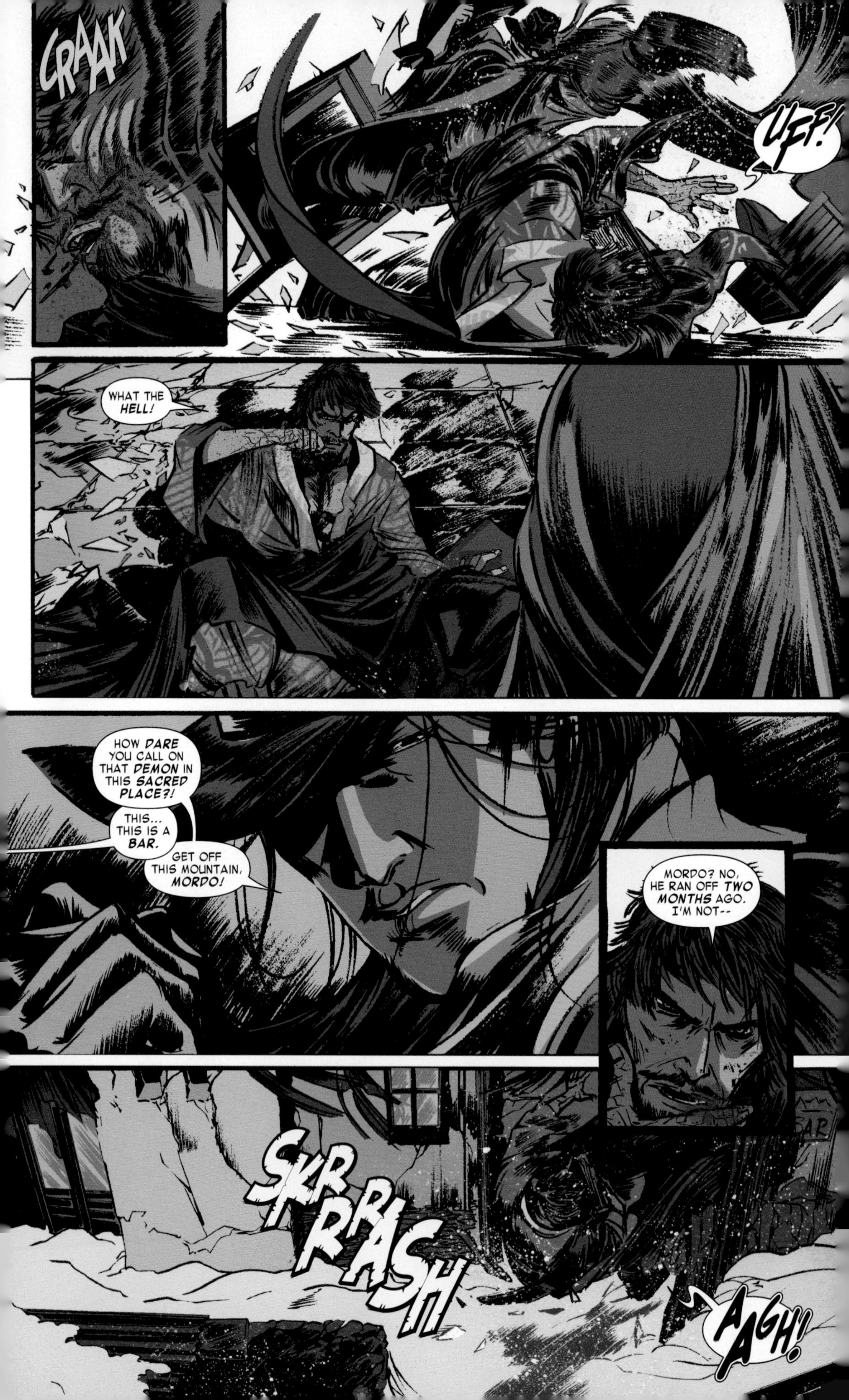
CRAAK
UFF!
WHAT THE HELL!
HOW DARE YOU CALL ON THAT DEMON IN THIS SACRED PLACE?!
THIS... THIS IS A BAR.
GET OFF THIS MOUNTAIN, MORDO!
MORDO? NO, HE RAN OFF TWO MONTHS AGO. I'M NOT--
SKRRASH
AAGH!

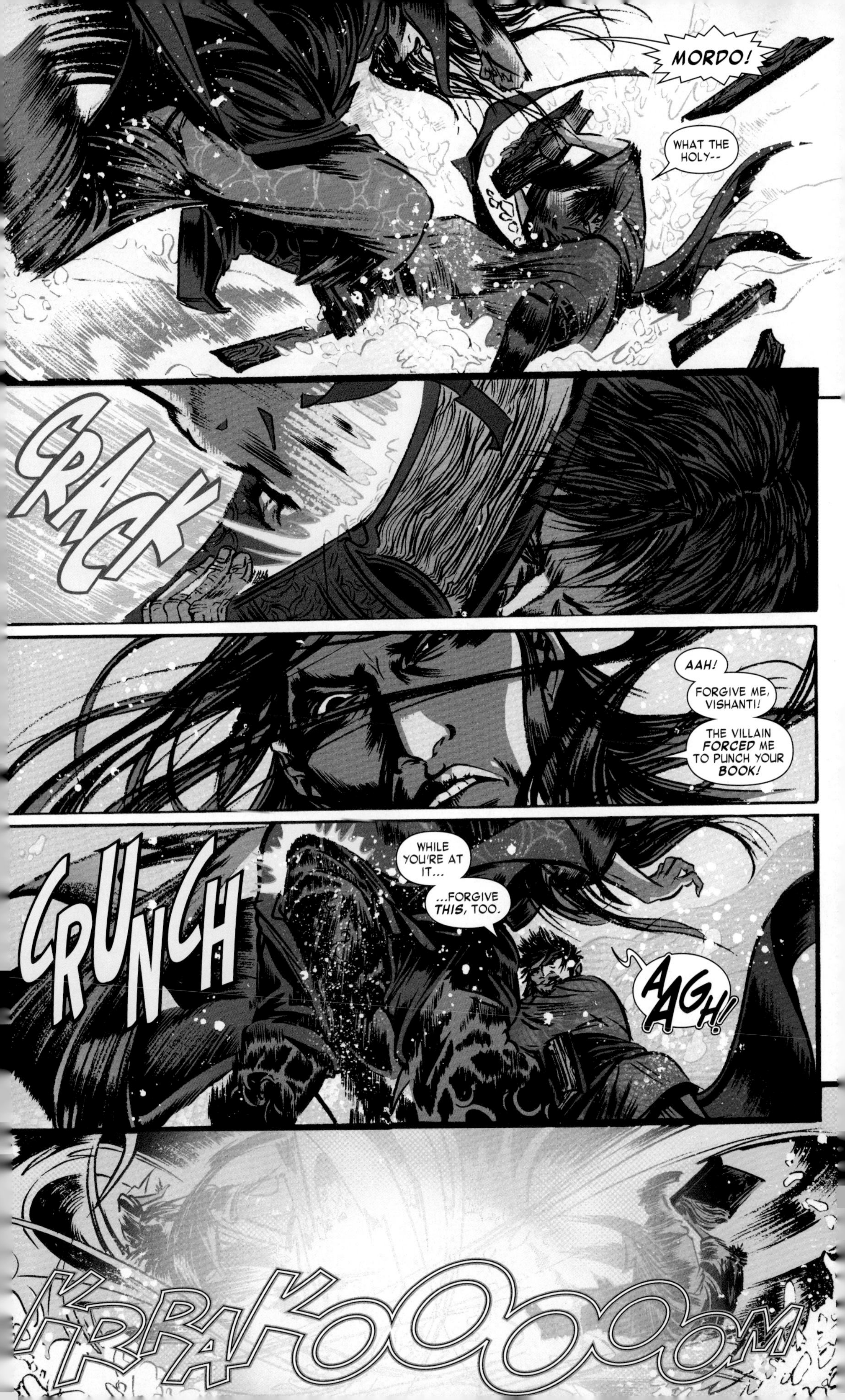
MORDO!
WHAT THE HOLY--
CRACK
AAH!
FORGIVE ME, VISHANTI!
THE VILLAIN FORCED ME TO PUNCH YOUR BOOK!
CRUNCH
WHILE YOU'RE AT IT...
...FORGIVE THIS, TOO.
AAGH!
KRRAKOOOOOM

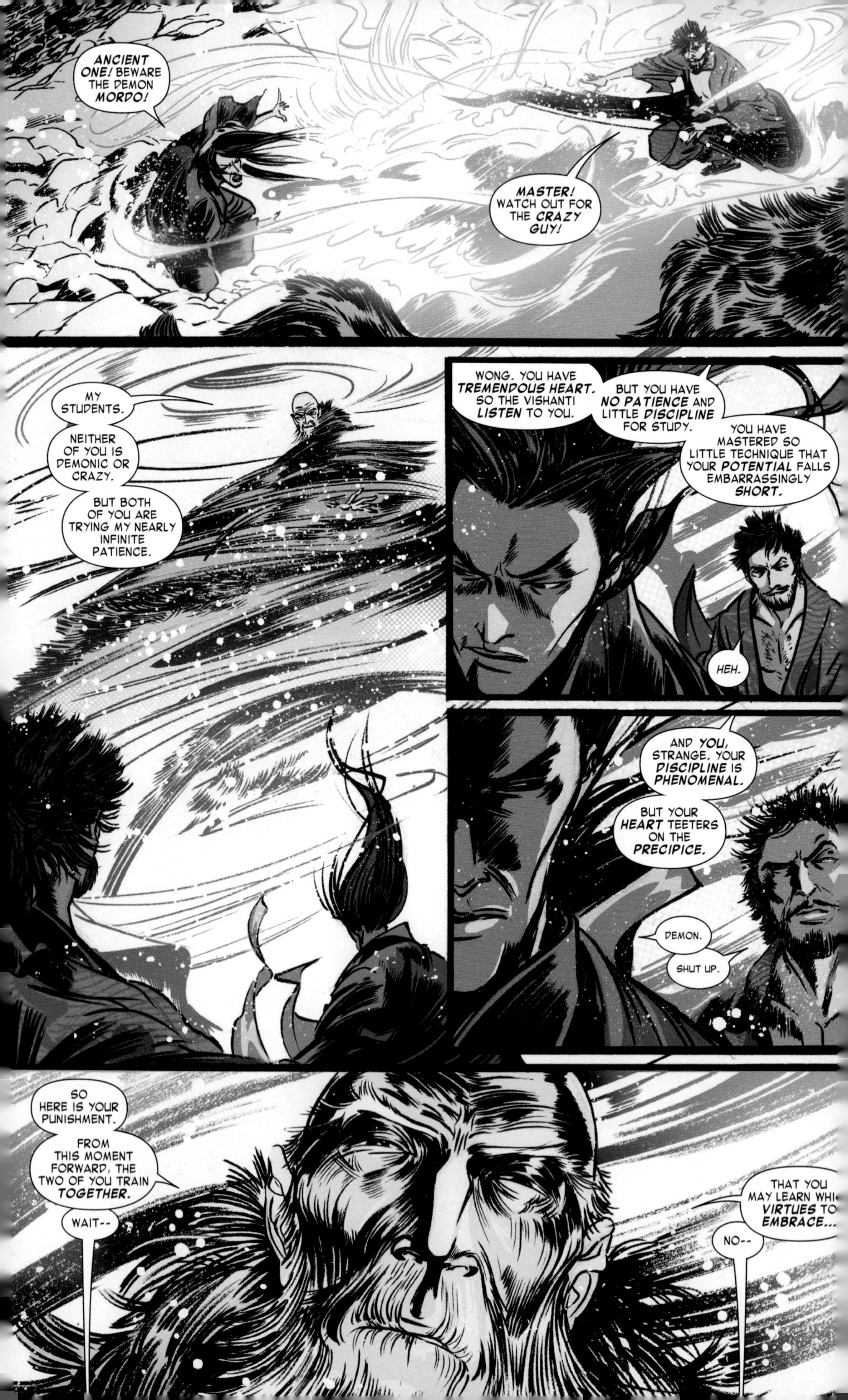
ANCIENT ONE! BEWARE THE DEMON MORDO!
MASTER! WATCH OUT FOR THE CRAZY GUY!
MY STUDENTS.
NEITHER OF YOU IS DEMONIC OR CRAZY.
BUT BOTH OF YOU ARE TRYING MY NEARLY INFINITE PATIENCE.
WONG. YOU HAVE TREMENDOUS HEART. SO THE VISHANTI LISTEN TO YOU.
BUT YOU HAVE NO PATIENCE AND LITTLE DISCIPLINE FOR STUDY.
YOU HAVE MASTERED SO LITTLE TECHNIQUE THAT YOUR POTENTIAL FALLS EMBARRASSINGLY SHORT.
HEH.
AND YOU, STRANGE. YOUR DISCIPLINE IS PHENOMENAL.
BUT YOUR HEART TEETERS ON THE PRECIPICE.
DEMON.
SHUT UP.
SO HERE IS YOUR PUNISHMENT.
FROM THIS MOMENT FORWARD, THE TWO OF YOU TRAIN TOGETHER.
WAIT--
THAT YOU MAY LEARN WHI
VIRTUES TO EMBRACE...
NO--

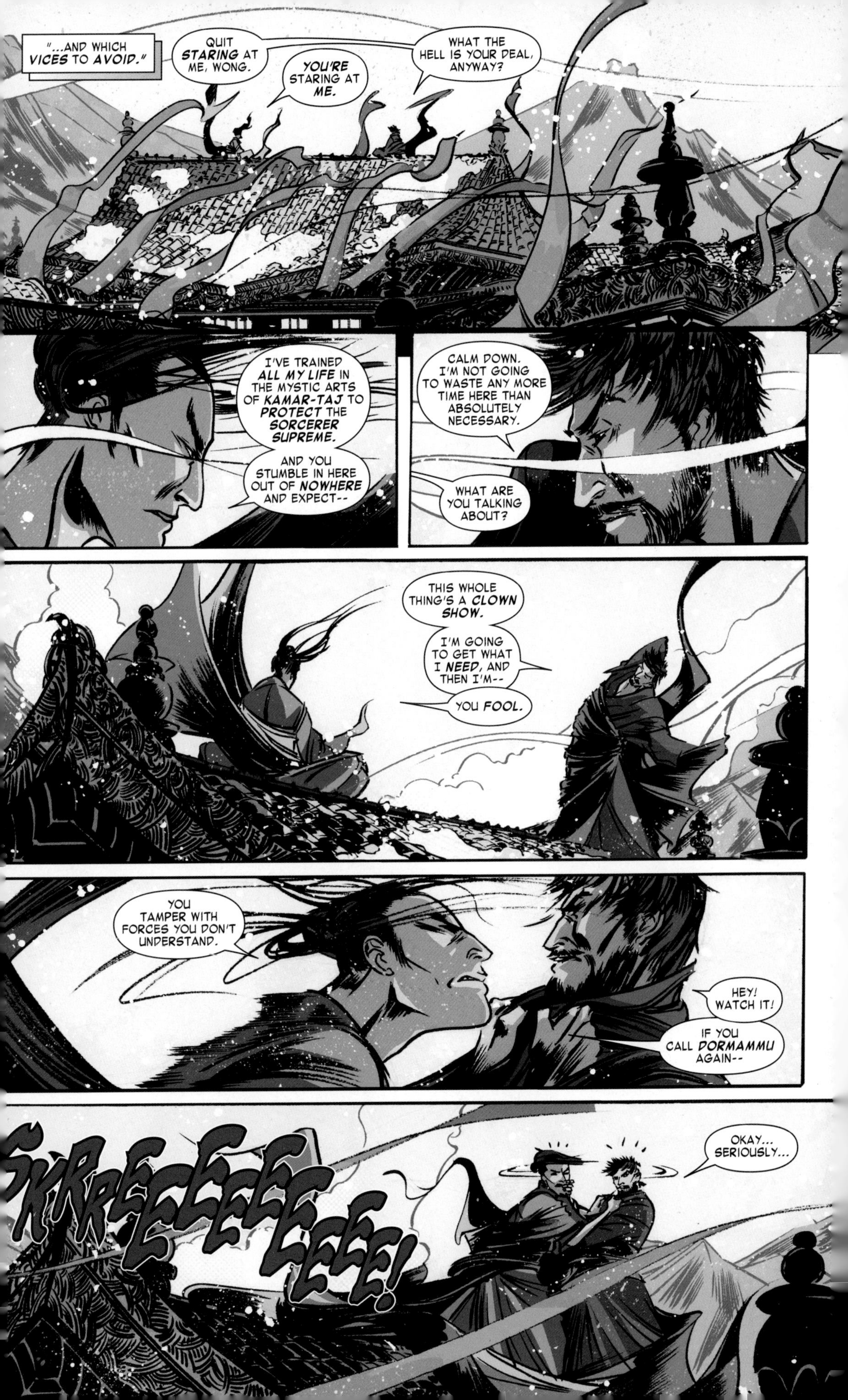
"...AND WHICH VICES TO AVOID."
QUIT STARING AT ME, WONG.
YOU'RE STARING AT ME.
WHAT THE HELL IS YOUR DEAL, ANYWAY?
I'VE TRAINED ALL MY LIFE IN THE MYSTIC ARTS OF KAMAR-TAJ TO PROTECT THE SORCERER SUPREME.
AND YOU STUMBLE IN HERE OUT OF NOWHERE AND EXPECT--
CALM DOWN. I'M NOT GOING TO WASTE ANY MORE TIME HERE THAN ABSOLUTELY NECESSARY.
WHAT ARE YOU TALKING ABOUT?
THIS WHOLE THING'S A CLOWN SHOW.
I'M GOING TO GET WHAT I NEED, AND THEN I'M--
YOU FOOL.
YOU TAMPER WITH FORCES YOU DON'T UNDERSTAND.
HEY! WATCH IT!
IF YOU CALL DORMAMMU AGAIN--
SKREEEEEEEEEEEE!
OKAY... SERIOUSLY...

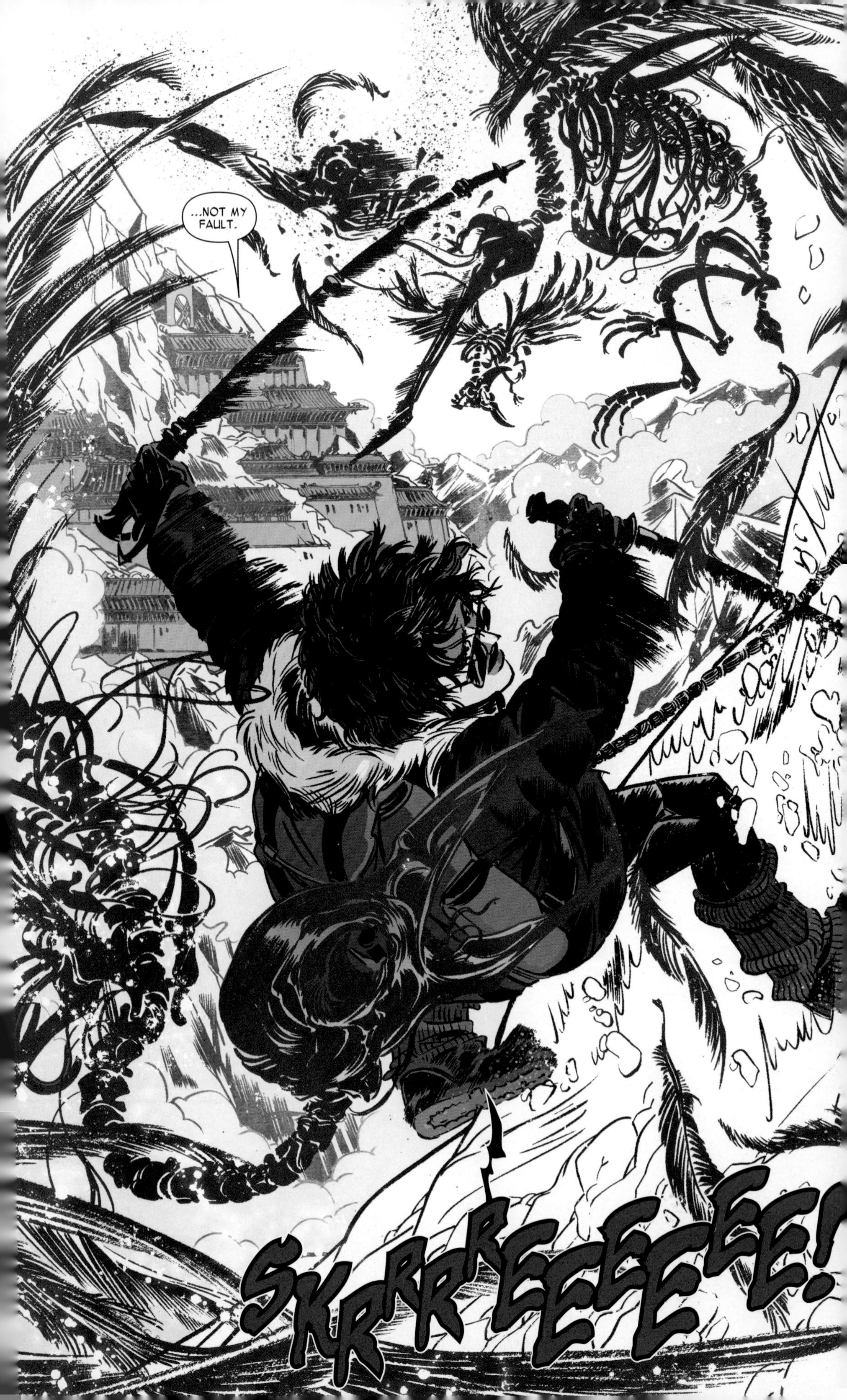
...NOT MY FAULT.
SKRRRREEEEEEEE!

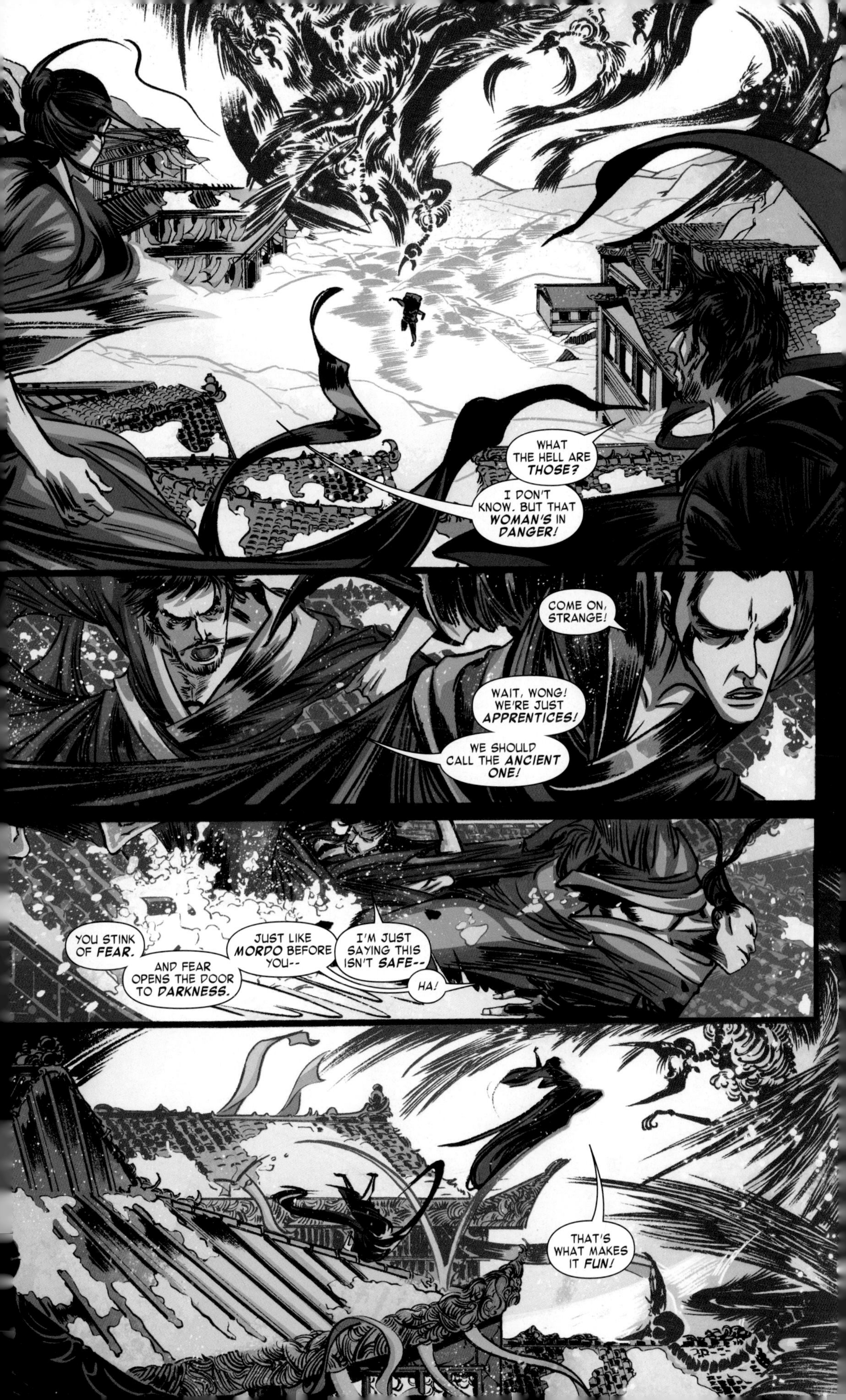
WHAT THE HELL ARE THOSE?
I DON'T KNOW. BUT THAT WOMAN'S IN DANGER!
COME ON, STRANGE!
WAIT, WONG! WE'RE JUST APPRENTICES!
WE SHOULD CALL THE ANCIENT ONE!
I'M JUST SAYING THIS ISN'T SAFE--
HA!
YOU STINK OF FEAR.
AND FEAR OPENS THE DOOR TO DARKNESS.
JUST LIKE MORDO BEFORE YOU--
THAT'S WHAT MAKES IT FUN!

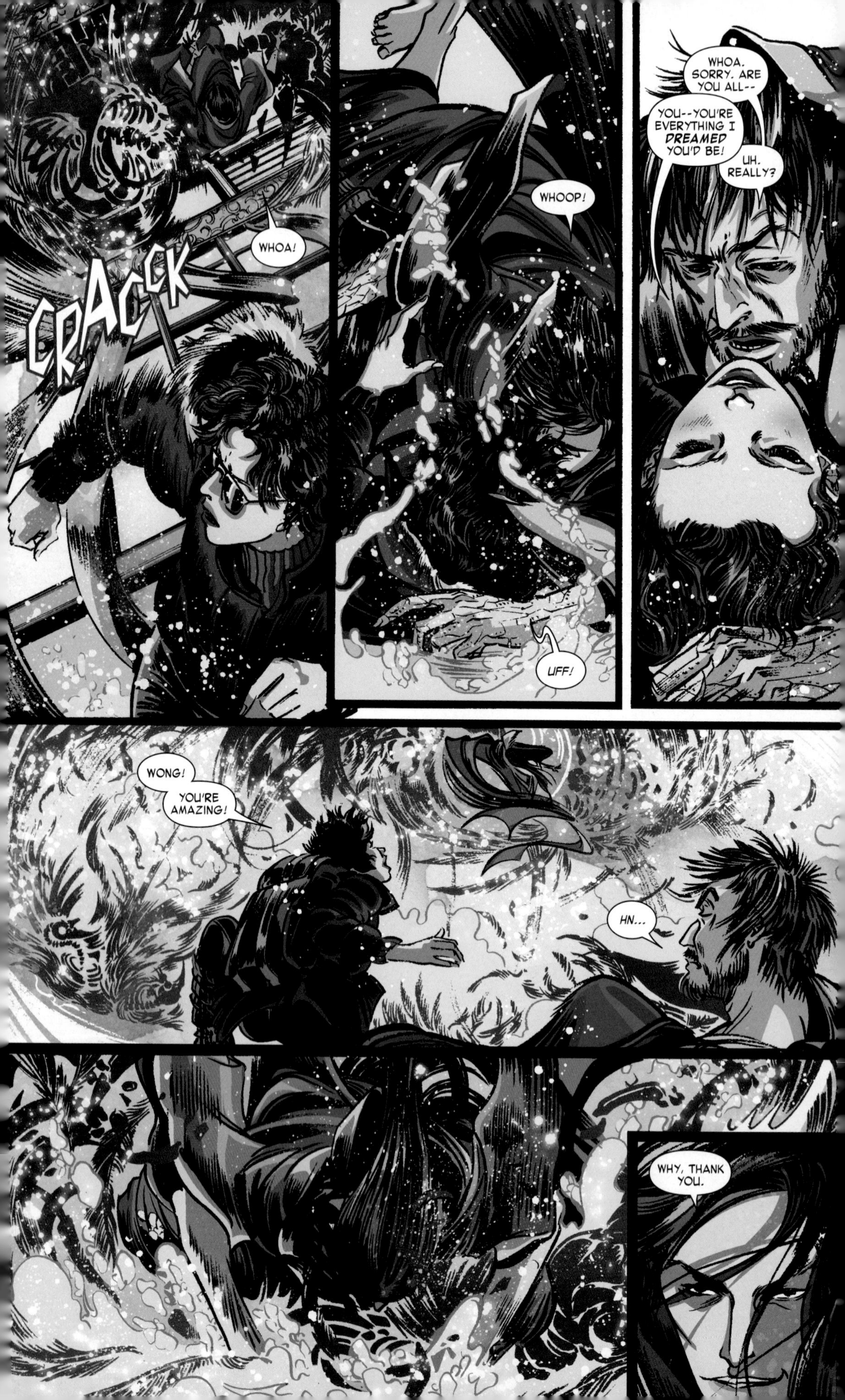
WHOA!
CRACCK
WHOOP!
UFF!
WHOA. SORRY. ARE YOU ALL--
YOU--YOU'RE EVERYTHING I DREAMED YOU'D BE!
UH. REALLY?
WONG!
YOU'RE AMAZING!
HN...
WHY, THANK YOU.

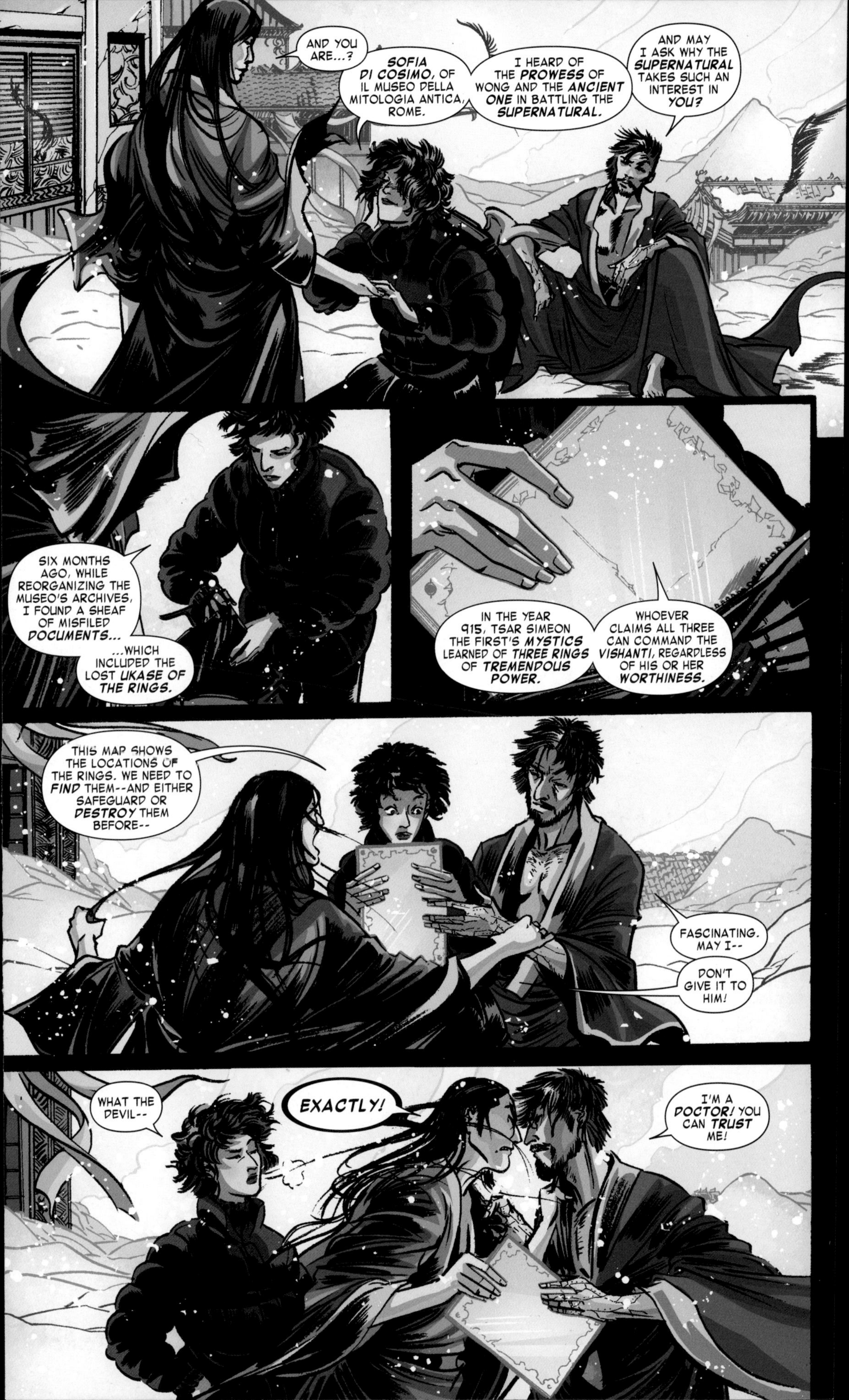
AND YOU ARE...?
SOFIA DI COSIMO, OF IL MUSEO DELLA MITOLOGIA ANTICA, ROME.
I HEARD OF THE PROWESS OF WONG AND THE ANCIENT ONE IN BATTLING THE SUPERNATURAL.
AND MAY I ASK WHY THE SUPERNATURAL TAKES SUCH AN INTEREST IN YOU?
SIX MONTHS AGO, WHILE REORGANIZING THE MUSEO'S ARCHIVES, I FOUND A SHEAF OF MISFILED DOCUMENTS...
...WHICH INCLUDED THE LOST UKASE OF THE RINGS.
IN THE YEAR 915, TSAR SIMEON THE FIRST'S MYSTICS LEARNED OF THREE RINGS OF TREMENDOUS POWER.
WHOEVER CLAIMS ALL THREE CAN COMMAND THE VISHANTI, REGARDLESS OF HIS OR HER WORTHINESS.
THIS MAP SHOWS THE LOCATIONS OF THE RINGS. WE NEED TO FIND THEM--AND EITHER SAFEGUARD OR DESTROY THEM BEFORE--
FASCINATING. MAY I--
DON'T GIVE IT TO HIM!
WHAT THE DEVIL--
EXACTLY!
I'M A DOCTOR! YOU CAN TRUST ME!

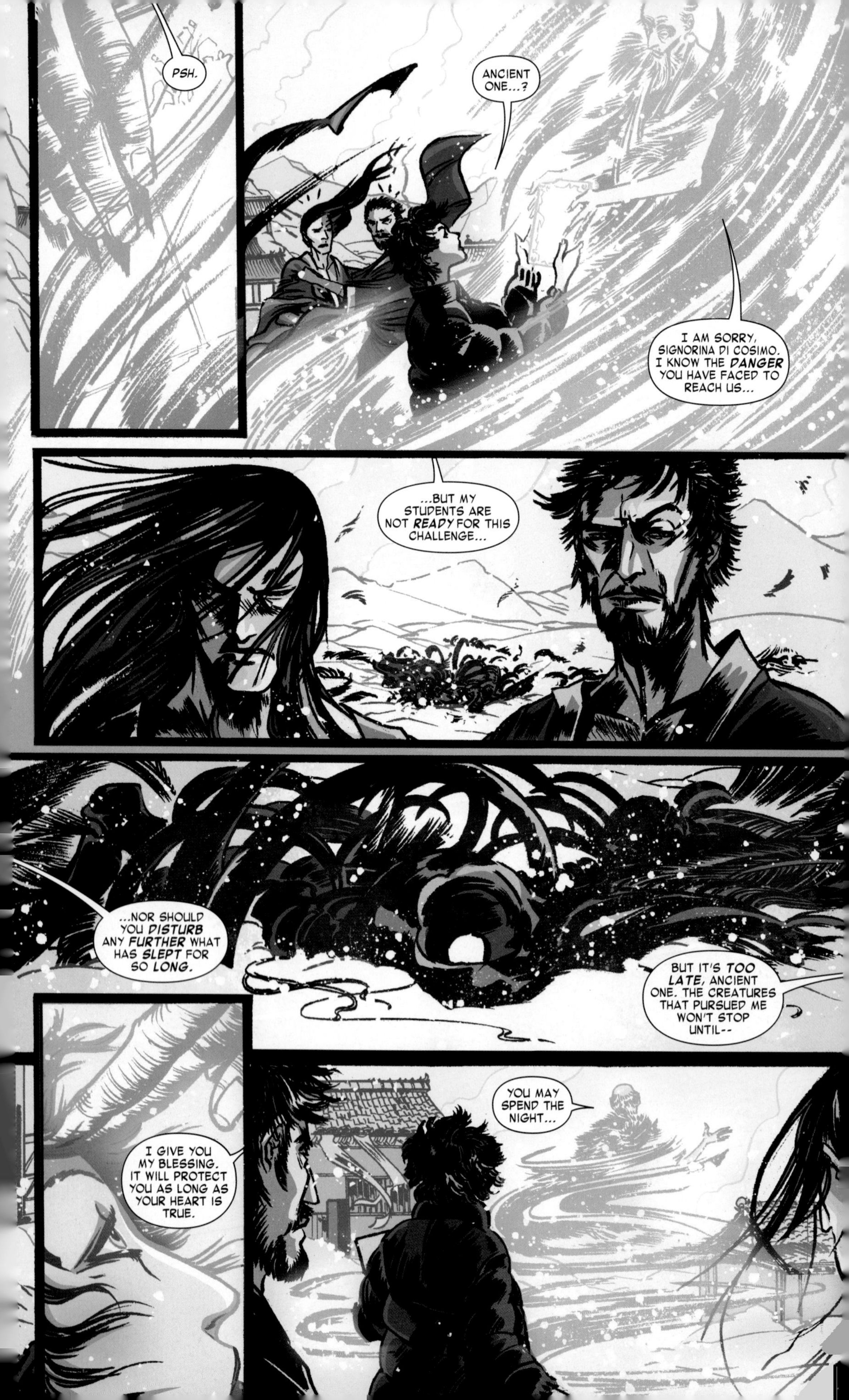
PSH.
ANCIENT ONE...?
I AM SORRY, SIGNORINA DI COSIMO. I KNOW THE DANGER YOU HAVE FACED TO REACH US...
...BUT MY STUDENTS ARE NOT READY FOR THIS CHALLENGE...
...NOR SHOULD YOU DISTURB ANY FURTHER WHAT HAS SLEPT FOR SO LONG.
BUT IT'S TOO LATE, ANCIENT ONE. THE CREATURES THAT PURSUED ME WON'T STOP UNTIL--
YOU MAY SPEND THE NIGHT...
I GIVE YOU MY BLESSING. IT WILL PROTECT YOU AS LONG AS YOUR HEART IS TRUE.

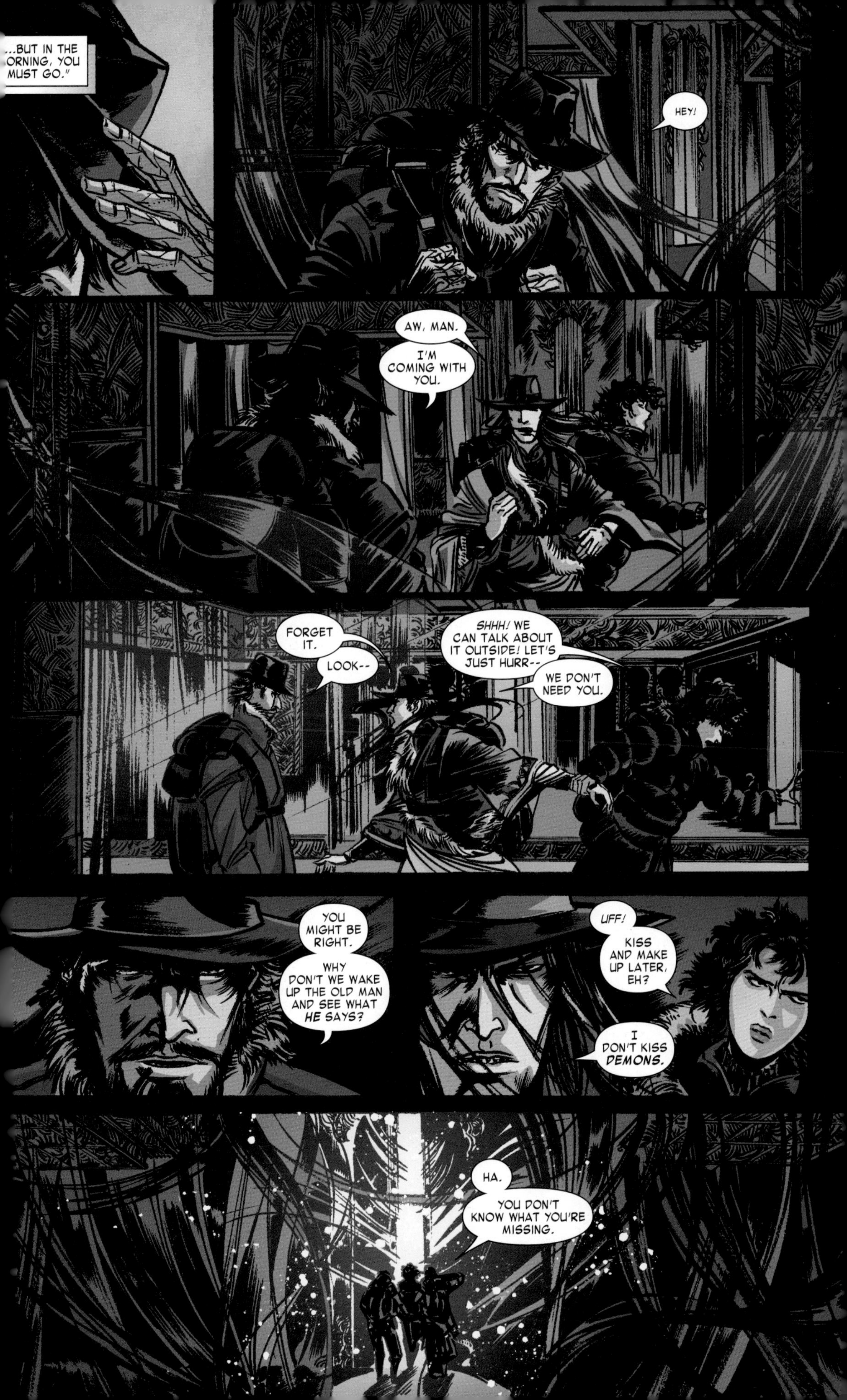

...BUT IN THE ORNING, YOU MUST GO."
HEY!
AW, MAN.
I'M COMING WITH YOU.
FORGET IT.
LOOK--
SHHH! WE CAN TALK ABOUT IT OUTSIDE! LET'S JUST HURR--
WE DON'T NEED YOU.
YOU MIGHT BE RIGHT.
WHY DON'T WE WAKE UP THE OLD MAN AND SEE WHAT HE SAYS?
UFF!
KISS AND MAKE UP LATER, EH?
I DON'T KISS DEMONS.
HA.
YOU DON'T KNOW WHAT YOU'RE MISSING.

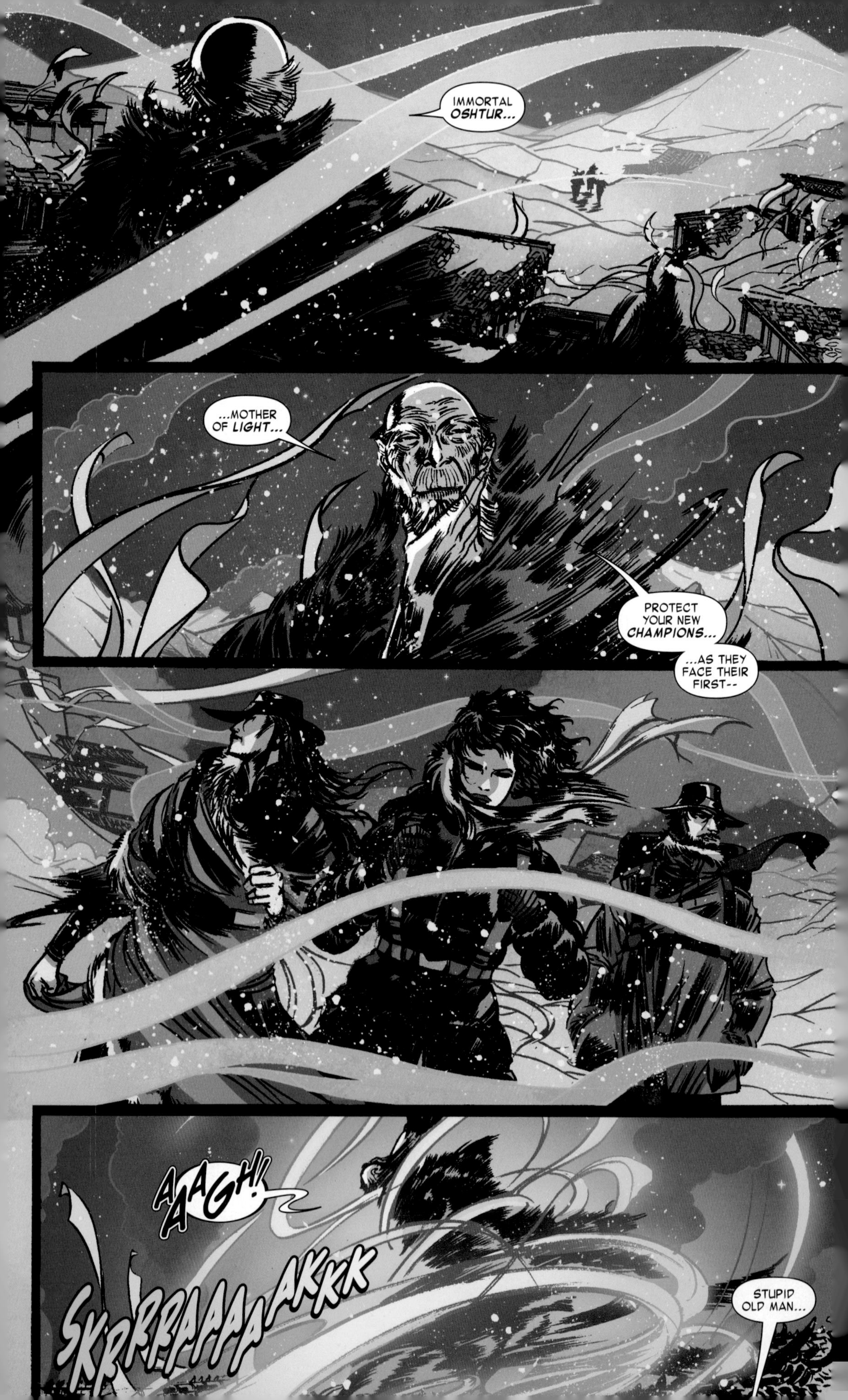
IMMORTAL OSHTUR...
...MOTHER OF LIGHT...
PROTECT YOUR NEW CHAMPIONS...
...AS THEY FACE THEIR FIRST--
AAAGH!
SKRRRAAAAAKKK
STUPID OLD MAN...

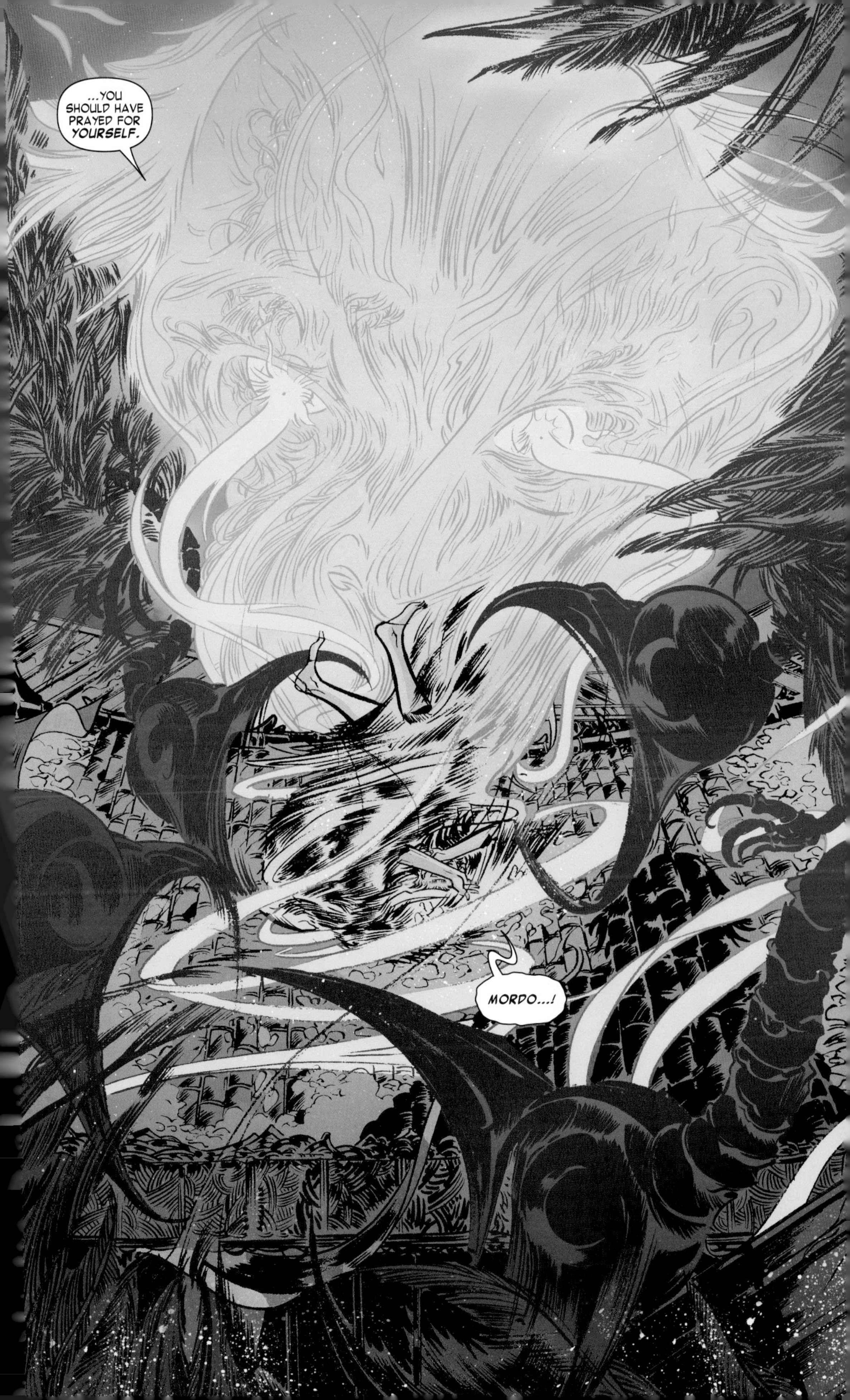
...YOU SHOULD HAVE PRAYED FOR YOURSELF.
MORDO...!

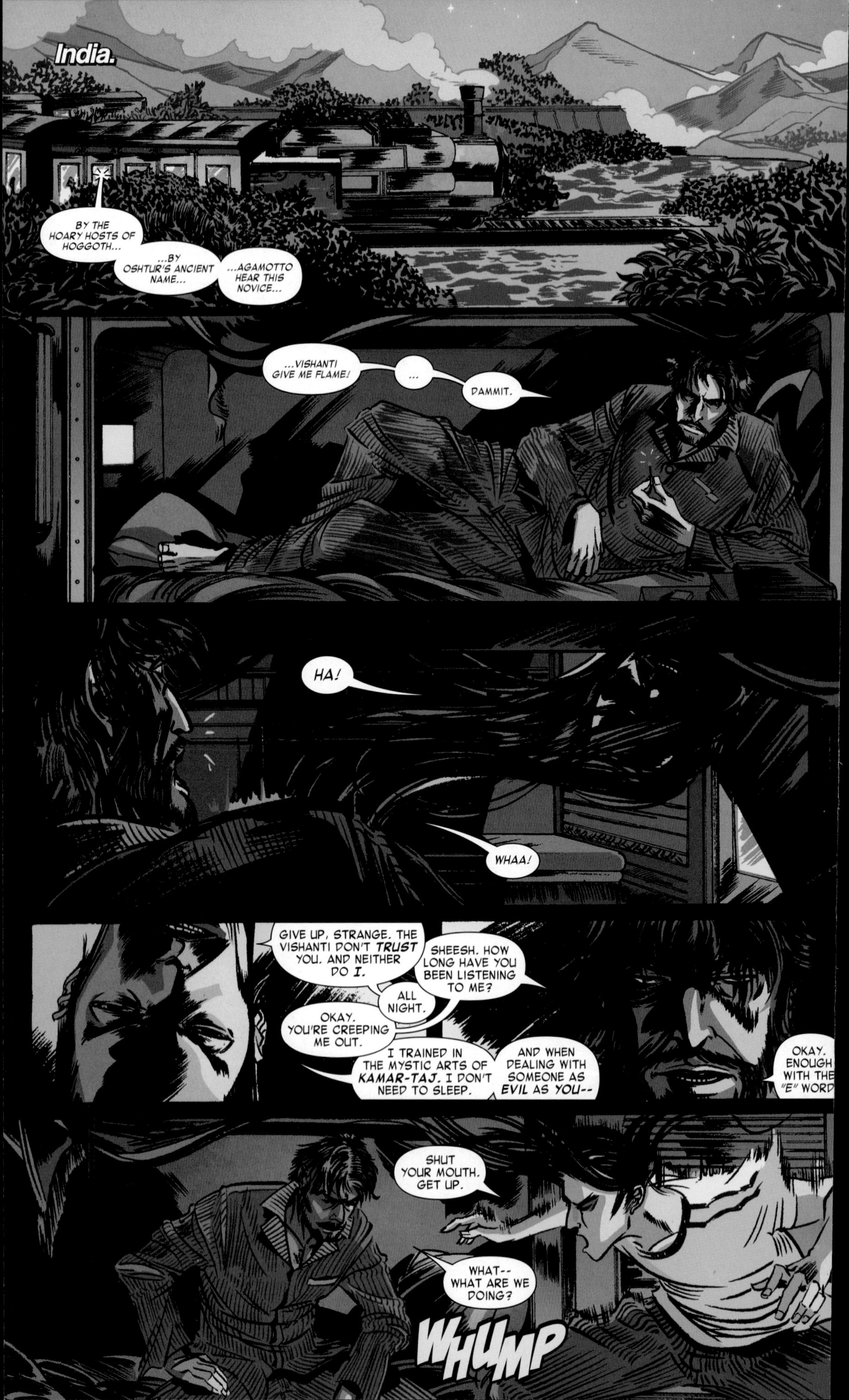
India.
BY THE HOARY HOSTS OF HOGGOTH...
...BY OSHTUR'S ANCIENT NAME...
...AGAMOTTO HEAR THIS NOVICE...
...VISHANTI GIVE ME FLAME!
...
DAMMIT.
HA!
WHAA!
GIVE UP, STRANGE. THE VISHANTI DON'T TRUST YOU. AND NEITHER DO I.
SHEESH. HOW LONG HAVE YOU BEEN LISTENING TO ME?
ALL NIGHT.
OKAY. YOU'RE CREEPING ME OUT.
I TRAINED IN THE MYSTIC ARTS OF KAMAR-TAJ. I DON'T NEED TO SLEEP.
AND WHEN DEALING WITH SOMEONE AS EVIL AS YOU--
OKAY. ENOUGH WITH THE "E" WORD
SHUT YOUR MOUTH. GET UP.
WHAT-- WHAT ARE WE DOING?
WHUMP

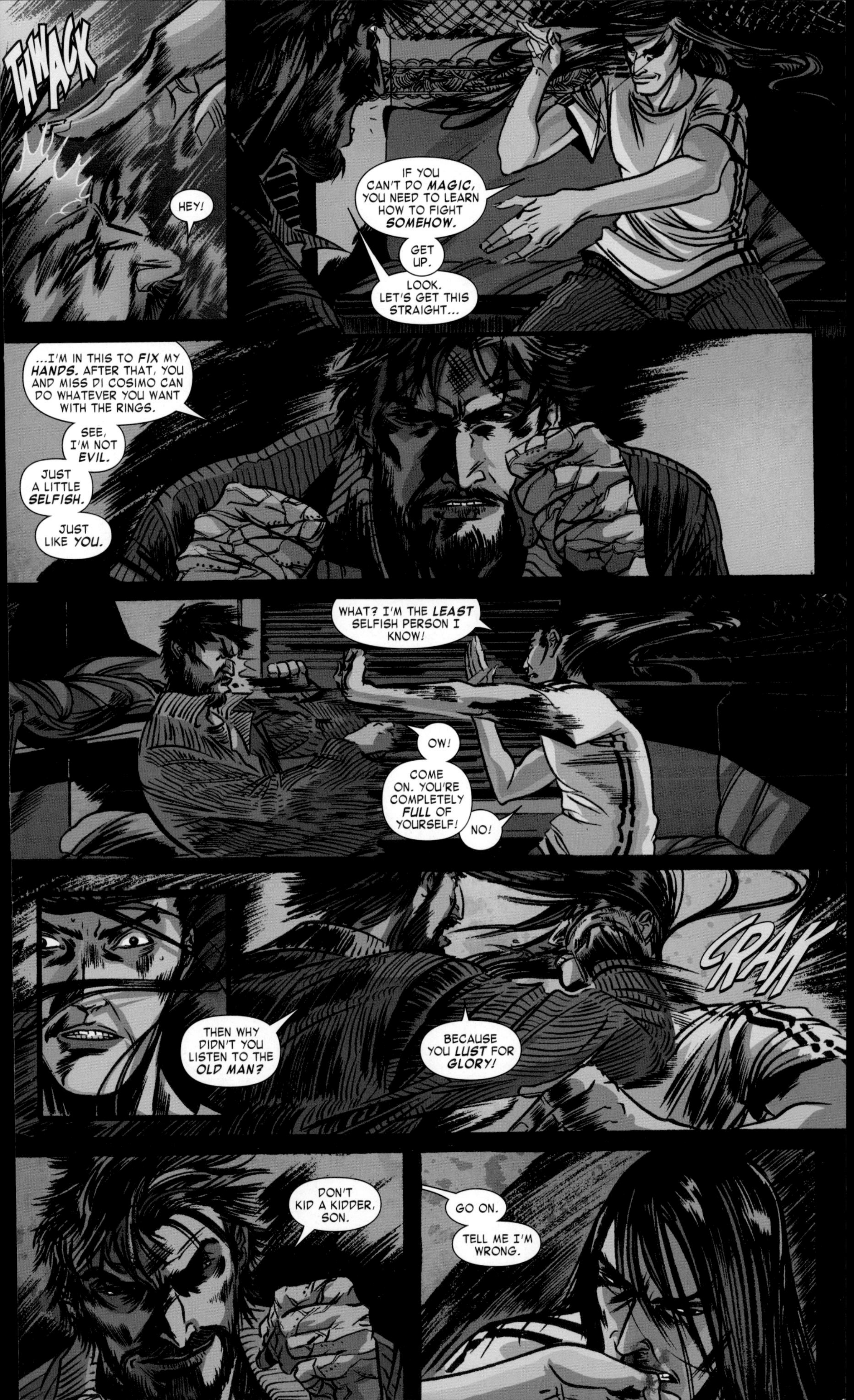

THWACK
HEY!
IF YOU CAN'T DO MAGIC, YOU NEED TO LEARN HOW TO FIGHT SOMEHOW.
GET UP.
LOOK. LET'S GET THIS STRAIGHT...
...I'M IN THIS TO FIX MY HANDS. AFTER THAT, YOU AND MISS DI COSIMO CAN DO WHATEVER YOU WANT WITH THE RINGS.
SEE, I'M NOT EVIL.
JUST A LITTLE SELFISH.
JUST LIKE YOU.
WHAT? I'M THE LEAST SELFISH PERSON I KNOW!
OW!
COME ON. YOU'RE COMPLETELY FULL OF YOURSELF!
NO!
THEN WHY DIDN'T YOU LISTEN TO THE OLD MAN?
BECAUSE YOU LUST FOR GLORY!
CRAK
DON'T KID A KIDDER, SON.
GO ON.
TELL ME I'M WRONG.

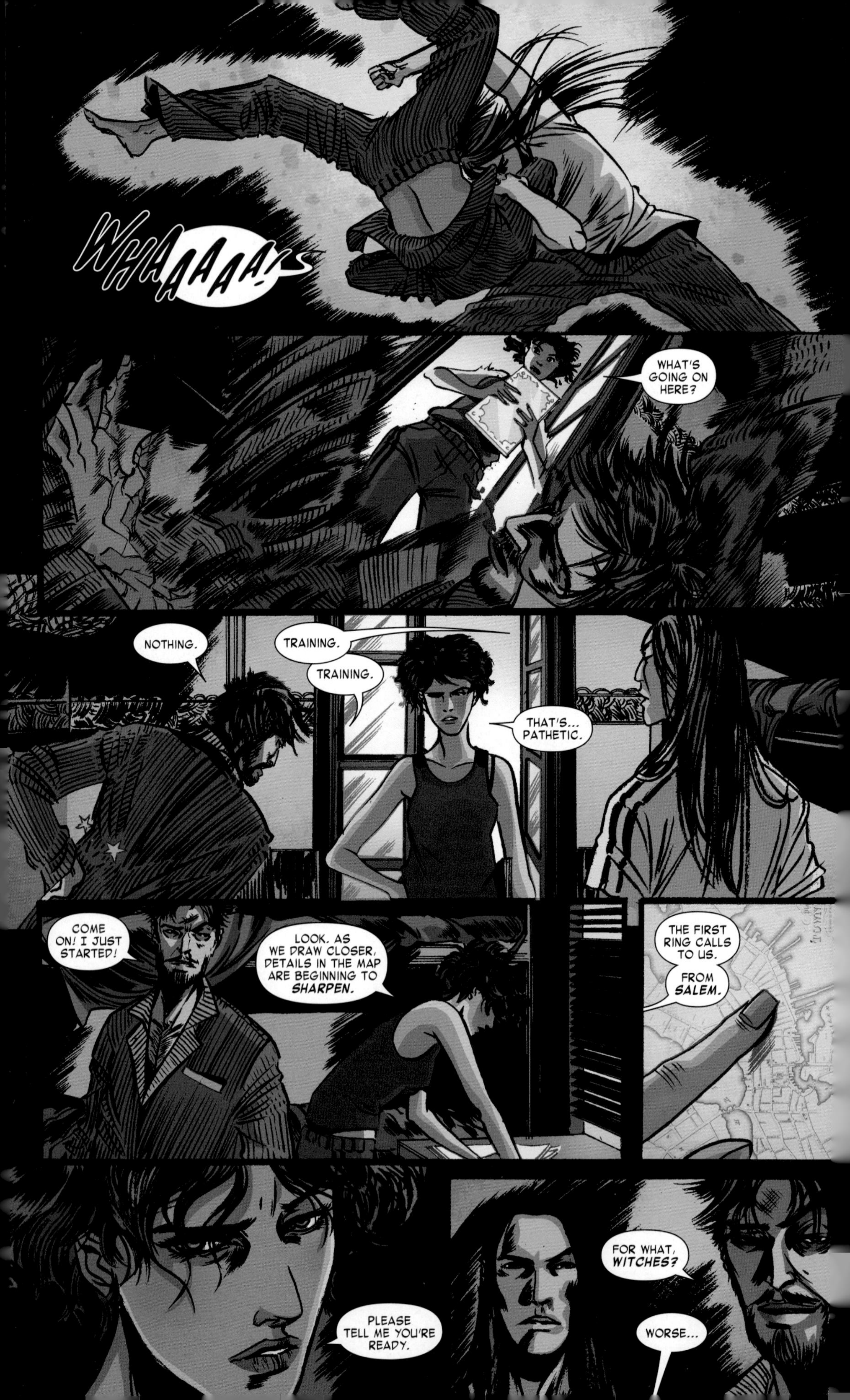
WHAAAAA!S
WHAT'S GOING ON HERE?
NOTHING.
TRAINING.
TRAINING.
THAT'S... PATHETIC.
COME ON! I JUST STARTED!
LOOK. AS WE DRAW CLOSER, DETAILS IN THE MAP ARE BEGINNING TO SHARPEN.
THE FIRST RING CALLS TO US.
FROM SALEM.
PLEASE TELL ME YOU'RE READY.
FOR WHAT, WITCHES?
WORSE...

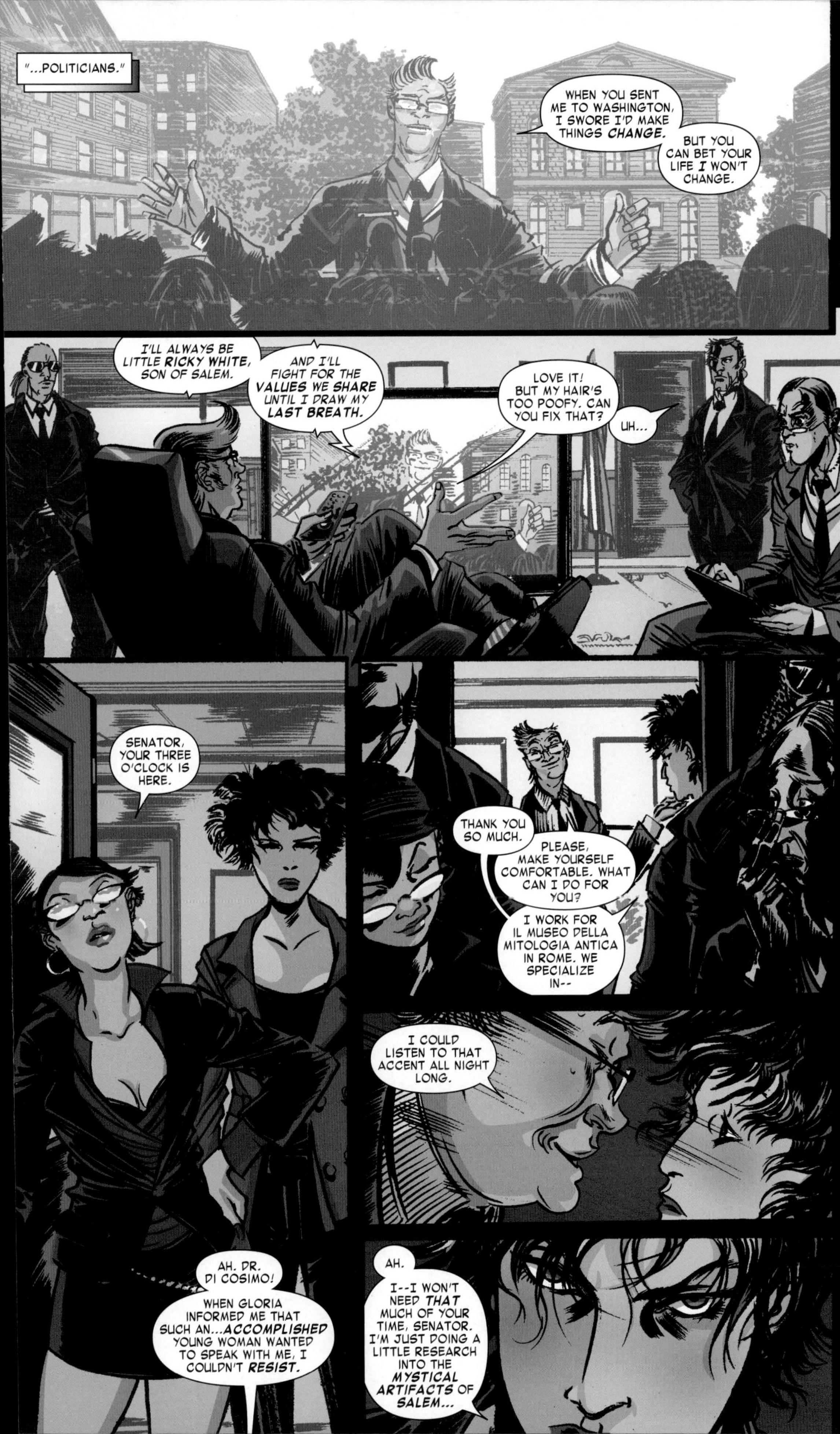
"...POLITICIANS."
WHEN YOU SENT ME TO WASHINGTON, I SWORE I'D MAKE THINGS CHANGE.
BUT YOU CAN BET YOUR LIFE I WON'T CHANGE.
I'LL ALWAYS BE LITTLE RICKY WHITE, SON OF SALEM.
AND I'LL FIGHT FOR THE VALUES WE SHARE UNTIL I DRAW MY LAST BREATH.
LOVE IT! BUT MY HAIR'S TOO POOFY. CAN YOU FIX THAT?
UH...
SENATOR, YOUR THREE O'CLOCK IS HERE.
THANK YOU SO MUCH.
PLEASE, MAKE YOURSELF COMFORTABLE. WHAT CAN I DO FOR YOU?
I WORK FOR IL MUSEO DELLA MITOLOGIA ANTICA IN ROME. WE SPECIALIZE IN--
I COULD LISTEN TO THAT ACCENT ALL NIGHT LONG.
AH. DR. DI COSIMO!
WHEN GLORIA INFORMED ME THAT SUCH AN...ACCOMPLISHED YOUNG WOMAN WANTED TO SPEAK WITH ME, I COULDN'T RESIST.
AH.
I--I WON'T NEED THAT MUCH OF YOUR TIME, SENATOR. I'M JUST DOING A LITTLE RESEARCH INTO THE MYSTICAL ARTIFACTS OF SALEM...

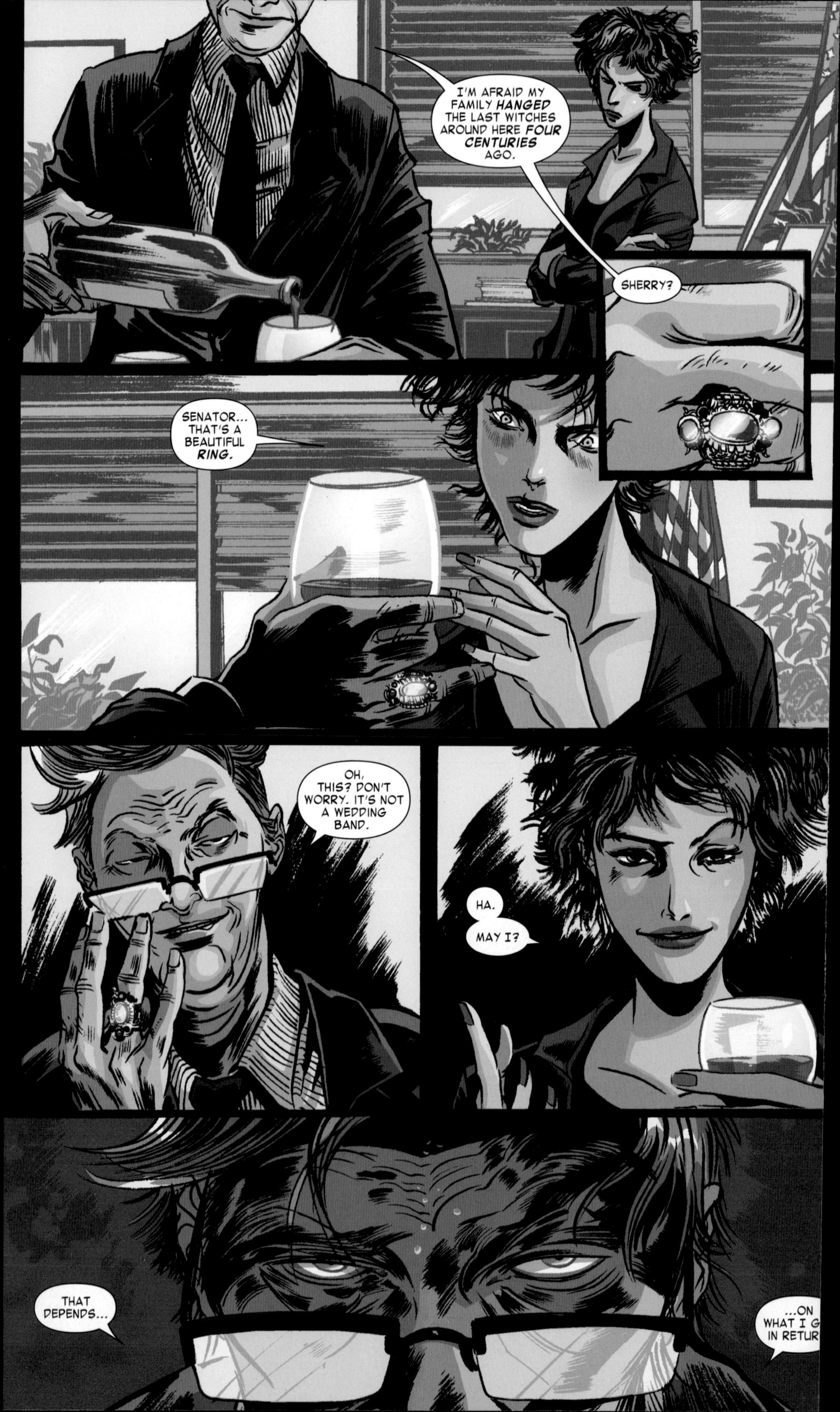
I'M AFRAID MY FAMILY HANGED THE LAST WITCHES AROUND HERE FOUR CENTURIES AGO.
SHERRY?
SENATOR... THAT'S A BEAUTIFUL RING.
OH, THIS? DON'T WORRY. IT'S NOT A WEDDING BAND.
HA.
MAY I?
THAT DEPENDS...
...ON WHAT I G
IN RETUR

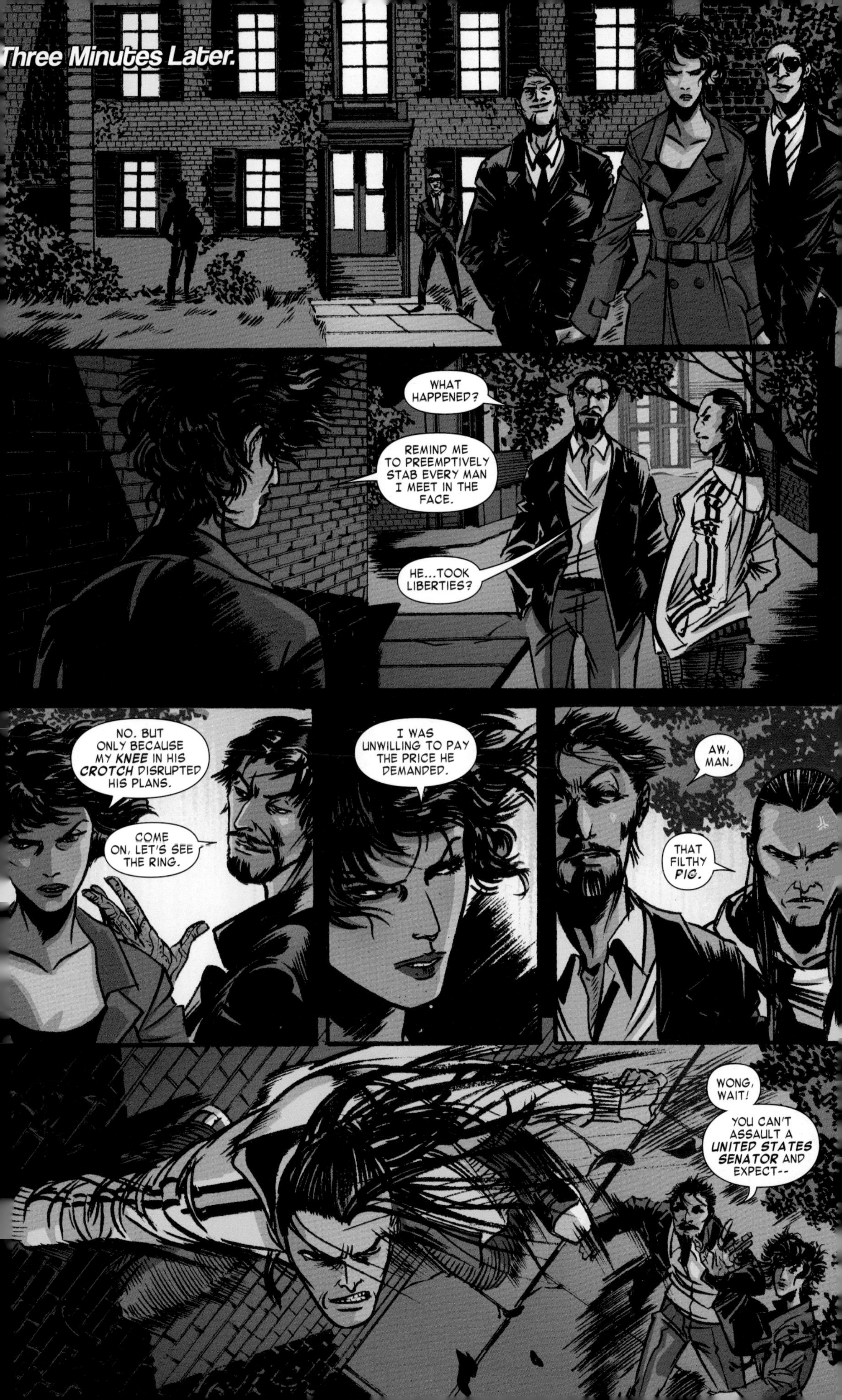
Three Minutes Later.
WHAT HAPPENED?
REMIND ME TO PREEMPTIVELY STAB EVERY MAN I MEET IN THE FACE.
HE...TOOK LIBERTIES?
NO. BUT ONLY BECAUSE MY KNEE IN HIS CROTCH DISRUPTED HIS PLANS.
COME ON, LET'S SEE THE RING.
I WAS UNWILLING TO PAY THE PRICE HE DEMANDED.
AW, MAN.
THAT FILTHY PIG.
WONG, WAIT!
YOU CAN'T ASSAULT A UNITED STATES SENATOR AND EXPECT--

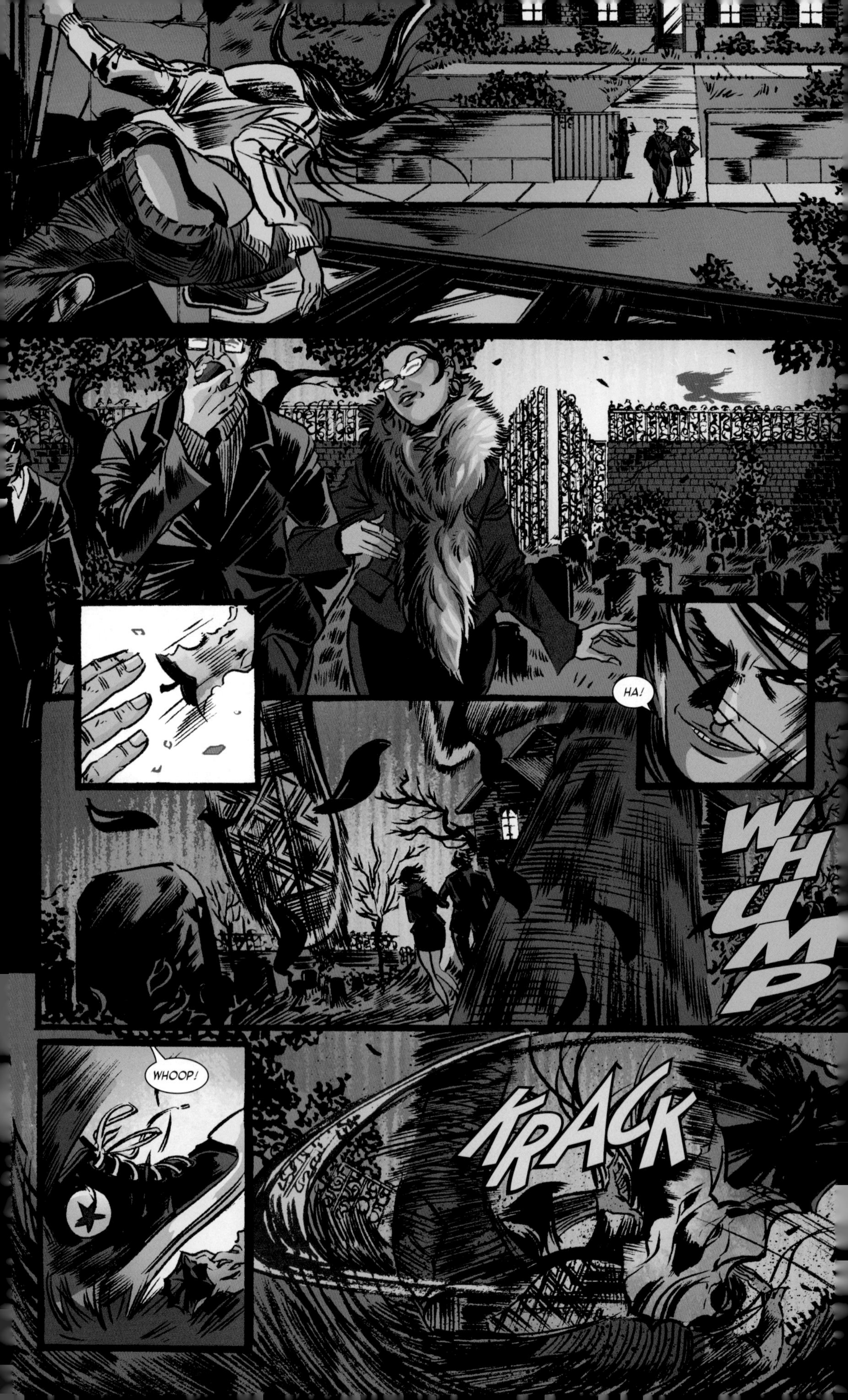
HA!
WHUMP
WHOOP!
KRACK

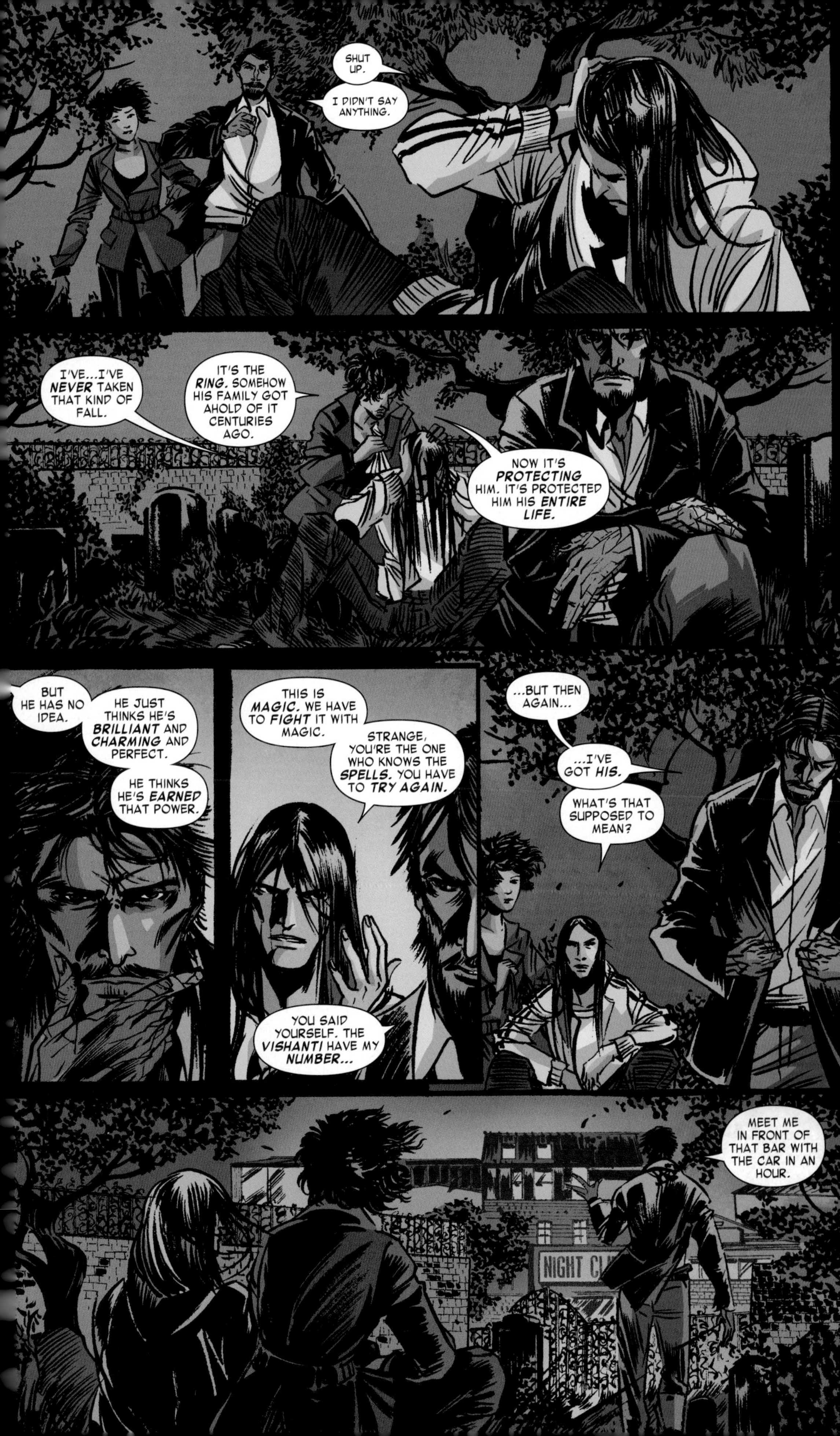
SHUT UP.
I DIDN'T SAY ANYTHING.
I'VE...I'VE NEVER TAKEN THAT KIND OF FALL.
IT'S THE RING. SOMEHOW HIS FAMILY GOT AHOLD OF IT CENTURIES AGO.
NOW IT'S PROTECTING HIM. IT'S PROTECTED HIM HIS ENTIRE LIFE.
BUT HE HAS NO IDEA.
HE JUST THINKS HE'S BRILLIANT AND CHARMING AND PERFECT.
HE THINKS HE'S EARNED THAT POWER.
THIS IS MAGIC. WE HAVE TO FIGHT IT WITH MAGIC.
STRANGE, YOU'RE THE ONE WHO KNOWS THE SPELLS. YOU HAVE TO TRY AGAIN.
YOU SAID YOURSELF. THE VISHANTI HAVE MY NUMBER...
...BUT THEN AGAIN...
...I'VE GOT HIS.
WHAT'S THAT SUPPOSED TO MEAN?
MEET ME IN FRONT OF THAT BAR WITH THE CAR IN AN HOUR.
NIGHT CL

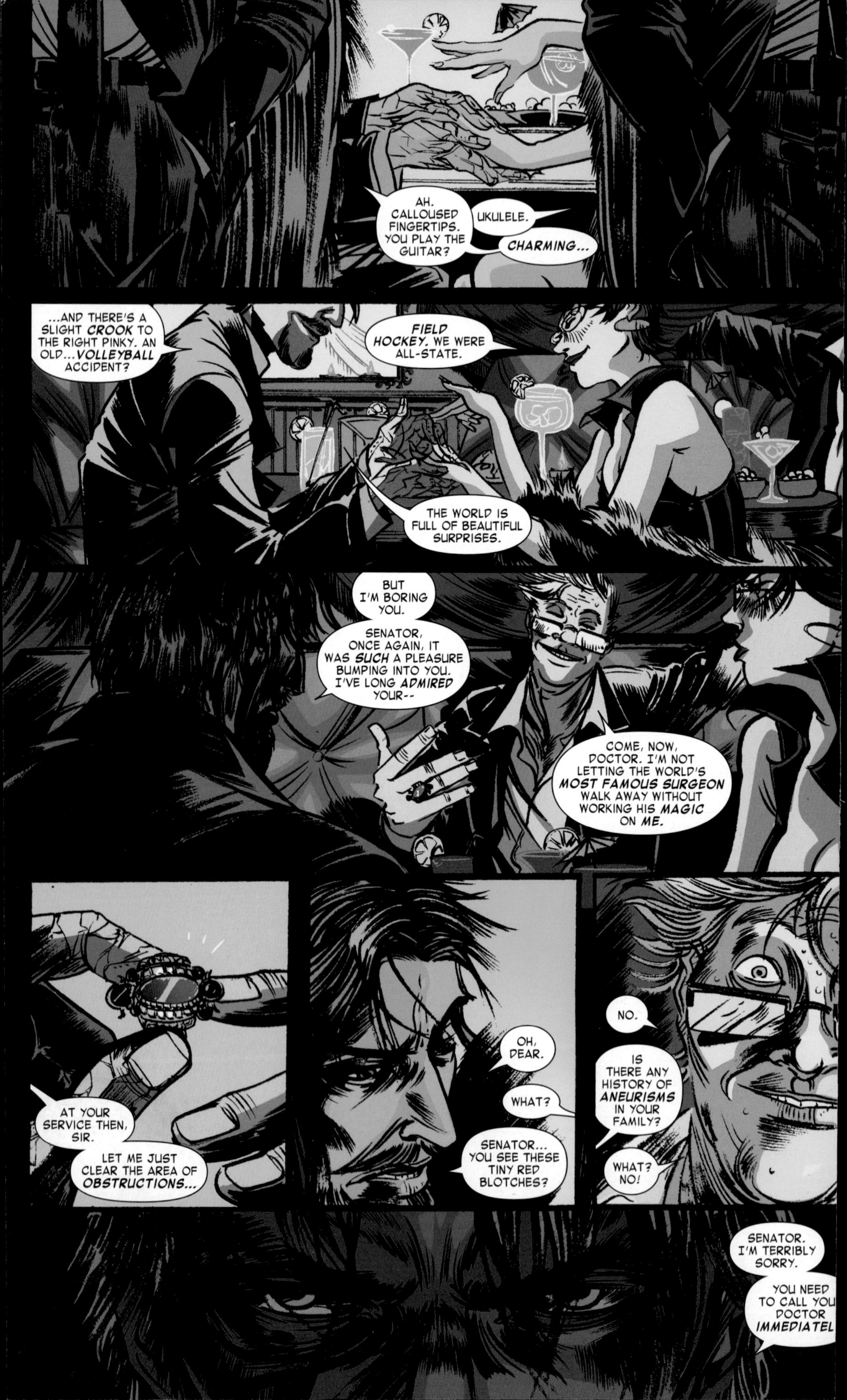
AH. CALLOUSED FINGERTIPS. YOU PLAY THE GUITAR?
UKULELE.
CHARMING...
...AND THERE'S A SLIGHT CROOK TO THE RIGHT PINKY. AN OLD...VOLLEYBALL ACCIDENT?
FIELD HOCKEY. WE WERE ALL-STATE.
THE WORLD IS FULL OF BEAUTIFUL SURPRISES.
BUT I'M BORING YOU.
SENATOR, ONCE AGAIN, IT WAS SUCH A PLEASURE BUMPING INTO YOU. I'VE LONG ADMIRED YOUR--
COME, NOW, DOCTOR. I'M NOT LETTING THE WORLD'S MOST FAMOUS SURGEON WALK AWAY WITHOUT WORKING HIS MAGIC ON ME.
AT YOUR SERVICE THEN, SIR.
LET ME JUST CLEAR THE AREA OF OBSTRUCTIONS...
OH, DEAR.
WHAT?
SENATOR... YOU SEE THESE TINY RED BLOTCHES?
NO.
IS THERE ANY HISTORY OF ANEURISMS IN YOUR FAMILY?
WHAT? NO!
SENATOR. I'M TERRIBLY SORRY.
YOU NEED TO CALL YOU DOCTOR IMMEDIATEL

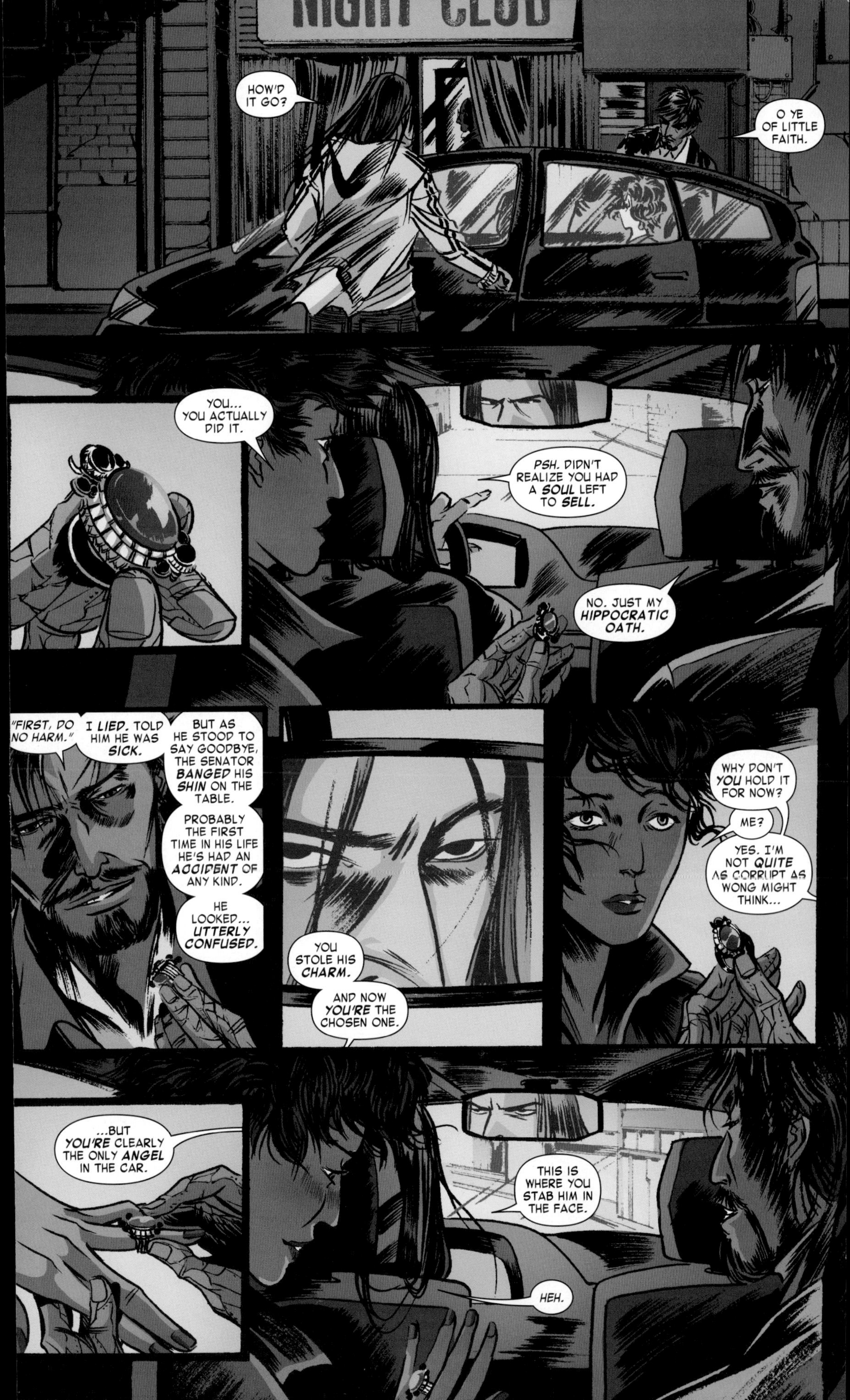
NIGHT CLUB
HOW'D IT GO?
O YE OF LITTLE FAITH.
YOU... YOU ACTUALLY DID IT.
PSH. DIDN'T REALIZE YOU HAD A SOUL LEFT TO SELL.
NO. JUST MY HIPPOCRATIC OATH.
"FIRST, DO NO HARM."
I LIED. TOLD HIM HE WAS SICK.
BUT AS HE STOOD TO SAY GOODBYE, THE SENATOR BANGED HIS SHIN ON THE TABLE.
PROBABLY THE FIRST TIME IN HIS LIFE HE'S HAD AN ACCIDENT OF ANY KIND.
HE LOOKED... UTTERLY CONFUSED.
YOU STOLE HIS CHARM.
AND NOW YOU'RE THE CHOSEN ONE.
WHY DON'T YOU HOLD IT FOR NOW?
ME?
YES. I'M NOT QUITE AS CORRUPT AS WONG MIGHT THINK...
...BUT YOU'RE CLEARLY THE ONLY ANGEL IN THE CAR.
THIS IS WHERE YOU STAB HIM IN THE FACE.
HEH.

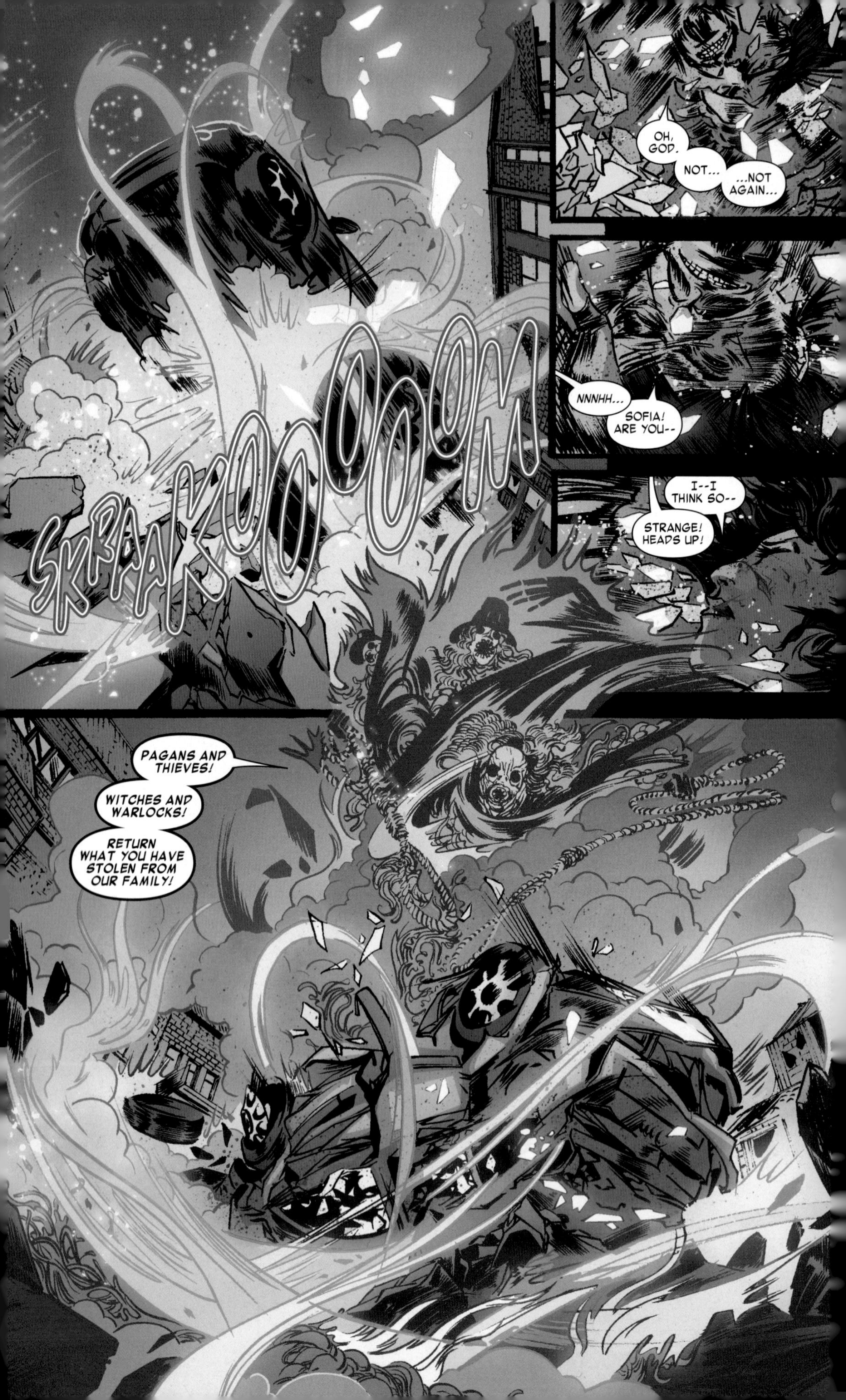
OH, GOD.
NOT...
...NOT AGAIN...
NNNHH...
SOFIA! ARE YOU--
I--I THINK SO--
STRANGE! HEADS UP!
SKRAAKOOOOOOOM
PAGANS AND THIEVES!
WITCHES AND WARLOCKS!
RETURN WHAT YOU HAVE STOLEN FROM OUR FAMILY!

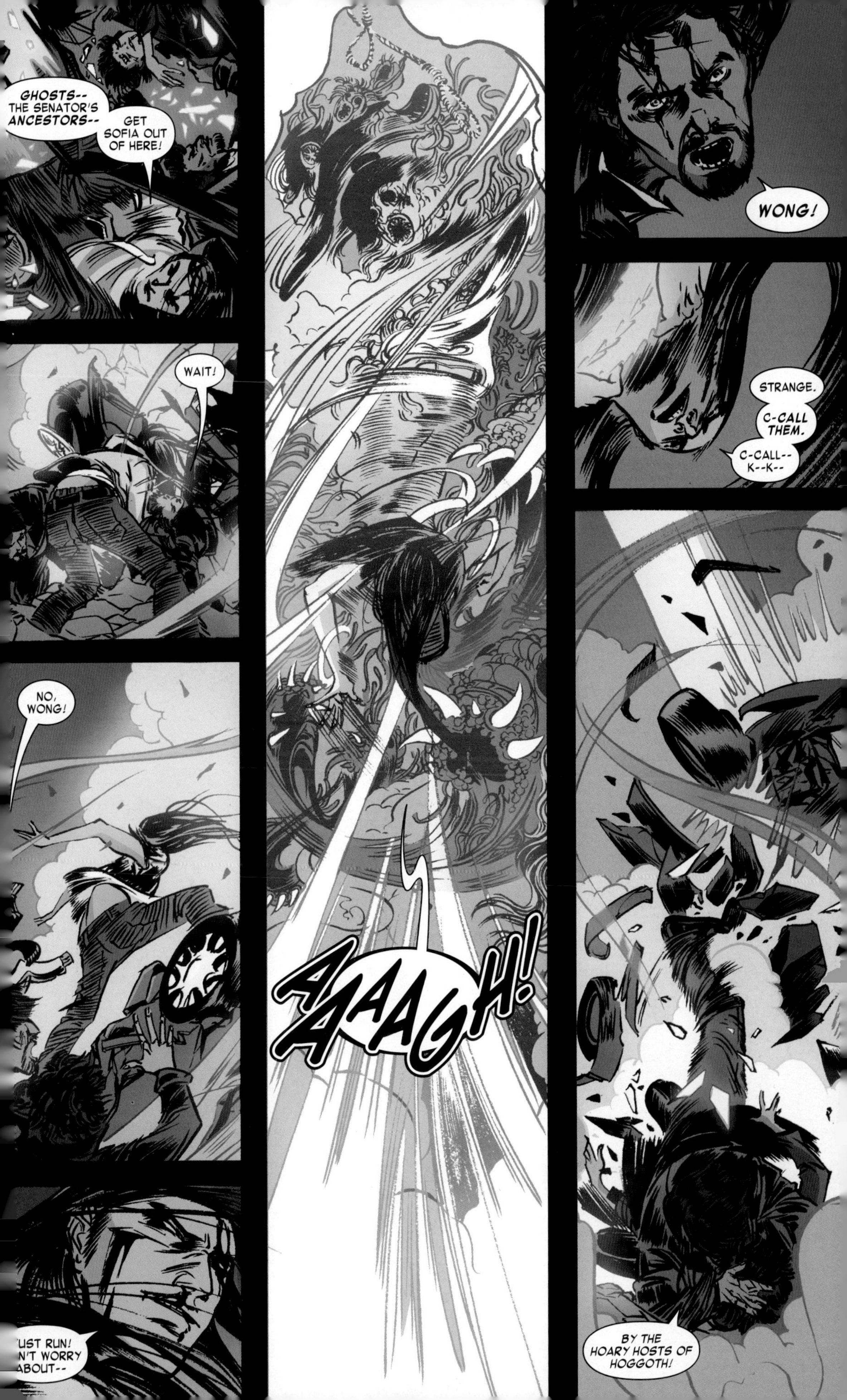
GHOSTS-- THE SENATOR'S ANCESTORS--
GET SOFIA OUT OF HERE!
WAIT!
NO, WONG!
UST RUN! N'T WORRY ABOUT--
AAAAGH!
WONG!
STRANGE.
C-CALL THEM.
C-CALL-- K--K--
BY THE HOARY HOSTS OF HOGGOTH!

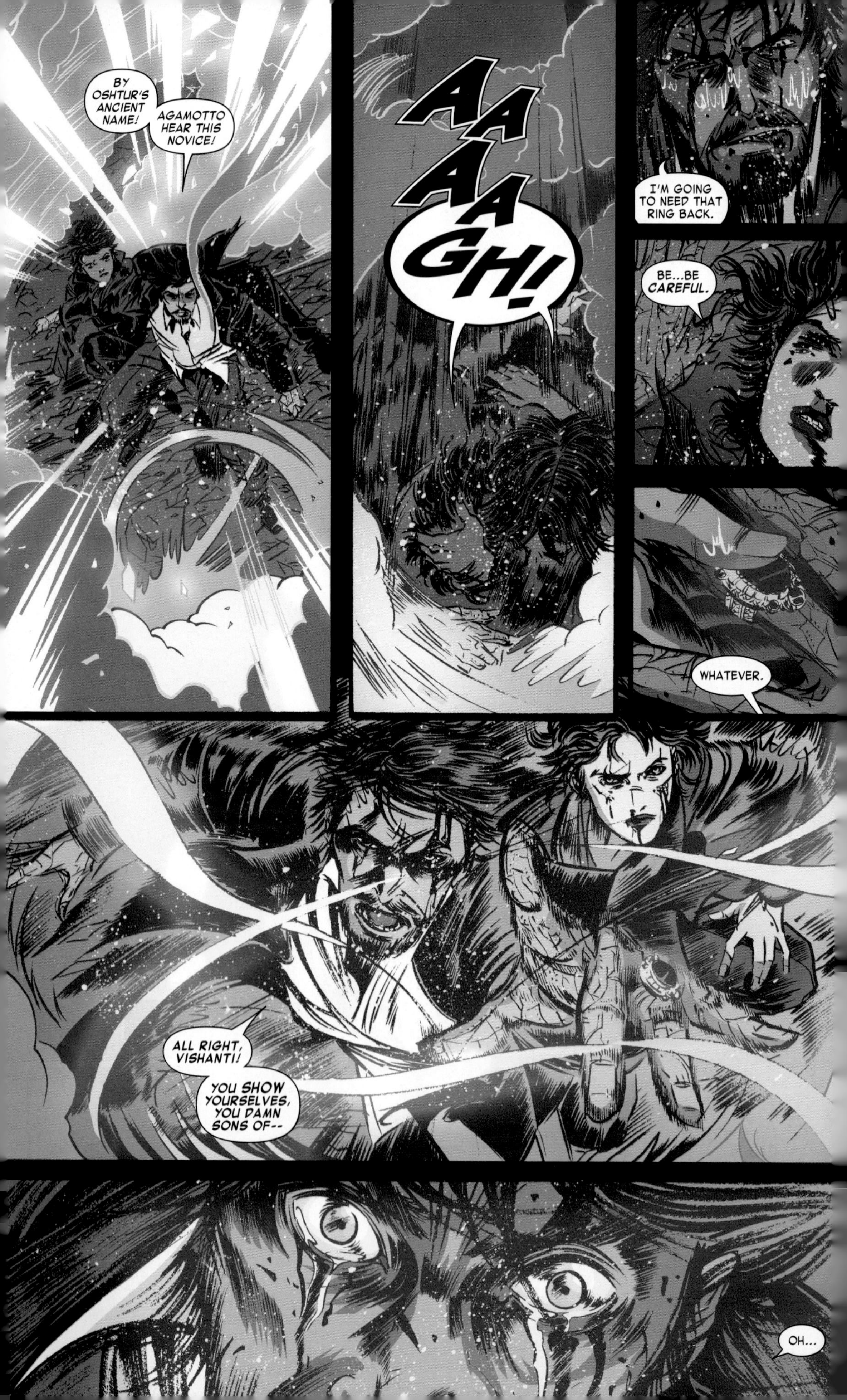
BY OSHTUR'S ANCIENT NAME!
AGAMOTTO HEAR THIS NOVICE!
AAAAAGH!
I'M GOING TO NEED THAT RING BACK.
BE...BE CAREFUL.
WHATEVER.
ALL RIGHT, VISHANTI!
YOU SHOW YOURSELVES, YOU DAMN SONS OF--
OH...

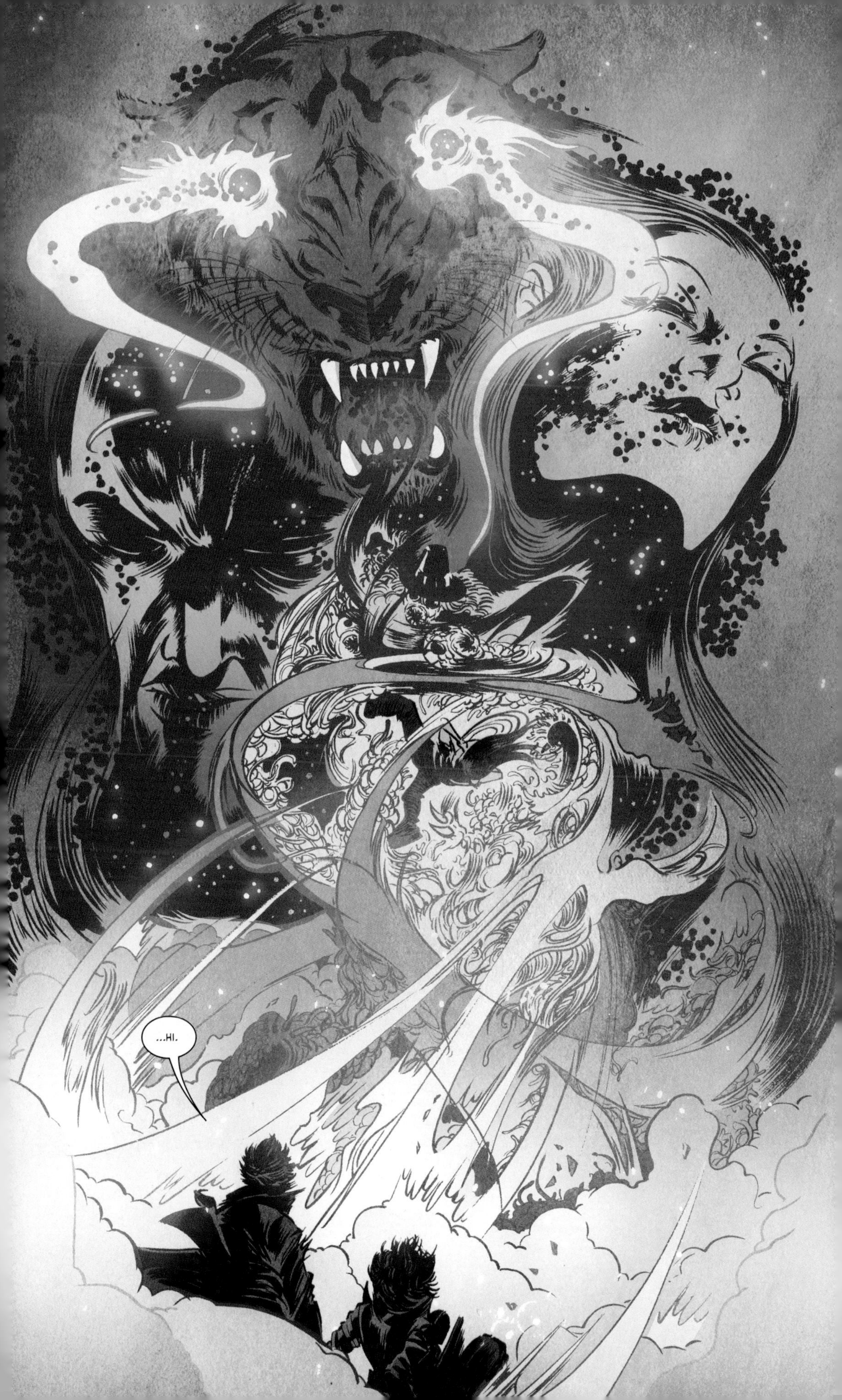
...HI.

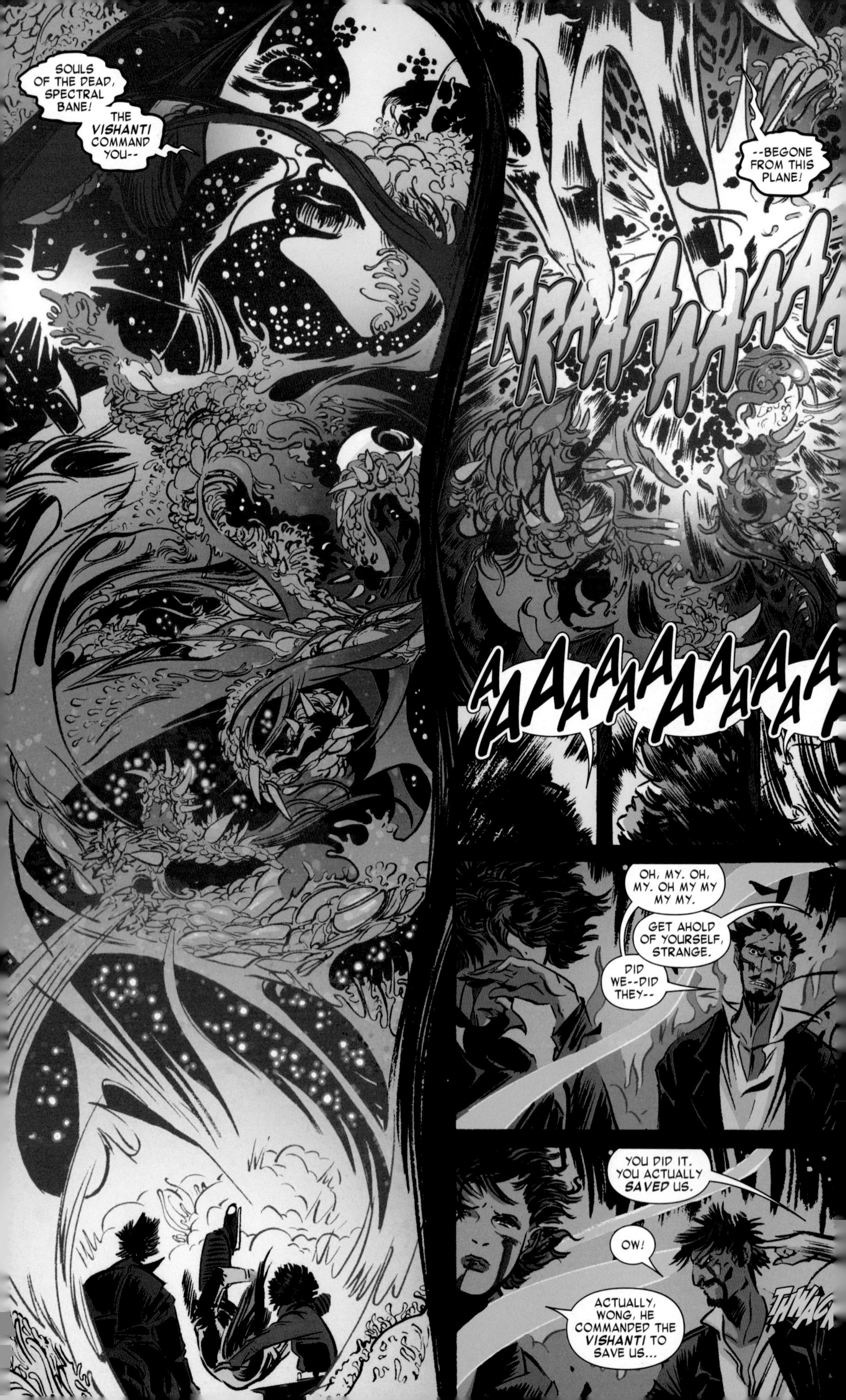
SOULS OF THE DEAD, SPECTRAL BANE!
THE VISHANTI COMMAND YOU--
--BEGONE FROM THIS PLANE!
RRAAAAAAAAAAA
AAAAAAAAAAAA
OH, MY. OH, MY. OH MY MY MY MY.
GET AHOLD OF YOURSELF, STRANGE.
DID WE--DID THEY--
YOU DID IT. YOU ACTUALLY SAVED US.
OW!
ACTUALLY, WONG, HE COMMANDED THE VISHANTI TO SAVE US...

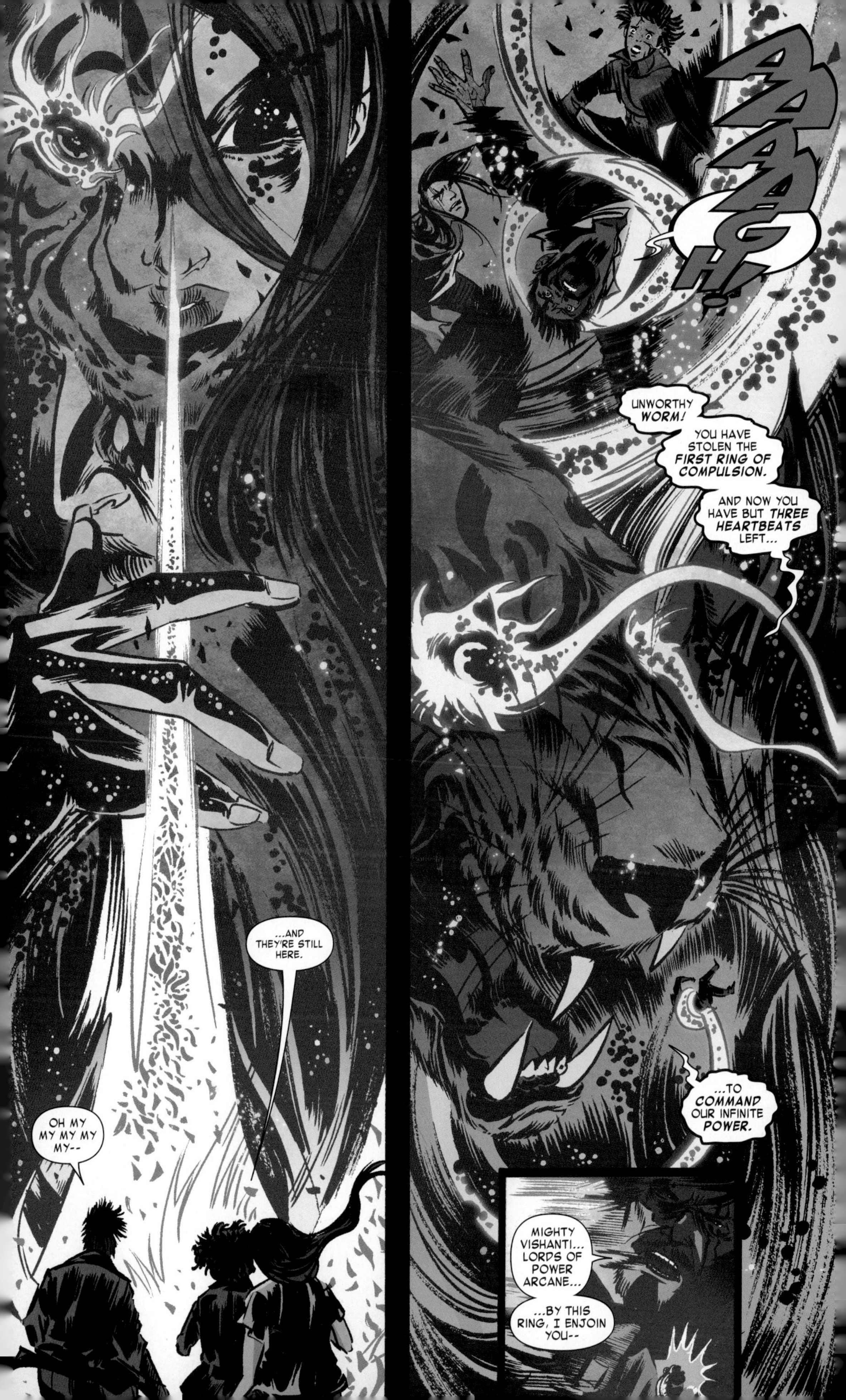

...AND THEY'RE STILL HERE.
OH MY MY MY MY MY--
AAAAGH!
UNWORTHY WORM!
YOU HAVE STOLEN THE FIRST RING OF COMPULSION.
AND NOW YOU HAVE BUT THREE HEARTBEATS LEFT...
...TO COMMAND OUR INFINITE POWER.
MIGHTY VISHANTI... LORDS OF POWER ARCANE...
...BY THIS RING, I ENJOIN YOU--

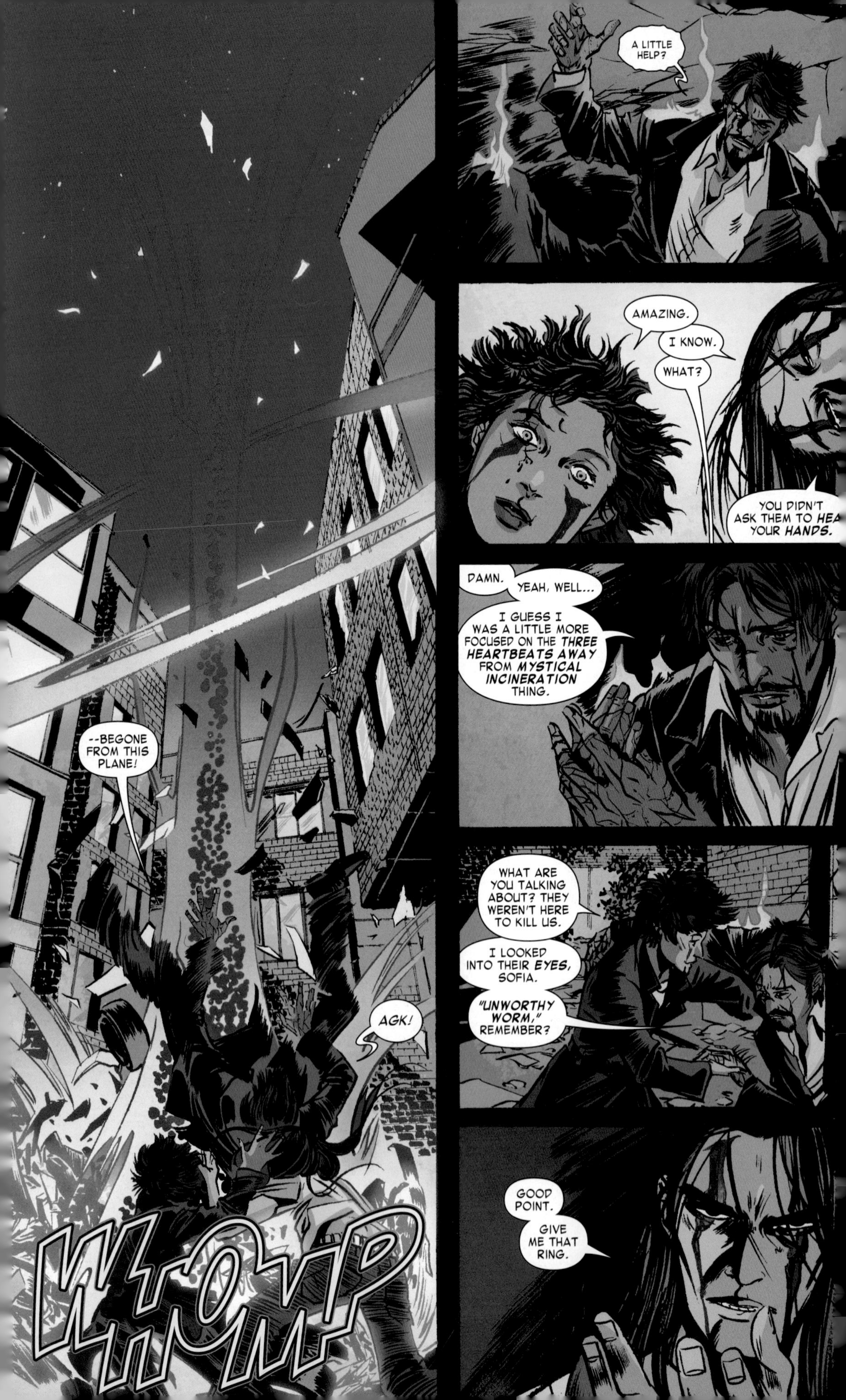
--BEGONE FROM THIS PLANE!
AGK!
WHOOMP
A LITTLE HELP?
AMAZING.
I KNOW.
WHAT?
YOU DIDN'T ASK THEM TO HEA YOUR HANDS.
DAMN.
YEAH, WELL...
I GUESS I WAS A LITTLE MORE FOCUSED ON THE THREE HEARTBEATS AWAY FROM MYSTICAL INCINERATION THING.
WHAT ARE YOU TALKING ABOUT? THEY WEREN'T HERE TO KILL US.
I LOOKED INTO THEIR EYES, SOFIA.
"UNWORTHY WORM," REMEMBER?
GOOD POINT.
GIVE ME THAT RING.

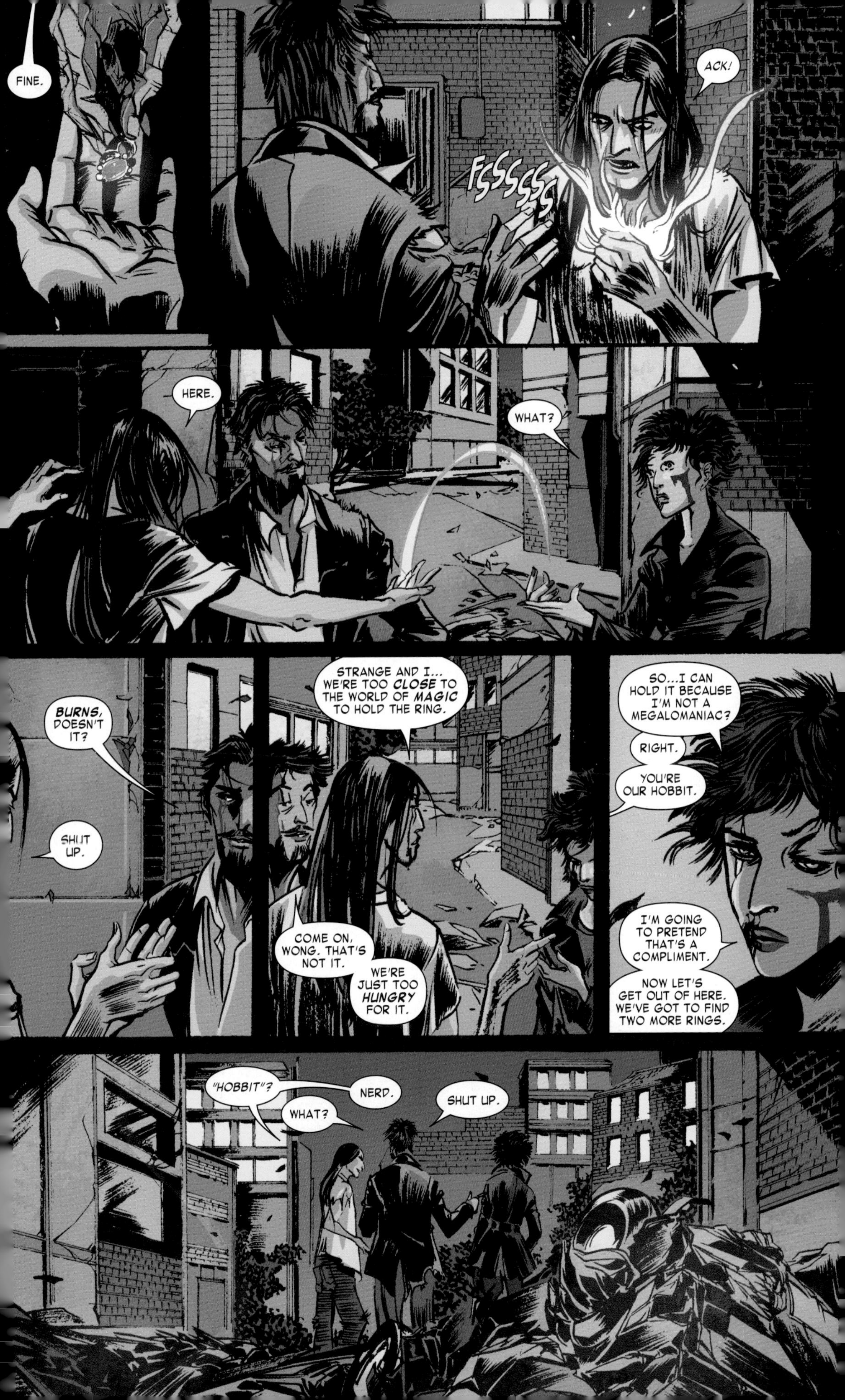
FINE.
ACK!
FSSSSSS
HERE.
WHAT?
BURNS, DOESN'T IT?
SHUT UP.
STRANGE AND I... WE'RE TOO CLOSE TO THE WORLD OF MAGIC TO HOLD THE RING.
COME ON, WONG. THAT'S NOT IT.
WE'RE JUST TOO HUNGRY FOR IT.
SO...I CAN HOLD IT BECAUSE I'M NOT A MEGALOMANIAC?
RIGHT.
YOU'RE OUR HOBBIT.
I'M GOING TO PRETEND THAT'S A COMPLIMENT.
NOW LET'S GET OUT OF HERE. WE'VE GOT TO FIND TWO MORE RINGS.
"HOBBIT"?
NERD.
WHAT?
SHUT UP.

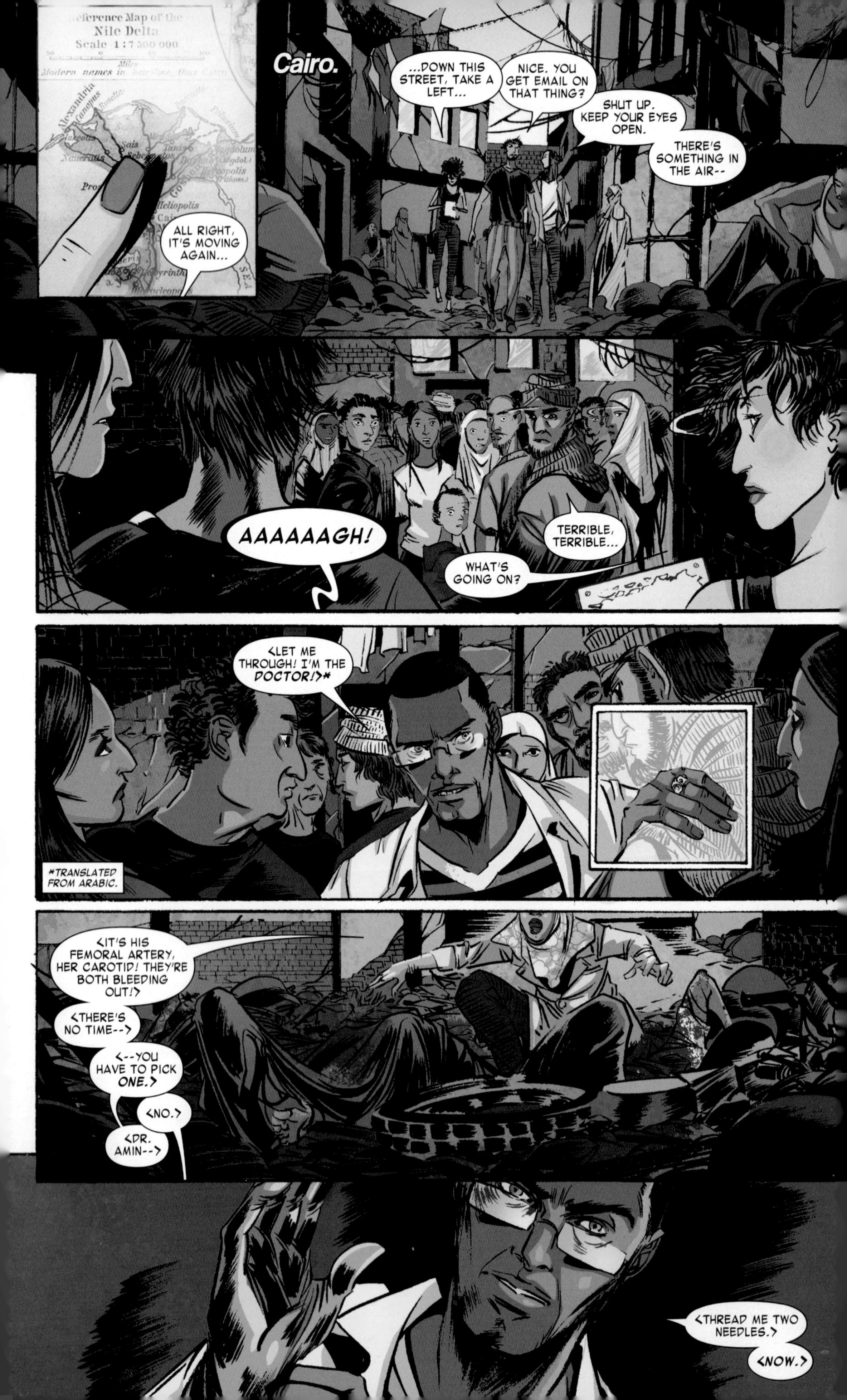
Nile Delta
Scale 1:7 500 000
Cairo.
ALL RIGHT, IT'S MOVING AGAIN...
...DOWN THIS STREET, TAKE A LEFT...
NICE. YOU GET EMAIL ON THAT THING?
SHUT UP. KEEP YOUR EYES OPEN.
THERE'S SOMETHING IN THE AIR--
AAAAAAGH!
TERRIBLE, TERRIBLE...
WHAT'S GOING ON?
<LET ME THROUGH! I'M THE *DOCTOR!*>*
*TRANSLATED FROM ARABIC.
<IT'S HIS FEMORAL ARTERY, HER CAROTID! THEY'RE BOTH BLEEDING OUT!>
<THERE'S NO TIME-->
<--YOU HAVE TO PICK *ONE.*>
<NO.>
<DR. AMIN-->
<THREAD ME TWO NEEDLES.>
<*NOW.*>

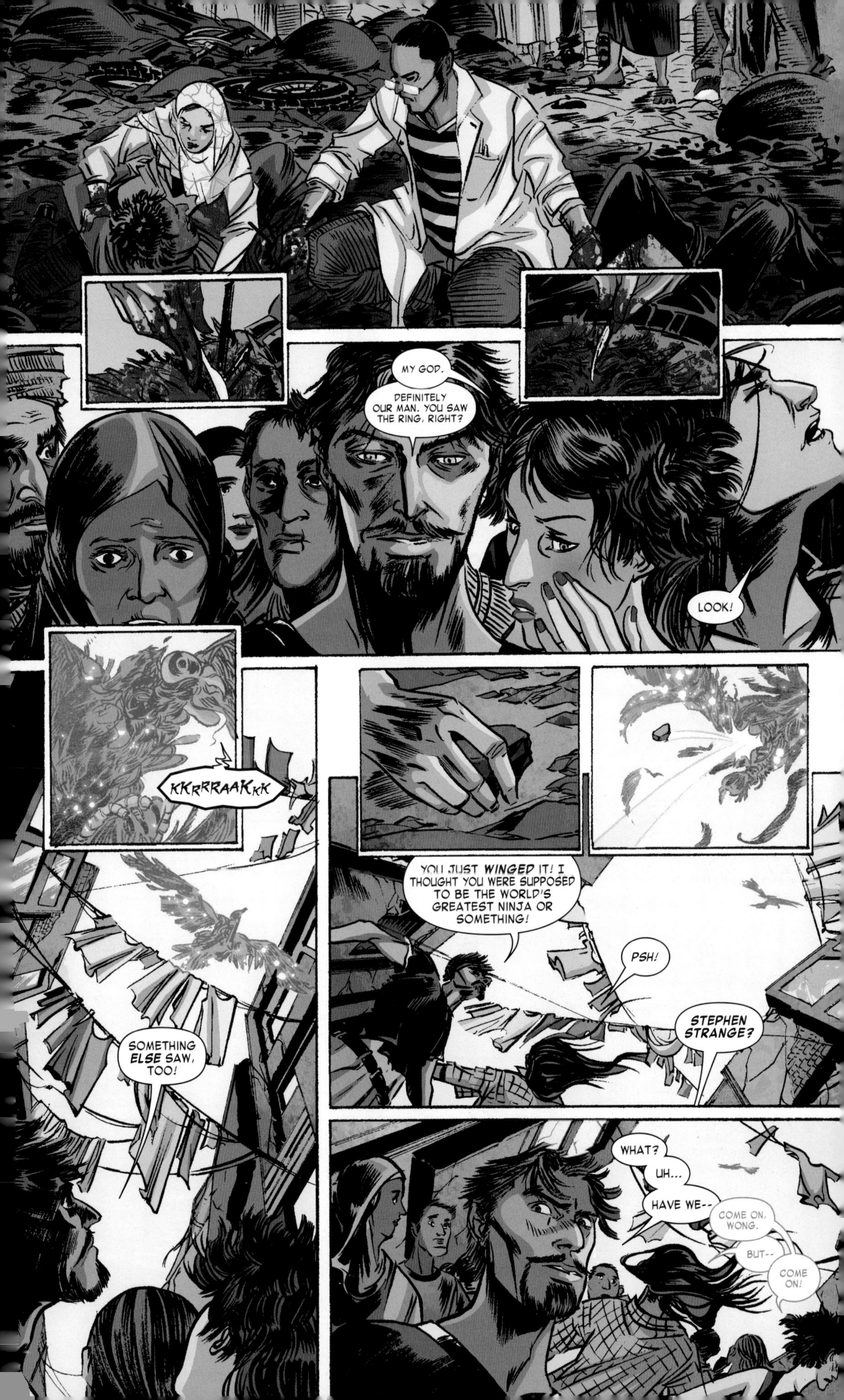
MY GOD.
DEFINITELY OUR MAN. YOU SAW THE RING, RIGHT?
LOOK!
KKRRRAAKKK
SOMETHING ELSE SAW, TOO!
YOU JUST WINGED IT! I THOUGHT YOU WERE SUPPOSED TO BE THE WORLD'S GREATEST NINJA OR SOMETHING!
PSH!
STEPHEN STRANGE?
WHAT?
UH...
HAVE WE--
COME ON, WONG.
BUT--
COME ON!

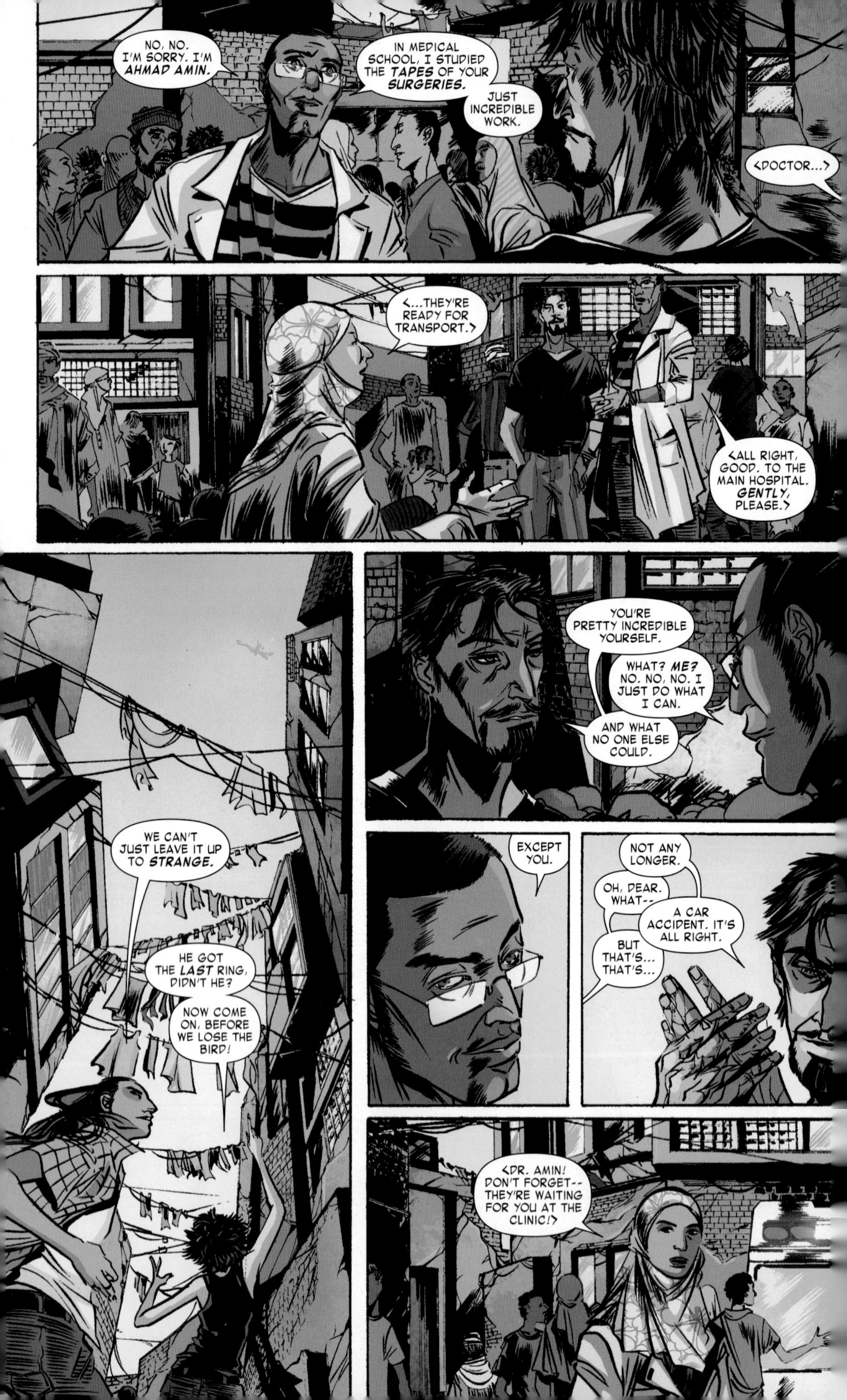

NO, NO. I'M SORRY. I'M AHMAD AMIN.
IN MEDICAL SCHOOL, I STUDIED THE TAPES OF YOUR SURGERIES.
JUST INCREDIBLE WORK.
<DOCTOR...>
<...THEY'RE READY FOR TRANSPORT.>
<ALL RIGHT, GOOD. TO THE MAIN HOSPITAL. GENTLY, PLEASE.>
WE CAN'T JUST LEAVE IT UP TO STRANGE.
HE GOT THE LAST RING, DIDN'T HE?
NOW COME ON, BEFORE WE LOSE THE BIRD!
YOU'RE PRETTY INCREDIBLE YOURSELF.
WHAT? ME? NO. NO, NO. I JUST DO WHAT I CAN.
AND WHAT NO ONE ELSE COULD.
EXCEPT YOU.
NOT ANY LONGER.
OH, DEAR. WHAT--
A CAR ACCIDENT. IT'S ALL RIGHT.
BUT THAT'S... THAT'S...
<DR. AMIN! DON'T FORGET-- THEY'RE WAITING FOR YOU AT THE CLINIC!>

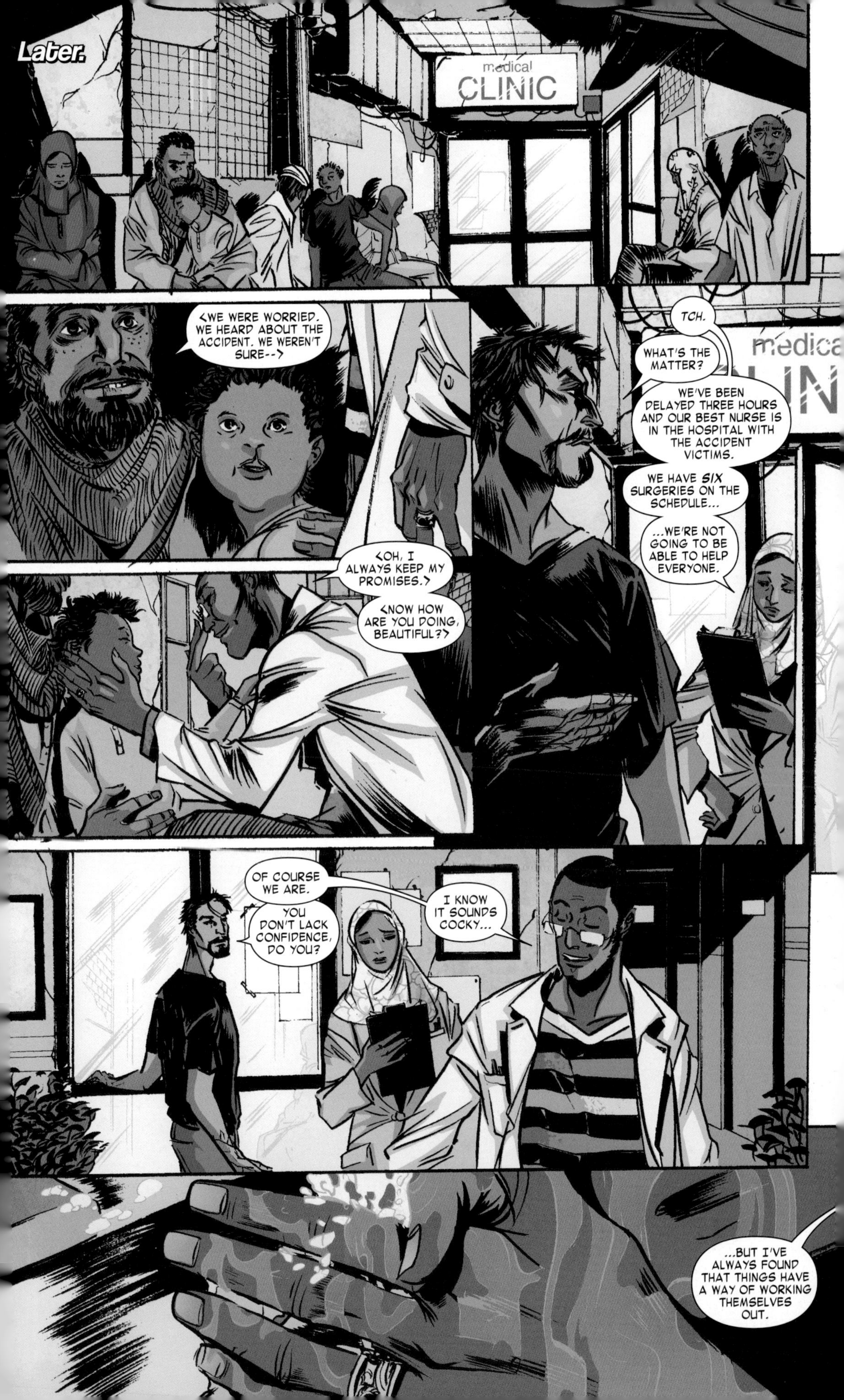
Later.
medical CLINIC
<WE WERE WORRIED. WE HEARD ABOUT THE ACCIDENT. WE WEREN'T SURE-->
<OH, I ALWAYS KEEP MY PROMISES.>
<NOW HOW ARE YOU DOING, BEAUTIFUL?>
TCH.
WHAT'S THE MATTER?
WE'VE BEEN DELAYED THREE HOURS AND OUR BEST NURSE IS IN THE HOSPITAL WITH THE ACCIDENT VICTIMS.
WE HAVE *SIX* SURGERIES ON THE SCHEDULE...
...WE'RE NOT GOING TO BE ABLE TO HELP EVERYONE.
OF COURSE WE ARE.
YOU DON'T LACK CONFIDENCE, DO YOU?
I KNOW IT SOUNDS COCKY...
...BUT I'VE ALWAYS FOUND THAT THINGS HAVE A WAY OF WORKING THEMSELVES OUT.

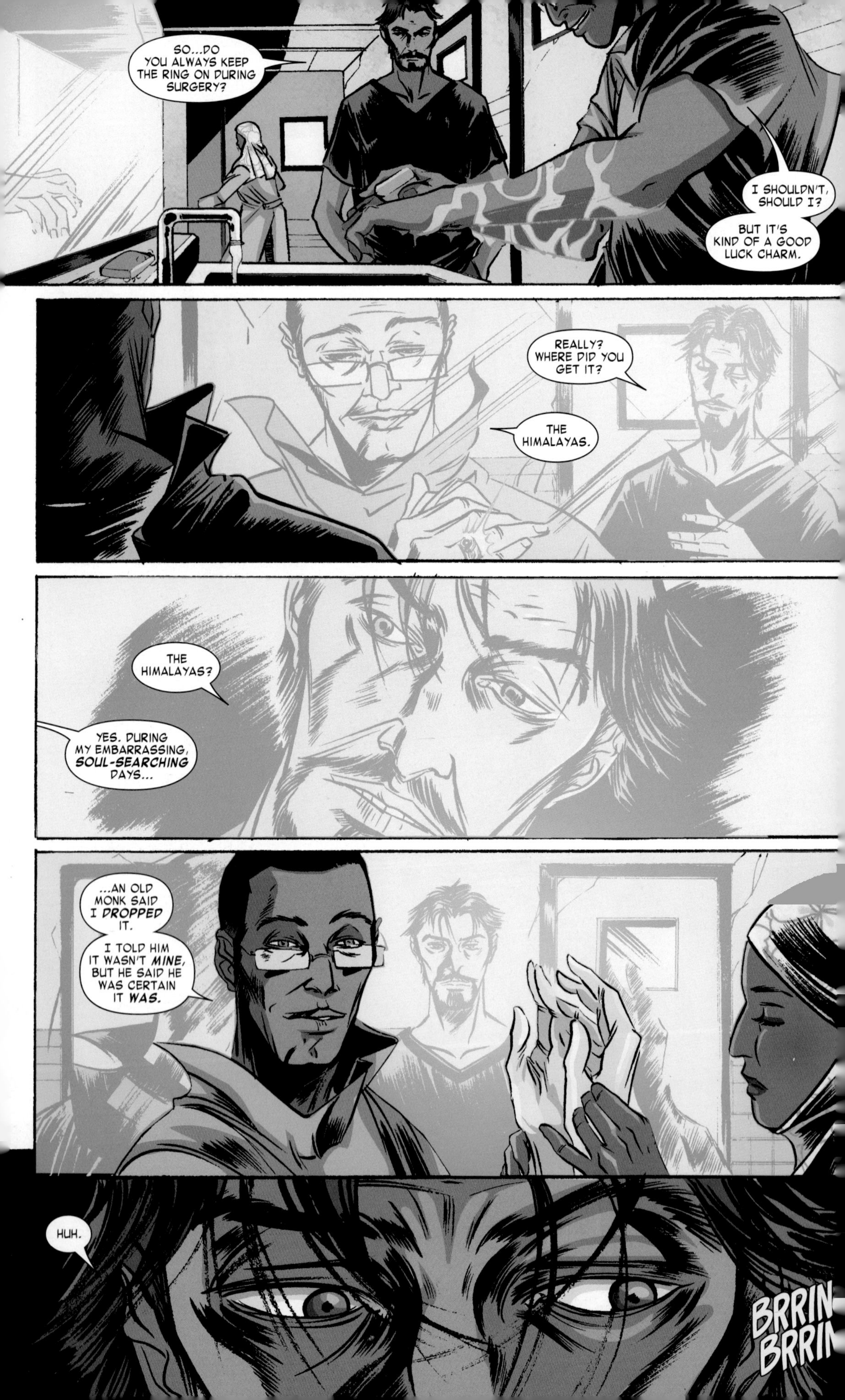
SO...DO YOU ALWAYS KEEP THE RING ON DURING SURGERY?
I SHOULDN'T, SHOULD I?
BUT IT'S KIND OF A GOOD LUCK CHARM.
REALLY? WHERE DID YOU GET IT?
THE HIMALAYAS.
THE HIMALAYAS?
YES. DURING MY EMBARRASSING, SOUL-SEARCHING DAYS...
...AN OLD MONK SAID I DROPPED IT.
I TOLD HIM IT WASN'T MINE, BUT HE SAID HE WAS CERTAIN IT WAS.
HUH.
BRRIN BRRIN

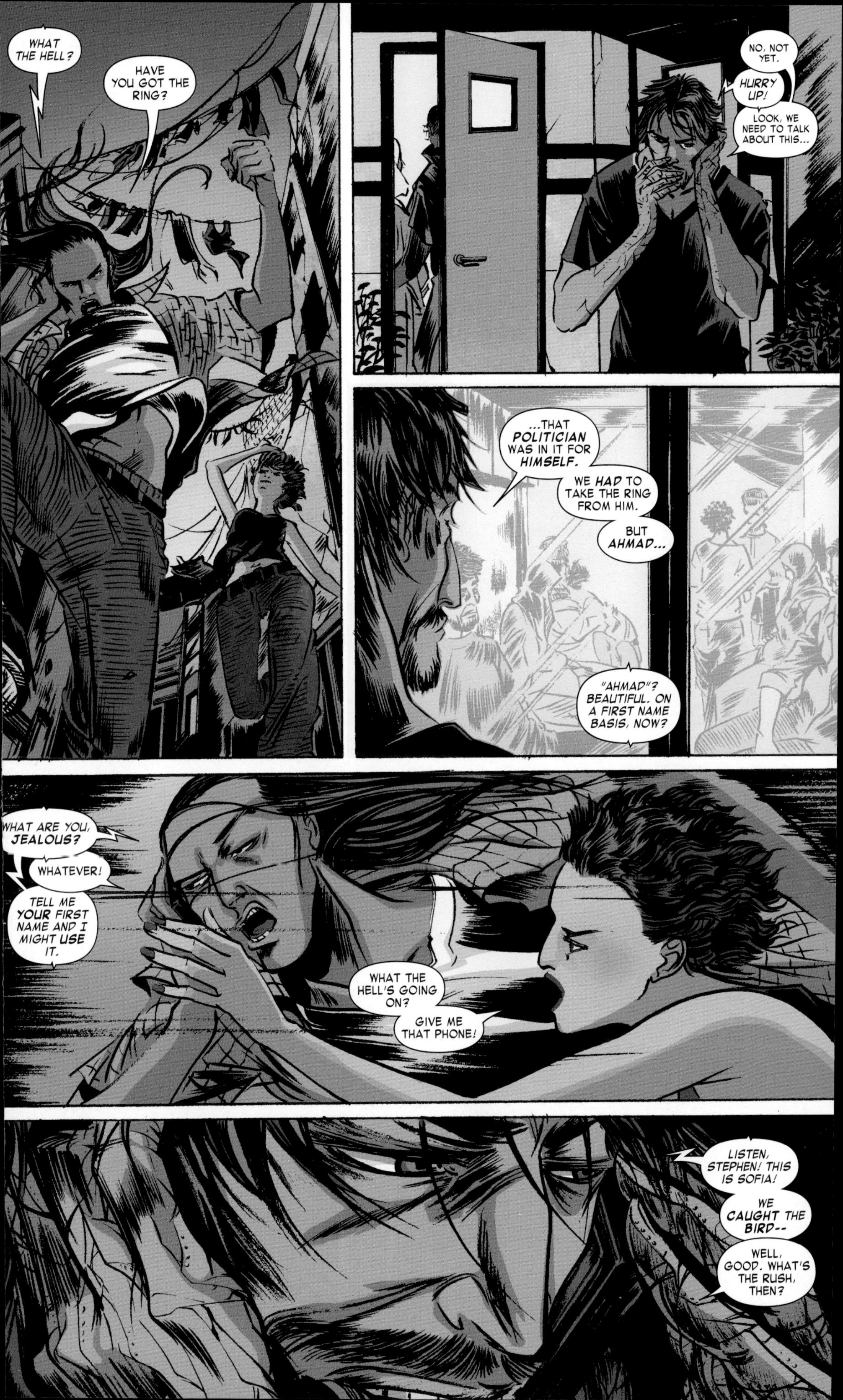
WHAT THE HELL?
HAVE YOU GOT THE RING?
NO, NOT YET.
HURRY UP!
LOOK, WE NEED TO TALK ABOUT THIS...
...THAT POLITICIAN WAS IN IT FOR HIMSELF.
WE HAD TO TAKE THE RING FROM HIM.
BUT AHMAD...
"AHMAD"? BEAUTIFUL. ON A FIRST NAME BASIS, NOW?
WHAT ARE YOU, JEALOUS?
WHATEVER!
TELL ME YOUR FIRST NAME AND I MIGHT USE IT.
WHAT THE HELL'S GOING ON?
GIVE ME THAT PHONE!
LISTEN, STEPHEN! THIS IS SOFIA!
WE CAUGHT THE BIRD--
WELL, GOOD. WHAT'S THE RUSH, THEN?

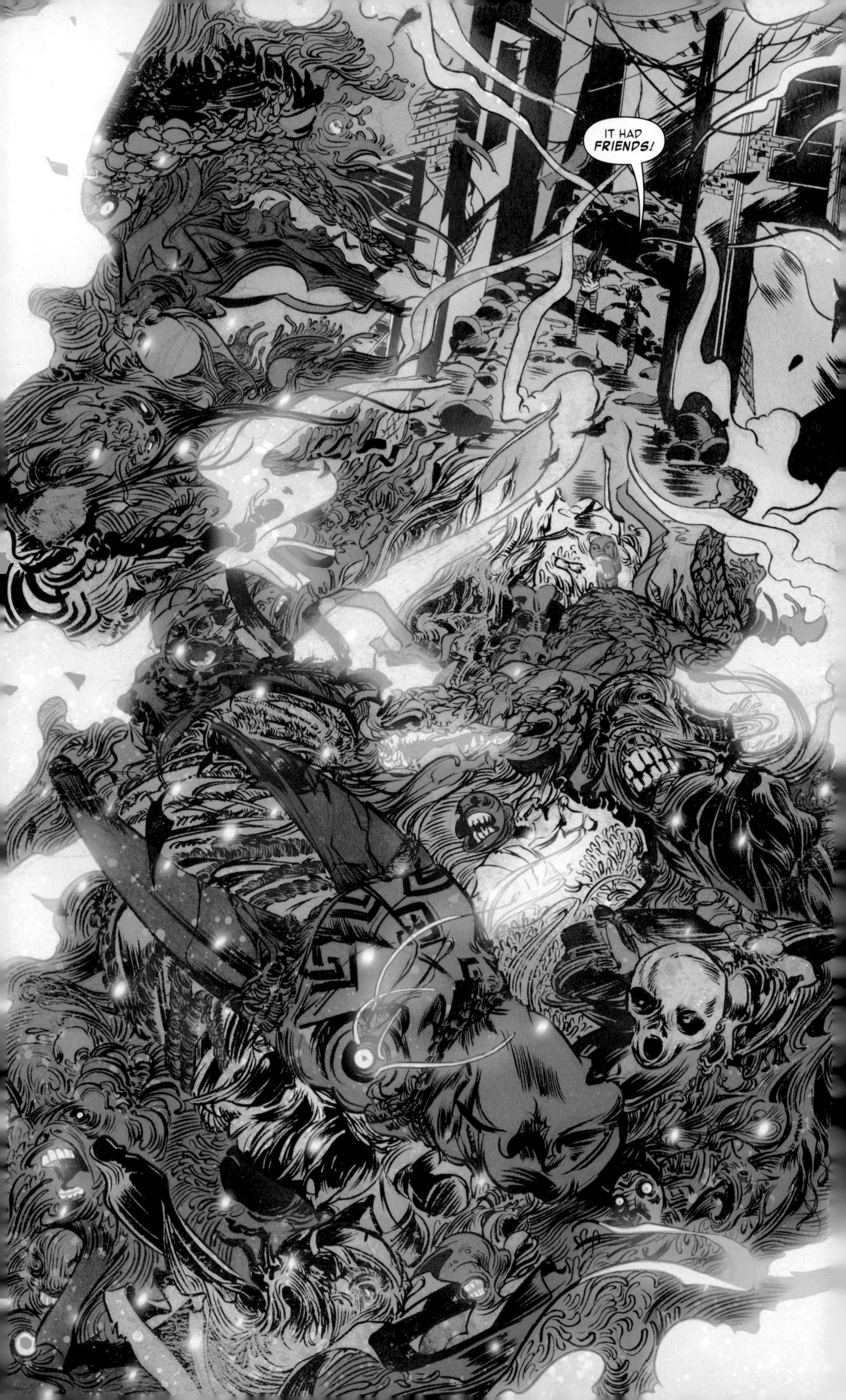
IT HAD FRIENDS!

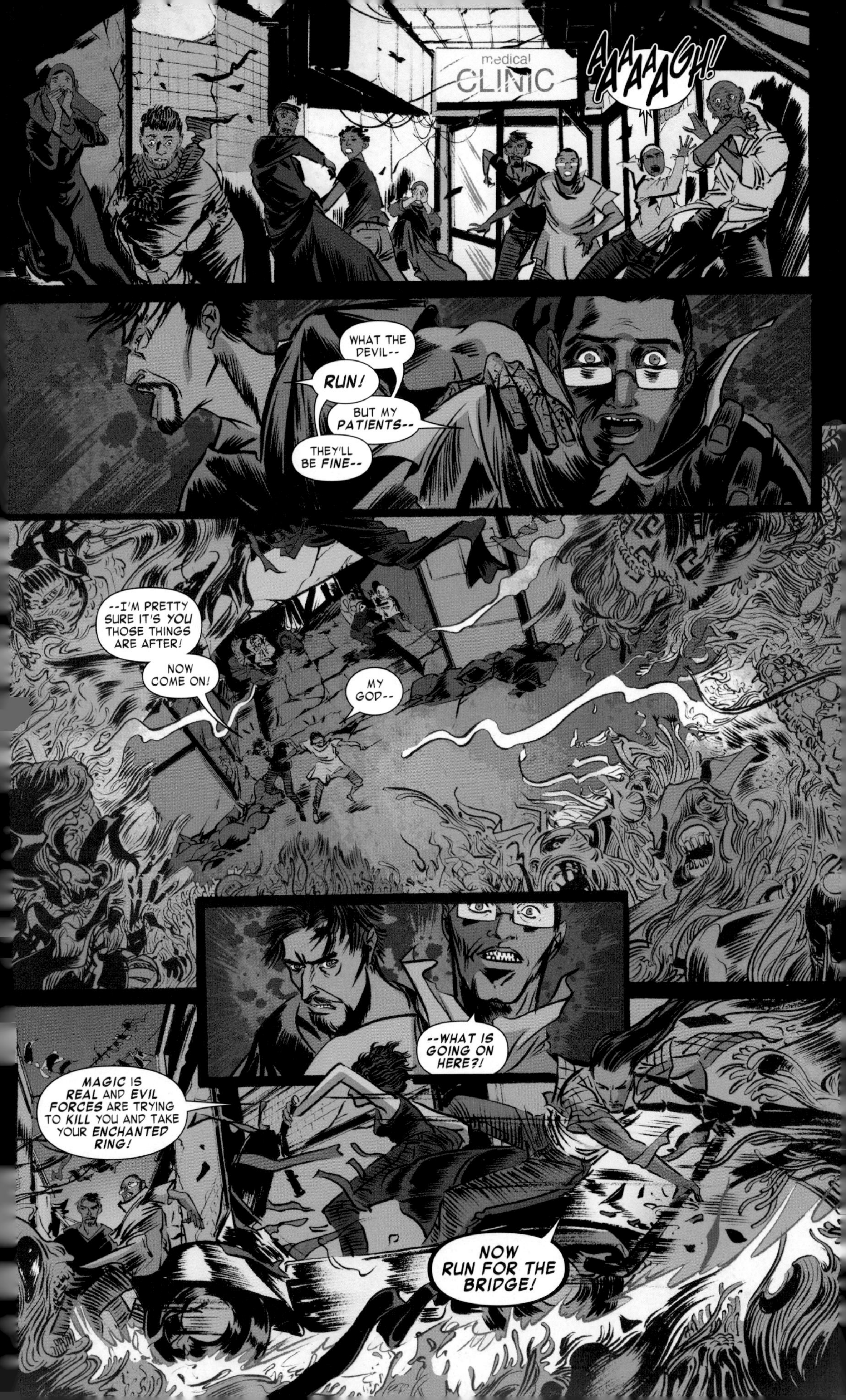
medical CLINIC
AAAAAAGH!
WHAT THE DEVIL--
RUN!
BUT MY PATIENTS--
THEY'LL BE FINE--
--I'M PRETTY SURE IT'S YOU THOSE THINGS ARE AFTER!
NOW COME ON!
MY GOD--
--WHAT IS GOING ON HERE?!
MAGIC IS REAL AND EVIL FORCES ARE TRYING TO KILL YOU AND TAKE YOUR ENCHANTED RING!
NOW RUN FOR THE BRIDGE!

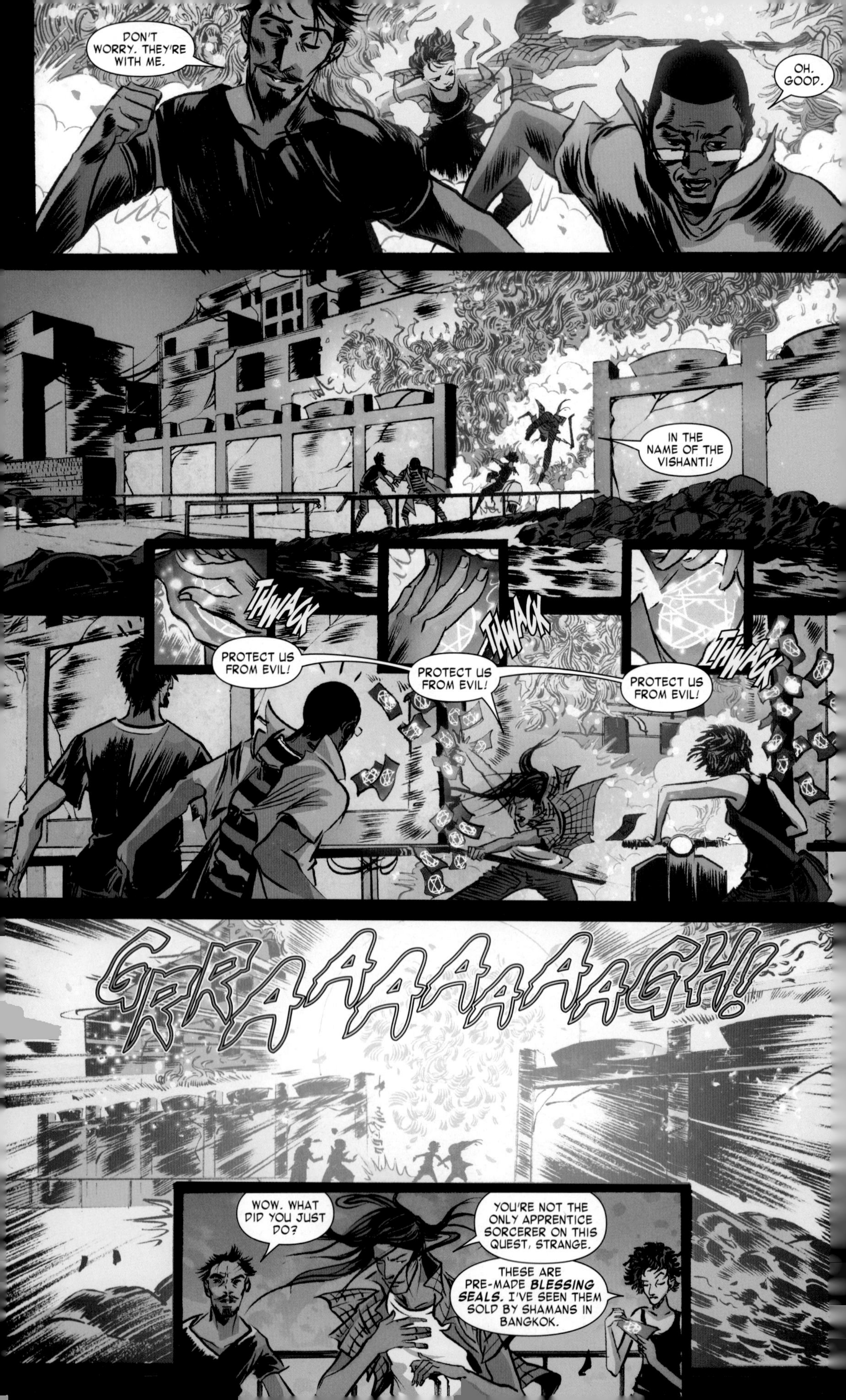
DON'T WORRY. THEY'RE WITH ME.
OH. GOOD.
IN THE NAME OF THE VISHANTI!
THWACK
PROTECT US FROM EVIL!
THWACK
PROTECT US FROM EVIL!
THWACK
PROTECT US FROM EVIL!
GRAAAAAAAGH!
WOW. WHAT DID YOU JUST DO?
YOU'RE NOT THE ONLY APPRENTICE SORCERER ON THIS QUEST, STRANGE.
THESE ARE PRE-MADE BLESSING SEALS. I'VE SEEN THEM SOLD BY SHAMANS IN BANGKOK.

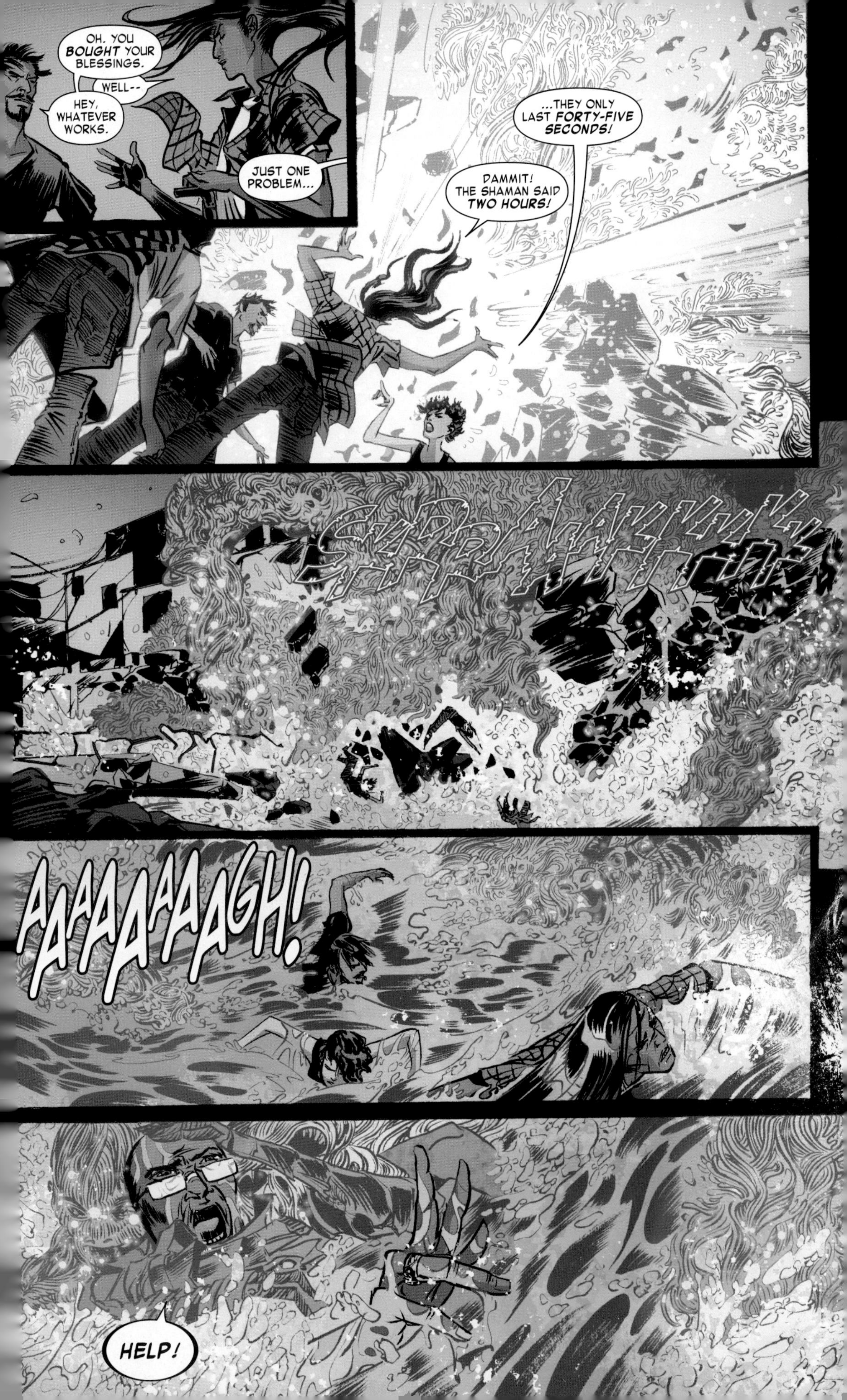
OH. YOU BOUGHT YOUR BLESSINGS.
WELL--
HEY, WHATEVER WORKS.
JUST ONE PROBLEM...
...THEY ONLY LAST FORTY-FIVE SECONDS!
DAMMIT! THE SHAMAN SAID TWO HOURS!
AAAAAAAGH!
HELP!

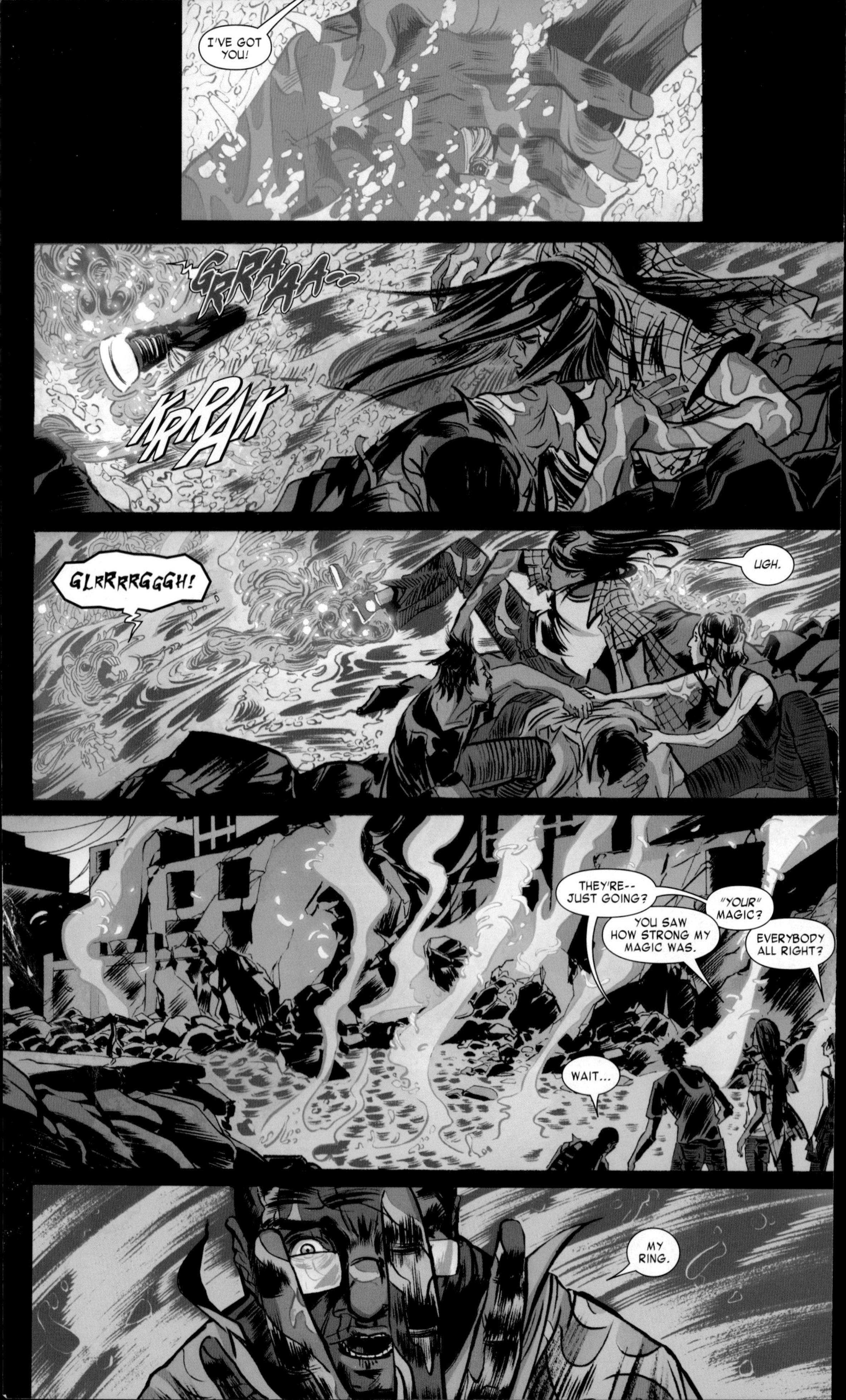
I'VE GOT YOU!
GRRAAA--
KRRAK
GLRRRRGGGH!
UGH.
THEY'RE-- JUST GOING?
"YOUR" MAGIC?
YOU SAW HOW STRONG MY MAGIC WAS.
EVERYBODY ALL RIGHT?
WAIT...
MY RING.

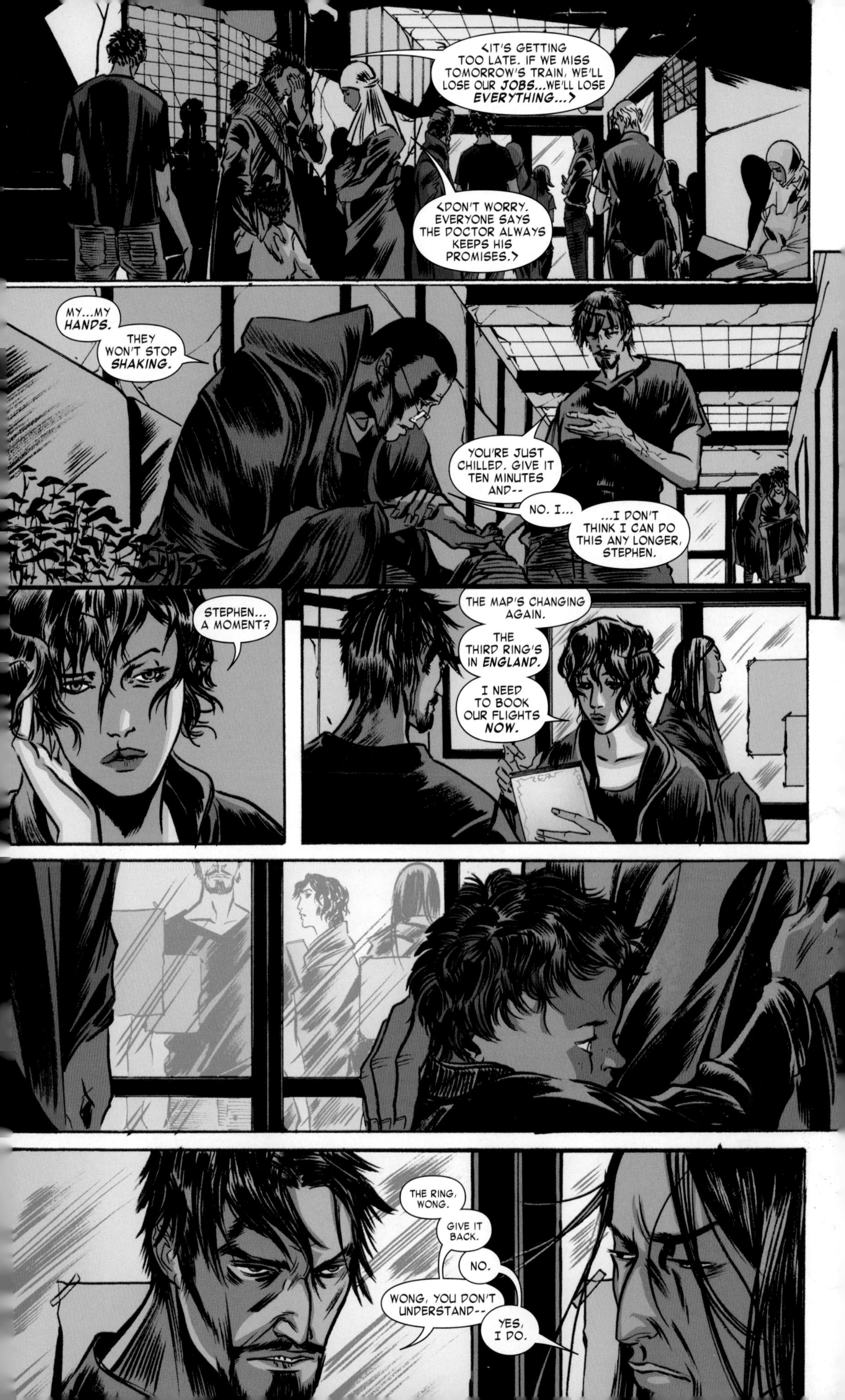

<IT'S GETTING TOO LATE. IF WE MISS TOMORROW'S TRAIN, WE'LL LOSE OUR JOBS...WE'LL LOSE EVERYTHING...>
<DON'T WORRY. EVERYONE SAYS THE DOCTOR ALWAYS KEEPS HIS PROMISES.>
MY...MY HANDS.
THEY WON'T STOP SHAKING.
YOU'RE JUST CHILLED. GIVE IT TEN MINUTES AND--
NO. I...
...I DON'T THINK I CAN DO THIS ANY LONGER, STEPHEN.
STEPHEN... A MOMENT?
THE MAP'S CHANGING AGAIN.
THE THIRD RING'S IN ENGLAND.
I NEED TO BOOK OUR FLIGHTS NOW.
THE RING, WONG.
GIVE IT BACK.
NO.
WONG, YOU DON'T UNDERSTAND--
YES, I DO.

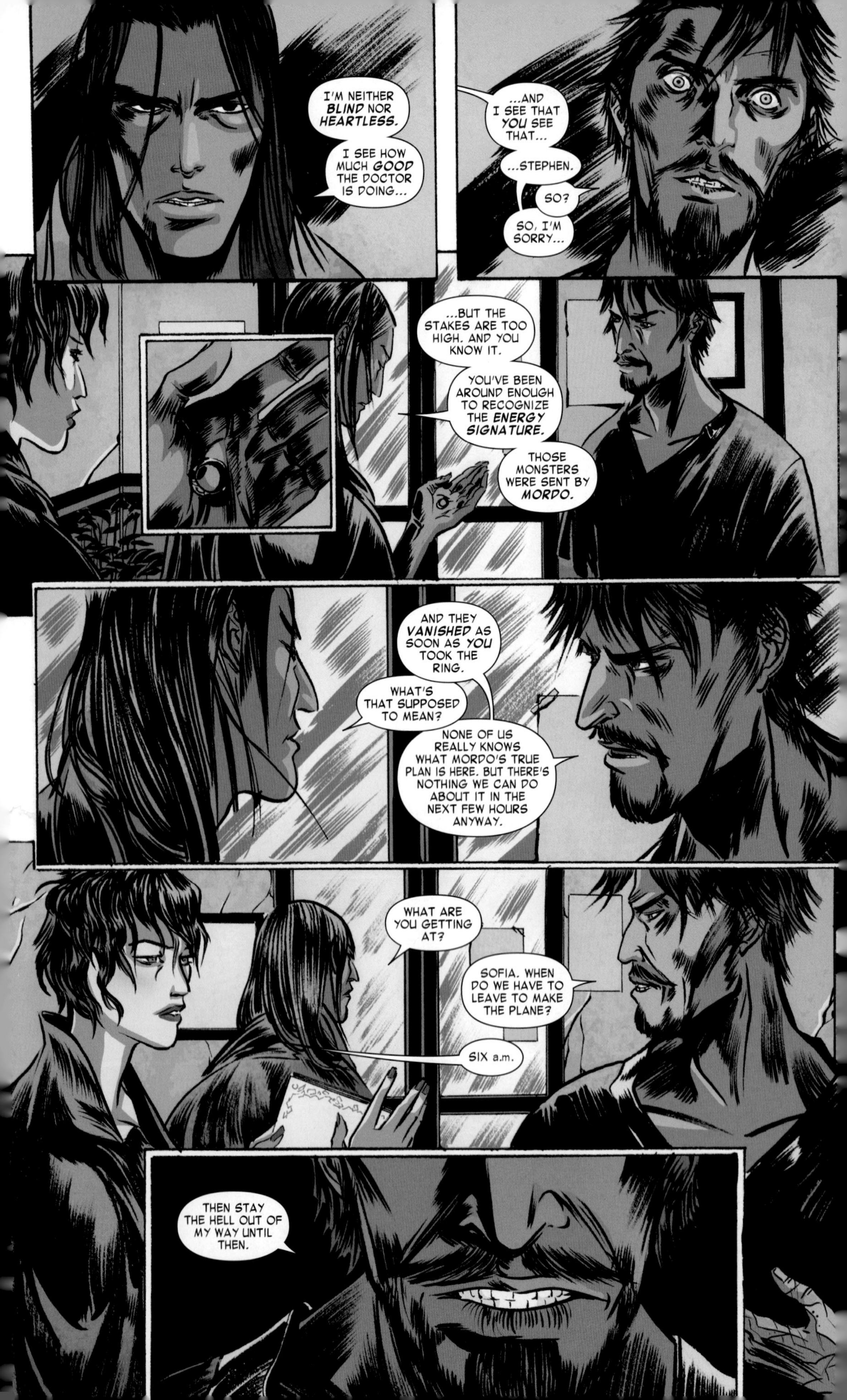
I'M NEITHER BLIND NOR HEARTLESS.
I SEE HOW MUCH GOOD THE DOCTOR IS DOING...
...AND I SEE THAT YOU SEE THAT...
...STEPHEN.
SO?
SO, I'M SORRY...
...BUT THE STAKES ARE TOO HIGH. AND YOU KNOW IT.
YOU'VE BEEN AROUND ENOUGH TO RECOGNIZE THE ENERGY SIGNATURE.
THOSE MONSTERS WERE SENT BY MORDO.
AND THEY VANISHED AS SOON AS YOU TOOK THE RING.
WHAT'S THAT SUPPOSED TO MEAN?
NONE OF US REALLY KNOWS WHAT MORDO'S TRUE PLAN IS HERE. BUT THERE'S NOTHING WE CAN DO ABOUT IT IN THE NEXT FEW HOURS ANYWAY.
WHAT ARE YOU GETTING AT?
SOFIA. WHEN DO WE HAVE TO LEAVE TO MAKE THE PLANE?
SIX a.m.
THEN STAY THE HELL OUT OF MY WAY UNTIL THEN.

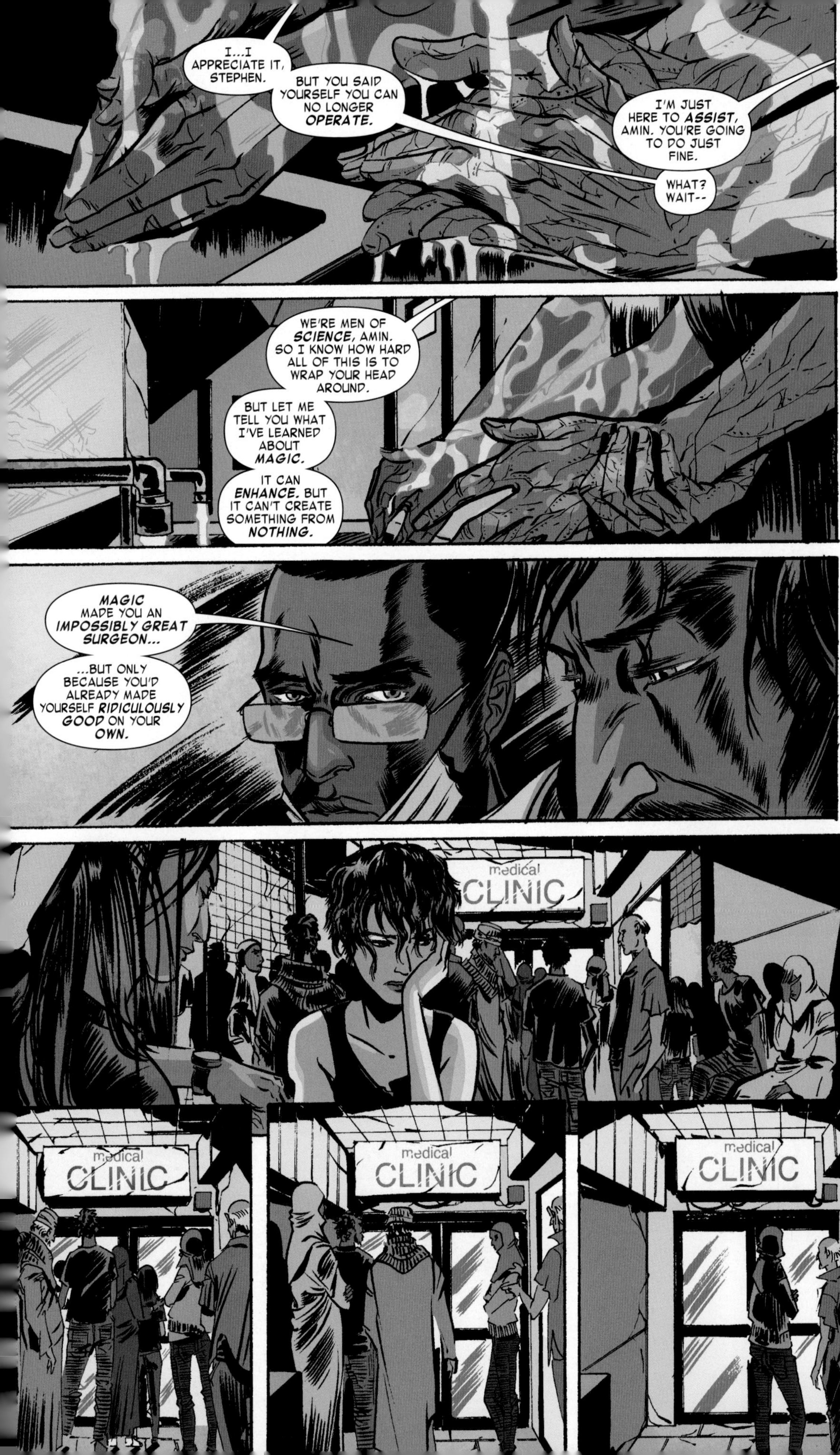
I...I APPRECIATE IT, STEPHEN.
BUT YOU SAID YOURSELF YOU CAN NO LONGER OPERATE.
I'M JUST HERE TO ASSIST, AMIN. YOU'RE GOING TO DO JUST FINE.
WHAT? WAIT--
WE'RE MEN OF SCIENCE, AMIN. SO I KNOW HOW HARD ALL OF THIS IS TO WRAP YOUR HEAD AROUND.
BUT LET ME TELL YOU WHAT I'VE LEARNED ABOUT MAGIC.
IT CAN ENHANCE. BUT IT CAN'T CREATE SOMETHING FROM NOTHING.
MAGIC MADE YOU AN IMPOSSIBLY GREAT SURGEON...
...BUT ONLY BECAUSE YOU'D ALREADY MADE YOURSELF RIDICULOUSLY GOOD ON YOUR OWN.
medical CLINIC
medical CLINIC
medical CLINIC
medical CLINIC

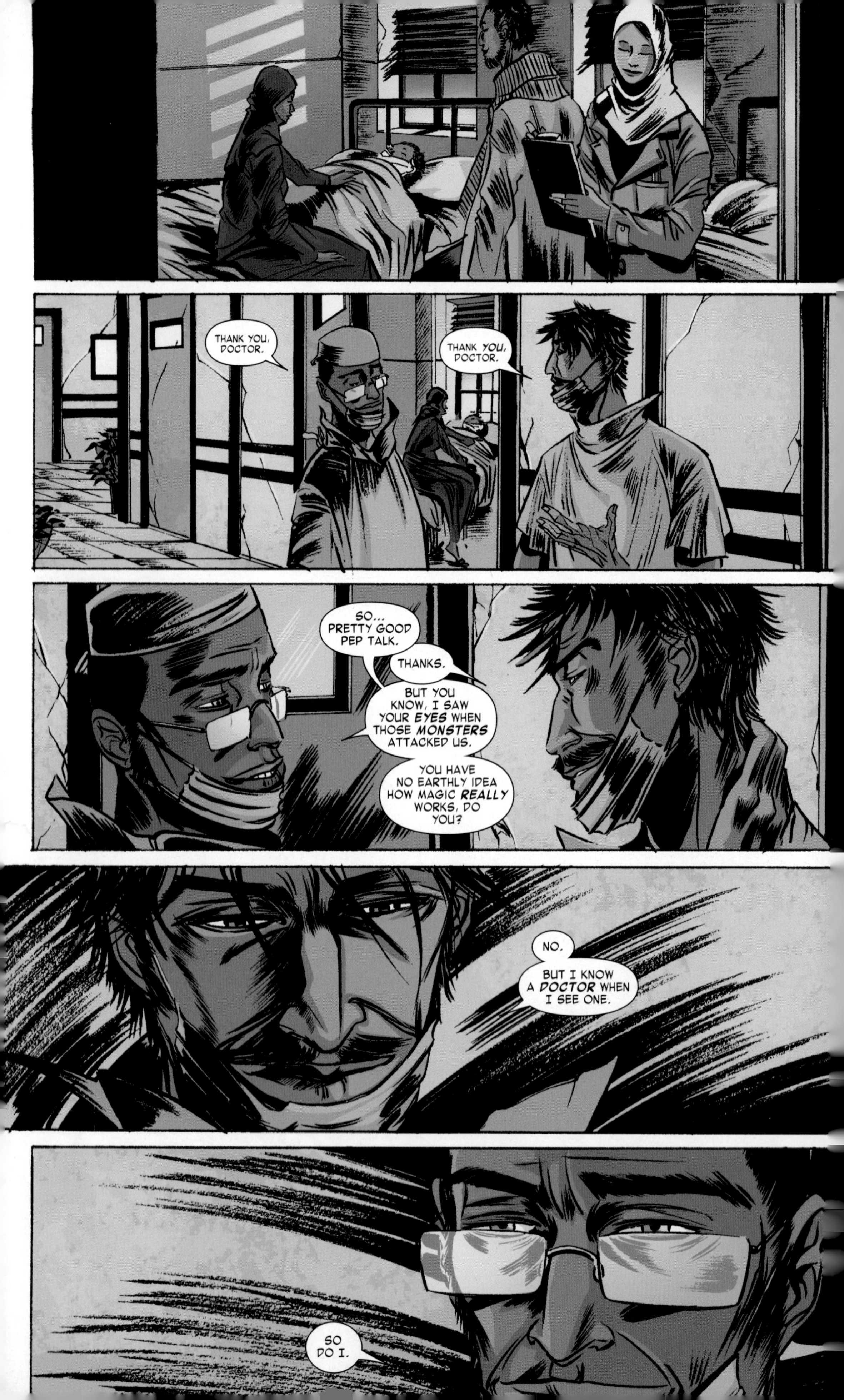
THANK YOU, DOCTOR.
THANK YOU, DOCTOR.
SO... PRETTY GOOD PEP TALK.
THANKS.
BUT YOU KNOW, I SAW YOUR EYES WHEN THOSE MONSTERS ATTACKED US.
YOU HAVE NO EARTHLY IDEA HOW MAGIC REALLY WORKS, DO YOU?
NO.
BUT I KNOW A DOCTOR WHEN I SEE ONE.
SO DO I.

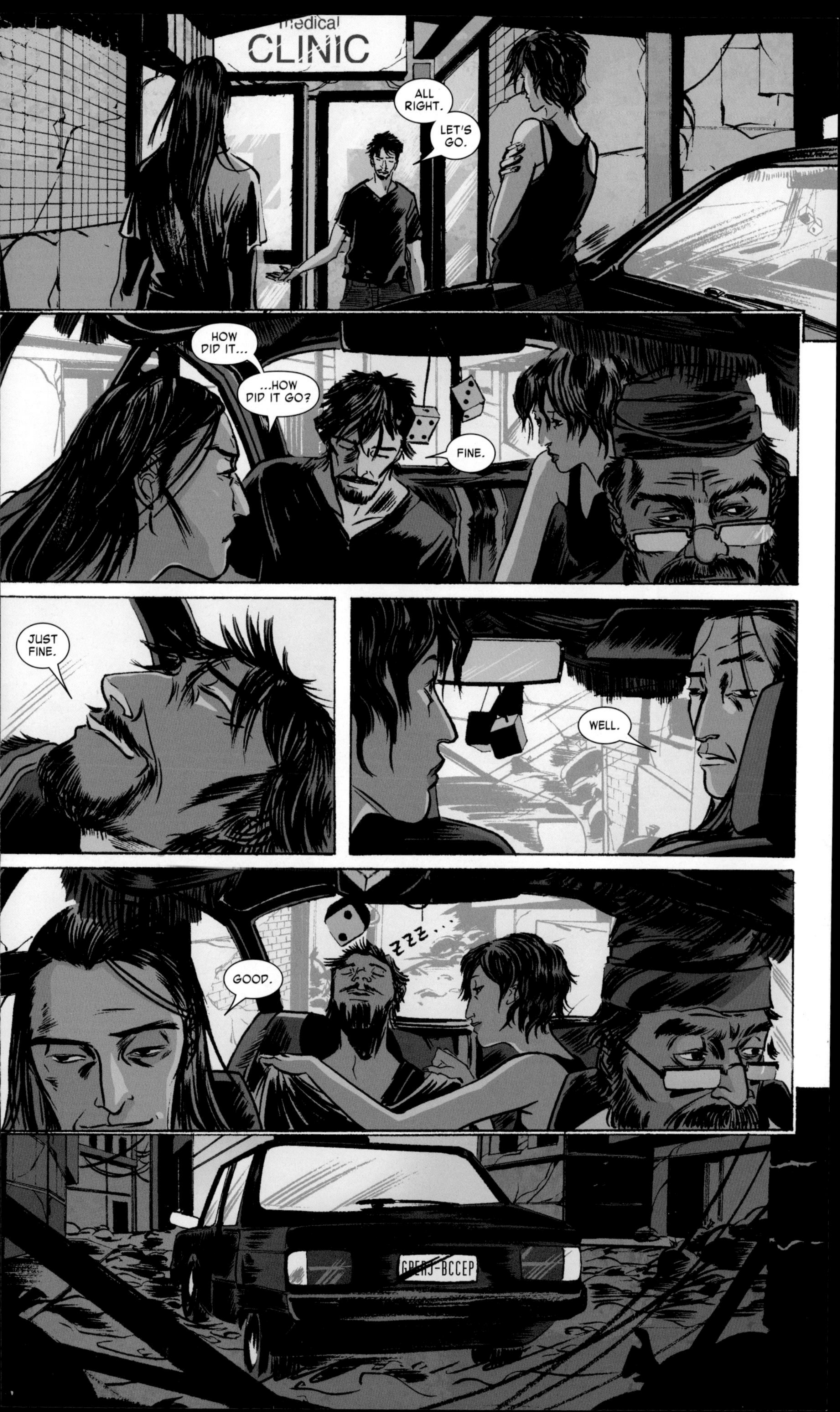
medical
CLINIC
ALL RIGHT.
LET'S GO.
HOW DID IT...
...HOW DID IT GO?
FINE.
JUST FINE.
WELL.
GOOD.
ZZZ...
GPERJ-BCCEP

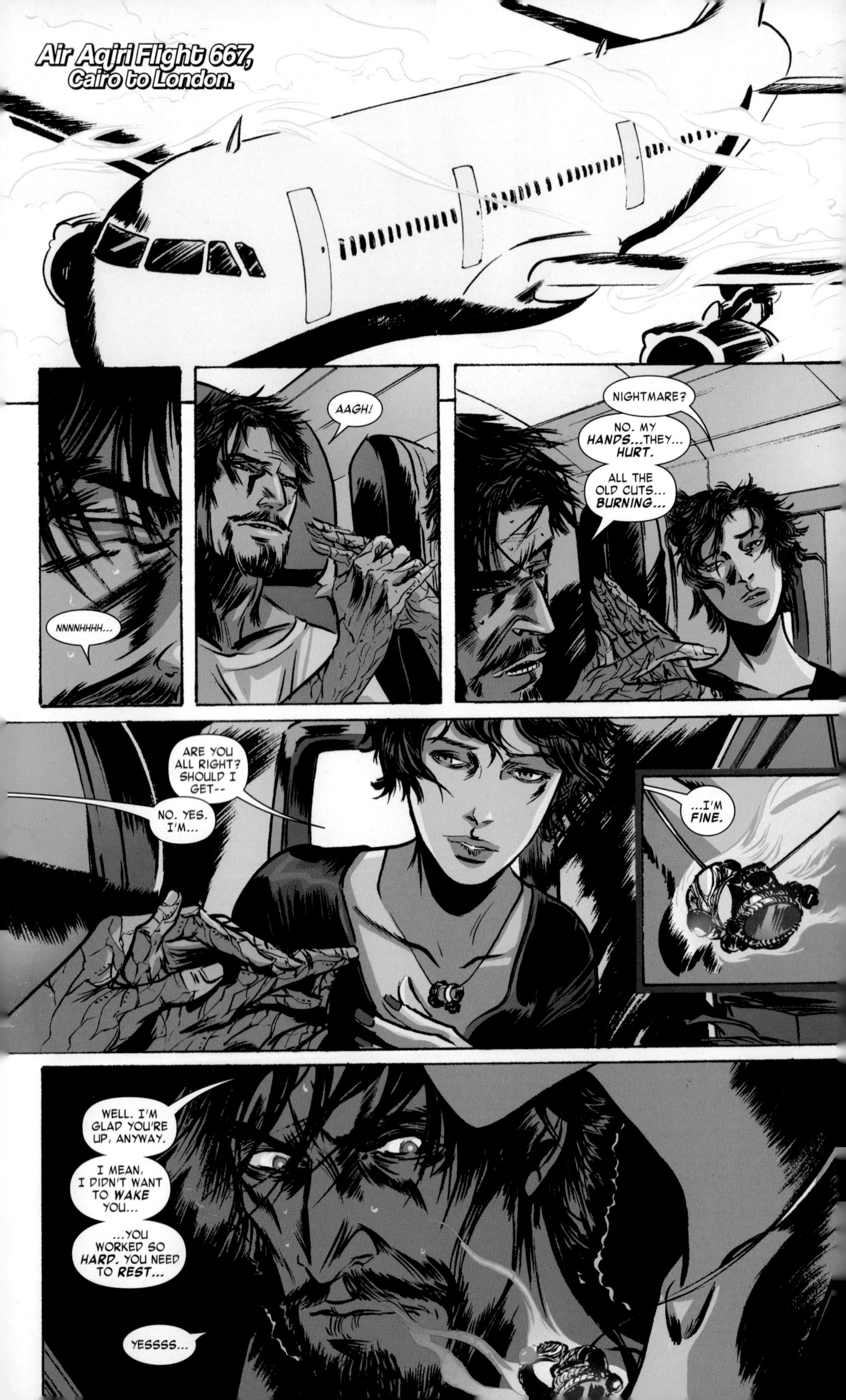

Air Aqjri Flight 667, Cairo to London.
NNNNHHHH...
AAGH!
NIGHTMARE?
NO. MY HANDS...THEY... HURT.
ALL THE OLD CUTS... BURNING...
ARE YOU ALL RIGHT? SHOULD I GET--
NO. YES. I'M...
...I'M FINE.
WELL. I'M GLAD YOU'RE UP, ANYWAY.
I MEAN, I DIDN'T WANT TO WAKE YOU...
...YOU WORKED SO HARD. YOU NEED TO REST...
YESSSS...

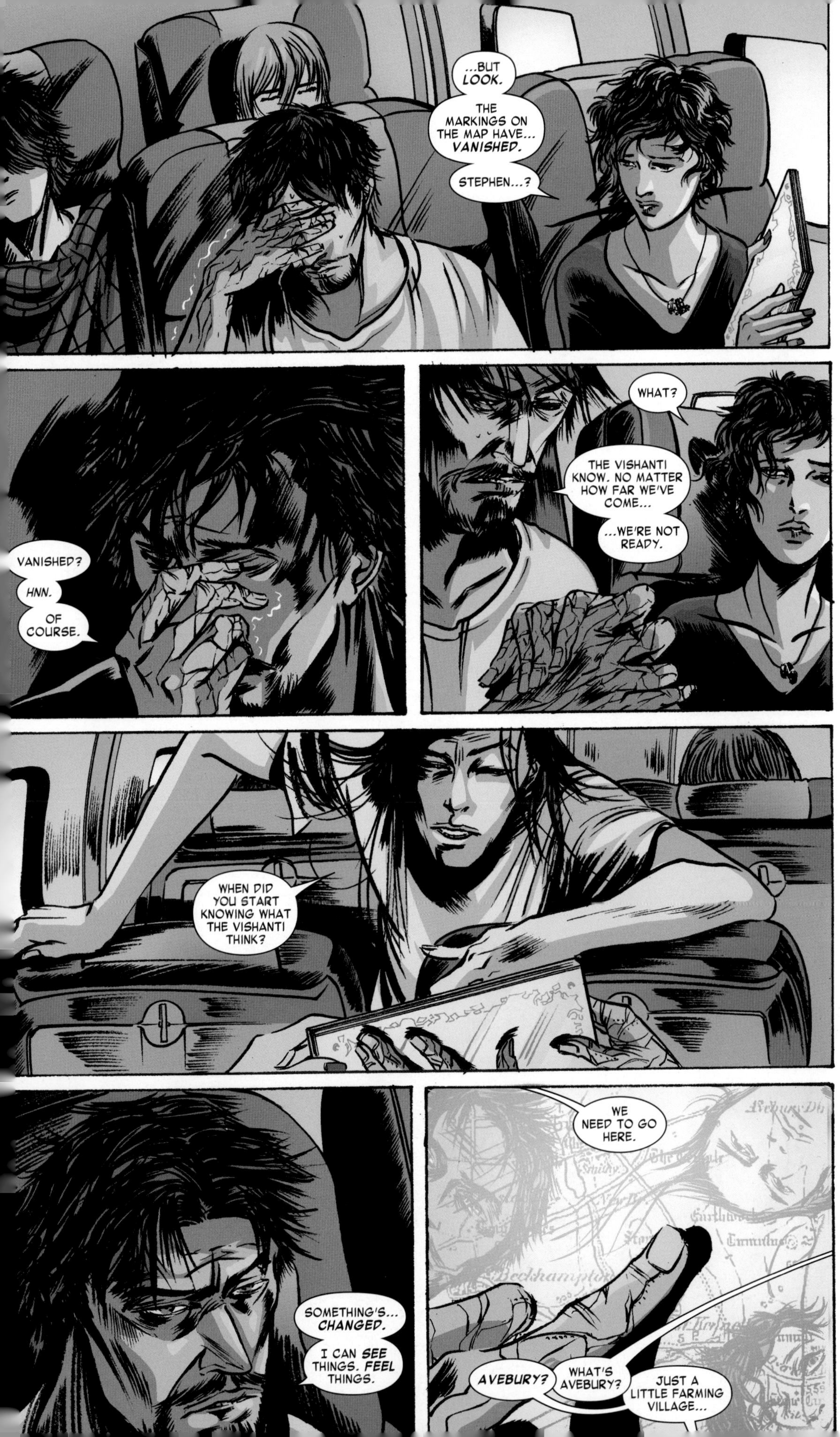
...BUT LOOK.
THE MARKINGS ON THE MAP HAVE... VANISHED.
STEPHEN...?
VANISHED?
HNN.
OF COURSE.
WHAT?
THE VISHANTI KNOW. NO MATTER HOW FAR WE'VE COME...
...WE'RE NOT READY.
WHEN DID YOU START KNOWING WHAT THE VISHANTI THINK?
SOMETHING'S... CHANGED.
I CAN SEE THINGS. FEEL THINGS.
WE NEED TO GO HERE.
AVEBURY?
WHAT'S AVEBURY?
JUST A LITTLE FARMING VILLAGE...
Beckhampton

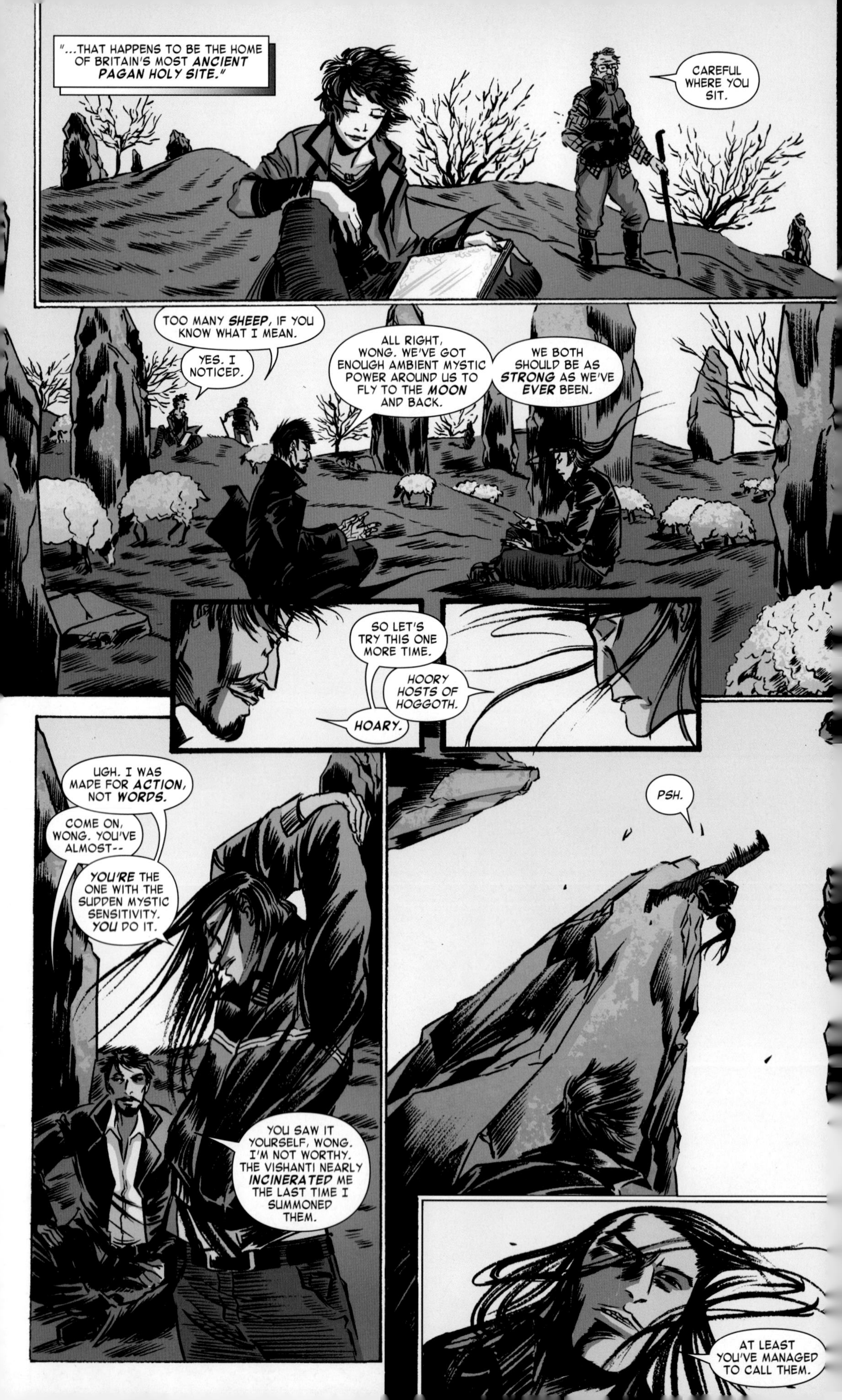
"...THAT HAPPENS TO BE THE HOME OF BRITAIN'S MOST ANCIENT PAGAN HOLY SITE."
CAREFUL WHERE YOU SIT.
TOO MANY SHEEP, IF YOU KNOW WHAT I MEAN.
YES. I NOTICED.
ALL RIGHT, WONG. WE'VE GOT ENOUGH AMBIENT MYSTIC POWER AROUND US TO FLY TO THE MOON AND BACK.
WE BOTH SHOULD BE AS STRONG AS WE'VE EVER BEEN.
SO LET'S TRY THIS ONE MORE TIME.
HOORY HOSTS OF HOGGOTH.
HOARY.
UGH. I WAS MADE FOR ACTION, NOT WORDS.
COME ON, WONG. YOU'VE ALMOST--
YOU'RE THE ONE WITH THE SUDDEN MYSTIC SENSITIVITY. YOU DO IT.
YOU SAW IT YOURSELF, WONG. I'M NOT WORTHY. THE VISHANTI NEARLY INCINERATED ME THE LAST TIME I SUMMONED THEM.
PSH.
AT LEAST YOU'VE MANAGED TO CALL THEM.

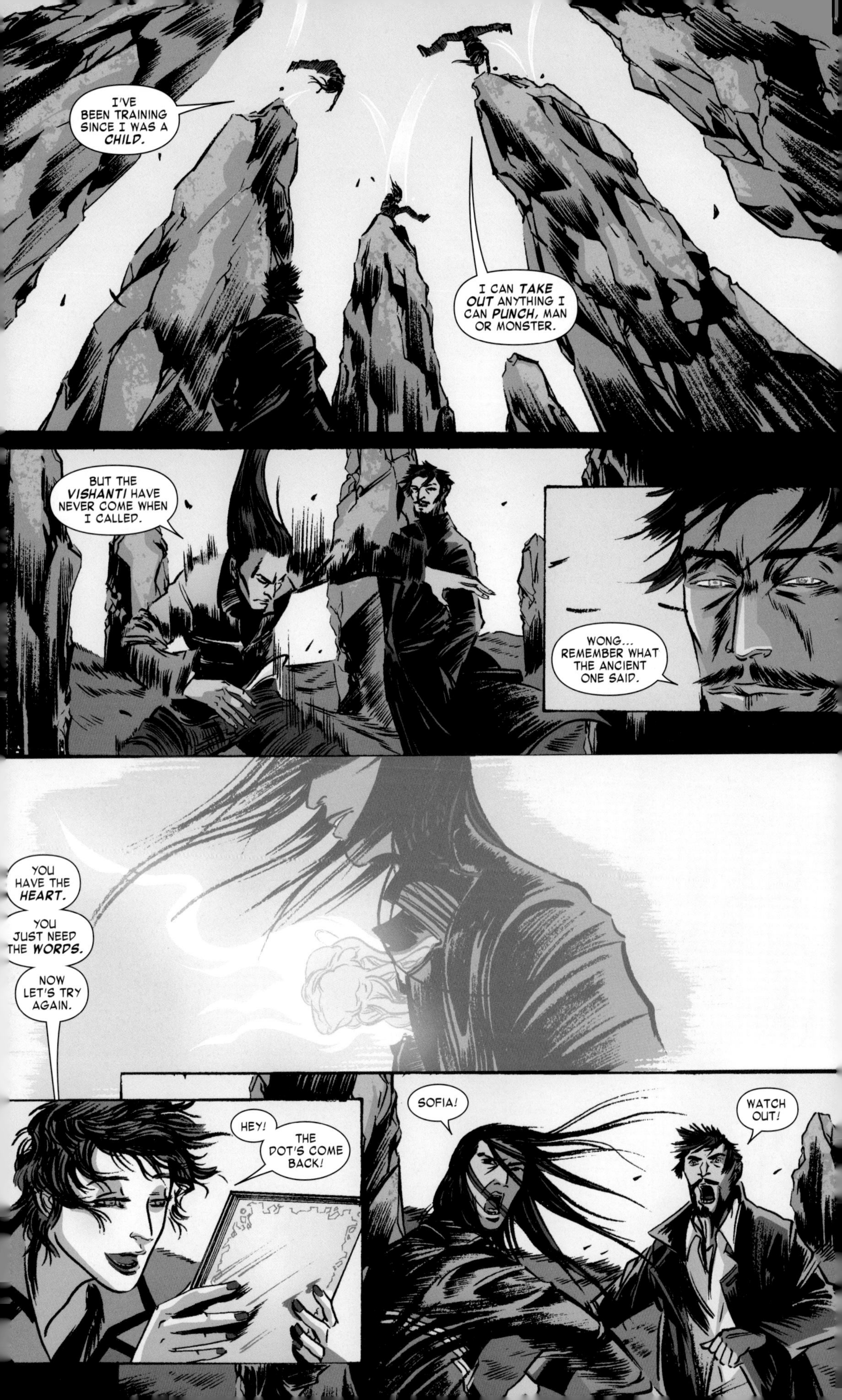
I'VE BEEN TRAINING SINCE I WAS A CHILD.
I CAN TAKE OUT ANYTHING I CAN PUNCH, MAN OR MONSTER.
BUT THE VISHANTI HAVE NEVER COME WHEN I CALLED.
WONG... REMEMBER WHAT THE ANCIENT ONE SAID.
YOU HAVE THE HEART.
YOU JUST NEED THE WORDS.
NOW LET'S TRY AGAIN.
HEY!
THE DOT'S COME BACK!
SOFIA!
WATCH OUT!

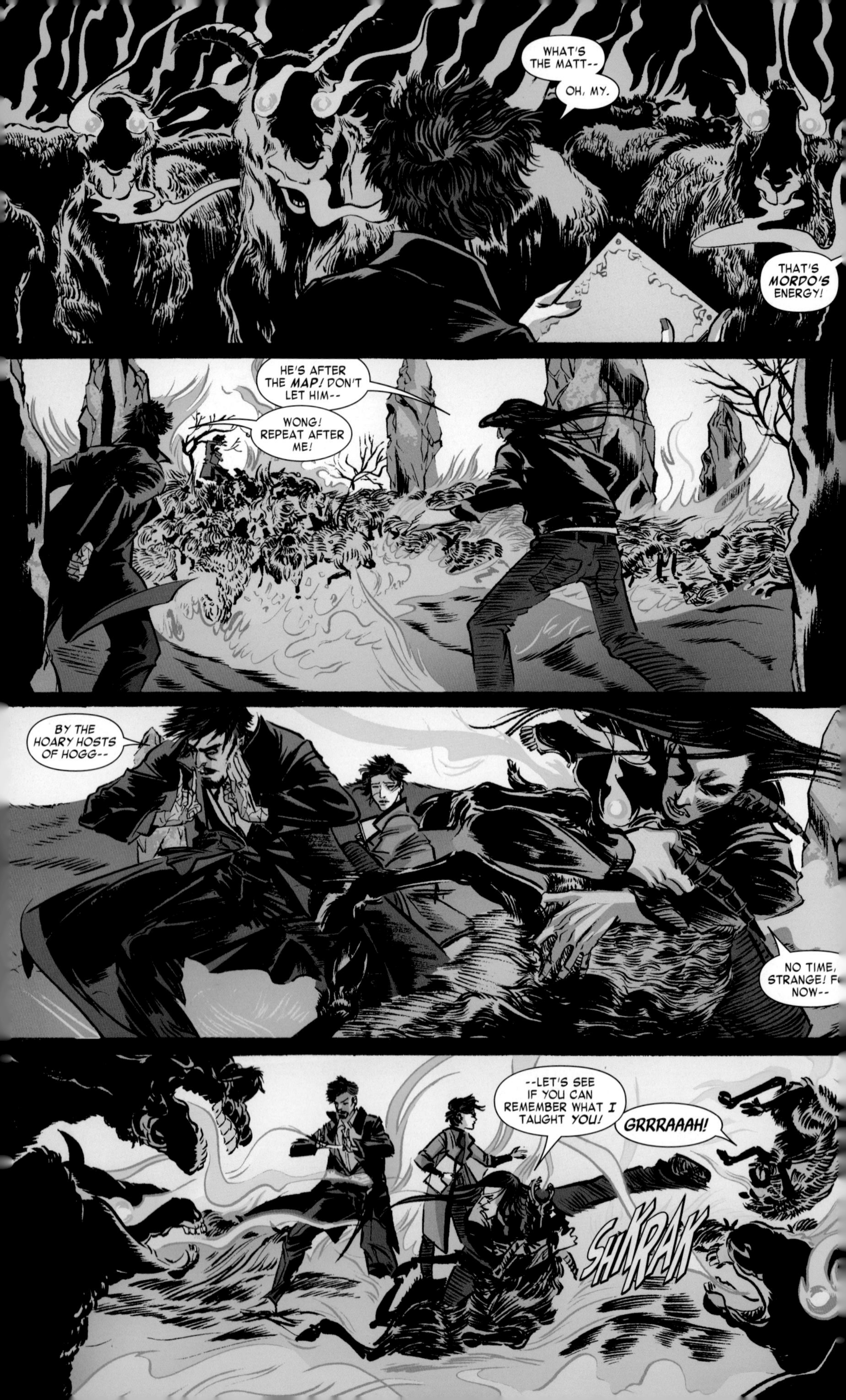
WHAT'S THE MATT--
OH, MY.
THAT'S MORDO'S ENERGY!
HE'S AFTER THE MAP! DON'T LET HIM--
WONG! REPEAT AFTER ME!
BY THE HOARY HOSTS OF HOGG--
NO TIME, STRANGE! F
NOW--
--LET'S SEE IF YOU CAN REMEMBER WHAT I TAUGHT YOU!
GRRRAAAH!
SHKRAK

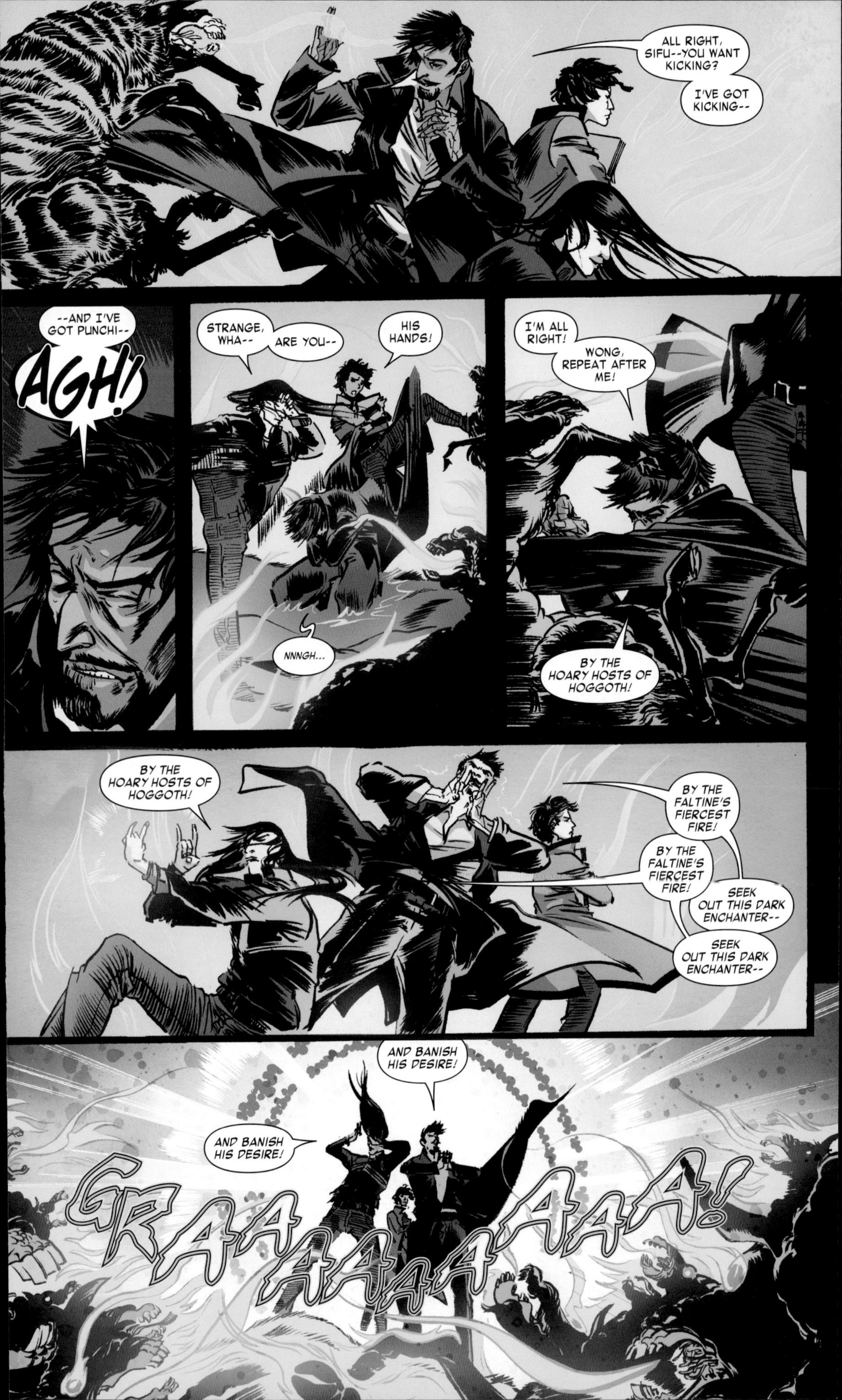
ALL RIGHT, SIFU--YOU WANT KICKING?
I'VE GOT KICKING--
--AND I'VE GOT PUNCHI--
AGH!
STRANGE, WHA--
ARE YOU--
HIS HANDS!
NNNGH...
I'M ALL RIGHT!
WONG, REPEAT AFTER ME!
BY THE HOARY HOSTS OF HOGGOTH!
BY THE HOARY HOSTS OF HOGGOTH!
BY THE FALTINE'S FIERCEST FIRE!
BY THE FALTINE'S FIERCEST FIRE!
SEEK OUT THIS DARK ENCHANTER--
SEEK OUT THIS DARK ENCHANTER--
AND BANISH HIS DESIRE!
AND BANISH HIS DESIRE!
GRAAAAAAAAAA!

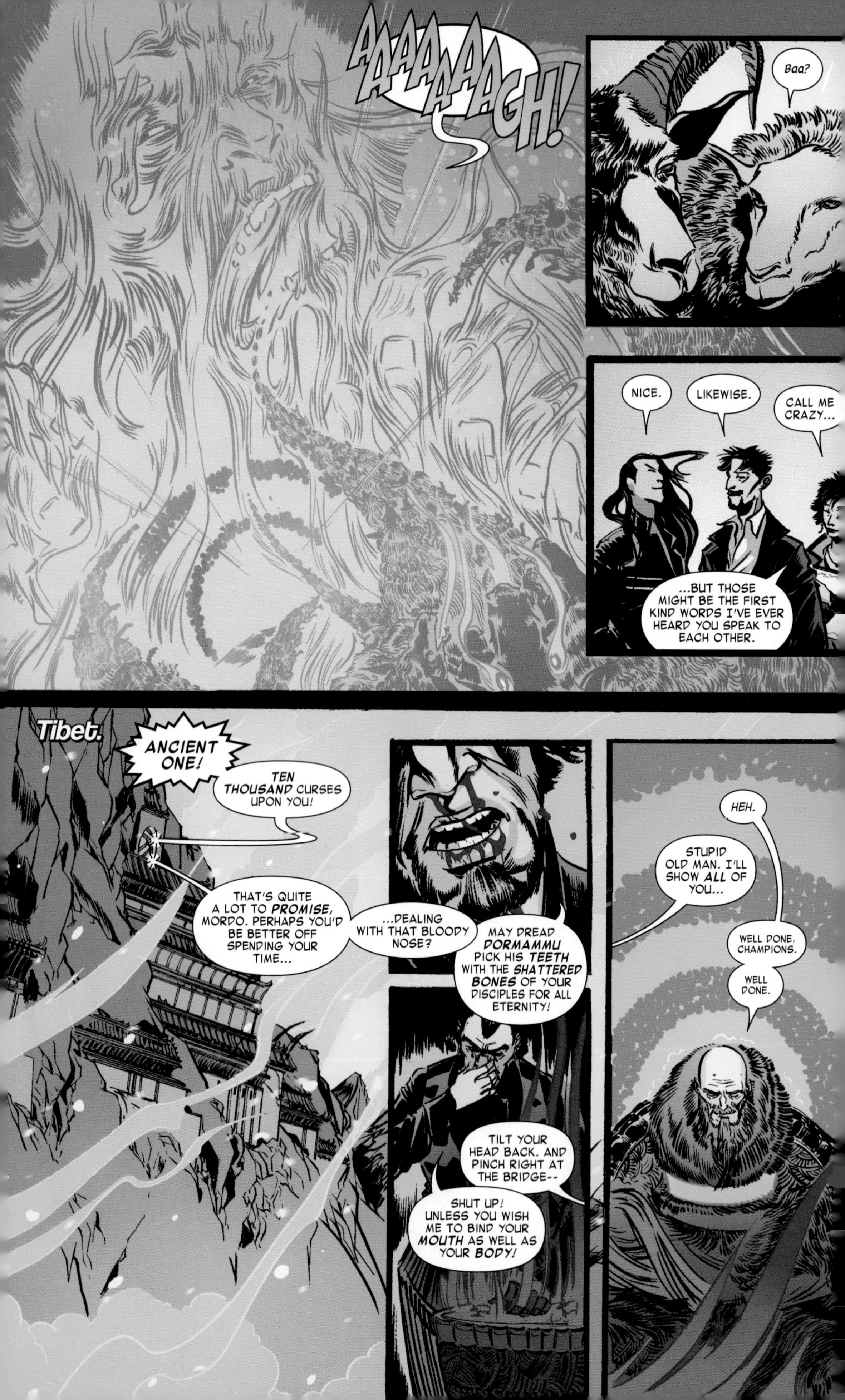
AAAAAAAGH!
Baa?
NICE.
LIKEWISE.
CALL ME CRAZY...
...BUT THOSE MIGHT BE THE FIRST KIND WORDS I'VE EVER HEARD YOU SPEAK TO EACH OTHER.
Tibet.
ANCIENT ONE!
TEN THOUSAND CURSES UPON YOU!
THAT'S QUITE A LOT TO PROMISE, MORDO. PERHAPS YOU'D BE BETTER OFF SPENDING YOUR TIME...
...DEALING WITH THAT BLOODY NOSE?
MAY DREAD DORMAMMU PICK HIS TEETH WITH THE SHATTERED BONES OF YOUR DISCIPLES FOR ALL ETERNITY!
TILT YOUR HEAD BACK. AND PINCH RIGHT AT THE BRIDGE--
SHUT UP! UNLESS YOU WISH ME TO BIND YOUR MOUTH AS WELL AS YOUR BODY!
HEH.
STUPID OLD MAN. I'LL SHOW ALL OF YOU...
WELL DONE, CHAMPIONS.
WELL DONE.

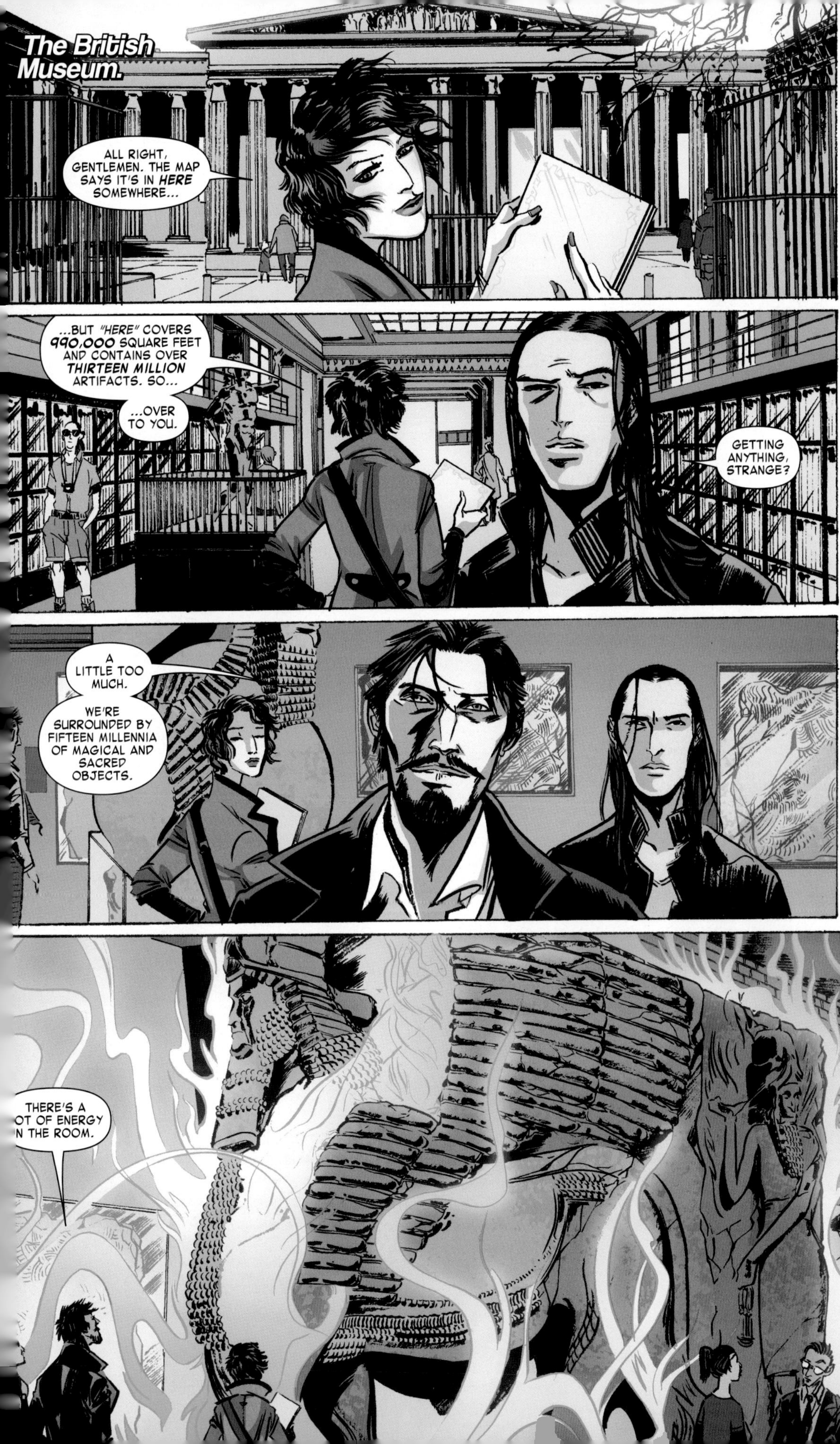
The British Museum.
ALL RIGHT, GENTLEMEN. THE MAP SAYS IT'S IN HERE SOMEWHERE...
...BUT "HERE" COVERS 990,000 SQUARE FEET AND CONTAINS OVER THIRTEEN MILLION ARTIFACTS. SO...
...OVER TO YOU.
GETTING ANYTHING, STRANGE?
A LITTLE TOO MUCH.
WE'RE SURROUNDED BY FIFTEEN MILLENNIA OF MAGICAL AND SACRED OBJECTS.
THERE'S A OT OF ENERGY N THE ROOM.

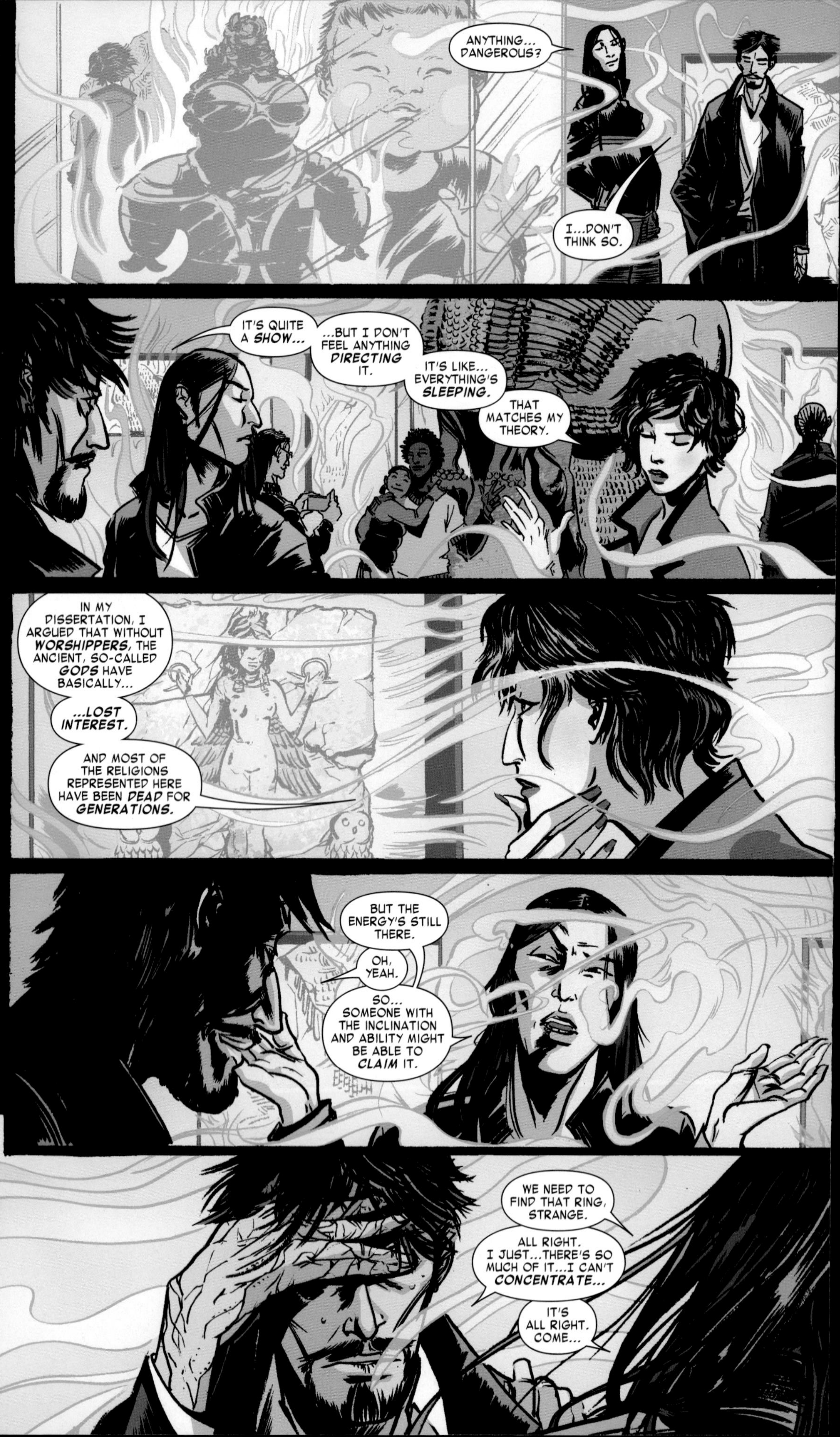
ANYTHING... DANGEROUS?
I...DON'T THINK SO.
IT'S QUITE A SHOW...
...BUT I DON'T FEEL ANYTHING DIRECTING IT.
IT'S LIKE... EVERYTHING'S SLEEPING.
THAT MATCHES MY THEORY.
IN MY DISSERTATION, I ARGUED THAT WITHOUT WORSHIPPERS, THE ANCIENT, SO-CALLED GODS HAVE BASICALLY...
...LOST INTEREST.
AND MOST OF THE RELIGIONS REPRESENTED HERE HAVE BEEN DEAD FOR GENERATIONS.
BUT THE ENERGY'S STILL THERE.
OH, YEAH.
SO... SOMEONE WITH THE INCLINATION AND ABILITY MIGHT BE ABLE TO CLAIM IT.
WE NEED TO FIND THAT RING, STRANGE.
ALL RIGHT. I JUST...THERE'S SO MUCH OF IT...I CAN'T CONCENTRATE...
IT'S ALL RIGHT. COME...

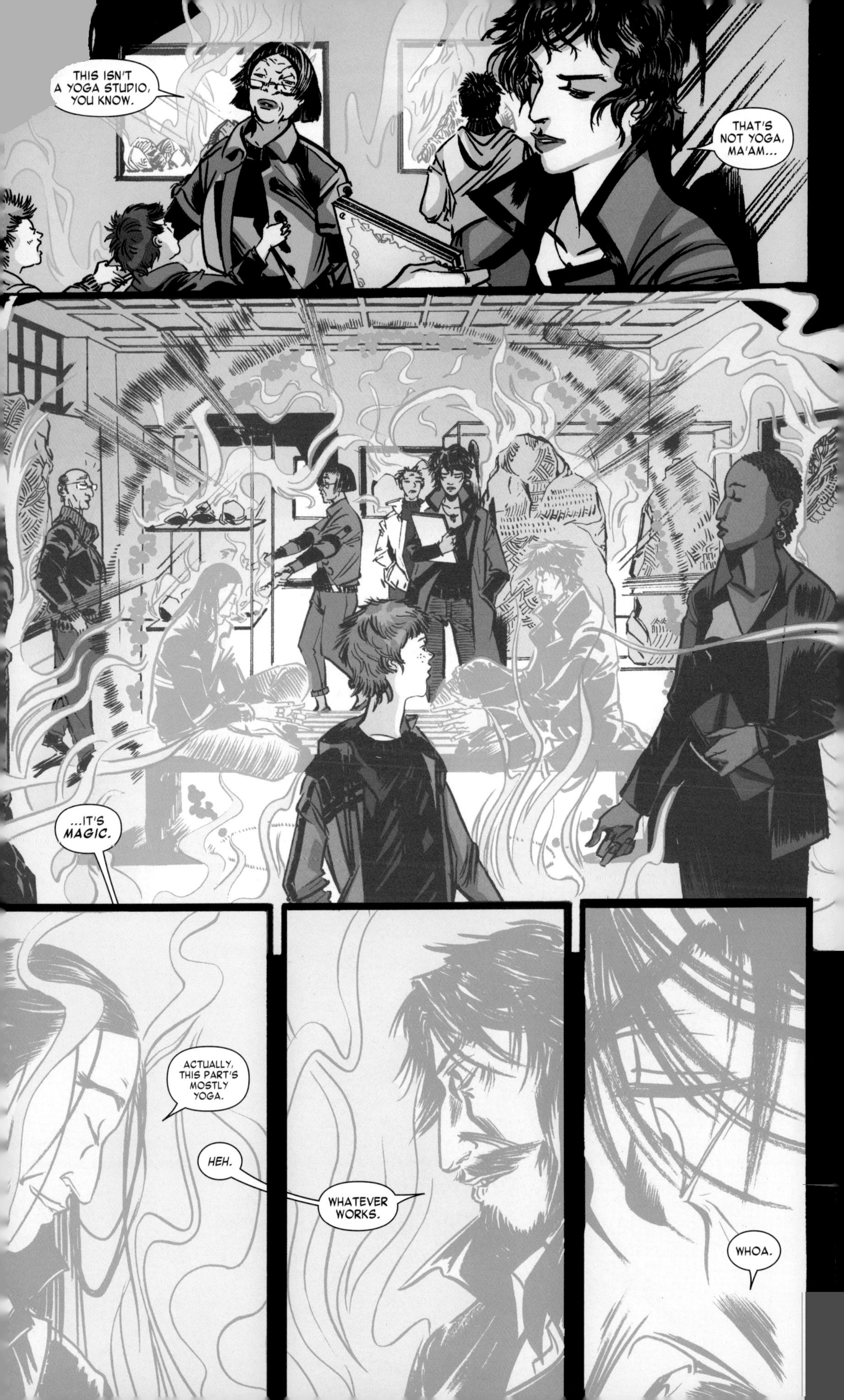
THIS ISN'T A YOGA STUDIO, YOU KNOW.
THAT'S NOT YOGA, MA'AM...
...IT'S MAGIC.
ACTUALLY, THIS PART'S MOSTLY YOGA.
HEH.
WHATEVER WORKS.
WHOA.

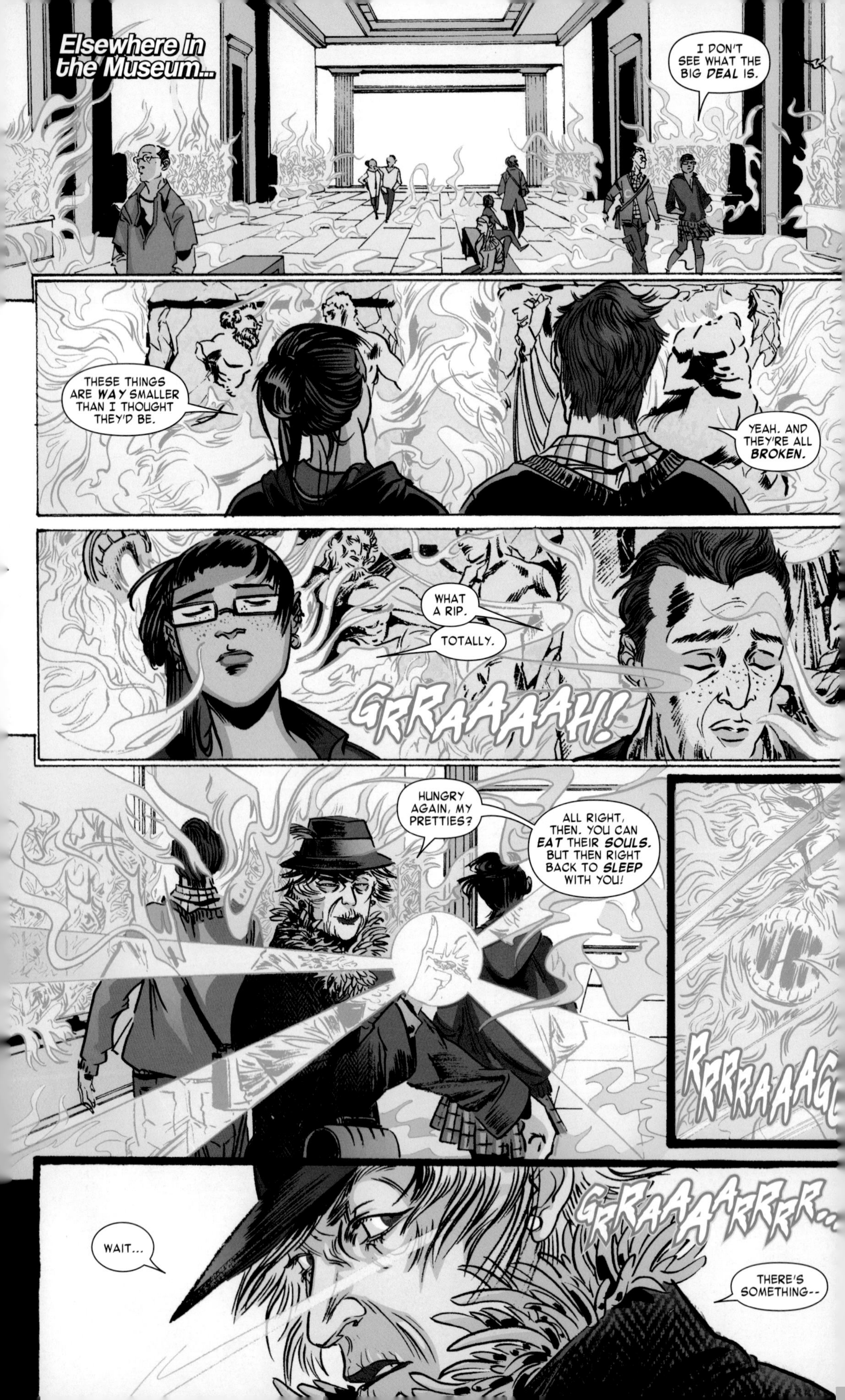
Elsewhere in the Museum...
I DON'T SEE WHAT THE BIG DEAL IS.
THESE THINGS ARE WAY SMALLER THAN I THOUGHT THEY'D BE.
YEAH. AND THEY'RE ALL BROKEN.
WHAT A RIP.
TOTALLY.
GRRAAAAAH!
HUNGRY AGAIN, MY PRETTIES?
ALL RIGHT, THEN. YOU CAN EAT THEIR SOULS. BUT THEN RIGHT BACK TO SLEEP WITH YOU!
RRRRAAAG
GRRAAAARRRR..
WAIT...
THERE'S SOMETHING--

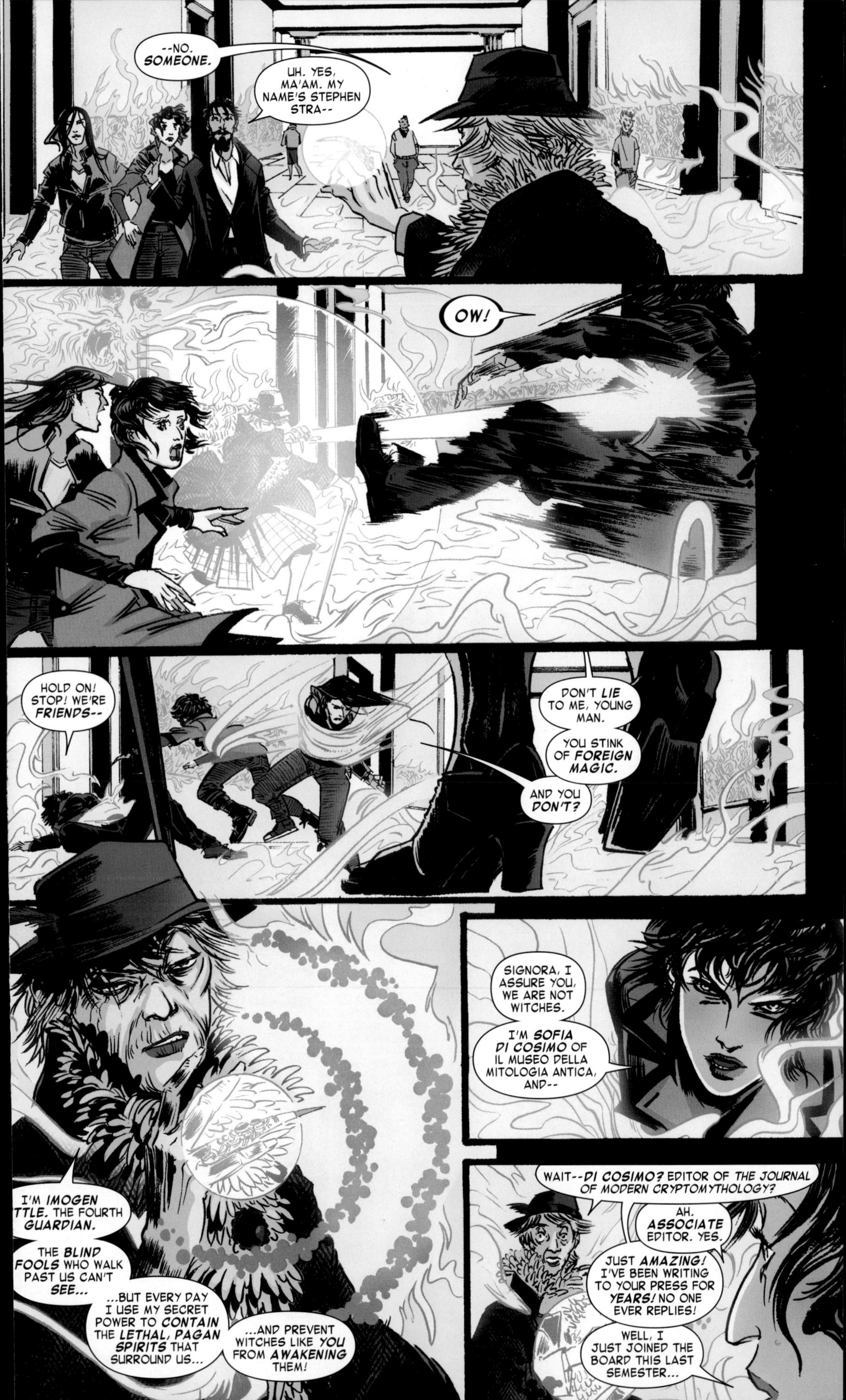

--NO. SOMEONE.
UH. YES, MA'AM. MY NAME'S STEPHEN STRA--
OW!
HOLD ON! STOP! WE'RE FRIENDS--
DON'T LIE TO ME, YOUNG MAN.
YOU STINK OF FOREIGN MAGIC.
AND YOU DON'T?
I'M IMOGEN TTLE. THE FOURTH GUARDIAN.
THE BLIND FOOLS WHO WALK PAST US CAN'T SEE...
...BUT EVERY DAY I USE MY SECRET POWER TO CONTAIN THE LETHAL, PAGAN SPIRITS THAT SURROUND US...
...AND PREVENT WITCHES LIKE YOU FROM AWAKENING THEM!
SIGNORA, I ASSURE YOU, WE ARE NOT WITCHES.
I'M SOFIA DI COSIMO OF IL MUSEO DELLA MITOLOGIA ANTICA, AND--
WAIT--DI COSIMO? EDITOR OF THE JOURNAL OF MODERN CRYPTOMYTHOLOGY?
AH. ASSOCIATE EDITOR. YES.
JUST AMAZING! I'VE BEEN WRITING TO YOUR PRESS FOR YEARS! NO ONE EVER REPLIES!
WELL, I JUST JOINED THE BOARD THIS LAST SEMESTER...

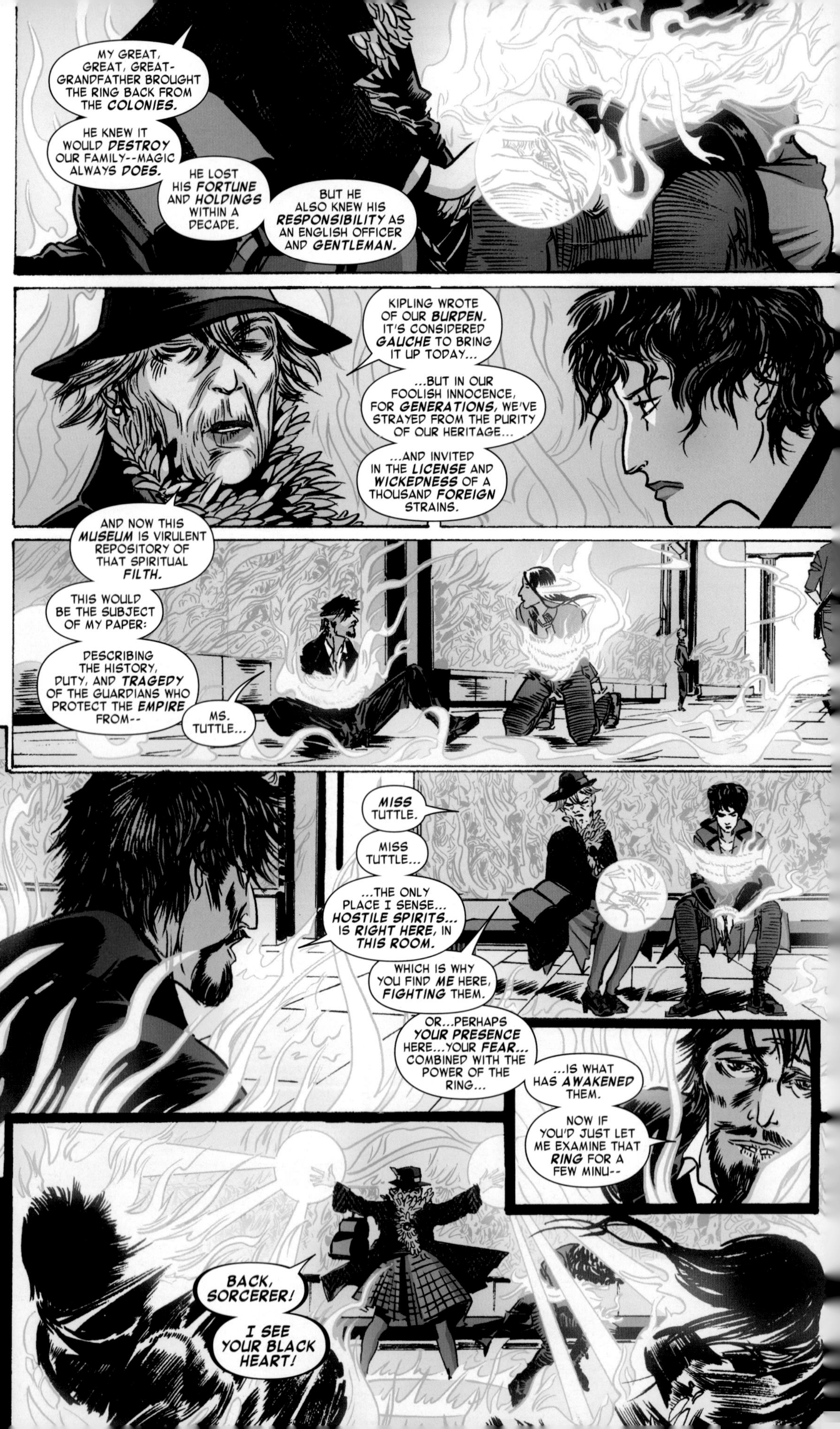
MY GREAT, GREAT, GREAT-GRANDFATHER BROUGHT THE RING BACK FROM THE COLONIES.
HE KNEW IT WOULD DESTROY OUR FAMILY--MAGIC ALWAYS DOES.
HE LOST HIS FORTUNE AND HOLDINGS WITHIN A DECADE.
BUT HE ALSO KNEW HIS RESPONSIBILITY AS AN ENGLISH OFFICER AND GENTLEMAN.
KIPLING WROTE OF OUR BURDEN. IT'S CONSIDERED GAUCHE TO BRING IT UP TODAY...
...BUT IN OUR FOOLISH INNOCENCE, FOR GENERATIONS, WE'VE STRAYED FROM THE PURITY OF OUR HERITAGE...
...AND INVITED IN THE LICENSE AND WICKEDNESS OF A THOUSAND FOREIGN STRAINS.
AND NOW THIS MUSEUM IS VIRULENT REPOSITORY OF THAT SPIRITUAL FILTH.
THIS WOULD BE THE SUBJECT OF MY PAPER:
DESCRIBING THE HISTORY, DUTY, AND TRAGEDY OF THE GUARDIANS WHO PROTECT THE EMPIRE FROM--
MS. TUTTLE...
MISS TUTTLE.
MISS TUTTLE...
...THE ONLY PLACE I SENSE... HOSTILE SPIRITS... IS RIGHT HERE, IN THIS ROOM.
WHICH IS WHY YOU FIND ME HERE, FIGHTING THEM.
OR...PERHAPS YOUR PRESENCE HERE...YOUR FEAR... COMBINED WITH THE POWER OF THE RING...
...IS WHAT HAS AWAKENED THEM.
NOW IF YOU'D JUST LET ME EXAMINE THAT RING FOR A FEW MINU--
BACK, SORCERER!
I SEE YOUR BLACK HEART!

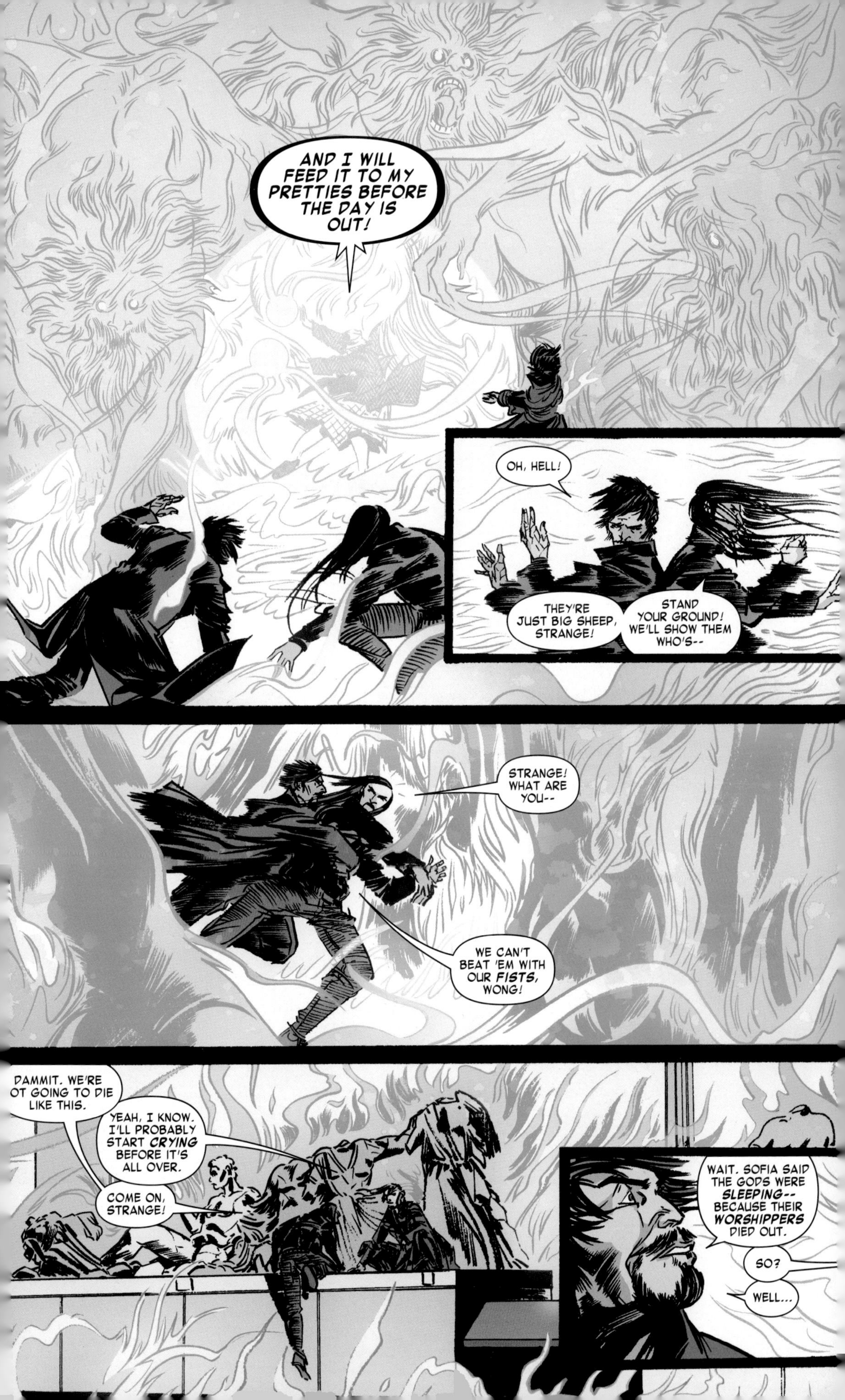
AND I WILL FEED IT TO MY PRETTIES BEFORE THE DAY IS OUT!
OH, HELL!
THEY'RE JUST BIG SHEEP, STRANGE!
STAND YOUR GROUND! WE'LL SHOW THEM WHO'S--
STRANGE! WHAT ARE YOU--
WE CAN'T BEAT 'EM WITH OUR FISTS, WONG!
DAMMIT. WE'RE OT GOING TO DIE LIKE THIS.
YEAH, I KNOW. I'LL PROBABLY START CRYING BEFORE IT'S ALL OVER.
COME ON, STRANGE!
WAIT. SOFIA SAID THE GODS WERE SLEEPING-- BECAUSE THEIR WORSHIPPERS DIED OUT.
SO?
WELL...

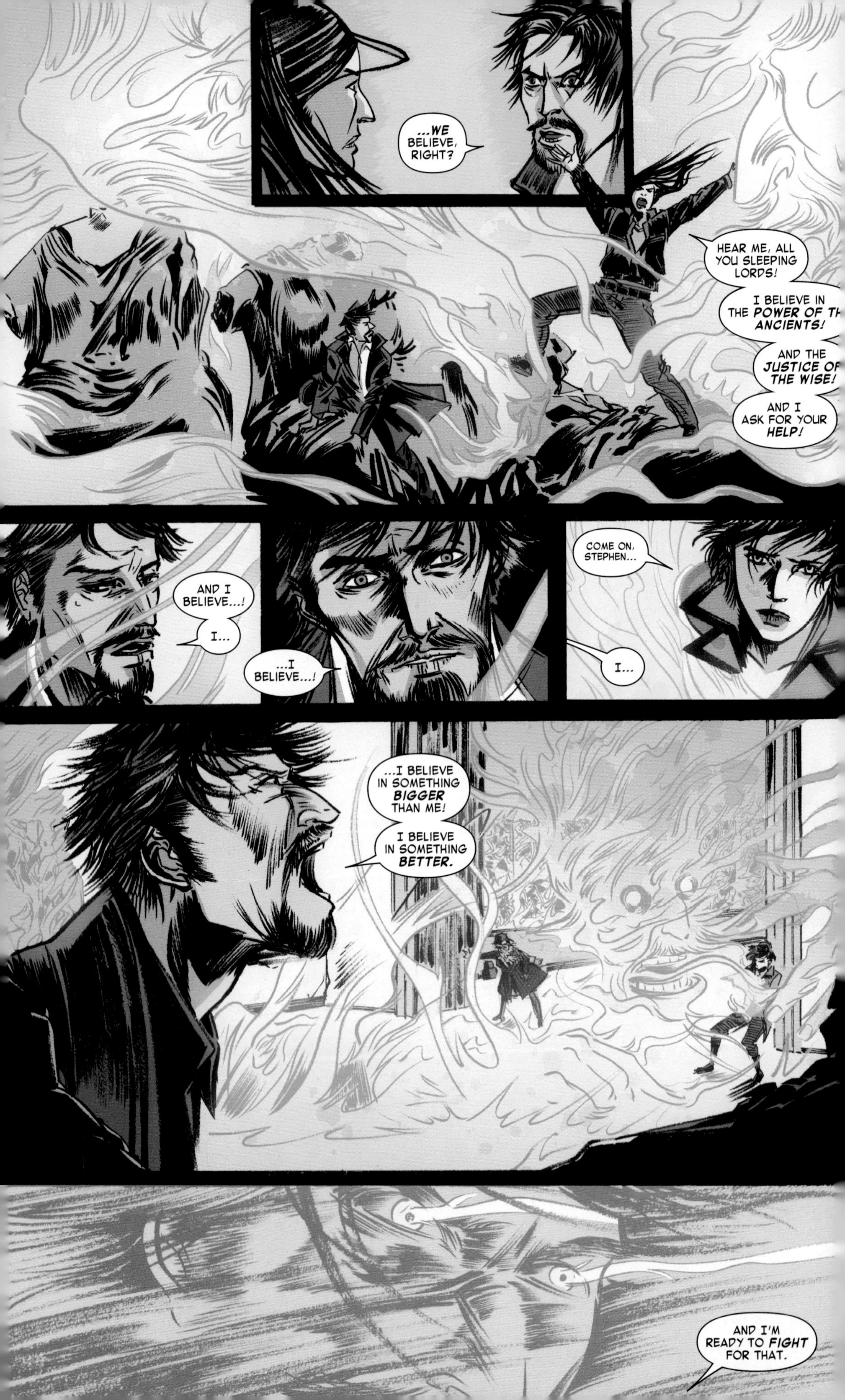
...WE BELIEVE, RIGHT?
HEAR ME, ALL YOU SLEEPING LORDS!
I BELIEVE IN THE POWER OF TH ANCIENTS!
AND THE JUSTICE OF THE WISE!
AND I ASK FOR YOUR HELP!
AND I BELIEVE...!
I...
...I BELIEVE...!
COME ON, STEPHEN...
I...
...I BELIEVE IN SOMETHING BIGGER THAN ME!
I BELIEVE IN SOMETHING BETTER.
AND I'M READY TO FIGHT FOR THAT.

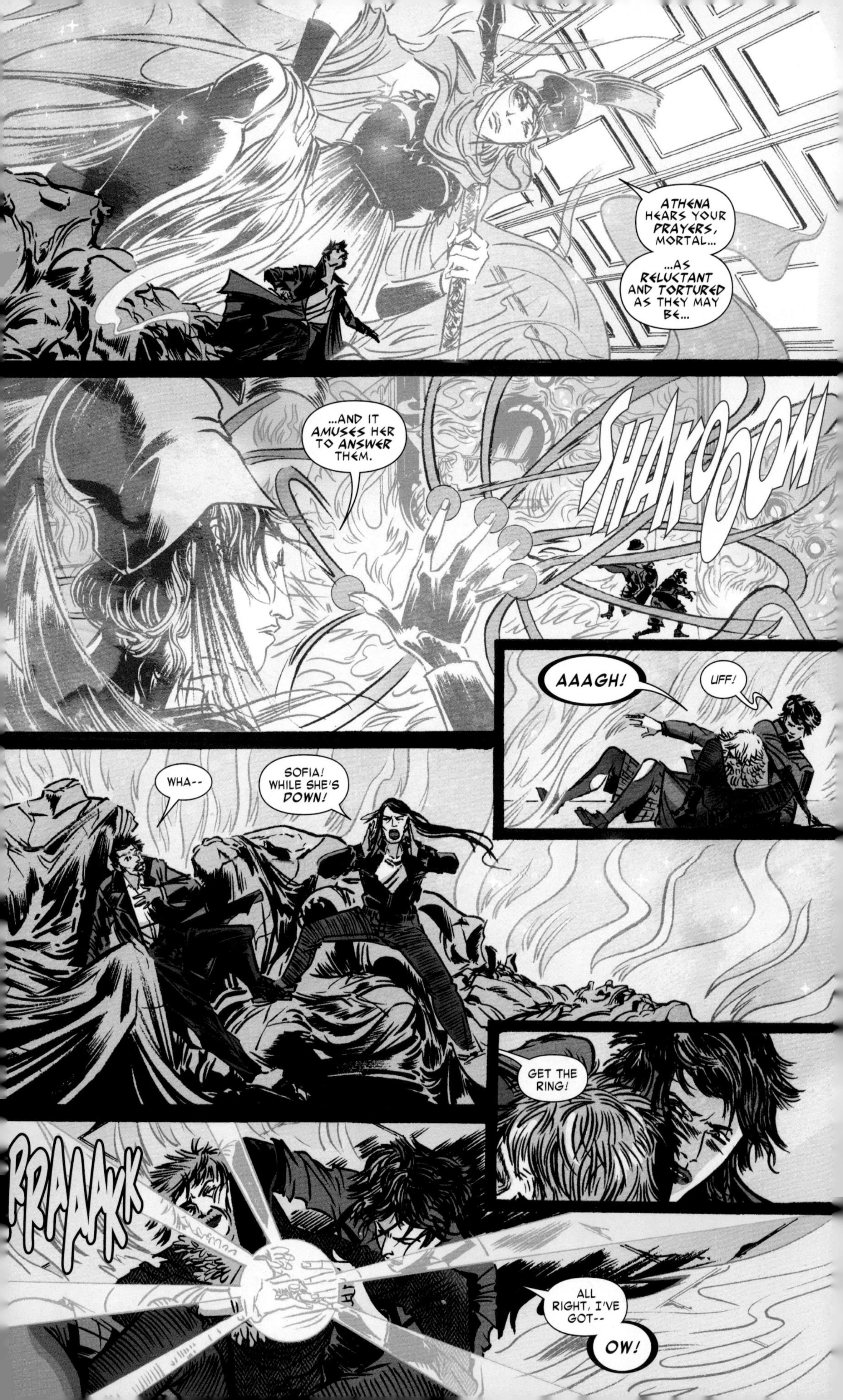
ATHENA HEARS YOUR PRAYERS, MORTAL...
...AS RELUCTANT AND TORTURED AS THEY MAY BE...
...AND IT AMUSES HER TO ANSWER THEM.
SHAKOOOOM
AAAGH!
UFF!
WHA--
SOFIA! WHILE SHE'S DOWN!
GET THE RING!
FRAAAKK
ALL RIGHT, I'VE GOT--
OW!

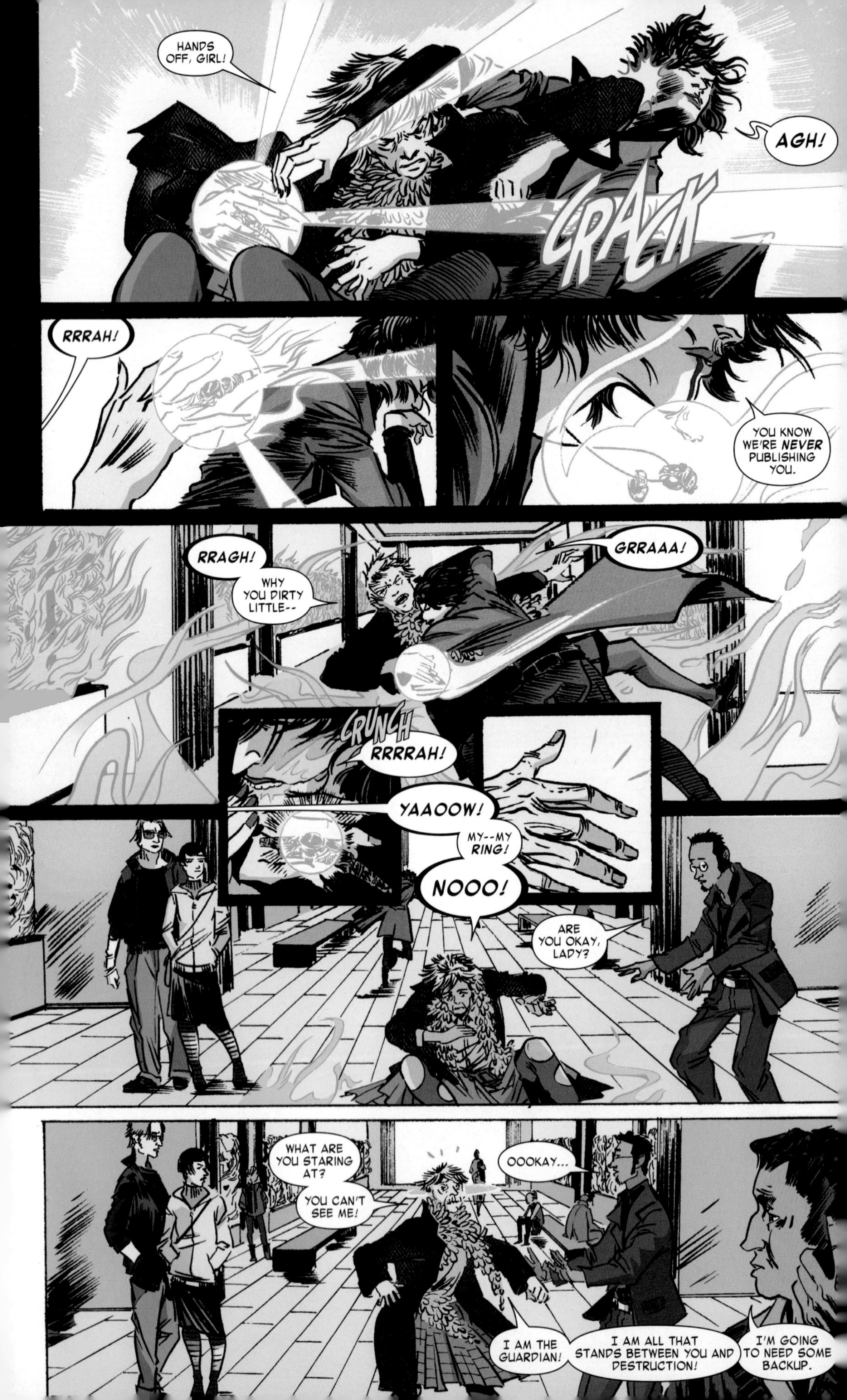
HANDS OFF, GIRL!
AGH!
CRACK
RRRAH!
YOU KNOW WE'RE NEVER PUBLISHING YOU.
RRAGH!
WHY YOU DIRTY LITTLE--
GRRAAA!
CRUNCH
RRRRAH!
YAAOOW!
MY--MY RING!
NOOO!
ARE YOU OKAY, LADY?
WHAT ARE YOU STARING AT?
YOU CAN'T SEE ME!
OOOKAY...
I AM THE GUARDIAN!
I AM ALL THAT STANDS BETWEEN YOU AND DESTRUCTION!
I'M GOING TO NEED SOME BACKUP.

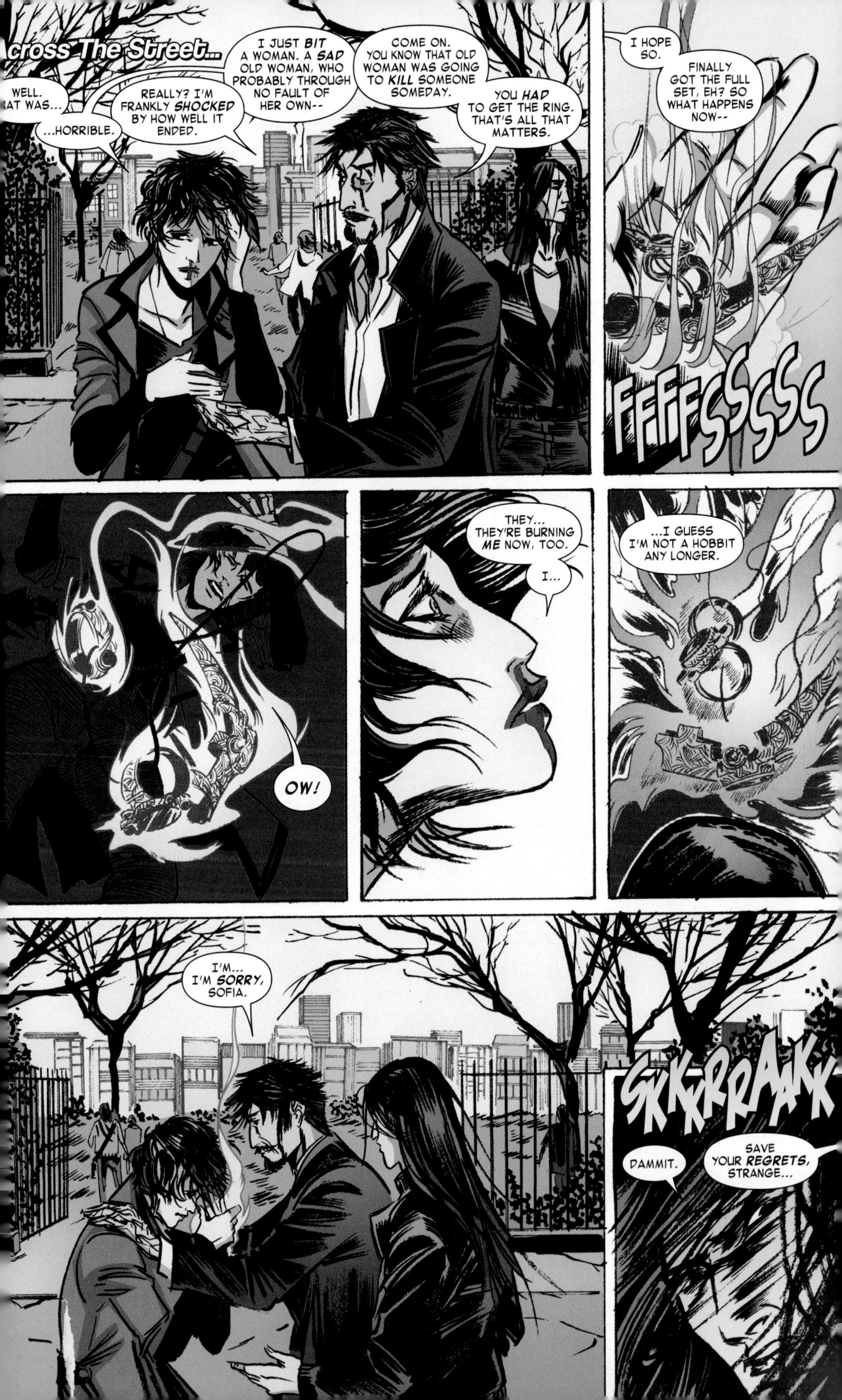

cross The Street...
WELL. AT WAS...
...HORRIBLE.
REALLY? I'M FRANKLY SHOCKED BY HOW WELL IT ENDED.
I JUST BIT A WOMAN. A SAD OLD WOMAN, WHO PROBABLY THROUGH NO FAULT OF HER OWN--
COME ON. YOU KNOW THAT OLD WOMAN WAS GOING TO KILL SOMEONE SOMEDAY.
YOU HAD TO GET THE RING. THAT'S ALL THAT MATTERS.
I HOPE SO.
FINALLY GOT THE FULL SET, EH? SO WHAT HAPPENS NOW--
FFFFSSSSS
OW!
THEY... THEY'RE BURNING ME NOW, TOO.
I...
...I GUESS I'M NOT A HOBBIT ANY LONGER.
I'M... I'M SORRY, SOFIA.
SKKRRAKK
DAMMIT.
SAVE YOUR REGRETS, STRANGE...

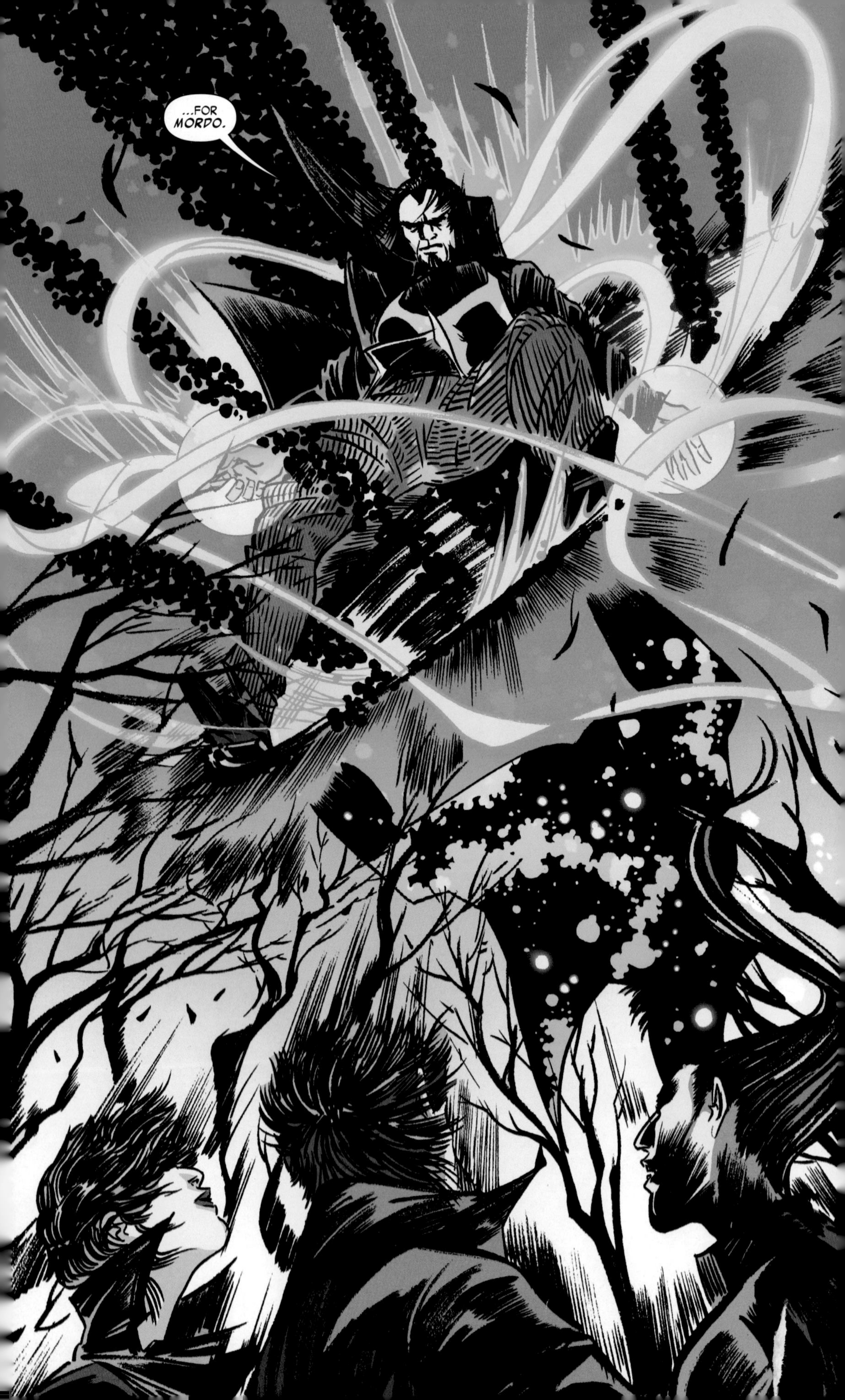
...FOR MORDO.

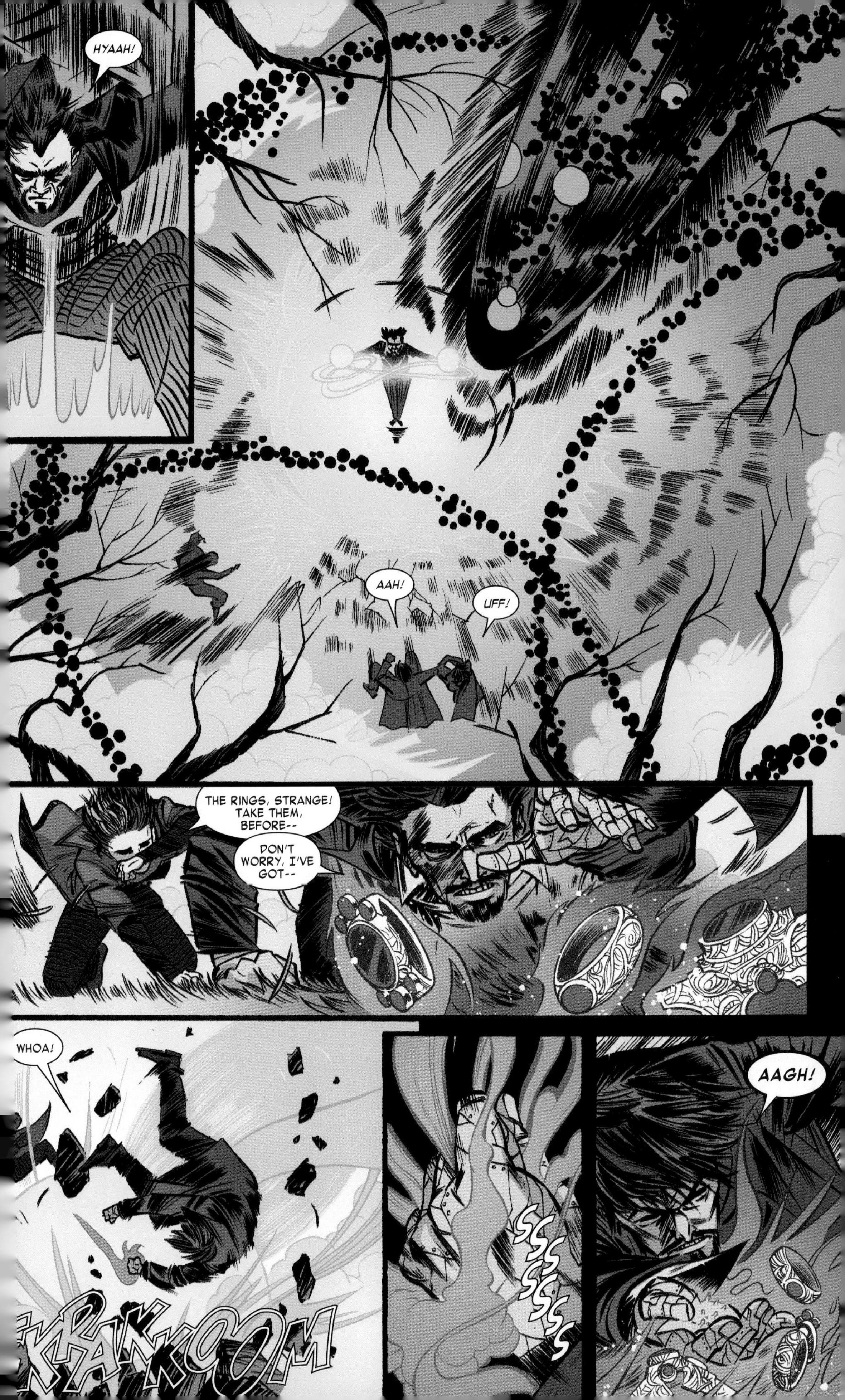
HYAAH!
AAH!
UFF!
THE RINGS, STRANGE! TAKE THEM, BEFORE--
DON'T WORRY, I'VE GOT--
WHOA!
KRAKOOM
SSSSSSS
AAGH!

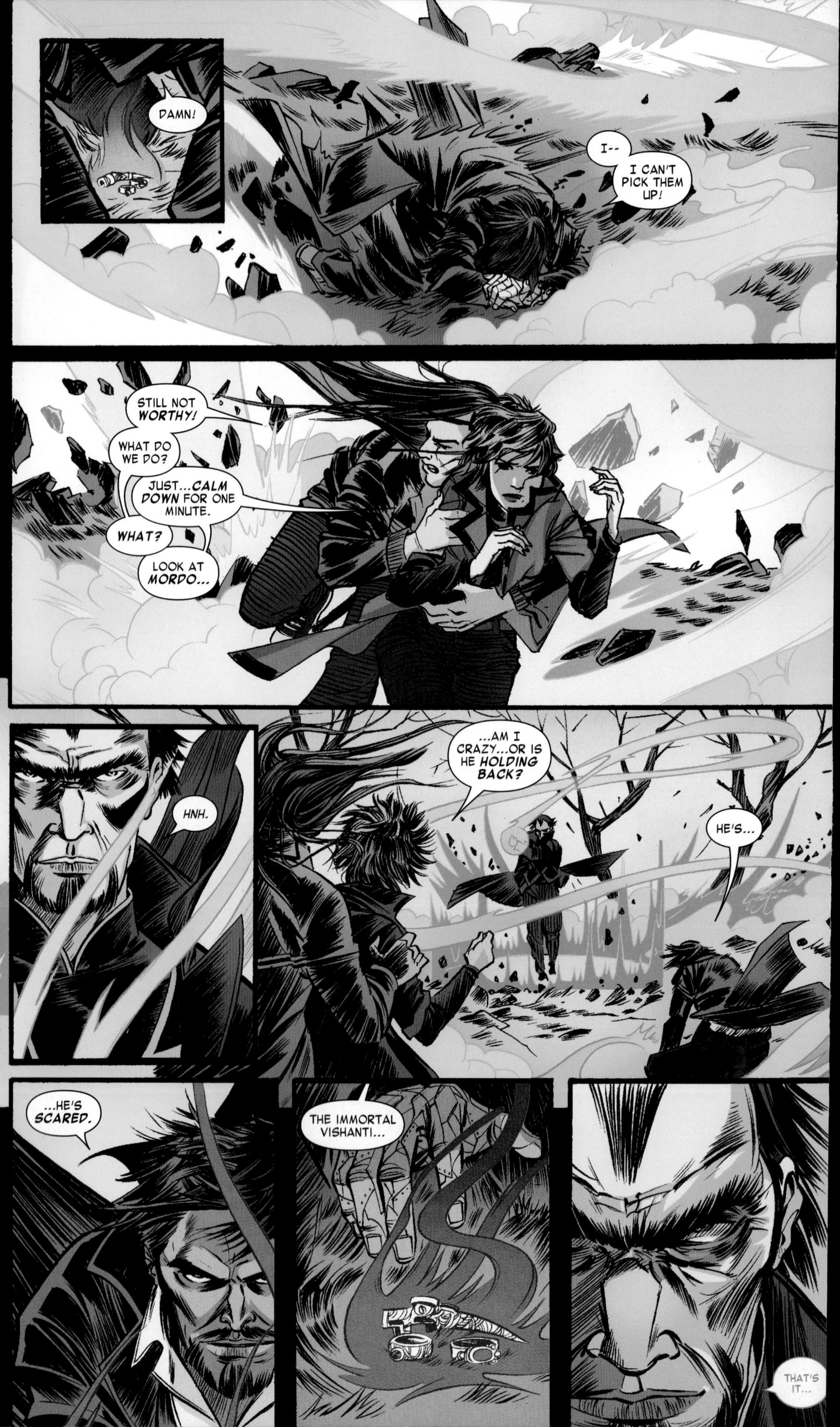

DAMN!
I--
I CAN'T PICK THEM UP!
STILL NOT WORTHY!
WHAT DO WE DO?
JUST...CALM DOWN FOR ONE MINUTE.
WHAT?
LOOK AT MORDO...
HNH.
...AM I CRAZY...OR IS HE HOLDING BACK?
HE'S...
...HE'S SCARED.
THE IMMORTAL VISHANTI...
THAT'S IT...

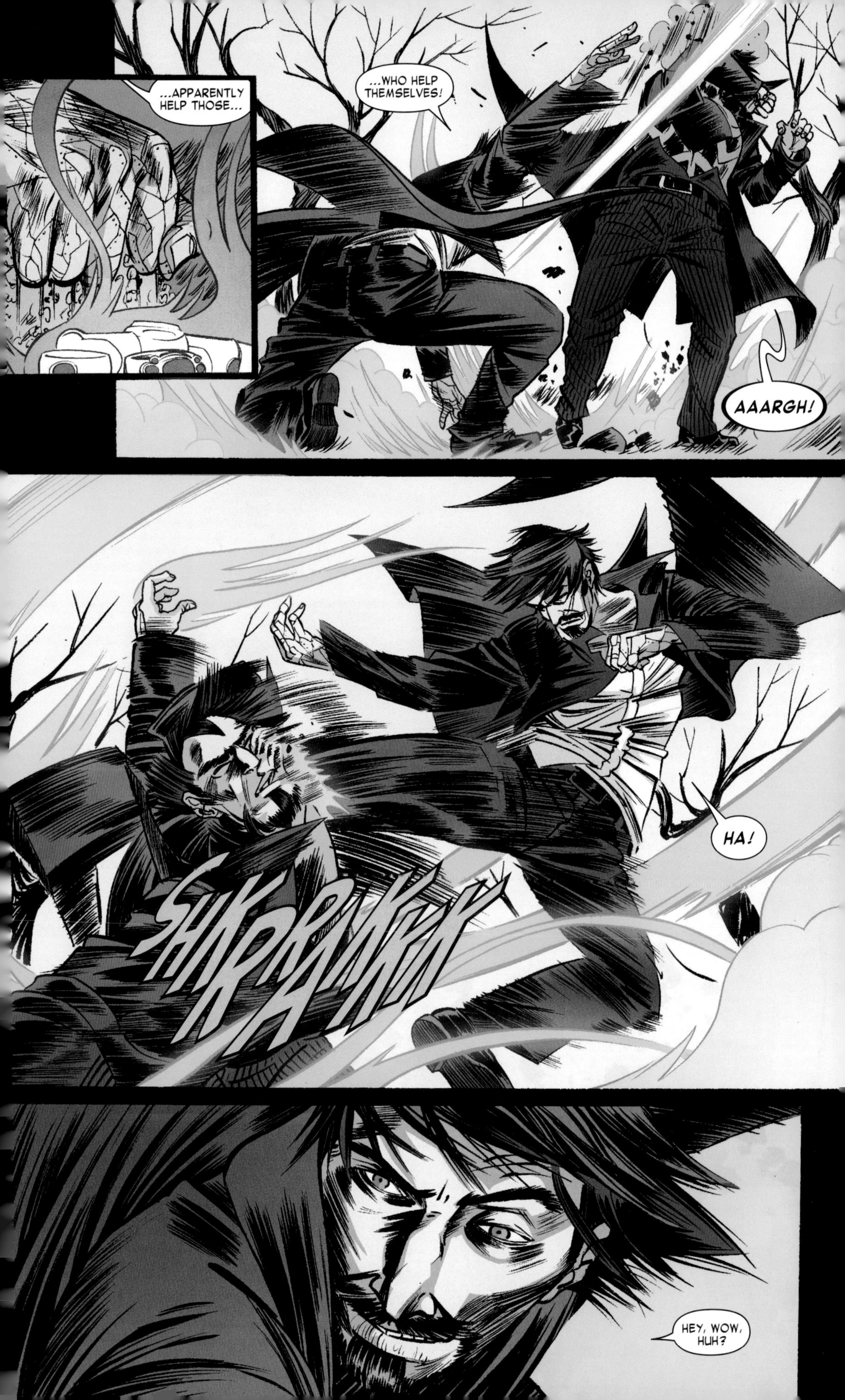
...APPARENTLY HELP THOSE...
...WHO HELP THEMSELVES!
AAARGH!
HA!
SHKRAAKKK
HEY, WOW, HUH?

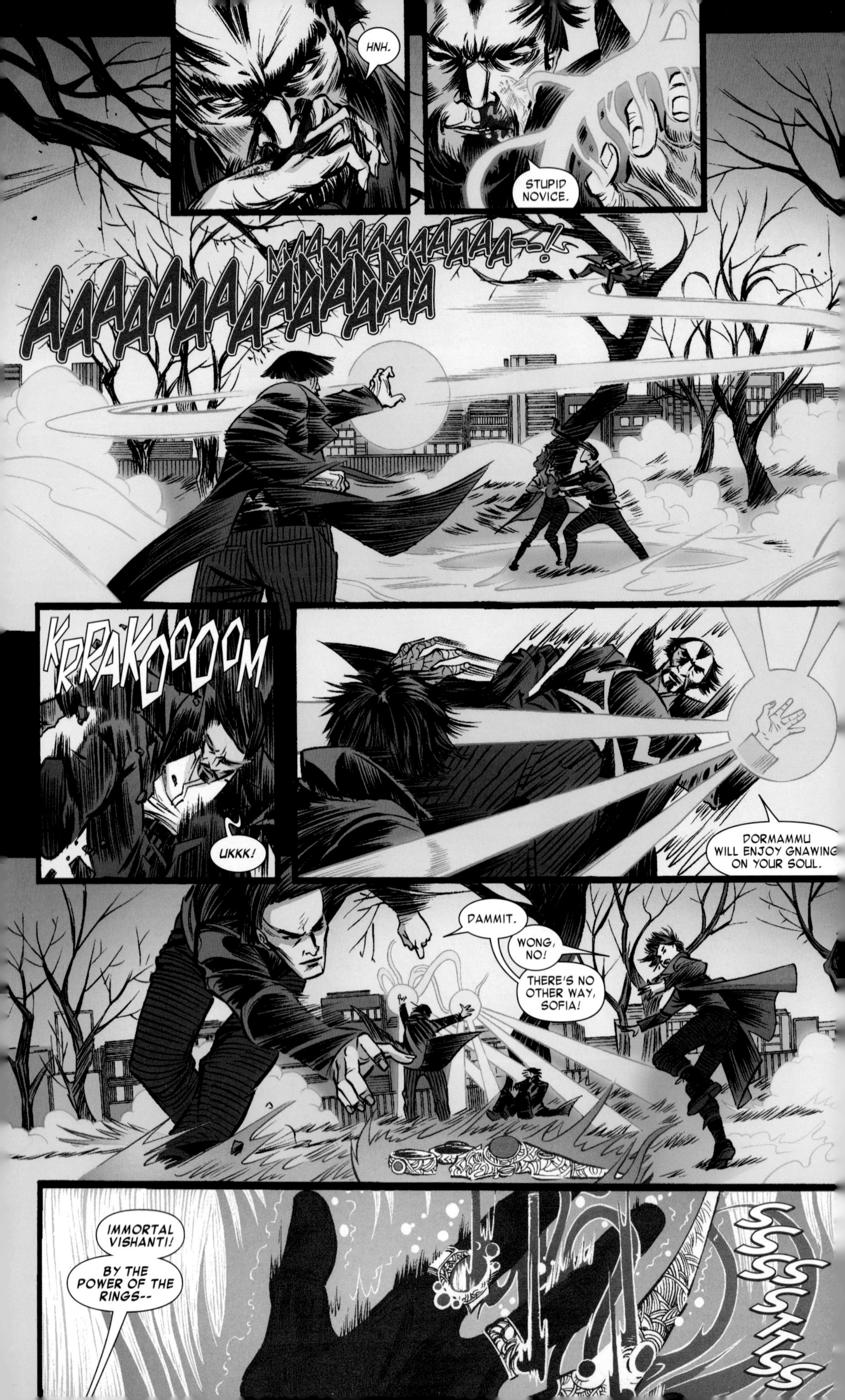
HNH.
STUPID NOVICE.
AAAAAAAAAAAAAA--!
AAAAAAAAAAAAAAAA
KRRAKOOOOOM
UKKK!
DORMAMMU WILL ENJOY GNAWING ON YOUR SOUL.
DAMMIT.
WONG, NO!
THERE'S NO OTHER WAY, SOFIA!
IMMORTAL VISHANTI!
BY THE POWER OF THE RINGS--
SSSSSTSSS

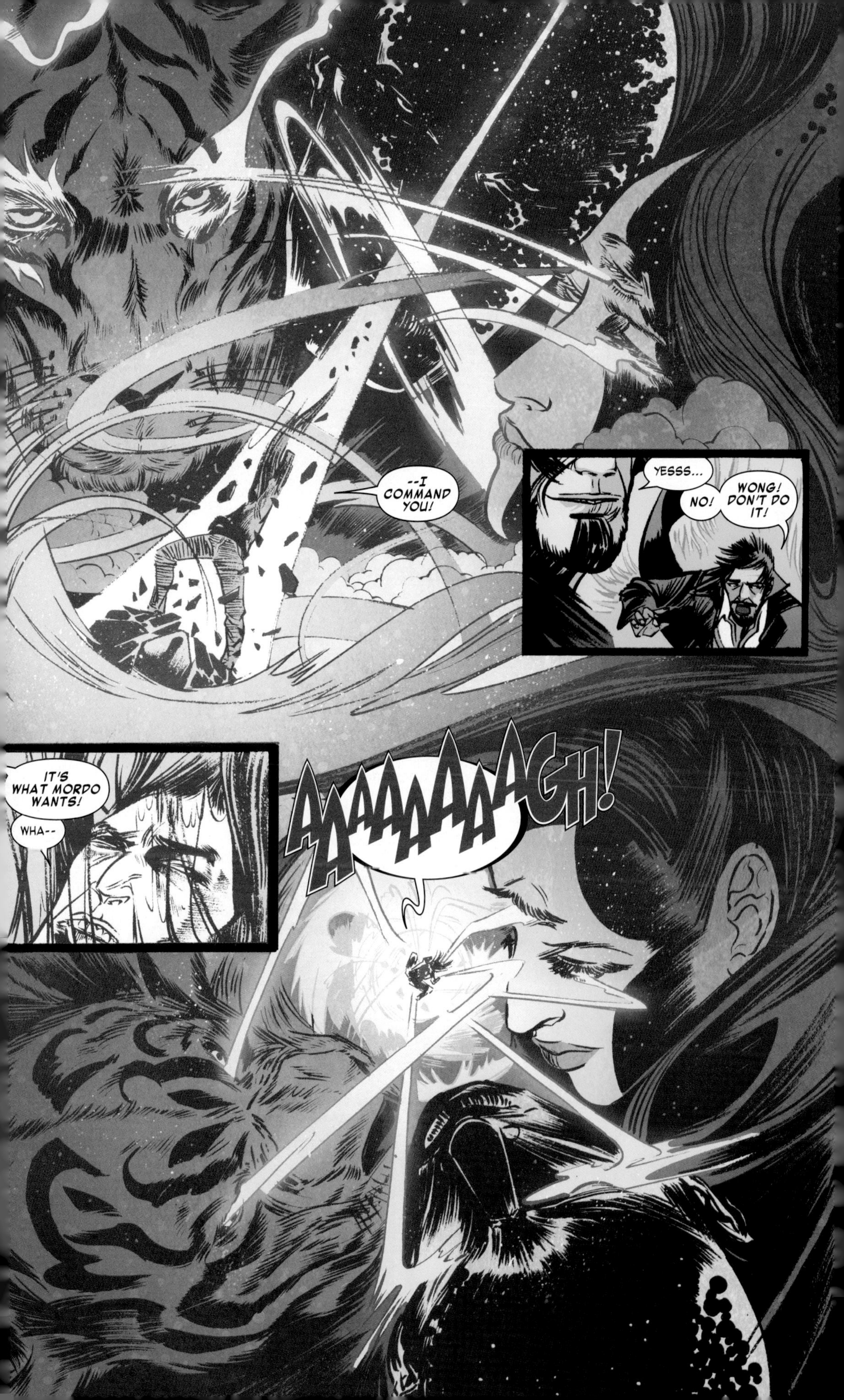
--I COMMAND YOU!
YESSS...
NO!
WONG! DON'T DO IT!
IT'S WHAT MORDO WANTS!
WHA--
AAAAAAAAAAGH!

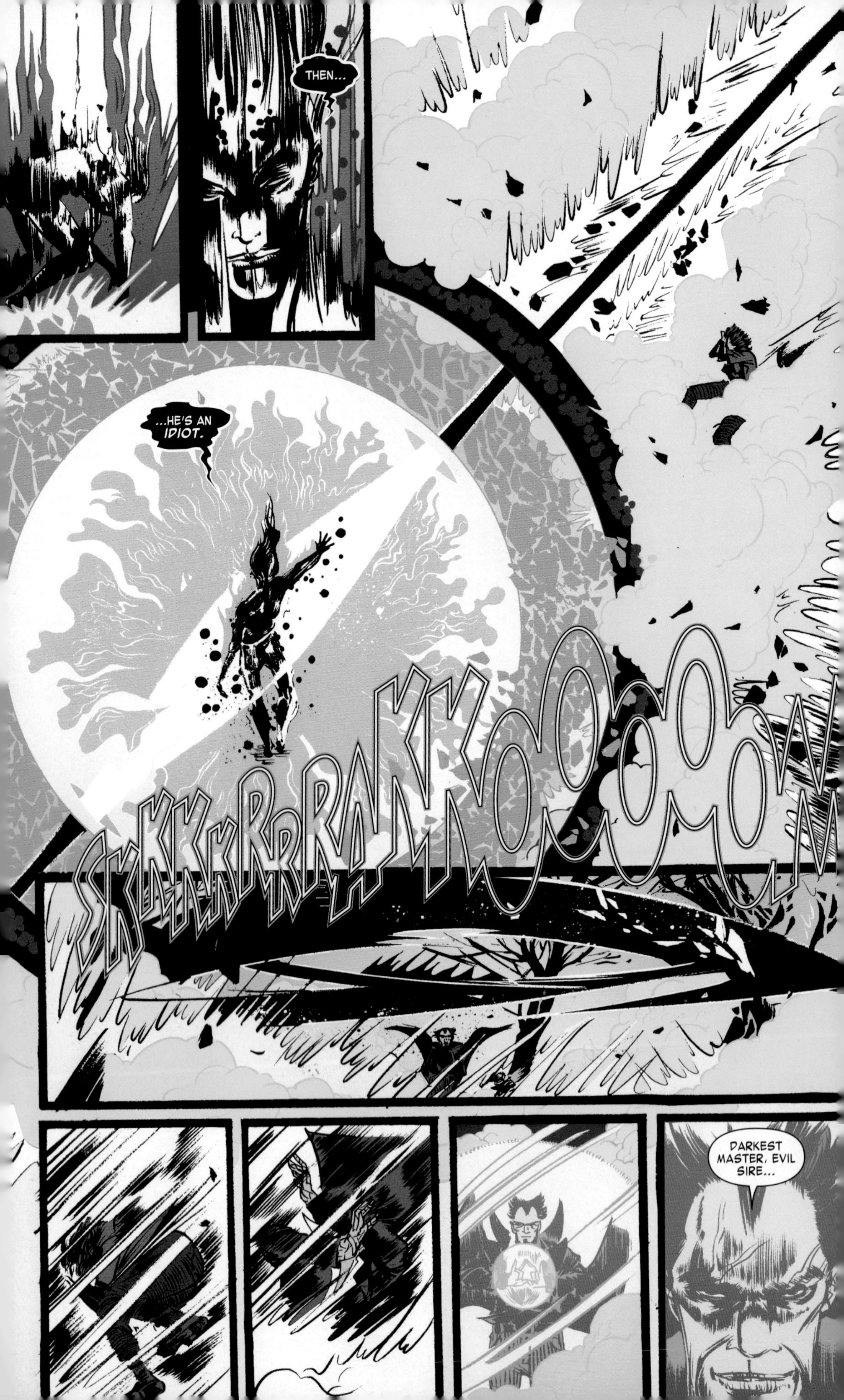
THEN...
...HE'S AN IDIOT.
SKKKKKRRRRAKKOOOOOOOM
DARKEST MASTER, EVIL SIRE...

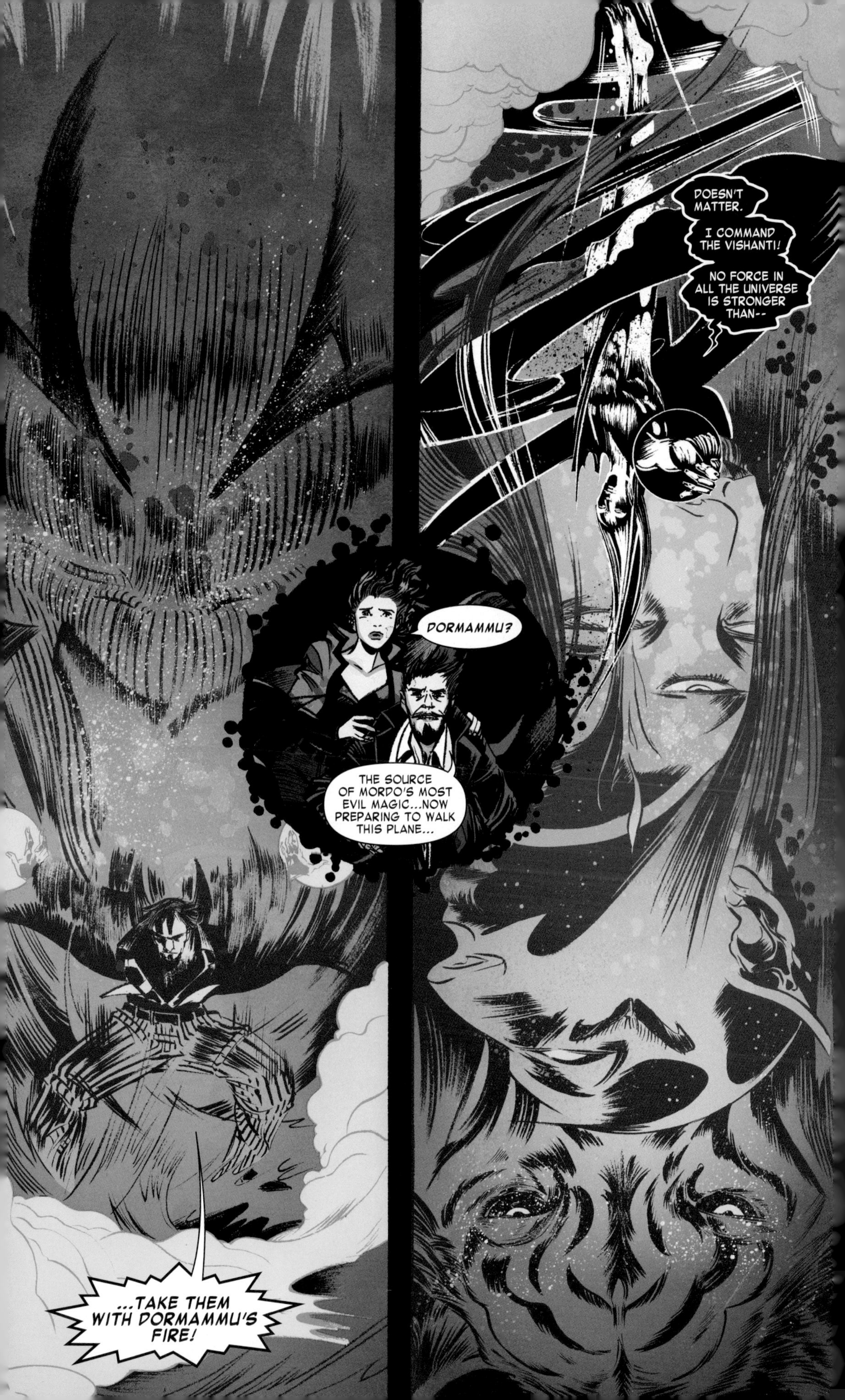
DOESN'T MATTER.
I COMMAND THE VISHANTI!
NO FORCE IN ALL THE UNIVERSE IS STRONGER THAN--
DORMAMMU?
THE SOURCE OF MORDO'S MOST EVIL MAGIC...NOW PREPARING TO WALK THIS PLANE...
...TAKE THEM WITH DORMAMMU'S FIRE!

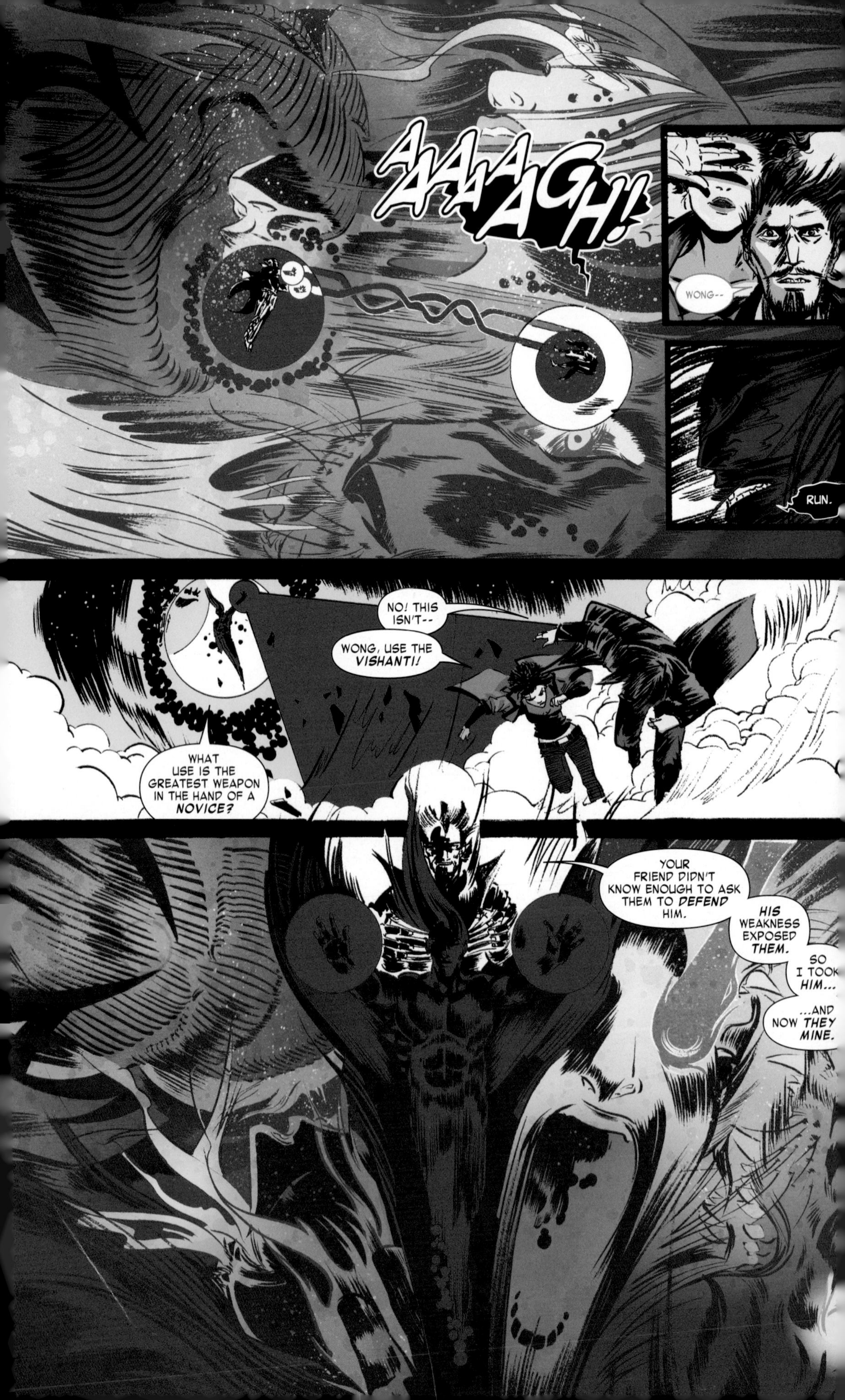

AAAAAAGH!
WONG--
RUN.
NO! THIS ISN'T--
WONG, USE THE VISHANTI!
WHAT USE IS THE GREATEST WEAPON IN THE HAND OF A NOVICE?
YOUR FRIEND DIDN'T KNOW ENOUGH TO ASK THEM TO DEFEND HIM.
HIS WEAKNESS EXPOSED THEM.
SO I TOOK HIM...
...AND NOW THEY MINE.

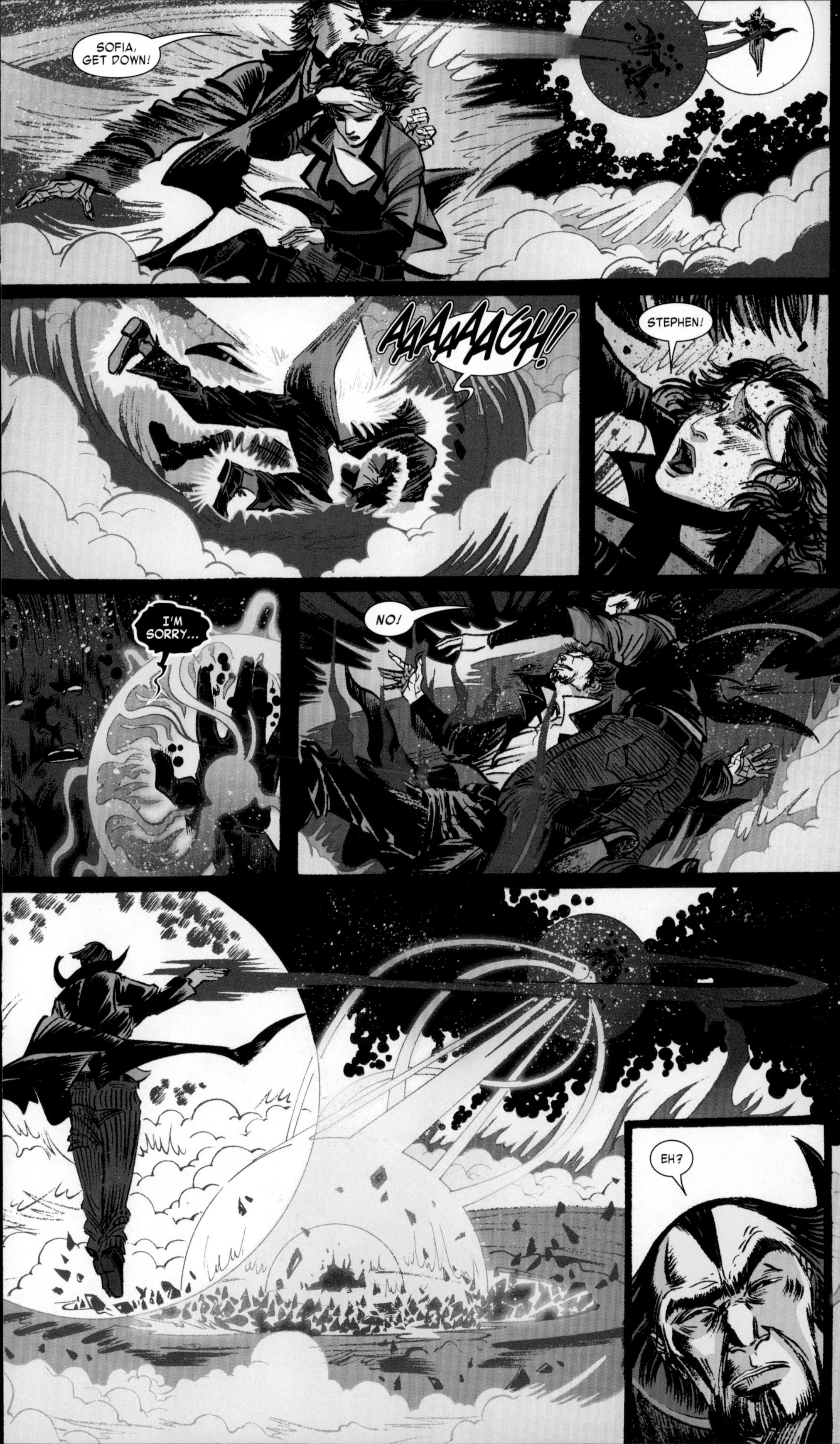

SOFIA, GET DOWN!
AAAAAAGH!
STEPHEN!
I'M SORRY...
NO!
EH?

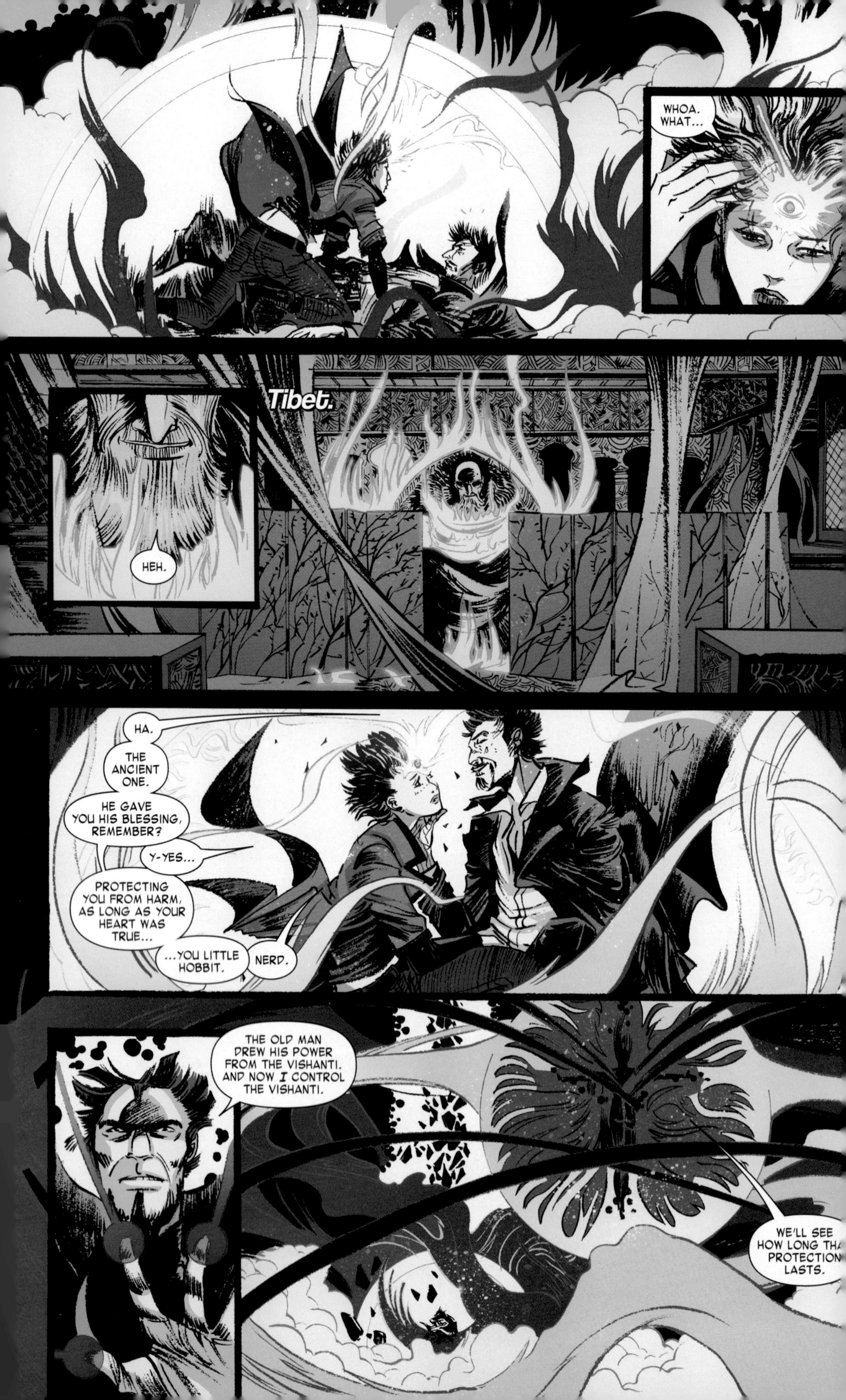
WHOA. WHAT...
Tibet.
HEH.
HA.
THE ANCIENT ONE.
HE GAVE YOU HIS BLESSING, REMEMBER?
Y-YES...
PROTECTING YOU FROM HARM, AS LONG AS YOUR HEART WAS TRUE...
...YOU LITTLE HOBBIT.
NERD.
THE OLD MAN DREW HIS POWER FROM THE VISHANTI. AND NOW I CONTROL THE VISHANTI.
WE'LL SEE HOW LONG THA PROTECTION LASTS.

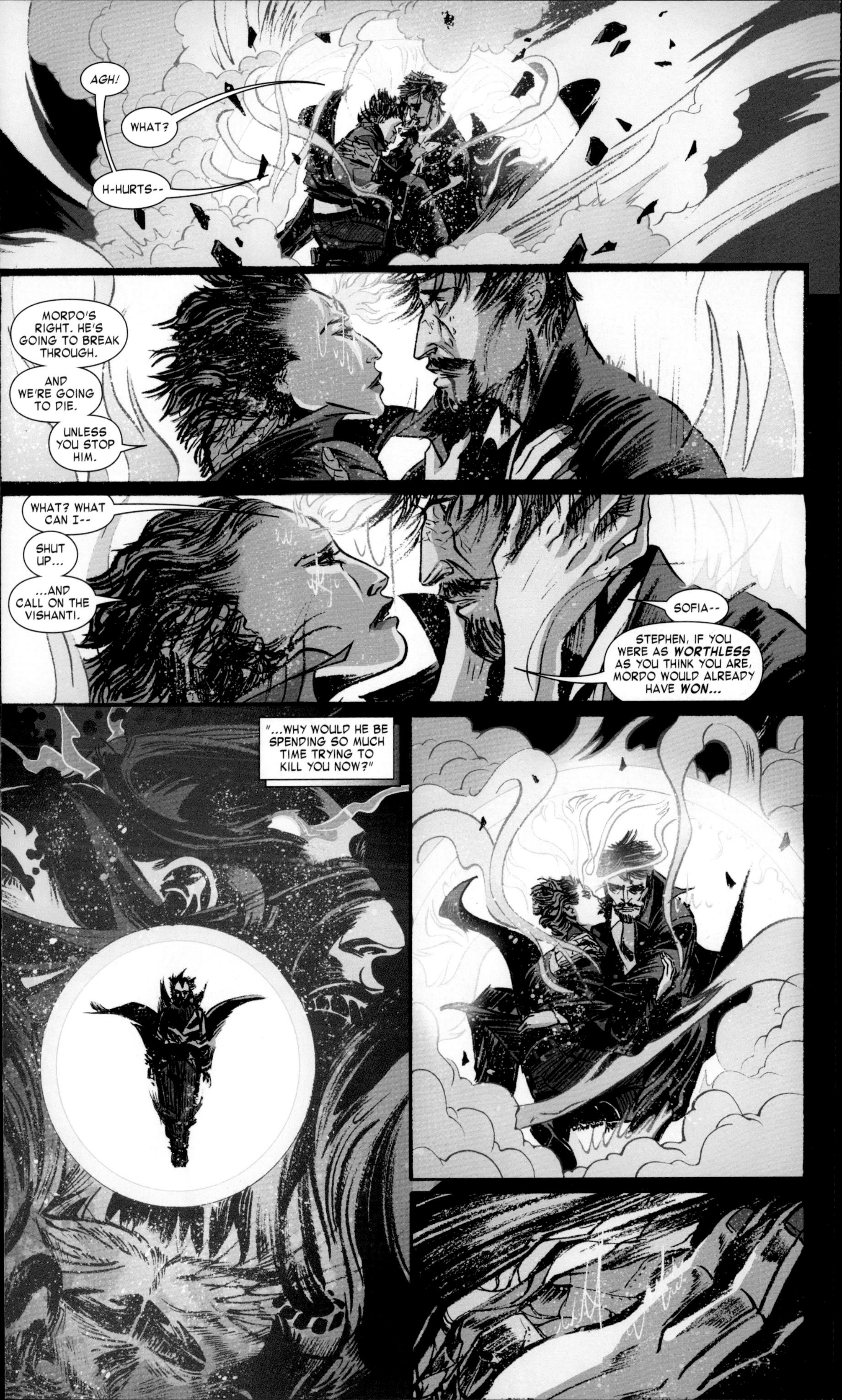
AGH!
WHAT?
H-HURTS--
MORDO'S RIGHT. HE'S GOING TO BREAK THROUGH.
AND WE'RE GOING TO DIE.
UNLESS YOU STOP HIM.
WHAT? WHAT CAN I--
SHUT UP...
...AND CALL ON THE VISHANTI.
SOFIA--
STEPHEN, IF YOU WERE AS WORTHLESS AS YOU THINK YOU ARE, MORDO WOULD ALREADY HAVE WON...
"...WHY WOULD HE BE SPENDING SO MUCH TIME TRYING TO KILL YOU NOW?"

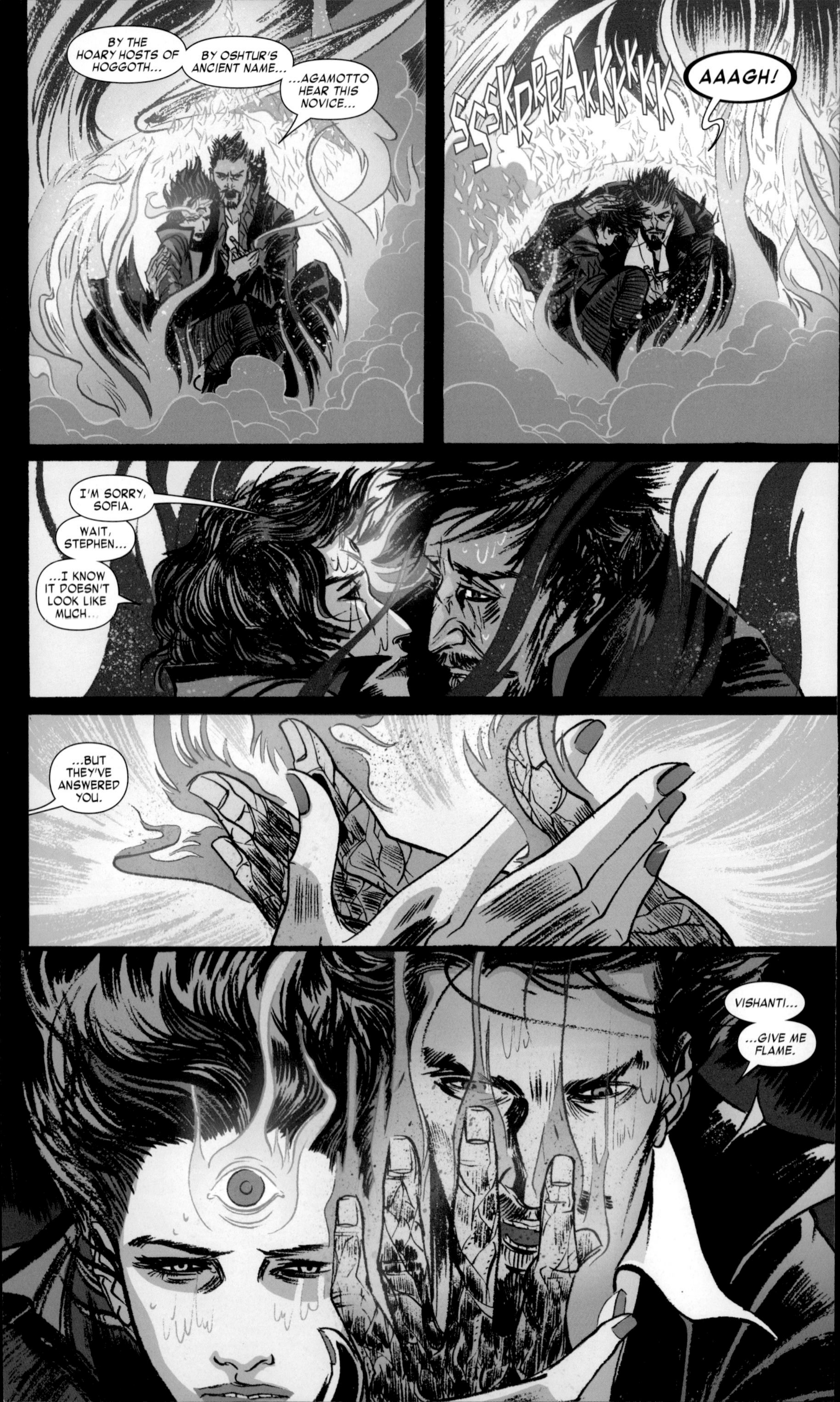
BY THE HOARY HOSTS OF HOGGOTH...
BY OSHTUR'S ANCIENT NAME...
...AGAMOTTO HEAR THIS NOVICE...
SCSKRRRAKKKKKK
AAAGH!
I'M SORRY, SOFIA.
WAIT, STEPHEN...
...I KNOW IT DOESN'T LOOK LIKE MUCH...
...BUT THEY'VE ANSWERED YOU.
VISHANTI...
...GIVE ME FLAME.

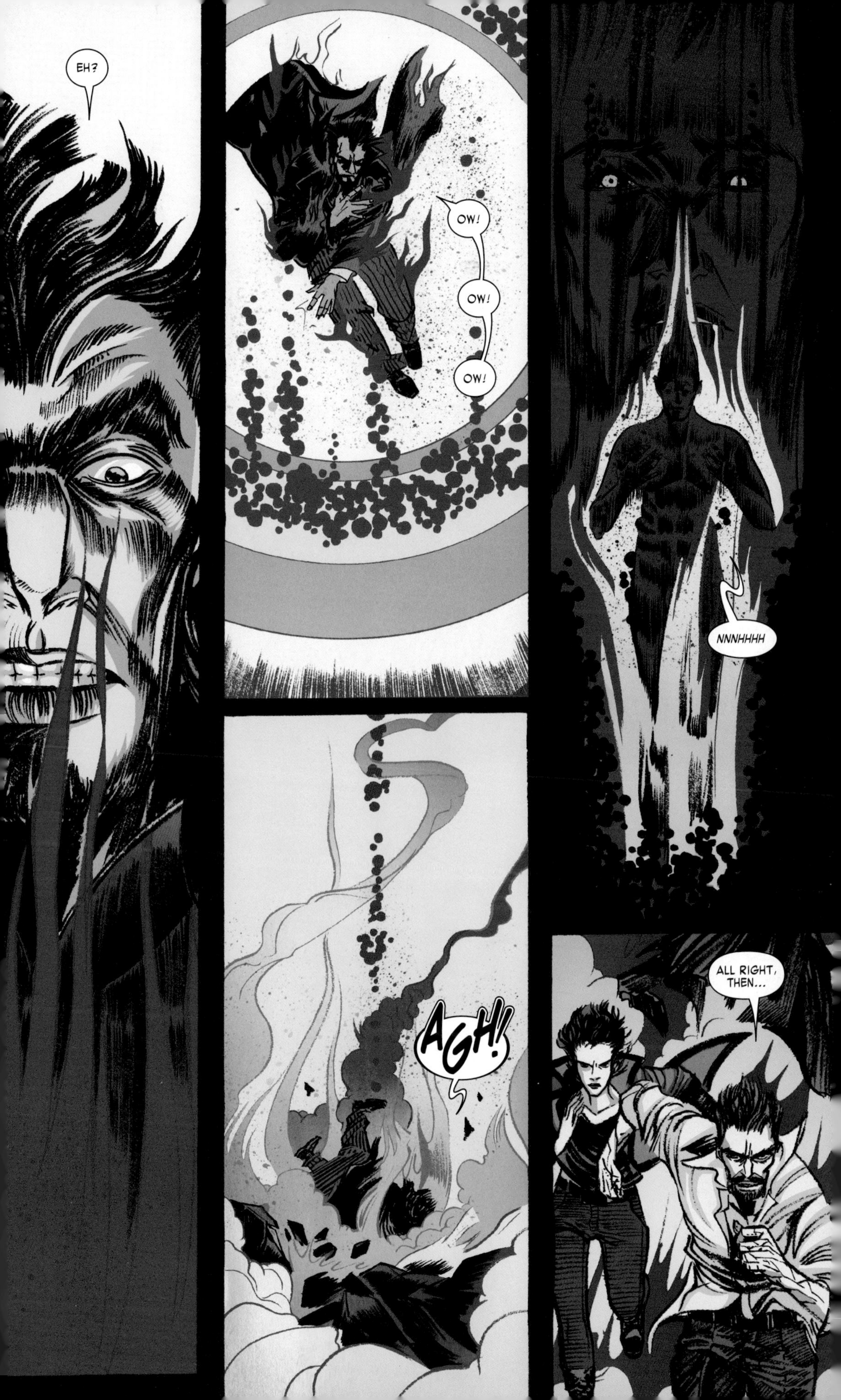
EH?
OW!
OW!
OW!
NNNHHHH
AGH!
ALL RIGHT, THEN...

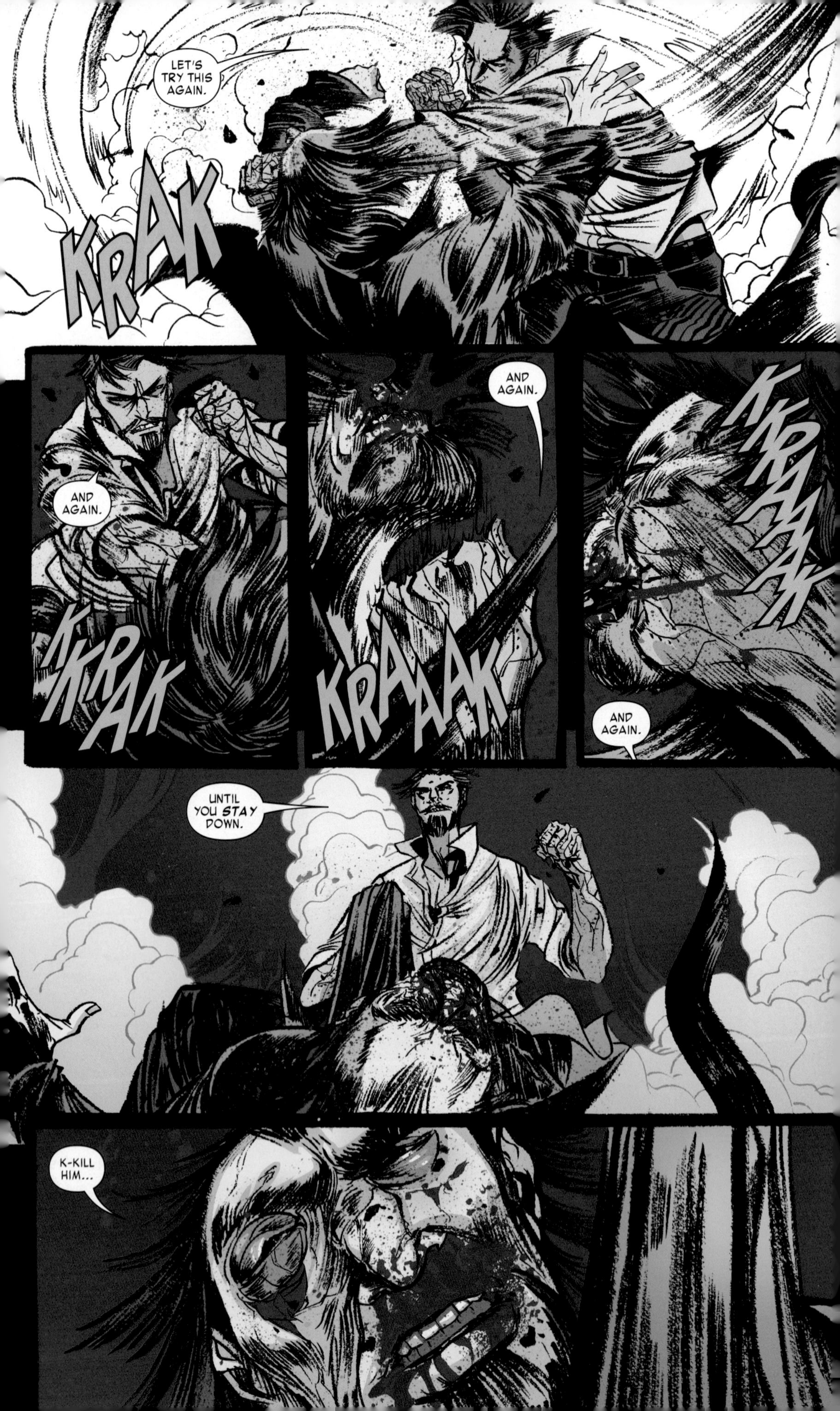

LET'S TRY THIS AGAIN.
KRAK
AND AGAIN.
KKRAK
AND AGAIN.
KRAAAK
KKRAAAAK
AND AGAIN.
UNTIL YOU STAY DOWN.
K-KILL HIM...

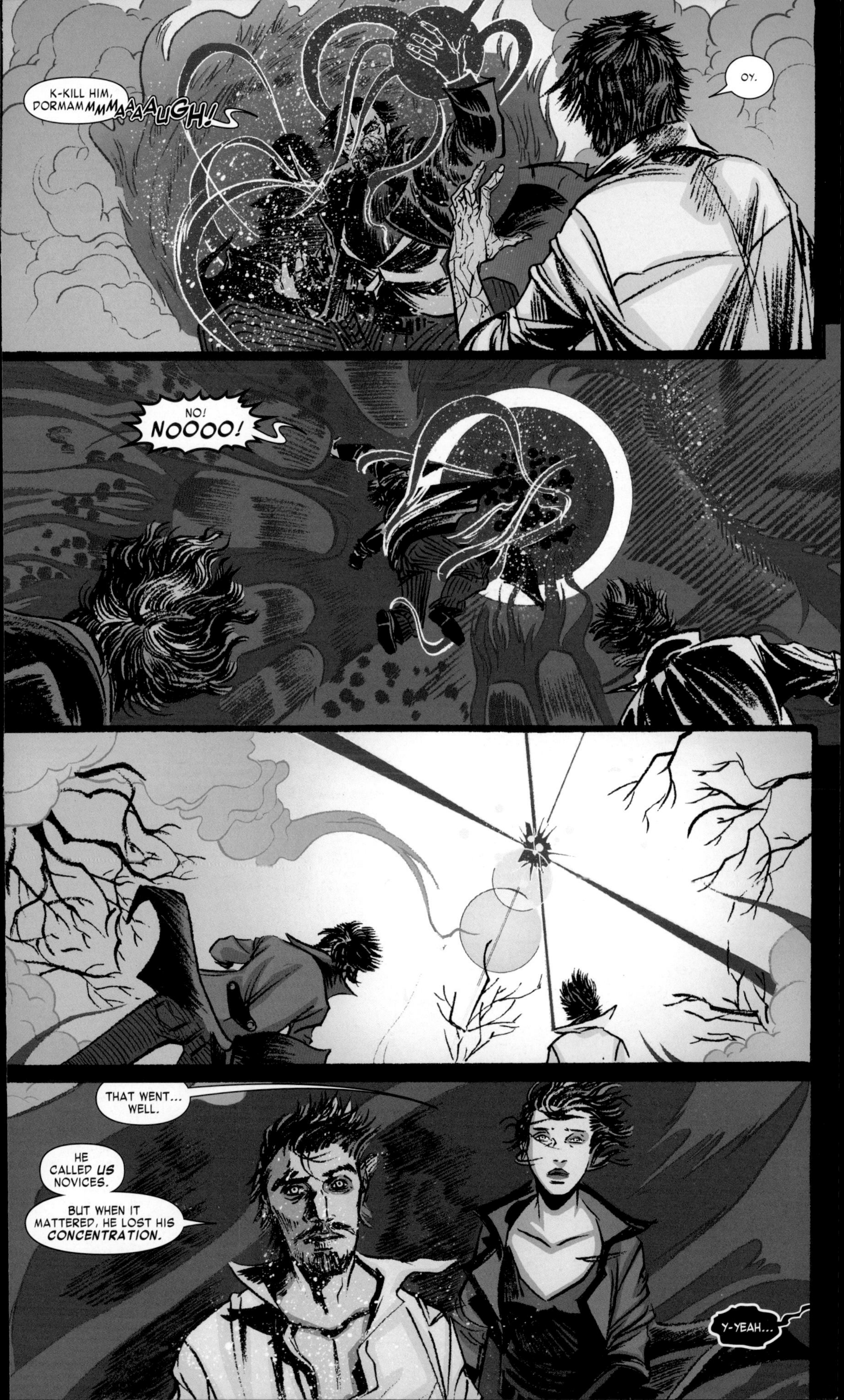
K-KILL HIM, DORMAMMMMAAAAUGH!
OY.
NO! NOOOO!
THAT WENT... WELL.
HE CALLED US NOVICES.
BUT WHEN IT MATTERED, HE LOST HIS CONCENTRATION.
Y-YEAH...

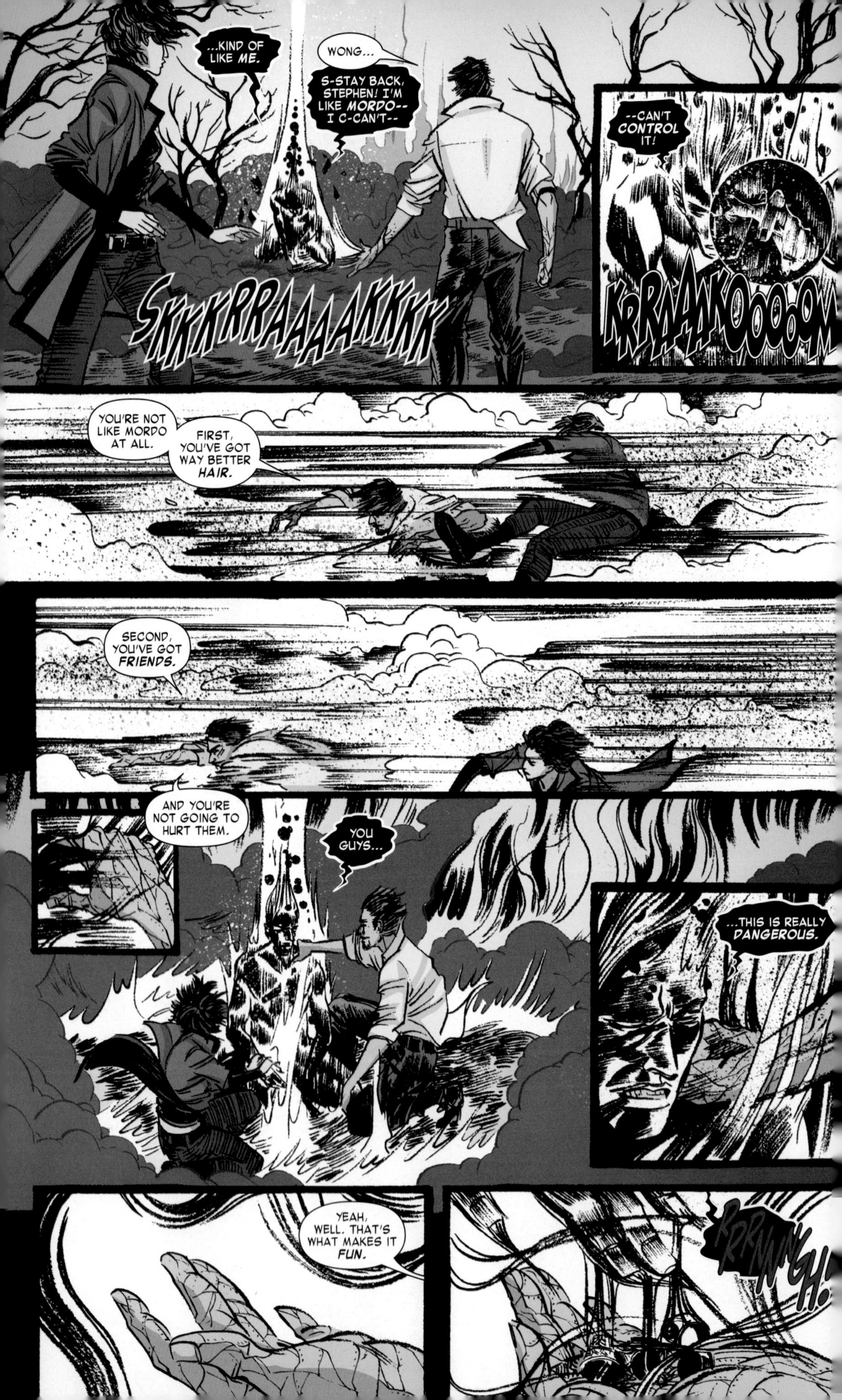

...KIND OF LIKE *ME.*
WONG...
S-STAY BACK, STEPHEN! I'M LIKE *MORDO*-- I C-CAN'T--
SKKKRRAAAAKKKK
--CAN'T *CONTROL* IT!
KRRAAAKOOOOOM
YOU'RE NOT LIKE MORDO AT ALL.
FIRST, YOU'VE GOT WAY BETTER *HAIR.*
SECOND, YOU'VE GOT *FRIENDS.*
AND YOU'RE NOT GOING TO HURT THEM.
YOU GUYS...
...THIS IS REALLY *DANGEROUS.*
YEAH, WELL. THAT'S WHAT MAKES IT *FUN.*
RRRNNNGH!

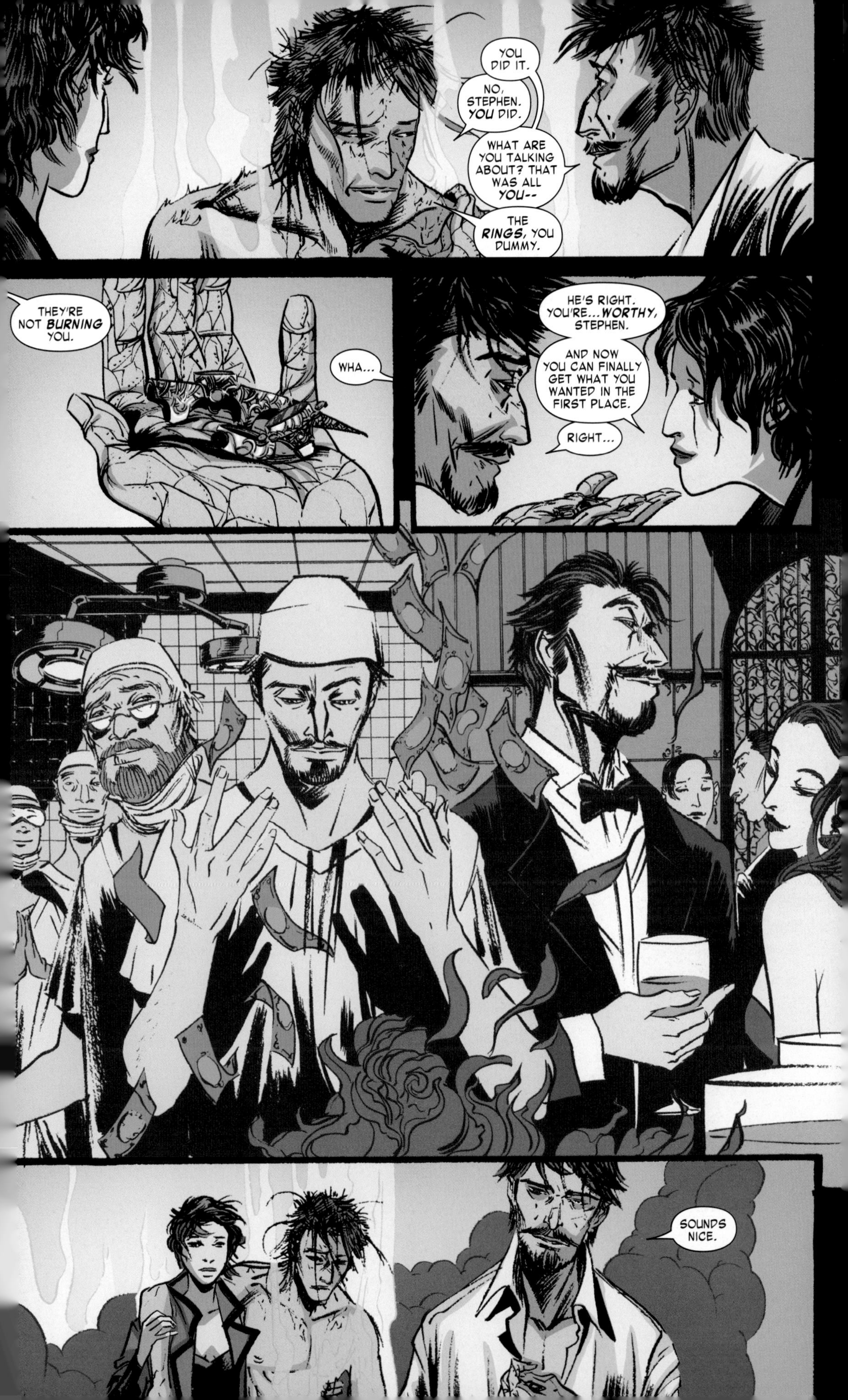
YOU DID IT.
NO, STEPHEN. YOU DID.
WHAT ARE YOU TALKING ABOUT? THAT WAS ALL YOU--
THE RINGS, YOU DUMMY.
THEY'RE NOT BURNING YOU.
WHA...
HE'S RIGHT. YOU'RE...WORTHY, STEPHEN.
AND NOW YOU CAN FINALLY GET WHAT YOU WANTED IN THE FIRST PLACE.
RIGHT...
SOUNDS NICE.

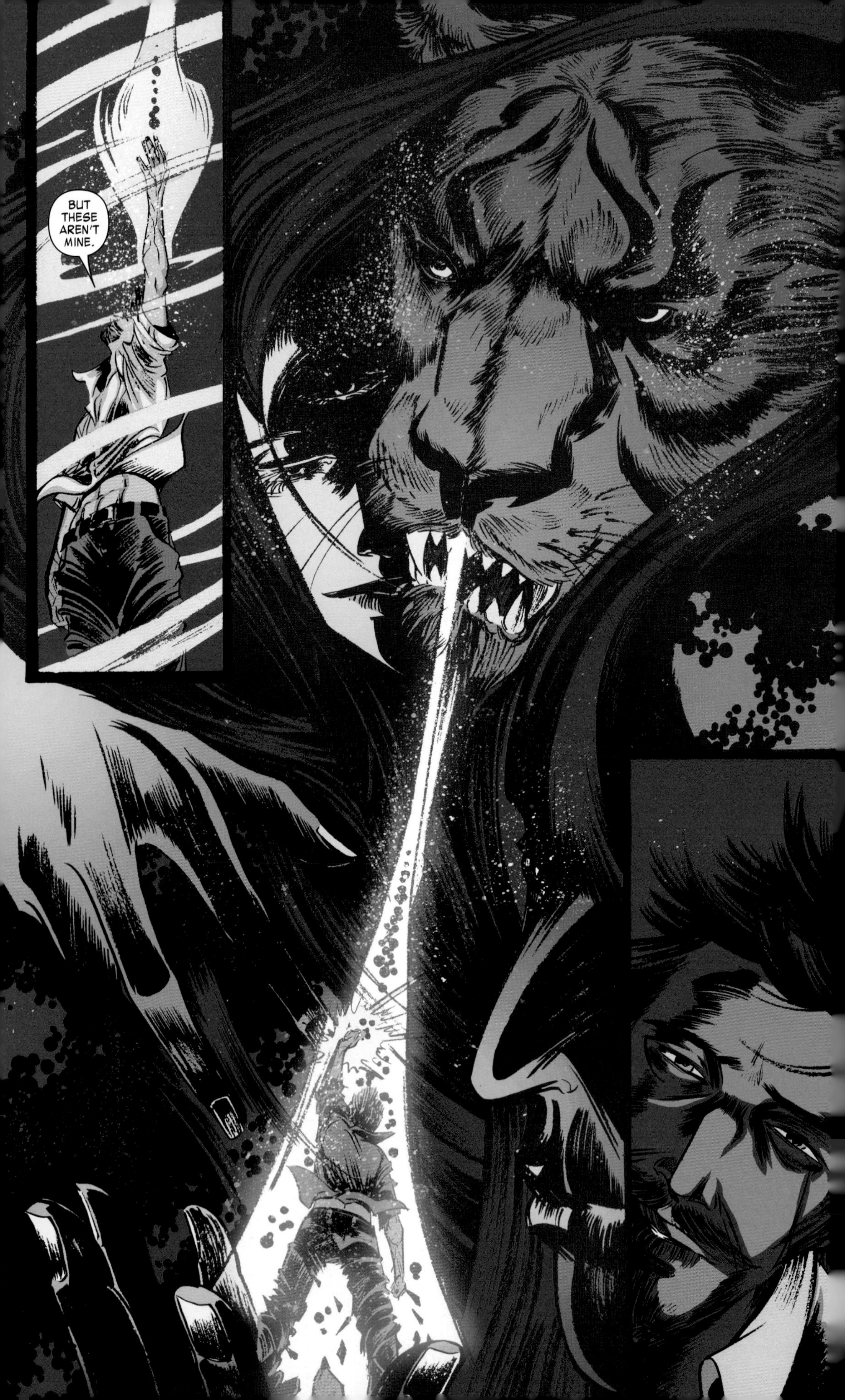
BUT THESE AREN'T MINE.

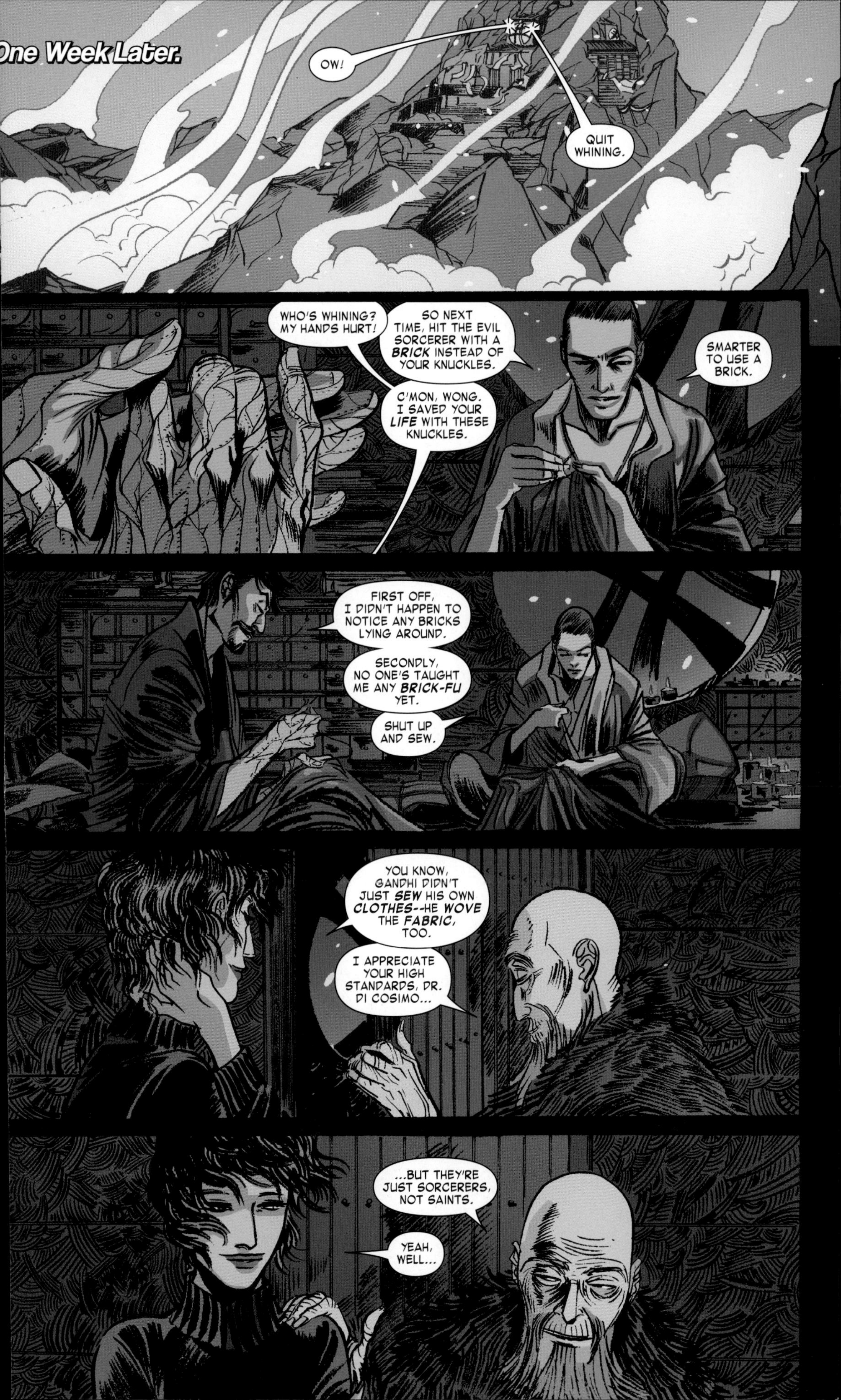

One Week Later.
OW!
QUIT WHINING.
WHO'S WHINING? MY HANDS HURT!
SO NEXT TIME, HIT THE EVIL SORCERER WITH A BRICK INSTEAD OF YOUR KNUCKLES.
SMARTER TO USE A BRICK.
C'MON, WONG. I SAVED YOUR LIFE WITH THESE KNUCKLES.
FIRST OFF, I DIDN'T HAPPEN TO NOTICE ANY BRICKS LYING AROUND.
SECONDLY, NO ONE'S TAUGHT ME ANY BRICK-FU YET.
SHUT UP AND SEW.
YOU KNOW, GANDHI DIDN'T JUST SEW HIS OWN CLOTHES--HE WOVE THE FABRIC, TOO.
I APPRECIATE YOUR HIGH STANDARDS, DR. DI COSIMO...
...BUT THEY'RE JUST SORCERERS, NOT SAINTS.
YEAH, WELL...

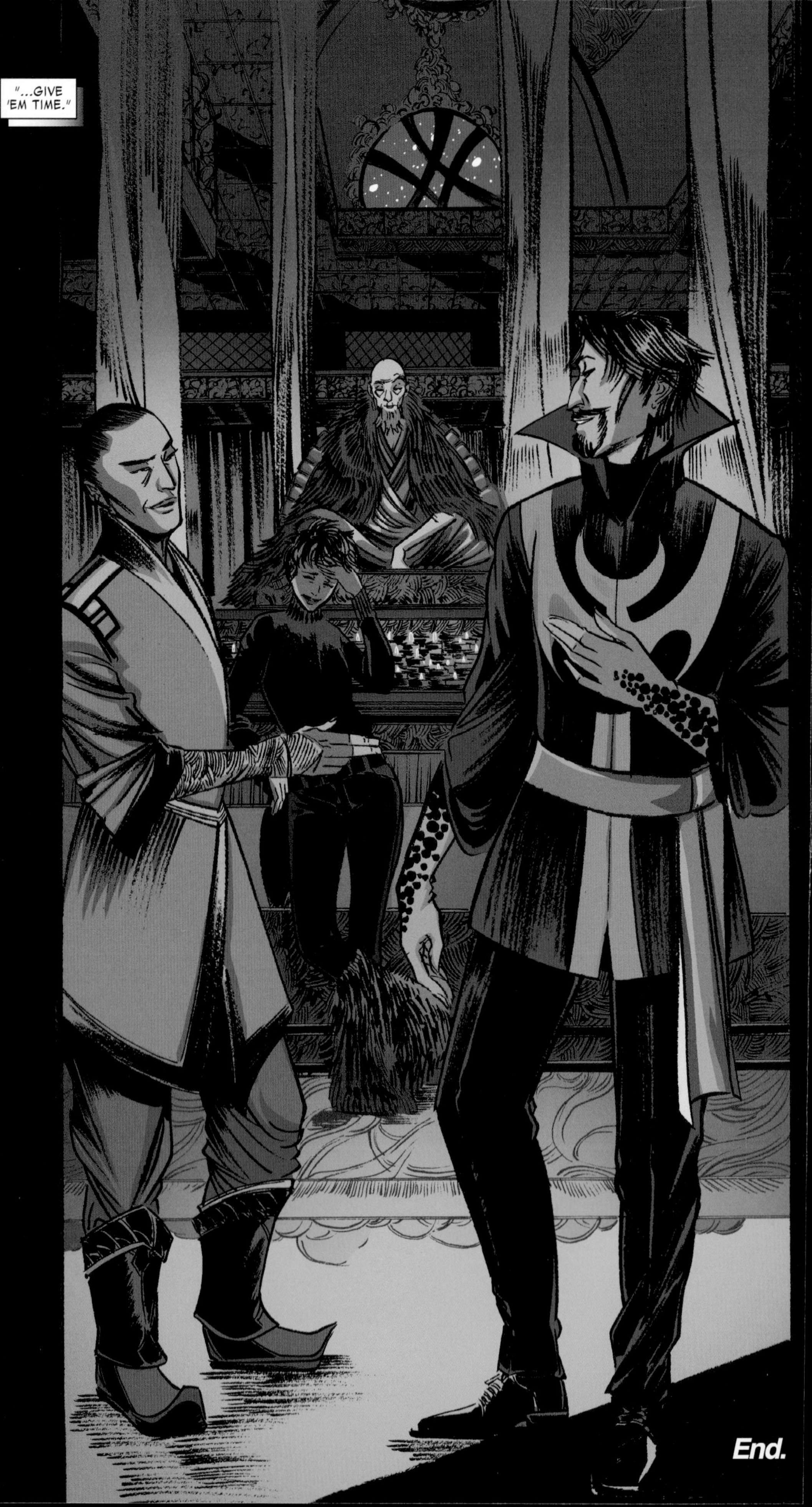
"...GIVE 'EM TIME."
End.

WHERE ARE THEY NOW? *DEFENDERS (2011) #1* EVERYONE'S FAVORITE MISFITS MUST BAND TOGETHER TO SOLVE A MYSTERIOUS CONSPIRACY DEEP AT THE HEART OF THE MARVEL UNIVERSE! THEY ARE THE ALL-NEW, ALL-DIFFERENT, ALL-DYNAMIC DEFENDERS — THE LAST LINE OF DEFENSE AGAINST THE FORCES OF THE UNKNOWN!

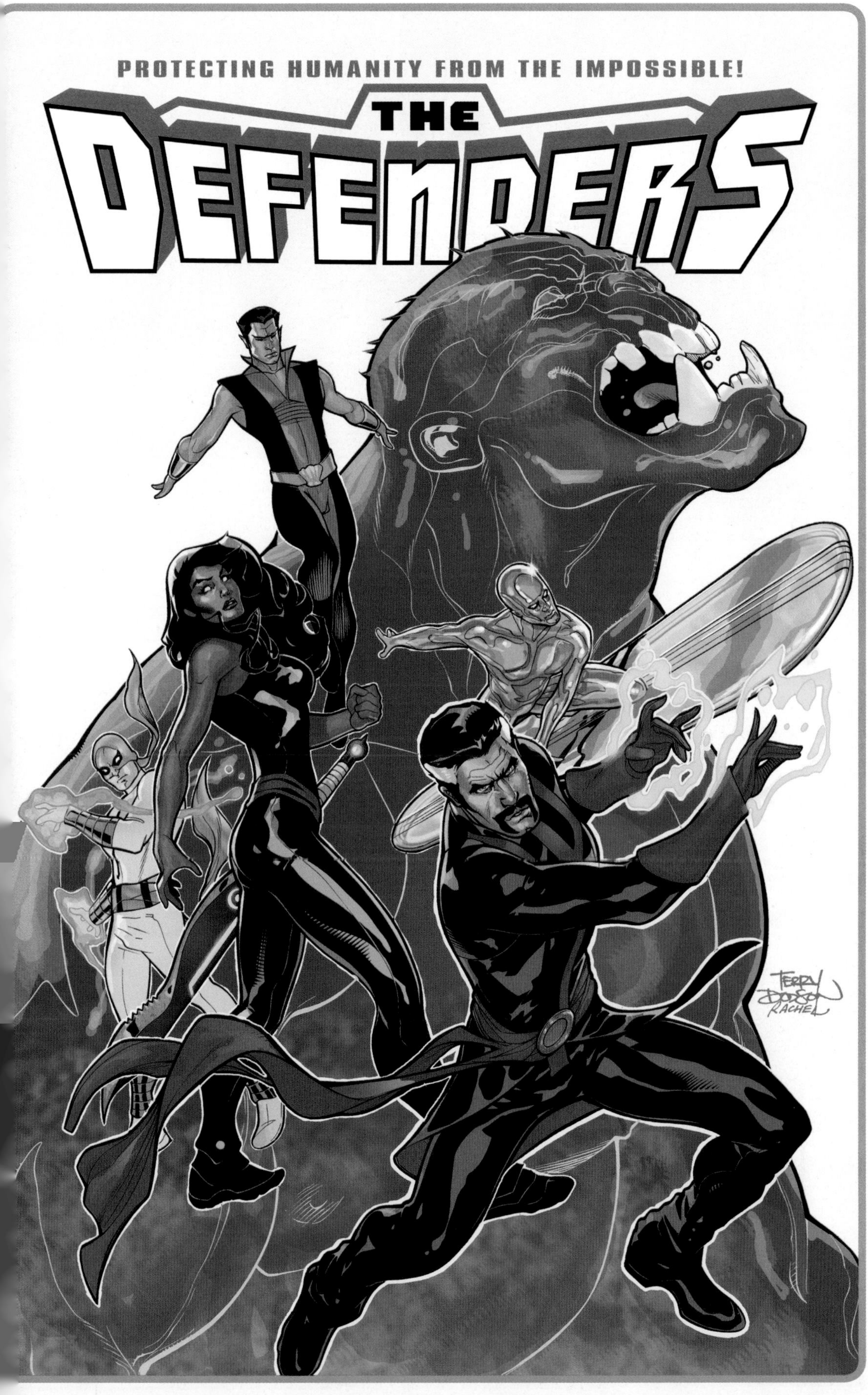
PROTECTING HUMANITY FROM THE IMPOSSIBLE!
THE DEFENDERS
TERRY DODSON RACHEL

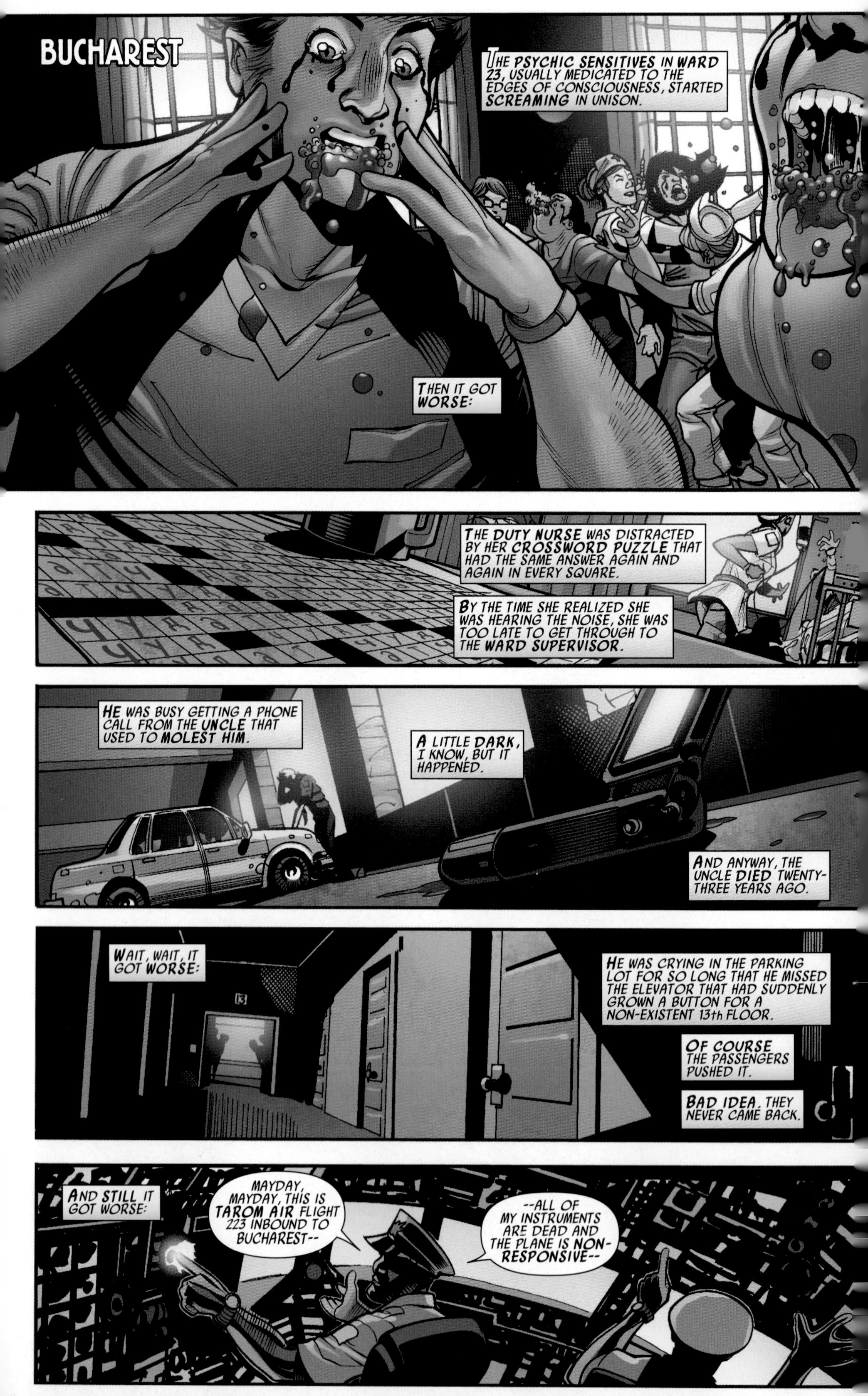
BUCHAREST
THE PSYCHIC SENSITIVES IN WARD 23, USUALLY MEDICATED TO THE EDGES OF CONSCIOUSNESS, STARTED SCREAMING IN UNISON.
THEN IT GOT WORSE:
THE DUTY NURSE WAS DISTRACTED BY HER CROSSWORD PUZZLE THAT HAD THE SAME ANSWER AGAIN AND AGAIN IN EVERY SQUARE.
BY THE TIME SHE REALIZED SHE WAS HEARING THE NOISE, SHE WAS TOO LATE TO GET THROUGH TO THE WARD SUPERVISOR.
HE WAS BUSY GETTING A PHONE CALL FROM THE UNCLE THAT USED TO MOLEST HIM.
A LITTLE DARK, I KNOW, BUT IT HAPPENED.
AND ANYWAY, THE UNCLE DIED TWENTY-THREE YEARS AGO.
WAIT, WAIT, IT GOT WORSE:
HE WAS CRYING IN THE PARKING LOT FOR SO LONG THAT HE MISSED THE ELEVATOR THAT HAD SUDDENLY GROWN A BUTTON FOR A NON-EXISTENT 13th FLOOR.
OF COURSE THE PASSENGERS PUSHED IT.
BAD IDEA. THEY NEVER CAME BACK.
AND STILL IT GOT WORSE:
MAYDAY, MAYDAY, THIS IS TAROM AIR FLIGHT 223 INBOUND TO BUCHAREST--
--ALL OF MY INSTRUMENTS ARE DEAD AND THE PLANE IS NON-RESPONSIVE--

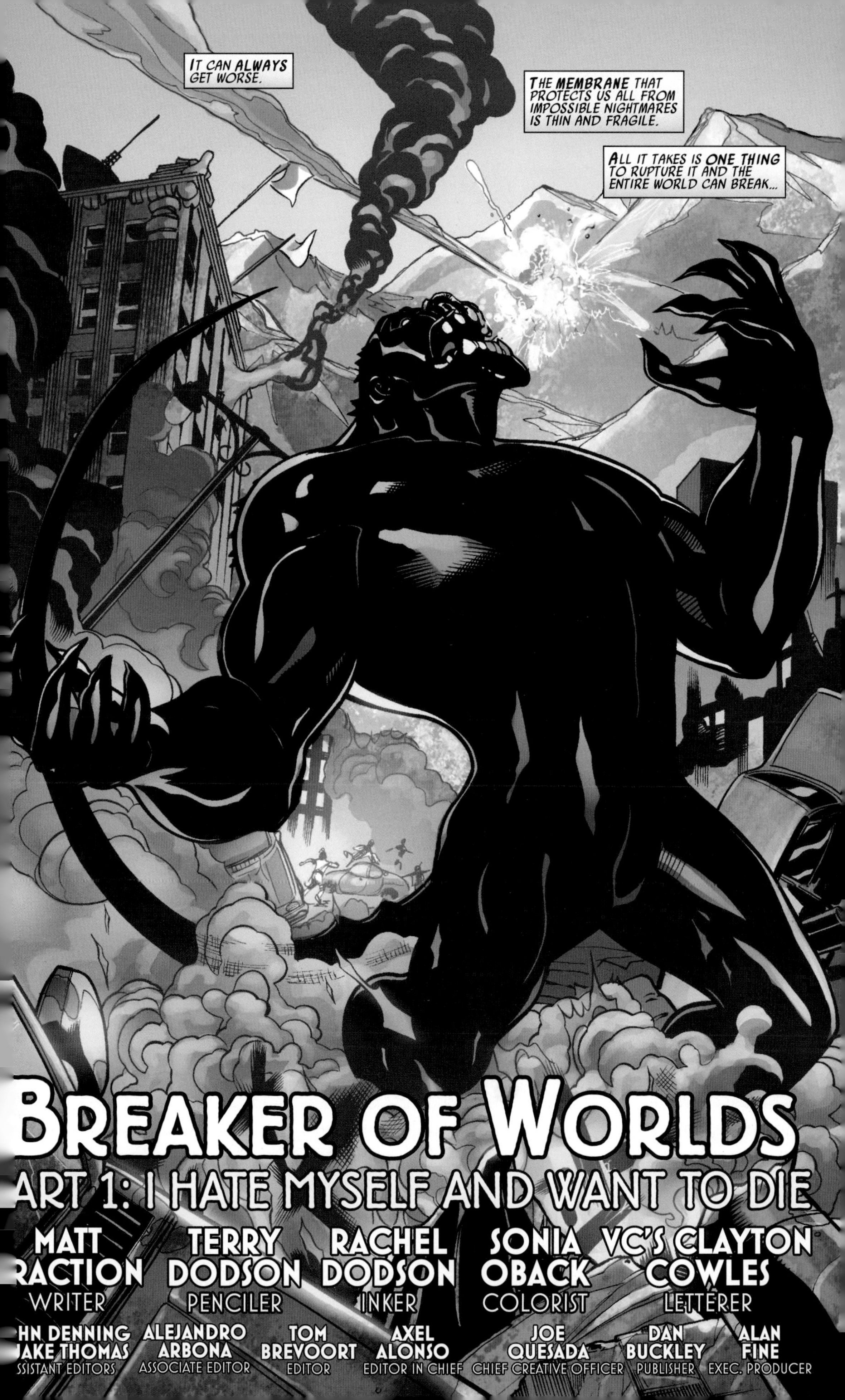
IT CAN ALWAYS GET WORSE.
THE MEMBRANE THAT PROTECTS US ALL FROM IMPOSSIBLE NIGHTMARES IS THIN AND FRAGILE.
ALL IT TAKES IS ONE THING TO RUPTURE IT AND THE ENTIRE WORLD CAN BREAK...
BREAKER OF WORLDS
ART 1: I HATE MYSELF AND WANT TO DIE
MATT RACTION WRITER
TERRY DODSON PENCILER
RACHEL DODSON INKER
SONIA OBACK COLORIST
VC'S CLAYTON COWLES LETTERER
HN DENNING JAKE THOMAS SSISTANT EDITORS
ALEJANDRO ARBONA ASSOCIATE EDITOR
TOM BREVOORT EDITOR
AXEL ALONSO EDITOR IN CHIEF
JOE QUESADA CHIEF CREATIVE OFFICER
DAN BUCKLEY PUBLISHER
ALAN FINE EXEC. PRODUCER

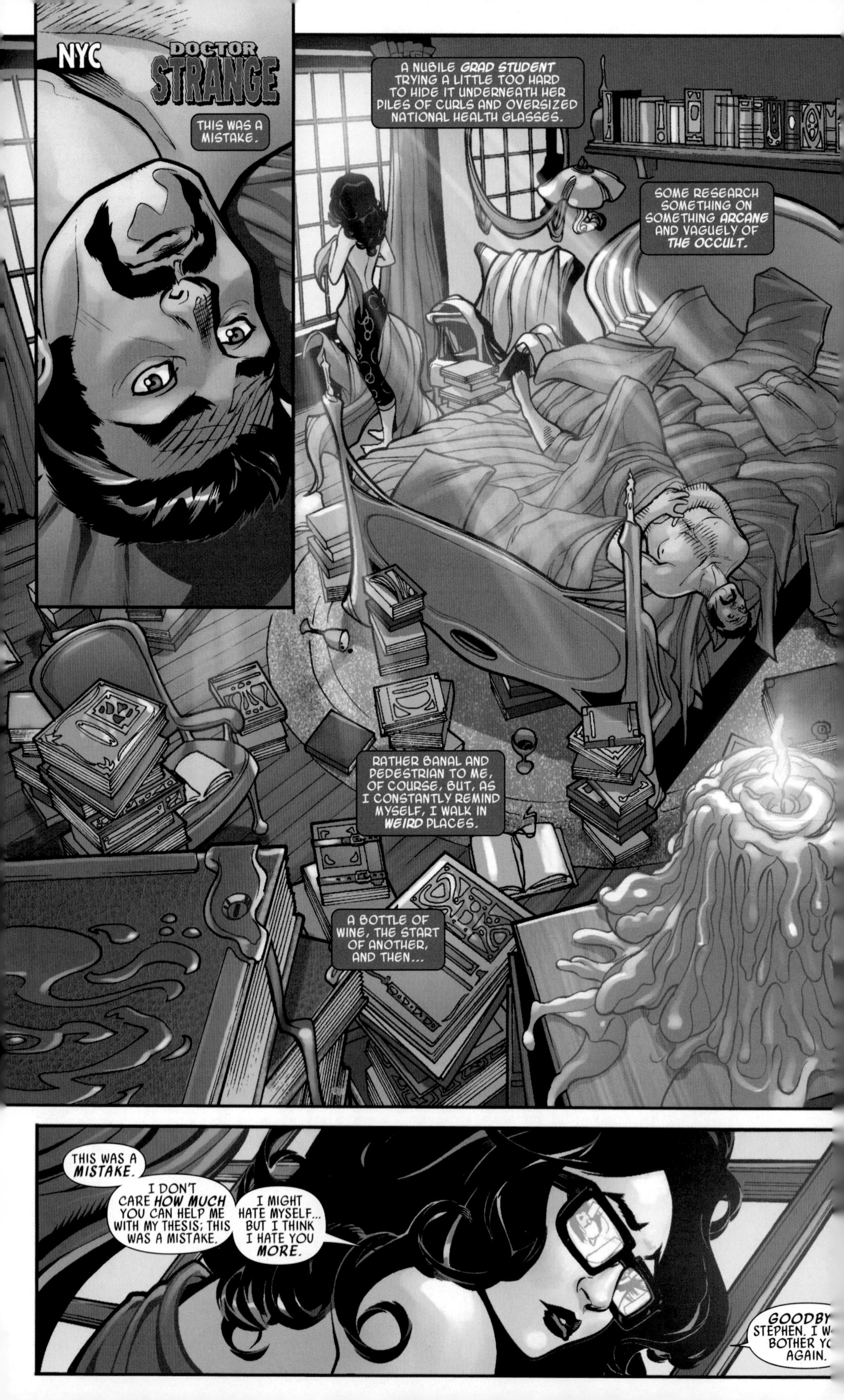
NYC
DOCTOR STRANGE
THIS WAS A MISTAKE.
A NUBILE GRAD STUDENT TRYING A LITTLE TOO HARD TO HIDE IT UNDERNEATH HER PILES OF CURLS AND OVERSIZED NATIONAL HEALTH GLASSES.
SOME RESEARCH SOMETHING ON SOMETHING ARCANE AND VAGUELY OF THE OCCULT.
RATHER BANAL AND PEDESTRIAN TO ME, OF COURSE, BUT, AS I CONSTANTLY REMIND MYSELF, I WALK IN WEIRD PLACES.
A BOTTLE OF WINE, THE START OF ANOTHER, AND THEN...
THIS WAS A MISTAKE.
I DON'T CARE HOW MUCH YOU CAN HELP ME WITH MY THESIS; THIS WAS A MISTAKE.
I MIGHT HATE MYSELF... BUT I THINK I HATE YOU MORE.
GOODBY STEPHEN. I W BOTHER YO AGAIN.

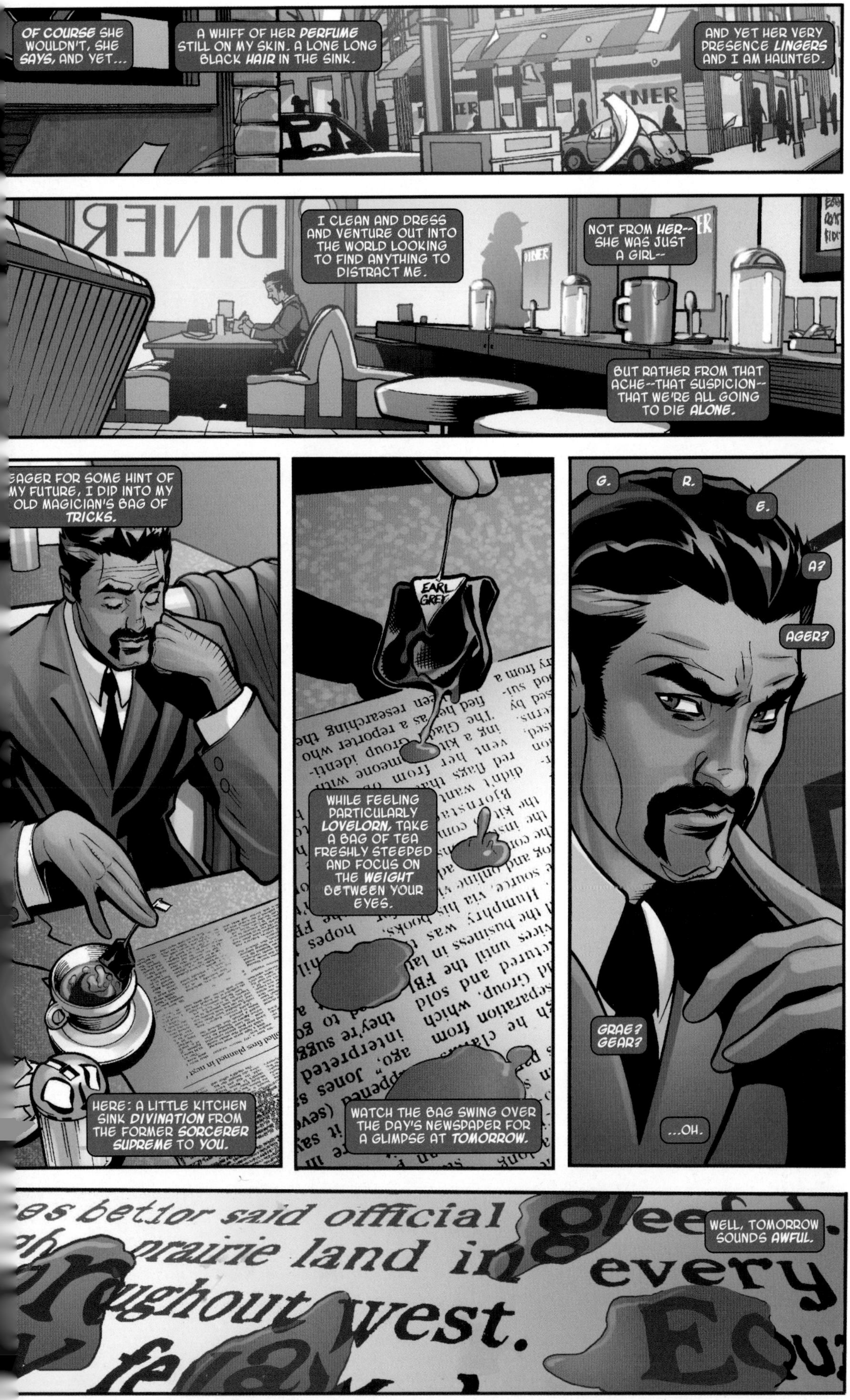
OF COURSE SHE WOULDN'T, SHE SAYS, AND YET...
A WHIFF OF HER PERFUME STILL ON MY SKIN. A LONE LONG BLACK HAIR IN THE SINK.
AND YET HER VERY PRESENCE LINGERS AND I AM HAUNTED.
I CLEAN AND DRESS AND VENTURE OUT INTO THE WORLD LOOKING TO FIND ANYTHING TO DISTRACT ME.
NOT FROM HER-- SHE WAS JUST A GIRL--
BUT RATHER FROM THAT ACHE--THAT SUSPICION-- THAT WE'RE ALL GOING TO DIE ALONE.
EAGER FOR SOME HINT OF MY FUTURE, I DIP INTO MY OLD MAGICIAN'S BAG OF TRICKS.
HERE: A LITTLE KITCHEN SINK DIVINATION FROM THE FORMER SORCERER SUPREME TO YOU.
EARL GREY
WHILE FEELING PARTICULARLY LOVELORN, TAKE A BAG OF TEA FRESHLY STEEPED AND FOCUS ON THE WEIGHT BETWEEN YOUR EYES.
WATCH THE BAG SWING OVER THE DAY'S NEWSPAPER FOR A GLIMPSE AT TOMORROW.
G.
R.
E.
A?
AGER?
GRAE? GEAR?
...OH.
WELL, TOMORROW SOUNDS AWFUL.

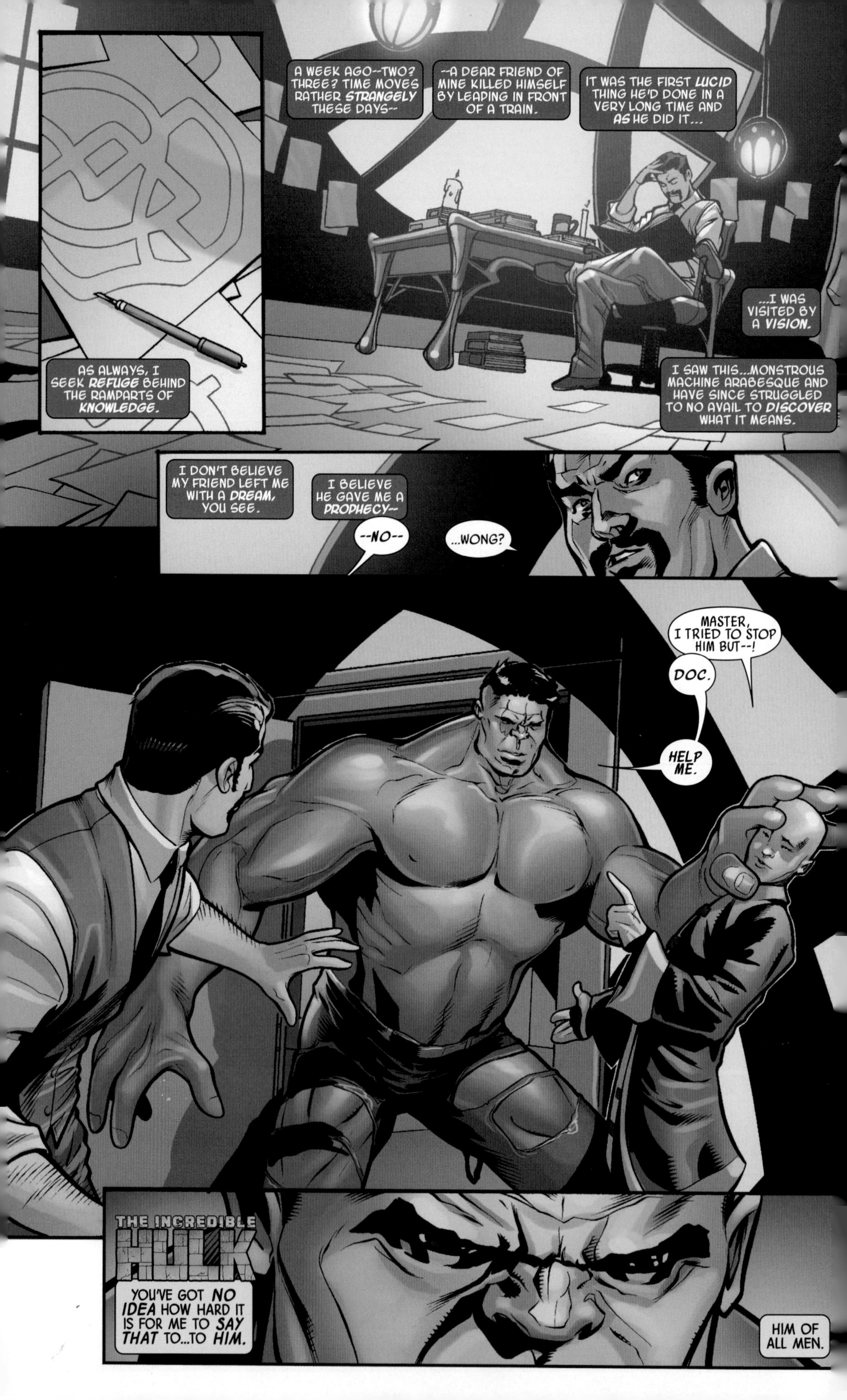

AS ALWAYS, I SEEK REFUGE BEHIND THE RAMPARTS OF KNOWLEDGE.
A WEEK AGO--TWO? THREE? TIME MOVES RATHER STRANGELY THESE DAYS--
--A DEAR FRIEND OF MINE KILLED HIMSELF BY LEAPING IN FRONT OF A TRAIN.
IT WAS THE FIRST LUCID THING HE'D DONE IN A VERY LONG TIME AND AS HE DID IT...
...I WAS VISITED BY A VISION.
I SAW THIS...MONSTROUS MACHINE ARABESQUE AND HAVE SINCE STRUGGLED TO NO AVAIL TO DISCOVER WHAT IT MEANS.
I DON'T BELIEVE MY FRIEND LEFT ME WITH A DREAM, YOU SEE.
I BELIEVE HE GAVE ME A PROPHECY--
--NO--
...WONG?
MASTER, I TRIED TO STOP HIM BUT--!
DOC.
HELP ME.
THE INCREDIBLE HULK
YOU'VE GOT NO IDEA HOW HARD IT IS FOR ME TO SAY THAT TO...TO HIM.
HIM OF ALL MEN.

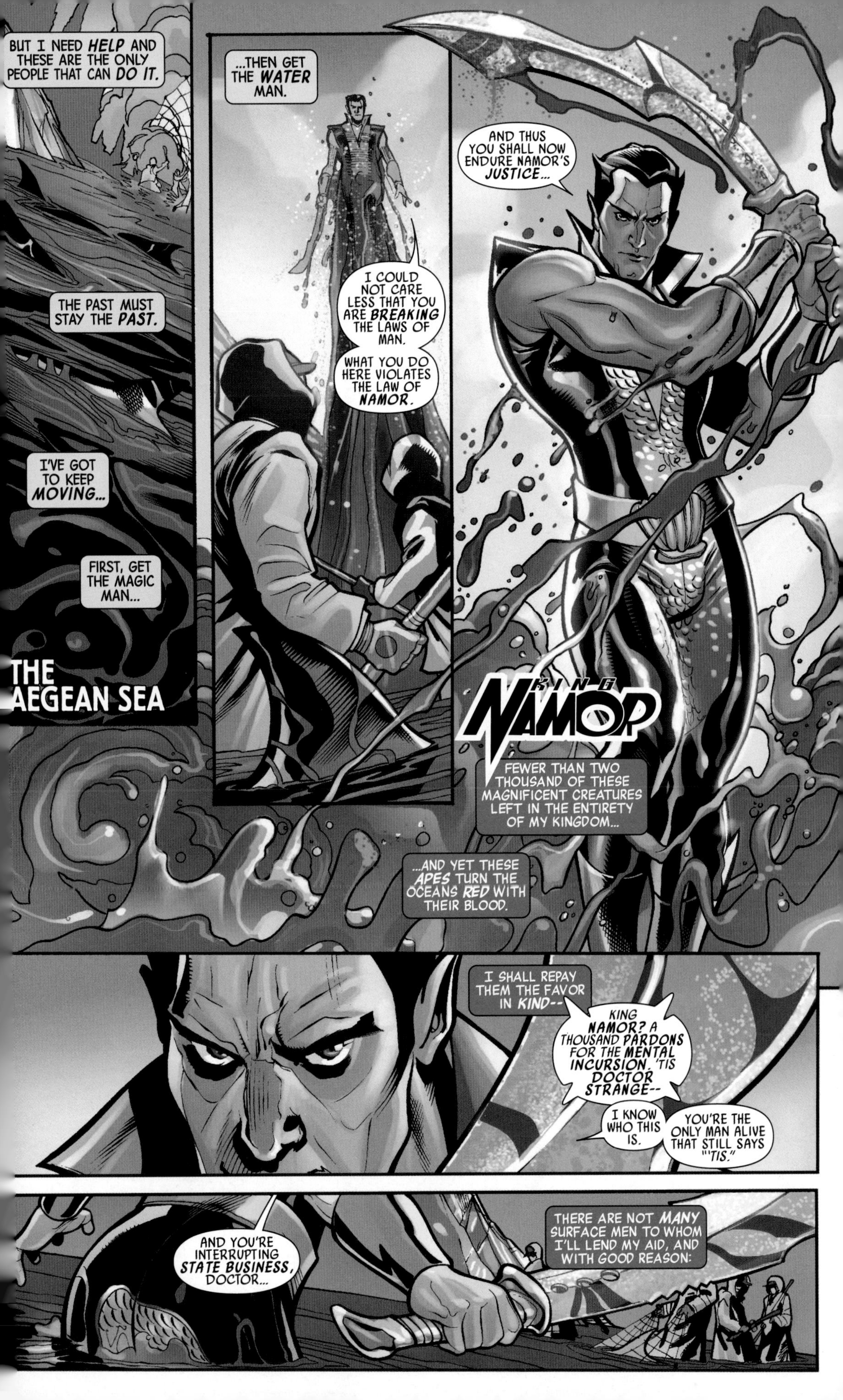

BUT I NEED HELP AND THESE ARE THE ONLY PEOPLE THAT CAN DO IT.
THE PAST MUST STAY THE PAST.
I'VE GOT TO KEEP MOVING...
FIRST, GET THE MAGIC MAN...
THE AEGEAN SEA
...THEN GET THE WATER MAN.
I COULD NOT CARE LESS THAT YOU ARE BREAKING THE LAWS OF MAN.
WHAT YOU DO HERE VIOLATES THE LAW OF NAMOR.
AND THUS YOU SHALL NOW ENDURE NAMOR'S JUSTICE...
KING NAMOR
FEWER THAN TWO THOUSAND OF THESE MAGNIFICENT CREATURES LEFT IN THE ENTIRETY OF MY KINGDOM...
...AND YET THESE APES TURN THE OCEANS RED WITH THEIR BLOOD.
I SHALL REPAY THEM THE FAVOR IN KIND--
KING NAMOR? A THOUSAND PARDONS FOR THE MENTAL INCURSION. 'TIS DOCTOR STRANGE--
I KNOW WHO THIS IS.
YOU'RE THE ONLY MAN ALIVE THAT STILL SAYS "'TIS."
AND YOU'RE INTERRUPTING STATE BUSINESS, DOCTOR...
THERE ARE NOT MANY SURFACE MEN TO WHOM I'LL LEND MY AID, AND WITH GOOD REASON:

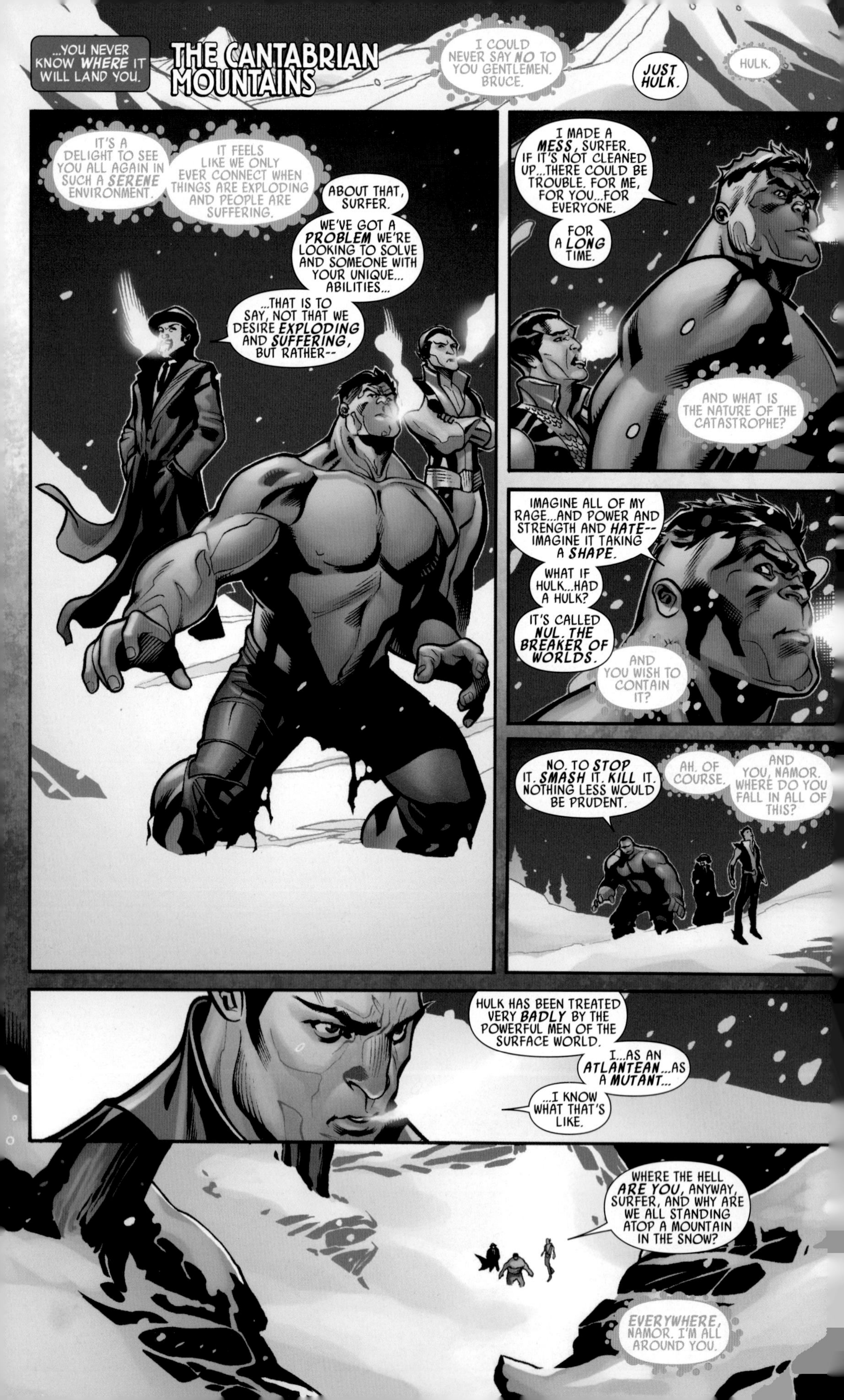
...YOU NEVER KNOW WHERE IT WILL LAND YOU.
THE CANTABRIAN MOUNTAINS
I COULD NEVER SAY NO TO YOU GENTLEMEN. BRUCE.
JUST HULK.
HULK.
IT'S A DELIGHT TO SEE YOU ALL AGAIN IN SUCH A SERENE ENVIRONMENT.
IT FEELS LIKE WE ONLY EVER CONNECT WHEN THINGS ARE EXPLODING AND PEOPLE ARE SUFFERING.
ABOUT THAT, SURFER.
WE'VE GOT A PROBLEM WE'RE LOOKING TO SOLVE AND SOMEONE WITH YOUR UNIQUE... ABILITIES...
...THAT IS TO SAY, NOT THAT WE DESIRE EXPLODING AND SUFFERING, BUT RATHER--
I MADE A MESS, SURFER. IF IT'S NOT CLEANED UP...THERE COULD BE TROUBLE. FOR ME, FOR YOU...FOR EVERYONE.
FOR A LONG TIME.
AND WHAT IS THE NATURE OF THE CATASTROPHE?
IMAGINE ALL OF MY RAGE...AND POWER AND STRENGTH AND HATE-- IMAGINE IT TAKING A SHAPE.
WHAT IF HULK...HAD A HULK?
IT'S CALLED NUL, THE BREAKER OF WORLDS.
AND YOU WISH TO CONTAIN IT?
NO. TO STOP IT. SMASH IT. KILL IT. NOTHING LESS WOULD BE PRUDENT.
AH, OF COURSE.
AND YOU, NAMOR. WHERE DO YOU FALL IN ALL OF THIS?
HULK HAS BEEN TREATED VERY BADLY BY THE POWERFUL MEN OF THE SURFACE WORLD.
I...AS AN ATLANTEAN...AS A MUTANT...
...I KNOW WHAT THAT'S LIKE.
WHERE THE HELL ARE YOU, ANYWAY, SURFER, AND WHY ARE WE ALL STANDING ATOP A MOUNTAIN IN THE SNOW?
EVERYWHERE, NAMOR. I'M ALL AROUND YOU.

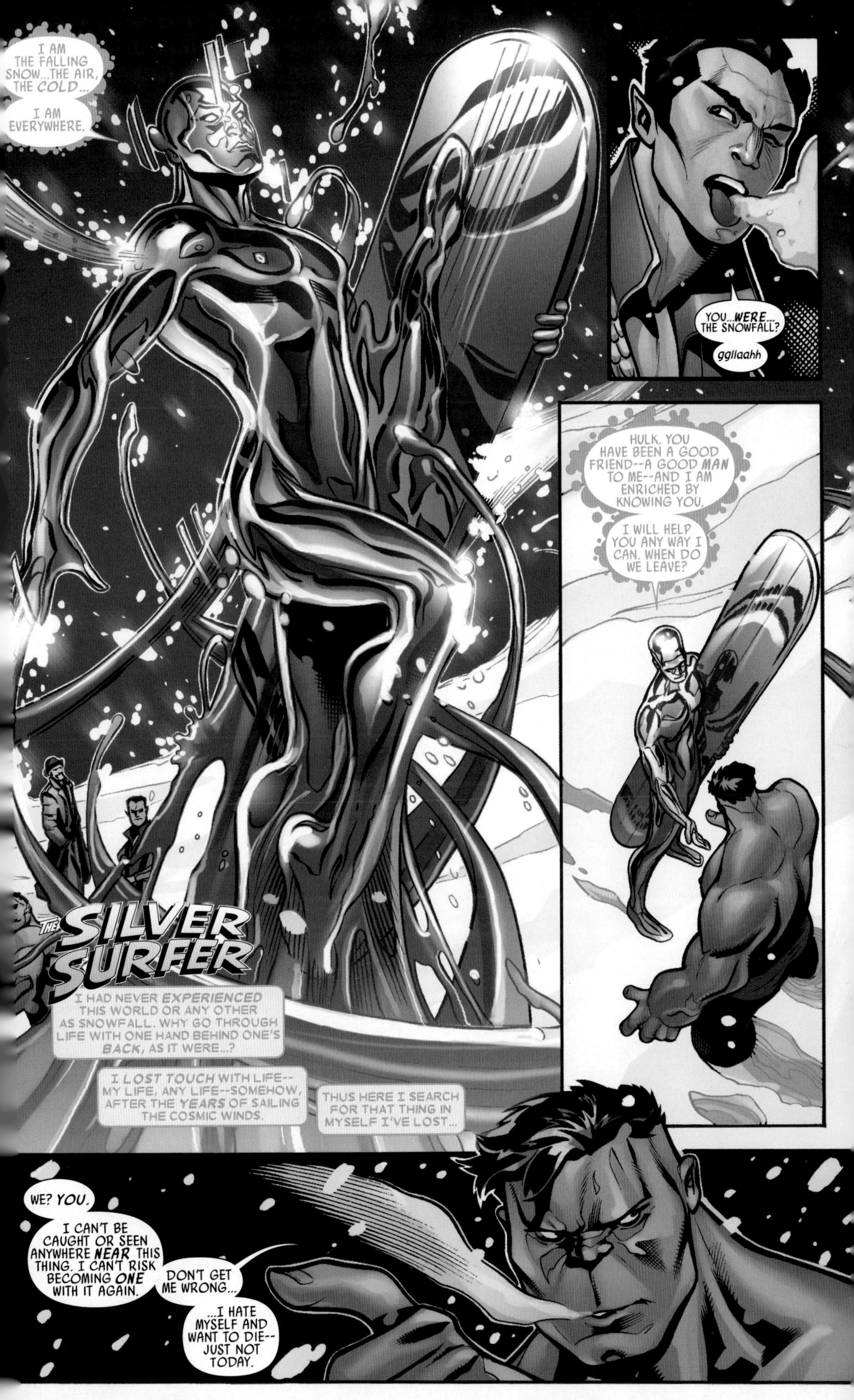
I AM THE FALLING SNOW...THE AIR, THE COLD...
I AM EVERYWHERE.
YOU...WERE... THE SNOWFALL?
ggllaahh
HULK. YOU HAVE BEEN A GOOD FRIEND--A GOOD MAN TO ME--AND I AM ENRICHED BY KNOWING YOU.
I WILL HELP YOU ANY WAY I CAN. WHEN DO WE LEAVE?
THE SILVER SURFER
I HAD NEVER EXPERIENCED THIS WORLD OR ANY OTHER AS SNOWFALL. WHY GO THROUGH LIFE WITH ONE HAND BEHIND ONE'S BACK, AS IT WERE...?
I LOST TOUCH WITH LIFE--MY LIFE, ANY LIFE--SOMEHOW, AFTER THE YEARS OF SAILING THE COSMIC WINDS.
THUS HERE I SEARCH FOR THAT THING IN MYSELF I'VE LOST...
WE? YOU.
I CAN'T BE CAUGHT OR SEEN ANYWHERE NEAR THIS THING. I CAN'T RISK BECOMING ONE WITH IT AGAIN.
DON'T GET ME WRONG...
...I HATE MYSELF AND WANT TO DIE--JUST NOT TODAY.

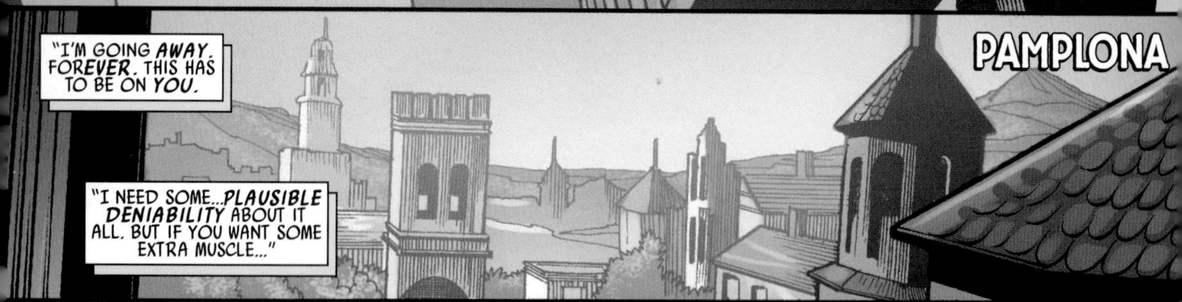
"I'M GOING AWAY. FOREVER. THIS HAS TO BE ON YOU.
PAMPLONA
"I NEED SOME...PLAUSIBLE DENIABILITY ABOUT IT ALL. BUT IF YOU WANT SOME EXTRA MUSCLE..."
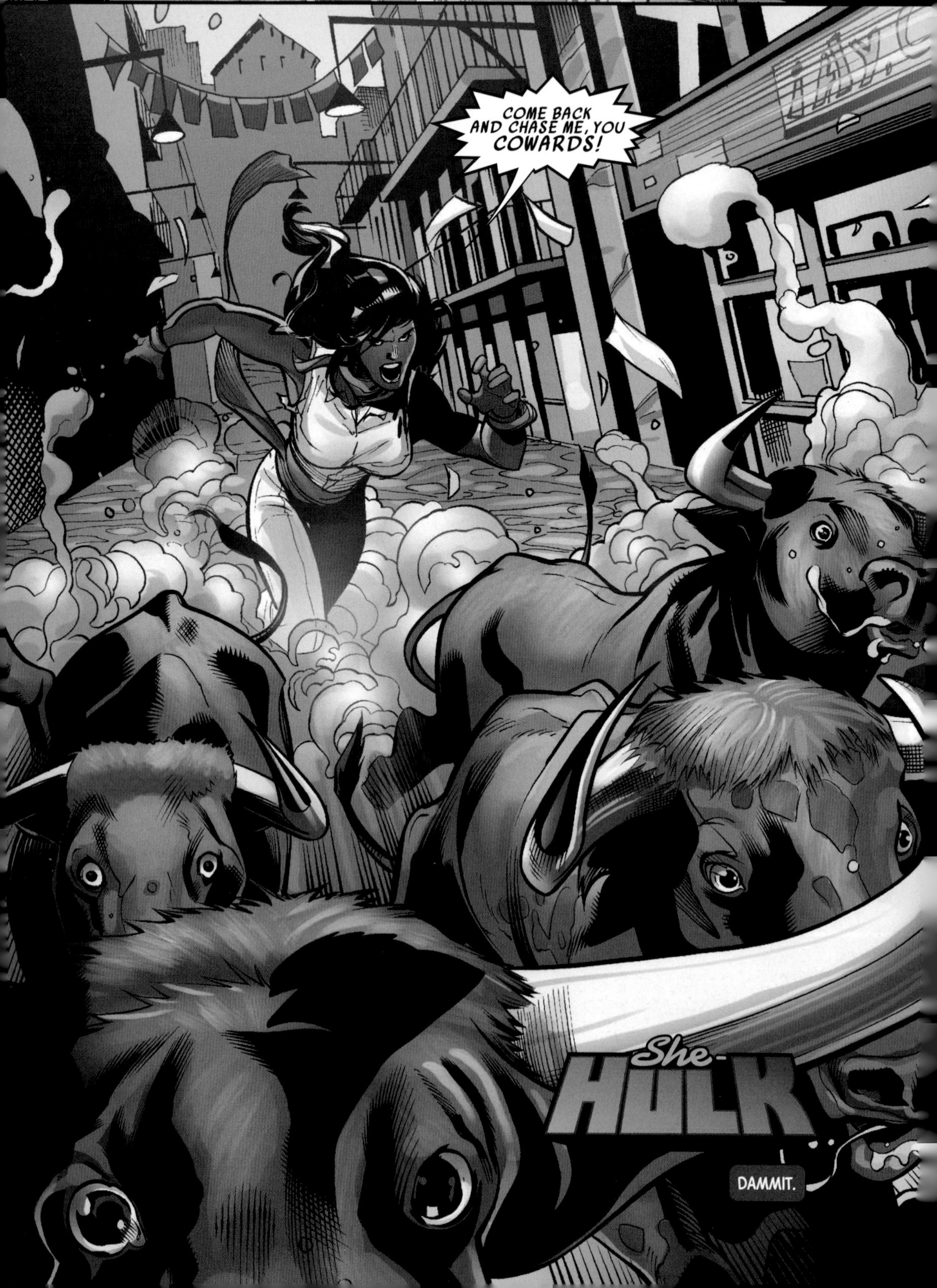
COME BACK AND CHASE ME, YOU COWARDS!
She-HULK
DAMMIT.

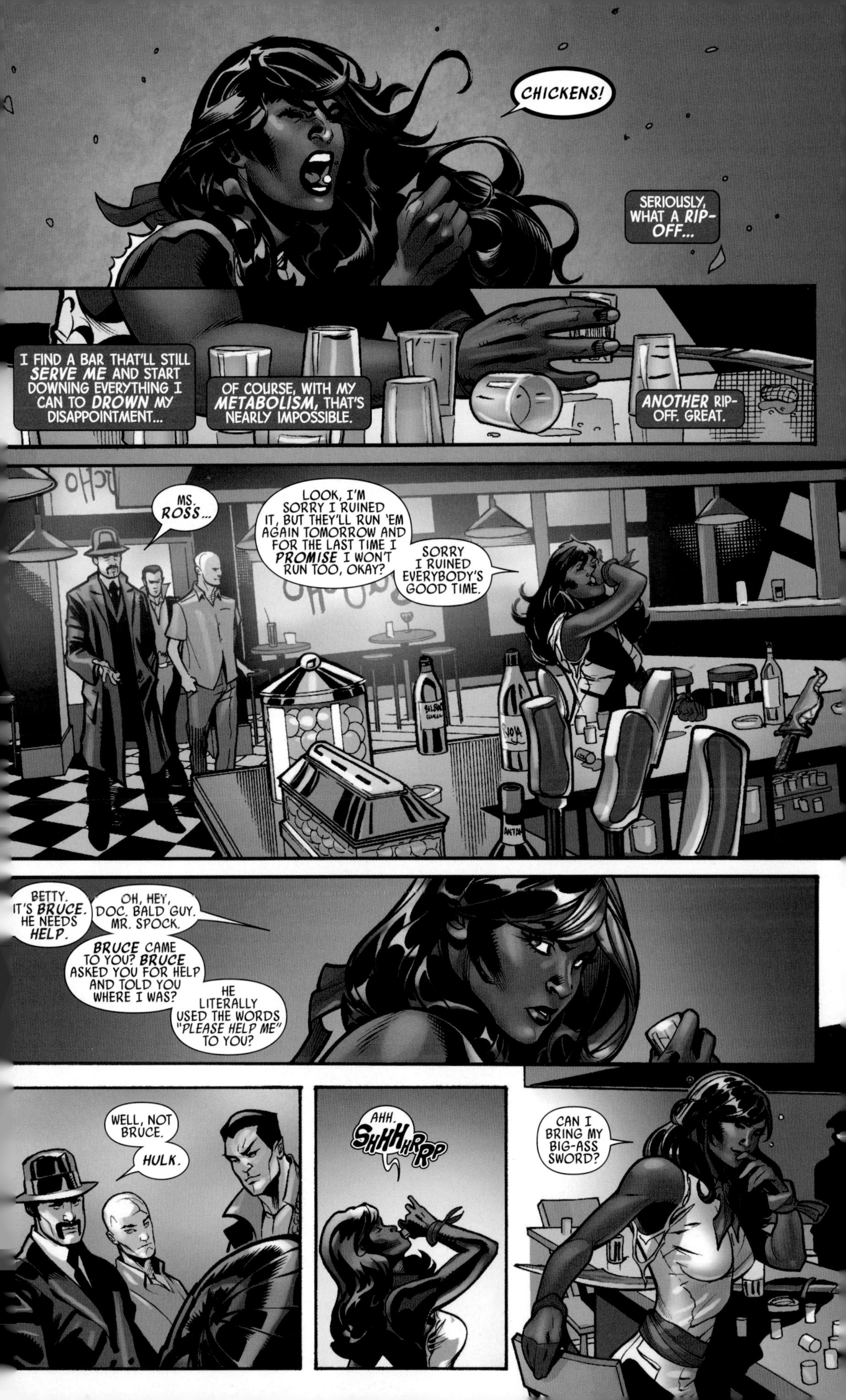
CHICKENS!
SERIOUSLY, WHAT A RIP-OFF...
I FIND A BAR THAT'LL STILL SERVE ME AND START DOWNING EVERYTHING I CAN TO DROWN MY DISAPPOINTMENT...
OF COURSE, WITH MY METABOLISM, THAT'S NEARLY IMPOSSIBLE.
ANOTHER RIP-OFF. GREAT.
MS. ROSS...
LOOK, I'M SORRY I RUINED IT, BUT THEY'LL RUN 'EM AGAIN TOMORROW AND FOR THE LAST TIME I PROMISE I WON'T RUN TOO, OKAY?
SORRY I RUINED EVERYBODY'S GOOD TIME.
BETTY. IT'S BRUCE. HE NEEDS HELP.
OH, HEY, DOC. BALD GUY. MR. SPOCK.
BRUCE CAME TO YOU? BRUCE ASKED YOU FOR HELP AND TOLD YOU WHERE I WAS?
HE LITERALLY USED THE WORDS "PLEASE HELP ME" TO YOU?
WELL, NOT BRUCE.
HULK.
AHH.
SHHHHRRP
CAN I BRING MY BIG-ASS SWORD?

HOW DID YOU LUNATICS ALL GET HERE, ANYWAY?

I FLEW TO THE *AEGEAN*, WHERE I FOUND NAMOR.

THE SURFER, BY *COINCIDENCE*, WAS IN THE CANTABRIANS NOT FAR FROM THERE.

FROM *THERE*, WE TOOK THE EURAIL *HERE*.

HOW'D *THAT* WORK OUT FOR YOU?

"IT WAS *AWKWARD*."

WE'LL NEED A PLANE BOTH *LARGE* AND *DISCREET* IF WE'RE TO HUNT THE *BLACK HULK* ACROSS EUROPE. STRANGE, DO YOU--

STRANGE.

SORRY-- ONE SECOND, I--

THERE'VE BEEN A HANDFUL OF *COINCIDENCES* AROUND ME LATELY AND I WANTED TO *JOT THEM DOWN.*

RECURRING *PHRASES.* OUR *PROXIMITIES.* REPEATING *NUMBERS,* IMAGES...

THE COINCIDENCE OF SEVERAL *COINCIDENCES.* THE WORLD IS POKING AT OUR *SUBCONSCIOUS...*

WHAT'S IT ALL *MEAN?*

*NOTHING.* IT MEANS ABSOLUTELY *NOTHING.* STEPHEN, STOP TRYING TO *SLEEP* WITH THE PRETTY GIRL BY SOUNDING LIKE A SPOOKY OLD *CONJURER.*

UNLESS, OF COURSE, YOU CONJURE US U[P?] A PLANE.

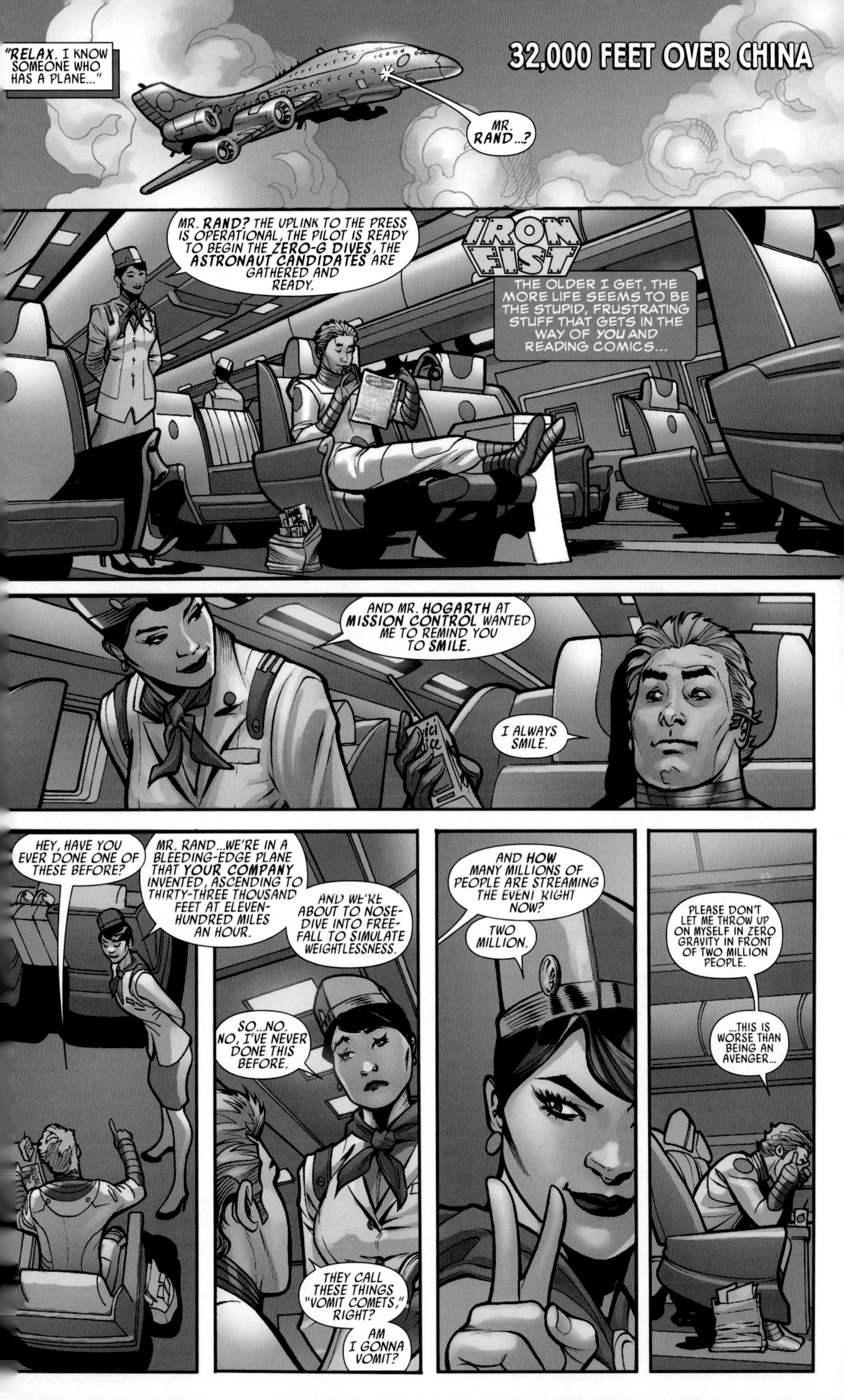

"RELAX. I KNOW SOMEONE WHO HAS A PLANE..."
32,000 FEET OVER CHINA
MR. RAND...?
MR. RAND? THE UPLINK TO THE PRESS IS OPERATIONAL, THE PILOT IS READY TO BEGIN THE ZERO-G DIVES, THE ASTRONAUT CANDIDATES ARE GATHERED AND READY.
IRON FIST
THE OLDER I GET, THE MORE LIFE SEEMS TO BE THE STUPID, FRUSTRATING STUFF THAT GETS IN THE WAY OF YOU AND READING COMICS...
AND MR. HOGARTH AT MISSION CONTROL WANTED ME TO REMIND YOU TO SMILE.
I ALWAYS SMILE.
HEY, HAVE YOU EVER DONE ONE OF THESE BEFORE?
MR. RAND...WE'RE IN A BLEEDING-EDGE PLANE THAT YOUR COMPANY INVENTED, ASCENDING TO THIRTY-THREE THOUSAND FEET AT ELEVEN-HUNDRED MILES AN HOUR.
AND WE'RE ABOUT TO NOSE-DIVE INTO FREE-FALL TO SIMULATE WEIGHTLESSNESS.
SO...NO. NO, I'VE NEVER DONE THIS BEFORE.
THEY CALL THESE THINGS "VOMIT COMETS," RIGHT?
AM I GONNA VOMIT?
AND HOW MANY MILLIONS OF PEOPLE ARE STREAMING THE EVENT RIGHT NOW?
TWO MILLION.
PLEASE DON'T LET ME THROW UP ON MYSELF IN ZERO GRAVITY IN FRONT OF TWO MILLION PEOPLE.
...THIS IS WORSE THAN BEING AN AVENGER...

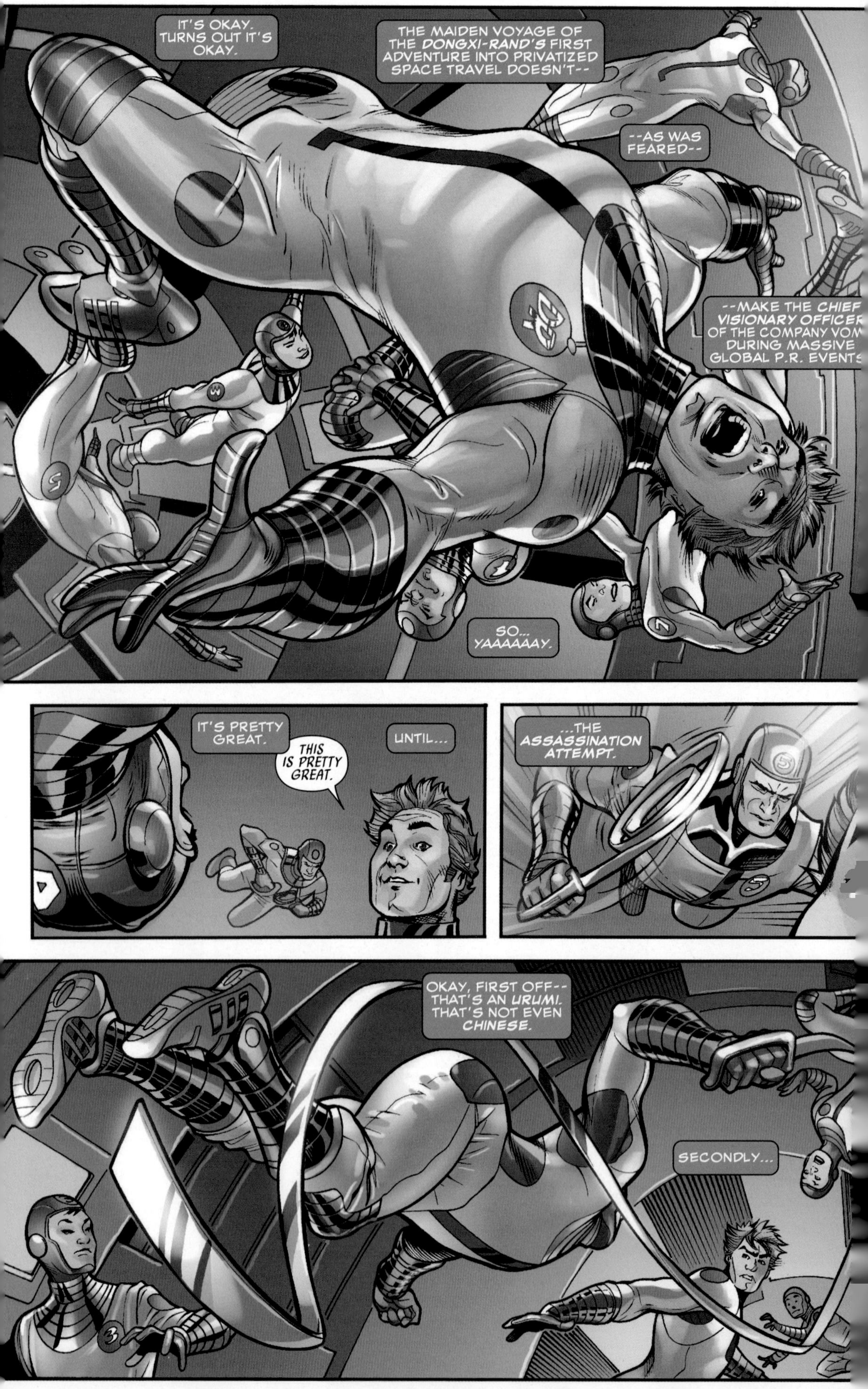
IT'S OKAY. TURNS OUT IT'S OKAY.
THE MAIDEN VOYAGE OF THE DONGXI-RAND'S FIRST ADVENTURE INTO PRIVATIZED SPACE TRAVEL DOESN'T--
--AS WAS FEARED--
--MAKE THE CHIEF VISIONARY OFFICER OF THE COMPANY VOMIT DURING MASSIVE GLOBAL P.R. EVENTS
SO... YAAAAAAY.
IT'S PRETTY GREAT.
THIS IS PRETTY GREAT.
UNTIL...
...THE ASSASSINATION ATTEMPT.
OKAY, FIRST OFF--THAT'S AN URUMI. THAT'S NOT EVEN CHINESE.
SECONDLY...

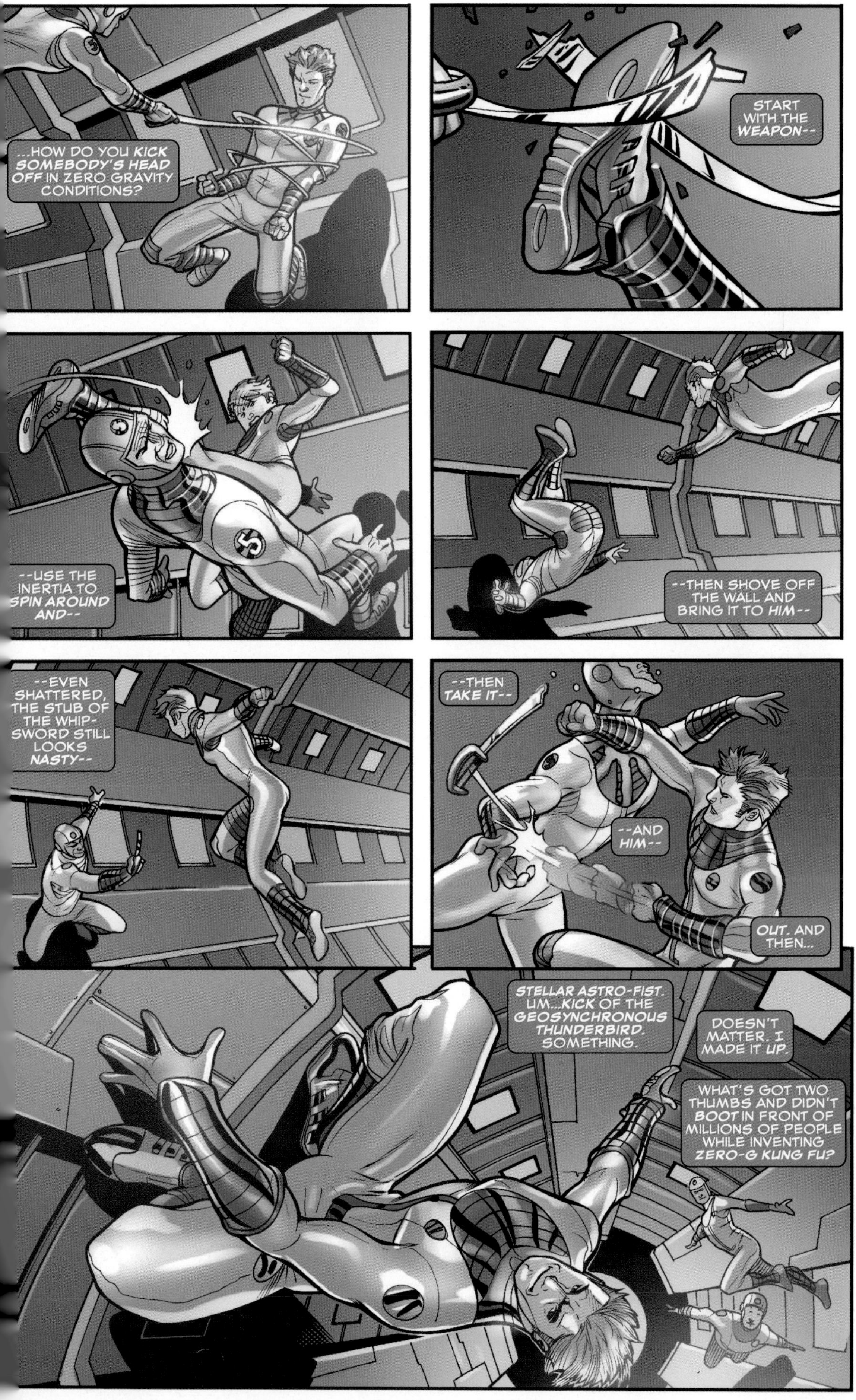
...HOW DO YOU KICK SOMEBODY'S HEAD OFF IN ZERO GRAVITY CONDITIONS?
START WITH THE WEAPON--
--USE THE INERTIA TO SPIN AROUND AND--
--THEN SHOVE OFF THE WALL AND BRING IT TO HIM--
--EVEN SHATTERED, THE STUB OF THE WHIP-SWORD STILL LOOKS NASTY--
--THEN TAKE IT--
--AND HIM--
OUT. AND THEN...
STELLAR ASTRO-FIST. UM...KICK OF THE GEOSYNCHRONOUS THUNDERBIRD. SOMETHING.
DOESN'T MATTER. I MADE IT UP.
WHAT'S GOT TWO THUMBS AND DIDN'T BOOT IN FRONT OF MILLIONS OF PEOPLE WHILE INVENTING ZERO-G KUNG FU?

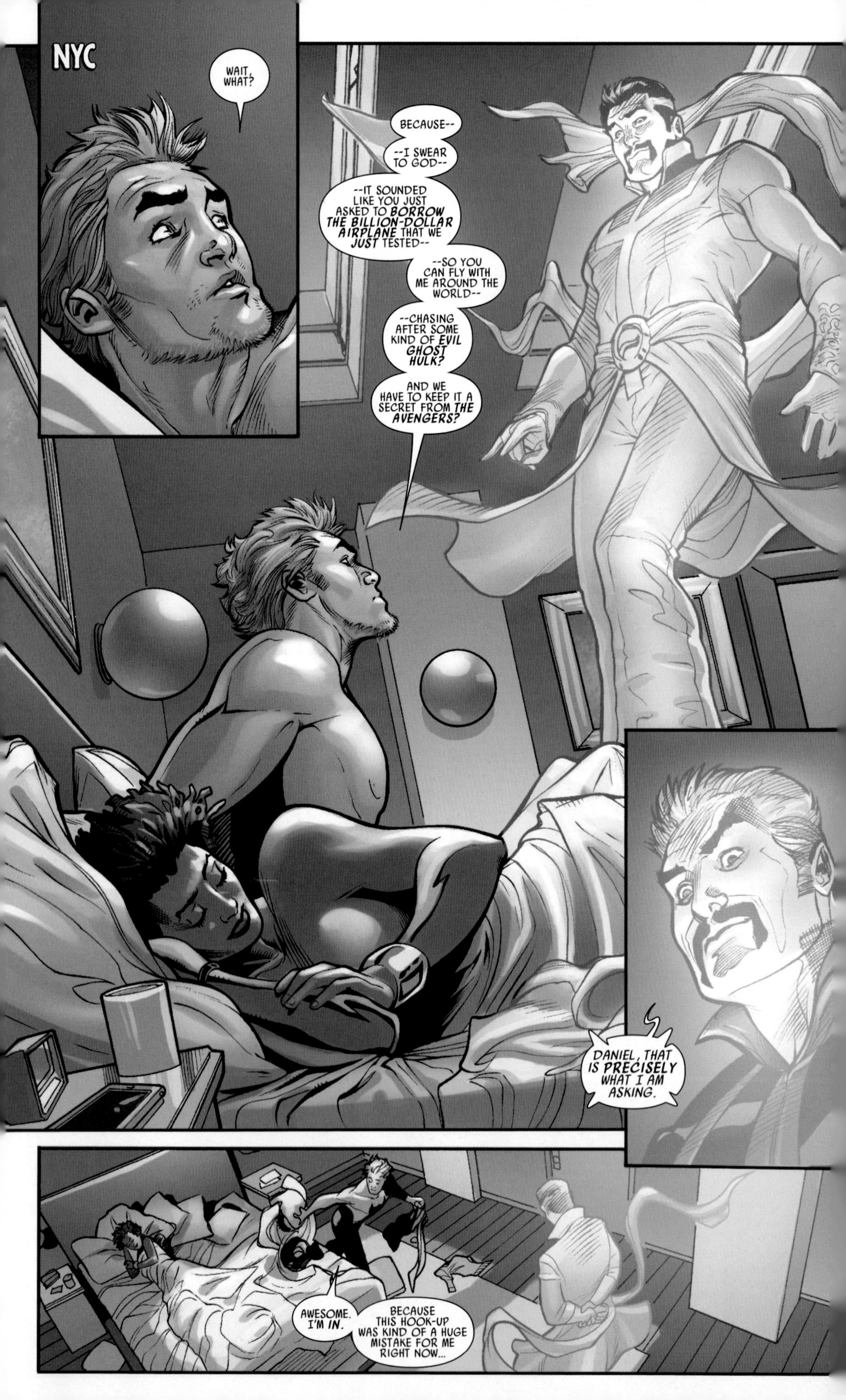
NYC
WAIT, WHAT?
BECAUSE--
--I SWEAR TO GOD--
--IT SOUNDED LIKE YOU JUST ASKED TO BORROW THE BILLION-DOLLAR AIRPLANE THAT WE JUST TESTED--
--SO YOU CAN FLY WITH ME AROUND THE WORLD--
--CHASING AFTER SOME KIND OF EVIL GHOST HULK?
AND WE HAVE TO KEEP IT A SECRET FROM THE AVENGERS?
DANIEL, THAT IS PRECISELY WHAT I AM ASKING.
AWESOME. I'M IN.
BECAUSE THIS HOOK-UP WAS KIND OF A HUGE MISTAKE FOR ME RIGHT NOW...

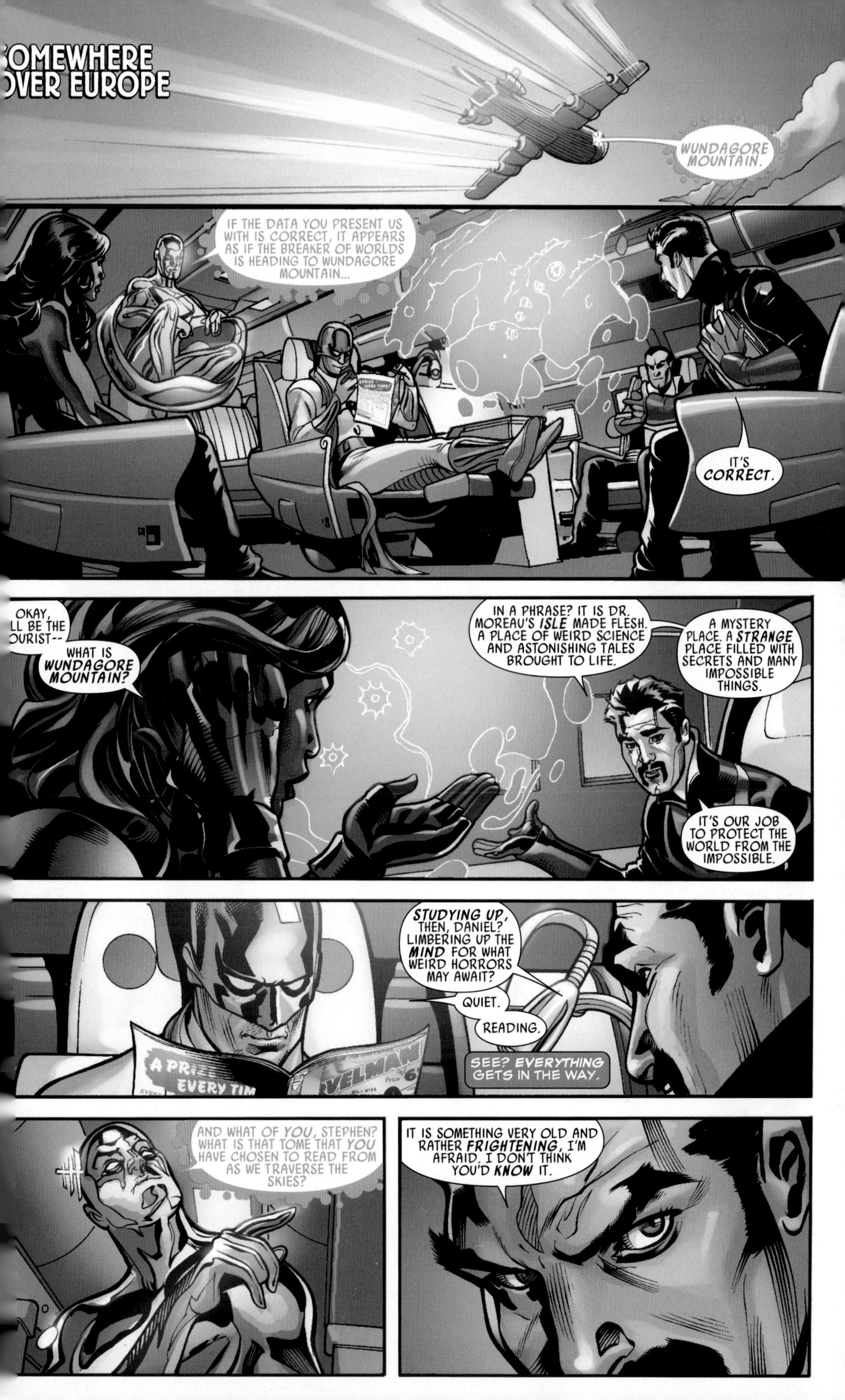

SOMEWHERE OVER EUROPE
WUNDAGORE MOUNTAIN.
IF THE DATA YOU PRESENT US WITH IS CORRECT, IT APPEARS AS IF THE BREAKER OF WORLDS IS HEADING TO WUNDAGORE MOUNTAIN...
IT'S CORRECT.
OKAY, I'LL BE THE TOURIST--
WHAT IS WUNDAGORE MOUNTAIN?
IN A PHRASE? IT IS DR. MOREAU'S ISLE MADE FLESH. A PLACE OF WEIRD SCIENCE AND ASTONISHING TALES BROUGHT TO LIFE.
A MYSTERY PLACE. A STRANGE PLACE FILLED WITH SECRETS AND MANY IMPOSSIBLE THINGS.
IT'S OUR JOB TO PROTECT THE WORLD FROM THE IMPOSSIBLE.
STUDYING UP, THEN, DANIEL? LIMBERING UP THE MIND FOR WHAT WEIRD HORRORS MAY AWAIT?
QUIET.
READING.
SEE? EVERYTHING GETS IN THE WAY.
AND WHAT OF YOU, STEPHEN? WHAT IS THAT TOME THAT YOU HAVE CHOSEN TO READ FROM AS WE TRAVERSE THE SKIES?
IT IS SOMETHING VERY OLD AND RATHER FRIGHTENING, I'M AFRAID. I DON'T THINK YOU'D KNOW IT.

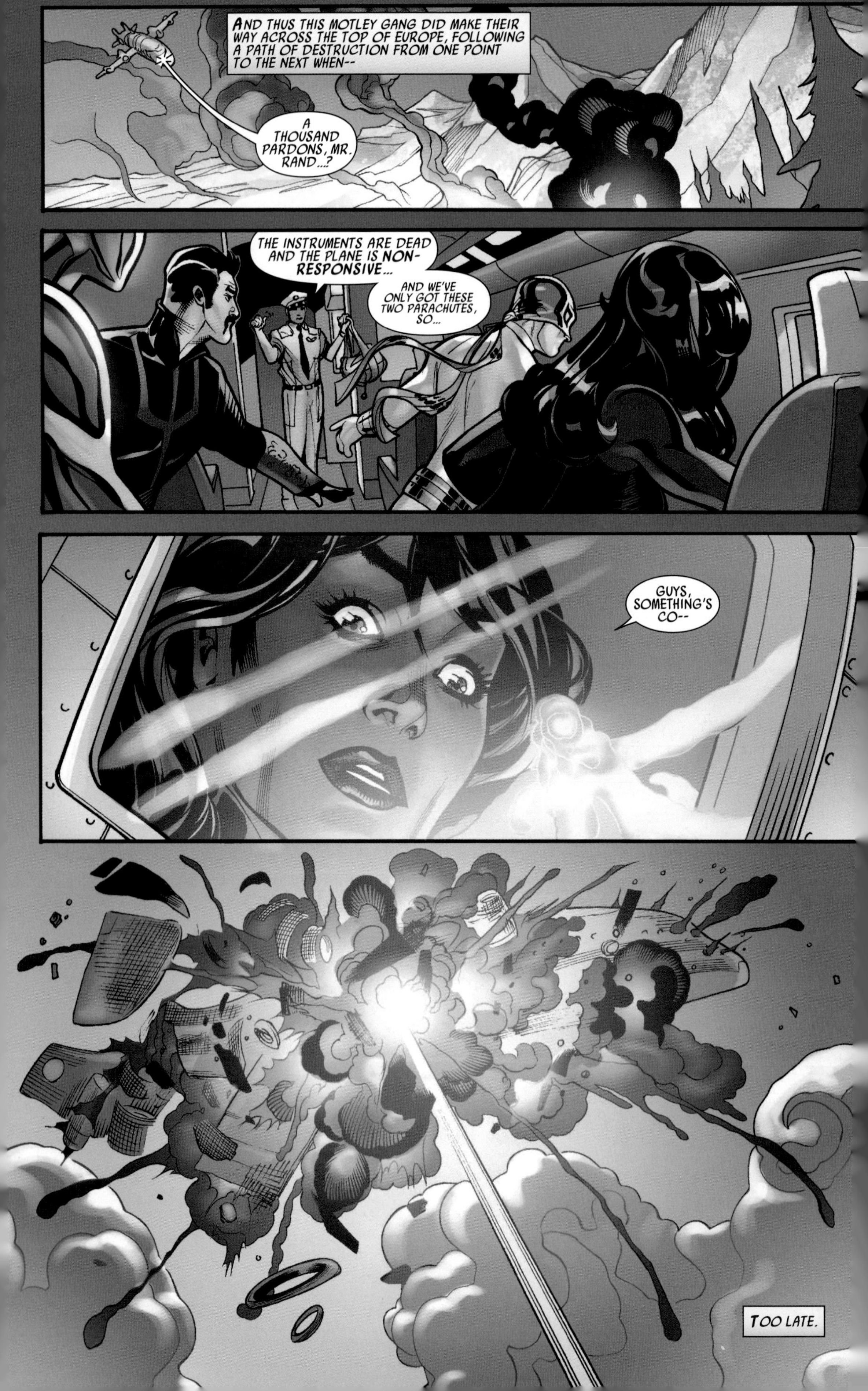
AND THUS THIS MOTLEY GANG DID MAKE THEIR WAY ACROSS THE TOP OF EUROPE, FOLLOWING A PATH OF DESTRUCTION FROM ONE POINT TO THE NEXT WHEN--
A THOUSAND PARDONS, MR. RAND...?
THE INSTRUMENTS ARE DEAD AND THE PLANE IS NON-RESPONSIVE...
AND WE'VE ONLY GOT THESE TWO PARACHUTES, SO...
GUYS, SOMETHING'S CO--
TOO LATE.

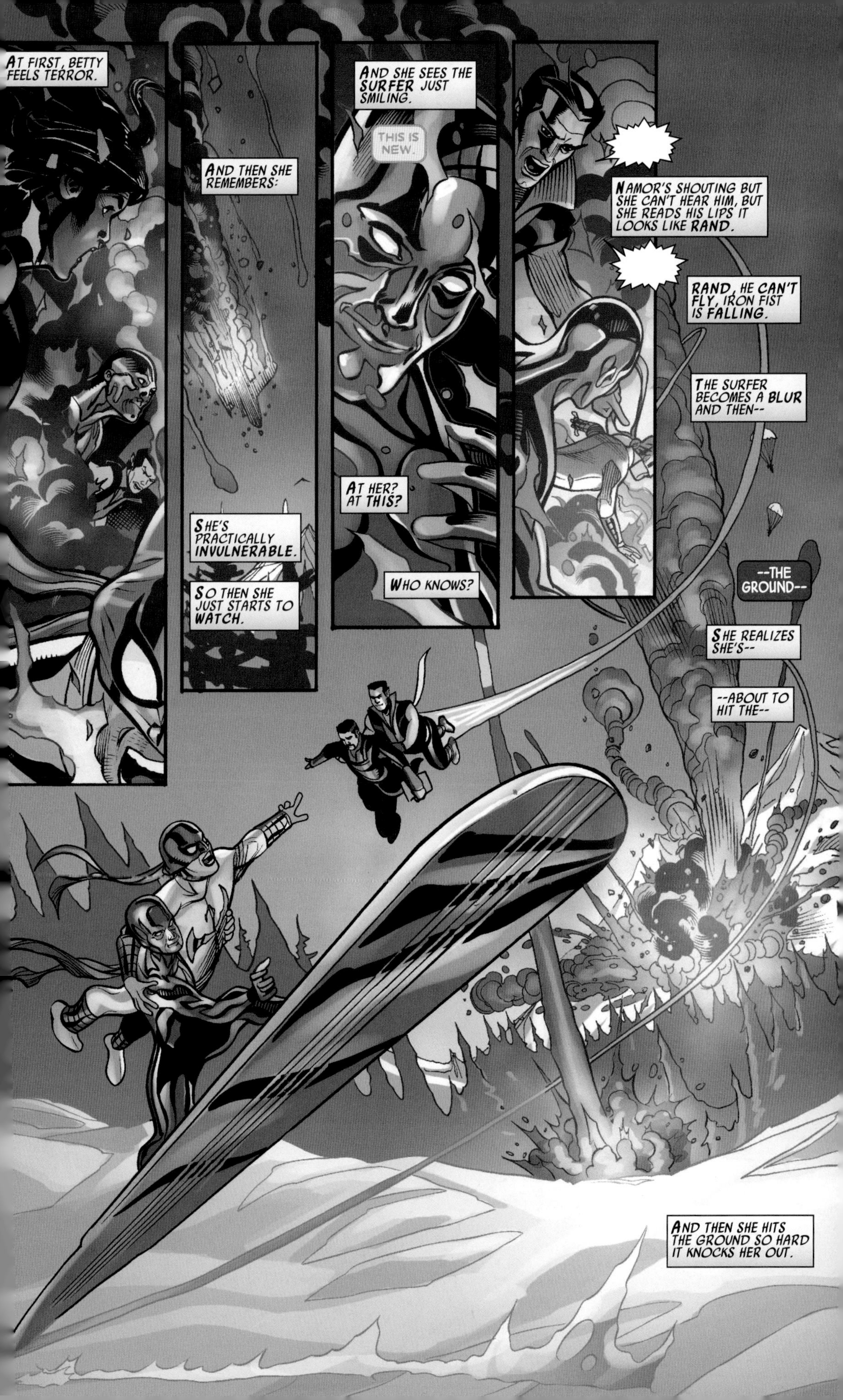

AT FIRST, BETTY FEELS TERROR.
AND THEN SHE REMEMBERS:
SHE'S PRACTICALLY INVULNERABLE.
SO THEN SHE JUST STARTS TO WATCH.
AND SHE SEES THE SURFER JUST SMILING.
THIS IS NEW.
AT HER? AT THIS?
WHO KNOWS?
NAMOR'S SHOUTING BUT SHE CAN'T HEAR HIM, BUT SHE READS HIS LIPS IT LOOKS LIKE RAND.
RAND, HE CAN'T FLY, IRON FIST IS FALLING.
THE SURFER BECOMES A BLUR AND THEN--
--THE GROUND--
SHE REALIZES SHE'S--
--ABOUT TO HIT THE--
AND THEN SHE HITS THE GROUND SO HARD IT KNOCKS HER OUT.

...FOR A SECOND, ANYWAY...

?!?

OW.

HEY. HELP YOU UP?

AND THEY SAY CHIVALRY IS *DEAD*.

SAW THE *PILOTS* AND THEIR CHUTES OPEN UP JUST FINE...

BUT THAT PLANE COST TEN FIGURES ALL-IN.

IF TODAY COULD *SUCK* ANY MORE, I'D SURE LIKE SOMEONE TO TELL ME *HOW*--

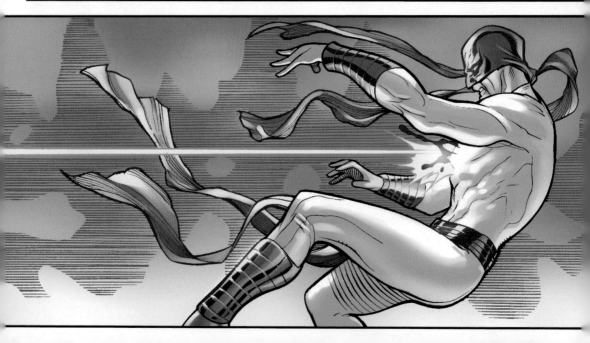

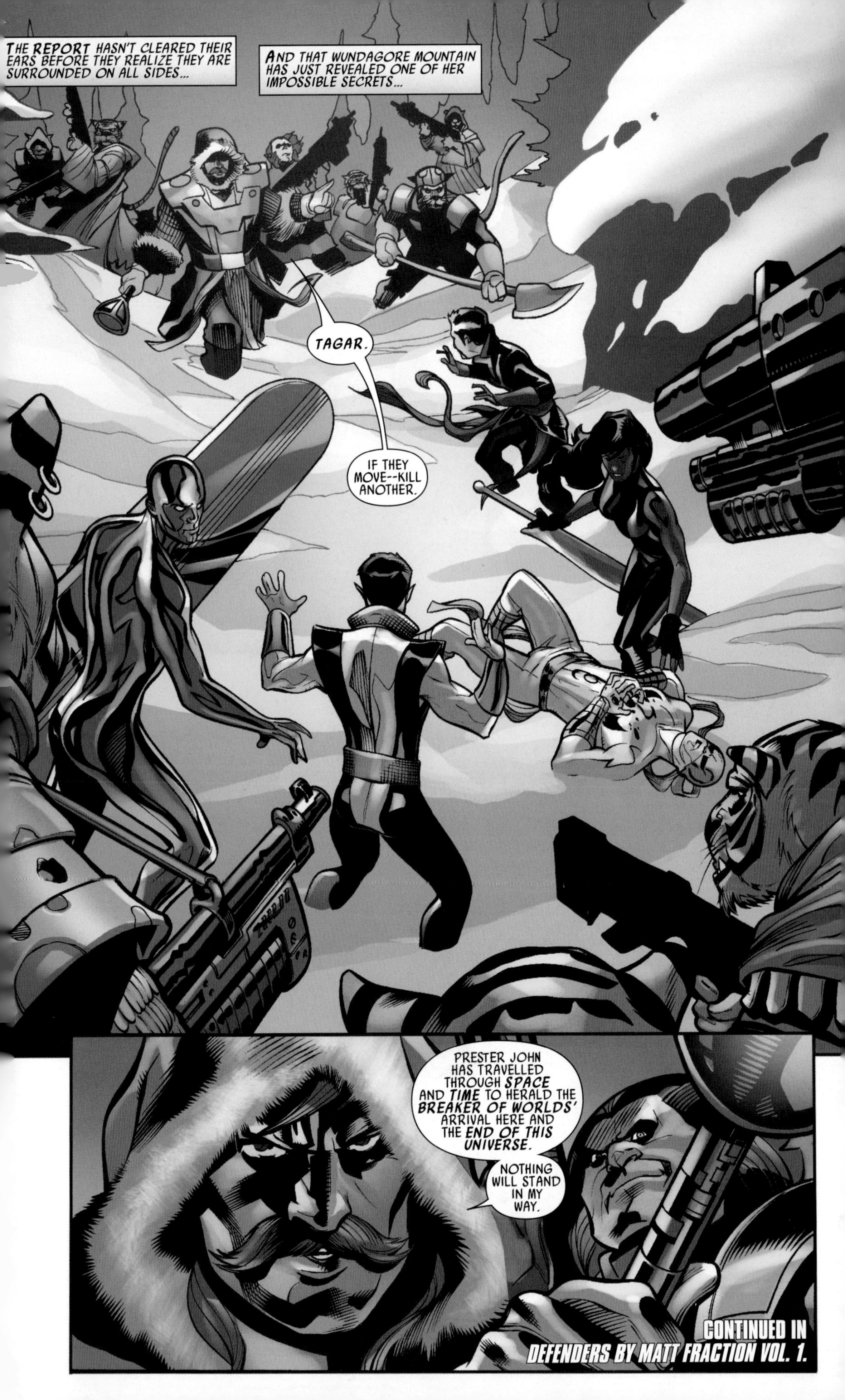

THE REPORT HASN'T CLEARED THEIR EARS BEFORE THEY REALIZE THEY ARE SURROUNDED ON ALL SIDES...
AND THAT WUNDAGORE MOUNTAIN HAS JUST REVEALED ONE OF HER IMPOSSIBLE SECRETS...
TAGAR.
IF THEY MOVE--KILL ANOTHER.
PRESTER JOHN HAS TRAVELLED THROUGH SPACE AND TIME TO HERALD THE BREAKER OF WORLDS' ARRIVAL HERE AND THE END OF THIS UNIVERSE.
NOTHING WILL STAND IN MY WAY.


CONTINUED IN
DEFENDERS BY MATT FRACTION VOL. 1.

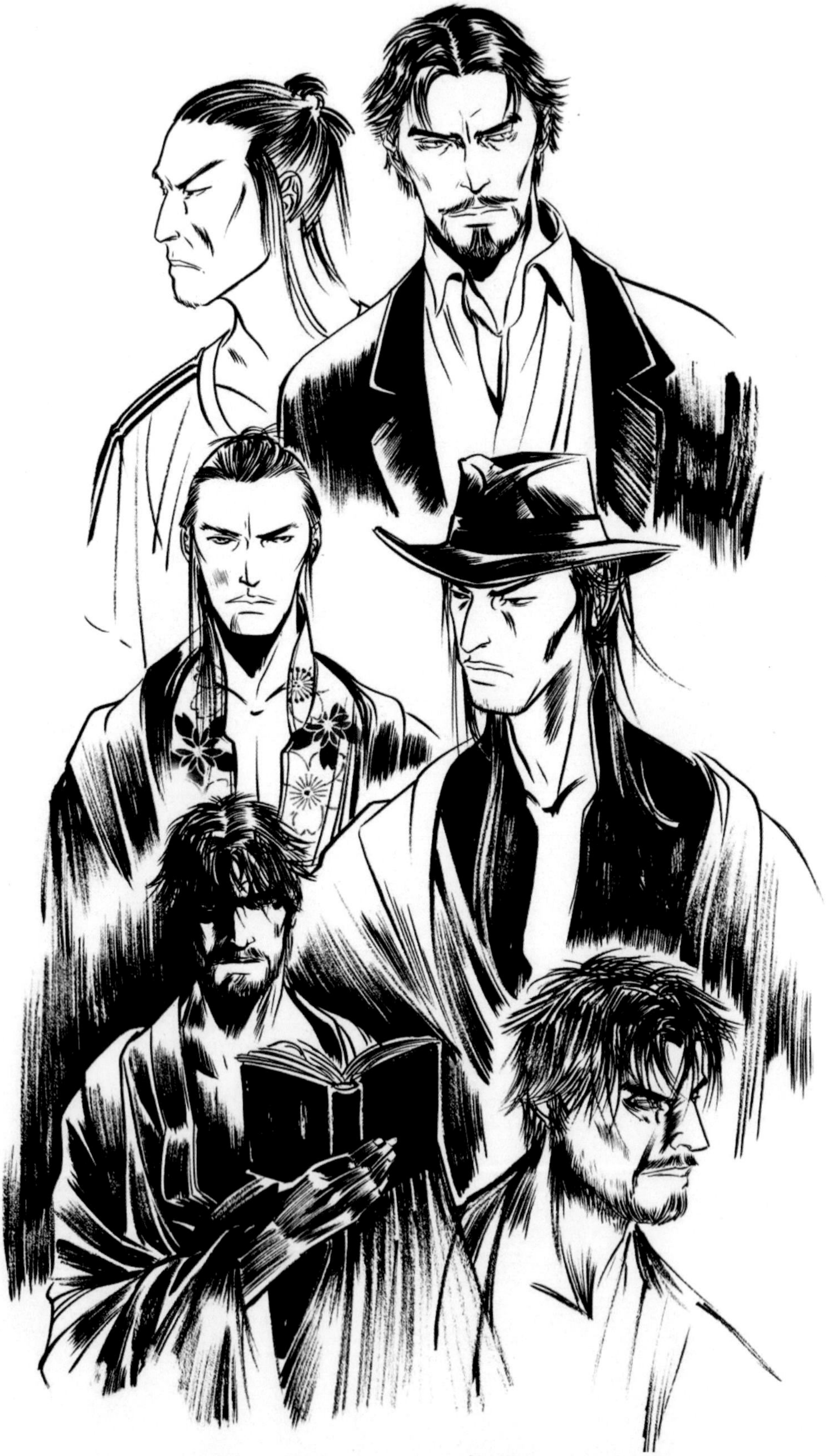

STEPHEN STRANGE AND WONG CHARACTER DESIGNS

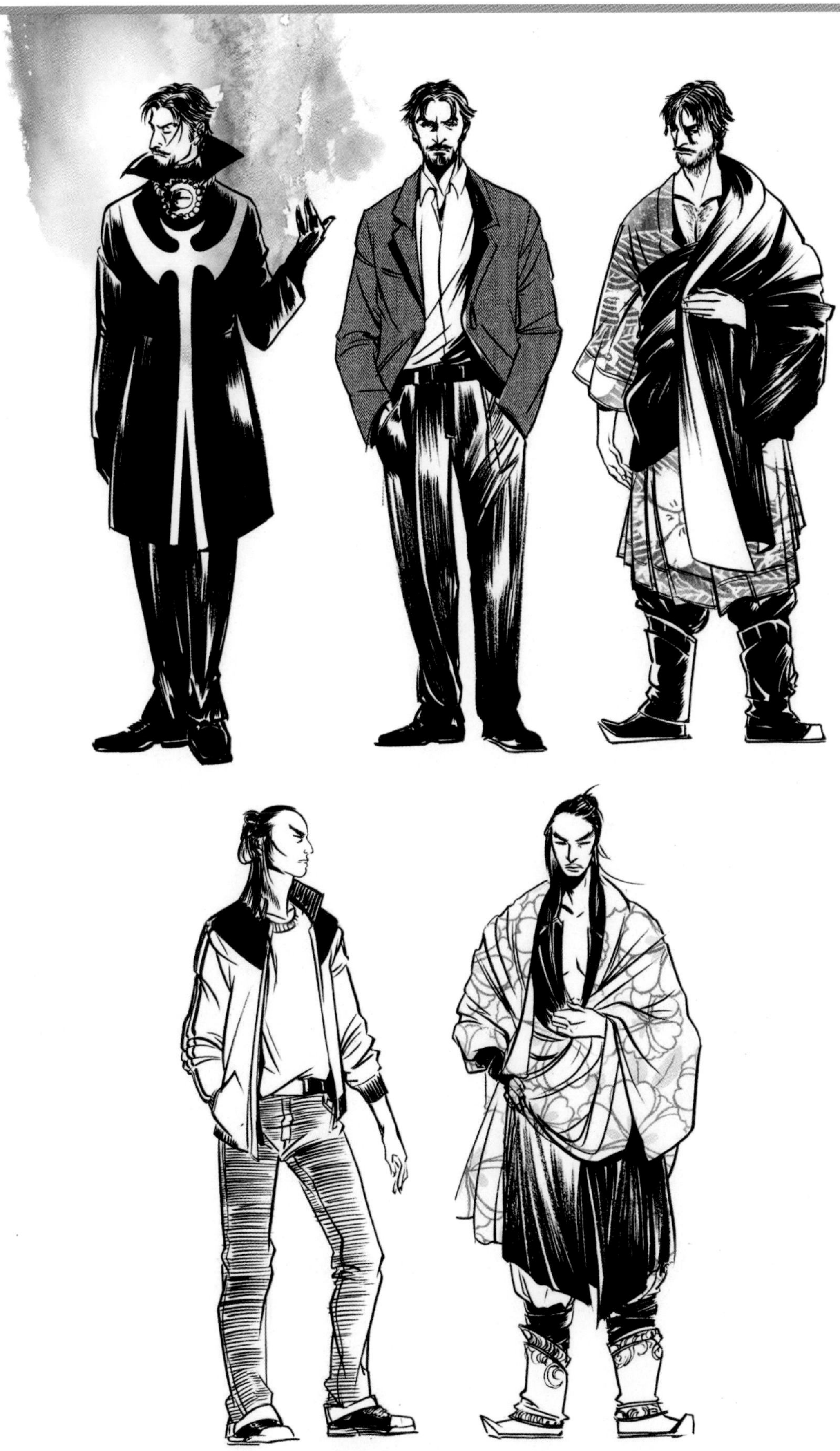

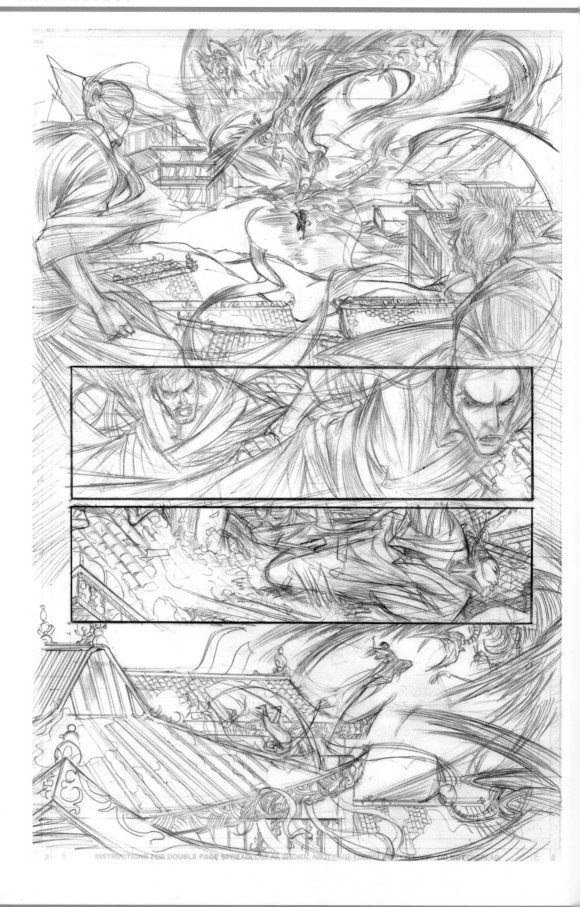

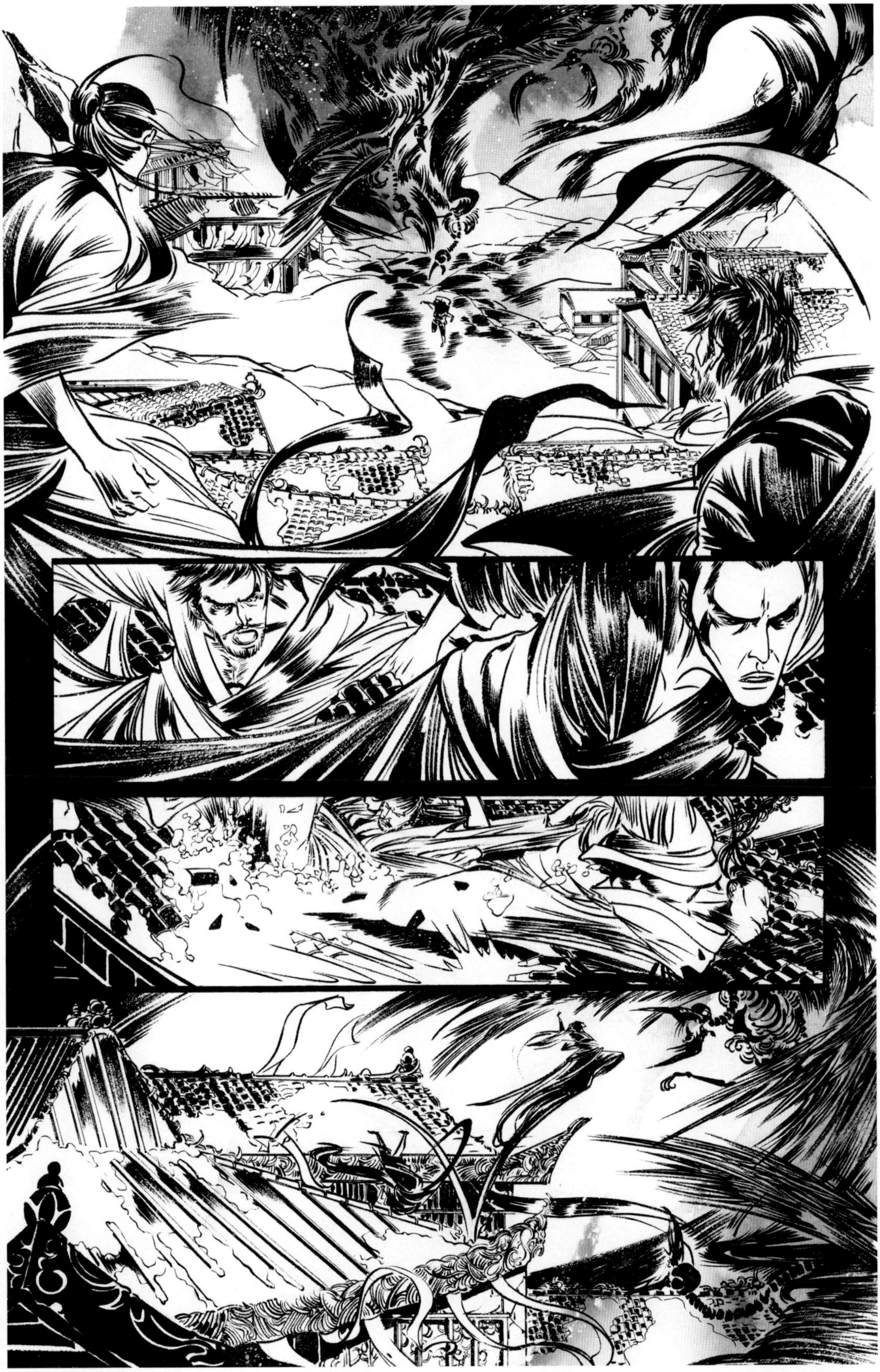

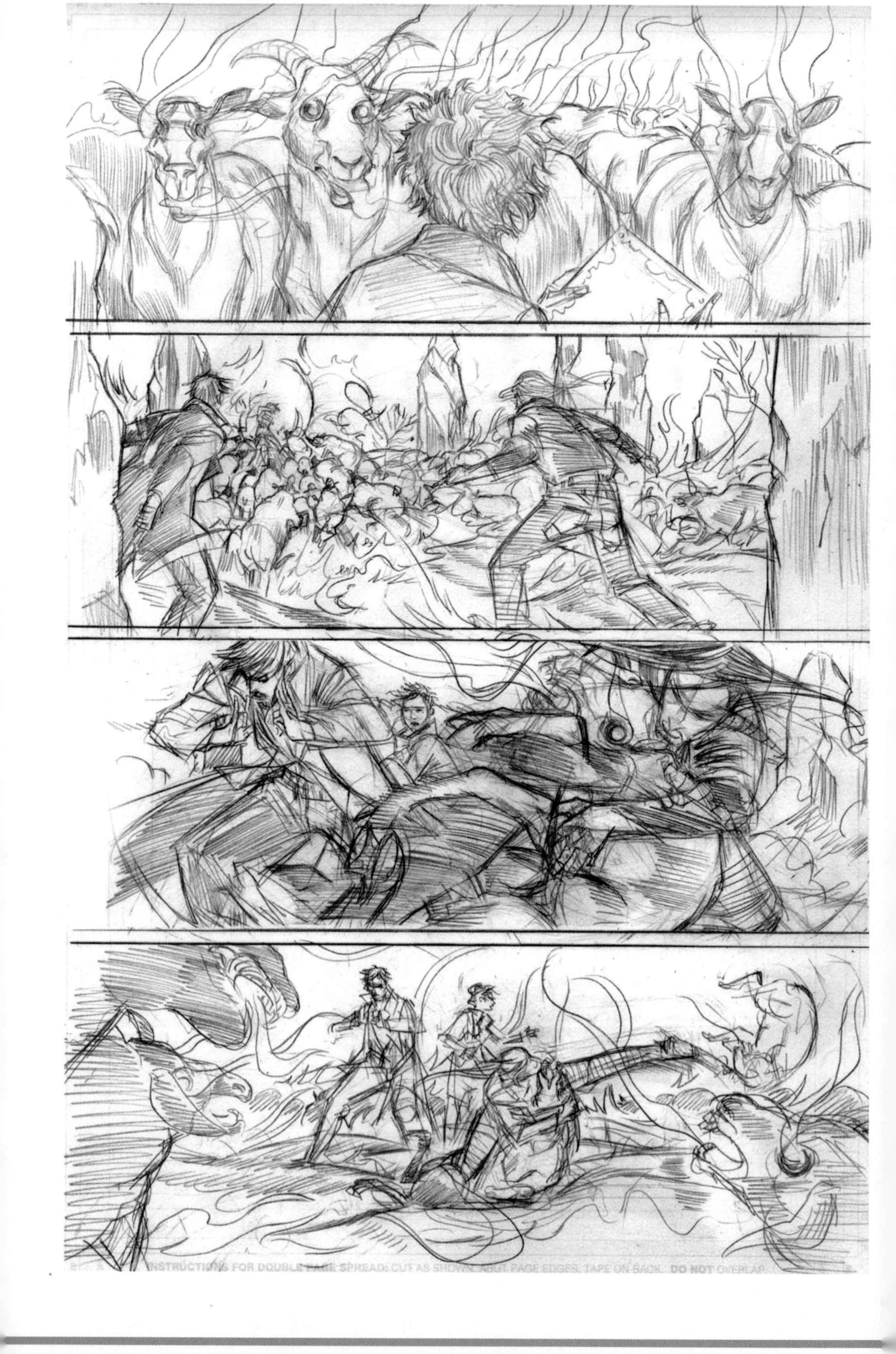
INSTRUCTIONS FOR DOUBLE PAGE SPREAD: CUT AS SHOWN. ABUT PAGE EDGES. TAPE ON BACK. DO NOT OVERLAP.

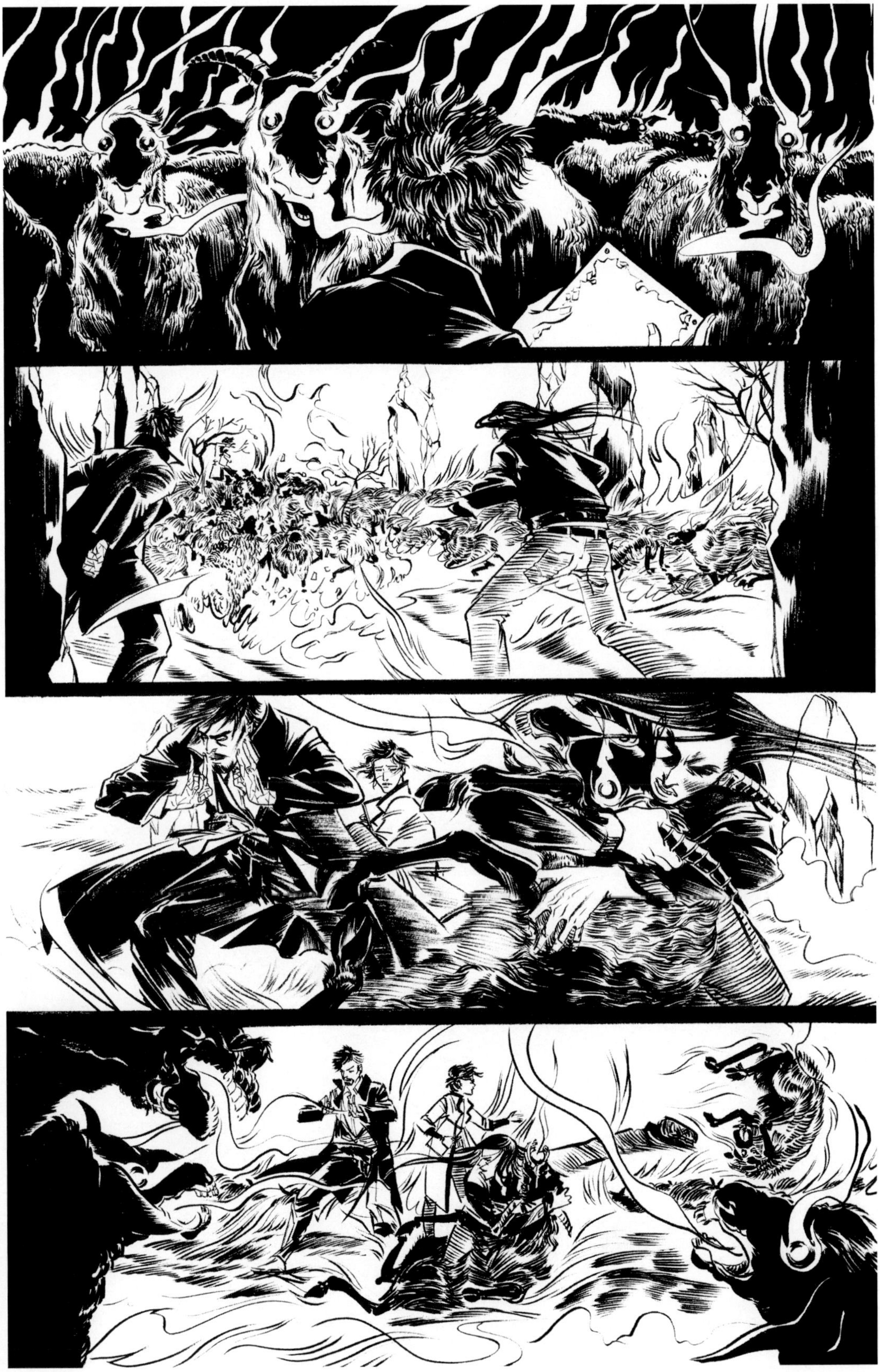

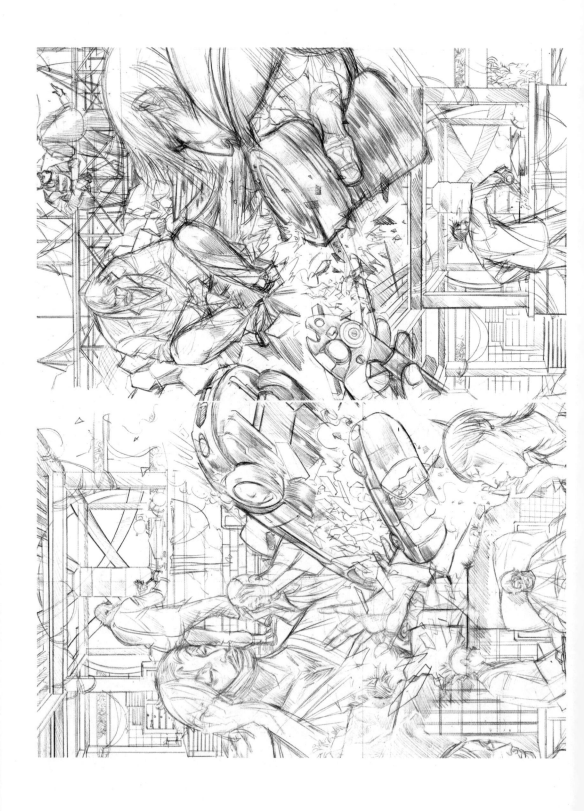

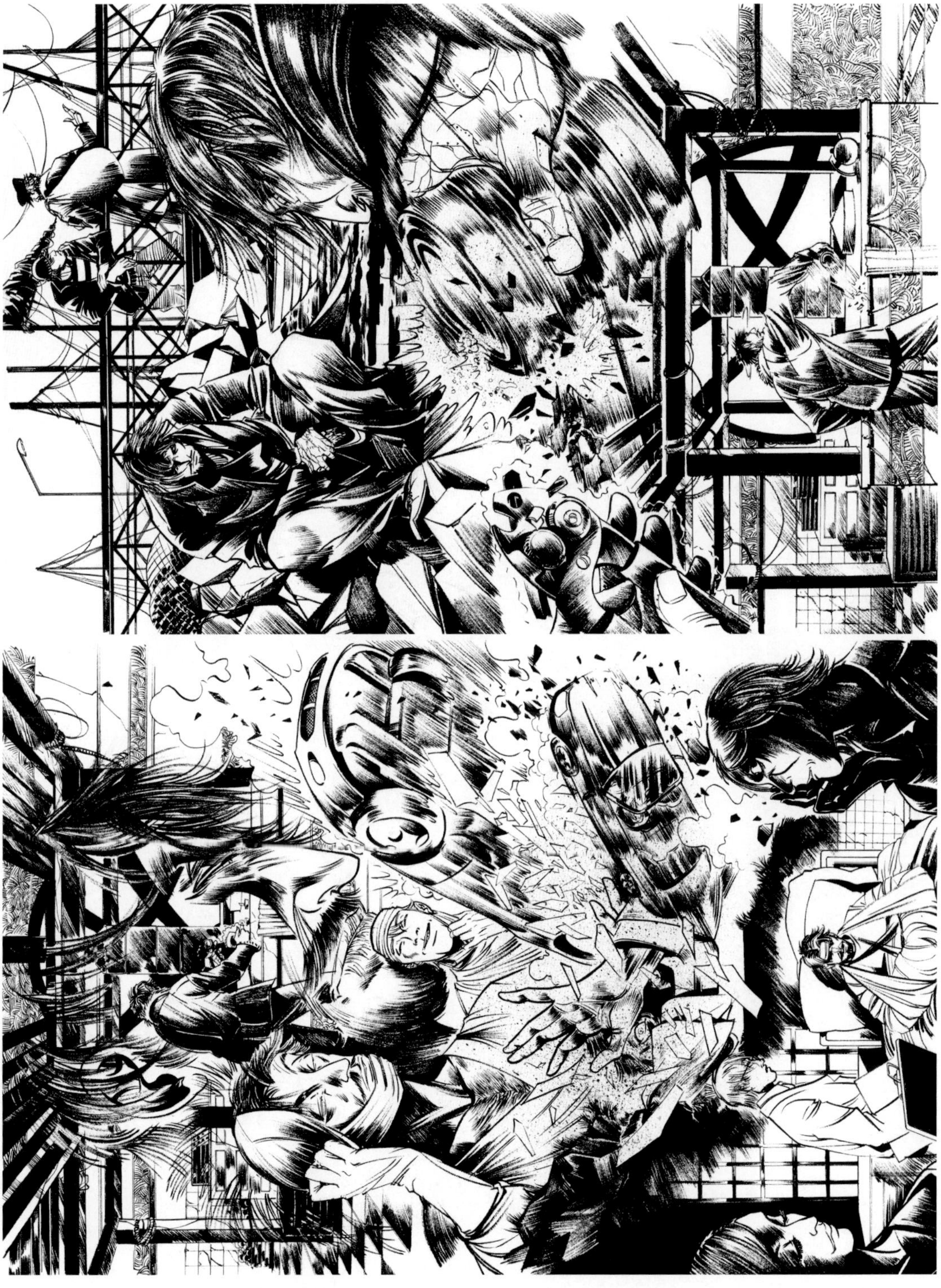

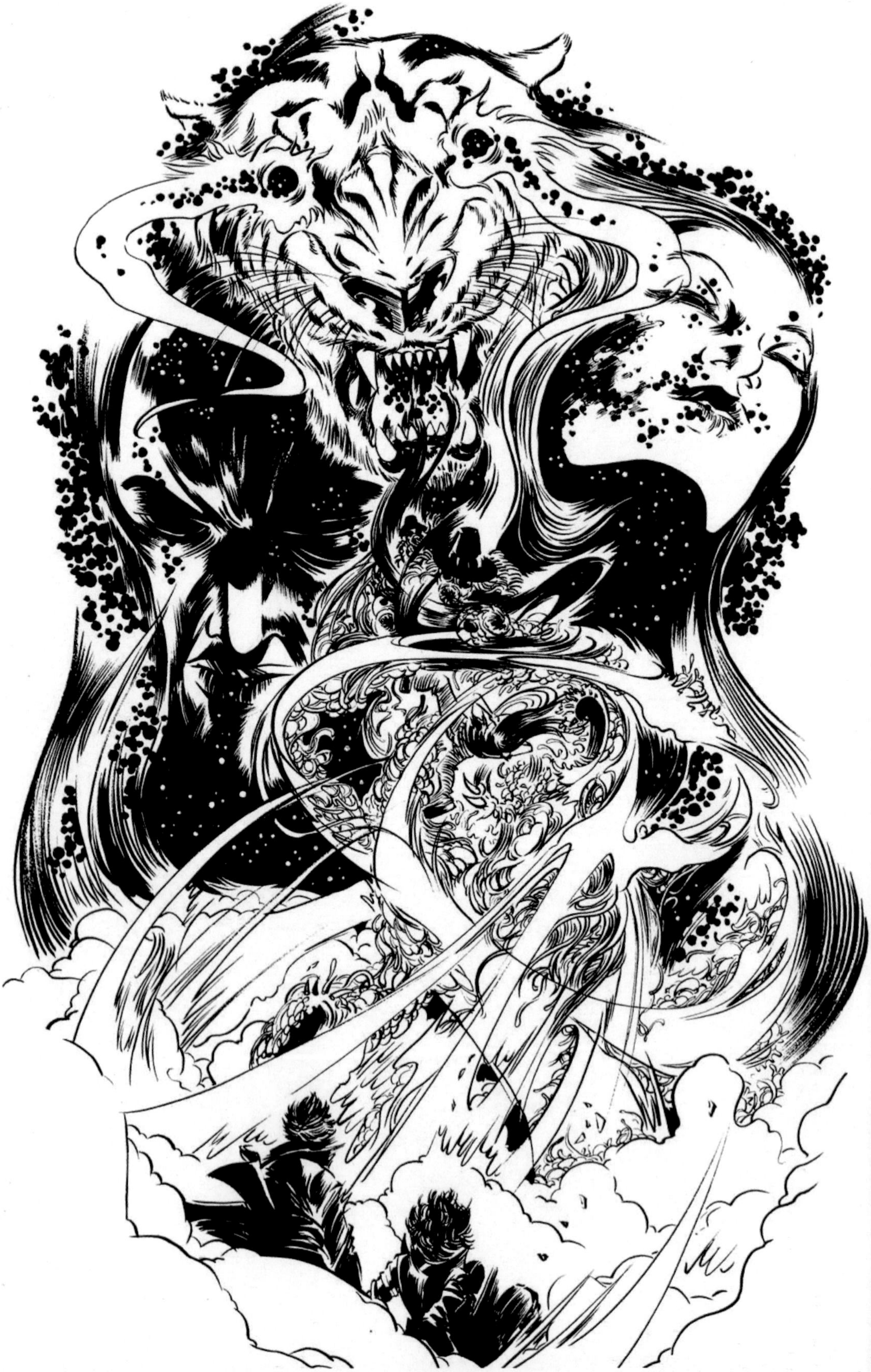

# MARVEL
# SEASON ONE

ROBERTO AGUIRRE-SACASA · DAVID MARQUEZ

**FANTASTIC FOUR**

MARVEL SEASON ONE

**ISBN # 978-0-7851-5641-3**

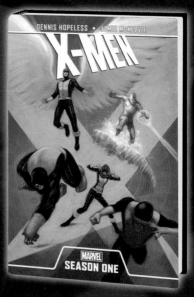

DENNIS HOPELESS · JAMIE McKELVIE

**X-MEN**

MARVEL SEASON ONE

**ISBN # 978-0-7851-5645-1**

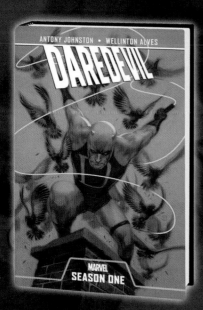

ANTONY JOHNSTON · WELLINTON ALVES

**DAREDEVIL**

MARVEL SEASON ONE

**ISBN # 978-0-7851-5643-7**

CULLEN BUNN · NEIL EDWARDS

**SPIDER-MAN**

MARVEL SEASON-ONE

**ISBN # 978-0-7851-5820-2**

## AVAILABLE WHEREVER BOOKS ARE SOLD.

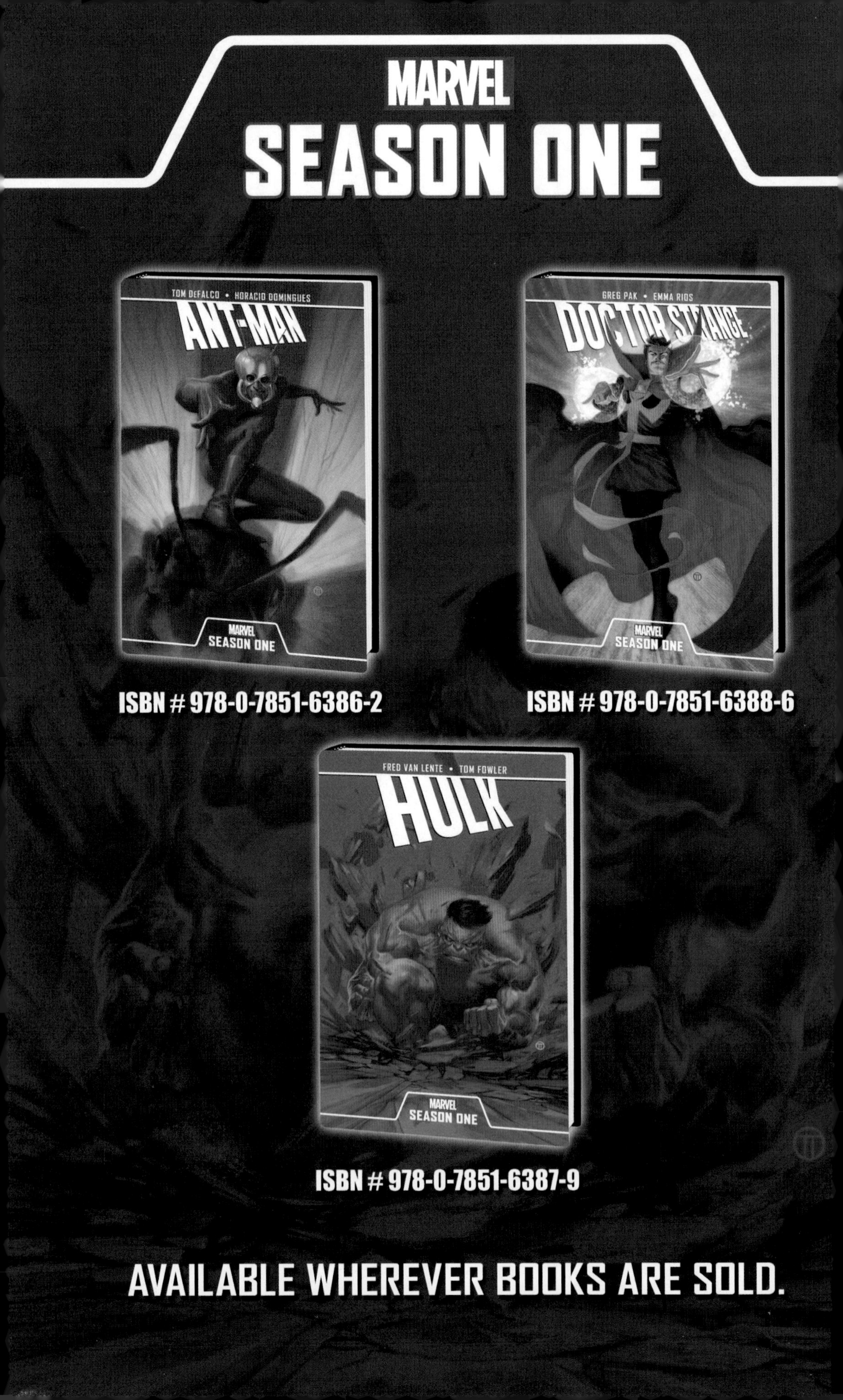
MARVEL
SEASON ONE
TOM DEFALCO • HORACIO DOMINGUES
ANT-MAN
MARVEL
SEASON ONE
ISBN # 978-0-7851-6386-2
GREG PAK • EMMA RIOS
DOCTOR STRANGE
MARVEL
SEASON ONE
ISBN # 978-0-7851-6388-6
FRED VAN LENTE • TOM FOWLER
HULK
MARVEL
SEASON ONE
ISBN # 978-0-7851-6387-9
AVAILABLE WHEREVER BOOKS ARE SOLD.

UNIVERSE ESSENTIALS

HELLBOY

Published by DARK HORSE BOOKS
A division of Dark Horse Comics LLC
10956 SE Main Street
Milwaukie, OR 97222

DarkHorse.com
Comic Shop Locator Service: Comicshoplocator.com

First edition: July 2021
Ebook ISBN 978-1-50672-677-9
Trade Paperback ISBN 978-1-50672-503-1

1 3 5 7 9 10 8 6 4 2
Printed in China

## HELLBOY UNIVERSE ESSENTIALS: HELLBOY

This book collects *Hellboy: The Chained Coffin, The Third Wish, Pancakes, The Nature of the Beast, The Corpse, The Baba Yaga, A Christmas Underground, The Ghoul,* and *The Troll Witch*, all previously published by Dark Horse Comics.

Library of Congress Cataloging-in-Publication Data

Names: Mignola, Mike, author, artist. | Stewart, Dave, colourist. |
  Hollingsworth, Matt, colourist. | Brosseau, Pat, letterer. | Robins,
  Clem, 1955- letterer.
Title: Hellboy universe essentials : Hellboy / stories and art by Mike
  Mignola ; with Dave Stewart, Matt Hollingsworth, Pat Brosseau, and Clem
  Robins.
Description: First edition. | Milwaukie, OR : Dark Horse Books, 2021. |
  Series: Hellboy universe essentials ; 1 | "This book collects Hellboy:
  The Chained Coffin, The Third Wish, Pancakes, The Nature of the Beast,
  The Corpse, The Baba Yaga, A Christmas Underground, The Ghoul, and The
  Troll Witch, all previously published by Dark Horse Comics." | Summary:
  "Confront the undead, swim to strange places, and encounter powerful fey
  in this introduction to the world of Hellboy. Newcomers to the series
  needn't have read the original stories to jump right in and see what
  Hellboy is all about thanks to this collection of short stories,
  selected by Mike Mignola himself as the perfect introduction to his most
  famous comic book character!"-- Provided by publisher.
Identifiers: LCCN 2021002406 (print) | LCCN 2021002407 (ebook) | ISBN
  9781506725031 (trade paperback) | ISBN 9781506726779 (ebook)
Subjects: LCSH: Comic books, strips, etc.
Classification: LCC PN6728.H3838 M456 2021  (print) | LCC PN6728.H3838
  (ebook) | DDC 741.5/973--dc23
LC record available at https://lccn.loc.gov/2021002406
LC ebook record available at https://lccn.loc.gov/2021002407

# UNIVERSE ESSENTIALS

## HELLBOY

*Stories and Art by*
MIKE MIGNOLA

*With*
DAVE STEWART, MATT HOLLINGSWORTH,
PAT BROSSEAU, *and* CLEM ROBINS

---

*President and Publisher*
MIKE RICHARDSON

*Editor*
KATII O'BRIEN

*Assistant Editor*
JENNY BLENK

*Collection Designer*
PATRICK SATTERFIELD

*Digital Art Technician*
ANN GRAY

**Dark Horse Books**

# FOREWORD

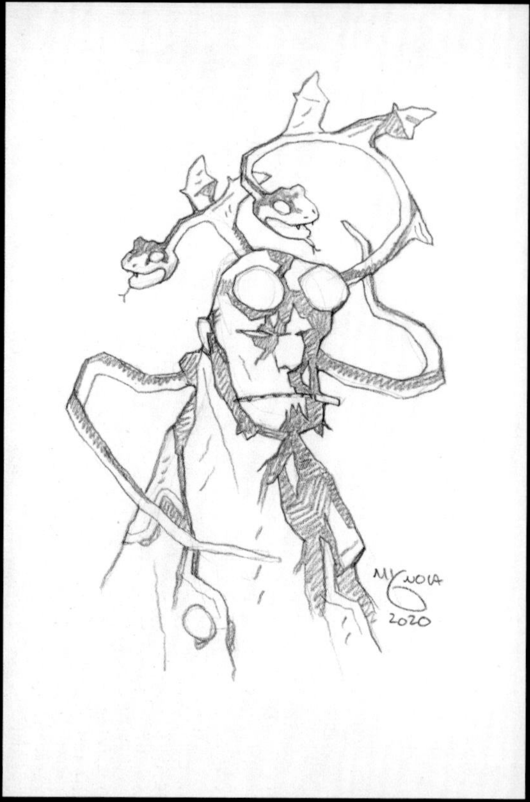
MIGNOLA
2020

Quite often people tell me they want to try out *Hellboy* (which is nice) and want to know where they should start. *Seed of Destruction* is the first book, where it all started, and it introduces most of the big ideas that will run through the series. It's a perfectly fine place to start if someone is sure they want to sign on for the big ride. But me, I usually recommend starting with a couple of the short stories—they're fun (most of them), they're short, and they're easy. Why commit before you see what you're in for? Anyway, that's what this book is—a sampler. Some of the stories here are included because they say something important about who Hellboy is, where he's from, and where he's going, but most are here just because they are my favorites. On the following pages you'll find fairies (the scary kind) and mermaids (also kind of scary), trolls, witches, vampires (both scary and sad), and a ghoul (kind of sad but mostly disgusting, even with the poetry). Also a little boy who likes noodles and one very talkative corpse.

For those of you already familiar with the *Hellboy* world, maybe there's something here you missed. Or maybe these will just be a pleasant reminder of Hellboy's less complicated days. For those of you new to the world, I hope you'll find something here you like and you'll choose to stick around.

To all you readers, whoever you are, thanks.

MIKE MIGNOLA

UNIVERSE ESSENTIALS

HELLBOY

———

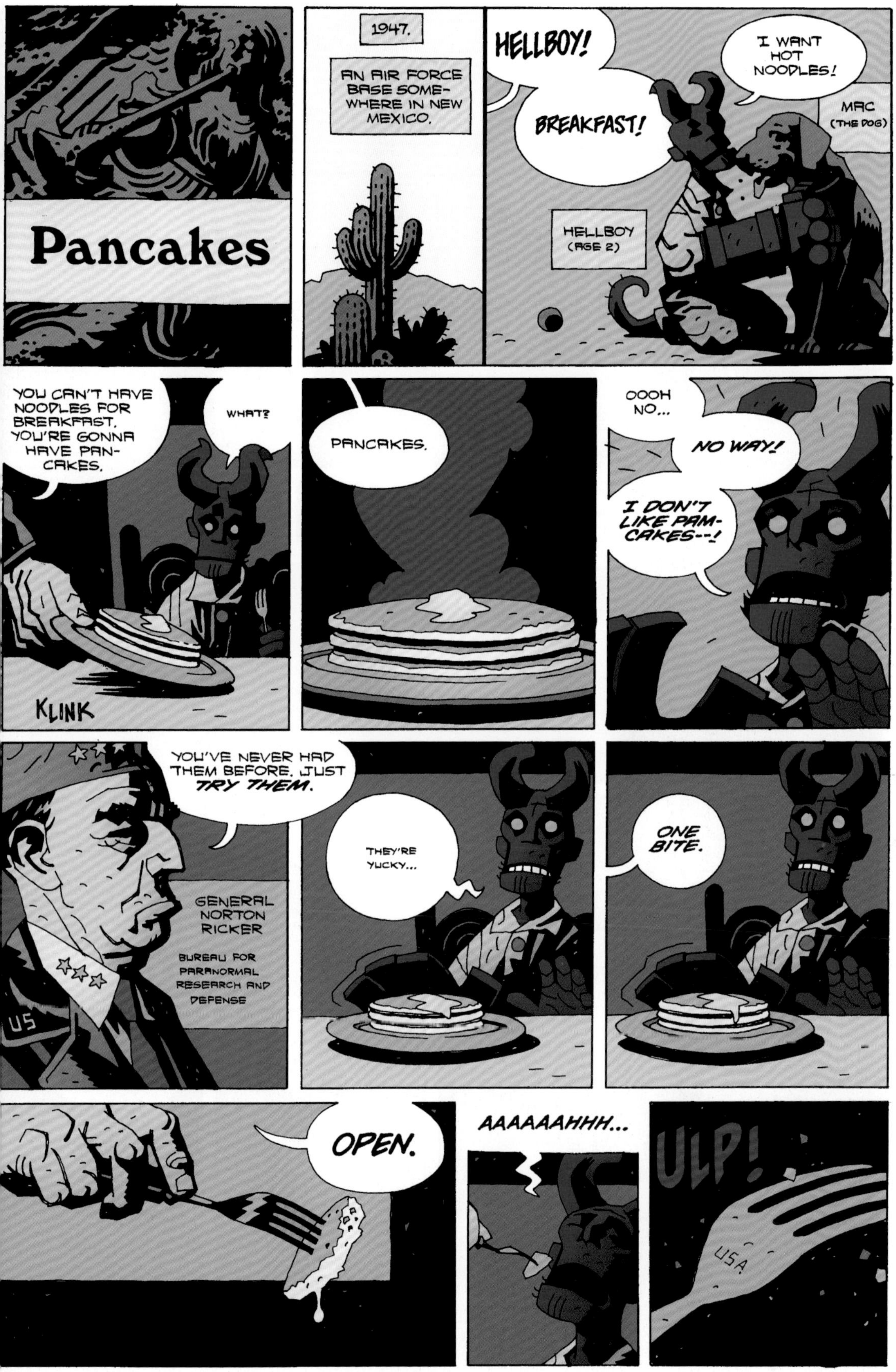
Pancakes
1947.
AN AIR FORCE BASE SOMEWHERE IN NEW MEXICO.
HELLBOY!
BREAKFAST!
I WANT HOT NOODLES!
MAC (THE DOG)
HELLBOY (AGE 2)
YOU CAN'T HAVE NOODLES FOR BREAKFAST. YOU'RE GONNA HAVE PANCAKES.
WHAT?
KLINK
PANCAKES.
OOOH NO...
NO WAY!
I DON'T LIKE PAMCAKES--!
YOU'VE NEVER HAD THEM BEFORE. JUST TRY THEM.
GENERAL NORTON RICKER
BUREAU FOR PARANORMAL RESEARCH AND DEFENSE
US
THEY'RE YUCKY...
ONE BITE.
OPEN.
AAAAAAHHH...
ULP!
USA

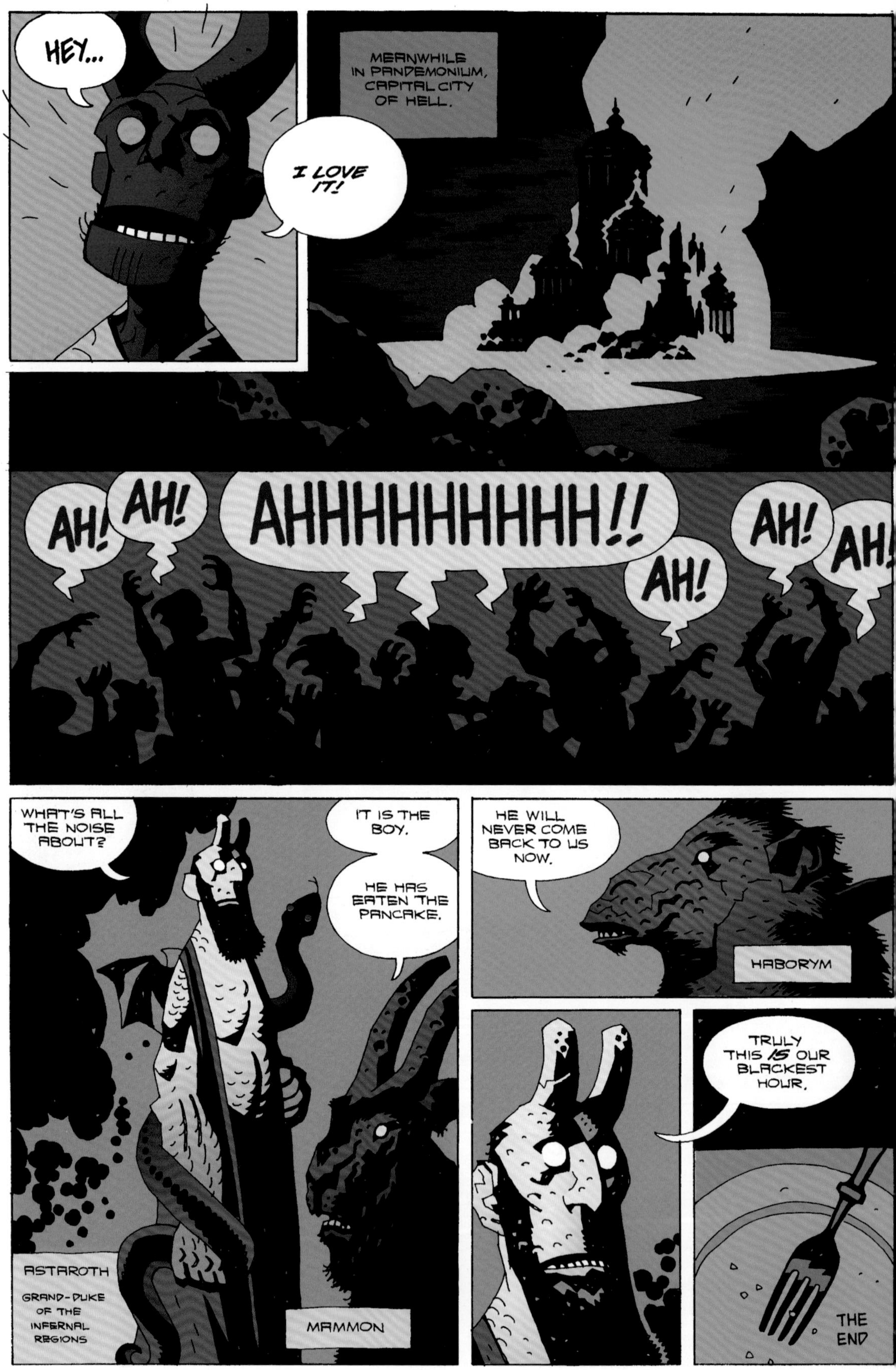
HEY...
I LOVE IT!
MEANWHILE IN PANDEMONIUM, CAPITAL CITY OF HELL.
AH!
AH!
AHHHHHHHHH!!
AH!
AH!
AH!
WHAT'S ALL THE NOISE ABOUT?
IT IS THE BOY.
HE HAS EATEN THE PANCAKE.
ASTAROTH
GRAND-DUKE OF THE INFERNAL REGIONS
MAMMON
HE WILL NEVER COME BACK TO US NOW.
HABORYM
TRULY THIS IS OUR BLACKEST HOUR.
THE END

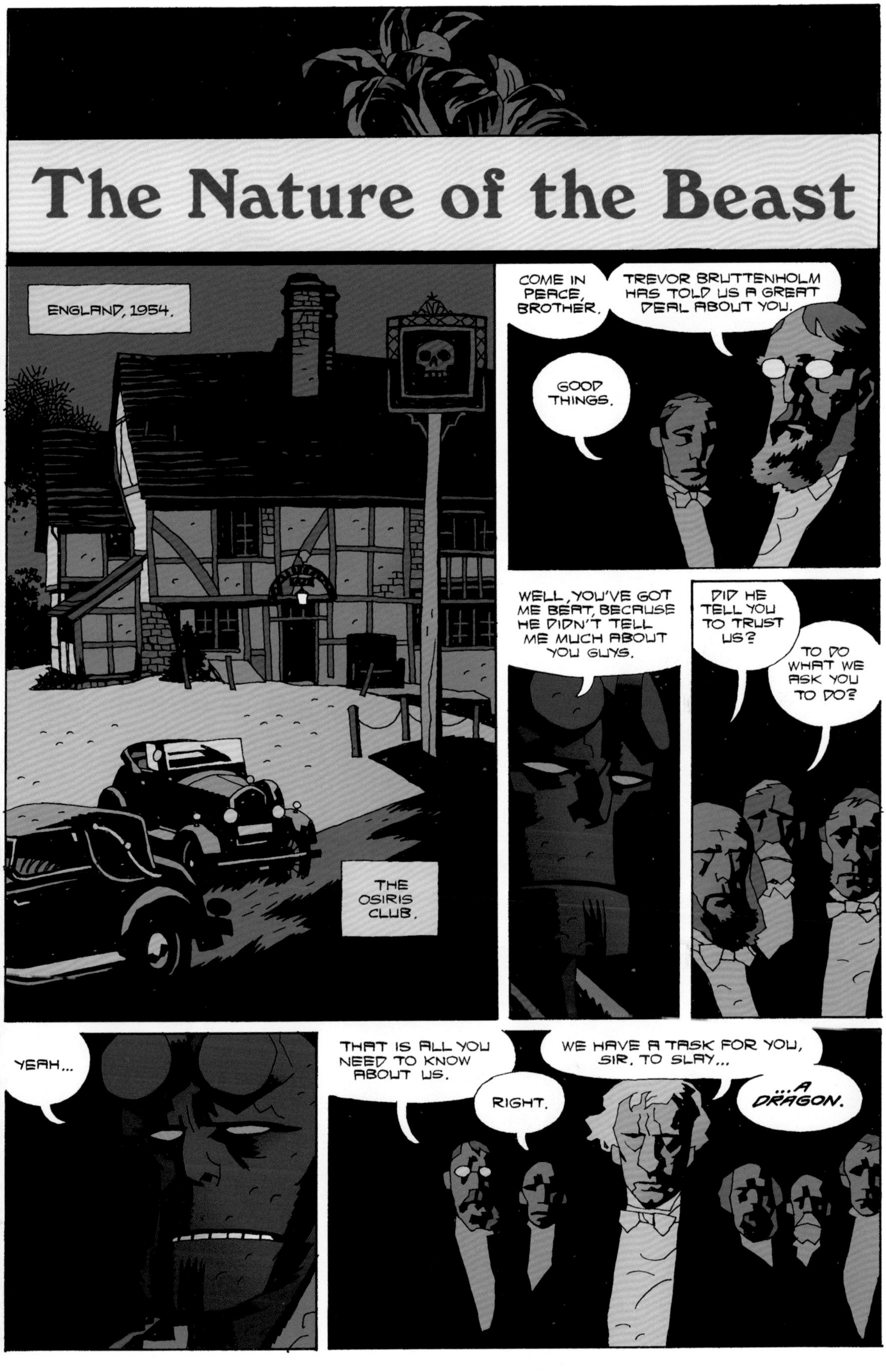
The Nature of the Beast
ENGLAND, 1954.
THE OSIRIS CLUB.
COME IN PEACE, BROTHER.
TREVOR BRUTTENHOLM HAS TOLD US A GREAT DEAL ABOUT YOU.
GOOD THINGS.
WELL, YOU'VE GOT ME BEAT, BECAUSE HE DIDN'T TELL ME MUCH ABOUT YOU GUYS.
DID HE TELL YOU TO TRUST US?
TO DO WHAT WE ASK YOU TO DO?
YEAH...
THAT IS ALL YOU NEED TO KNOW ABOUT US.
RIGHT.
WE HAVE A TASK FOR YOU, SIR. TO SLAY...
...A DRAGON.

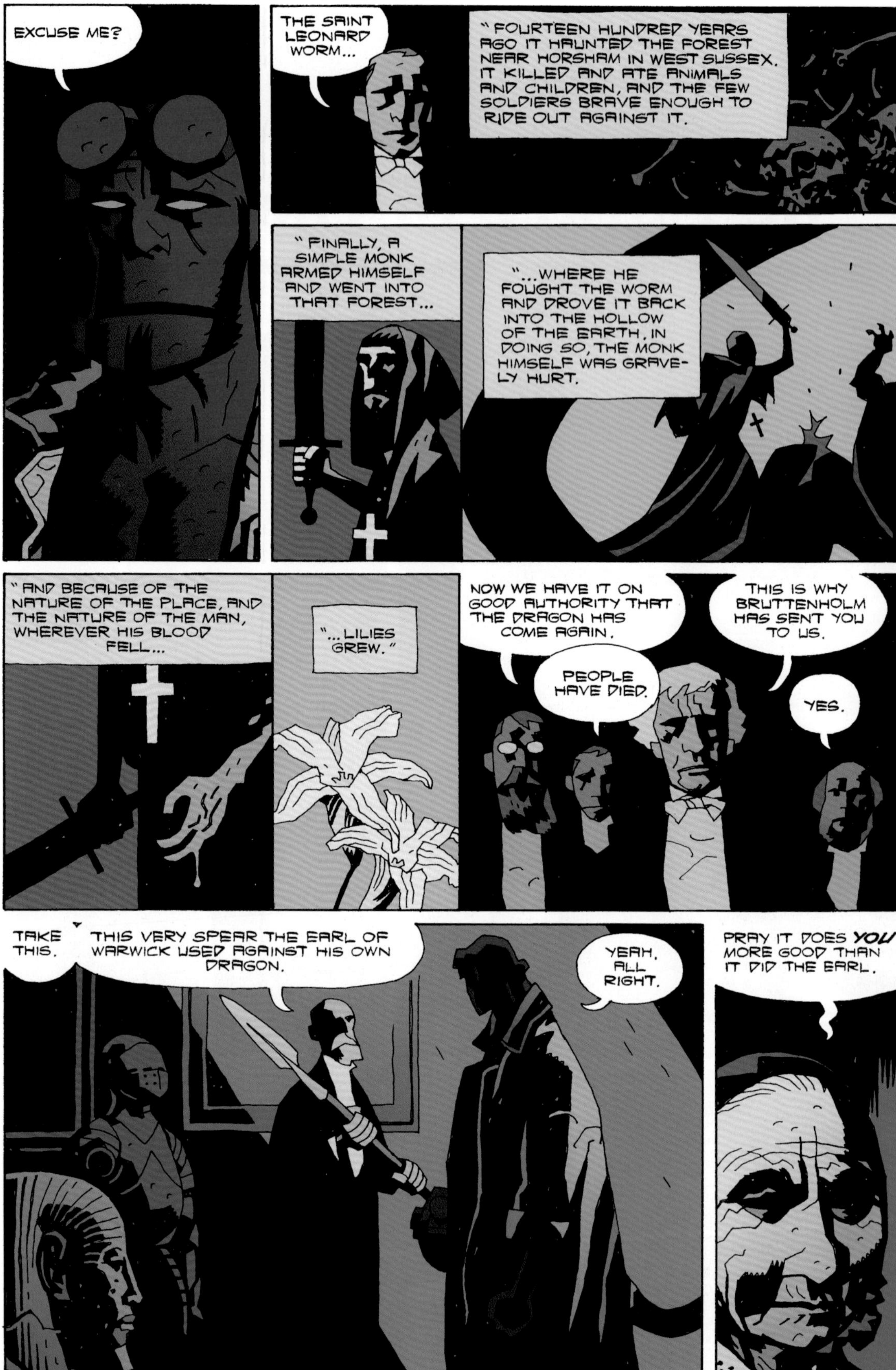
EXCUSE ME?
THE SAINT LEONARD WORM...
"FOURTEEN HUNDRED YEARS AGO IT HAUNTED THE FOREST NEAR HORSHAM IN WEST SUSSEX. IT KILLED AND ATE ANIMALS AND CHILDREN, AND THE FEW SOLDIERS BRAVE ENOUGH TO RIDE OUT AGAINST IT.
"FINALLY, A SIMPLE MONK ARMED HIMSELF AND WENT INTO THAT FOREST...
"...WHERE HE FOUGHT THE WORM AND DROVE IT BACK INTO THE HOLLOW OF THE EARTH. IN DOING SO, THE MONK HIMSELF WAS GRAVELY HURT.
"AND BECAUSE OF THE NATURE OF THE PLACE, AND THE NATURE OF THE MAN, WHEREVER HIS BLOOD FELL...
"...LILIES GREW."
NOW WE HAVE IT ON GOOD AUTHORITY THAT THE DRAGON HAS COME AGAIN.
PEOPLE HAVE DIED.
THIS IS WHY BRUTTENHOLM HAS SENT YOU TO US.
YES.
TAKE THIS.
THIS VERY SPEAR THE EARL OF WARWICK USED AGAINST HIS OWN DRAGON.
YEAH. ALL RIGHT.
PRAY IT DOES ***YOU*** MORE GOOD THAN IT DID THE EARL.

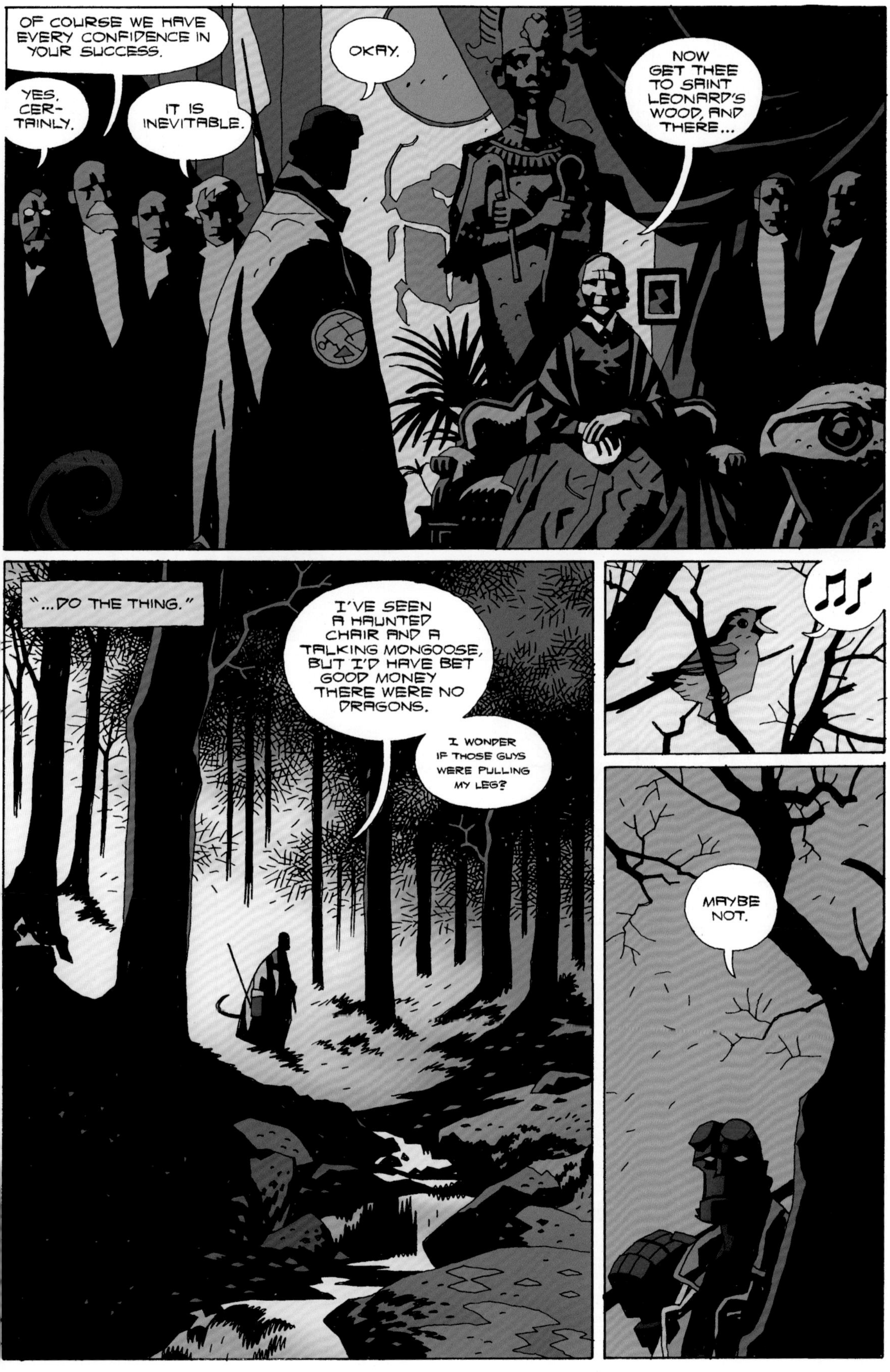
OF COURSE WE HAVE EVERY CONFIDENCE IN YOUR SUCCESS.
YES, CER-TAINLY.
IT IS INEVITABLE.
OKAY.
NOW GET THEE TO SAINT LEONARD'S WOOD, AND THERE...
"...DO THE THING."
I'VE SEEN A HAUNTED CHAIR AND A TALKING MONGOOSE, BUT I'D HAVE BET GOOD MONEY THERE WERE NO DRAGONS.
I WONDER IF THOSE GUYS WERE PULLING MY LEG?
MAYBE NOT.

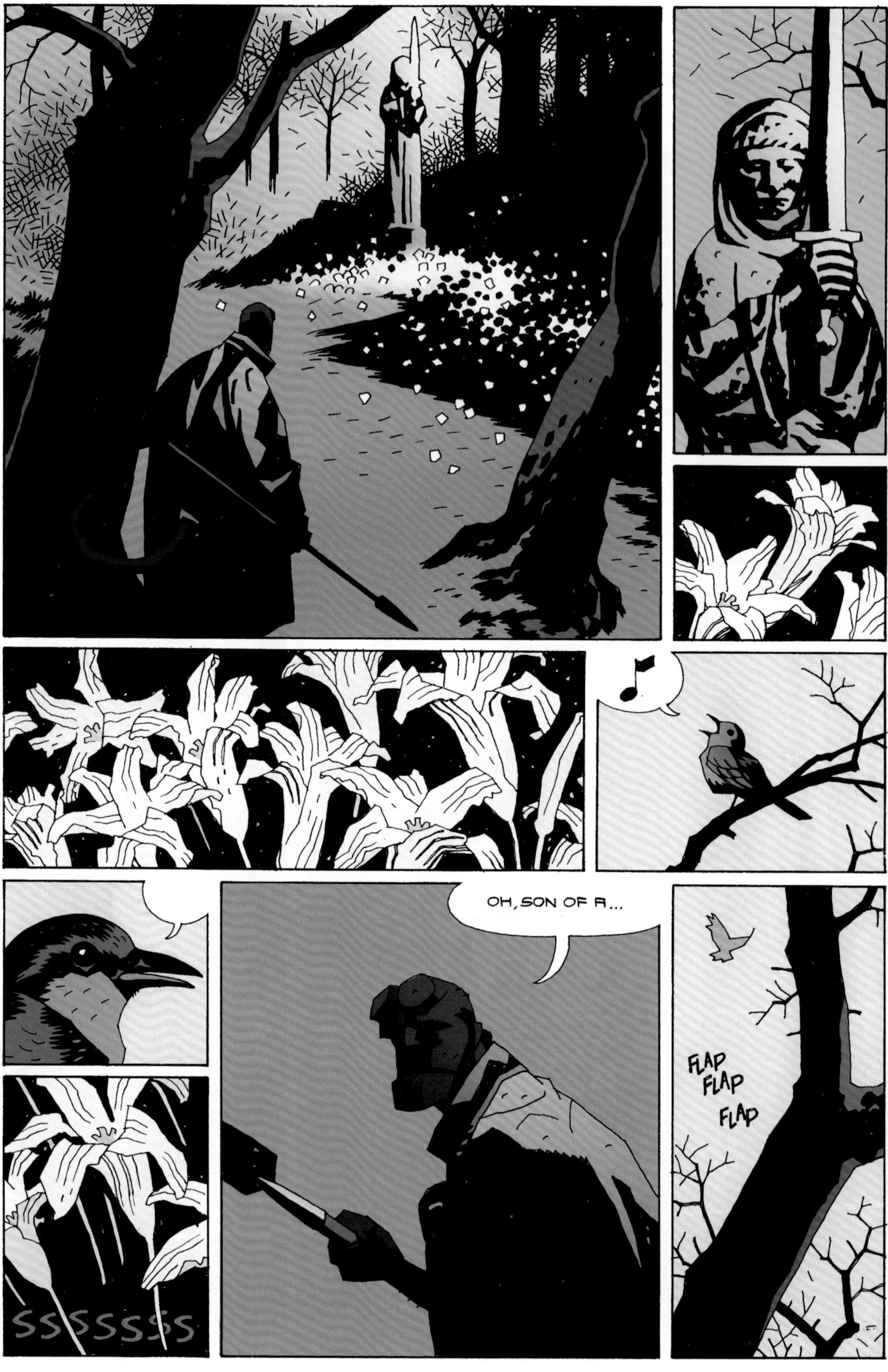
OH, SON OF A...
FLAP
FLAP
FLAP
SSSSSSS

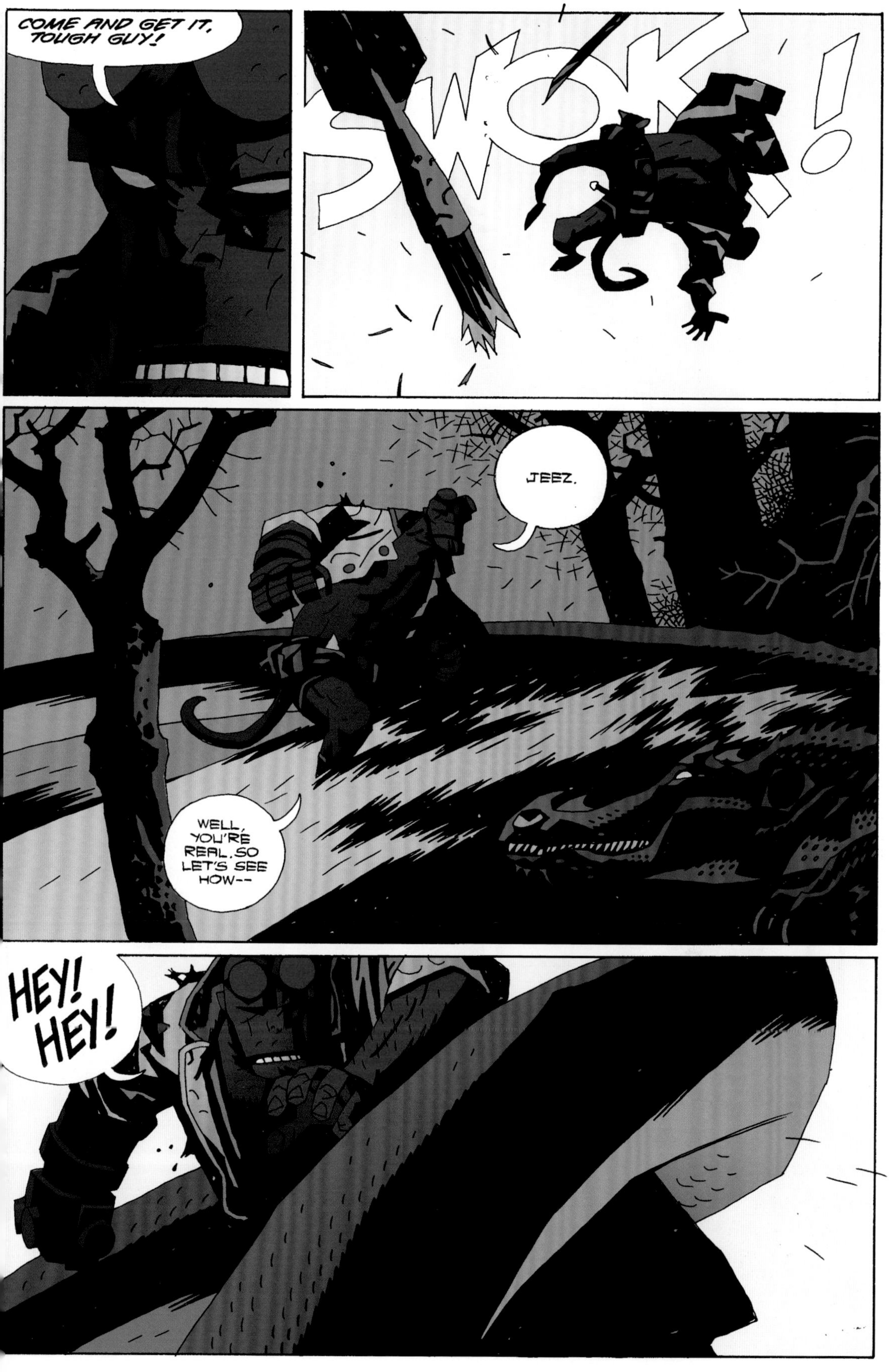
COME AND GET IT, TOUGH GUY!
SWOK!
JEEZ.
WELL, YOU'RE REAL. SO LET'S SEE HOW--
HEY! HEY!

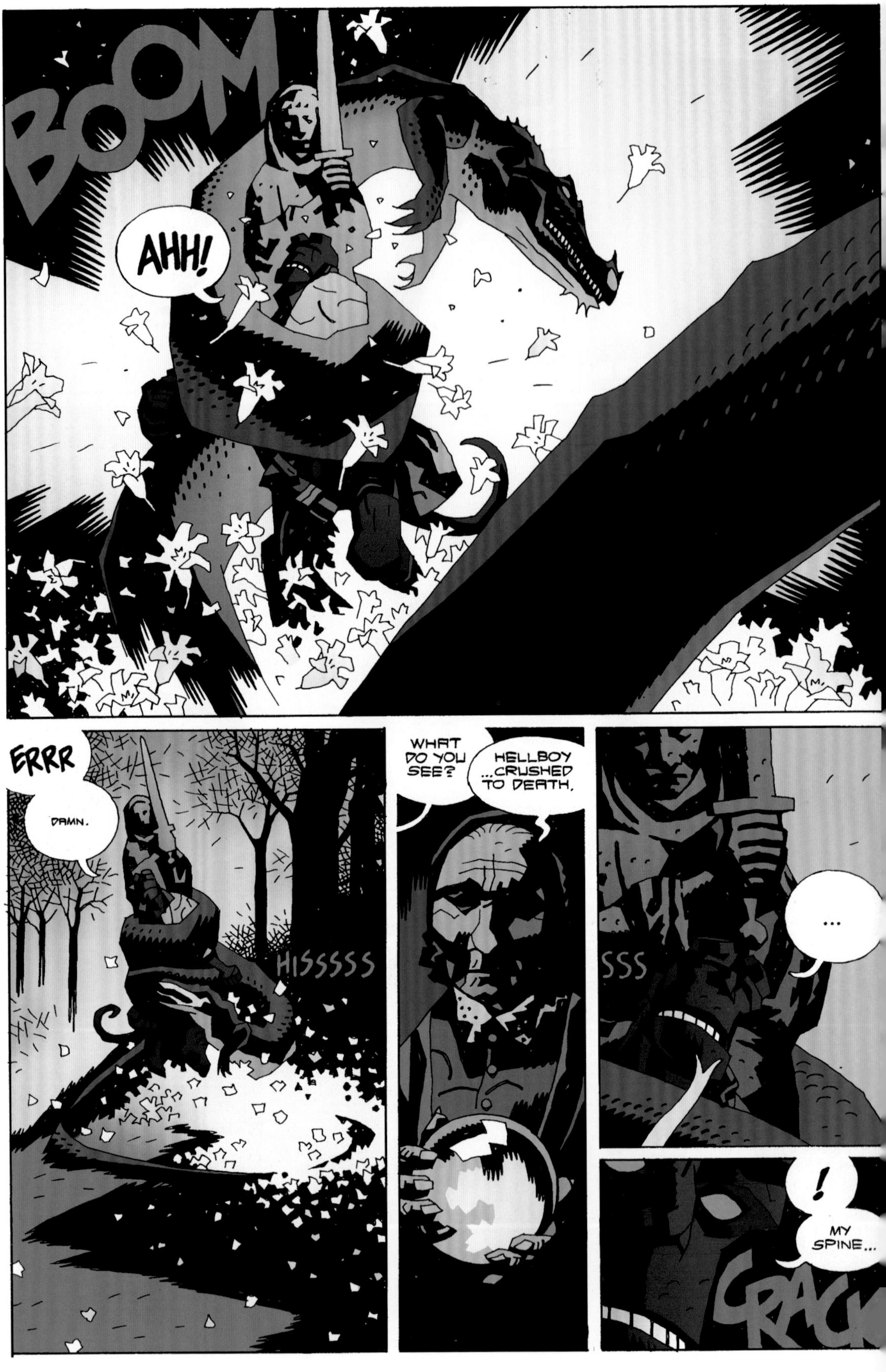
BOOM
AHH!
ERRR
DAMN.
HISSSSS
WHAT DO YOU SEE?
HELLBOY ...CRUSHED TO DEATH.
SSS
...
!
MY SPINE...
CRACK

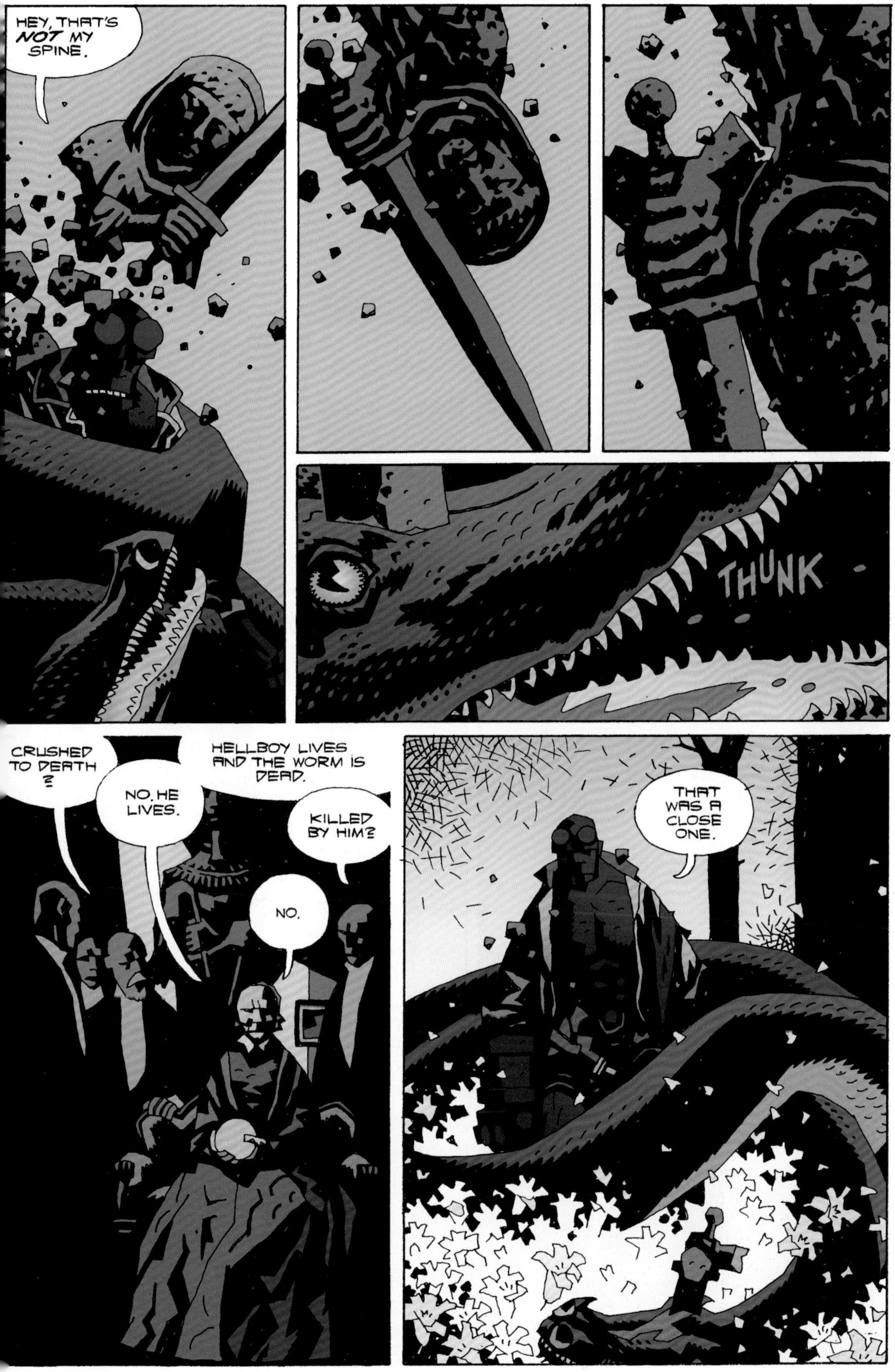
HEY, THAT'S NOT MY SPINE.
THUNK
CRUSHED TO DEATH?
NO, HE LIVES.
HELLBOY LIVES AND THE WORM IS DEAD.
KILLED BY HIM?
NO.
THAT WAS A CLOSE ONE.

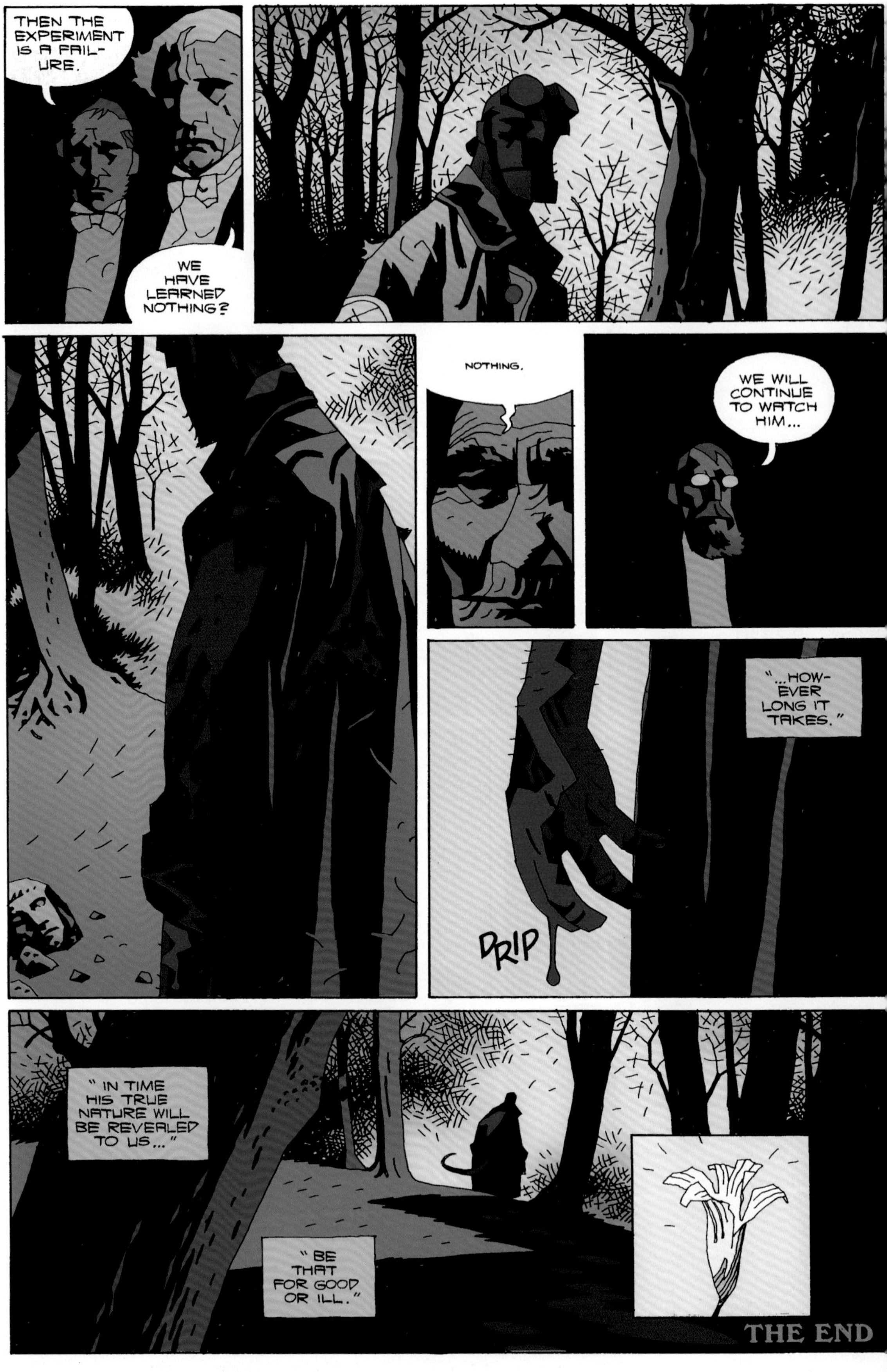
THEN THE EXPERIMENT IS A FAIL-URE.
WE HAVE LEARNED NOTHING?
NOTHING.
WE WILL CONTINUE TO WATCH HIM...
"...HOW-EVER LONG IT TAKES."
DRIP
" IN TIME HIS TRUE NATURE WILL BE REVEALED TO US..."
" BE THAT FOR GOOD OR ILL."
THE END

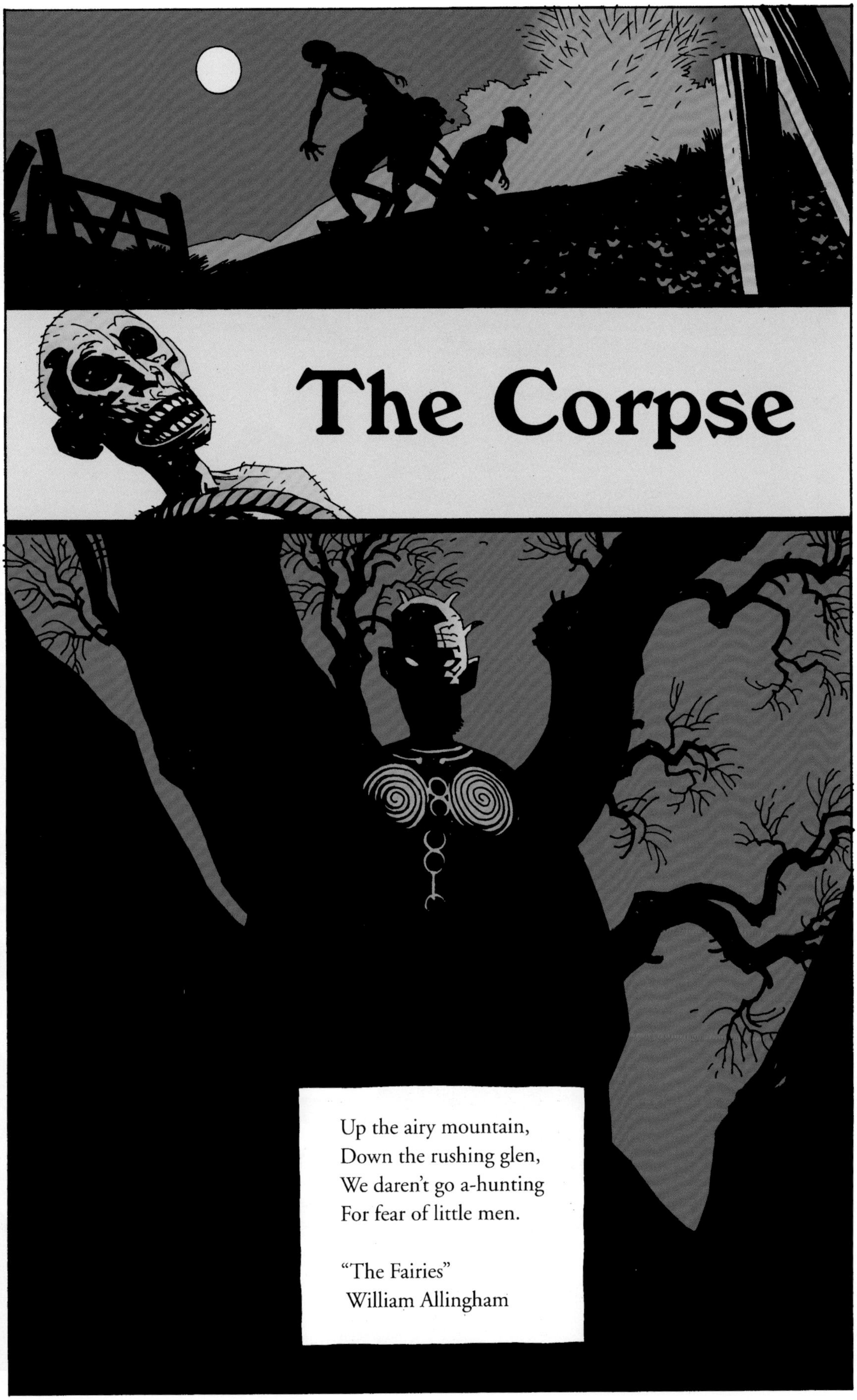
The Corpse
Up the airy mountain,
Down the rushing glen,
We daren't go a-hunting
For fear of little men.
"The Fairies"
William Allingham

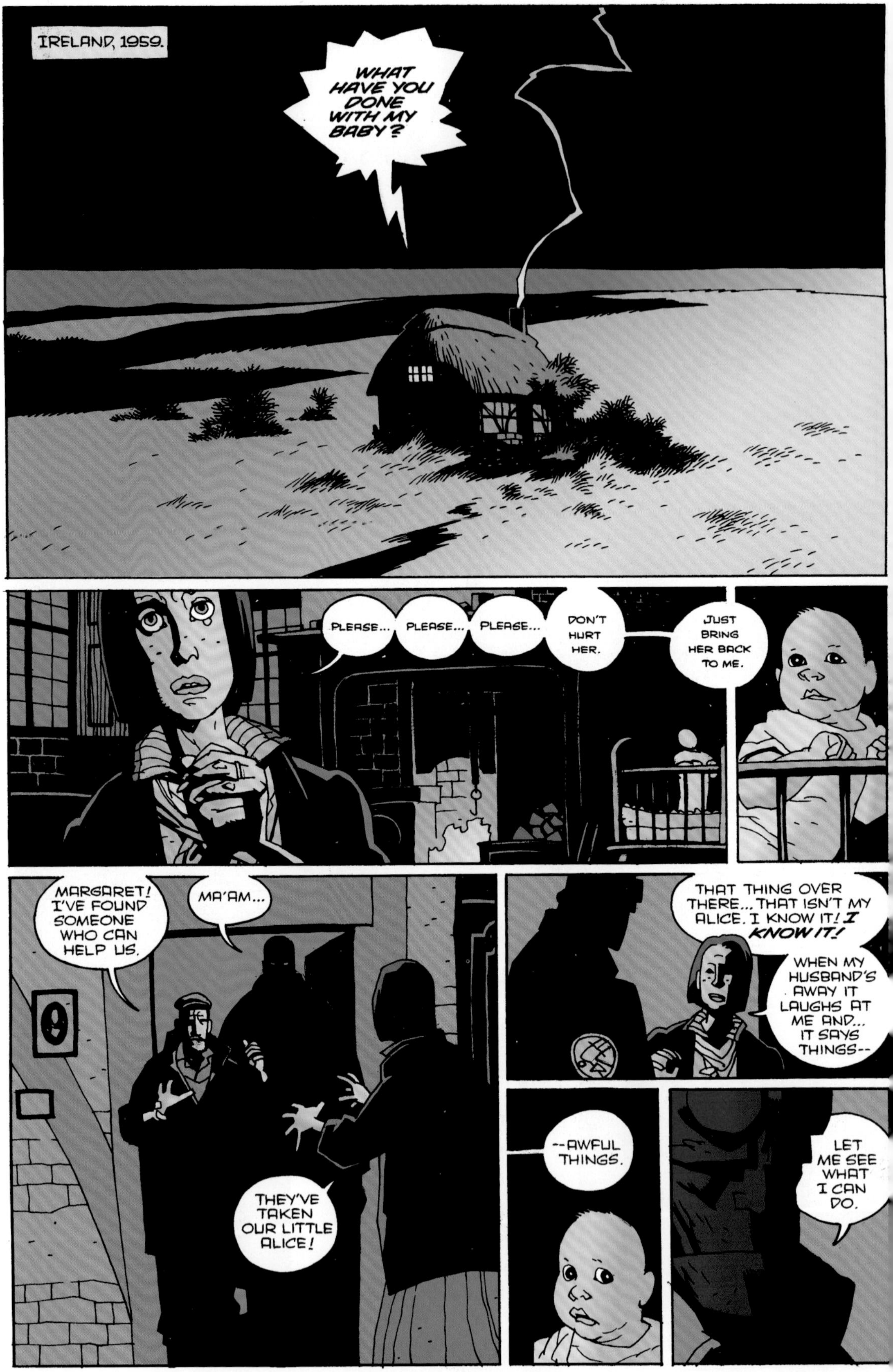
IRELAND, 1959.
WHAT HAVE YOU DONE WITH MY BABY?
PLEASE...
PLEASE...
PLEASE...
DON'T HURT HER.
JUST BRING HER BACK TO ME.
MARGARET! I'VE FOUND SOMEONE WHO CAN HELP US.
MA'AM...
THEY'VE TAKEN OUR LITTLE ALICE!
THAT THING OVER THERE... THAT ISN'T MY ALICE. I KNOW IT! I KNOW IT!
WHEN MY HUSBAND'S AWAY IT LAUGHS AT ME AND... IT SAYS THINGS--
--AWFUL THINGS.
LET ME SEE WHAT I CAN DO.

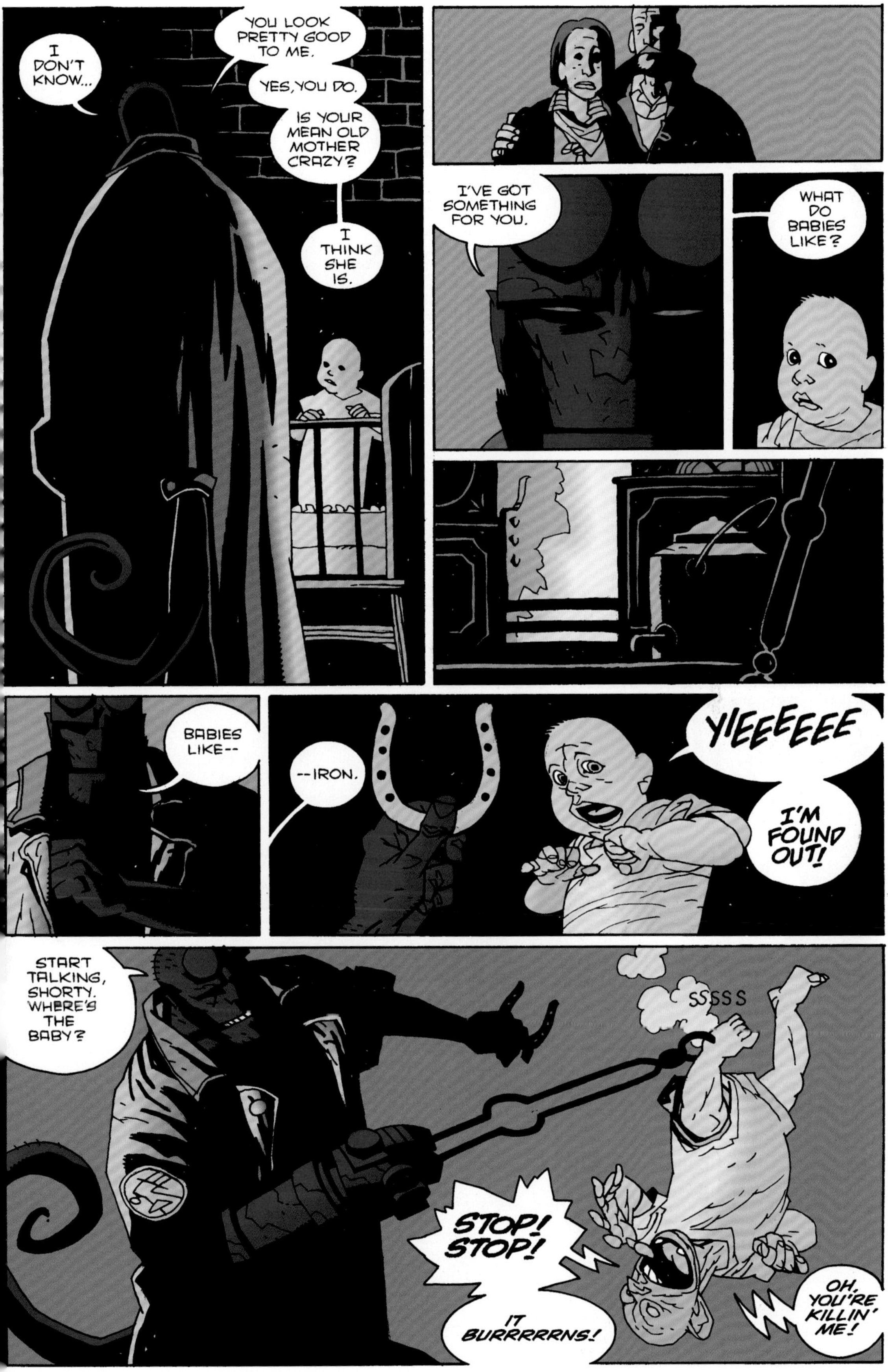

I DON'T KNOW...
YOU LOOK PRETTY GOOD TO ME.
YES, YOU DO.
IS YOUR MEAN OLD MOTHER CRAZY?
I THINK SHE IS.
I'VE GOT SOMETHING FOR YOU.
WHAT DO BABIES LIKE?
BABIES LIKE--
--IRON.
YIEEEEEE
I'M FOUND OUT!
START TALKING, SHORTY. WHERE'S THE BABY?
SSSSS
STOP! STOP!
IT BURRRRRNS!
OH, YOU'RE KILLIN' ME!

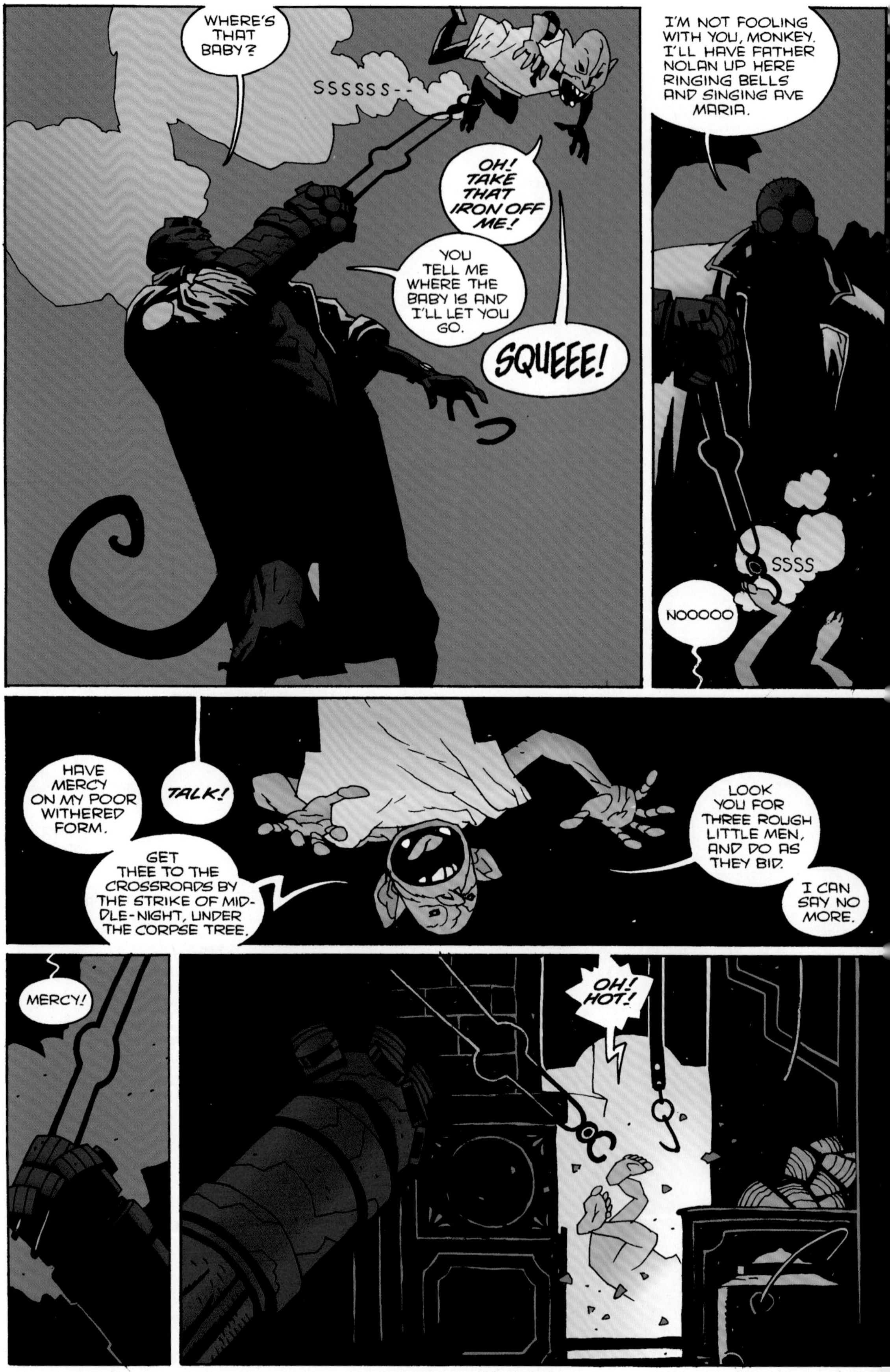
WHERE'S THAT BABY?
SSSSSS--
OH! TAKE THAT IRON OFF ME!
YOU TELL ME WHERE THE BABY IS AND I'LL LET YOU GO.
SQUEEE!
I'M NOT FOOLING WITH YOU, MONKEY. I'LL HAVE FATHER NOLAN UP HERE RINGING BELLS AND SINGING AVE MARIA.
SSSS
NOOOOO
HAVE MERCY ON MY POOR WITHERED FORM.
TALK!
GET THEE TO THE CROSSROADS BY THE STRIKE OF MID-DLE-NIGHT, UNDER THE CORPSE TREE.
LOOK YOU FOR THREE ROUGH LITTLE MEN, AND DO AS THEY BID.
I CAN SAY NO MORE.
MERCY!
OH! HOT!

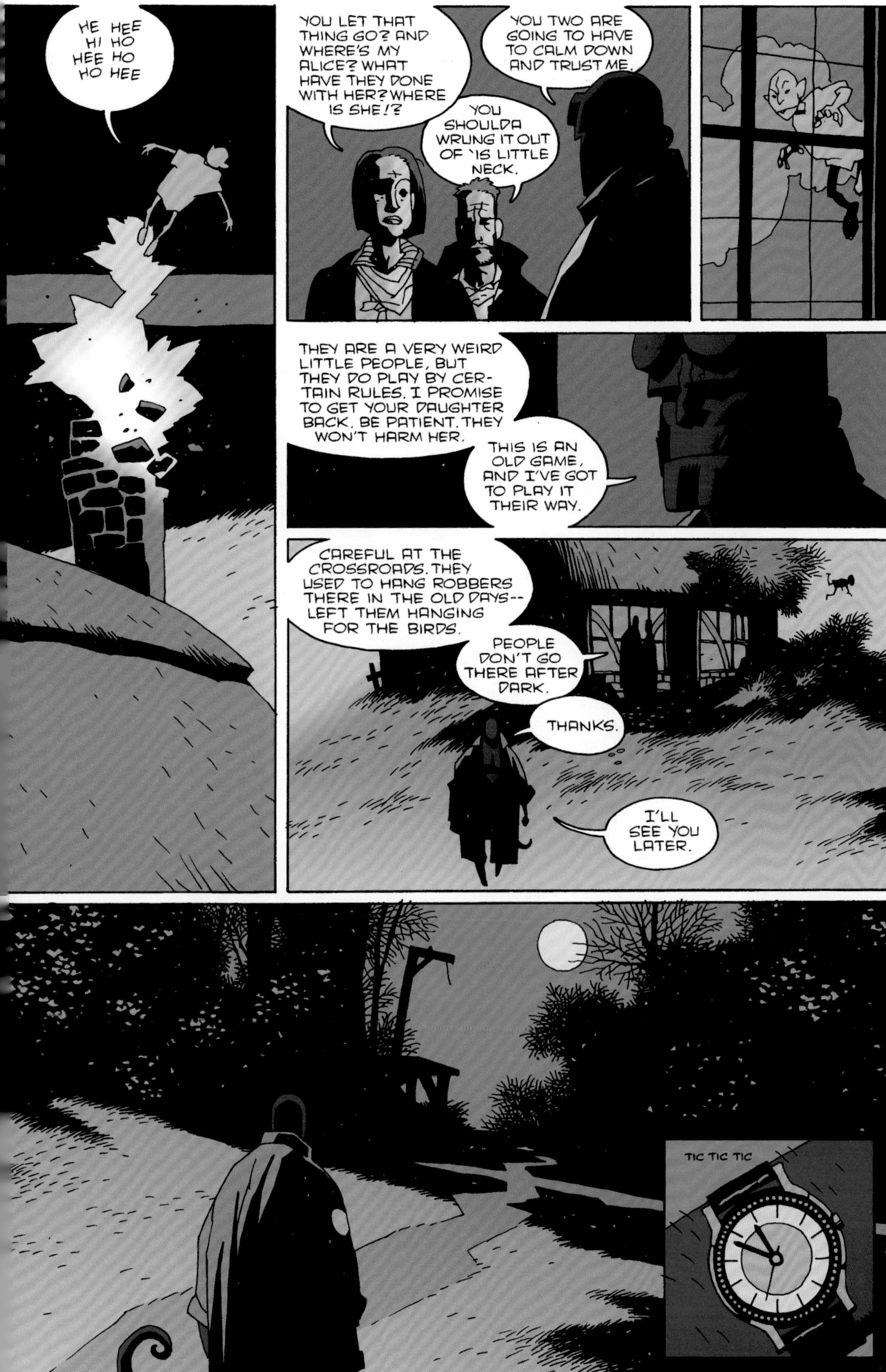
HE HEE HI HO HEE HO HO HEE
YOU LET THAT THING GO? AND WHERE'S MY ALICE? WHAT HAVE THEY DONE WITH HER? WHERE IS SHE!?
YOU TWO ARE GOING TO HAVE TO CALM DOWN AND TRUST ME.
YOU SHOULDA WRUNG IT OUT OF 'IS LITTLE NECK.
THEY ARE A VERY WEIRD LITTLE PEOPLE, BUT THEY DO PLAY BY CERTAIN RULES. I PROMISE TO GET YOUR DAUGHTER BACK. BE PATIENT. THEY WON'T HARM HER.
THIS IS AN OLD GAME, AND I'VE GOT TO PLAY IT THEIR WAY.
CAREFUL AT THE CROSSROADS. THEY USED TO HANG ROBBERS THERE IN THE OLD DAYS-- LEFT THEM HANGING FOR THE BIRDS.
PEOPLE DON'T GO THERE AFTER DARK.
THANKS.
I'LL SEE YOU LATER.
TIC TIC TIC

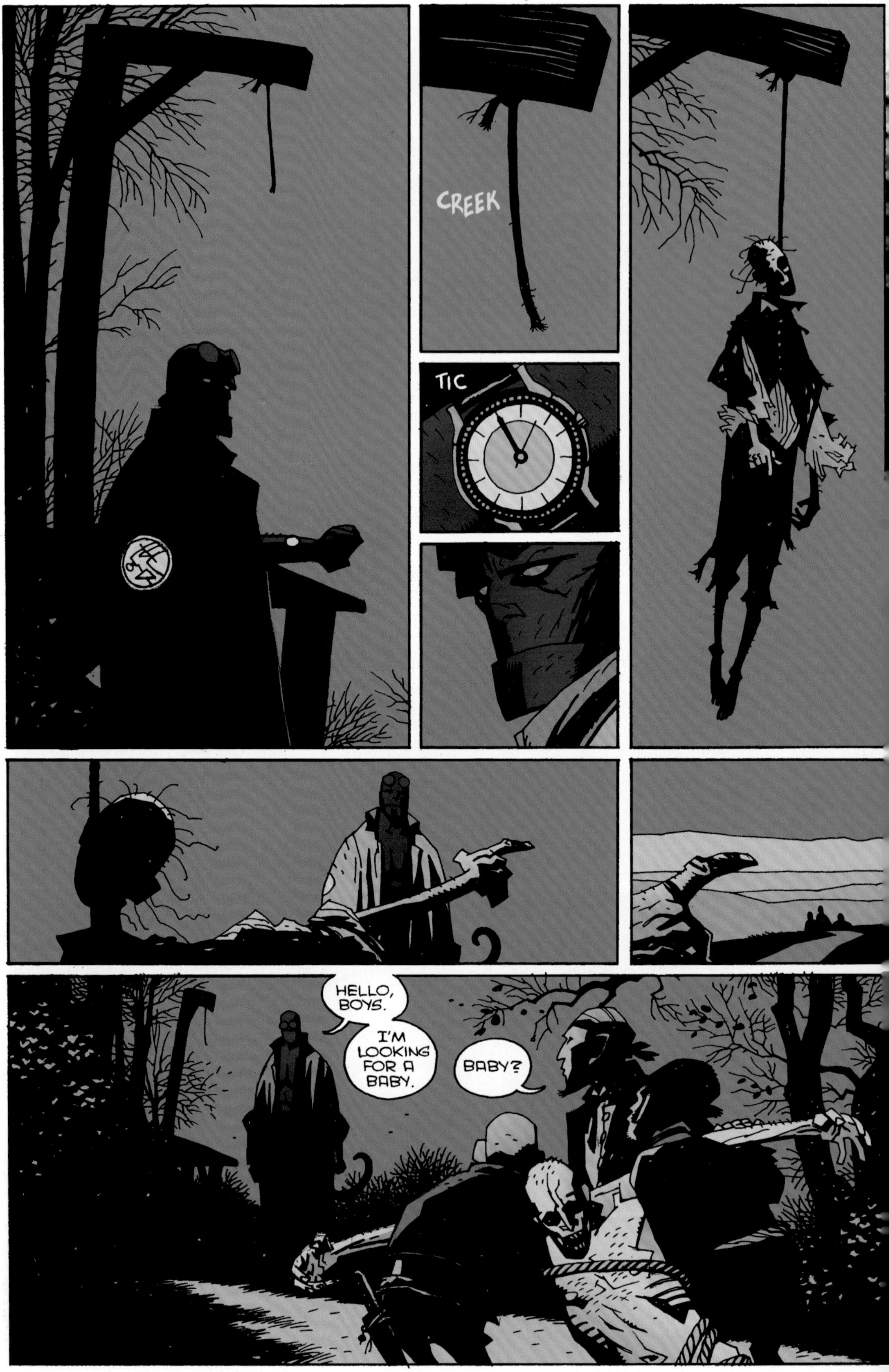
CREEK
TIC
HELLO, BOYS.
I'M LOOKING FOR A BABY.
BABY?

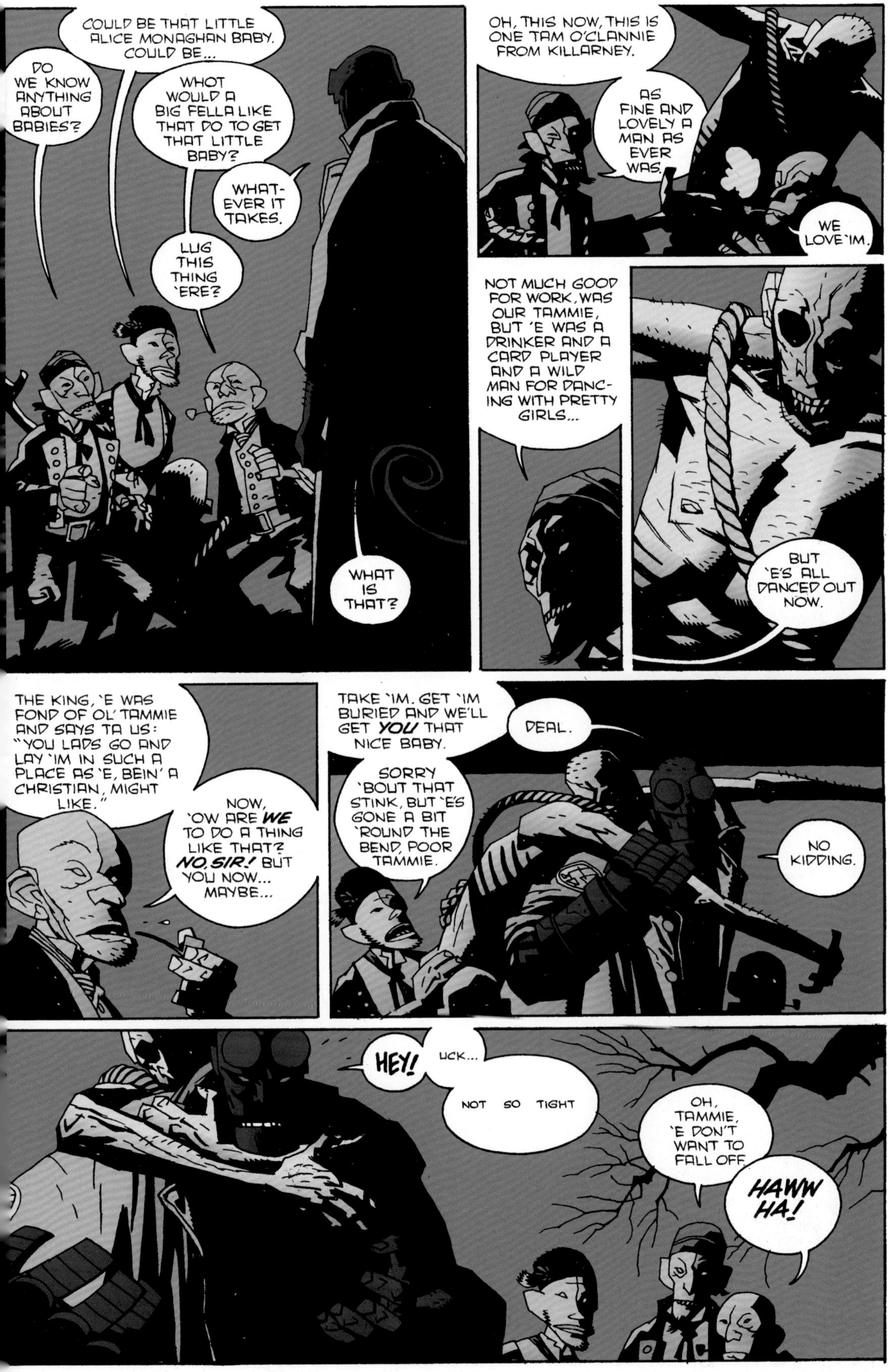
COULD BE THAT LITTLE ALICE MONAGHAN BABY. COULD BE...
DO WE KNOW ANYTHING ABOUT BABIES?
WHOT WOULD A BIG FELLA LIKE THAT DO TO GET THAT LITTLE BABY?
WHAT-EVER IT TAKES.
LUG THIS THING 'ERE?
WHAT IS THAT?
OH, THIS NOW, THIS IS ONE TAM O'CLANNIE FROM KILLARNEY.
AS FINE AND LOVELY A MAN AS EVER WAS.
WE LOVE 'IM.
NOT MUCH GOOD FOR WORK, WAS OUR TAMMIE, BUT 'E WAS A DRINKER AND A CARD PLAYER AND A WILD MAN FOR DANCING WITH PRETTY GIRLS...
BUT 'E'S ALL DANCED OUT NOW.
THE KING, 'E WAS FOND OF OL' TAMMIE AND SAYS TA US: "YOU LADS GO AND LAY 'IM IN SUCH A PLACE AS 'E, BEIN' A CHRISTIAN, MIGHT LIKE."
NOW, 'OW ARE WE TO DO A THING LIKE THAT? NO, SIR! BUT YOU NOW... MAYBE...
TAKE 'IM. GET 'IM BURIED AND WE'LL GET YOU THAT NICE BABY.
DEAL.
SORRY 'BOUT THAT STINK, BUT 'E'S GONE A BIT 'ROUND THE BEND, POOR TAMMIE.
NO KIDDING.
HEY!
UCK...
NOT SO TIGHT
OH, TAMMIE, 'E DON'T WANT TO FALL OFF.
HAWW HA!

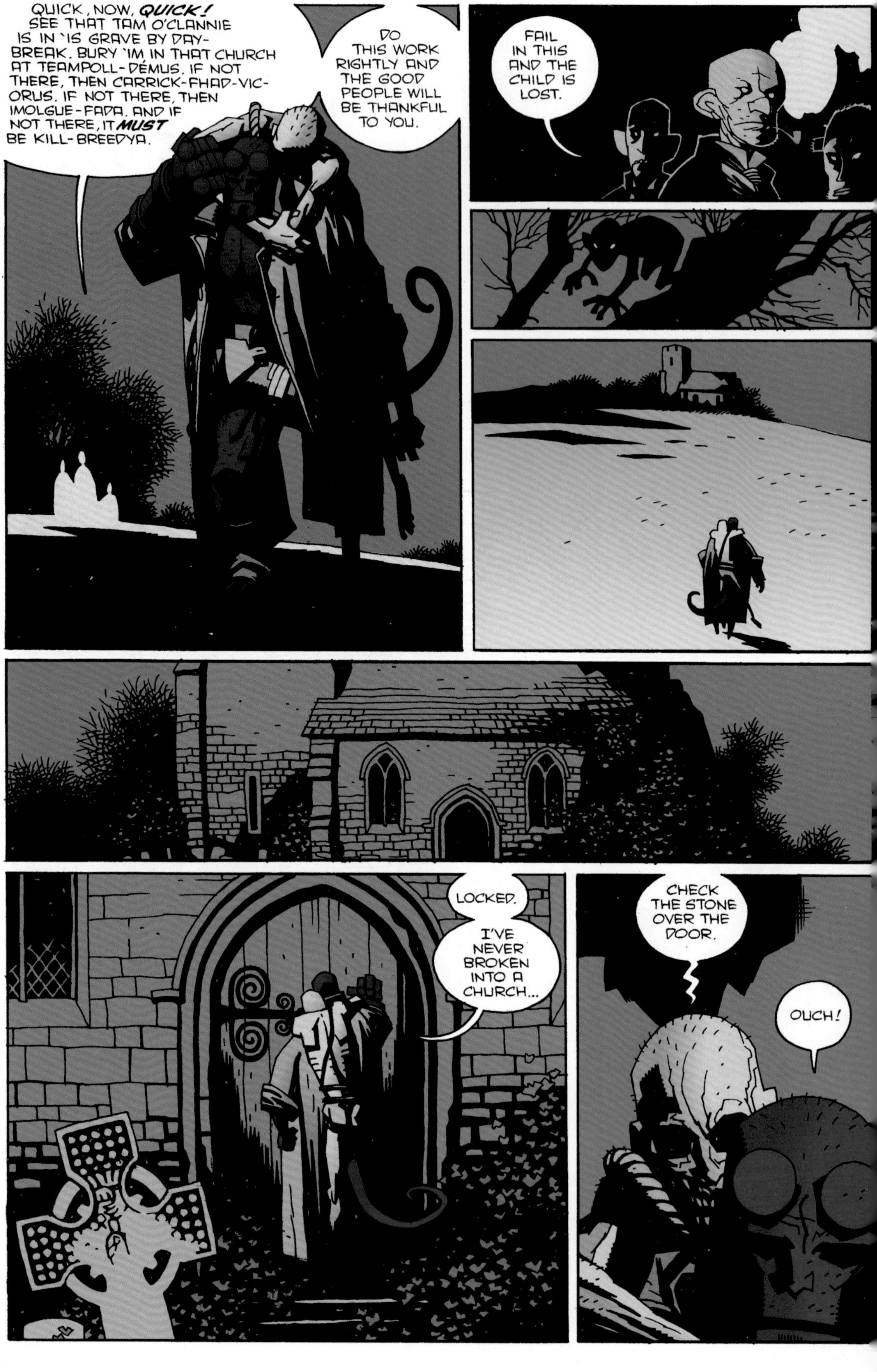
QUICK, NOW, QUICK! SEE THAT TAM O'CLANNIE IS IN 'IS GRAVE BY DAY-BREAK. BURY 'IM IN THAT CHURCH AT TEAMPOLL-DÉMUS. IF NOT THERE, THEN CARRICK-FHAD-VIC-ORUS. IF NOT THERE, THEN IMOLGUE-FADA. AND IF NOT THERE, IT MUST BE KILL-BREEDYA.
DO THIS WORK RIGHTLY AND THE GOOD PEOPLE WILL BE THANKFUL TO YOU.
FAIL IN THIS AND THE CHILD IS LOST.
LOCKED.
I'VE NEVER BROKEN INTO A CHURCH...
CHECK THE STONE OVER THE DOOR.
OUCH!

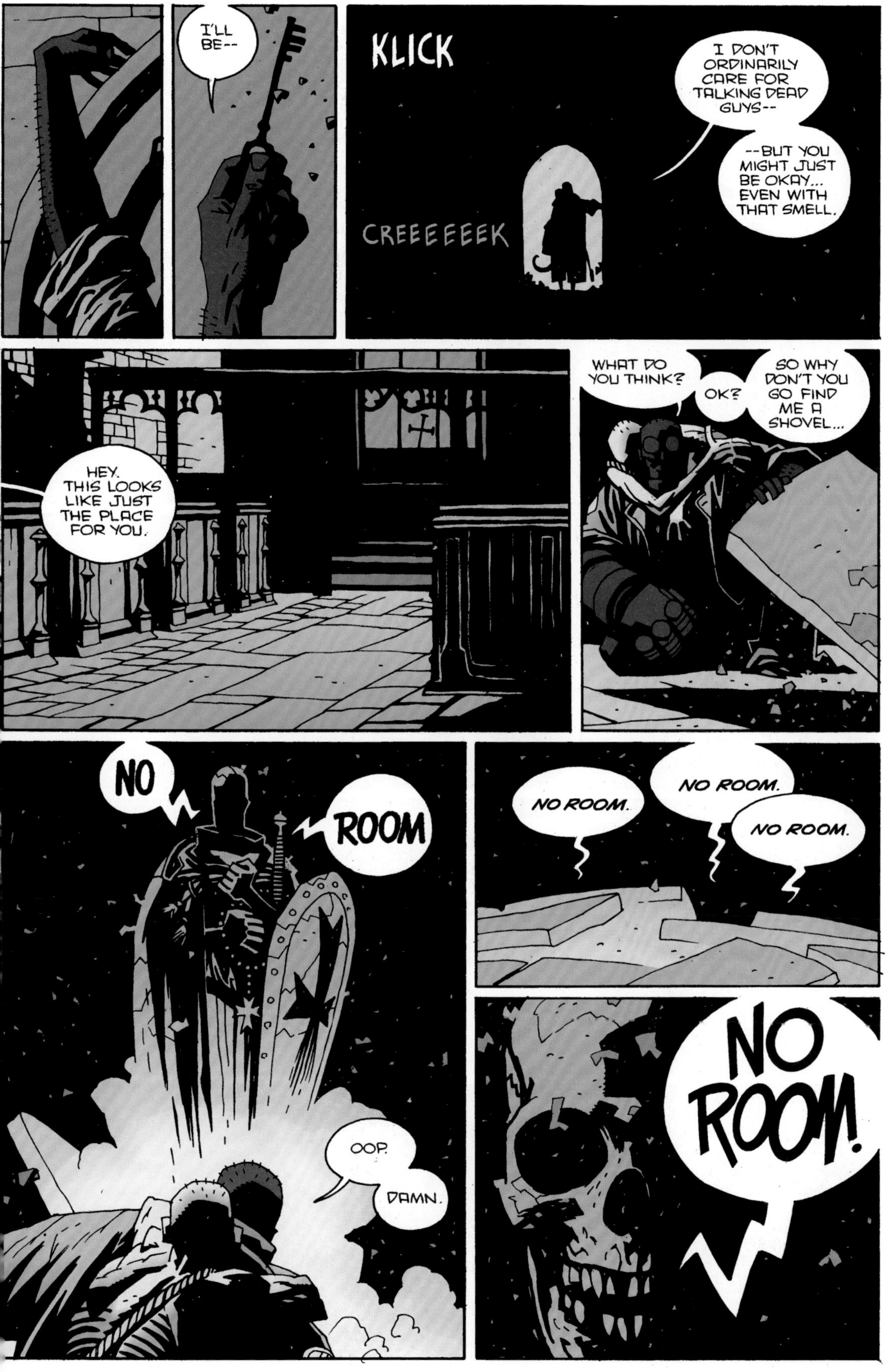
I'LL BE--
KLICK
CREEEEEEK
I DON'T ORDINARILY CARE FOR TALKING DEAD GUYS--
--BUT YOU MIGHT JUST BE OKAY... EVEN WITH THAT SMELL.
HEY. THIS LOOKS LIKE JUST THE PLACE FOR YOU.
WHAT DO YOU THINK?
OK?
SO WHY DON'T YOU GO FIND ME A SHOVEL...
NO
ROOM
OOP.
DAMN.
NO ROOM.
NO ROOM.
NO ROOM.
NO ROOM!

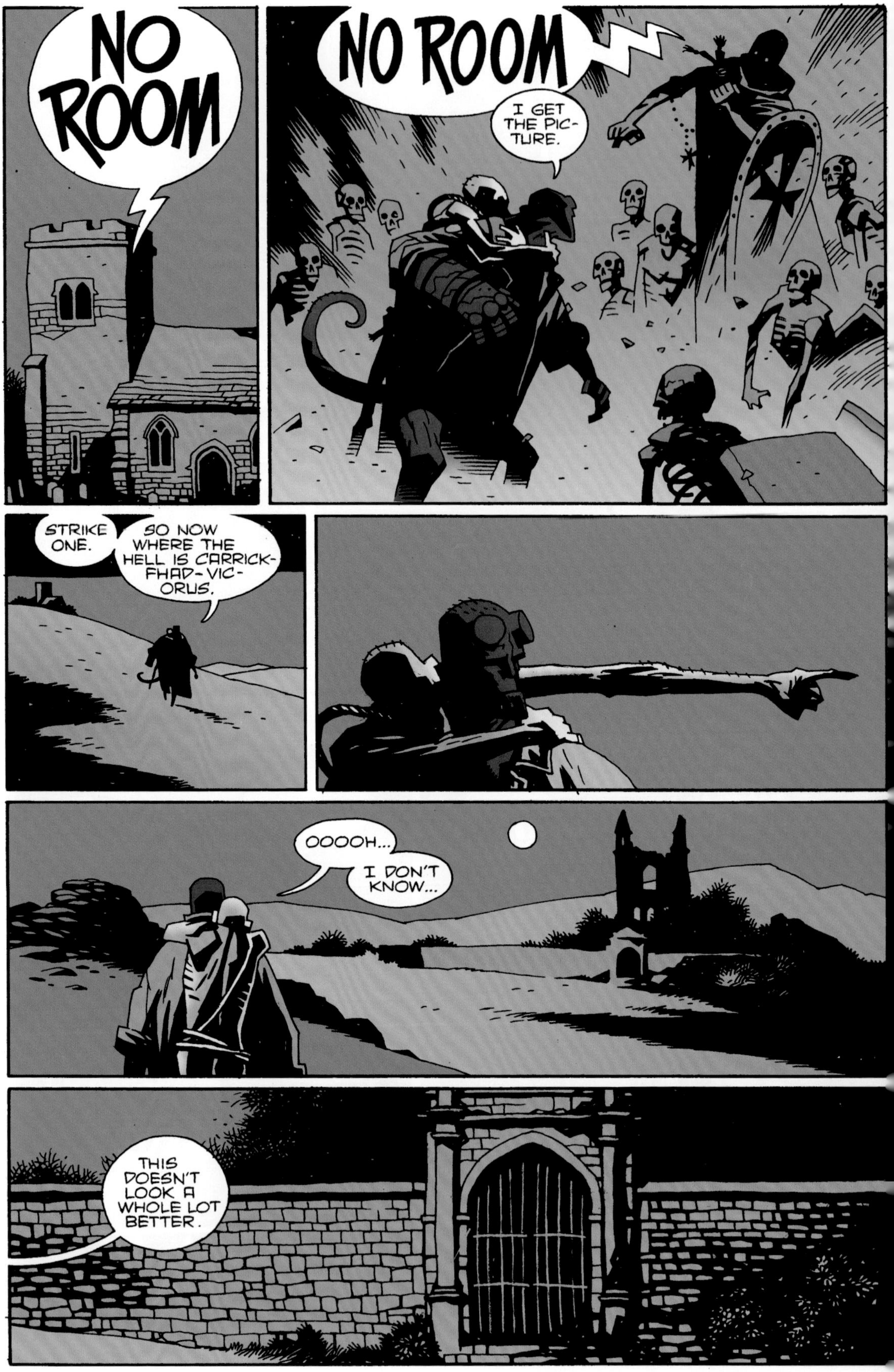
NO ROOM
NO ROOM
I GET THE PIC- TURE.
STRIKE ONE.
SO NOW WHERE THE HELL IS CARRICK- FHAD-VIC- ORUS.
OOOOH...
I DON'T KNOW...
THIS DOESN'T LOOK A WHOLE LOT BETTER.

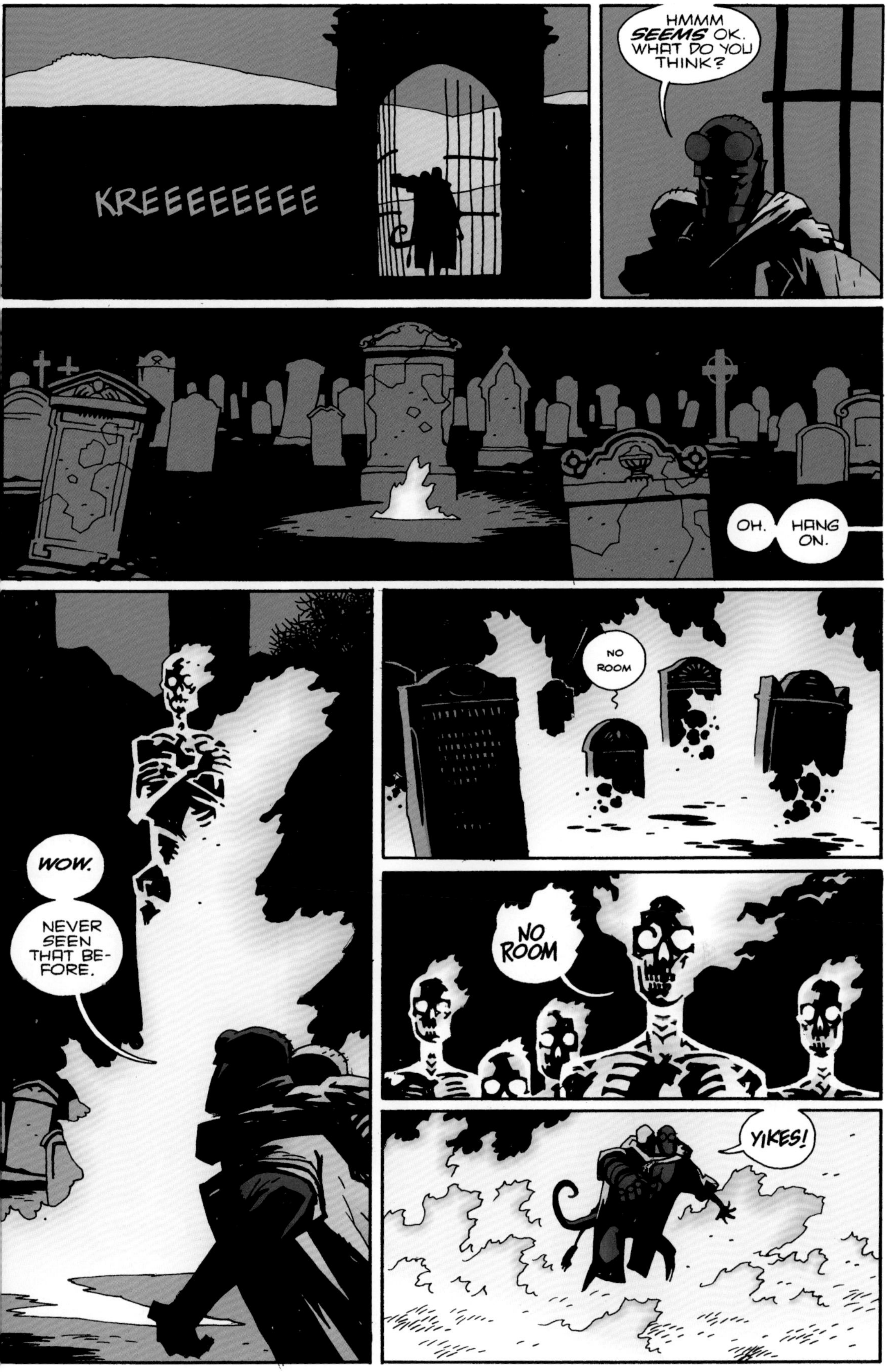
KREEEEEEEEE
HMMM SEEMS OK. WHAT DO YOU THINK?
OH.
HANG ON.
WOW.
NEVER SEEN THAT BE-FORE.
NO ROOM
NO ROOM
YIKES!

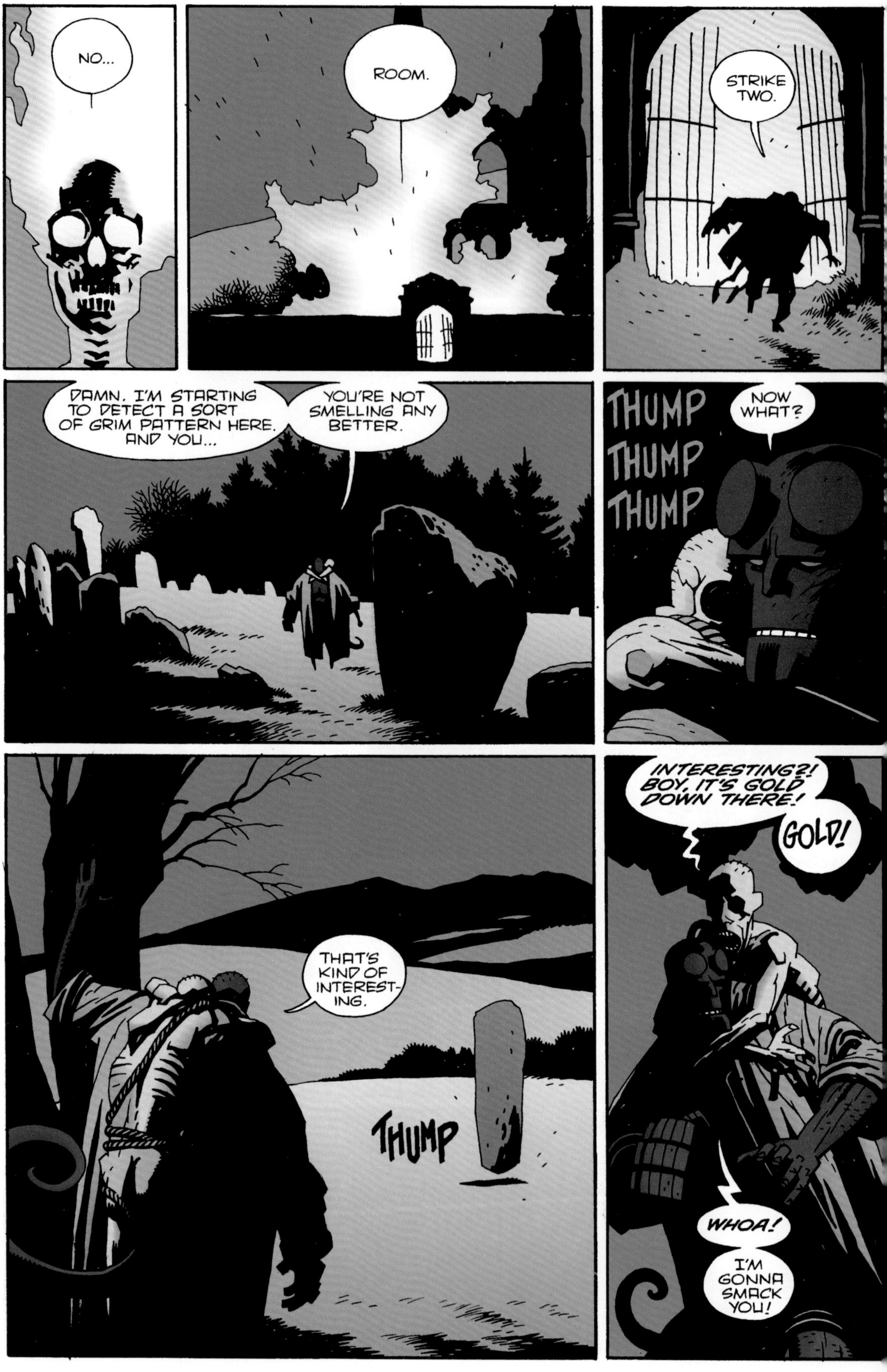
NO...
ROOM.
STRIKE TWO.
DAMN. I'M STARTING TO DETECT A SORT OF GRIM PATTERN HERE. AND YOU...
YOU'RE NOT SMELLING ANY BETTER.
THUMP THUMP THUMP
NOW WHAT?
THAT'S KIND OF INTEREST-ING.
THUMP
INTERESTING?! BOY, IT'S GOLD DOWN THERE!
GOLD!
WHOA!
I'M GONNA SMACK YOU!

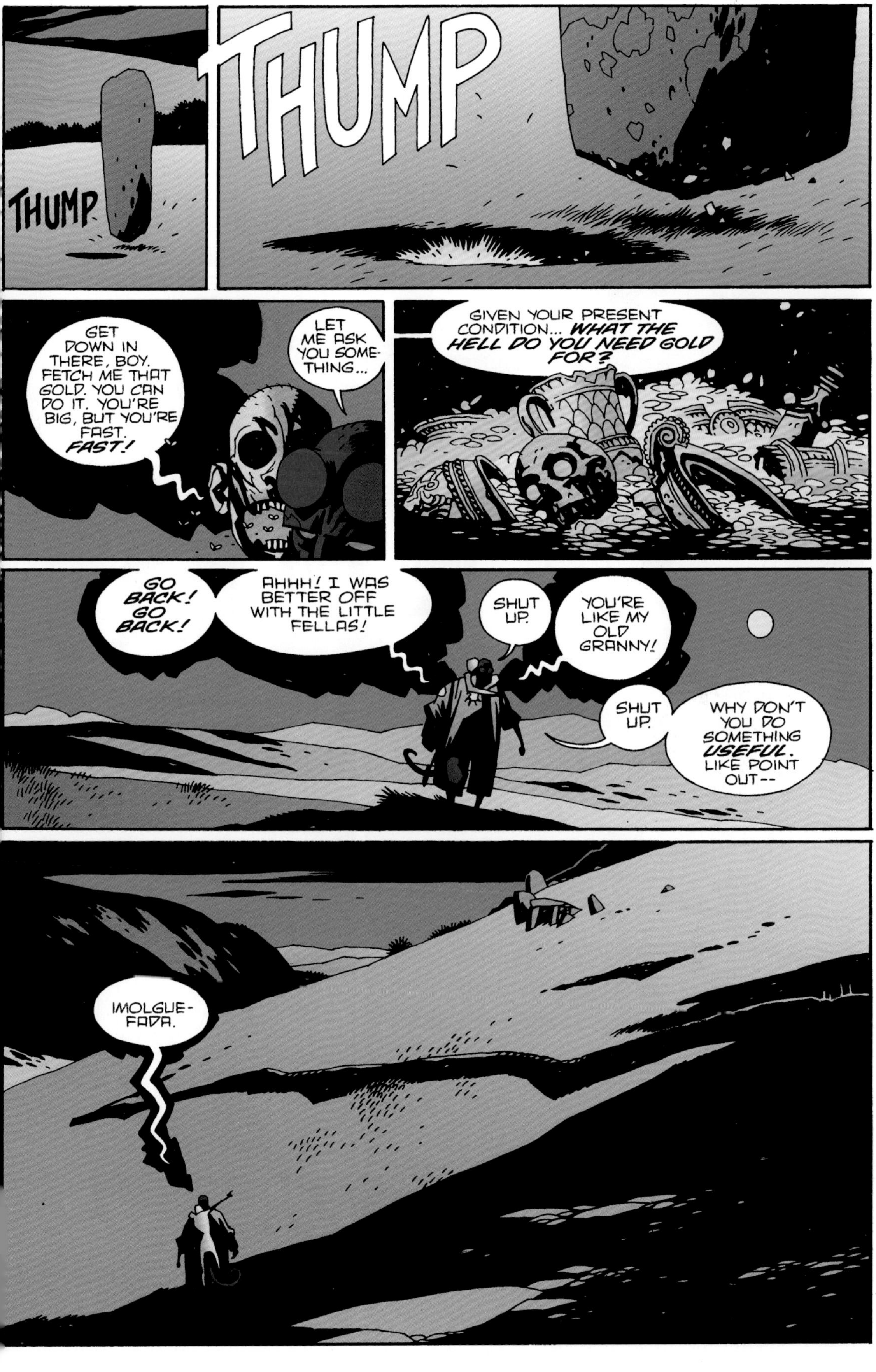
THUMP
THUMP
GET DOWN IN THERE, BOY. FETCH ME THAT GOLD. YOU CAN DO IT. YOU'RE BIG, BUT YOU'RE FAST. FAST!
LET ME ASK YOU SOME-THING...
GIVEN YOUR PRESENT CONDITION... WHAT THE HELL DO YOU NEED GOLD FOR?
GO BACK! GO BACK!
AHHH! I WAS BETTER OFF WITH THE LITTLE FELLAS!
SHUT UP.
YOU'RE LIKE MY OLD GRANNY!
SHUT UP.
WHY DON'T YOU DO SOMETHING USEFUL. LIKE POINT OUT--
IMOLGUE-FADA.

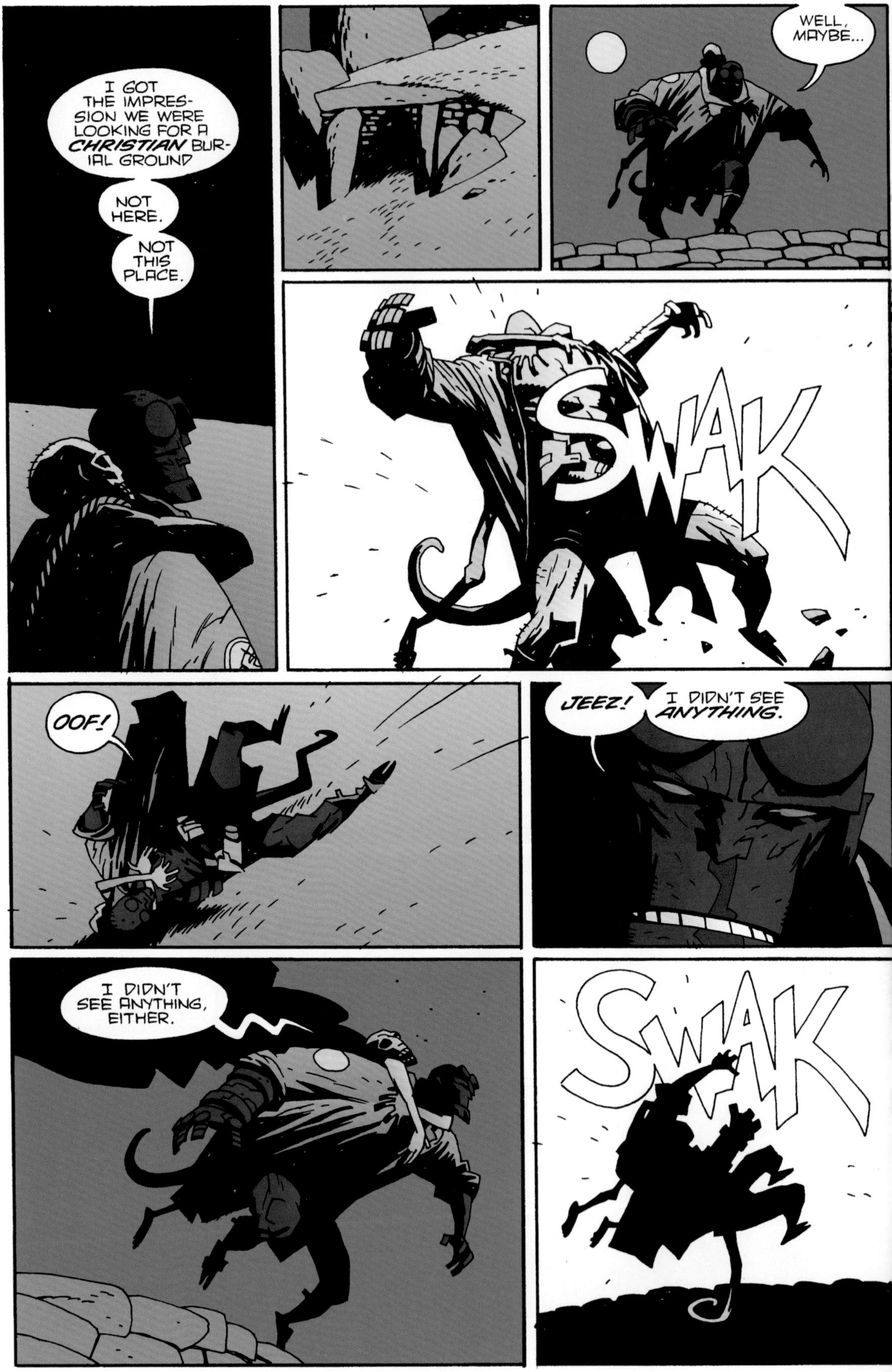

I GOT THE IMPRESSION WE WERE LOOKING FOR A *CHRISTIAN* BURIAL GROUND
NOT HERE.
NOT THIS PLACE.
WELL, MAYBE...
SWAK
OOF!
JEEZ!
I DIDN'T SEE *ANYTHING*.
I DIDN'T SEE ANYTHING, EITHER.
SWAK

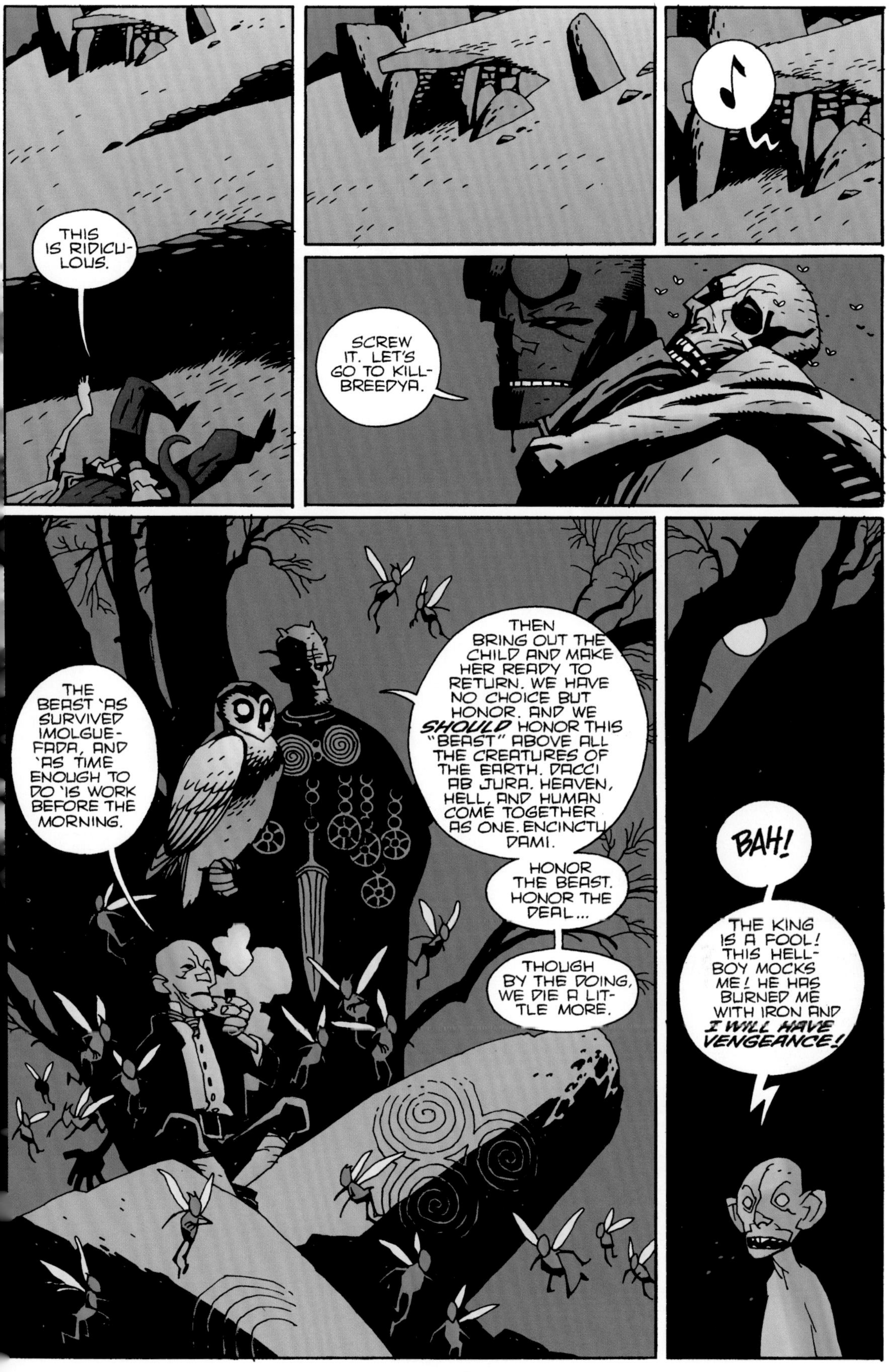
THIS IS RIDICU-LOUS.
SCREW IT. LET'S GO TO KILL-BREEDYA.
THE BEAST 'AS SURVIVED IMOLGUE-FADA, AND 'AS TIME ENOUGH TO DO 'IS WORK BEFORE THE MORNING.
THEN BRING OUT THE CHILD AND MAKE HER READY TO RETURN. WE HAVE NO CHOICE BUT HONOR. AND WE *SHOULD* HONOR THIS "BEAST" ABOVE ALL THE CREATURES OF THE EARTH. DACCI AB JURA. HEAVEN, HELL, AND HUMAN COME TOGETHER AS ONE. ENCINCTU DAMI.
HONOR THE BEAST. HONOR THE DEAL...
THOUGH BY THE DOING, WE DIE A LIT-TLE MORE.
BAH!
THE KING IS A FOOL! THIS HELL-BOY MOCKS ME! HE HAS BURNED ME WITH IRON AND *I WILL HAVE VENGEANCE!*

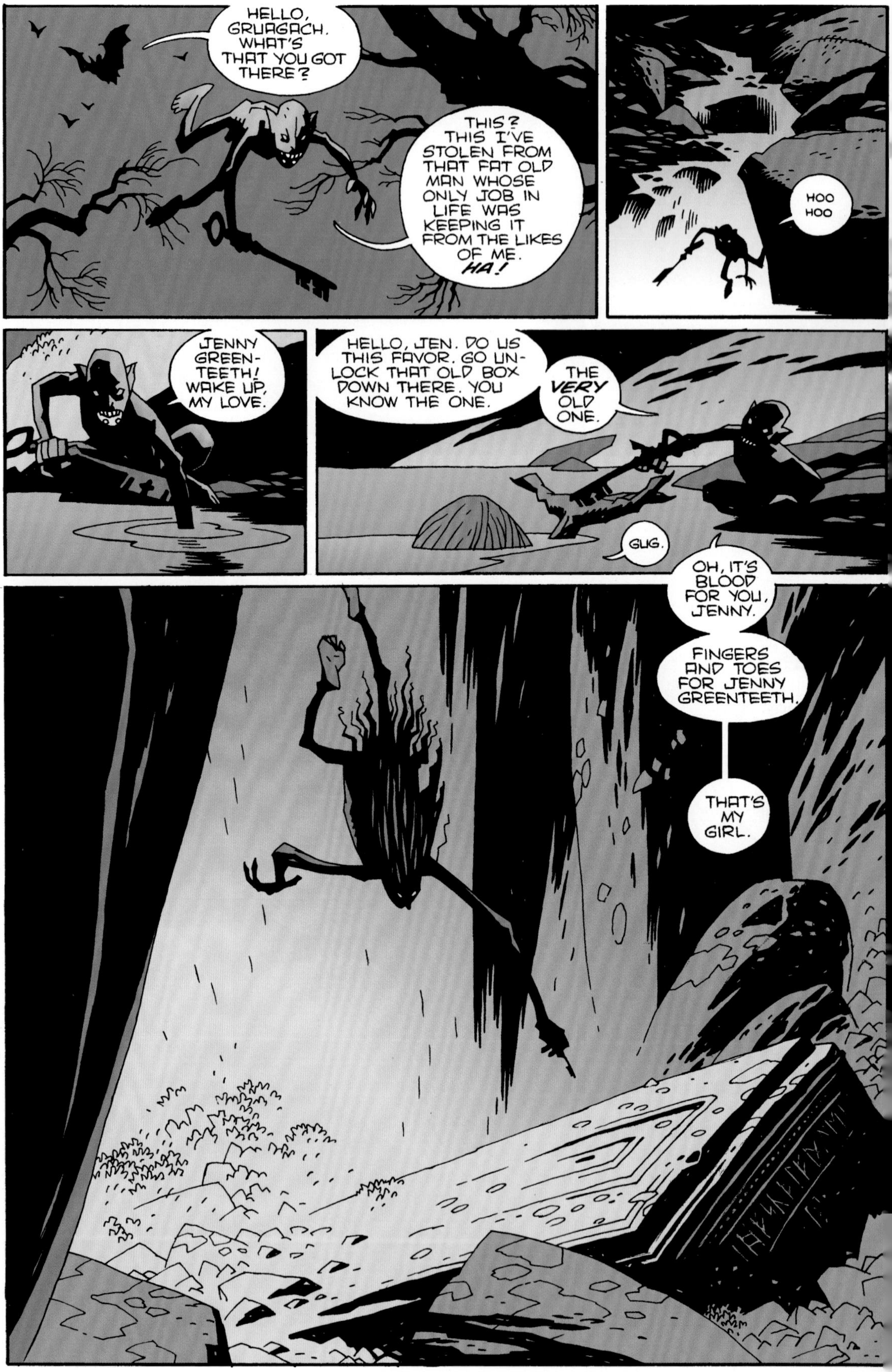
HELLO, GRUAGACH. WHAT'S THAT YOU GOT THERE?
THIS? THIS I'VE STOLEN FROM THAT FAT OLD MAN WHOSE ONLY JOB IN LIFE WAS KEEPING IT FROM THE LIKES OF ME. HA!
HOO HOO
JENNY GREEN-TEETH! WAKE UP, MY LOVE.
HELLO, JEN. DO US THIS FAVOR. GO UN-LOCK THAT OLD BOX DOWN THERE. YOU KNOW THE ONE.
THE VERY OLD ONE.
GUG.
OH, IT'S BLOOD FOR YOU, JENNY.
FINGERS AND TOES FOR JENNY GREENTEETH.
THAT'S MY GIRL.

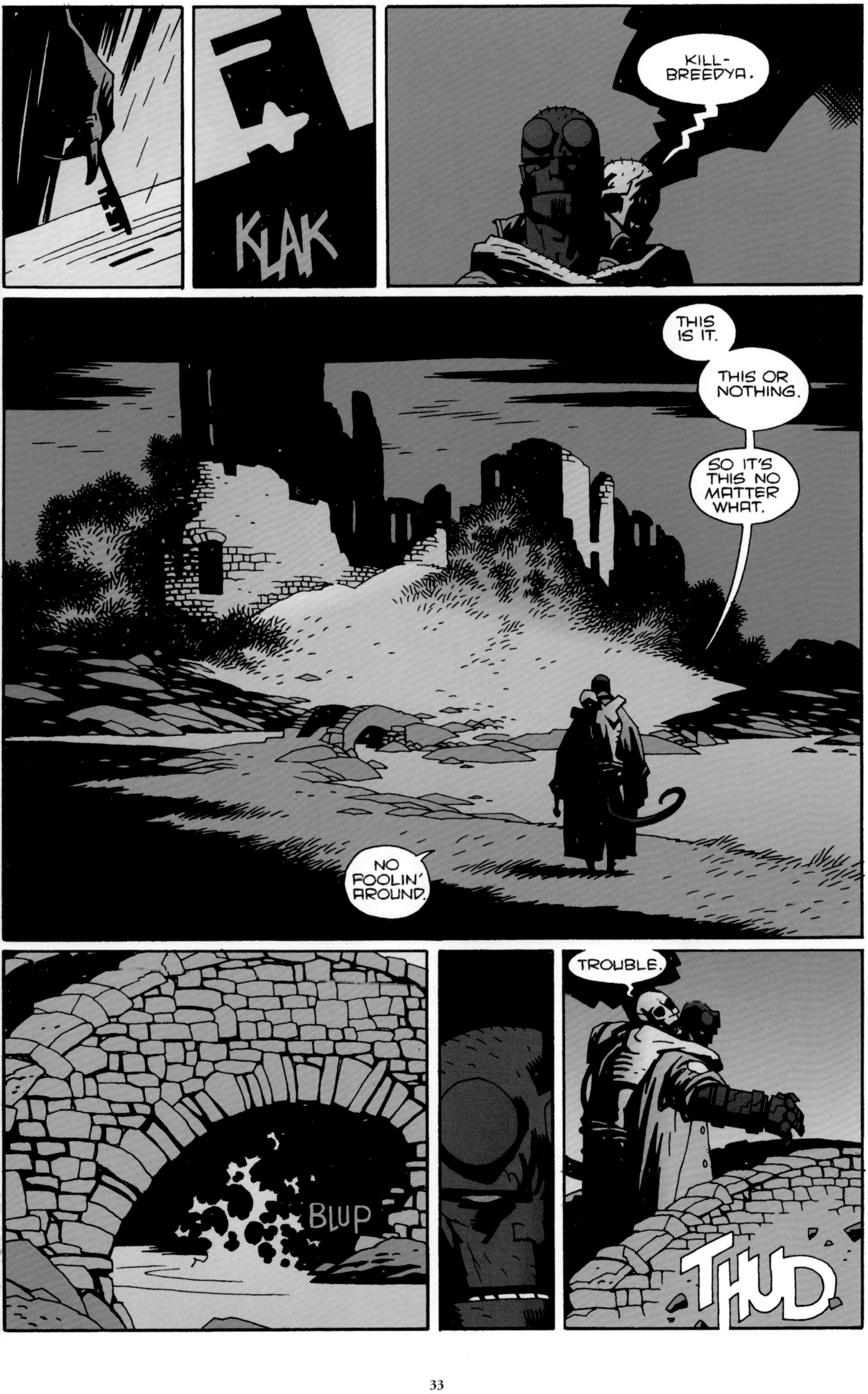
KLAK
KILL-BREEDYA.
THIS IS IT.
THIS OR NOTHING.
SO IT'S THIS NO MATTER WHAT.
NO FOOLIN' AROUND.
BLUP
TROUBLE.
THUD.

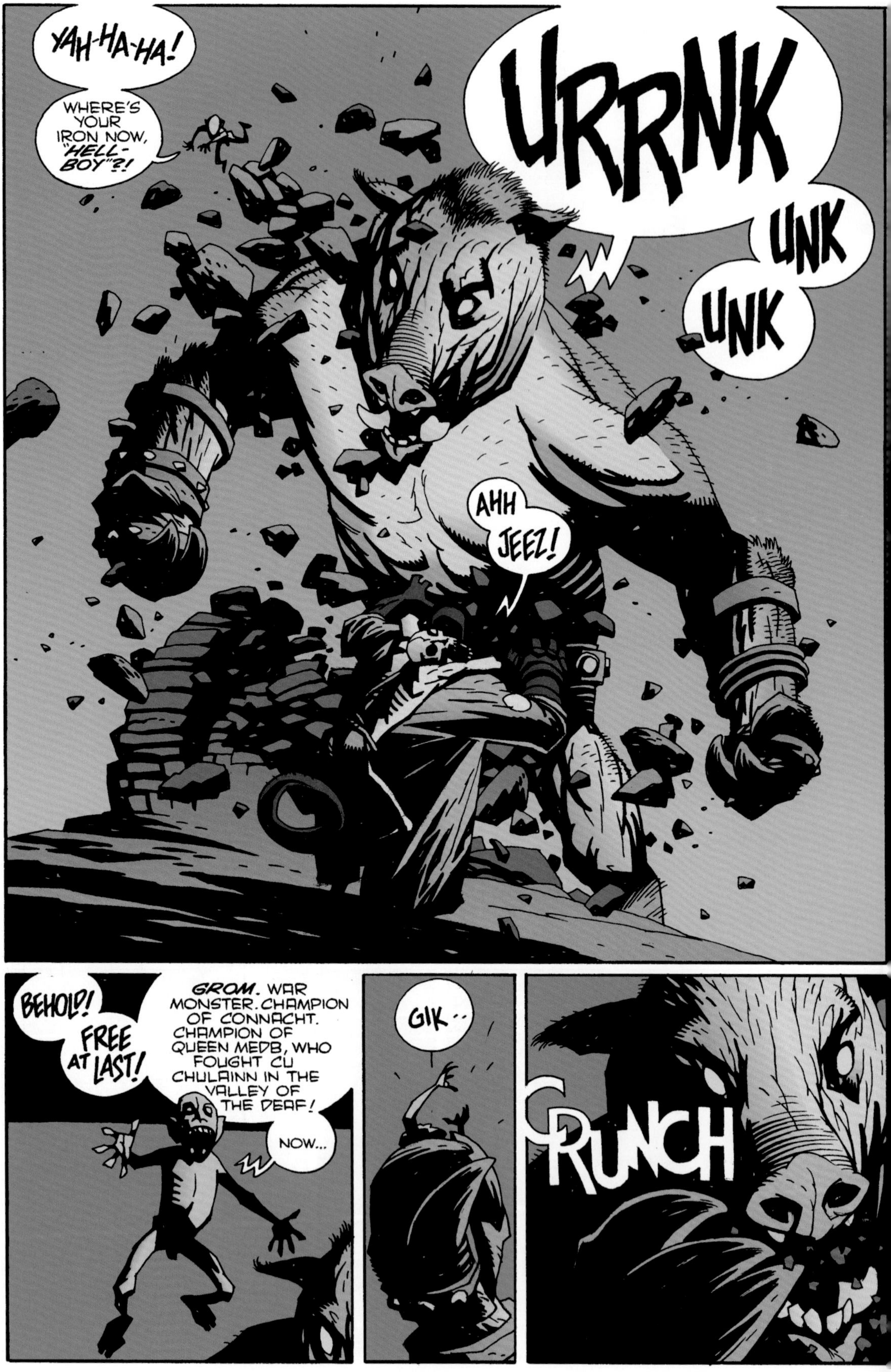

YAH-HA-HA!
WHERE'S YOUR IRON NOW, "HELL-BOY"?!
URRNK
UNK
UNK
AHH JEEZ!
BEHOLD!
FREE AT LAST!
GROM. WAR MONSTER. CHAMPION OF CONNACHT. CHAMPION OF QUEEN MEDB, WHO FOUGHT CU CHULAINN IN THE VALLEY OF THE DEAF!
NOW...
GIK..
CRUNCH

URNK

SO MUCH FOR THAT LITTLE GUY.

GAA!

WAK

Oooh...

WE DON'T HAVE TIME FOR THIS. THAT SUN'S COMING UP IN A COUPLE OF MINUTES...

HEY. I JUST THOUGHT OF SOMETHING.

WHERE IS IT?

SAW IT THE OTHER DAY...

HERE WE GO. CORNELIUS AGRIPPA'S CHARM AGAINST DEMONIC ANIMALS. SORT OF "ON LOAN" FROM THE VATICAN LIBRARY.

WORKED GREAT ON THE GIANT VAMPIRE CAT OF KYOTO.

URNK

THING IS...

THIS IS A GIANT PIG-*MAN* SITUATION.

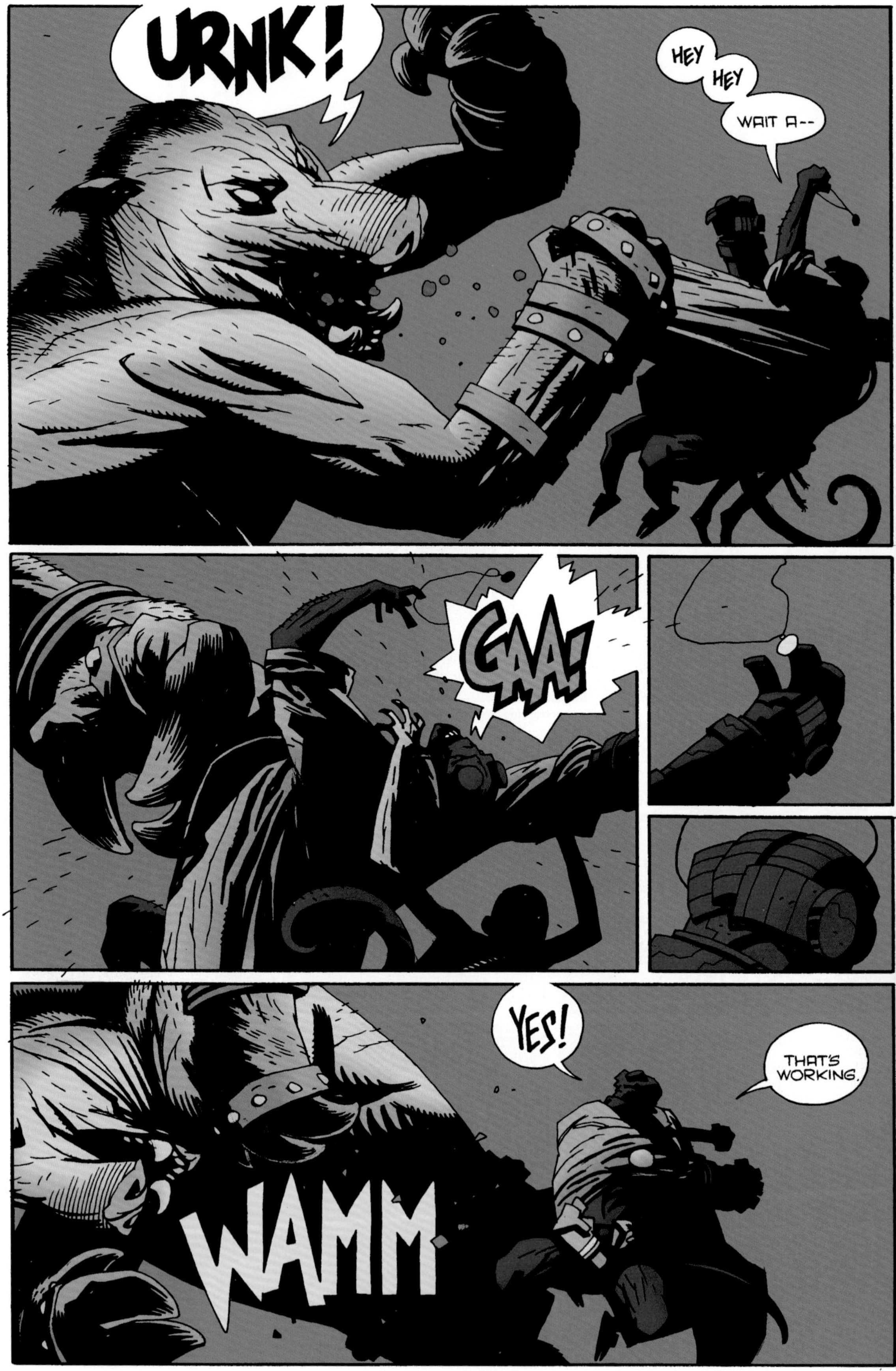
URNK!
HEY
HEY
WAIT A--
GAA!
YES!
THAT'S WORKING.
WAMM

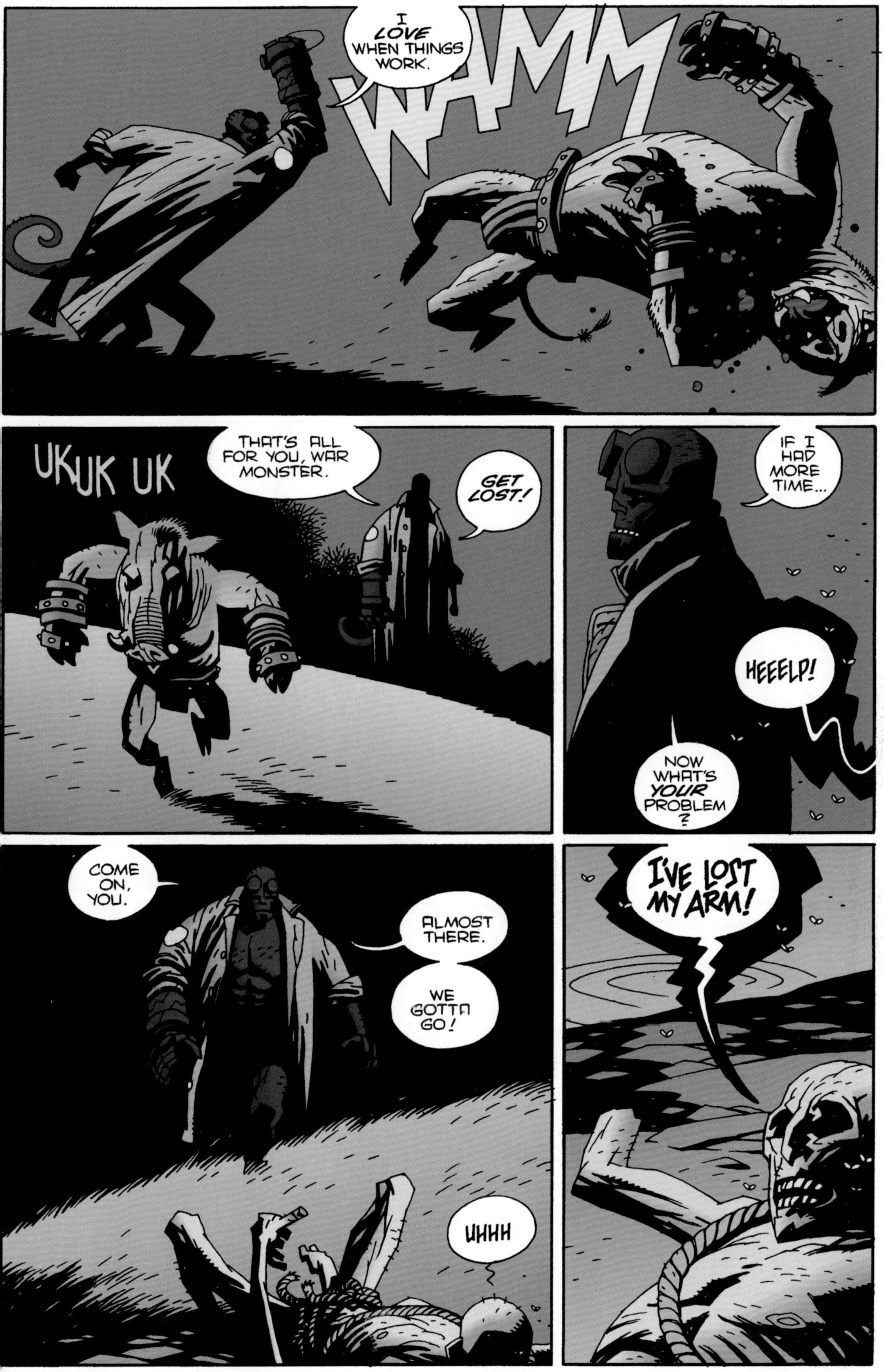
I LOVE WHEN THINGS WORK.
WAMM
UK UK UK
THAT'S ALL FOR YOU, WAR MONSTER.
GET LOST!
IF I HAD MORE TIME...
HEEELP!
NOW WHAT'S YOUR PROBLEM?
COME ON, YOU.
ALMOST THERE.
WE GOTTA GO!
UHHH
I'VE LOST MY ARM!

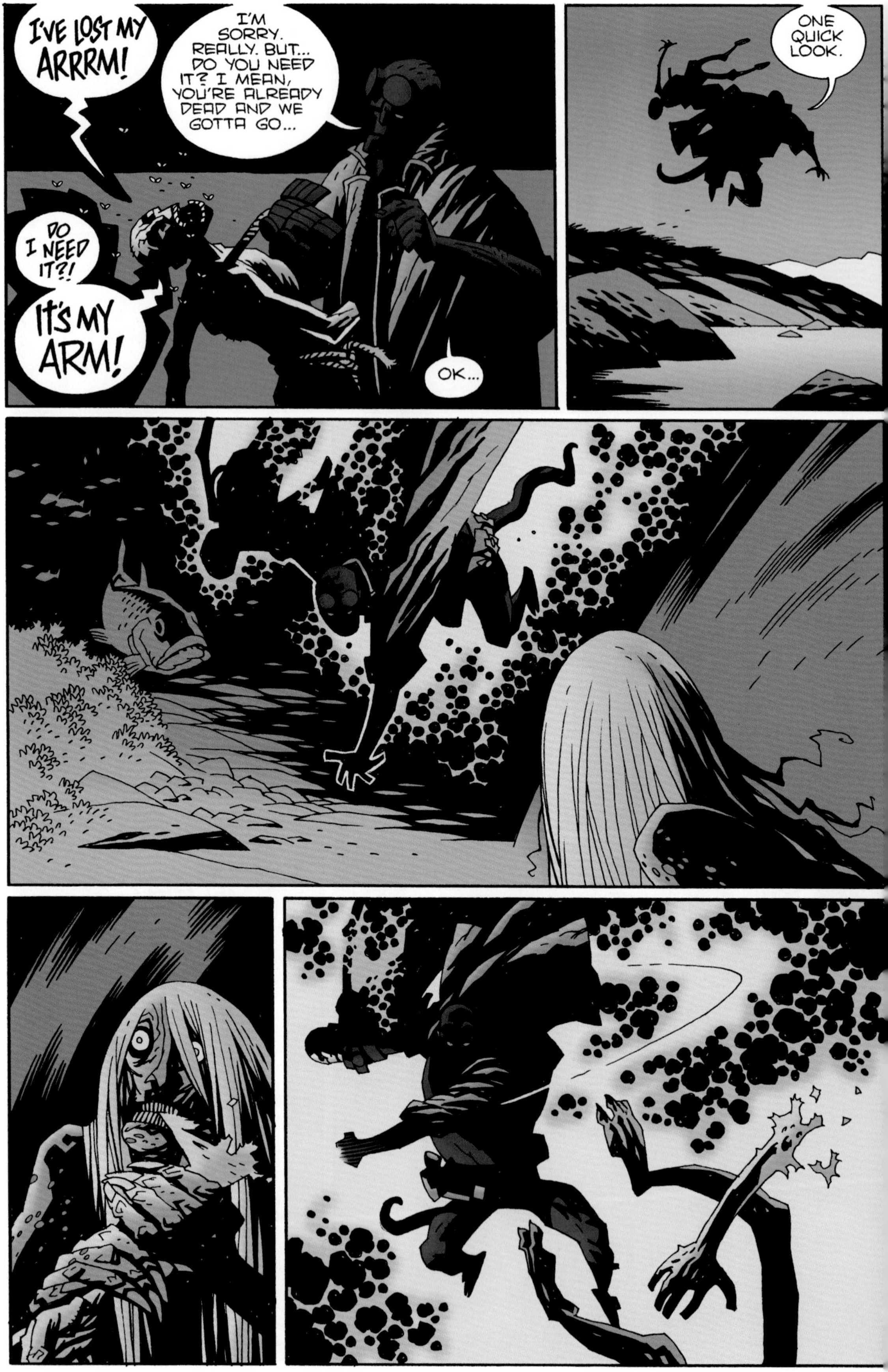
I'VE LOST MY ARRRM!
I'M SORRY. REALLY. BUT... DO YOU NEED IT? I MEAN, YOU'RE ALREADY DEAD AND WE GOTTA GO...
DO I NEED IT?!
IT'S MY ARM!
OK...
ONE QUICK LOOK.

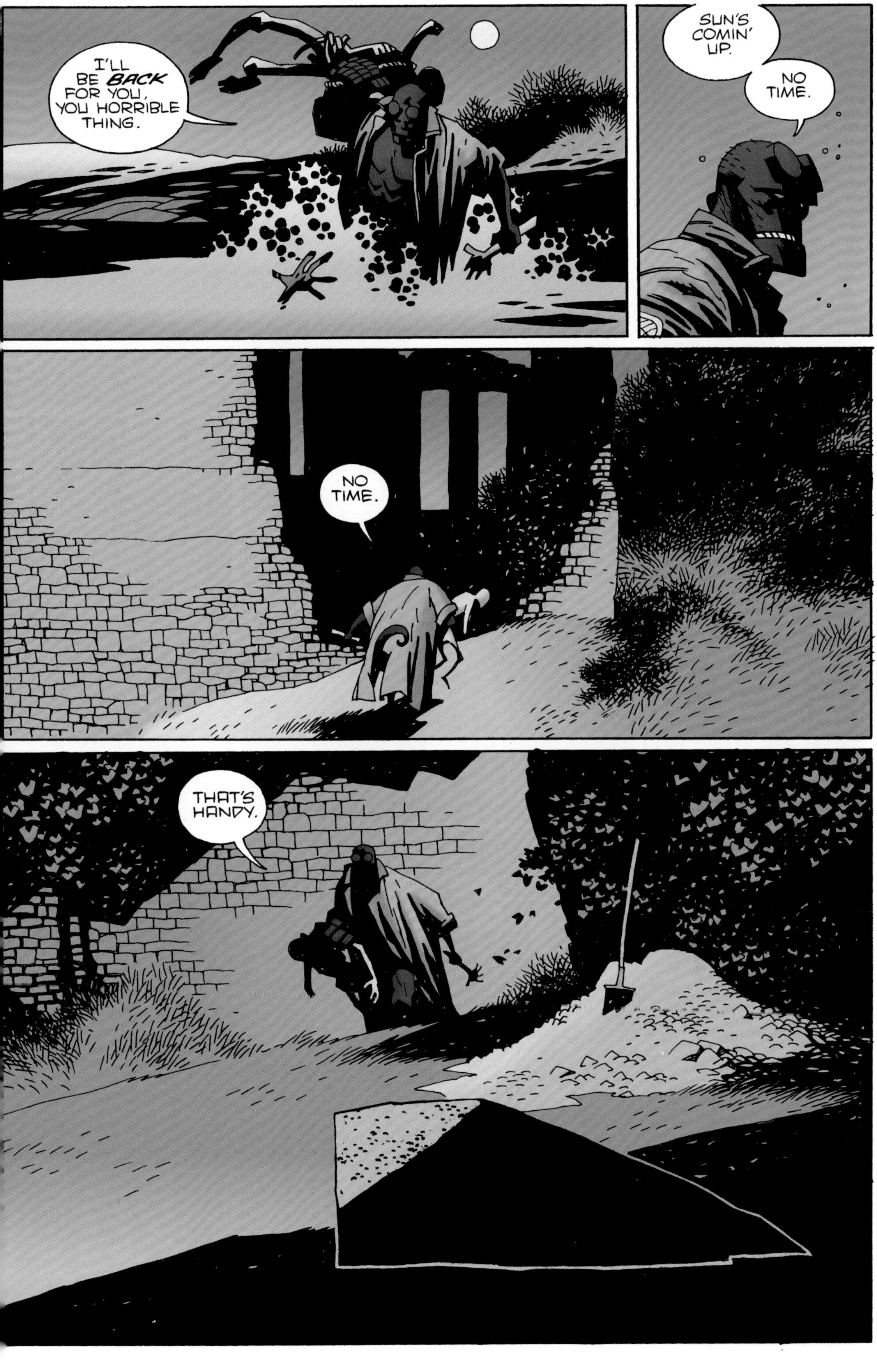
I'LL BE BACK FOR YOU, YOU HORRIBLE THING.
SUN'S COMIN' UP.
NO TIME.
NO TIME.
THAT'S HANDY.

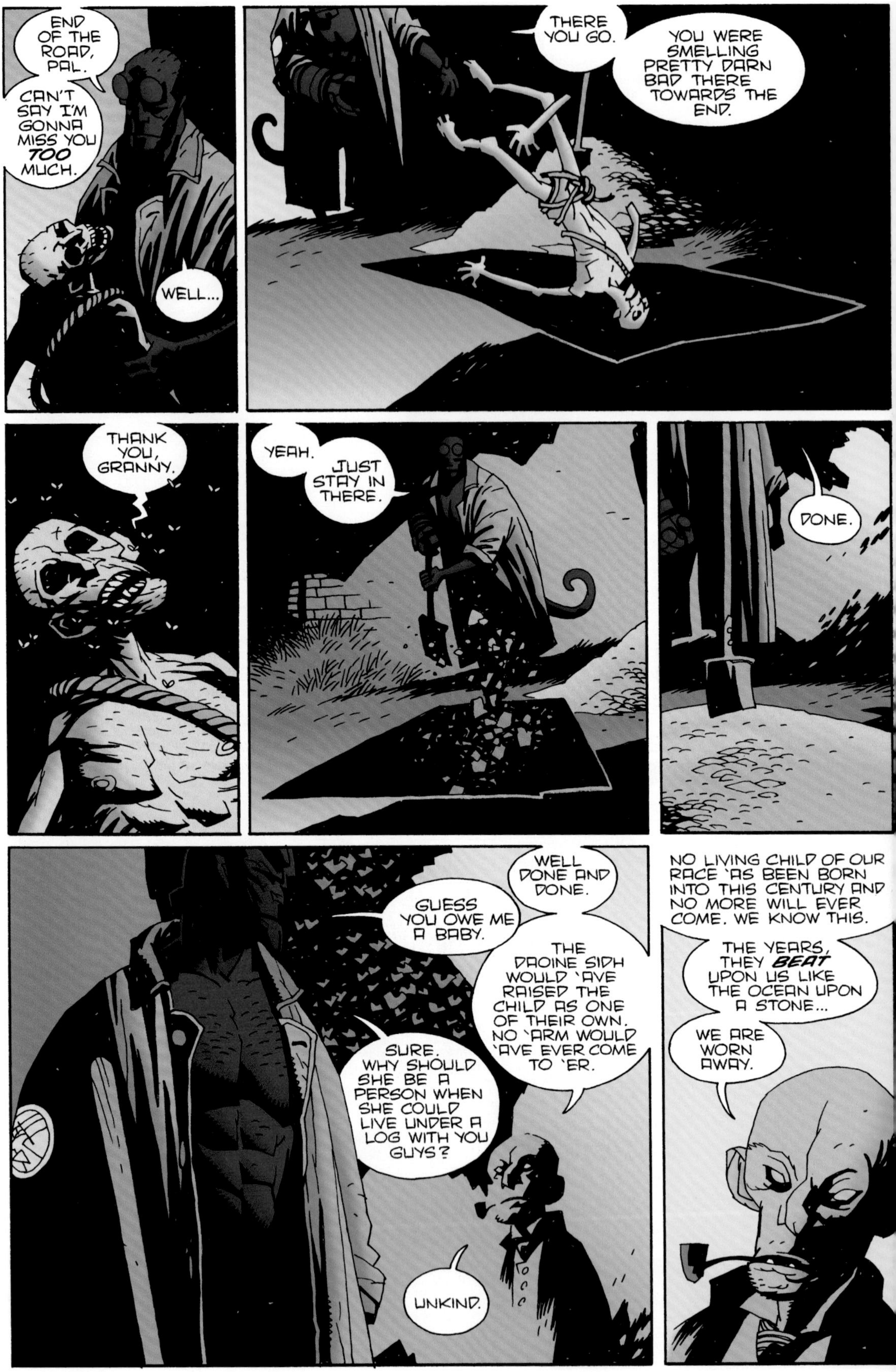
END OF THE ROAD, PAL.
CAN'T SAY I'M GONNA MISS YOU *TOO* MUCH.
WELL...
THERE YOU GO.
YOU WERE SMELLING PRETTY DARN BAD THERE TOWARDS THE END.
THANK YOU, GRANNY.
YEAH.
JUST STAY IN THERE.
DONE.
GUESS YOU OWE ME A BABY.
WELL DONE AND DONE.
THE DAOINE SIDH WOULD 'AVE RAISED THE CHILD AS ONE OF THEIR OWN. NO 'ARM WOULD 'AVE EVER COME TO 'ER.
SURE. WHY SHOULD SHE BE A PERSON WHEN SHE COULD LIVE UNDER A LOG WITH YOU GUYS?
UNKIND.
NO LIVING CHILD OF OUR RACE 'AS BEEN BORN INTO THIS CENTURY AND NO MORE WILL EVER COME. WE KNOW THIS.
THE YEARS, THEY *BEAT* UPON US LIKE THE OCEAN UPON A STONE...
WE ARE WORN AWAY.

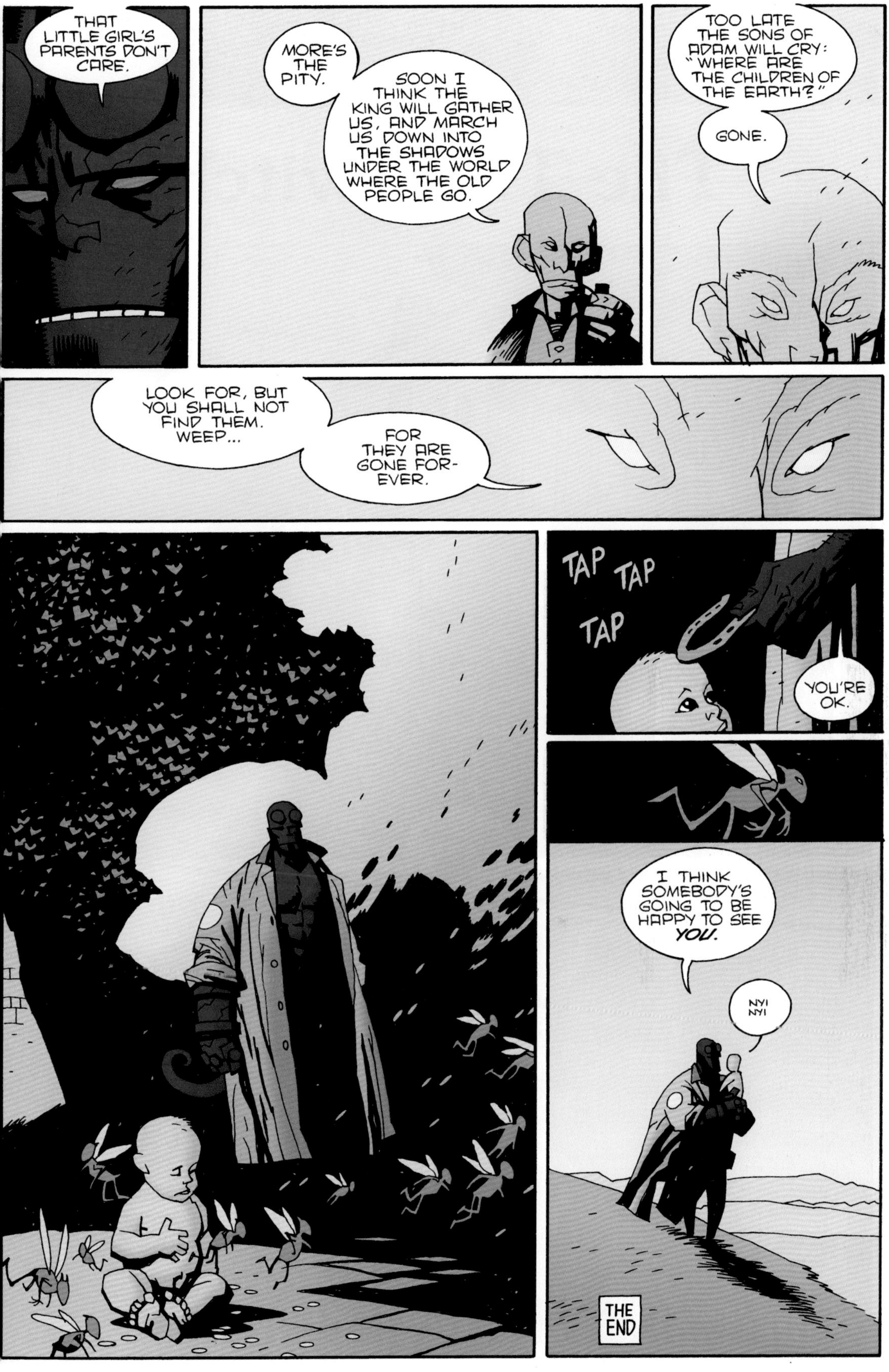
THAT LITTLE GIRL'S PARENTS DON'T CARE.
MORE'S THE PITY.
SOON I THINK THE KING WILL GATHER US, AND MARCH US DOWN INTO THE SHADOWS UNDER THE WORLD WHERE THE OLD PEOPLE GO.
TOO LATE THE SONS OF ADAM WILL CRY: "WHERE ARE THE CHILDREN OF THE EARTH?"
GONE.
LOOK FOR, BUT YOU SHALL NOT FIND THEM. WEEP...
FOR THEY ARE GONE FOR-EVER.
TAP TAP
TAP
YOU'RE OK.
I THINK SOMEBODY'S GOING TO BE HAPPY TO SEE *YOU*.
NYI NYI
THE END

# The Troll-witch

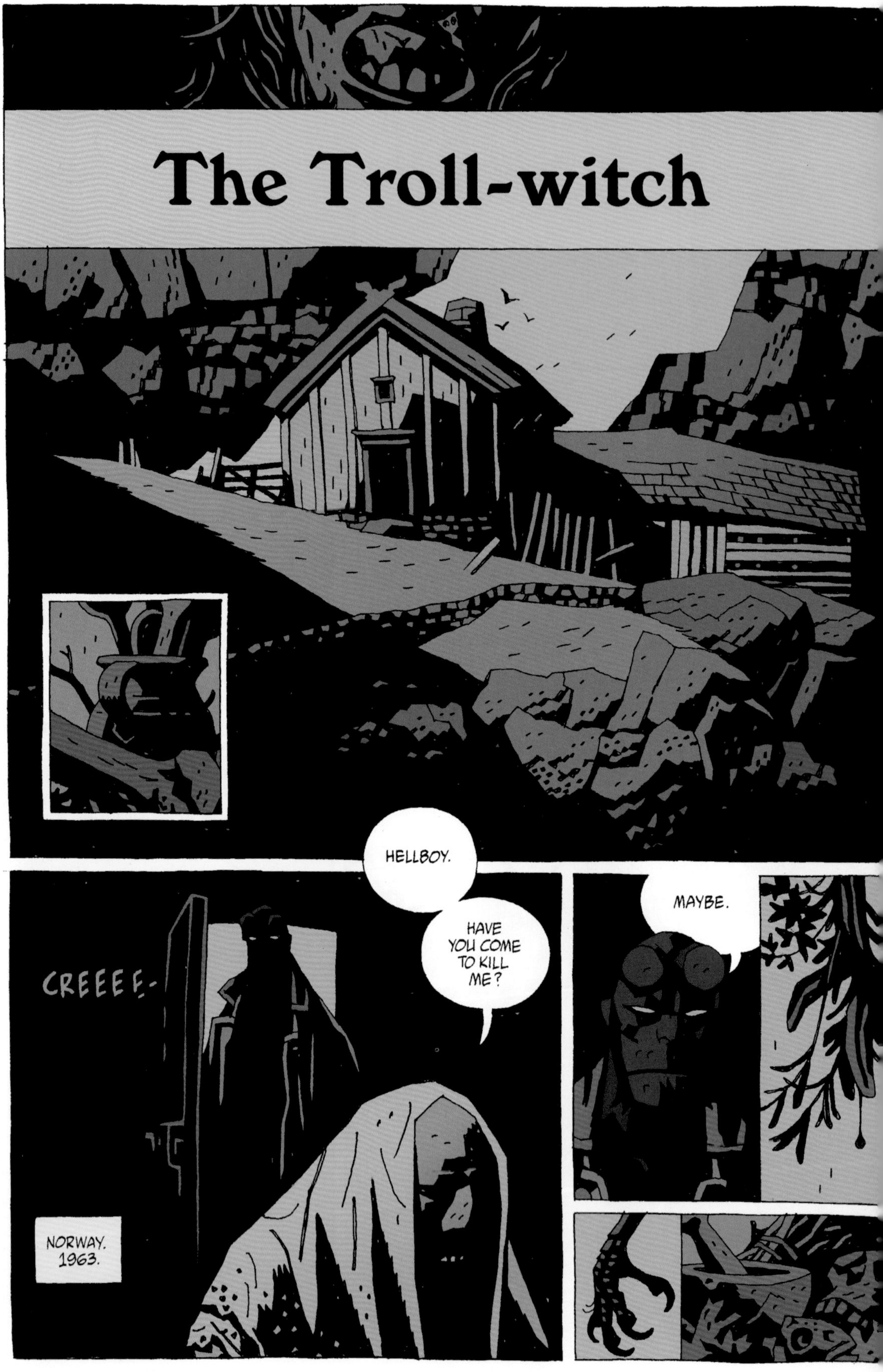

HELLBOY.
HAVE YOU COME TO KILL ME?
CREEEEE-
NORWAY. 1963.
MAYBE.

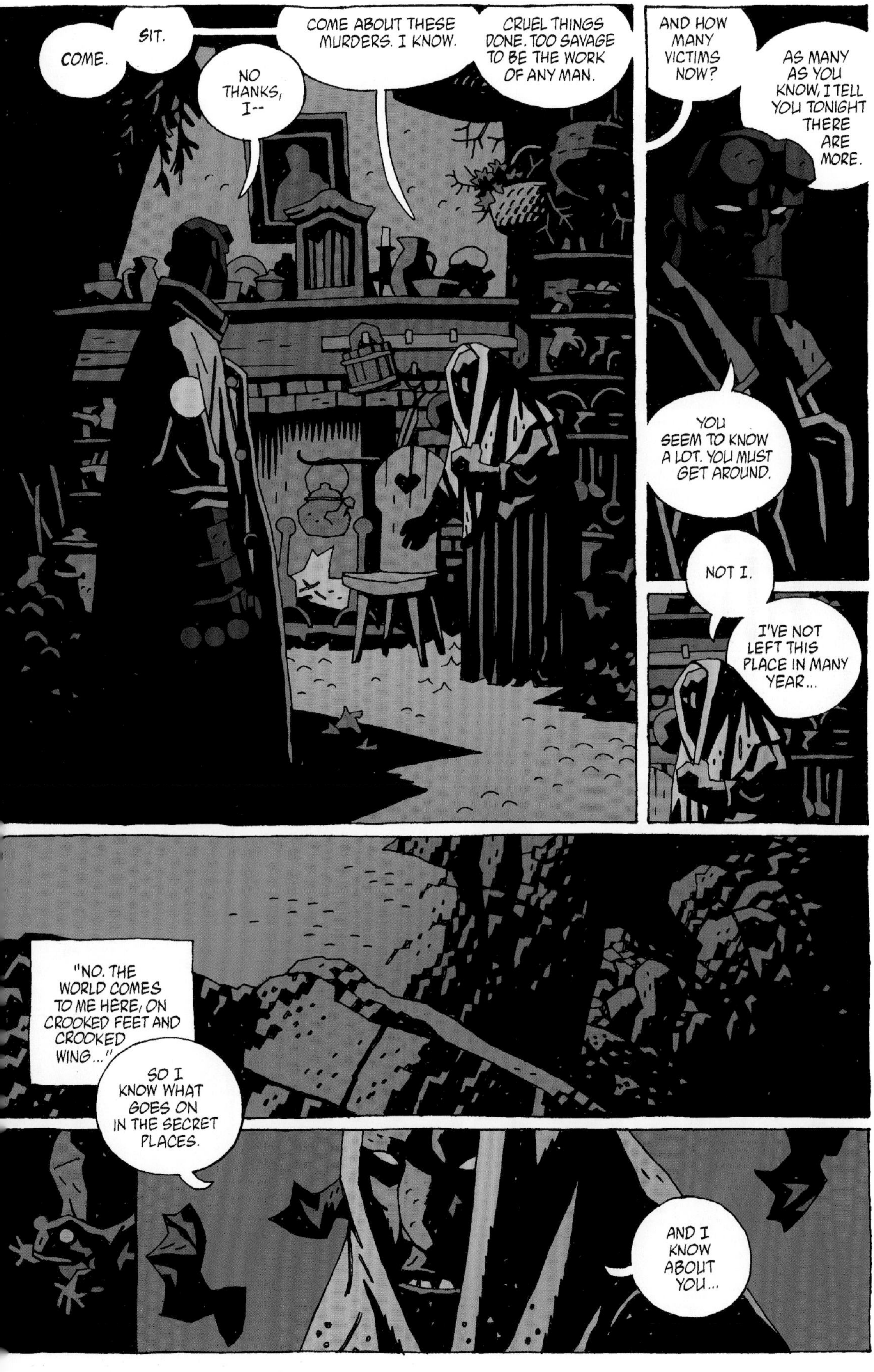

COME.
SIT.
NO THANKS, I--
COME ABOUT THESE MURDERS. I KNOW.
CRUEL THINGS DONE. TOO SAVAGE TO BE THE WORK OF ANY MAN.
AND HOW MANY VICTIMS NOW?
AS MANY AS YOU KNOW, I TELL YOU TONIGHT THERE ARE MORE.
YOU SEEM TO KNOW A LOT. YOU MUST GET AROUND.
NOT I.
I'VE NOT LEFT THIS PLACE IN MANY YEAR...
"NO. THE WORLD COMES TO ME HERE, ON CROOKED FEET AND CROOKED WING..."
SO I KNOW WHAT GOES ON IN THE SECRET PLACES.
AND I KNOW ABOUT YOU...

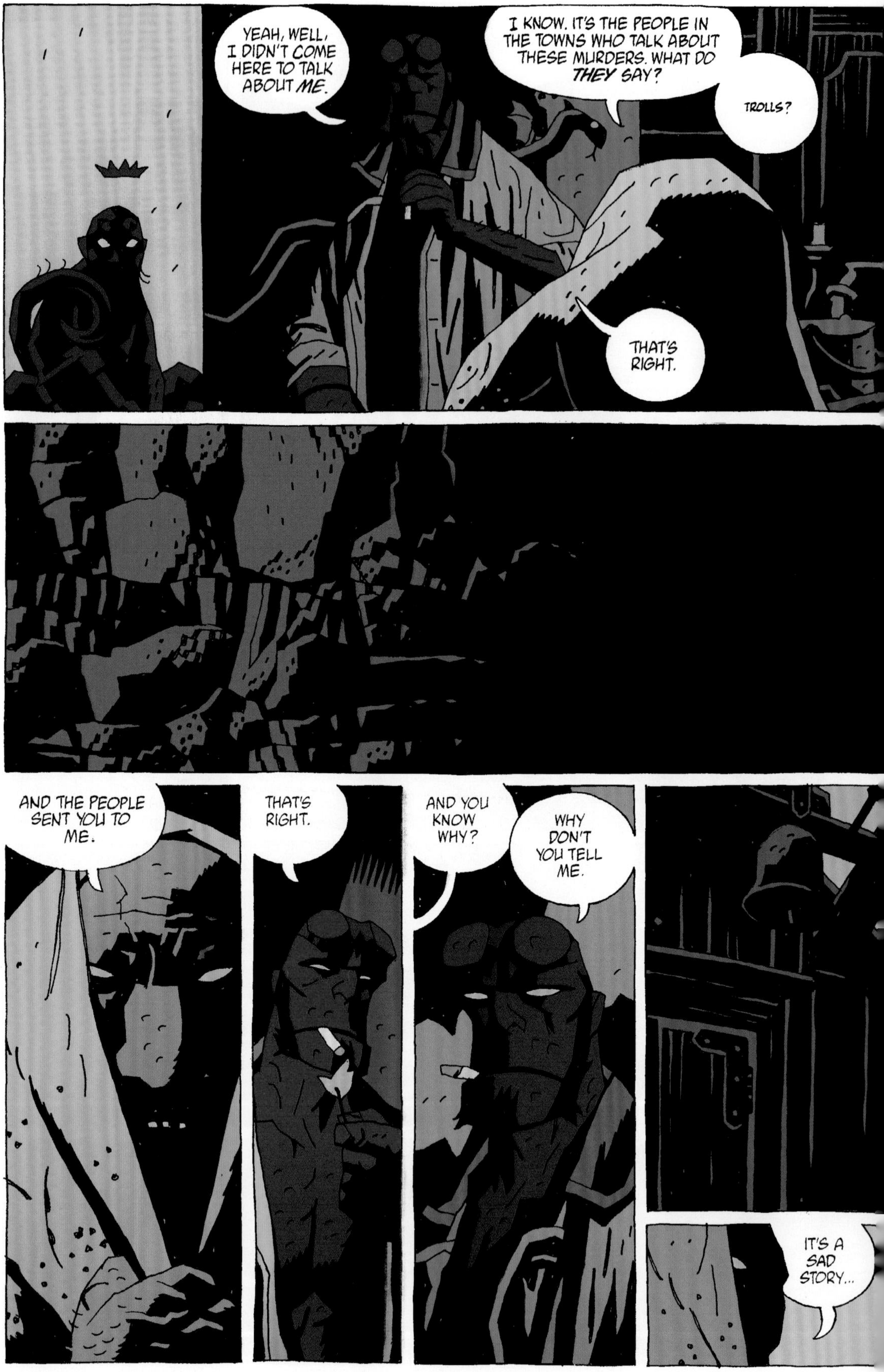
YEAH, WELL, I DIDN'T COME HERE TO TALK ABOUT *ME*.
I KNOW. IT'S THE PEOPLE IN THE TOWNS WHO TALK ABOUT THESE MURDERS. WHAT DO *THEY* SAY?
TROLLS?
THAT'S RIGHT.
AND THE PEOPLE SENT YOU TO ME.
THAT'S RIGHT.
AND YOU KNOW WHY?
WHY DON'T YOU TELL ME.
IT'S A SAD STORY...

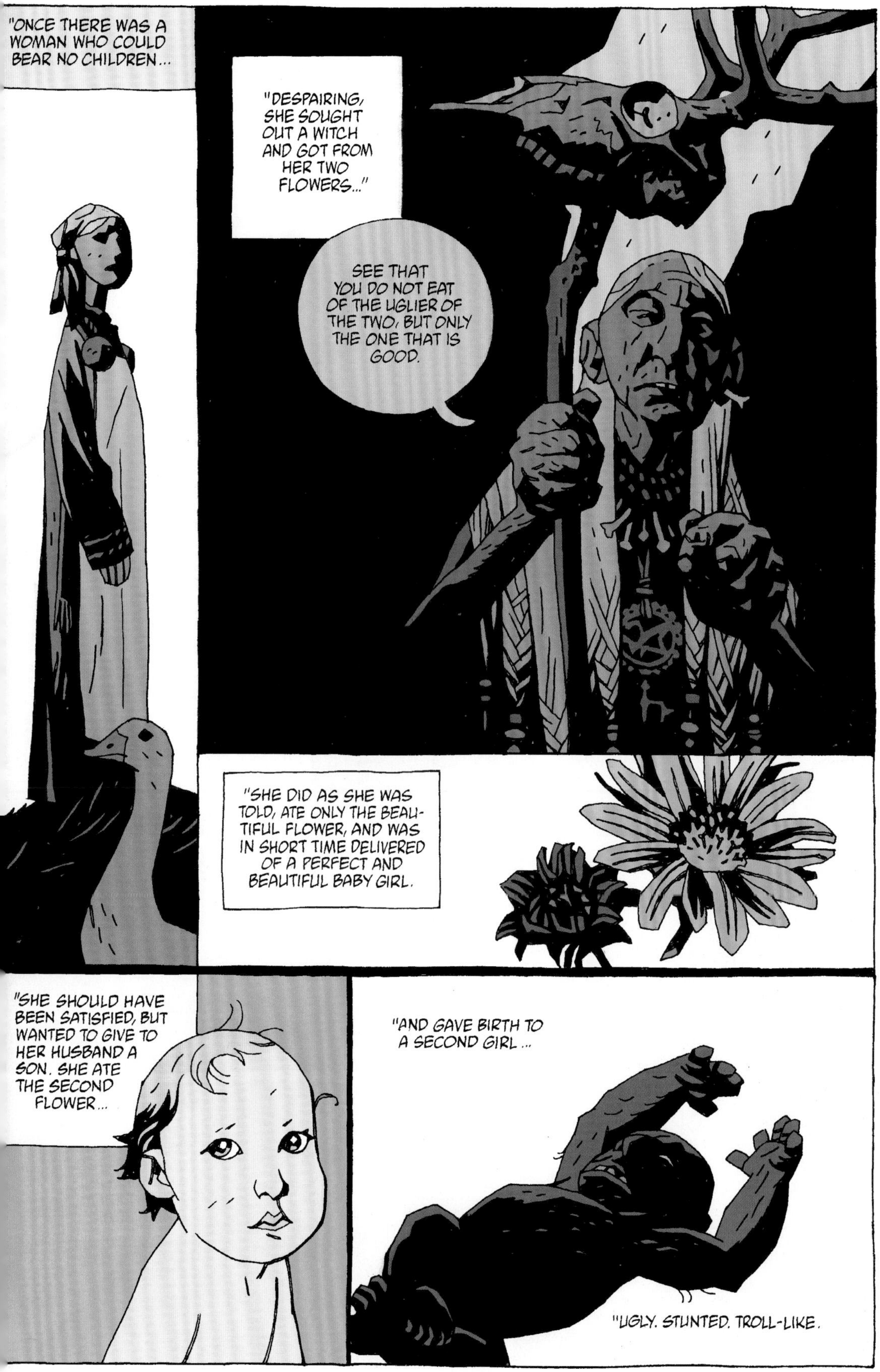
"ONCE THERE WAS A WOMAN WHO COULD BEAR NO CHILDREN...
"DESPAIRING, SHE SOUGHT OUT A WITCH AND GOT FROM HER TWO FLOWERS..."
SEE THAT YOU DO NOT EAT OF THE UGLIER OF THE TWO, BUT ONLY THE ONE THAT IS GOOD.
"SHE DID AS SHE WAS TOLD, ATE ONLY THE BEAUTIFUL FLOWER, AND WAS IN SHORT TIME DELIVERED OF A PERFECT AND BEAUTIFUL BABY GIRL.
"SHE SHOULD HAVE BEEN SATISFIED, BUT WANTED TO GIVE TO HER HUSBAND A SON. SHE ATE THE SECOND FLOWER...
"AND GAVE BIRTH TO A SECOND GIRL...
"UGLY. STUNTED. TROLL-LIKE.

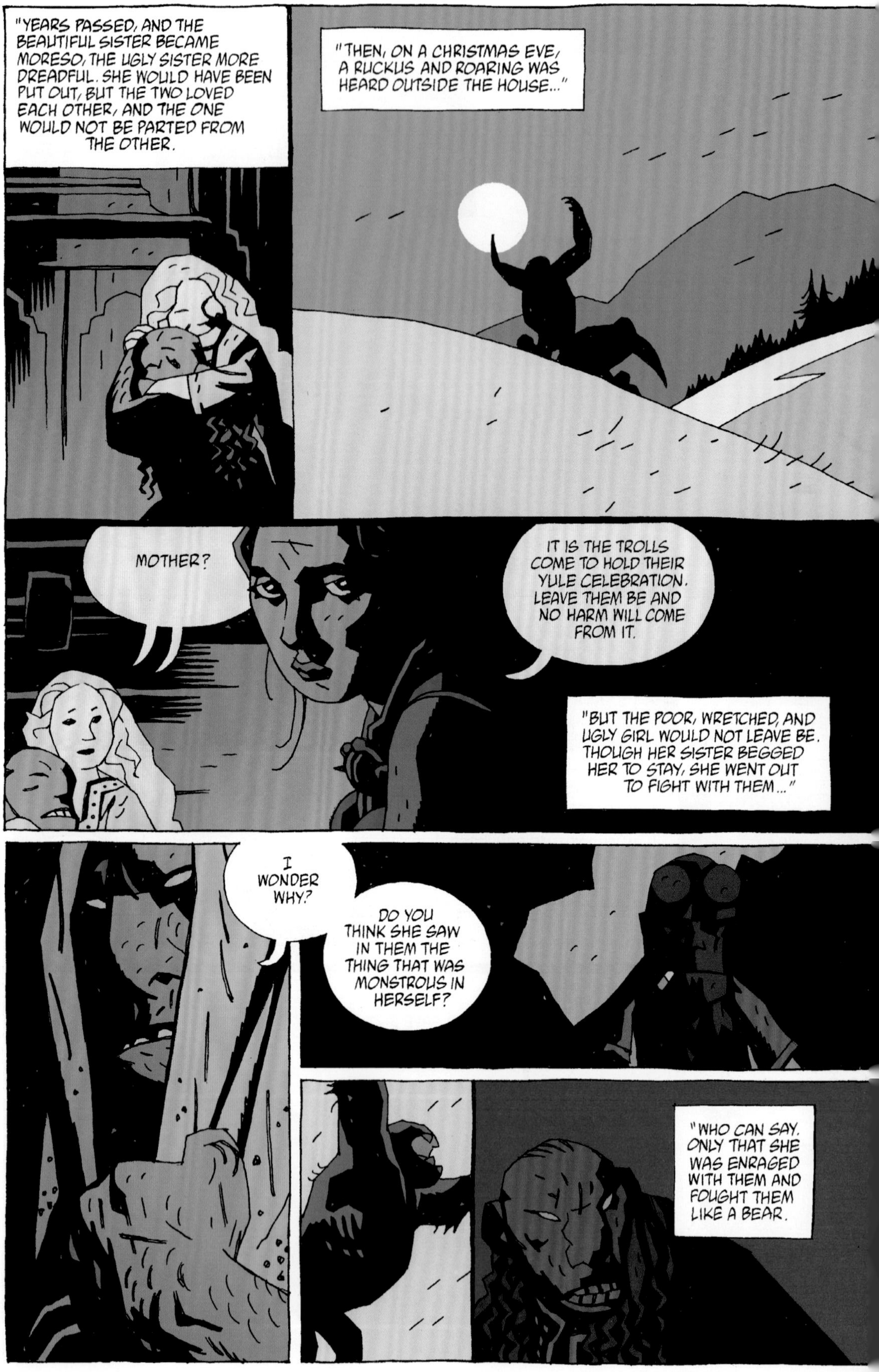
"YEARS PASSED, AND THE BEAUTIFUL SISTER BECAME MORESO, THE UGLY SISTER MORE DREADFUL. SHE WOULD HAVE BEEN PUT OUT, BUT THE TWO LOVED EACH OTHER, AND THE ONE WOULD NOT BE PARTED FROM THE OTHER.
"THEN, ON A CHRISTMAS EVE, A RUCKUS AND ROARING WAS HEARD OUTSIDE THE HOUSE..."
MOTHER?
IT IS THE TROLLS COME TO HOLD THEIR YULE CELEBRATION. LEAVE THEM BE AND NO HARM WILL COME FROM IT.
"BUT THE POOR, WRETCHED, AND UGLY GIRL WOULD NOT LEAVE BE. THOUGH HER SISTER BEGGED HER TO STAY, SHE WENT OUT TO FIGHT WITH THEM..."
I WONDER WHY?
DO YOU THINK SHE SAW IN THEM THE THING THAT WAS MONSTROUS IN HERSELF?
"WHO CAN SAY. ONLY THAT SHE WAS ENRAGED WITH THEM AND FOUGHT THEM LIKE A BEAR.

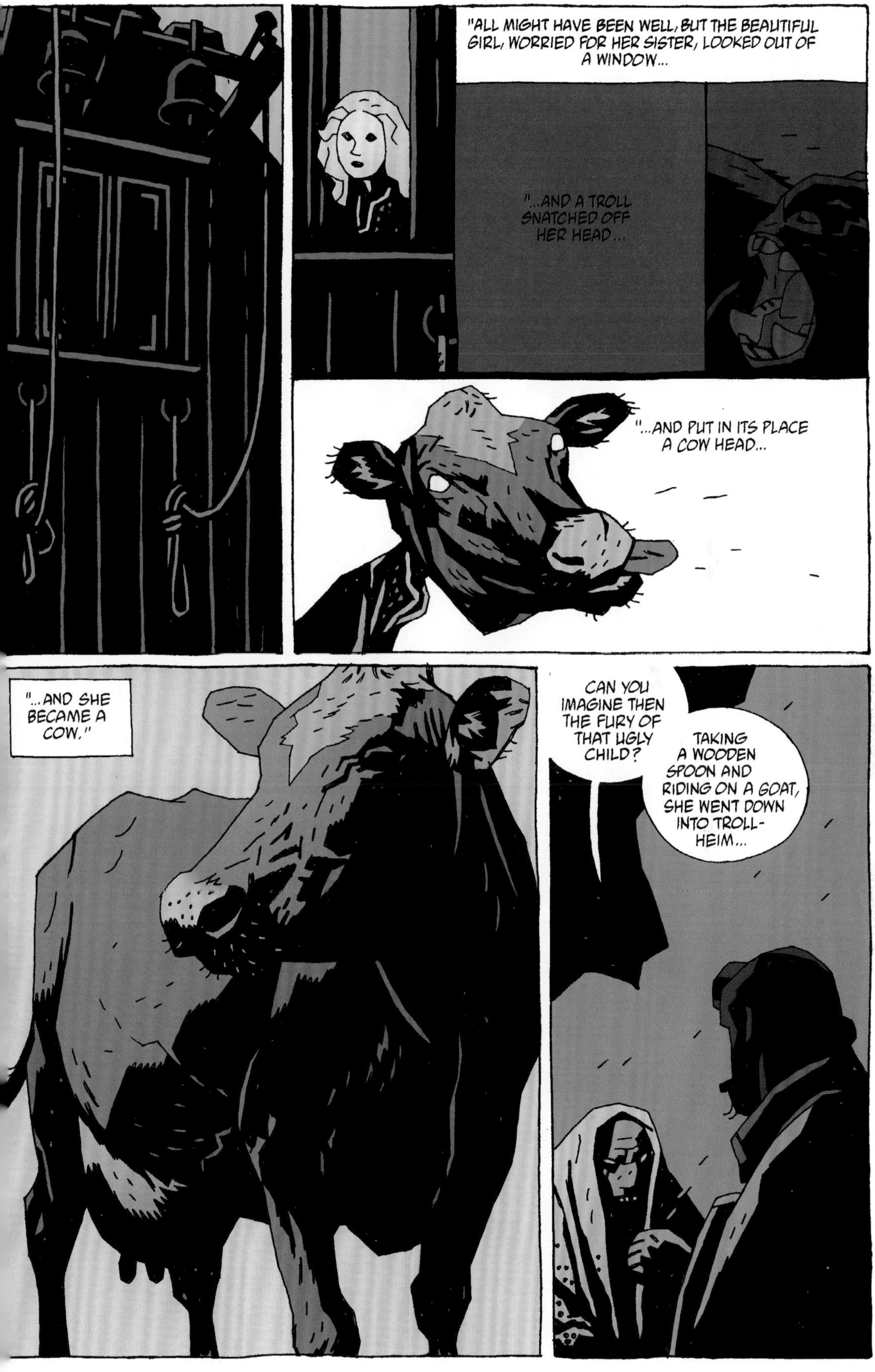
"ALL MIGHT HAVE BEEN WELL, BUT THE BEAUTIFUL GIRL, WORRIED FOR HER SISTER, LOOKED OUT OF A WINDOW...
"...AND A TROLL SNATCHED OFF HER HEAD...
"...AND PUT IN ITS PLACE A COW HEAD...
"...AND SHE BECAME A COW."
CAN YOU IMAGINE THEN THE FURY OF THAT UGLY CHILD?
TAKING A WOODEN SPOON AND RIDING ON A GOAT, SHE WENT DOWN INTO TROLL-HEIM...

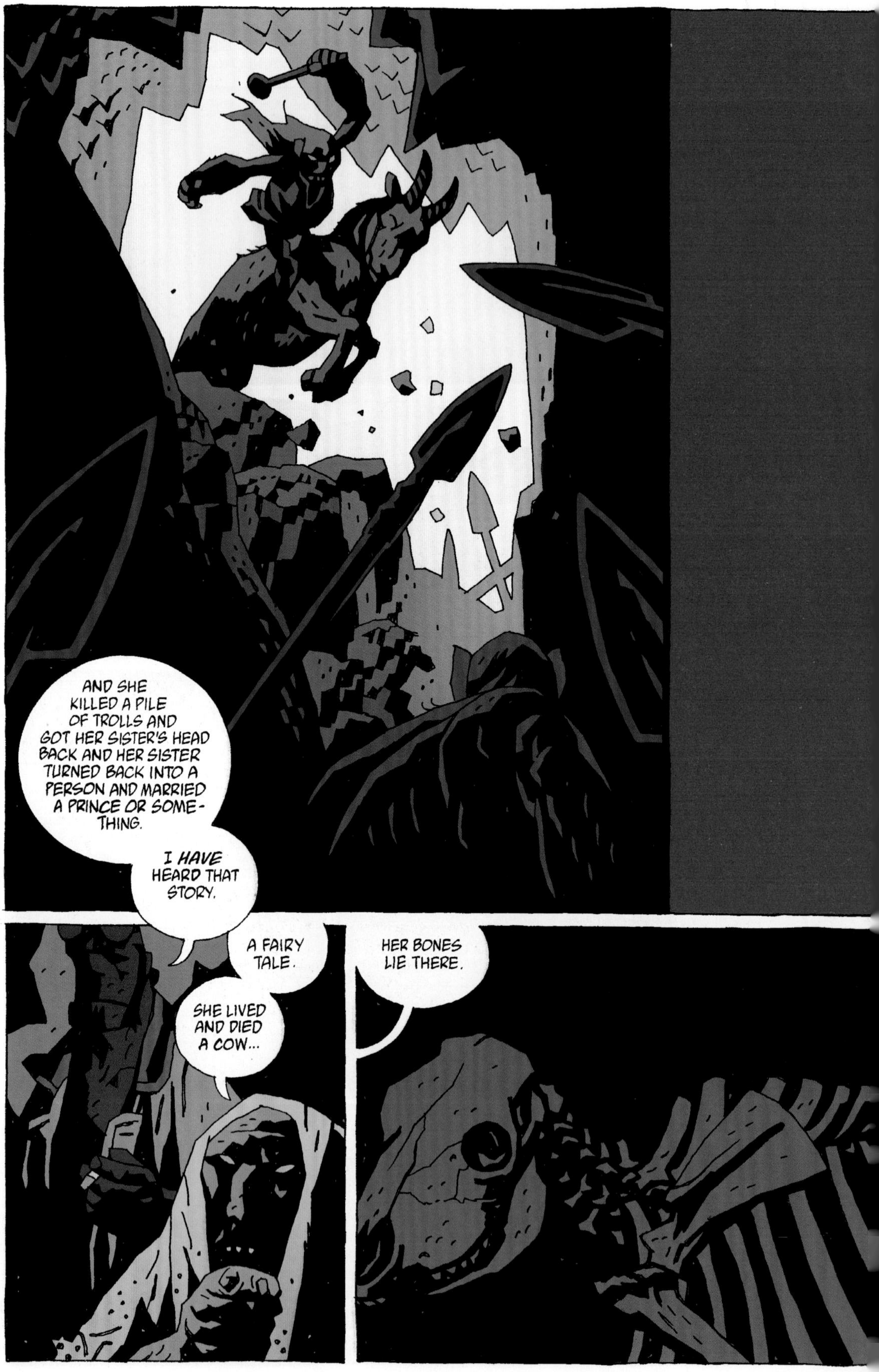
AND SHE KILLED A PILE OF TROLLS AND GOT HER SISTER'S HEAD BACK AND HER SISTER TURNED BACK INTO A PERSON AND MARRIED A PRINCE OR SOME-THING.
I *HAVE* HEARD THAT STORY.
A FAIRY TALE.
SHE LIVED AND DIED A COW...
HER BONES LIE THERE.

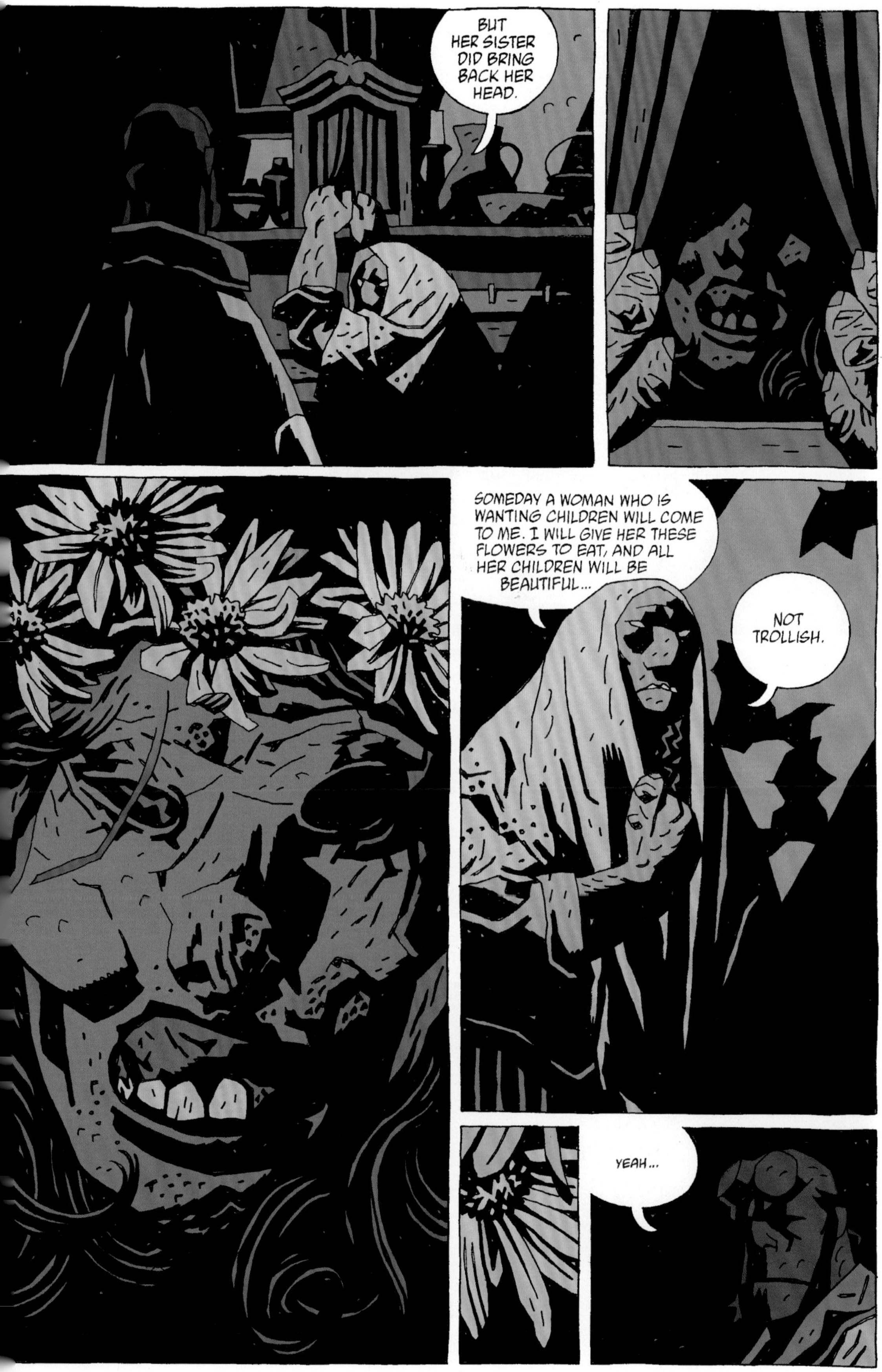
BUT HER SISTER DID BRING BACK HER HEAD.
SOMEDAY A WOMAN WHO IS WANTING CHILDREN WILL COME TO ME. I WILL GIVE HER THESE FLOWERS TO EAT, AND ALL HER CHILDREN WILL BE BEAUTIFUL...
NOT TROLLISH.
YEAH...

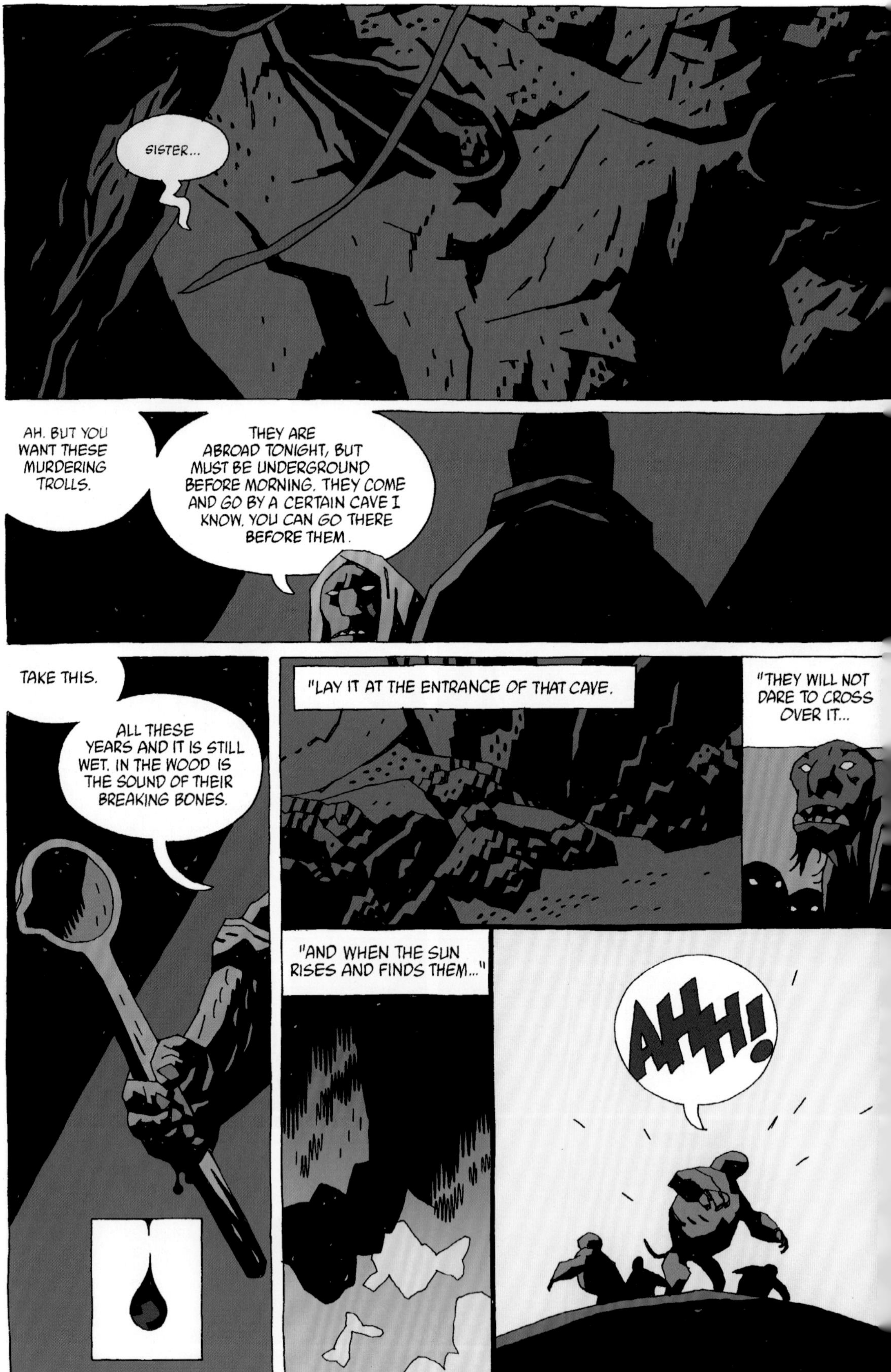
SISTER...
AH. BUT YOU WANT THESE MURDERING TROLLS.
THEY ARE ABROAD TONIGHT, BUT MUST BE UNDERGROUND BEFORE MORNING. THEY COME AND GO BY A CERTAIN CAVE I KNOW. YOU CAN GO THERE BEFORE THEM.
TAKE THIS.
ALL THESE YEARS AND IT IS STILL WET. IN THE WOOD IS THE SOUND OF THEIR BREAKING BONES.
"LAY IT AT THE ENTRANCE OF THAT CAVE.
"THEY WILL NOT DARE TO CROSS OVER IT...
"AND WHEN THE SUN RISES AND FINDS THEM..."
AHH!

"THEY WILL TURN TO STONE.

"NO BLOW STRUCK...

"NO DROP OF BLOOD SPILLED..."

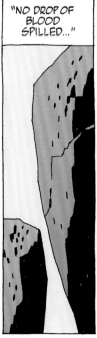

AND I WONDER... HOW WILL YOU FEEL ABOUT THAT?

THE END

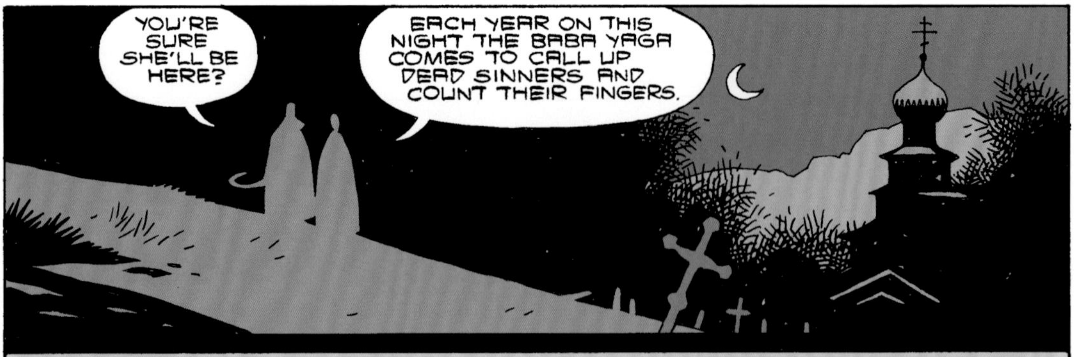
YOU'RE SURE SHE'LL BE HERE?
EACH YEAR ON THIS NIGHT THE BABA YAGA COMES TO CALL UP DEAD SINNERS AND COUNT THEIR FINGERS.

# The Baba Yaga

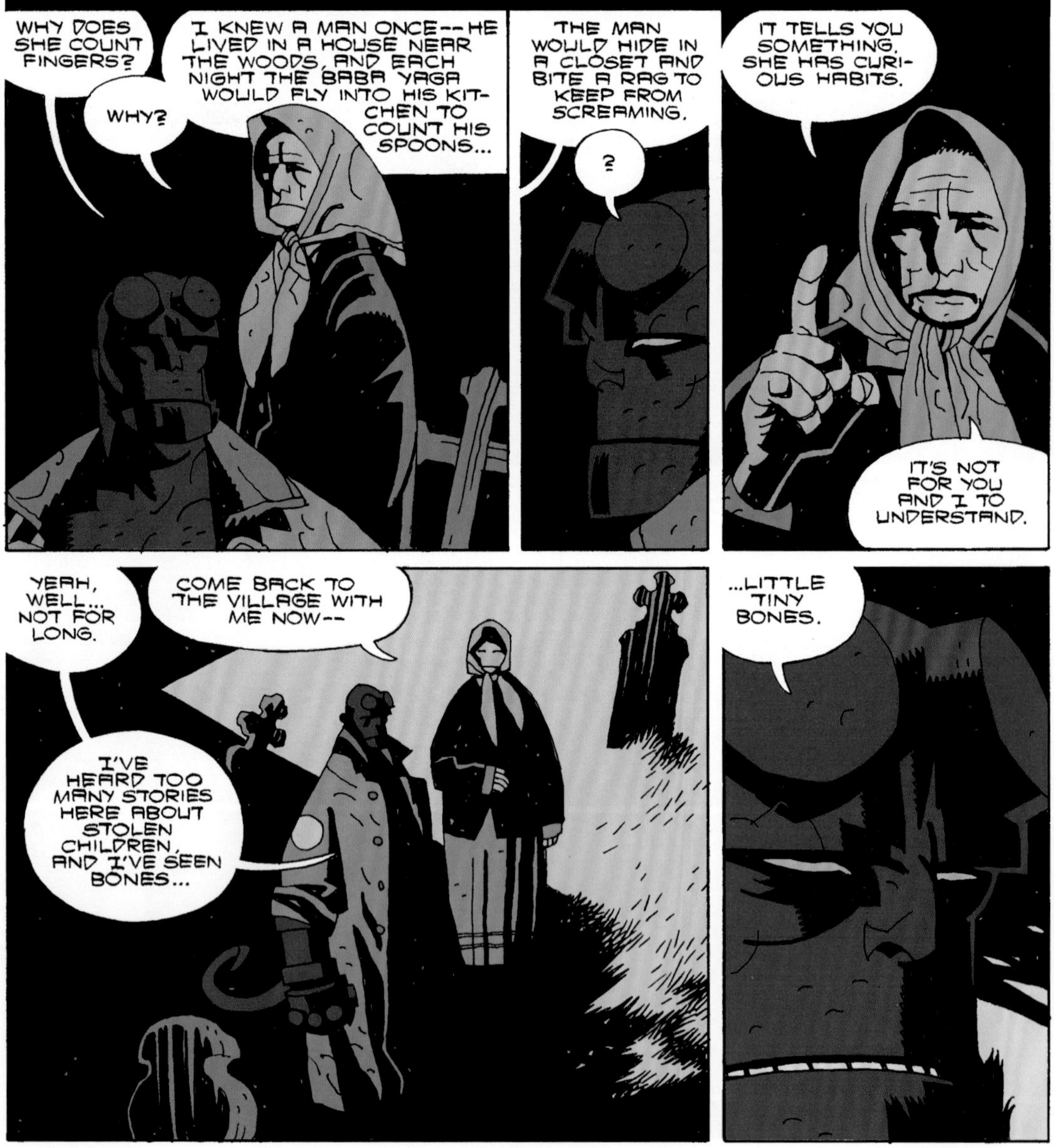
WHY DOES SHE COUNT FINGERS?
I KNEW A MAN ONCE--HE LIVED IN A HOUSE NEAR THE WOODS, AND EACH NIGHT THE BABA YAGA WOULD FLY INTO HIS KITCHEN TO COUNT HIS SPOONS...
WHY?
THE MAN WOULD HIDE IN A CLOSET AND BITE A RAG TO KEEP FROM SCREAMING.
?
IT TELLS YOU SOMETHING. SHE HAS CURIOUS HABITS.
IT'S NOT FOR YOU AND I TO UNDERSTAND.
YEAH, WELL... NOT FOR LONG.
COME BACK TO THE VILLAGE WITH ME NOW--
I'VE HEARD TOO MANY STORIES HERE ABOUT STOLEN CHILDREN, AND I'VE SEEN BONES...
...LITTLE TINY BONES.

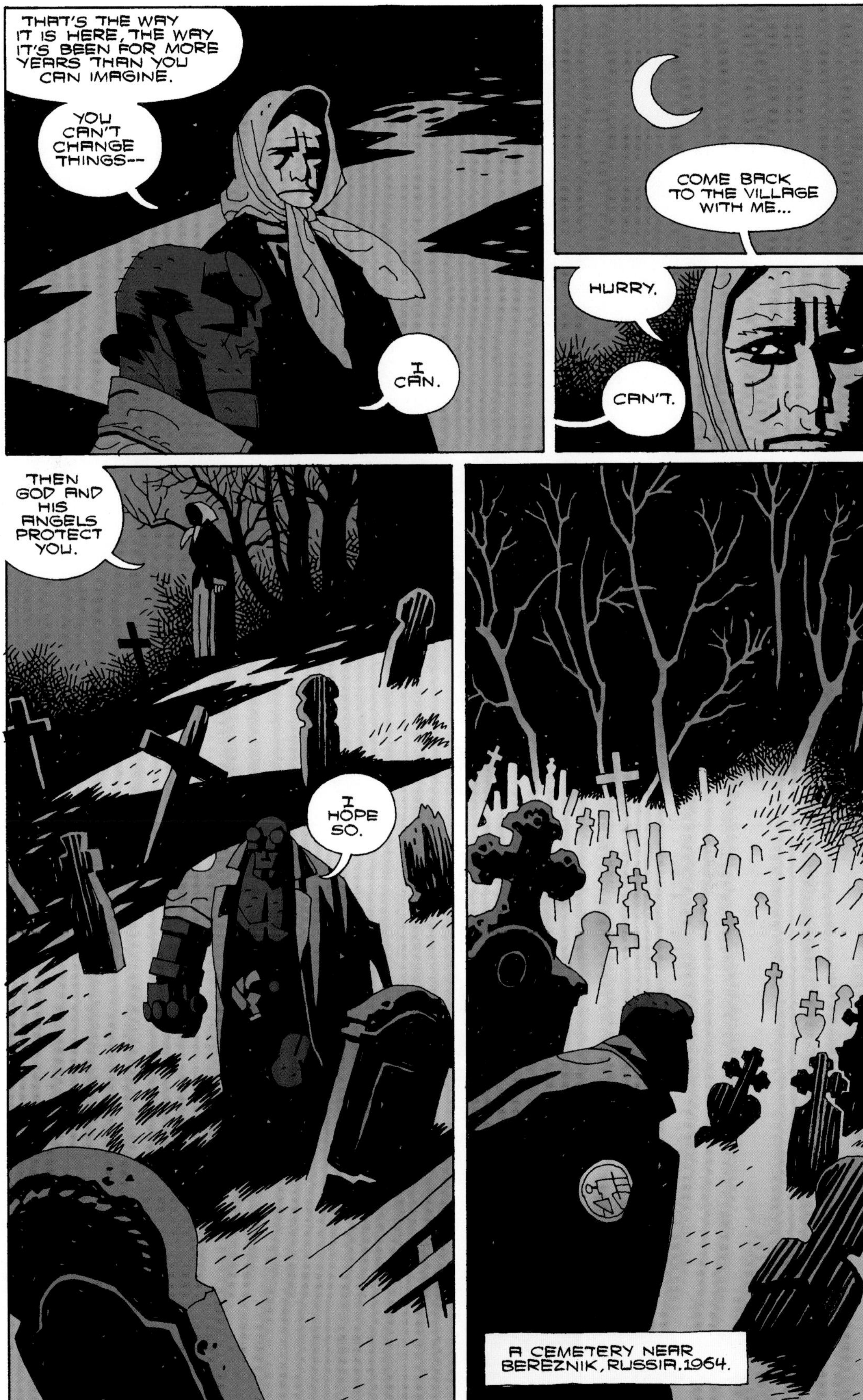
THAT'S THE WAY IT IS HERE, THE WAY IT'S BEEN FOR MORE YEARS THAN YOU CAN IMAGINE.
YOU CAN'T CHANGE THINGS--
I CAN.
COME BACK TO THE VILLAGE WITH ME...
HURRY.
CAN'T.
THEN GOD AND HIS ANGELS PROTECT YOU.
I HOPE SO.
A CEMETERY NEAR BEREZNIK, RUSSIA. 1964.

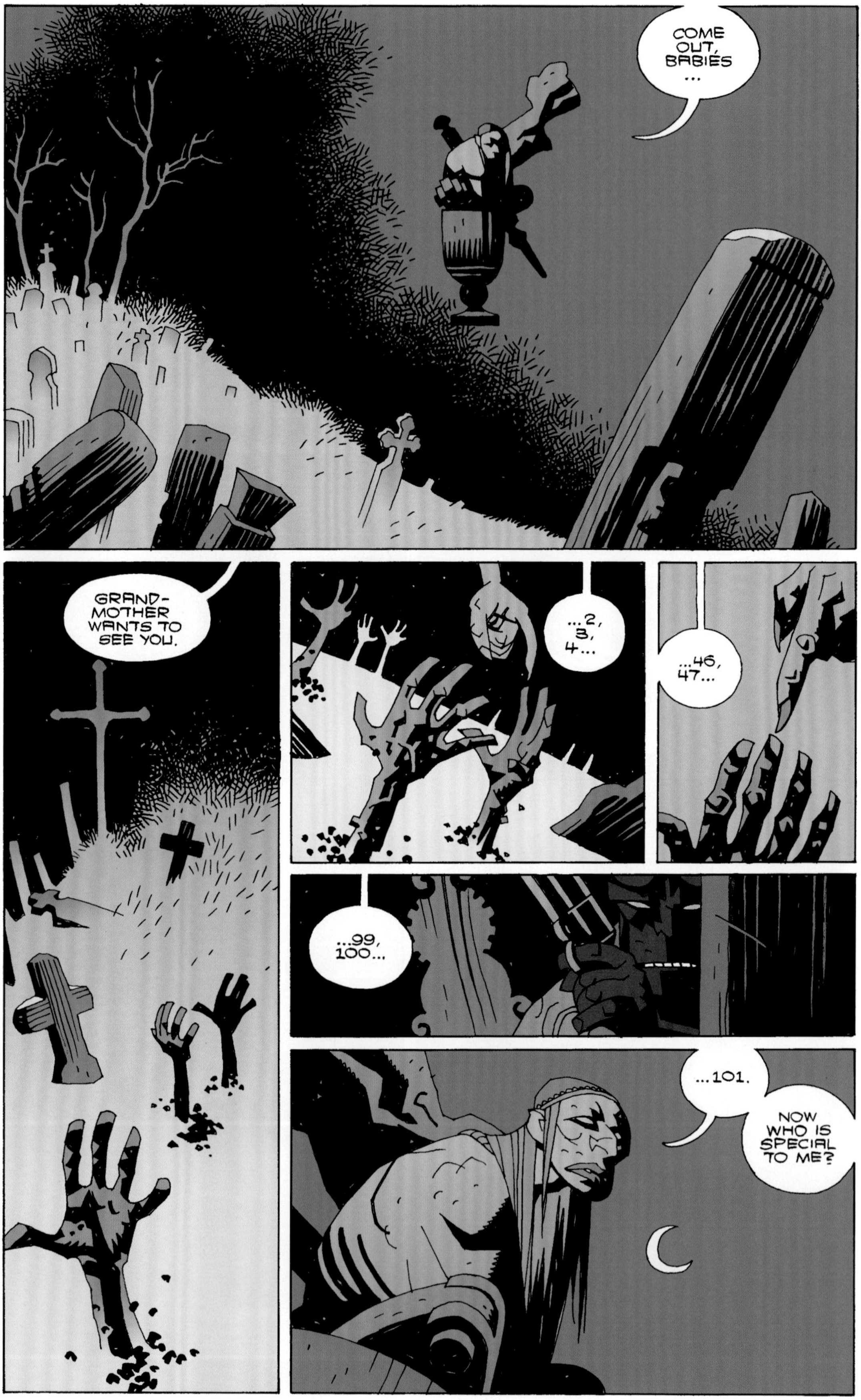
COME OUT, BABIES ...
GRAND-MOTHER WANTS TO SEE YOU.
...2, 3, 4...
...46, 47...
...99, 100...
...101.
NOW WHO IS SPECIAL TO ME?

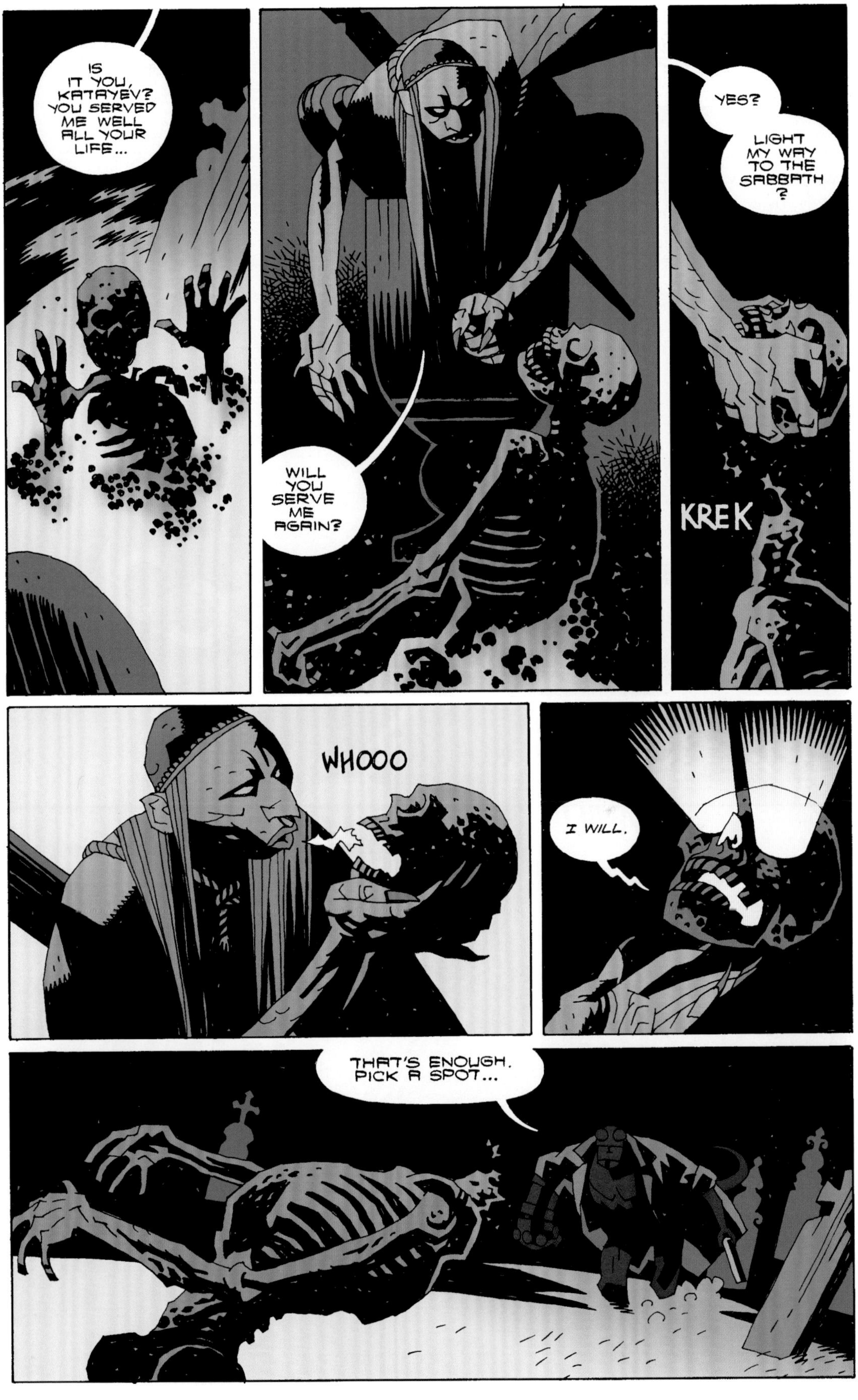
IS IT YOU, KATAYEV? YOU SERVED ME WELL ALL YOUR LIFE...
WILL YOU SERVE ME AGAIN?
YES?
LIGHT MY WAY TO THE SABBATH ?
KREK
WHOOO
I WILL.
THAT'S ENOUGH. PICK A SPOT...

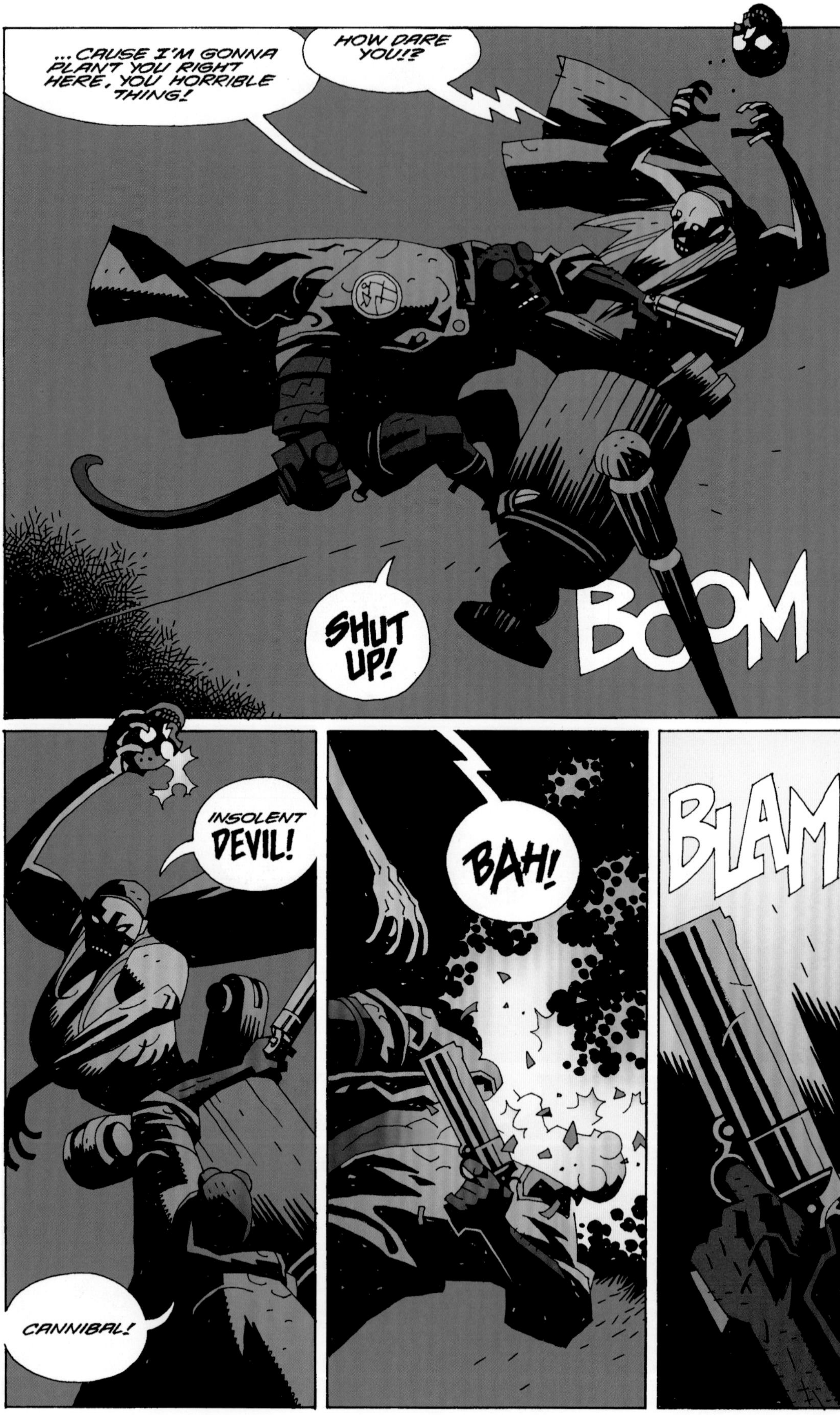
...CAUSE I'M GONNA PLANT YOU RIGHT HERE, YOU HORRIBLE THING!
HOW DARE YOU!?
SHUT UP!
BOOM
INSOLENT DEVIL!
CANNIBAL!
BAH!
BLAM

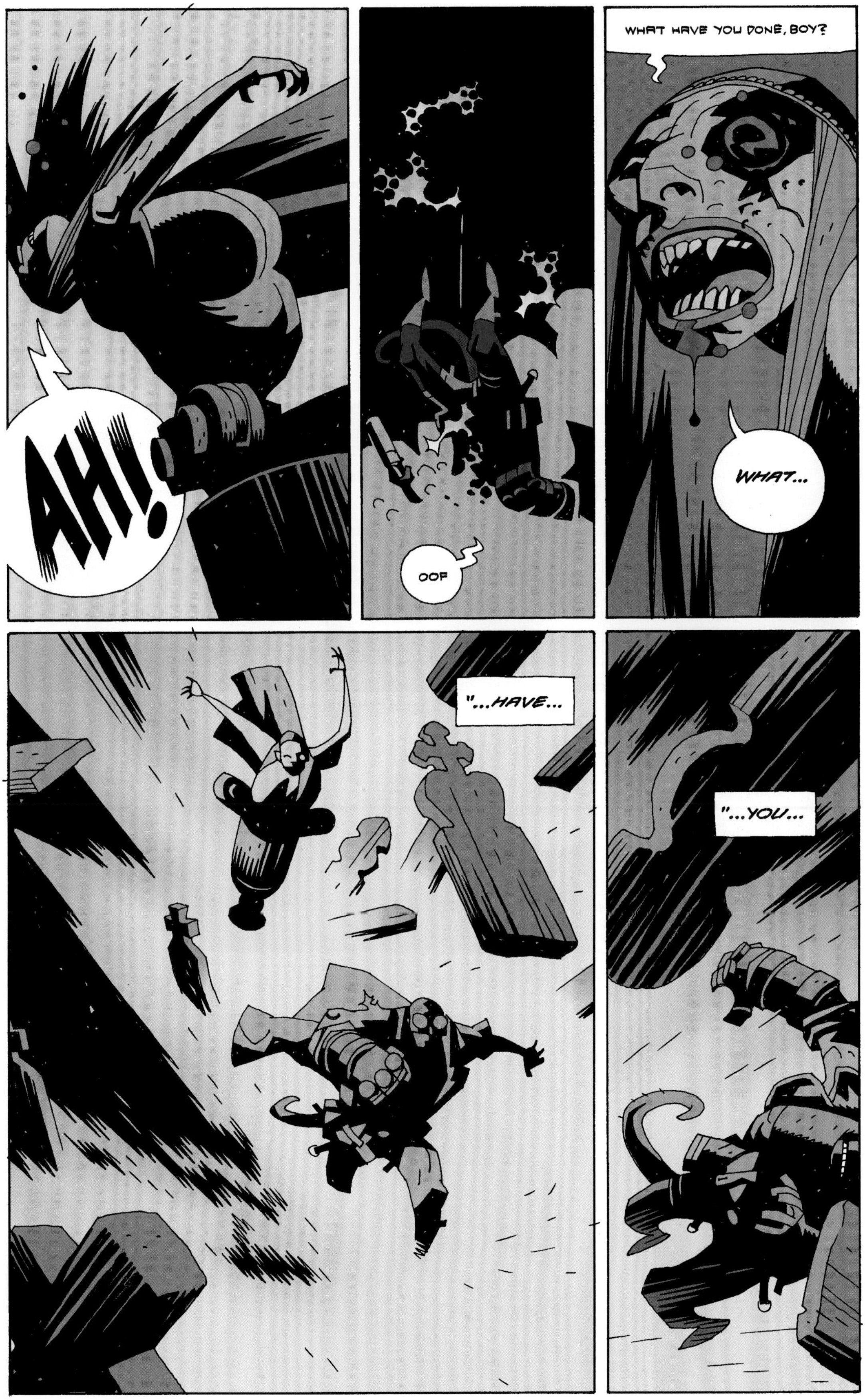
AH!
OOF
WHAT HAVE YOU DONE, BOY?
WHAT...
"...HAVE...
"...YOU...

"...DONE?"

THE BABA YAGA IS DEAD.

WHAT?

I FLEW PAST THE PLACE WHERE HER CHICKEN-LEG HOUSE HAS STOOD. TODAY IT'S GONE. IN ITS PLACE IS LEFT ONLY A FENCE OF OLD SKULLS...

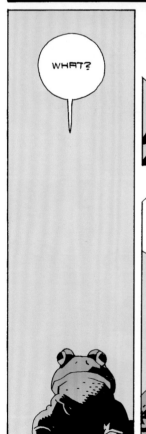

...AND A POOL OF BLOOD.

BUT SHE CANNOT BE DEAD.

SHE IS.

IN THE WOODS TODAY I FOUND A WOODEN BOWL AND A BROKEN STAFF, AND THERE ALSO WAS THE STAIN OF HER BLOOD.

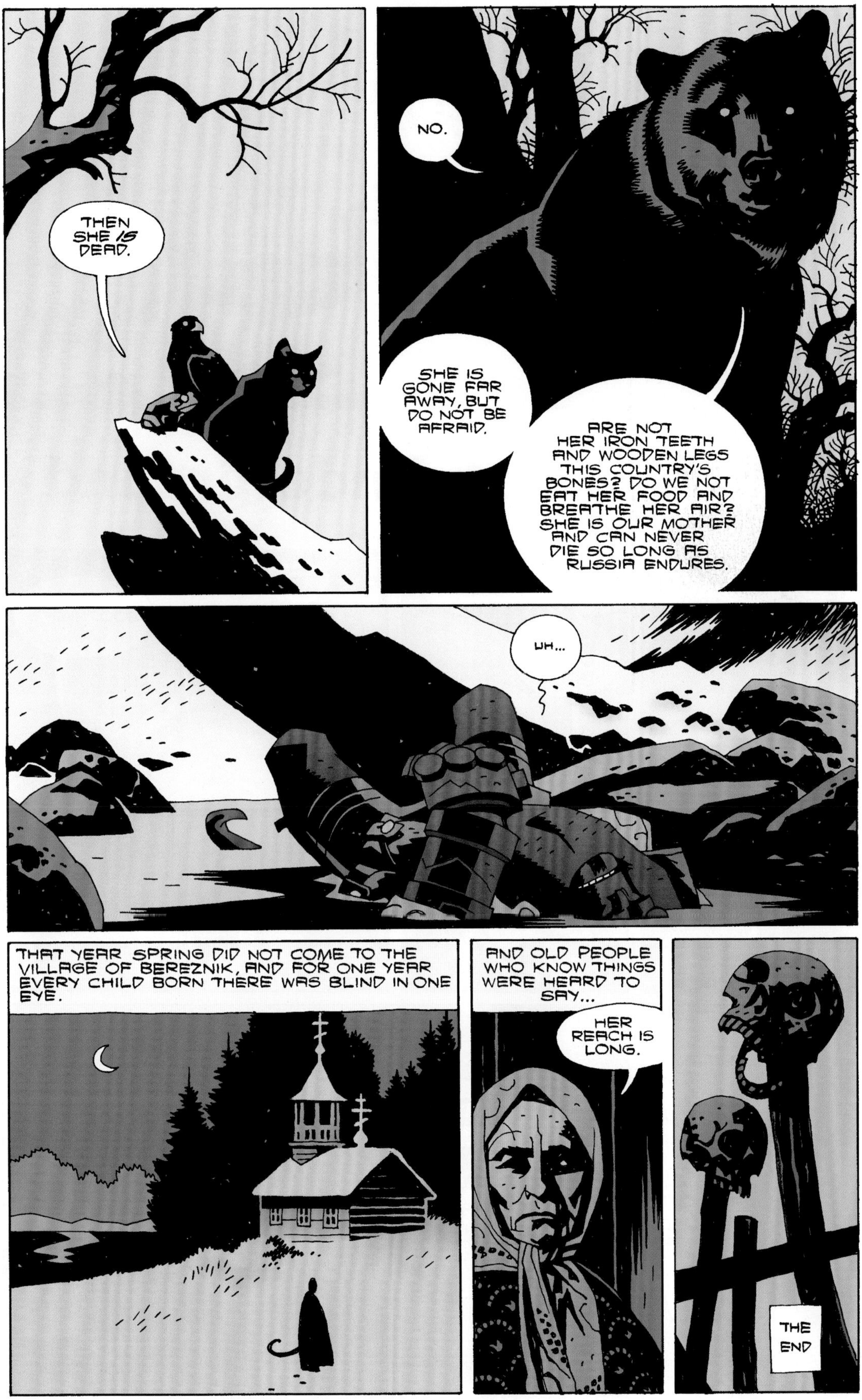
THEN SHE IS DEAD.
NO.
SHE IS GONE FAR AWAY, BUT DO NOT BE AFRAID.
ARE NOT HER IRON TEETH AND WOODEN LEGS THIS COUNTRY'S BONES? DO WE NOT EAT HER FOOD AND BREATHE HER AIR? SHE IS OUR MOTHER AND CAN NEVER DIE SO LONG AS RUSSIA ENDURES.
UH...
THAT YEAR SPRING DID NOT COME TO THE VILLAGE OF BEREZNIK, AND FOR ONE YEAR EVERY CHILD BORN THERE WAS BLIND IN ONE EYE.
AND OLD PEOPLE WHO KNOW THINGS WERE HEARD TO SAY...
HER REACH IS LONG.
THE END

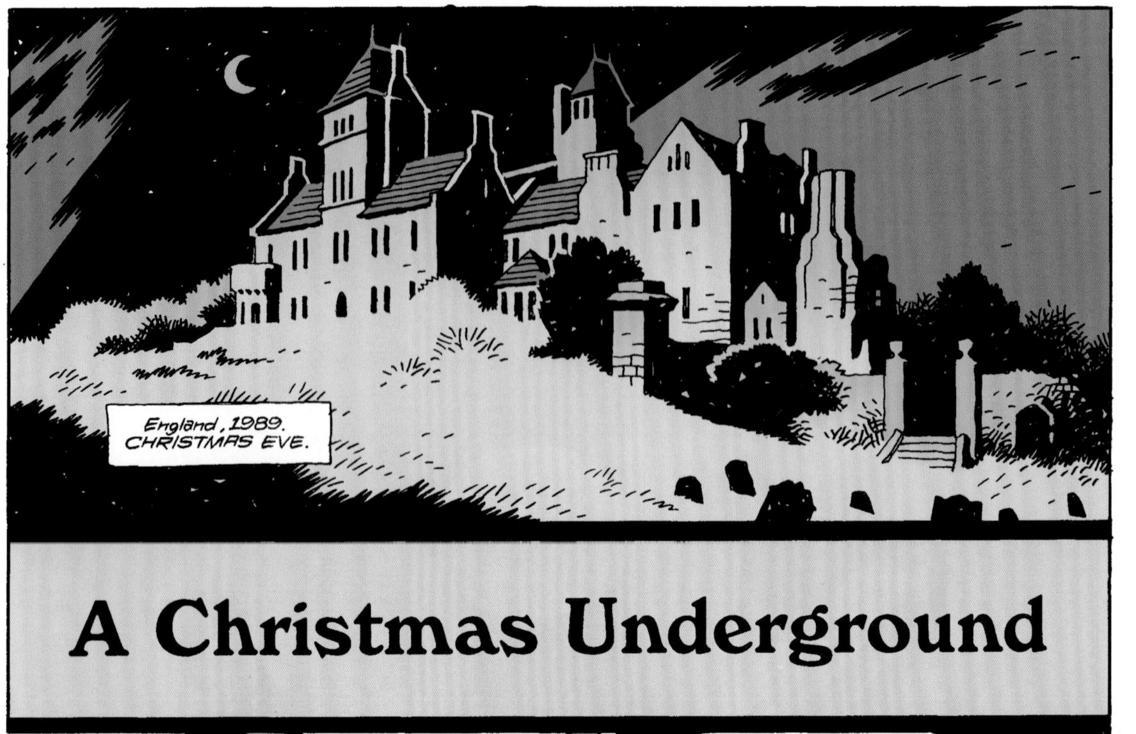
England, 1989.
CHRISTMAS EVE.

# A Christmas Underground

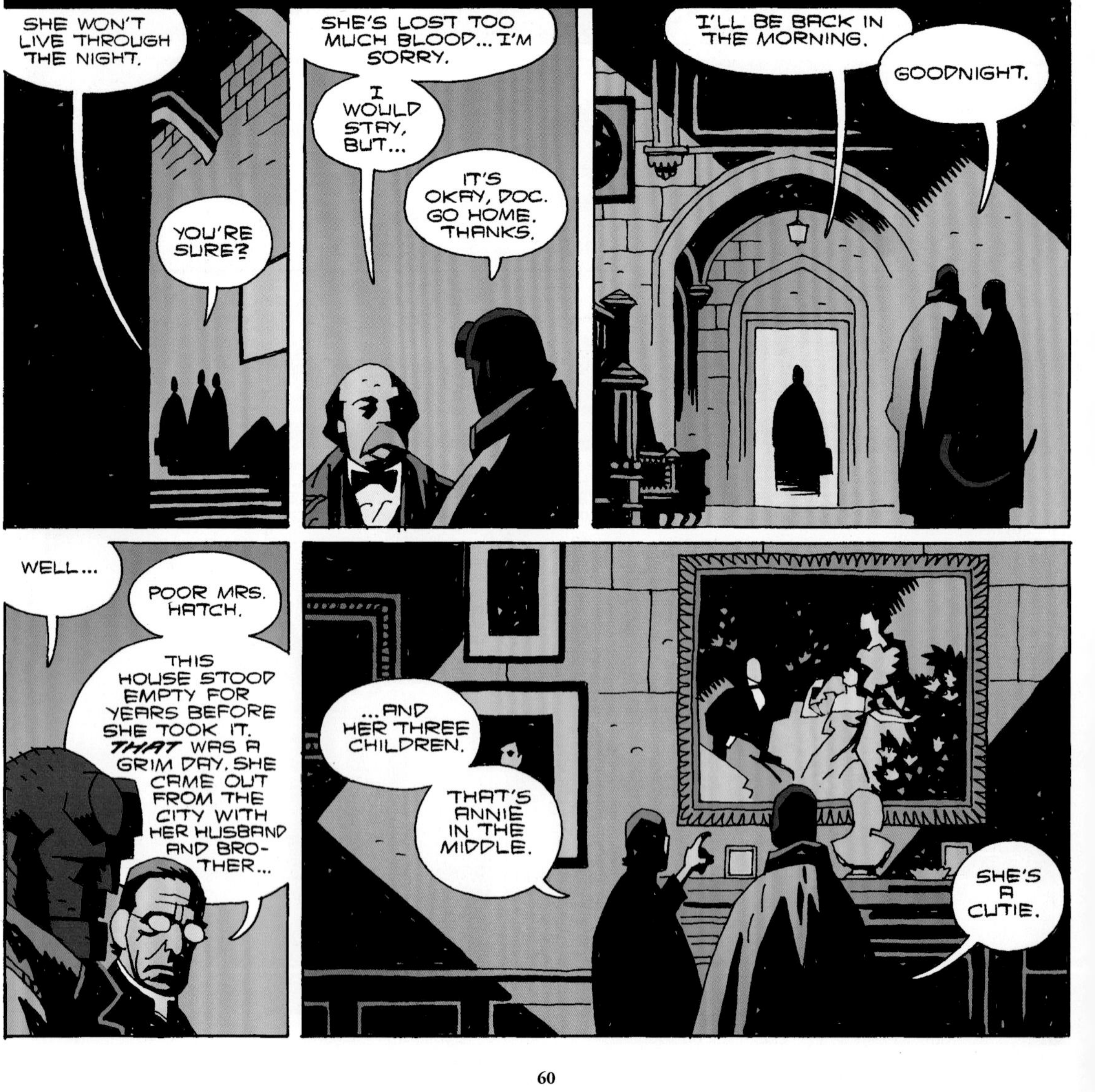
SHE WON'T LIVE THROUGH THE NIGHT.
YOU'RE SURE?
SHE'S LOST TOO MUCH BLOOD... I'M SORRY.
I WOULD STAY, BUT...
IT'S OKAY, DOC. GO HOME. THANKS.
I'LL BE BACK IN THE MORNING.
GOODNIGHT.
WELL...
POOR MRS. HATCH.
THIS HOUSE STOOD EMPTY FOR YEARS BEFORE SHE TOOK IT. THAT WAS A GRIM DAY. SHE CAME OUT FROM THE CITY WITH HER HUSBAND AND BROTHER...
...AND HER THREE CHILDREN.
THAT'S ANNIE IN THE MIDDLE.
SHE'S A CUTIE.

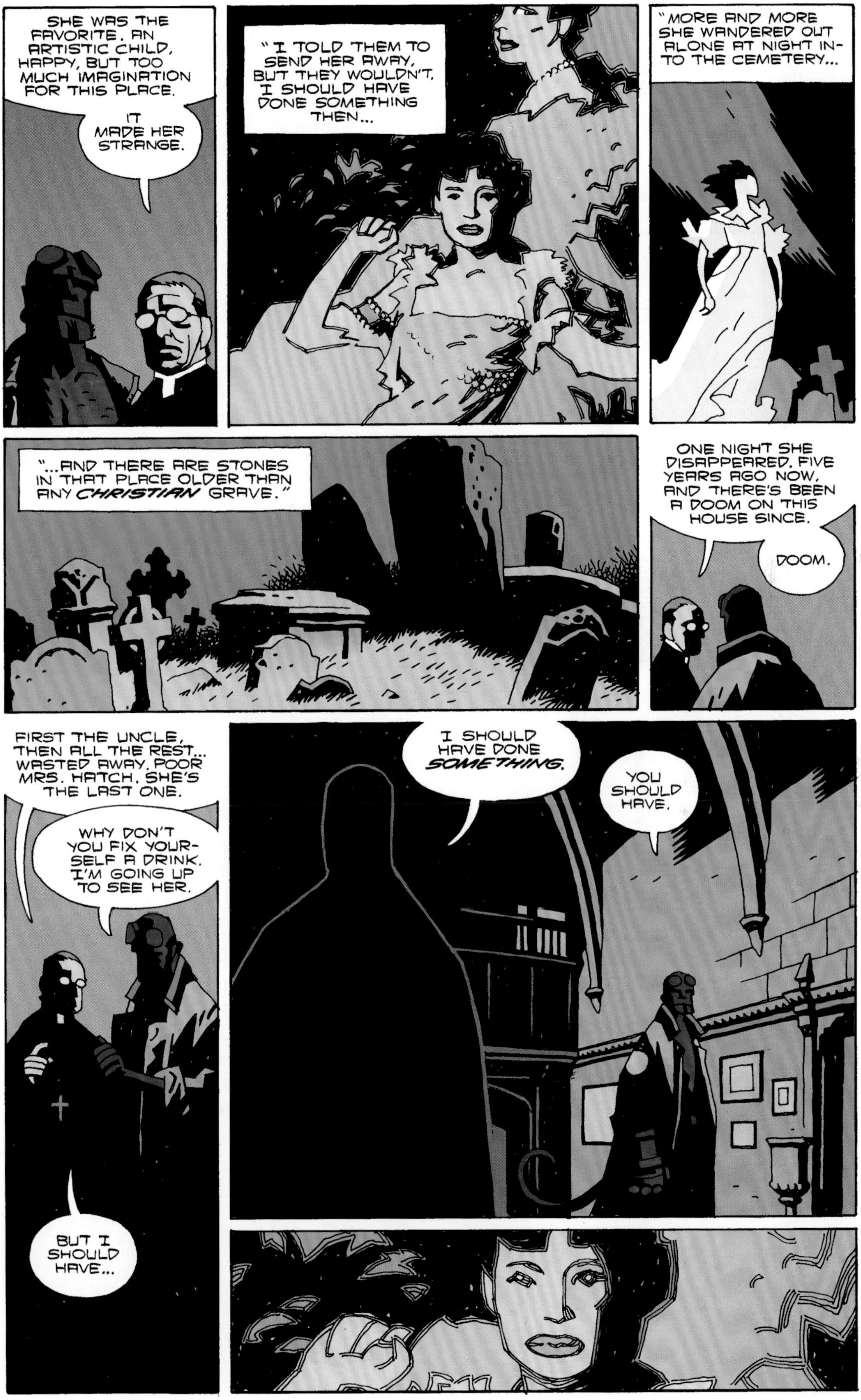
SHE WAS THE FAVORITE. AN ARTISTIC CHILD, HAPPY, BUT TOO MUCH IMAGINATION FOR THIS PLACE.
IT MADE HER STRANGE.
"I TOLD THEM TO SEND HER AWAY, BUT THEY WOULDN'T. I SHOULD HAVE DONE SOMETHING THEN...
"MORE AND MORE SHE WANDERED OUT ALONE AT NIGHT INTO THE CEMETERY...
"...AND THERE ARE STONES IN THAT PLACE OLDER THAN ANY *CHRISTIAN* GRAVE."
ONE NIGHT SHE DISAPPEARED. FIVE YEARS AGO NOW, AND THERE'S BEEN A DOOM ON THIS HOUSE SINCE.
DOOM.
FIRST THE UNCLE, THEN ALL THE REST... WASTED AWAY. POOR MRS. HATCH. SHE'S THE LAST ONE.
WHY DON'T YOU FIX YOURSELF A DRINK. I'M GOING UP TO SEE HER.
BUT I SHOULD HAVE...
I SHOULD HAVE DONE *SOMETHING.*
YOU SHOULD HAVE.

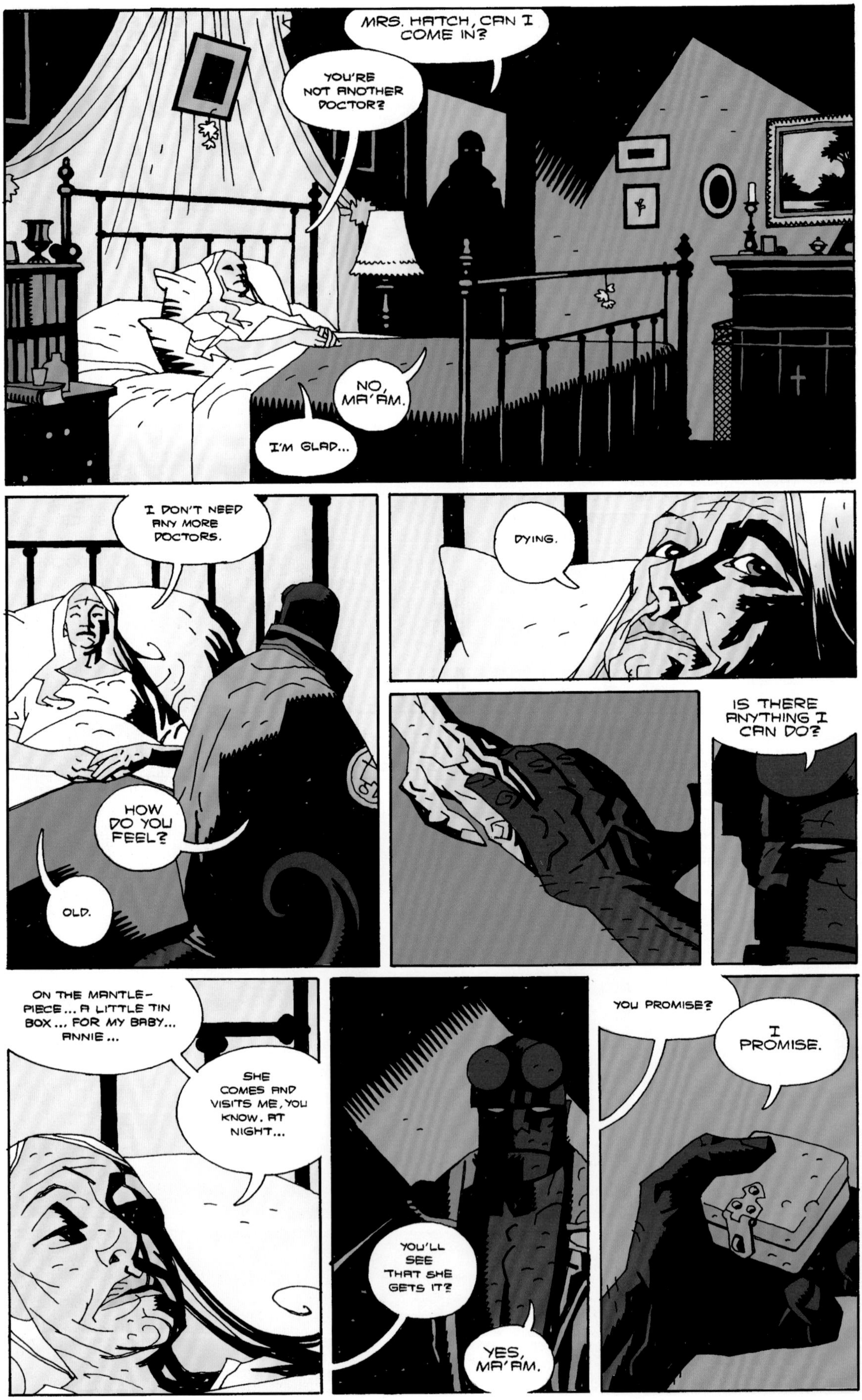
MRS. HATCH, CAN I COME IN?
YOU'RE NOT ANOTHER DOCTOR?
NO, MA'AM.
I'M GLAD...
I DON'T NEED ANY MORE DOCTORS.
HOW DO YOU FEEL?
OLD.
DYING.
IS THERE ANYTHING I CAN DO?
ON THE MANTLE-PIECE... A LITTLE TIN BOX... FOR MY BABY... ANNIE...
SHE COMES AND VISITS ME, YOU KNOW. AT NIGHT...
YOU'LL SEE THAT SHE GETS IT?
YES, MA'AM.
YOU PROMISE?
I PROMISE.

I KNEW YOU WOULD.

YOU THOUGHT I DIDN'T RECOGNIZE YOU...

MA'AM?

YOU'RE FATHER CHRISTMAS.

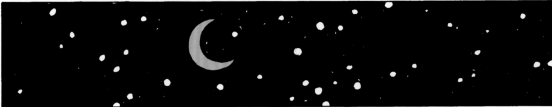

HERE.

A LIST OF THINGS YOU'RE GONNA HAVE TO DO WHEN SHE DIES. THERE'S ALSO A NUMBER FOR YOU TO CALL IF I DON'T COME BACK.

BUT I'LL COME BACK.

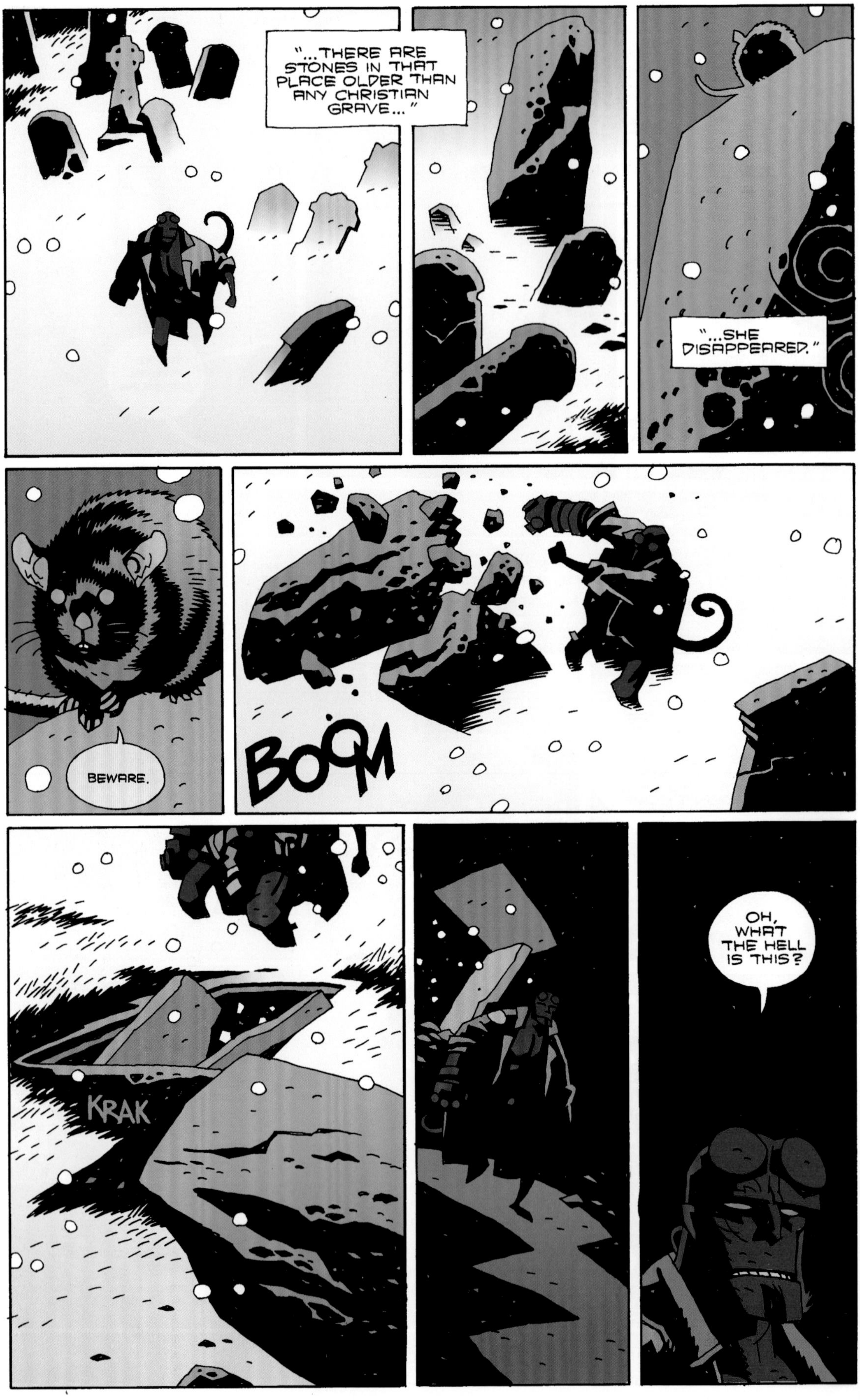
"...THERE ARE STONES IN THAT PLACE OLDER THAN ANY CHRISTIAN GRAVE..."
"...SHE DISAPPEARED."
BEWARE.
BOOM
KRAK
OH, WHAT THE HELL IS THIS?

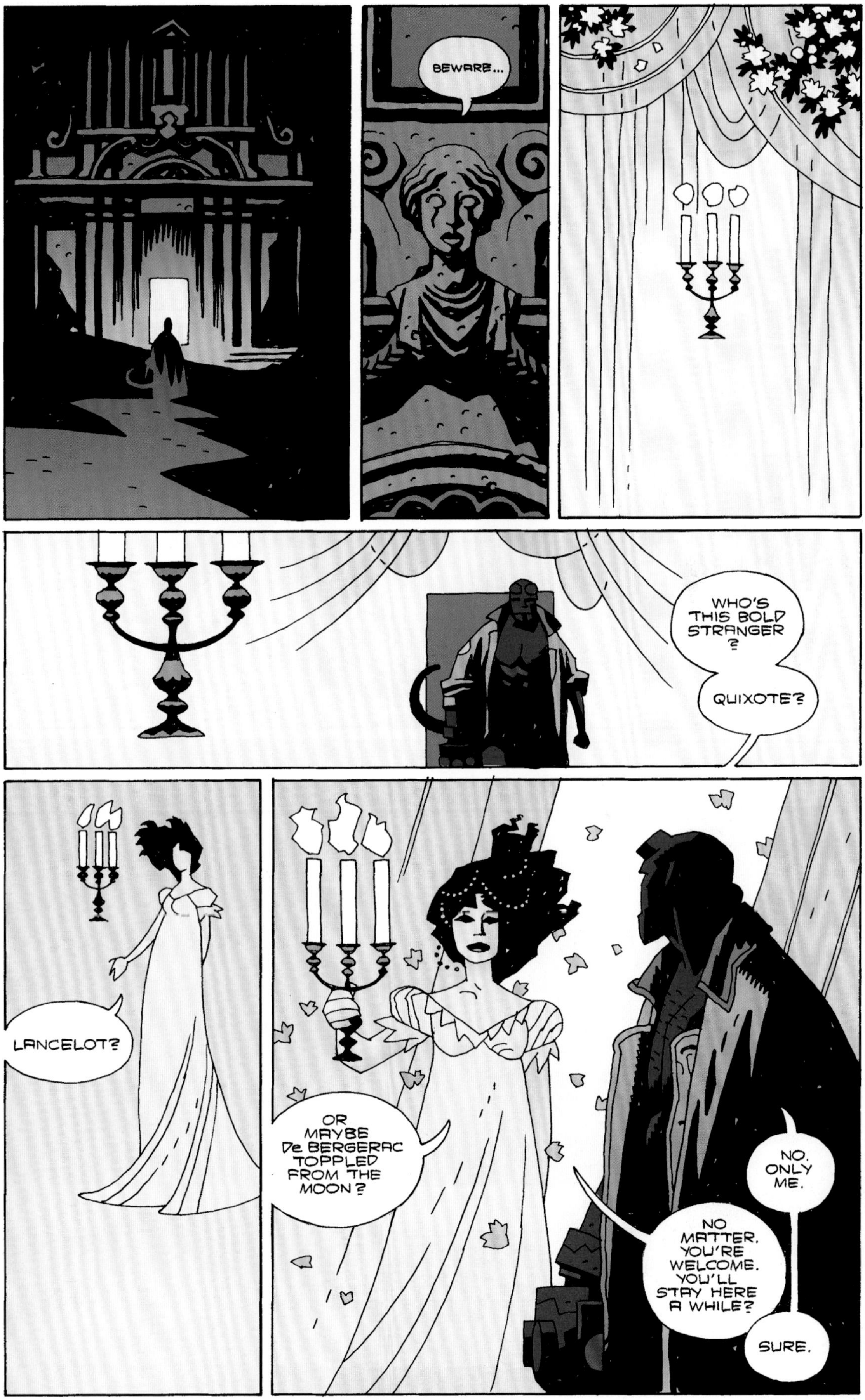
BEWARE...
WHO'S THIS BOLD STRANGER?
QUIXOTE?
LANCELOT?
OR MAYBE De BERGERAC TOPPLED FROM THE MOON?
NO. ONLY ME.
NO MATTER. YOU'RE WELCOME. YOU'LL STAY HERE A WHILE?
SURE.

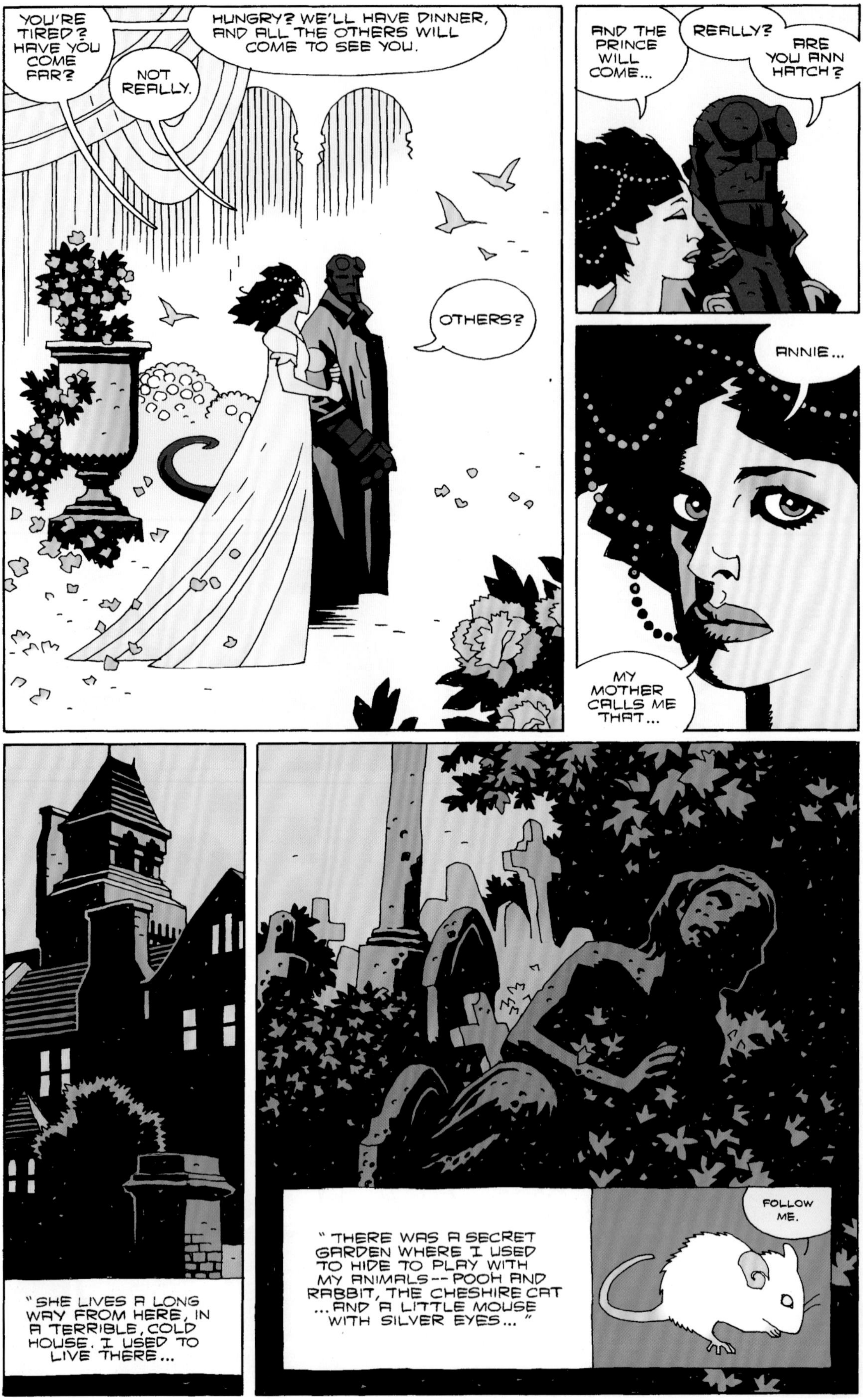
YOU'RE TIRED? HAVE YOU COME FAR?
NOT REALLY.
HUNGRY? WE'LL HAVE DINNER, AND ALL THE OTHERS WILL COME TO SEE YOU.
OTHERS?
AND THE PRINCE WILL COME...
REALLY?
ARE YOU ANN HATCH?
ANNIE...
MY MOTHER CALLS ME THAT...
"SHE LIVES A LONG WAY FROM HERE, IN A TERRIBLE, COLD HOUSE. I USED TO LIVE THERE...
"THERE WAS A SECRET GARDEN WHERE I USED TO HIDE TO PLAY WITH MY ANIMALS--POOH AND RABBIT, THE CHESHIRE CAT ...AND A LITTLE MOUSE WITH SILVER EYES..."
FOLLOW ME.

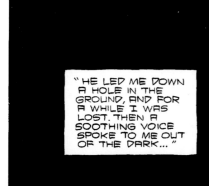

"HE LED ME DOWN A HOLE IN THE GROUND, AND FOR A WHILE I WAS LOST. THEN A SOOTHING VOICE SPOKE TO ME OUT OF THE DARK..."

ABIDE WITH ME AND BE MY BRIDE, AND THOU SHALT HAVE ALL THY HEART'S DESIRES.

WHO ARE YOU?

THE SECOND SON OF A KING.

"AND THAT'S ALL HE WOULD SAY."

"HE TOOK ME TO HIS PALACE AND GAVE ME EVERYTHING I COULD WANT."

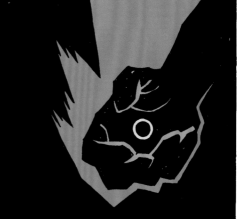

"I BELONG TO HIM."

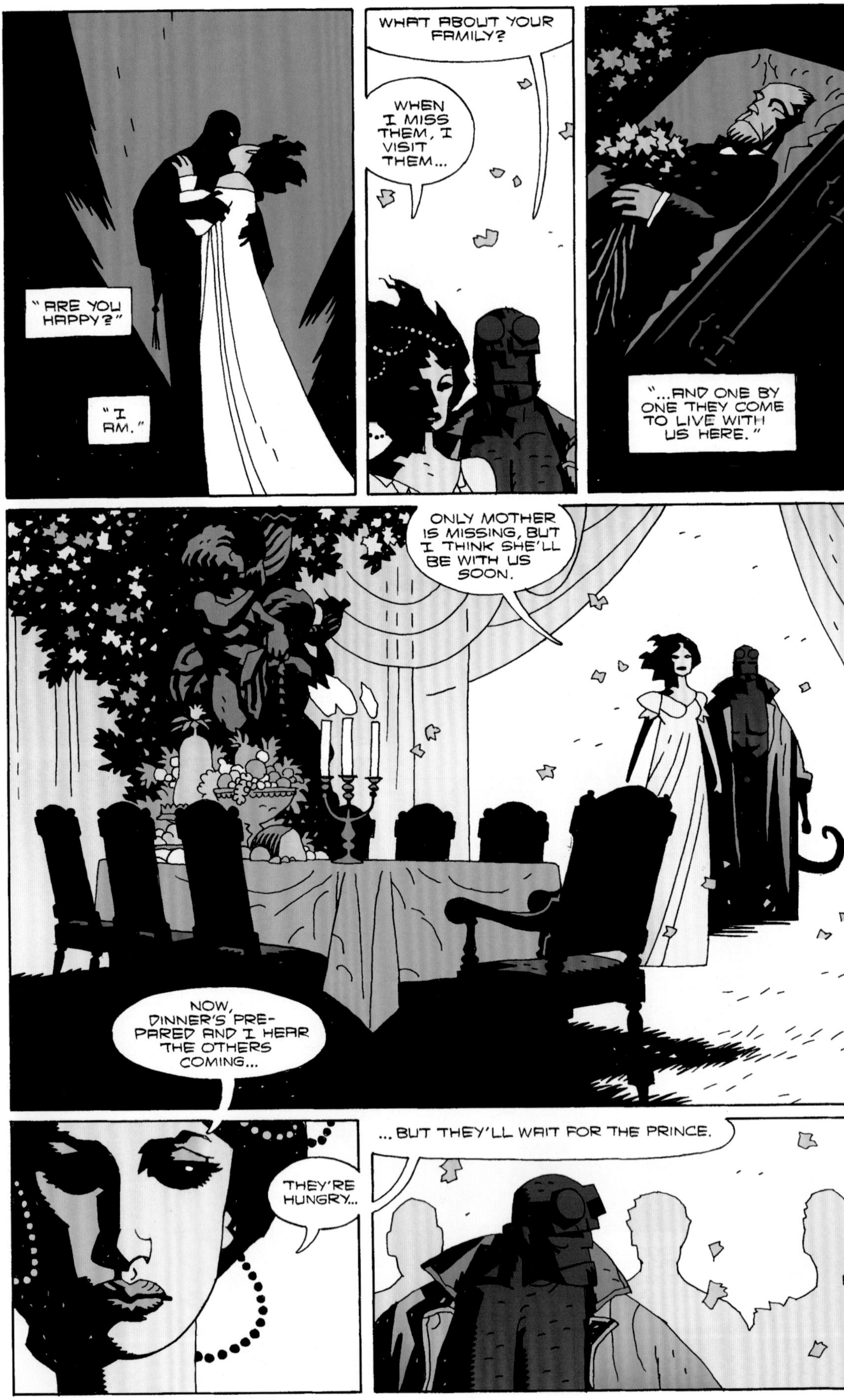

"ARE YOU HAPPY?"
"I AM."
WHAT ABOUT YOUR FAMILY?
WHEN I MISS THEM, I VISIT THEM...
"...AND ONE BY ONE THEY COME TO LIVE WITH US HERE."
ONLY MOTHER IS MISSING, BUT I THINK SHE'LL BE WITH US SOON.
NOW, DINNER'S PRE-PARED AND I HEAR THE OTHERS COMING...
THEY'RE HUNGRY...
... BUT THEY'LL WAIT FOR THE PRINCE.

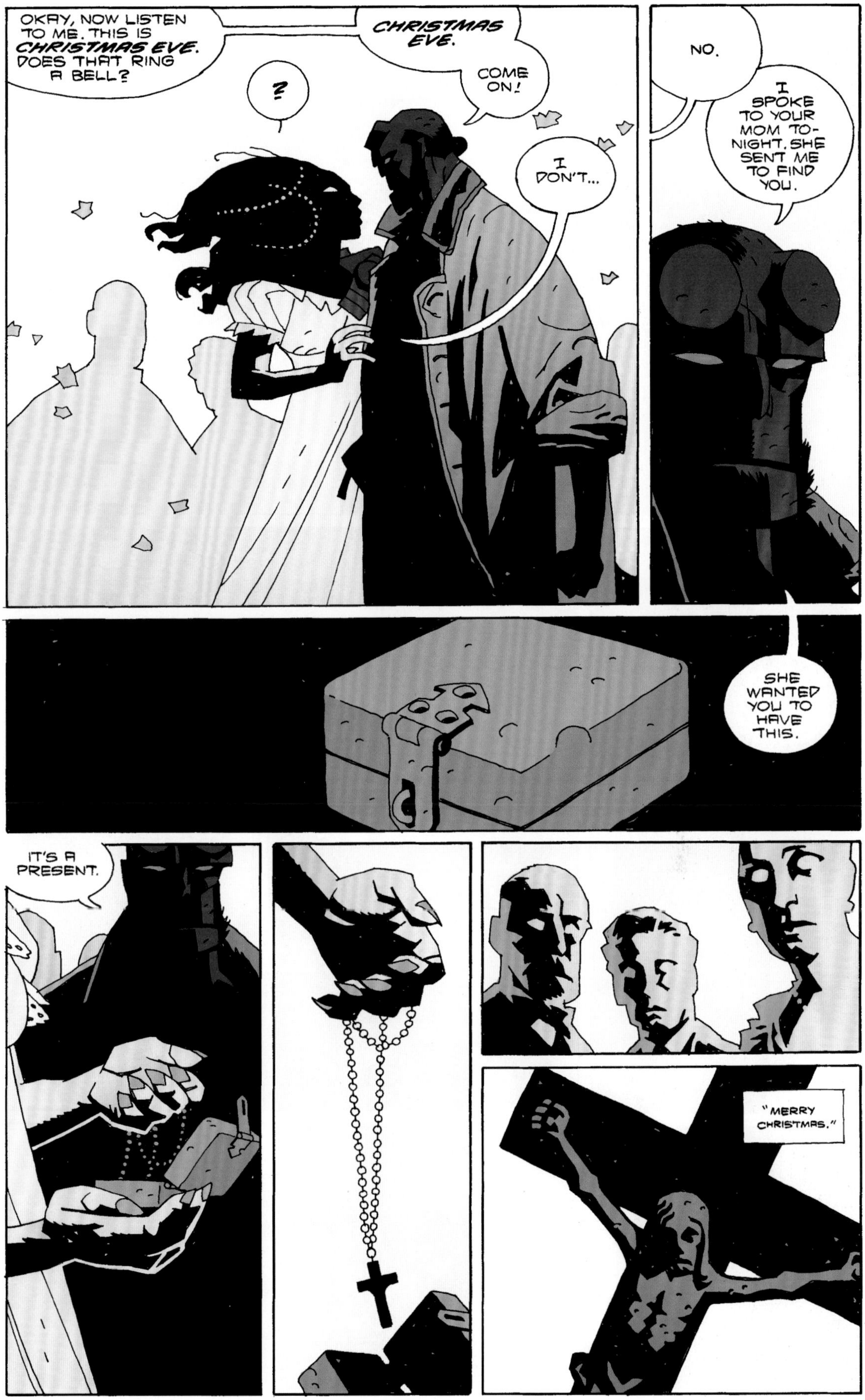
OKAY, NOW LISTEN TO ME. THIS IS CHRISTMAS EVE. DOES THAT RING A BELL?
CHRISTMAS EVE.
COME ON!
?
I DON'T...
NO.
I SPOKE TO YOUR MOM TO-NIGHT. SHE SENT ME TO FIND YOU.
SHE WANTED YOU TO HAVE THIS.
IT'S A PRESENT.
"MERRY CHRISTMAS."

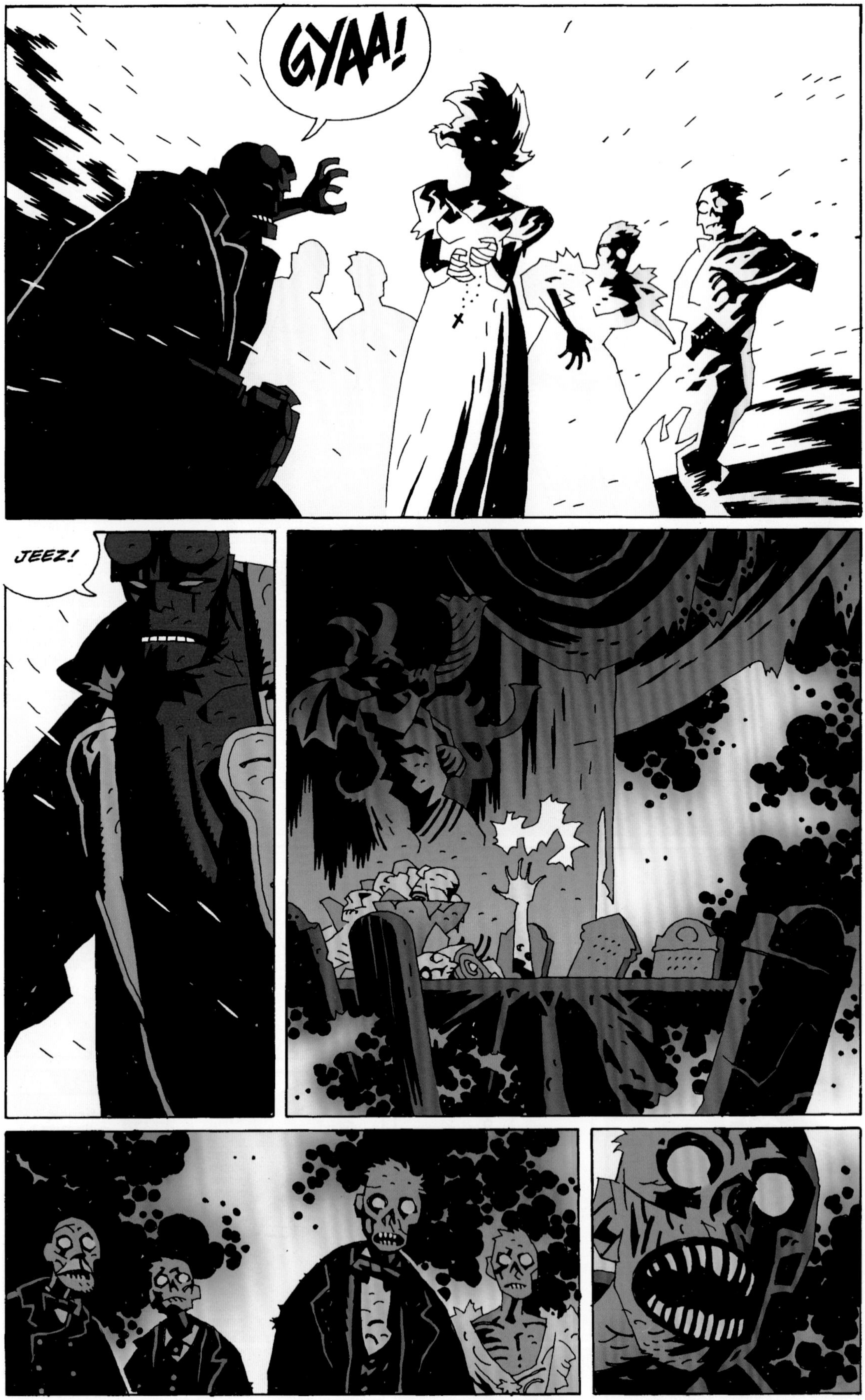
GYAA!
JEEZ!

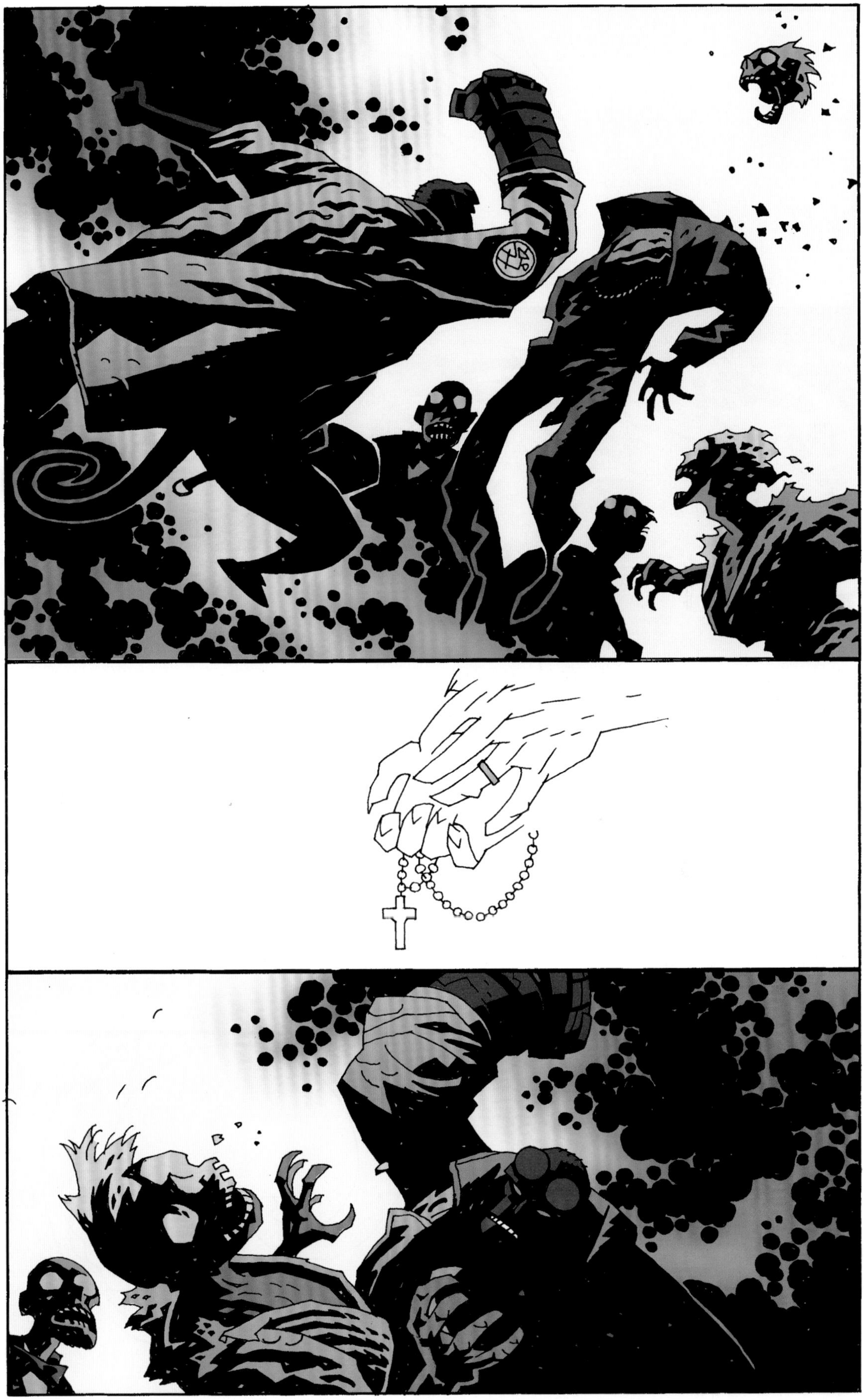

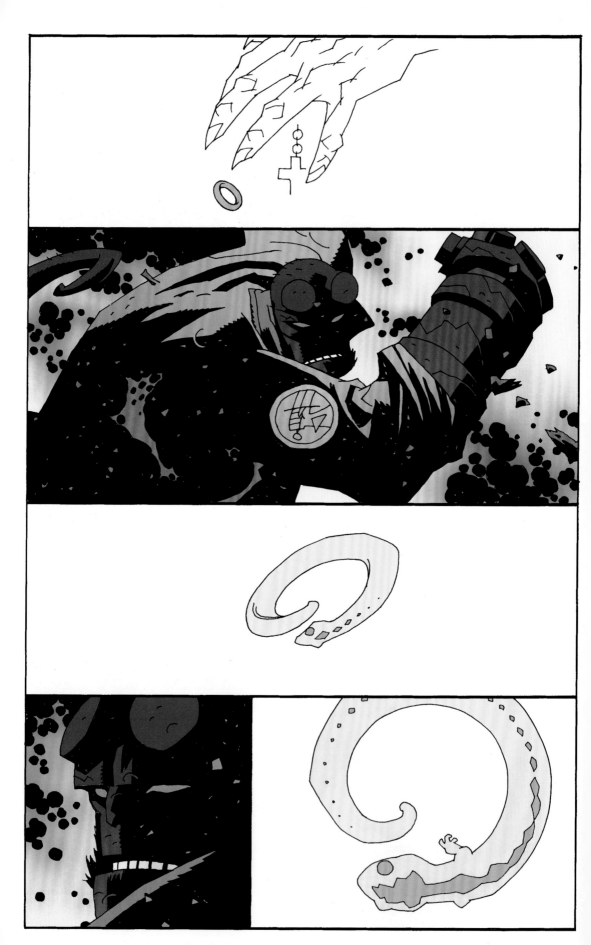

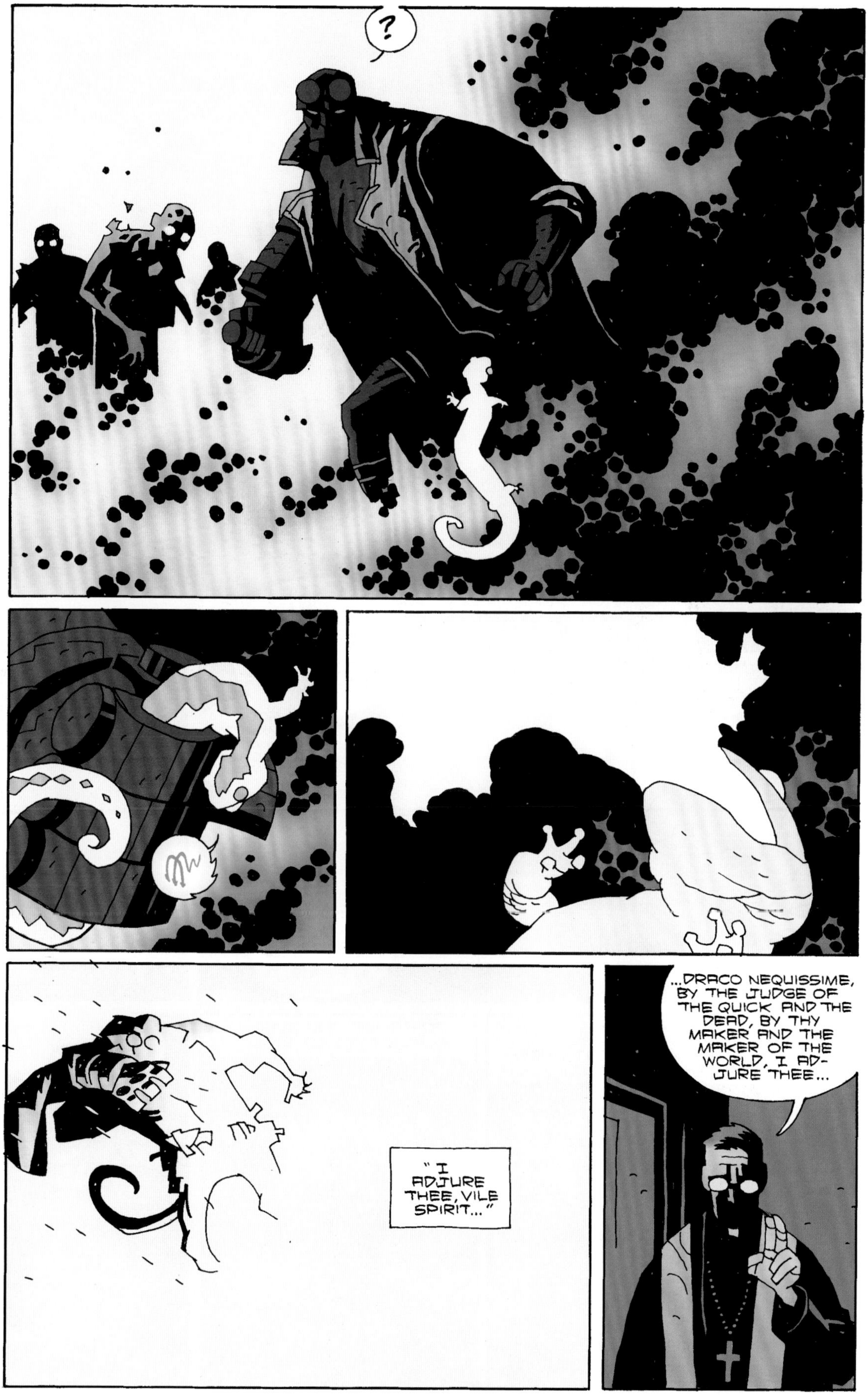
?
"I ADJURE THEE, VILE SPIRIT..."
...DRACO NEQUISSIME, BY THE JUDGE OF THE QUICK AND THE DEAD, BY THY MAKER AND THE MAKER OF THE WORLD, I ADJURE THEE...

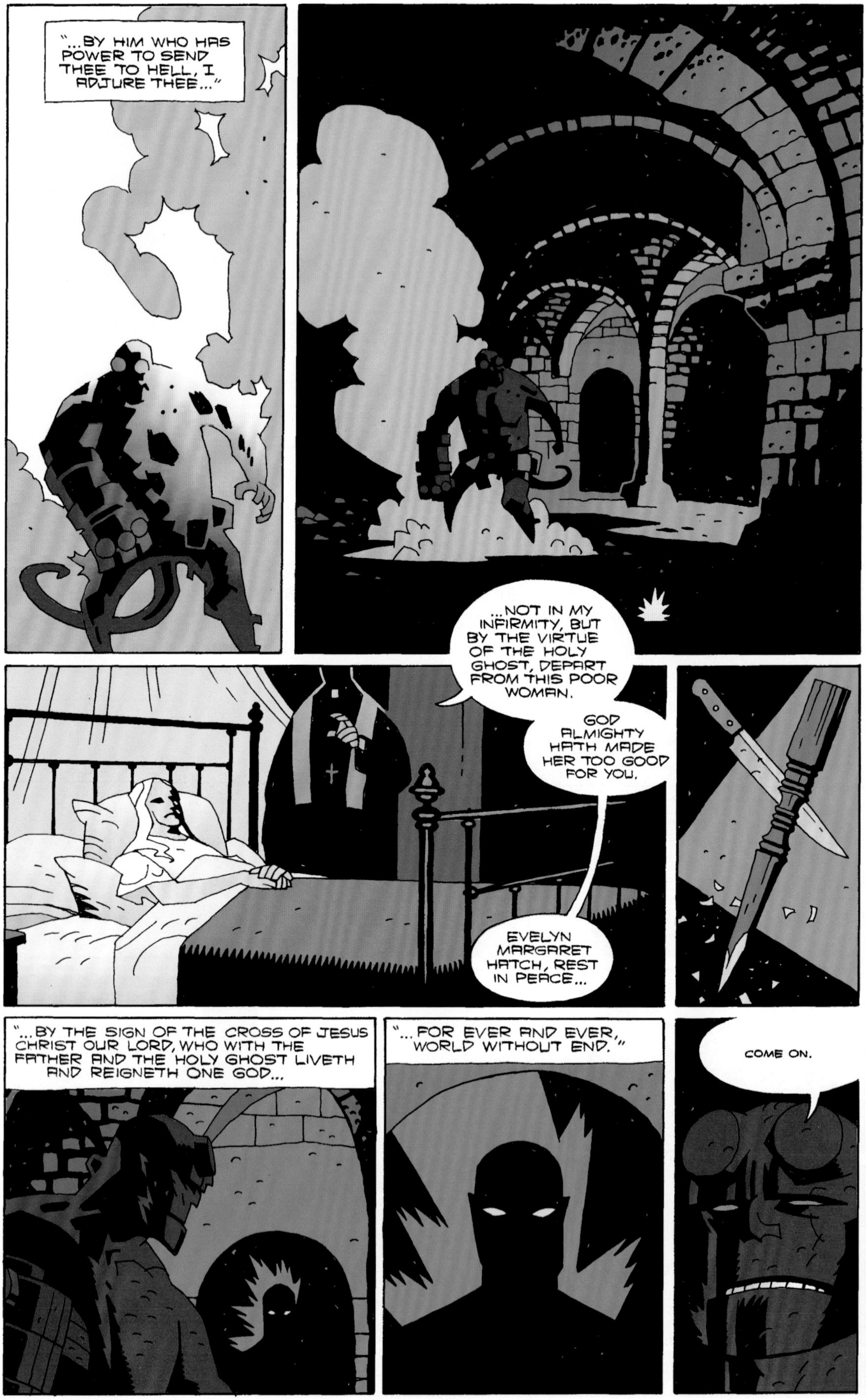
"...BY HIM WHO HAS POWER TO SEND THEE TO HELL, I ADJURE THEE..."
...NOT IN MY INFIRMITY, BUT BY THE VIRTUE OF THE HOLY GHOST, DEPART FROM THIS POOR WOMAN.
GOD ALMIGHTY HATH MADE HER TOO GOOD FOR YOU.
EVELYN MARGARET HATCH, REST IN PEACE...
"...BY THE SIGN OF THE CROSS OF JESUS CHRIST OUR LORD, WHO WITH THE FATHER AND THE HOLY GHOST LIVETH AND REIGNETH ONE GOD...
"...FOR EVER AND EVER, WORLD WITHOUT END."
COME ON.

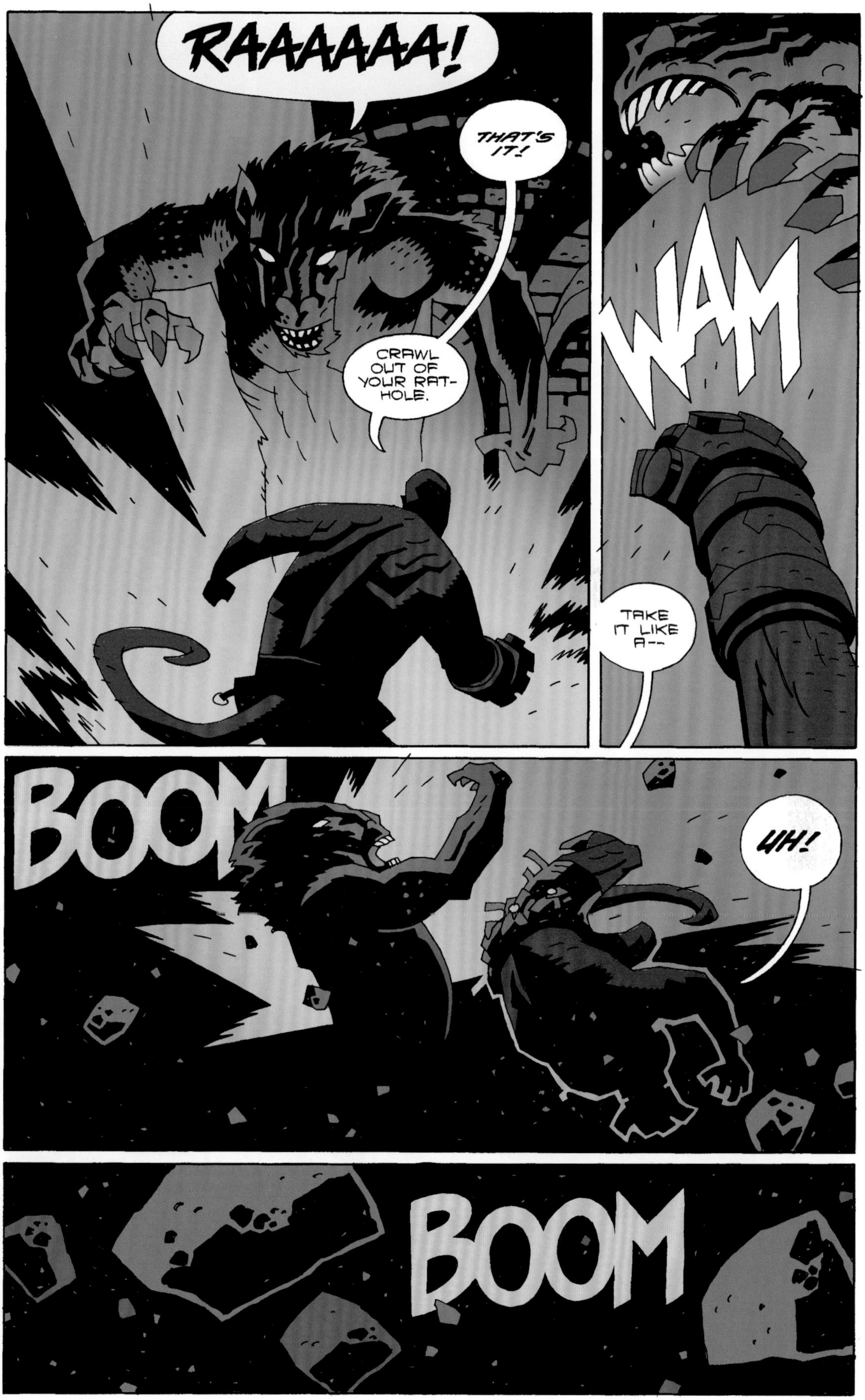
RAAAAAA!
THAT'S IT!
CRAWL OUT OF YOUR RAT-HOLE.
WAM
TAKE IT LIKE A--
BOOM
UH!
BOOM

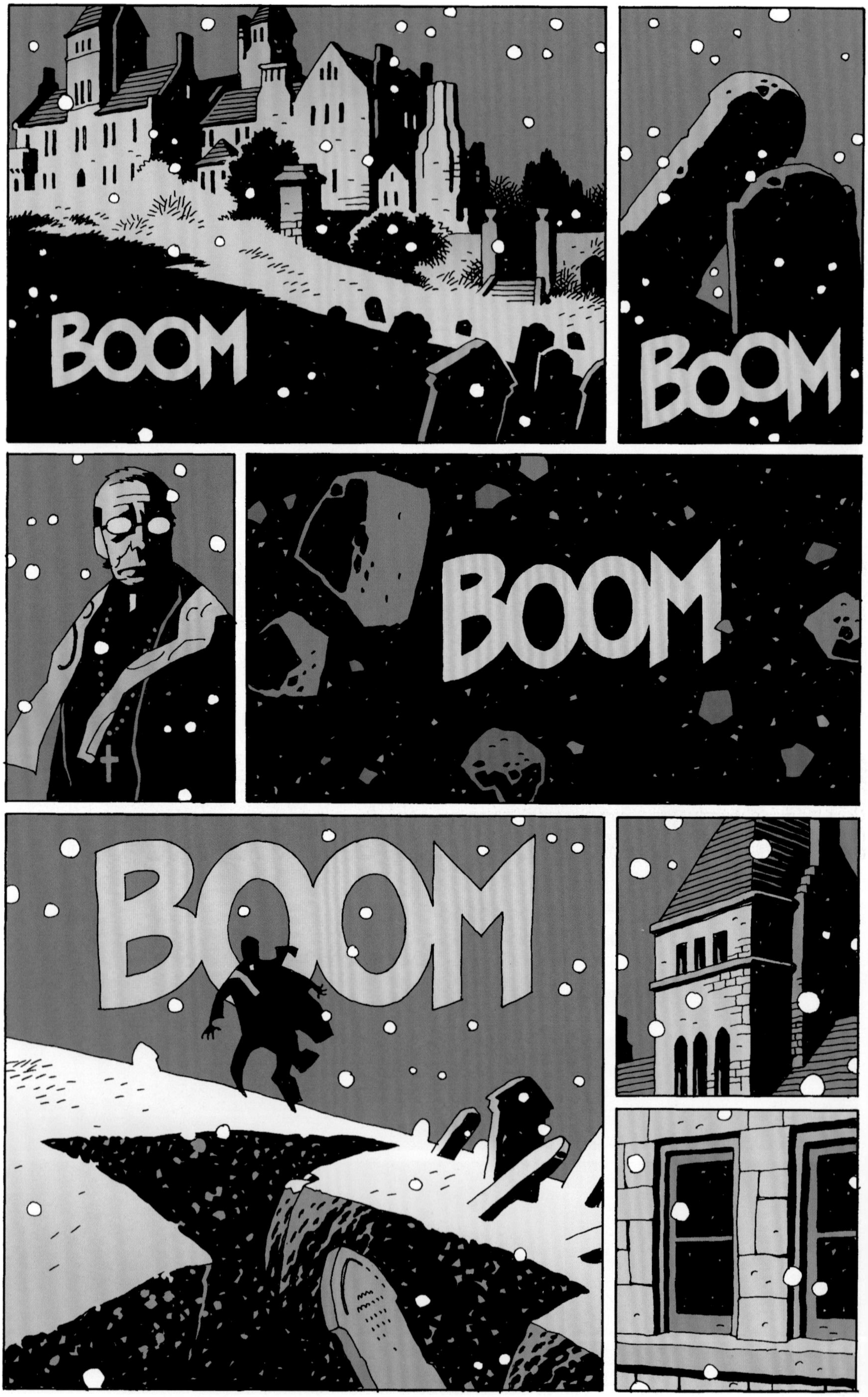
BOOM
BOOM
BOOM
BOOM

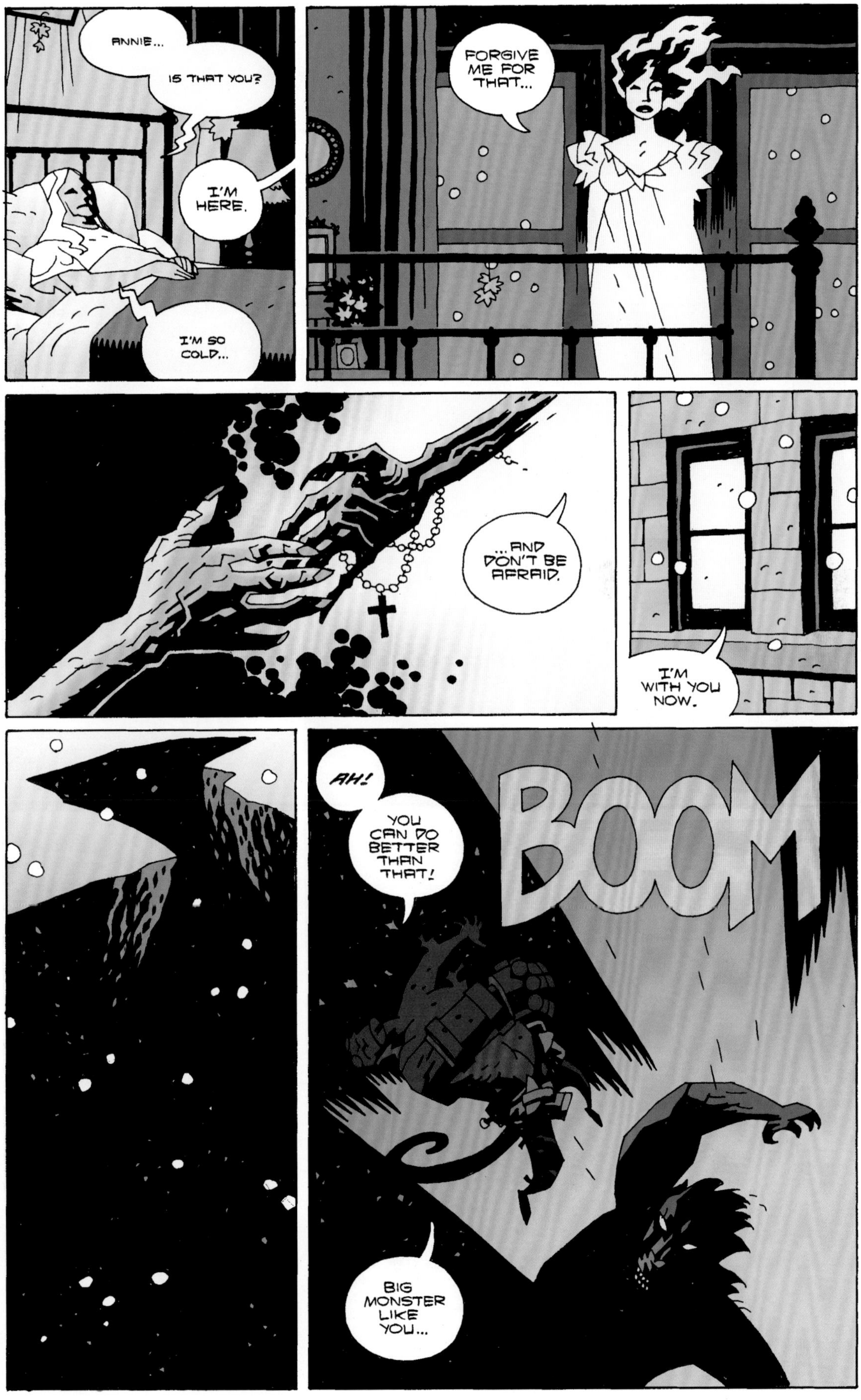
ANNIE...
IS THAT YOU?
I'M HERE.
I'M SO COLD...
FORGIVE ME FOR THAT...
...AND DON'T BE AFRAID.
I'M WITH YOU NOW.
AH!
YOU CAN DO BETTER THAN THAT!
BOOM
BIG MONSTER LIKE YOU...

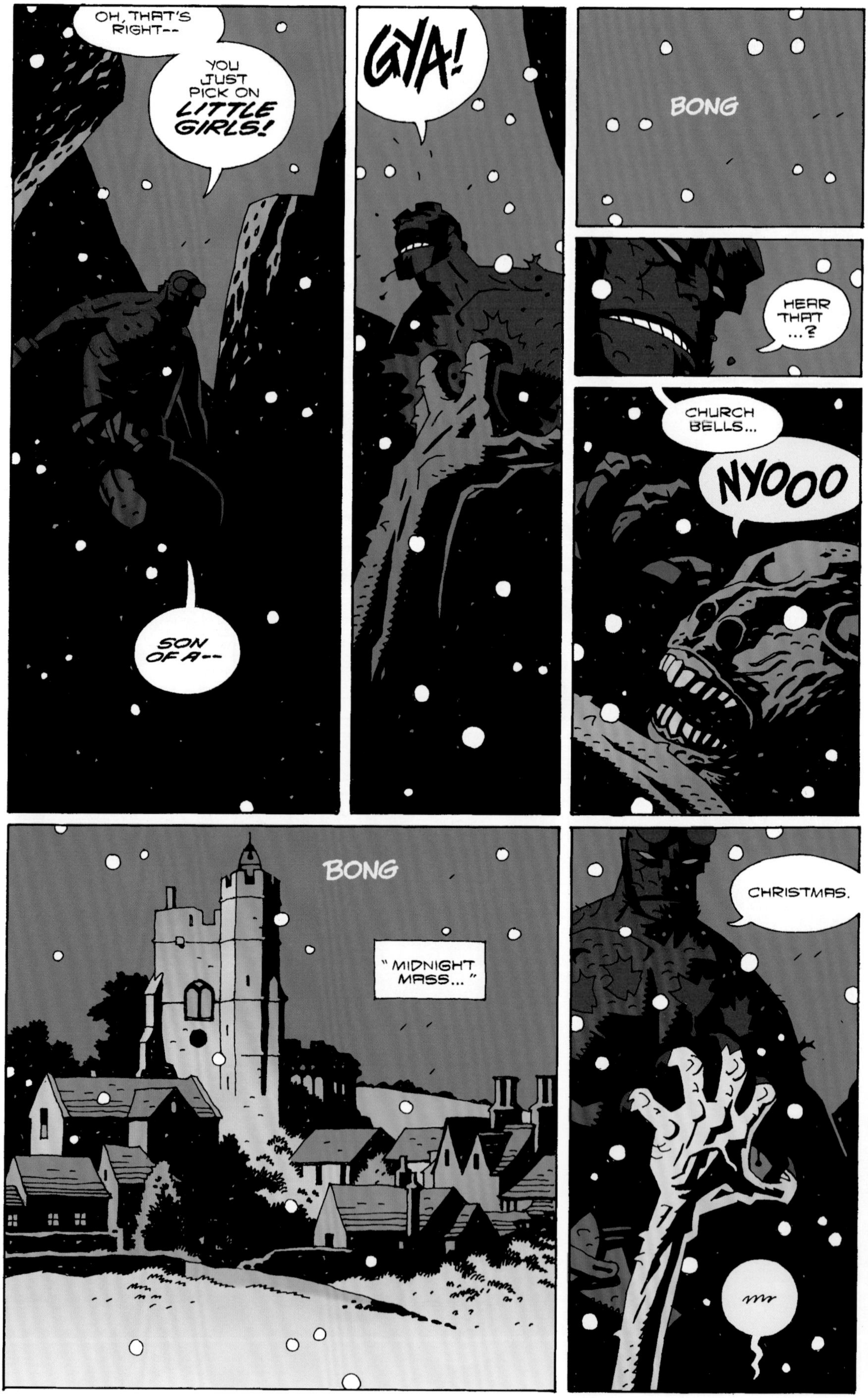
OH, THAT'S RIGHT--
YOU JUST PICK ON LITTLE GIRLS!
SON OF A--
GYA!
BONG
HEAR THAT ...?
CHURCH BELLS...
NYOOO
BONG
"MIDNIGHT MASS..."
CHRISTMAS.

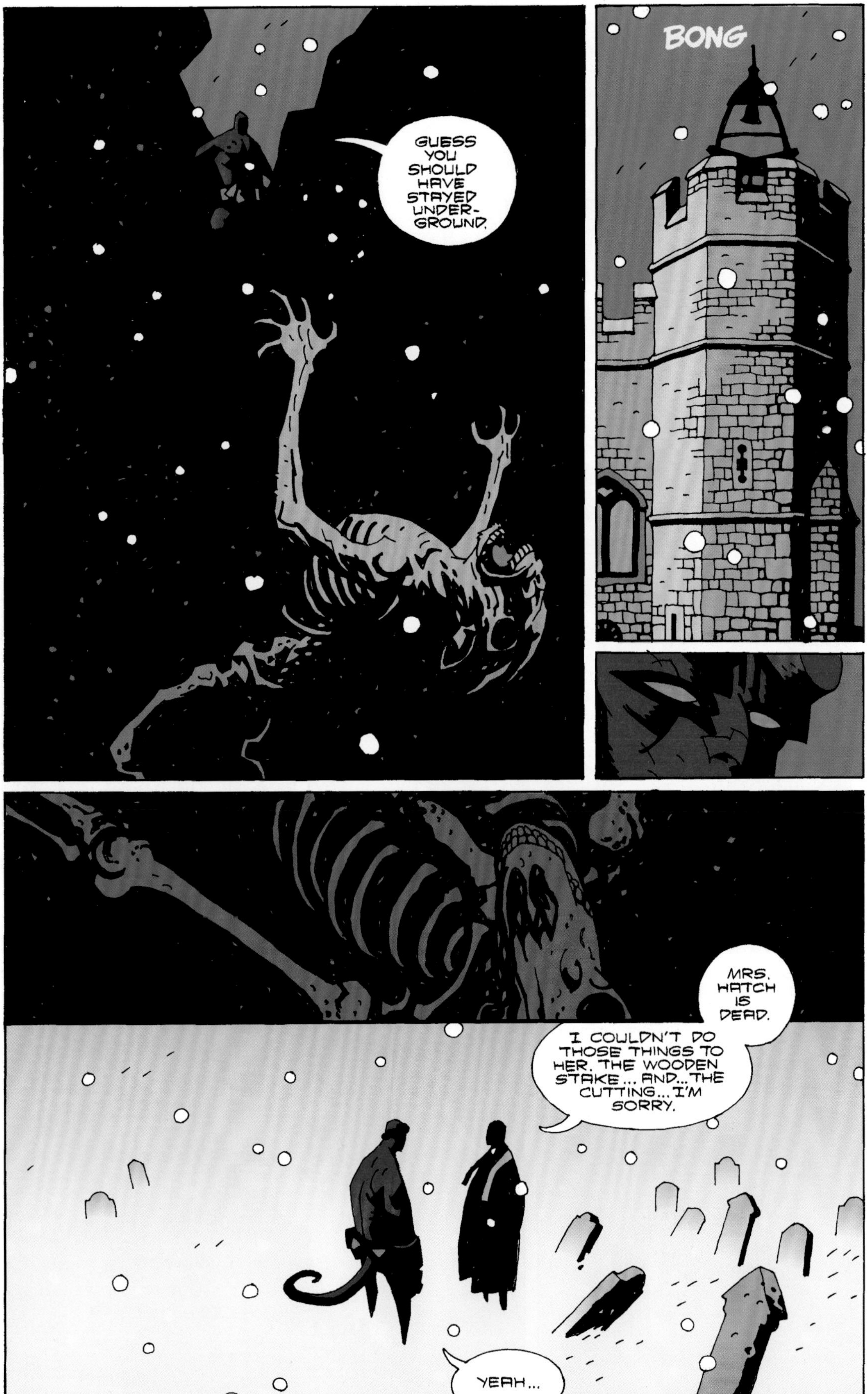
GUESS YOU SHOULD HAVE STAYED UNDER-GROUND.
BONG
MRS. HATCH IS DEAD.
I COULDN'T DO THOSE THINGS TO HER. THE WOODEN STAKE ... AND... THE CUTTING... I'M SORRY.
YEAH...

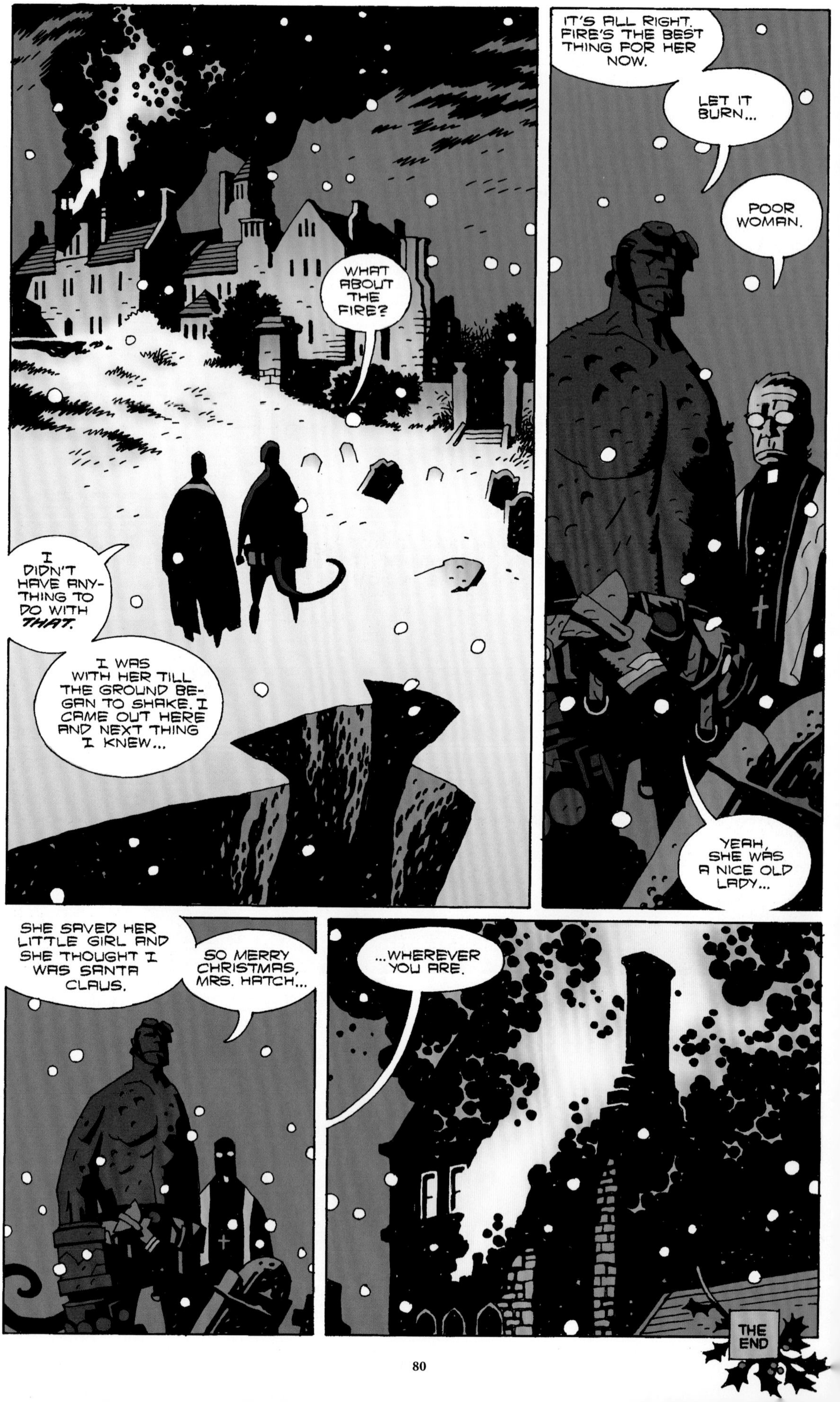
WHAT ABOUT THE FIRE?
I DIDN'T HAVE ANY-THING TO DO WITH THAT.
I WAS WITH HER TILL THE GROUND BE-GAN TO SHAKE. I CAME OUT HERE AND NEXT THING I KNEW...
IT'S ALL RIGHT. FIRE'S THE BEST THING FOR HER NOW.
LET IT BURN...
POOR WOMAN.
YEAH, SHE WAS A NICE OLD LADY...
SHE SAVED HER LITTLE GIRL AND SHE THOUGHT I WAS SANTA CLAUS.
SO MERRY CHRISTMAS, MRS. HATCH...
...WHEREVER YOU ARE.
THE END

# The Ghoul
*or*
## Reflections On Death
*and*
## The Poetry Of Worms

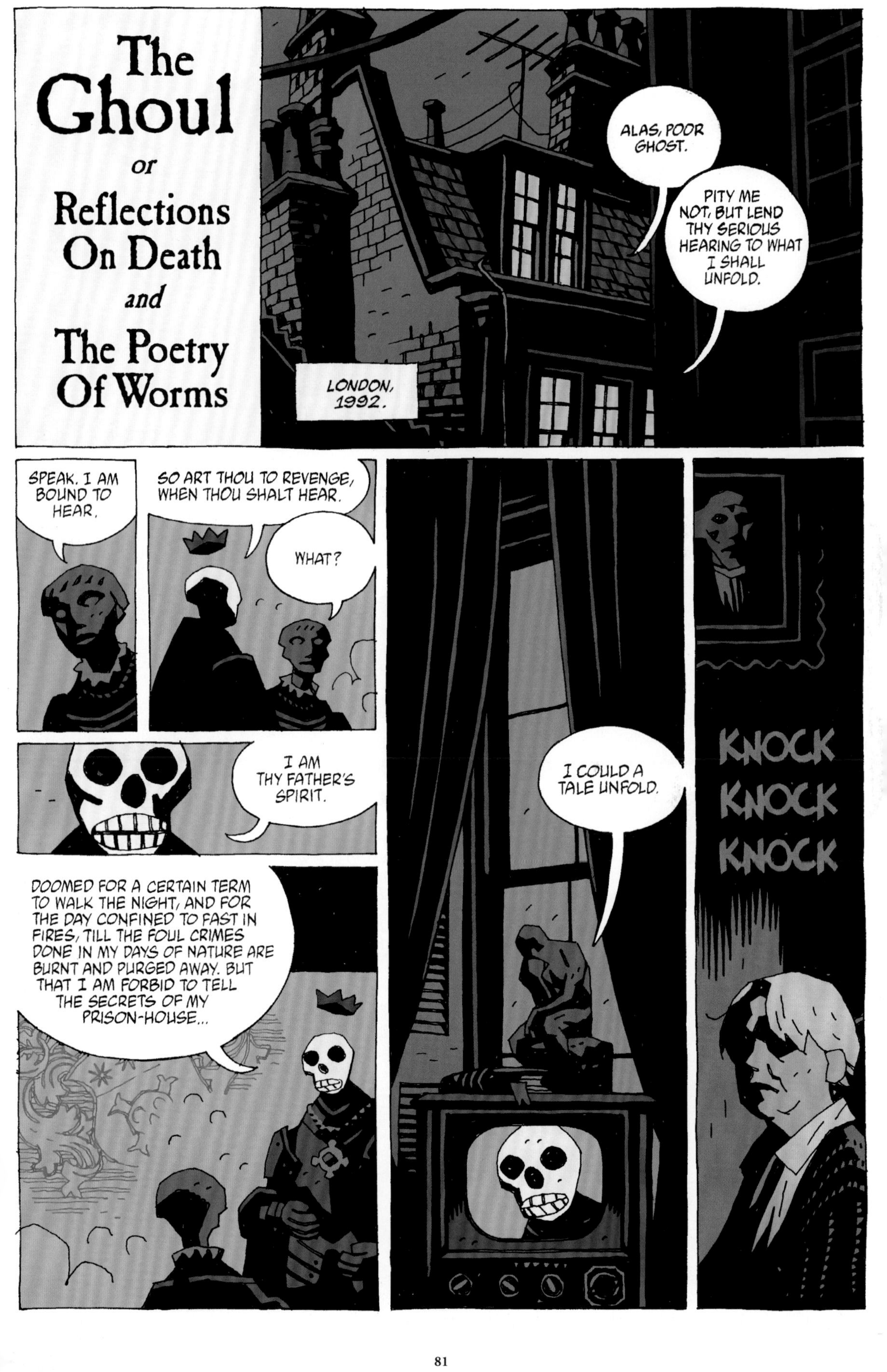

LONDON, 1992.
ALAS, POOR GHOST.
PITY ME NOT, BUT LEND THY SERIOUS HEARING TO WHAT I SHALL UNFOLD.
SPEAK. I AM BOUND TO HEAR.
SO ART THOU TO REVENGE, WHEN THOU SHALT HEAR.
WHAT?
I AM THY FATHER'S SPIRIT.
DOOMED FOR A CERTAIN TERM TO WALK THE NIGHT, AND FOR THE DAY CONFINED TO FAST IN FIRES, TILL THE FOUL CRIMES DONE IN MY DAYS OF NATURE ARE BURNT AND PURGED AWAY. BUT THAT I AM FORBID TO TELL THE SECRETS OF MY PRISON-HOUSE...
I COULD A TALE UNFOLD.
KNOCK
KNOCK
KNOCK

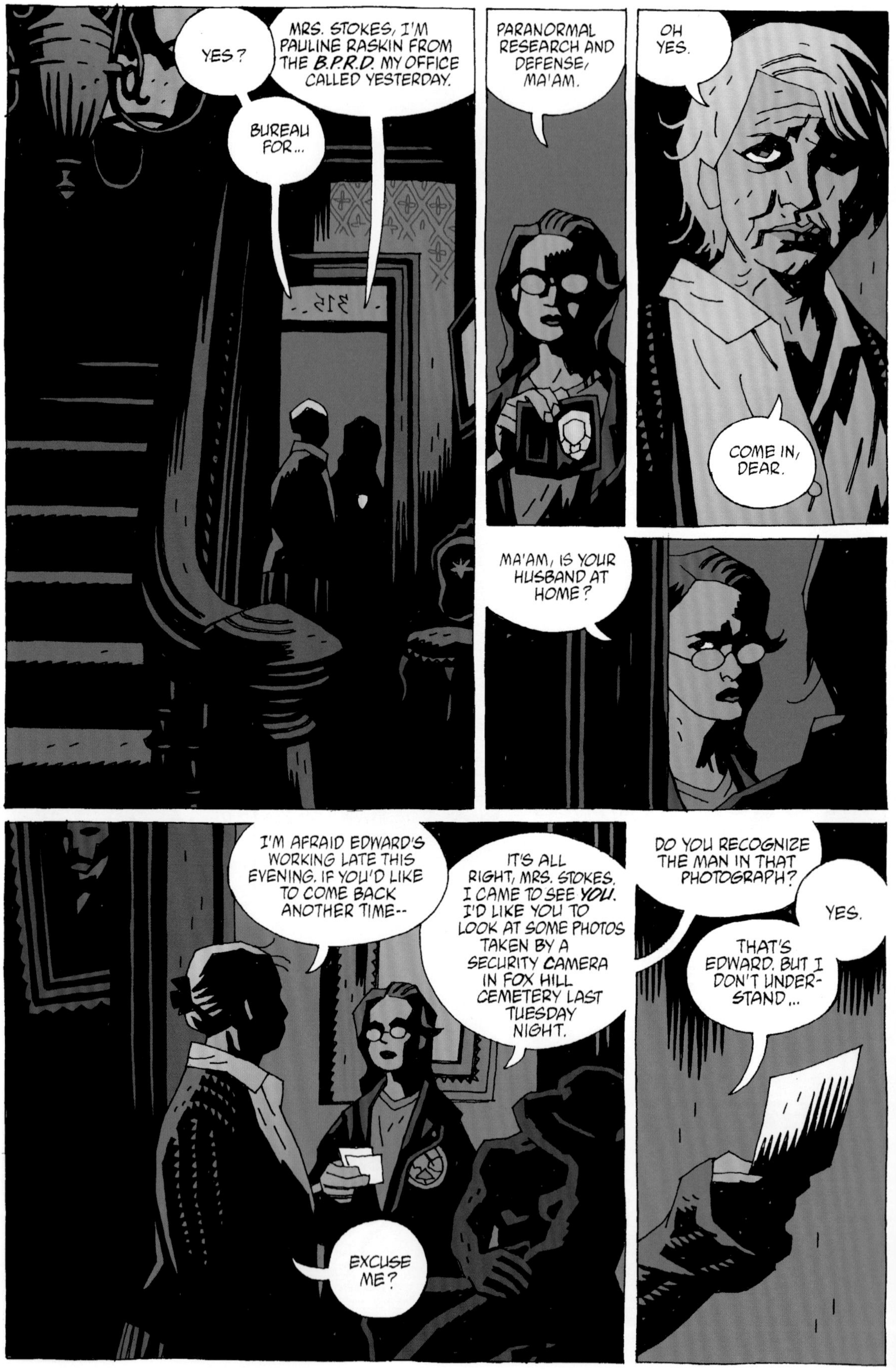
YES?
MRS. STOKES, I'M PAULINE RASKIN FROM THE B.P.R.D. MY OFFICE CALLED YESTERDAY.
BUREAU FOR...
315
PARANORMAL RESEARCH AND DEFENSE, MA'AM.
OH YES.
COME IN, DEAR.
MA'AM, IS YOUR HUSBAND AT HOME?
I'M AFRAID EDWARD'S WORKING LATE THIS EVENING. IF YOU'D LIKE TO COME BACK ANOTHER TIME--
IT'S ALL RIGHT, MRS. STOKES. I CAME TO SEE YOU. I'D LIKE YOU TO LOOK AT SOME PHOTOS TAKEN BY A SECURITY CAMERA IN FOX HILL CEMETERY LAST TUESDAY NIGHT.
EXCUSE ME?
DO YOU RECOGNIZE THE MAN IN THAT PHOTOGRAPH?
YES.
THAT'S EDWARD. BUT I DON'T UNDER-STAND...

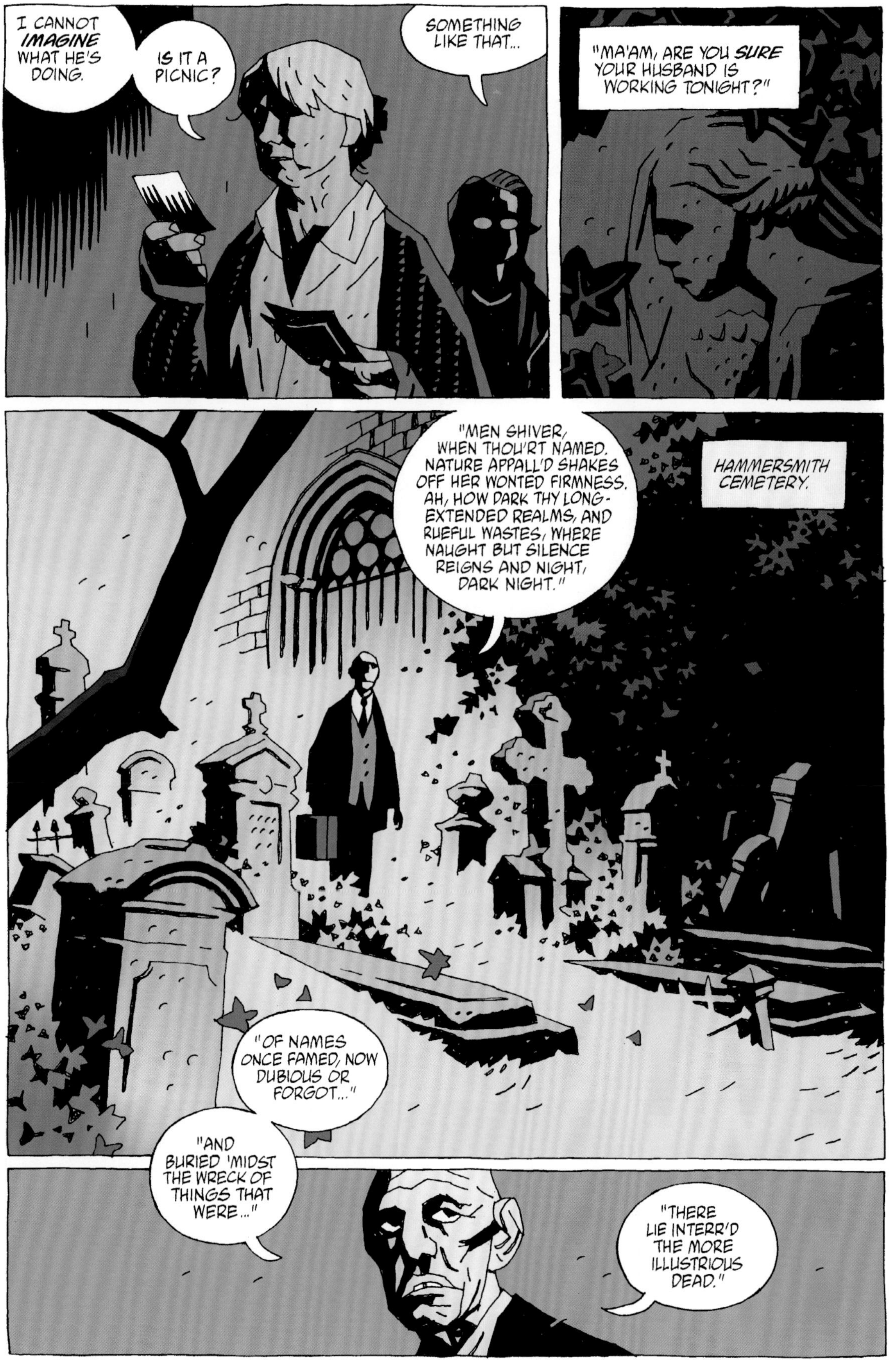
I CANNOT *IMAGINE* WHAT HE'S DOING.
IS IT A PICNIC?
SOMETHING LIKE THAT...
"MA'AM, ARE YOU *SURE* YOUR HUSBAND IS WORKING TONIGHT?"
HAMMERSMITH CEMETERY.
"MEN SHIVER, WHEN THOU'RT NAMED. NATURE APPALL'D SHAKES OFF HER WONTED FIRMNESS. AH, HOW DARK THY LONG-EXTENDED REALMS, AND RUEFUL WASTES, WHERE NAUGHT BUT SILENCE REIGNS AND NIGHT, DARK NIGHT."
"OF NAMES ONCE FAMED, NOW DUBIOUS OR FORGOT..."
"AND BURIED 'MIDST THE WRECK OF THINGS THAT WERE..."
"THERE LIE INTERR'D THE MORE ILLUSTRIOUS DEAD."

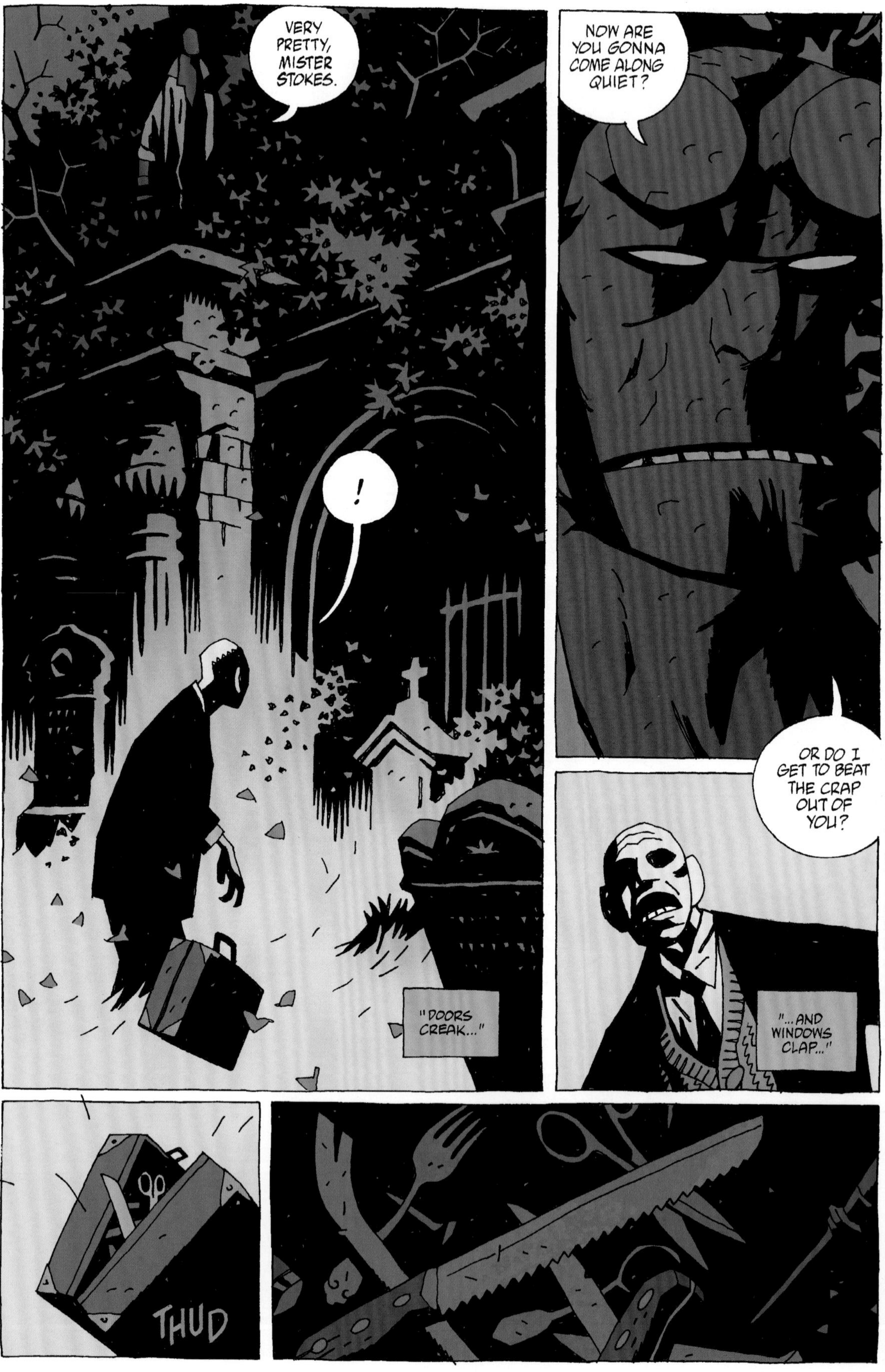
VERY PRETTY, MISTER STOKES.
!
"DOORS CREAK..."
NOW ARE YOU GONNA COME ALONG QUIET?
OR DO I GET TO BEAT THE CRAP OUT OF YOU?
"...AND WINDOWS CLAP..."
THUD

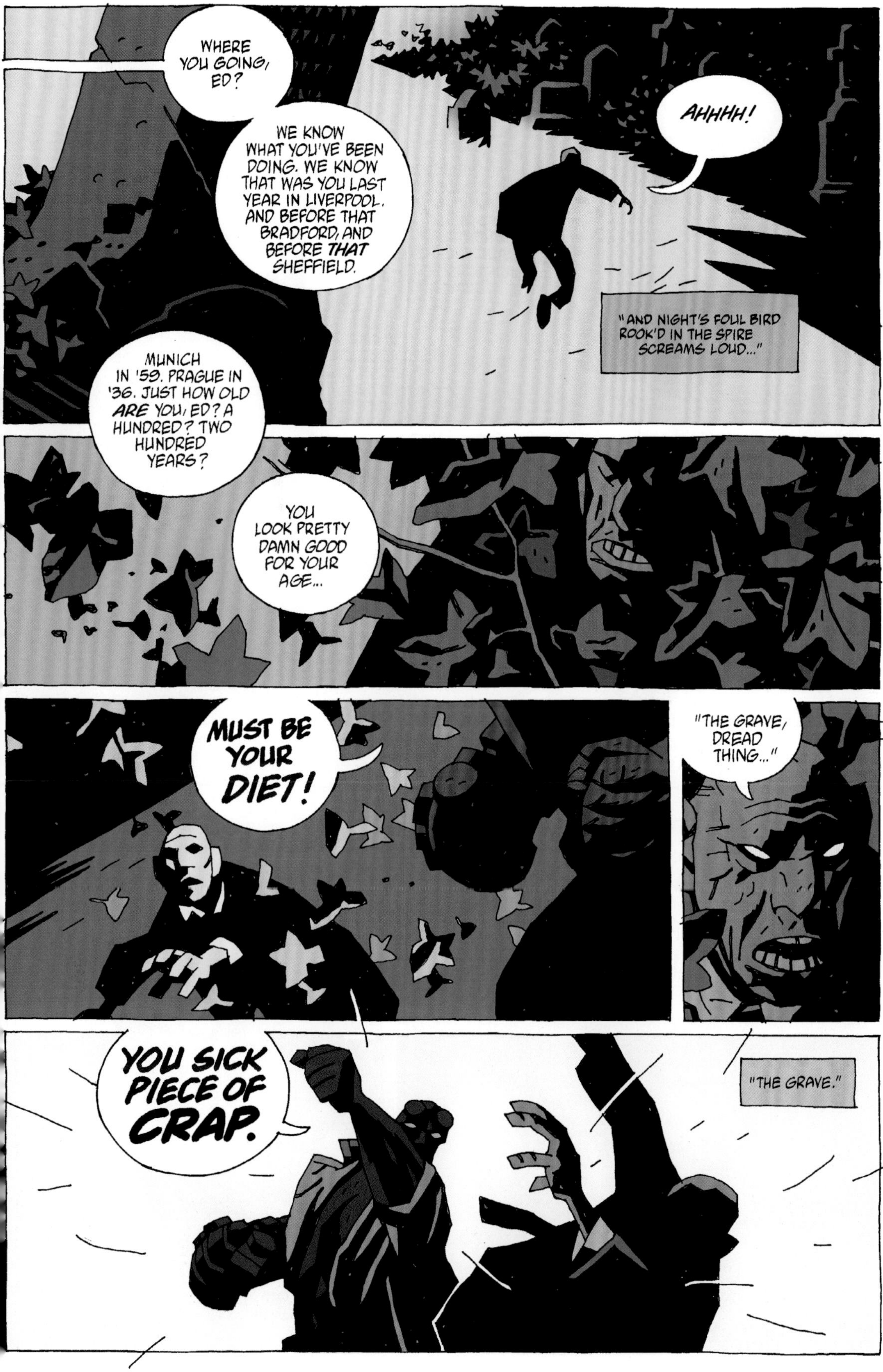
WHERE YOU GOING, ED?
WE KNOW WHAT YOU'VE BEEN DOING. WE KNOW THAT WAS YOU LAST YEAR IN LIVERPOOL, AND BEFORE THAT BRADFORD, AND BEFORE THAT SHEFFIELD.
AHHHH!
"AND NIGHT'S FOUL BIRD ROOK'D IN THE SPIRE SCREAMS LOUD..."
MUNICH IN '59. PRAGUE IN '36. JUST HOW OLD ARE YOU, ED? A HUNDRED? TWO HUNDRED YEARS?
YOU LOOK PRETTY DAMN GOOD FOR YOUR AGE...
MUST BE YOUR DIET!
"THE GRAVE, DREAD THING..."
YOU SICK PIECE OF CRAP.
"THE GRAVE."

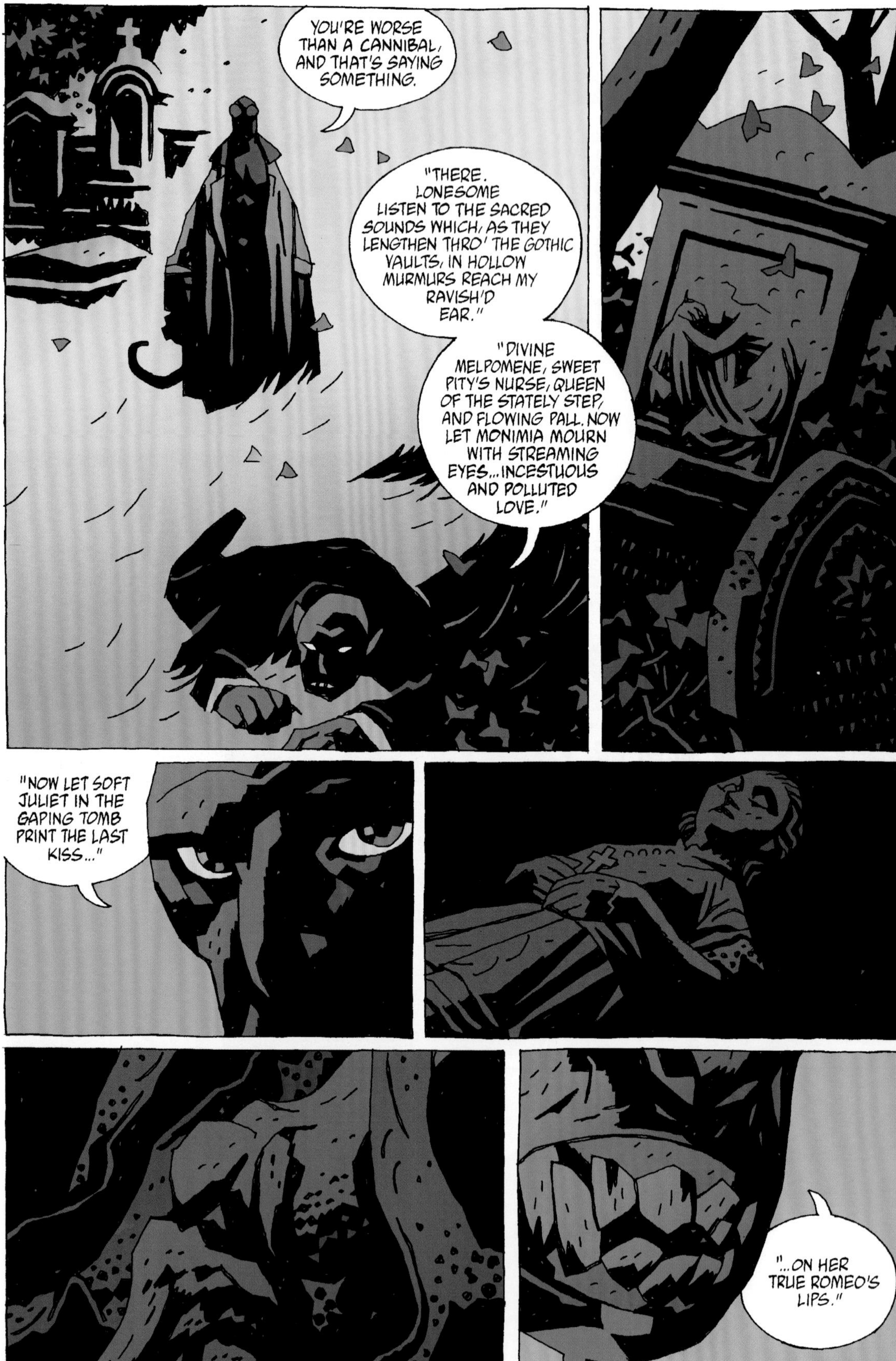
YOU'RE WORSE THAN A CANNIBAL, AND THAT'S SAYING SOMETHING.
"THERE. LONESOME LISTEN TO THE SACRED SOUNDS WHICH, AS THEY LENGTHEN THRO' THE GOTHIC VAULTS, IN HOLLOW MURMURS REACH MY RAVISH'D EAR."
"DIVINE MELPOMENE, SWEET PITY'S NURSE, QUEEN OF THE STATELY STEP, AND FLOWING PALL. NOW LET MONIMIA MOURN WITH STREAMING EYES... INCESTUOUS AND POLLUTED LOVE."
"NOW LET SOFT JULIET IN THE GAPING TOMB PRINT THE LAST KISS..."
"...ON HER TRUE ROMEO'S LIPS."

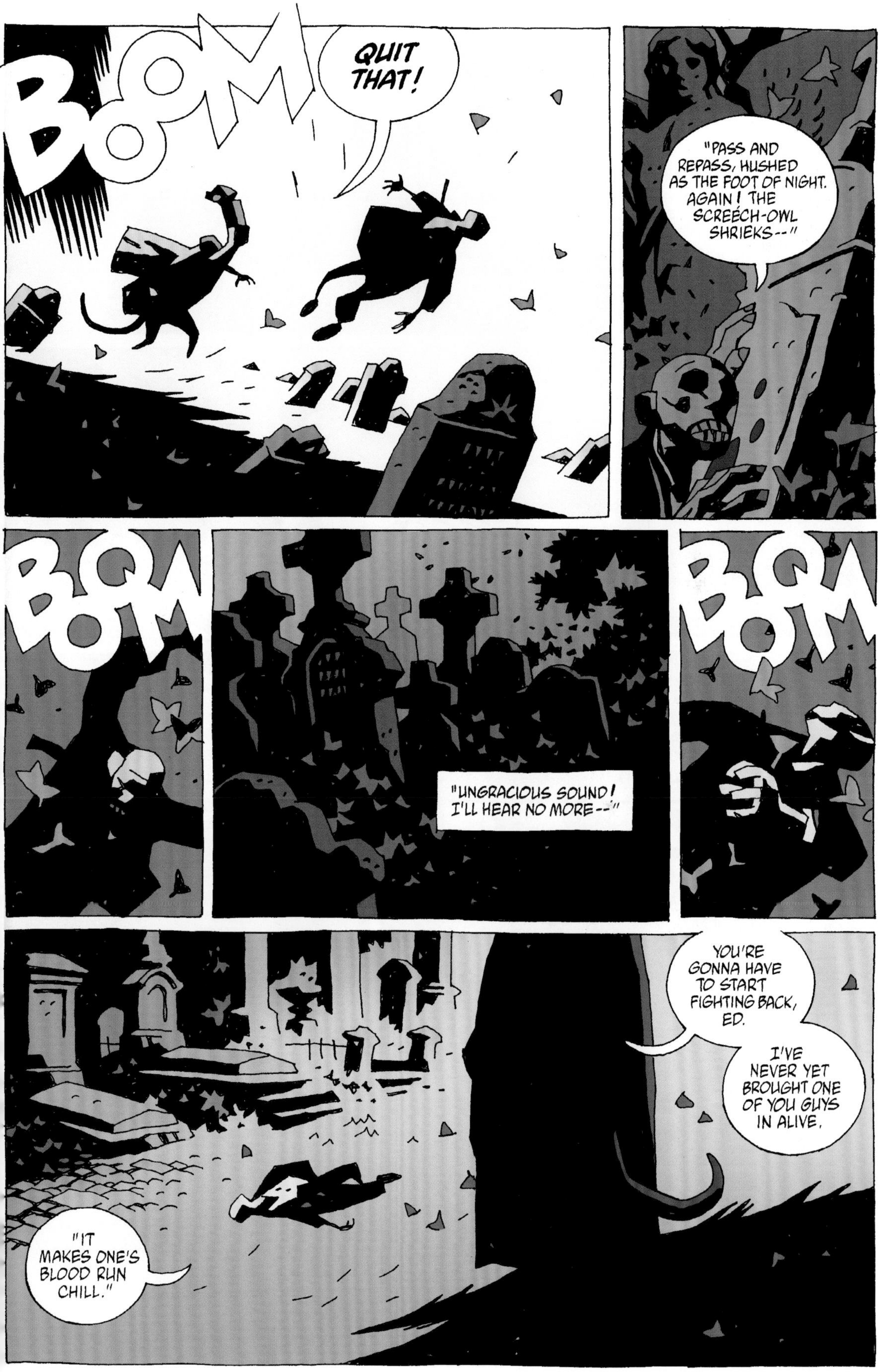
BOOM
QUIT THAT!
"PASS AND REPASS, HUSHED AS THE FOOT OF NIGHT. AGAIN! THE SCREECH-OWL SHRIEKS--"
BOOM
"UNGRACIOUS SOUND! I'LL HEAR NO MORE--"
BOOM
YOU'RE GONNA HAVE TO START FIGHTING BACK, ED.
I'VE NEVER YET BROUGHT ONE OF YOU GUYS IN ALIVE.
"IT MAKES ONE'S BLOOD RUN CHILL."

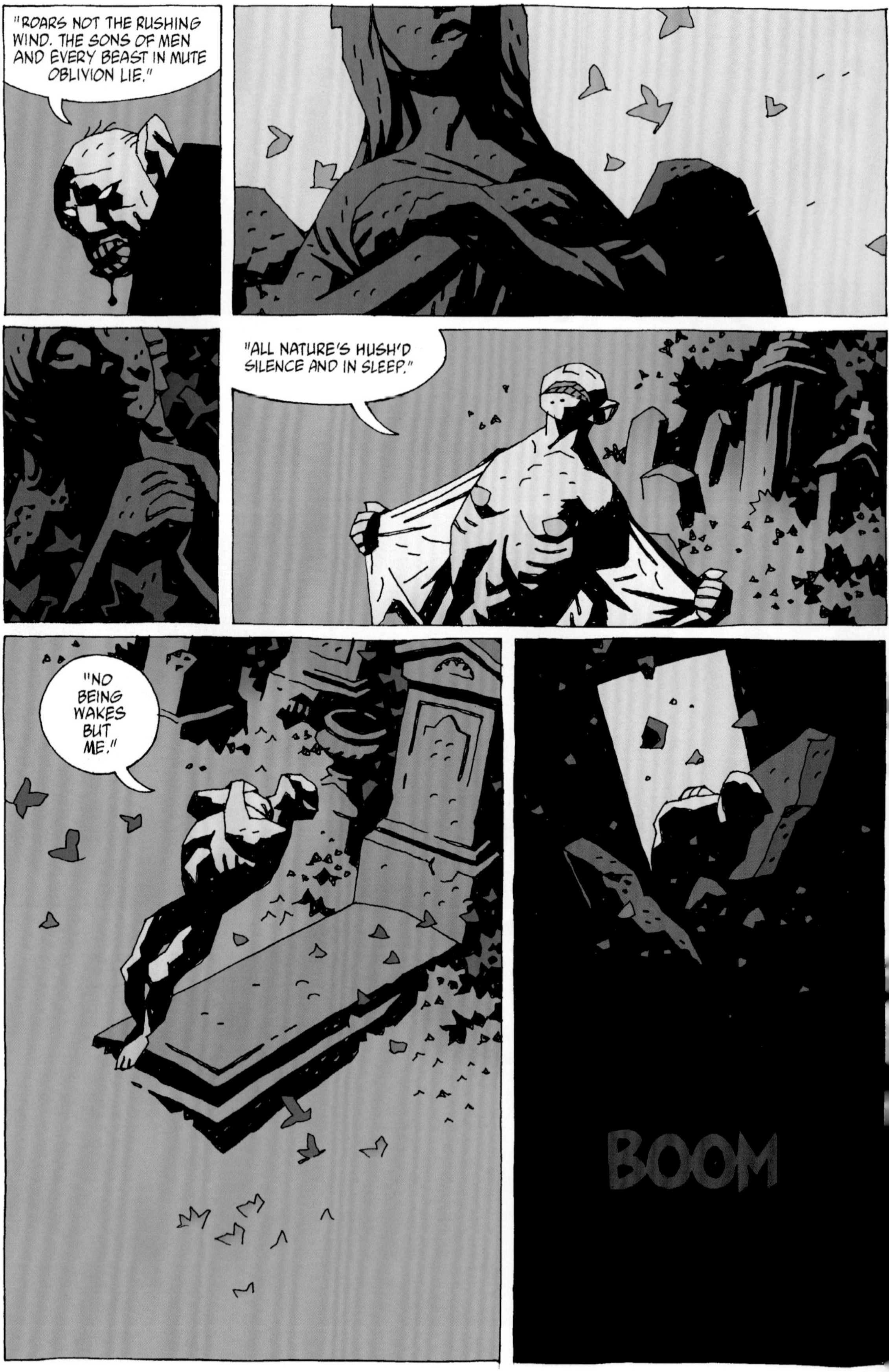
"ROARS NOT THE RUSHING WIND. THE SONS OF MEN AND EVERY BEAST IN MUTE OBLIVION LIE."
"ALL NATURE'S HUSH'D SILENCE AND IN SLEEP."
"NO BEING WAKES BUT ME."
BOOM

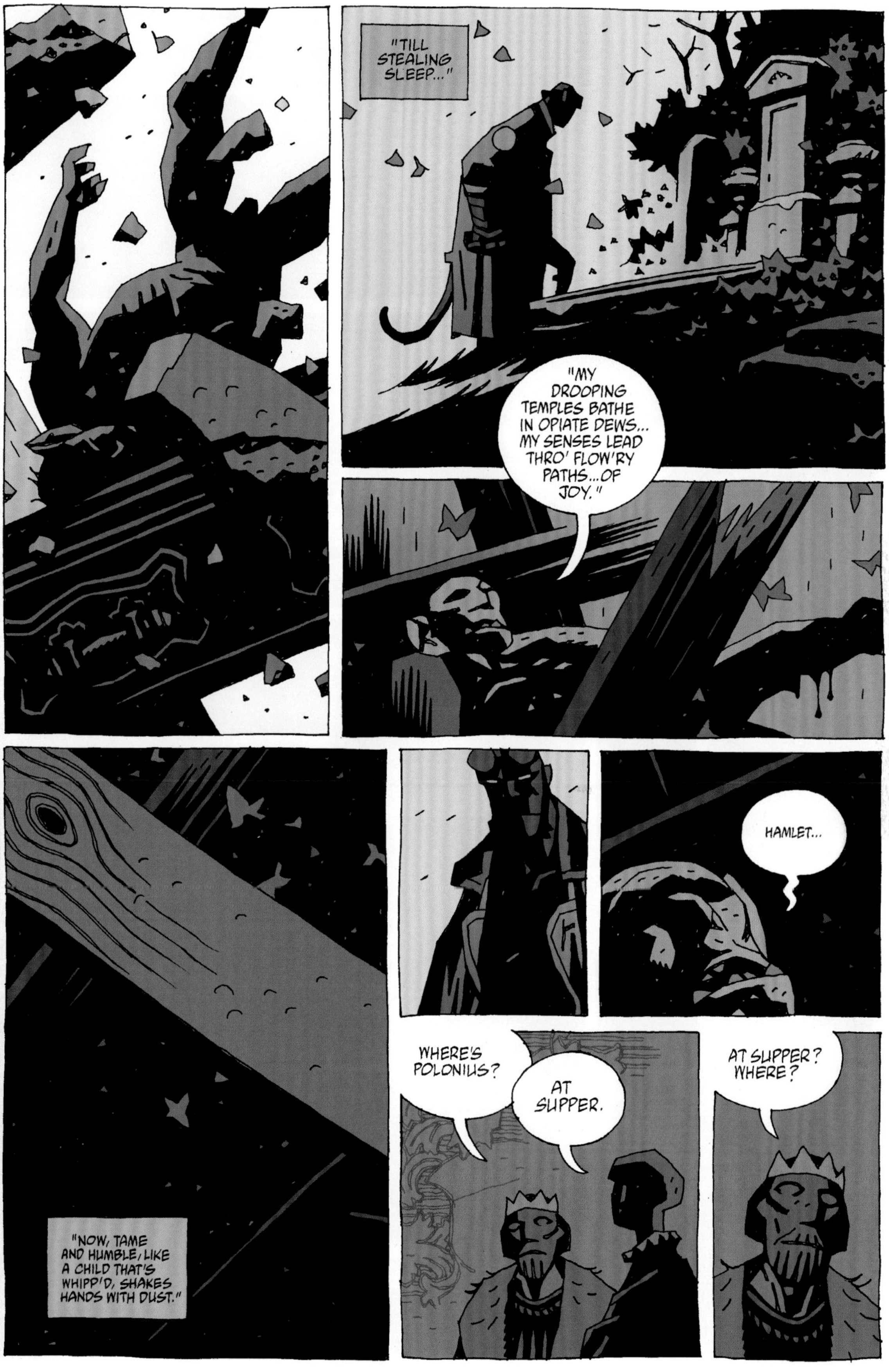

"TILL STEALING SLEEP..."
"MY DROOPING TEMPLES BATHE IN OPIATE DEWS... MY SENSES LEAD THRO' FLOW'RY PATHS...OF JOY."
"NOW, TAME AND HUMBLE, LIKE A CHILD THAT'S WHIPP'D, SHAKES HANDS WITH DUST."
HAMLET...
WHERE'S POLONIUS?
AT SUPPER.
AT SUPPER? WHERE?

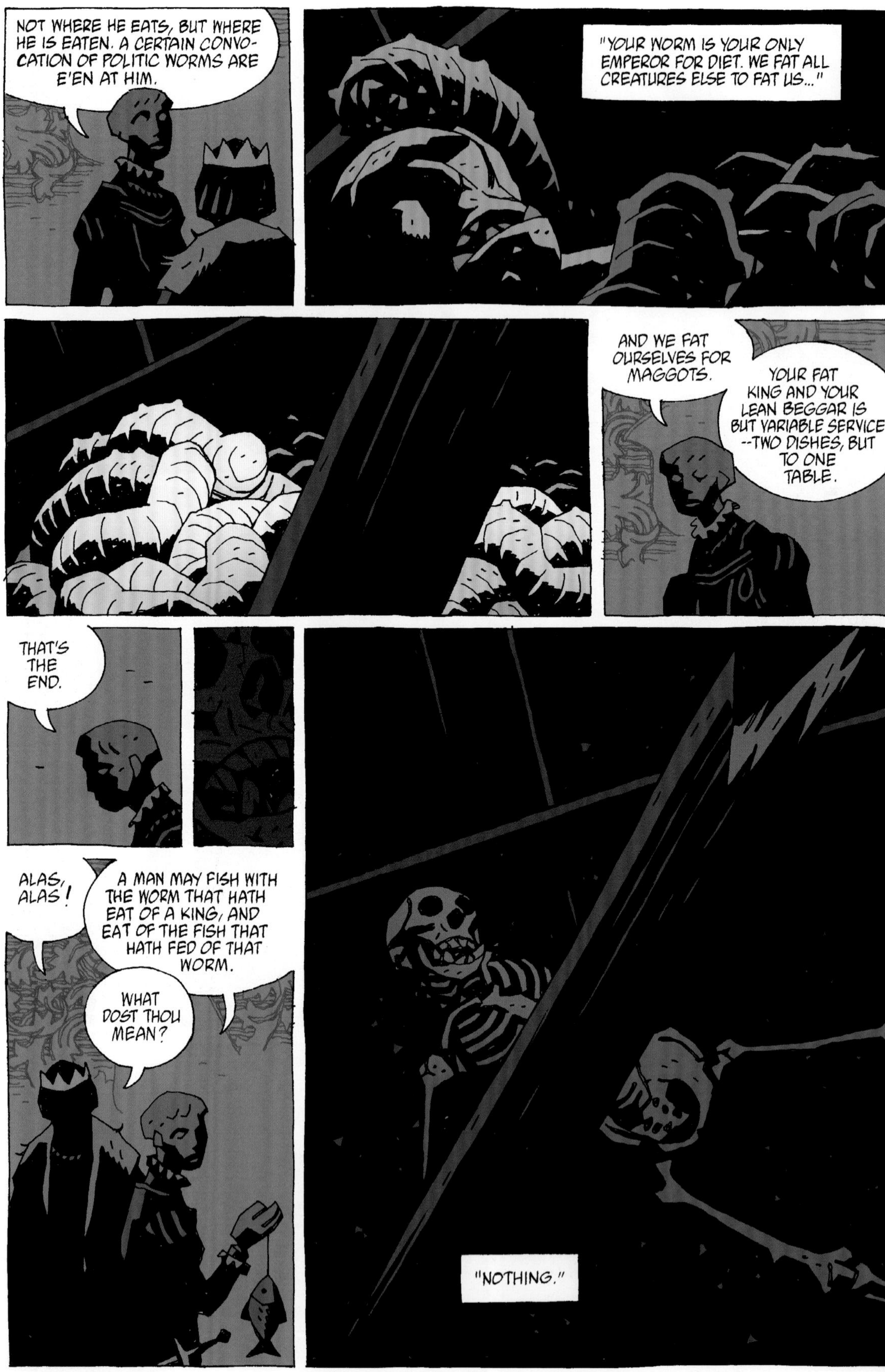
NOT WHERE HE EATS, BUT WHERE HE IS EATEN. A CERTAIN CONVOCATION OF POLITIC WORMS ARE E'EN AT HIM.
"YOUR WORM IS YOUR ONLY EMPEROR FOR DIET. WE FAT ALL CREATURES ELSE TO FAT US..."
AND WE FAT OURSELVES FOR MAGGOTS.
YOUR FAT KING AND YOUR LEAN BEGGAR IS BUT VARIABLE SERVICE --TWO DISHES, BUT TO ONE TABLE.
THAT'S THE END.
ALAS, ALAS!
A MAN MAY FISH WITH THE WORM THAT HATH EAT OF A KING, AND EAT OF THE FISH THAT HATH FED OF THAT WORM.
WHAT DOST THOU MEAN?
"NOTHING."

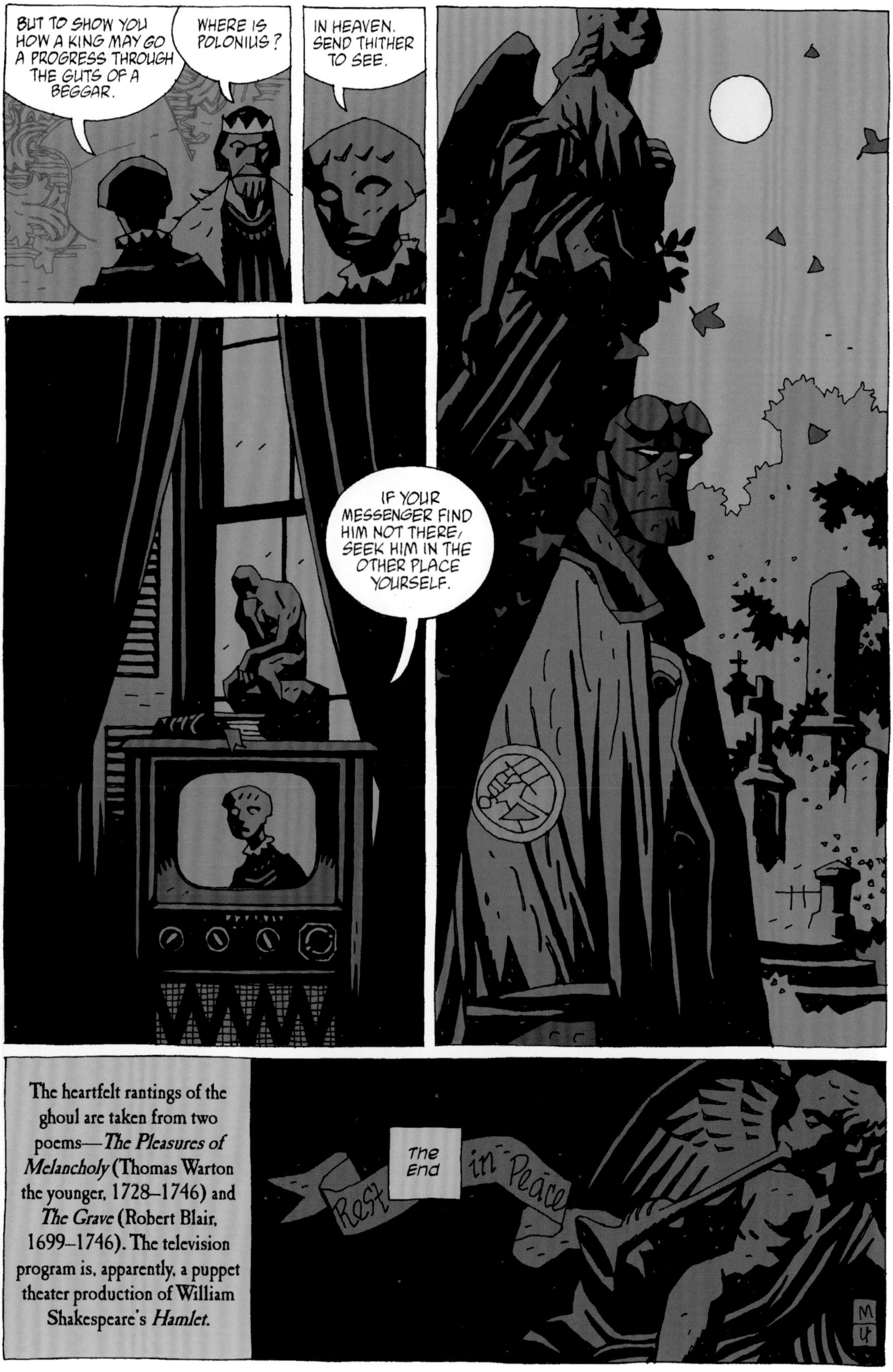
BUT TO SHOW YOU HOW A KING MAY GO A PROGRESS THROUGH THE GUTS OF A BEGGAR.
WHERE IS POLONIUS?
IN HEAVEN. SEND THITHER TO SEE.
IF YOUR MESSENGER FIND HIM NOT THERE, SEEK HIM IN THE OTHER PLACE YOURSELF.
The heartfelt rantings of the ghoul are taken from two poems—*The Pleasures of Melancholy* (Thomas Warton the younger, 1728–1746) and *The Grave* (Robert Blair, 1699–1746). The television program is, apparently, a puppet theater production of William Shakespeare's *Hamlet*.
Rest in Peace
The End

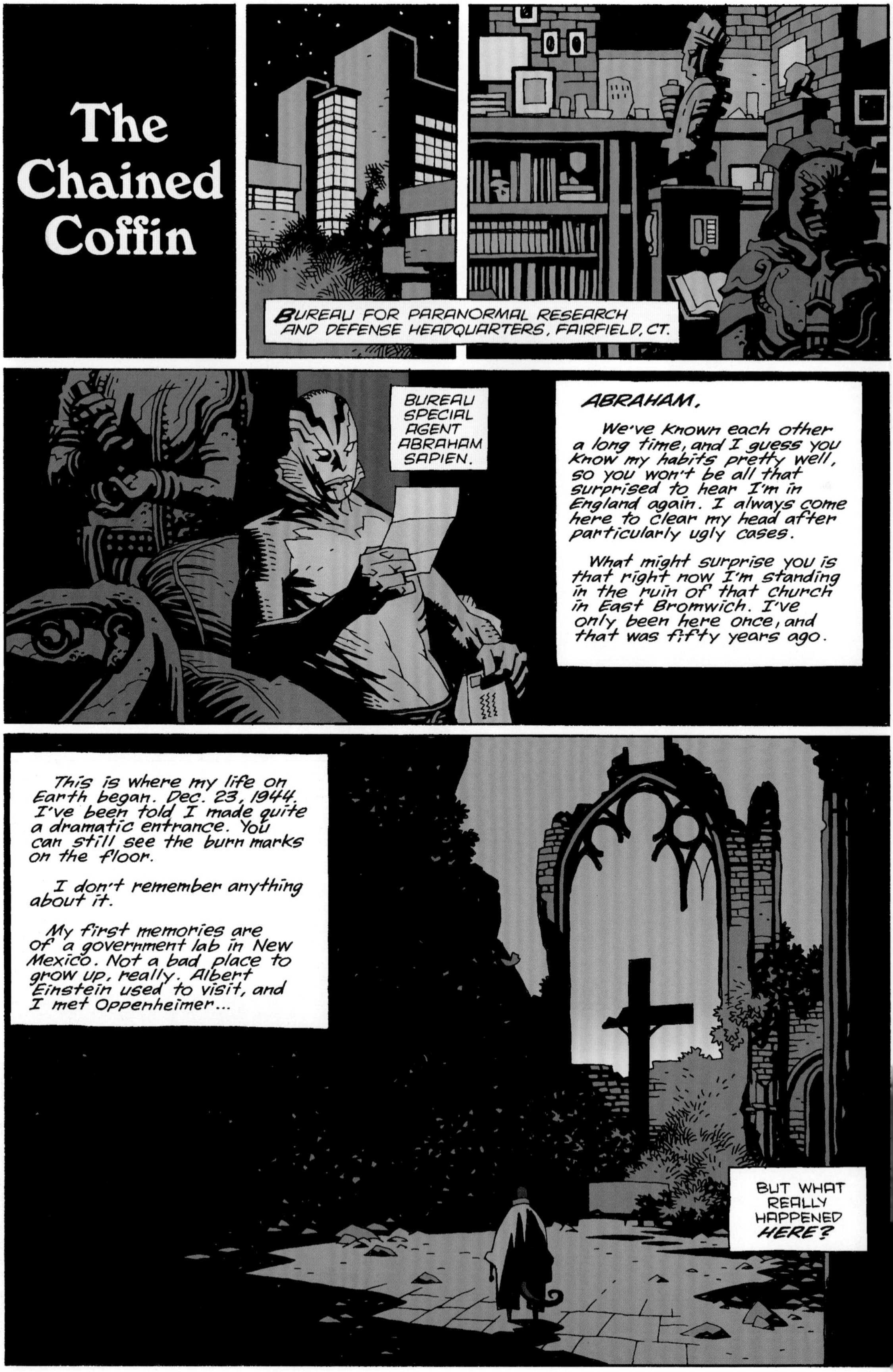
The Chained Coffin
BUREAU FOR PARANORMAL RESEARCH AND DEFENSE HEADQUARTERS, FAIRFIELD, CT.
BUREAU SPECIAL AGENT ABRAHAM SAPIEN.
ABRAHAM,
We've known each other a long time, and I guess you know my habits pretty well, so you won't be all that surprised to hear I'm in England again. I always come here to clear my head after particularly ugly cases.
What might surprise you is that right now I'm standing in the ruin of that church in East Bromwich. I've only been here once, and that was fifty years ago.
This is where my life on Earth began. Dec. 23, 1944. I've been told I made quite a dramatic entrance. You can still see the burn marks on the floor.
I don't remember anything about it.
My first memories are of a government lab in New Mexico. Not a bad place to grow up, really. Albert Einstein used to visit, and I met Oppenheimer...
BUT WHAT REALLY HAPPENED HERE?

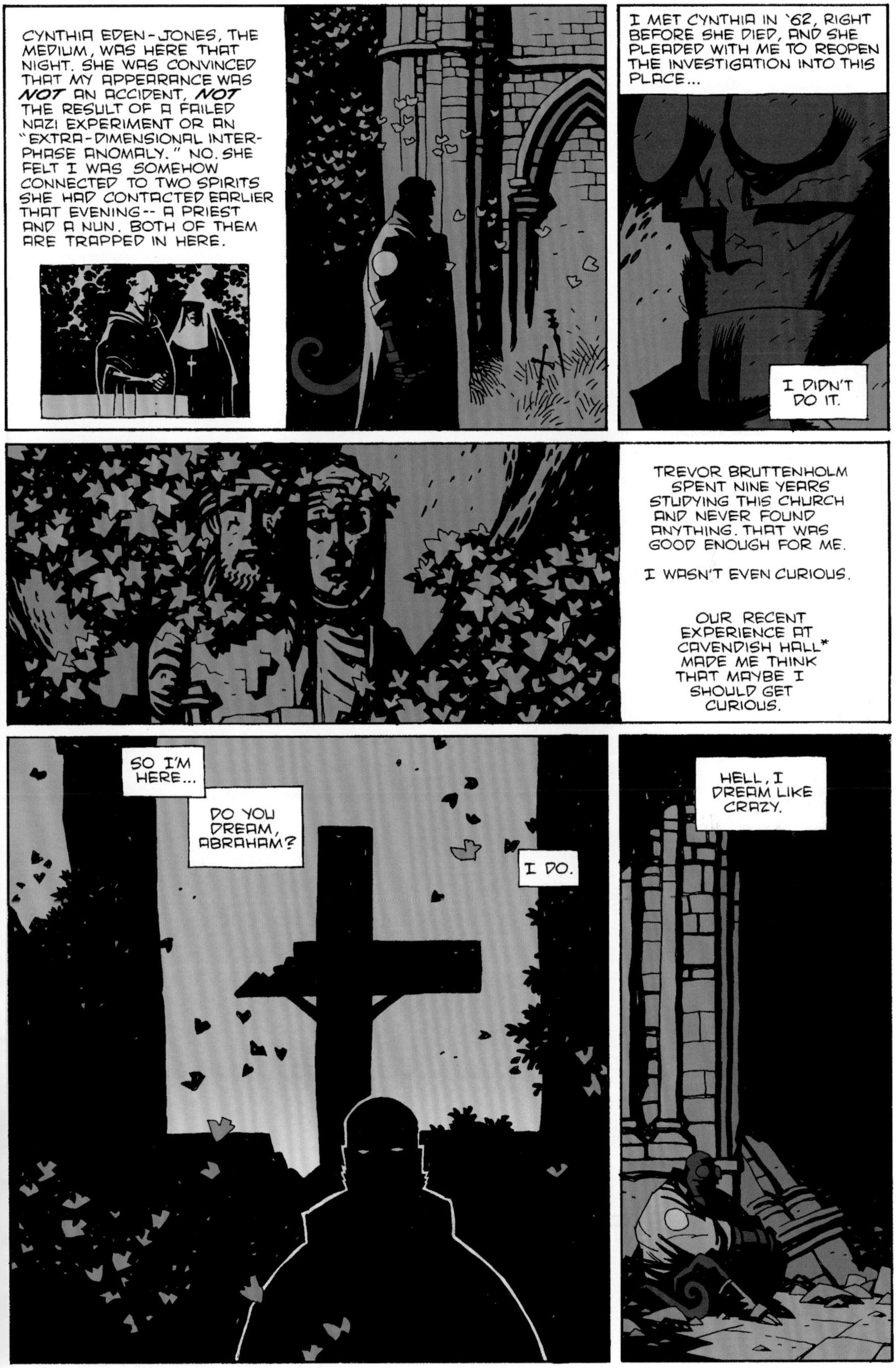
CYNTHIA EDEN-JONES, THE MEDIUM, WAS HERE THAT NIGHT. SHE WAS CONVINCED THAT MY APPEARANCE WAS NOT AN ACCIDENT, NOT THE RESULT OF A FAILED NAZI EXPERIMENT OR AN "EXTRA-DIMENSIONAL INTER-PHASE ANOMALY." NO. SHE FELT I WAS SOMEHOW CONNECTED TO TWO SPIRITS SHE HAD CONTACTED EARLIER THAT EVENING-- A PRIEST AND A NUN. BOTH OF THEM ARE TRAPPED IN HERE.
I MET CYNTHIA IN '62, RIGHT BEFORE SHE DIED, AND SHE PLEADED WITH ME TO REOPEN THE INVESTIGATION INTO THIS PLACE...
I DIDN'T DO IT.
TREVOR BRUTTENHOLM SPENT NINE YEARS STUDYING THIS CHURCH AND NEVER FOUND ANYTHING. THAT WAS GOOD ENOUGH FOR ME.
I WASN'T EVEN CURIOUS.
OUR RECENT EXPERIENCE AT CAVENDISH HALL* MADE ME THINK THAT MAYBE I SHOULD GET CURIOUS.
SO I'M HERE...
DO YOU DREAM, ABRAHAM?
I DO.
HELL, I DREAM LIKE CRAZY.

* *HELLBOY: SEED OF DESTRUCTION*

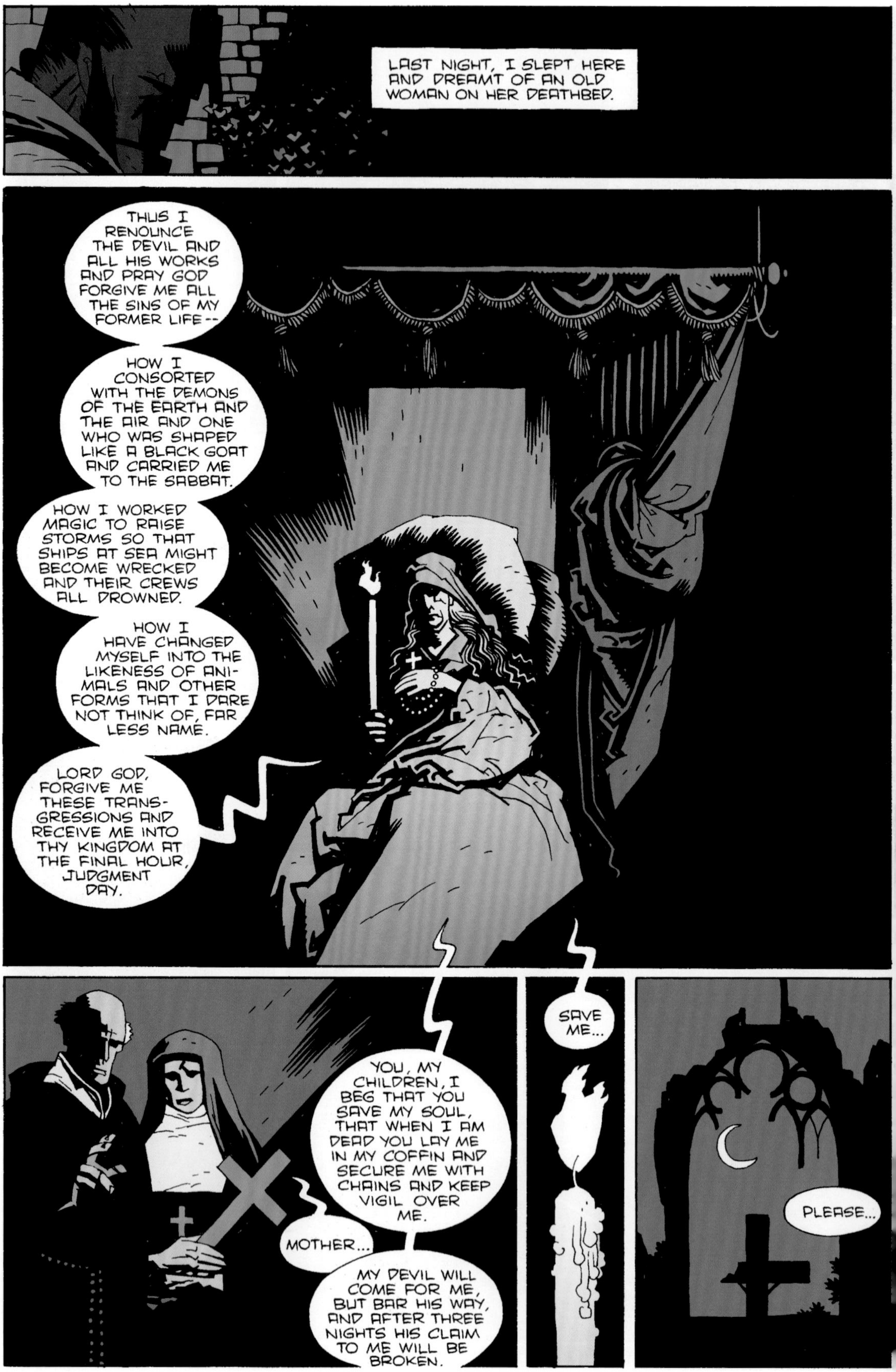
LAST NIGHT, I SLEPT HERE AND DREAMT OF AN OLD WOMAN ON HER DEATHBED.
THUS I RENOUNCE THE DEVIL AND ALL HIS WORKS AND PRAY GOD FORGIVE ME ALL THE SINS OF MY FORMER LIFE--
HOW I CONSORTED WITH THE DEMONS OF THE EARTH AND THE AIR AND ONE WHO WAS SHAPED LIKE A BLACK GOAT AND CARRIED ME TO THE SABBAT.
HOW I WORKED MAGIC TO RAISE STORMS SO THAT SHIPS AT SEA MIGHT BECOME WRECKED AND THEIR CREWS ALL DROWNED.
HOW I HAVE CHANGED MYSELF INTO THE LIKENESS OF ANI-MALS AND OTHER FORMS THAT I DARE NOT THINK OF, FAR LESS NAME.
LORD GOD, FORGIVE ME THESE TRANS-GRESSIONS AND RECEIVE ME INTO THY KINGDOM AT THE FINAL HOUR, JUDGMENT DAY.
YOU, MY CHILDREN, I BEG THAT YOU SAVE MY SOUL, THAT WHEN I AM DEAD YOU LAY ME IN MY COFFIN AND SECURE ME WITH CHAINS AND KEEP VIGIL OVER ME.
MOTHER...
MY DEVIL WILL COME FOR ME, BUT BAR HIS WAY, AND AFTER THREE NIGHTS HIS CLAIM TO ME WILL BE BROKEN.
SAVE ME...
PLEASE...

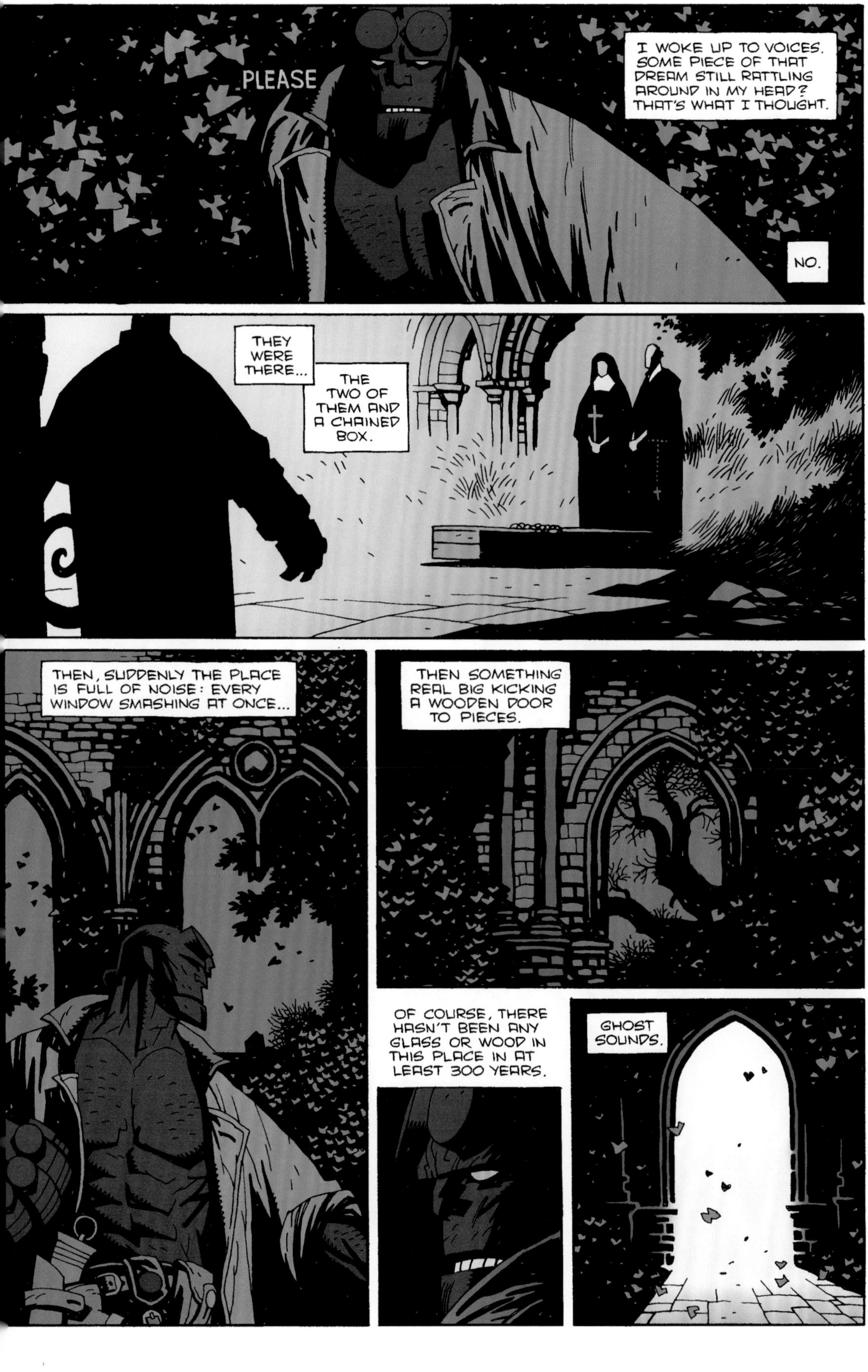
PLEASE
I WOKE UP TO VOICES. SOME PIECE OF THAT DREAM STILL RATTLING AROUND IN MY HEAD? THAT'S WHAT I THOUGHT.
NO.
THEY WERE THERE...
THE TWO OF THEM AND A CHAINED BOX.
THEN, SUDDENLY THE PLACE IS FULL OF NOISE: EVERY WINDOW SMASHING AT ONCE...
THEN SOMETHING REAL BIG KICKING A WOODEN DOOR TO PIECES.
OF COURSE, THERE HASN'T BEEN ANY GLASS OR WOOD IN THIS PLACE IN AT LEAST 300 YEARS.
GHOST SOUNDS.

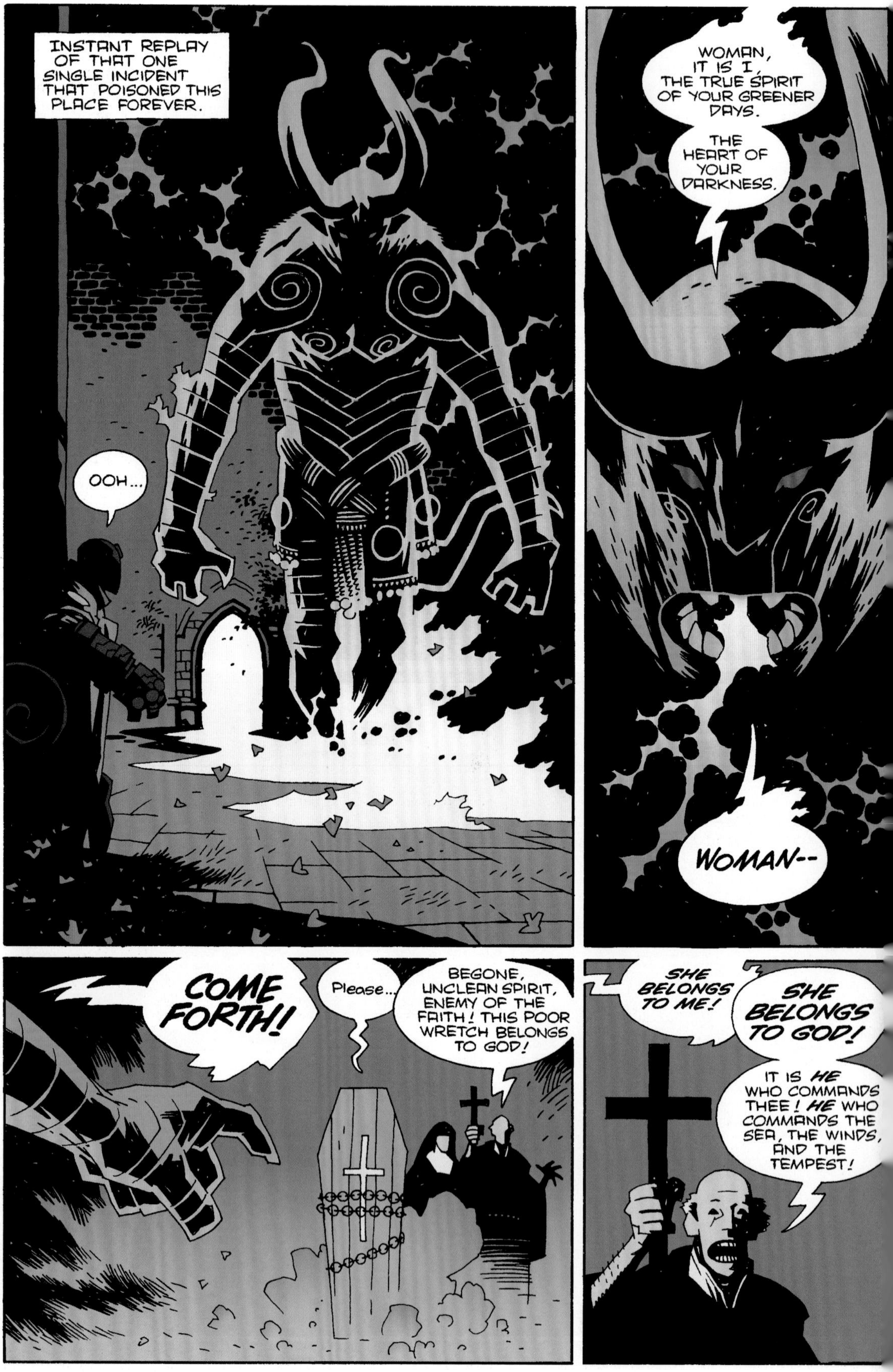
INSTANT REPLAY OF THAT ONE SINGLE INCIDENT THAT POISONED THIS PLACE FOREVER.
OOH...
WOMAN, IT IS I, THE TRUE SPIRIT OF YOUR GREENER DAYS.
THE HEART OF YOUR DARKNESS.
WOMAN--
COME FORTH!
Please...
BEGONE, UNCLEAN SPIRIT, ENEMY OF THE FAITH! THIS POOR WRETCH BELONGS TO GOD!
SHE BELONGS TO ME!
SHE BELONGS TO GOD!
IT IS HE WHO COMMANDS THEE! HE WHO COMMANDS THE SEA, THE WINDS, AND THE TEMPEST!

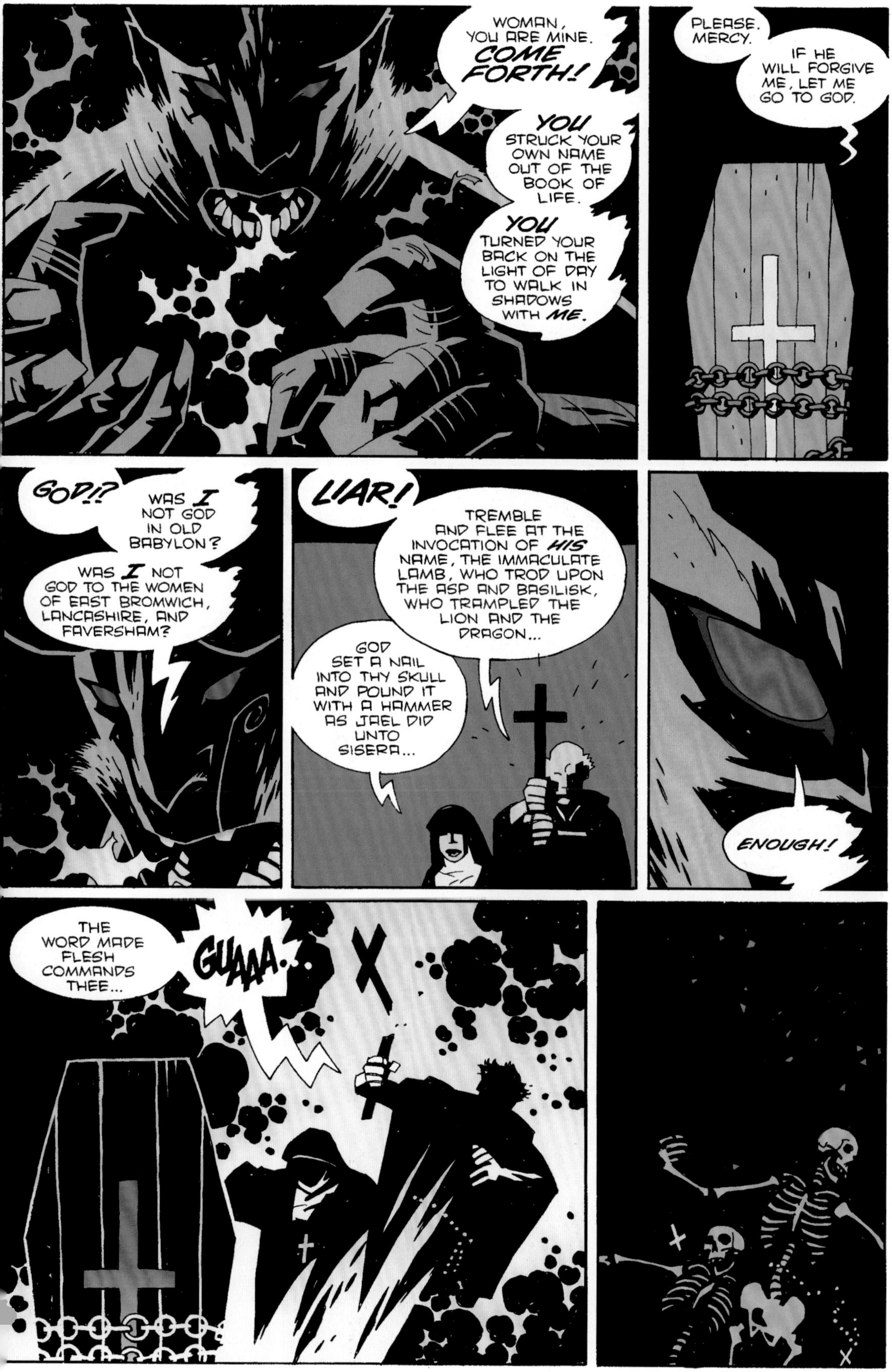
WOMAN, YOU ARE MINE. COME FORTH!
YOU STRUCK YOUR OWN NAME OUT OF THE BOOK OF LIFE.
YOU TURNED YOUR BACK ON THE LIGHT OF DAY TO WALK IN SHADOWS WITH ME.
PLEASE. MERCY.
IF HE WILL FORGIVE ME, LET ME GO TO GOD.
GOD!?
WAS I NOT GOD IN OLD BABYLON?
WAS I NOT GOD TO THE WOMEN OF EAST BROMWICH, LANCASHIRE, AND FAVERSHAM?
LIAR!
TREMBLE AND FLEE AT THE INVOCATION OF HIS NAME, THE IMMACULATE LAMB, WHO TROD UPON THE ASP AND BASILISK, WHO TRAMPLED THE LION AND THE DRAGON...
GOD SET A NAIL INTO THY SKULL AND POUND IT WITH A HAMMER AS JAEL DID UNTO SISERA...
ENOUGH!
THE WORD MADE FLESH COMMANDS THEE...
GUAAA...

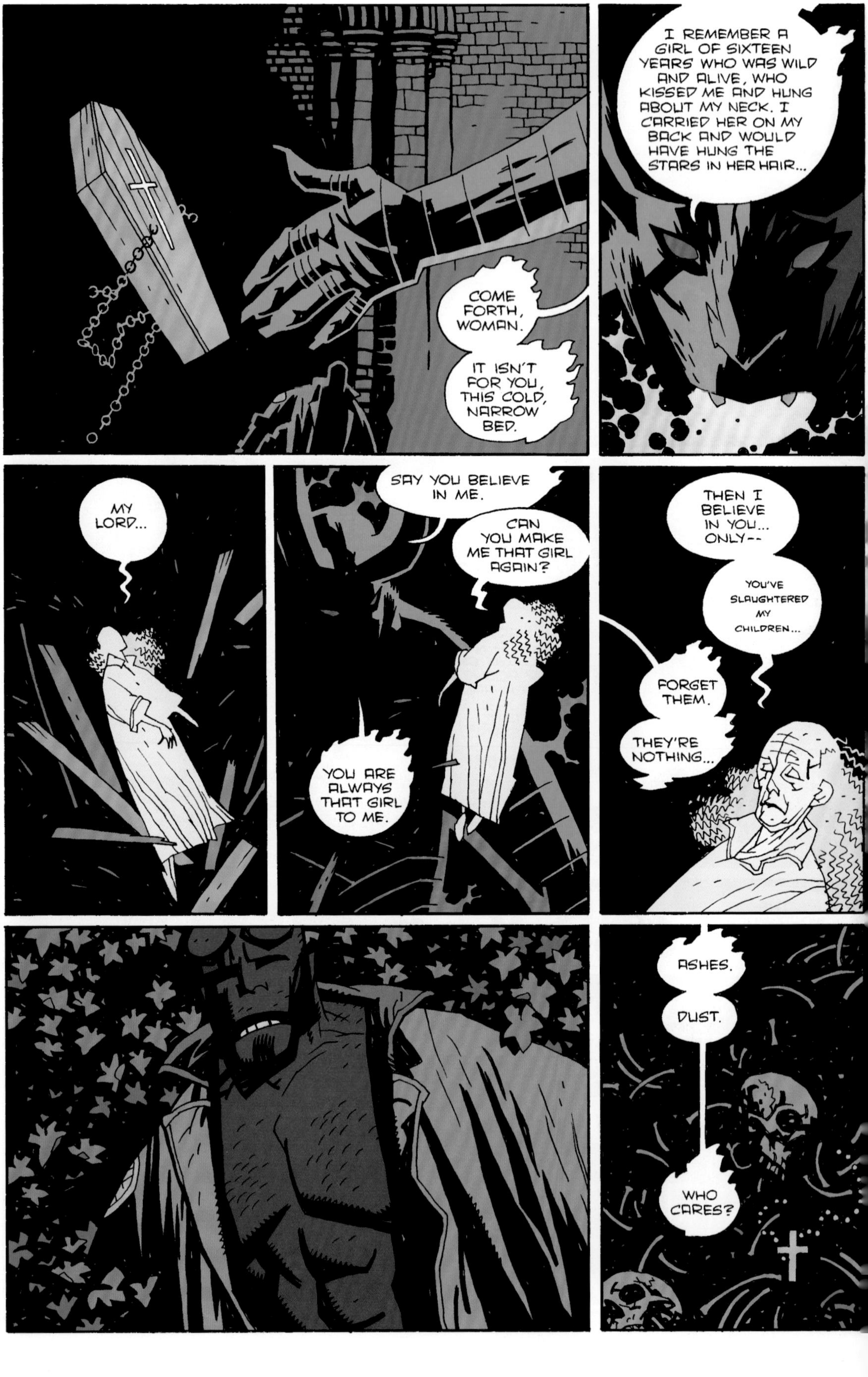
I REMEMBER A GIRL OF SIXTEEN YEARS WHO WAS WILD AND ALIVE, WHO KISSED ME AND HUNG ABOUT MY NECK. I CARRIED HER ON MY BACK AND WOULD HAVE HUNG THE STARS IN HER HAIR...
COME FORTH, WOMAN.
IT ISN'T FOR YOU, THIS COLD, NARROW BED.
MY LORD...
SAY YOU BELIEVE IN ME.
CAN YOU MAKE ME THAT GIRL AGAIN?
YOU ARE ALWAYS THAT GIRL TO ME.
THEN I BELIEVE IN YOU... ONLY--
YOU'VE SLAUGHTERED MY CHILDREN...
FORGET THEM.
THEY'RE NOTHING...
ASHES.
DUST.
WHO CARES?

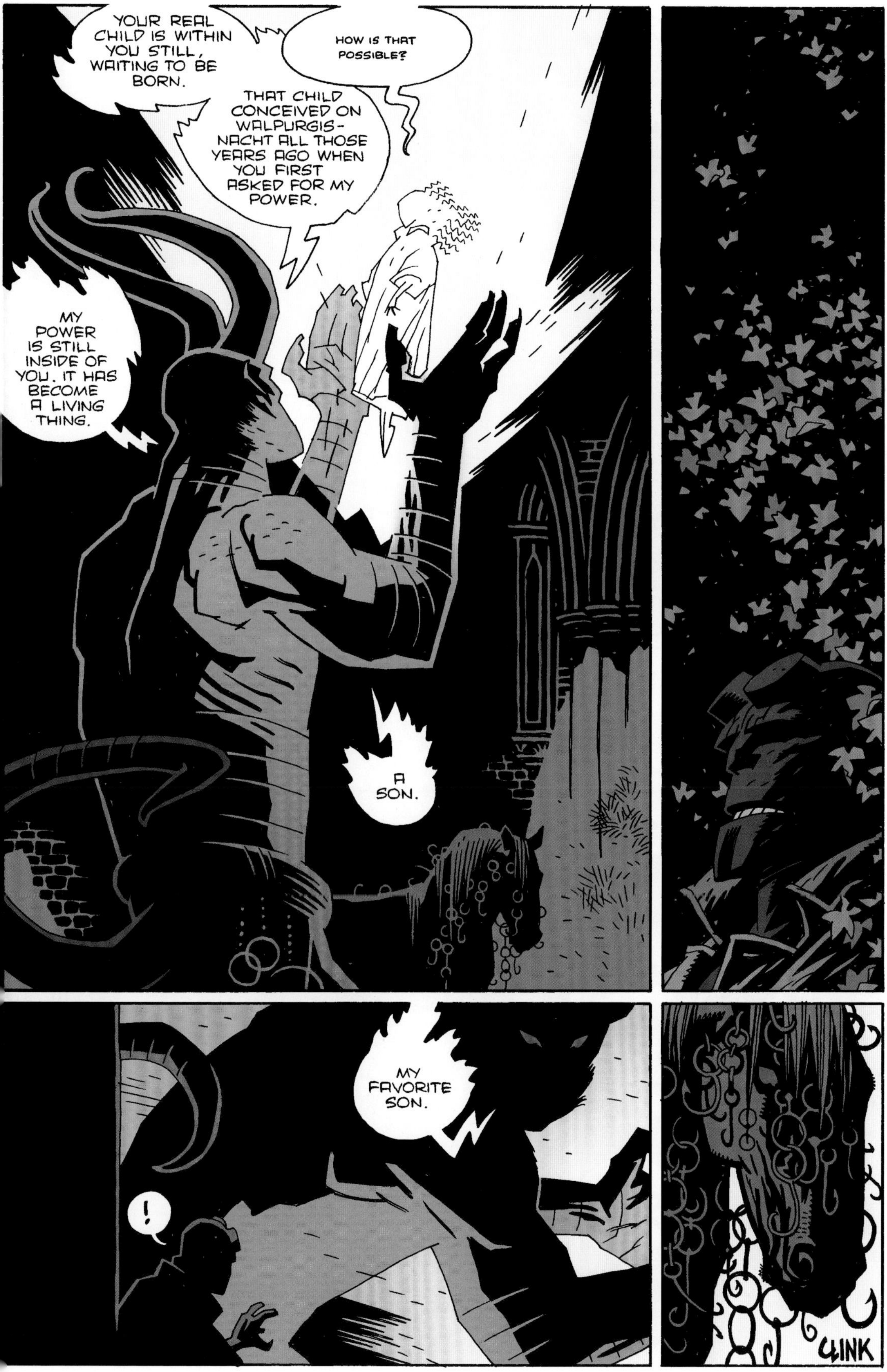
YOUR REAL CHILD IS WITHIN YOU STILL, WAITING TO BE BORN.
HOW IS THAT POSSIBLE?
THAT CHILD CONCEIVED ON WALPURGIS-NACHT ALL THOSE YEARS AGO WHEN YOU FIRST ASKED FOR MY POWER.
MY POWER IS STILL INSIDE OF YOU. IT HAS BECOME A LIVING THING.
A SON.
MY FAVORITE SON.
!
CLINK

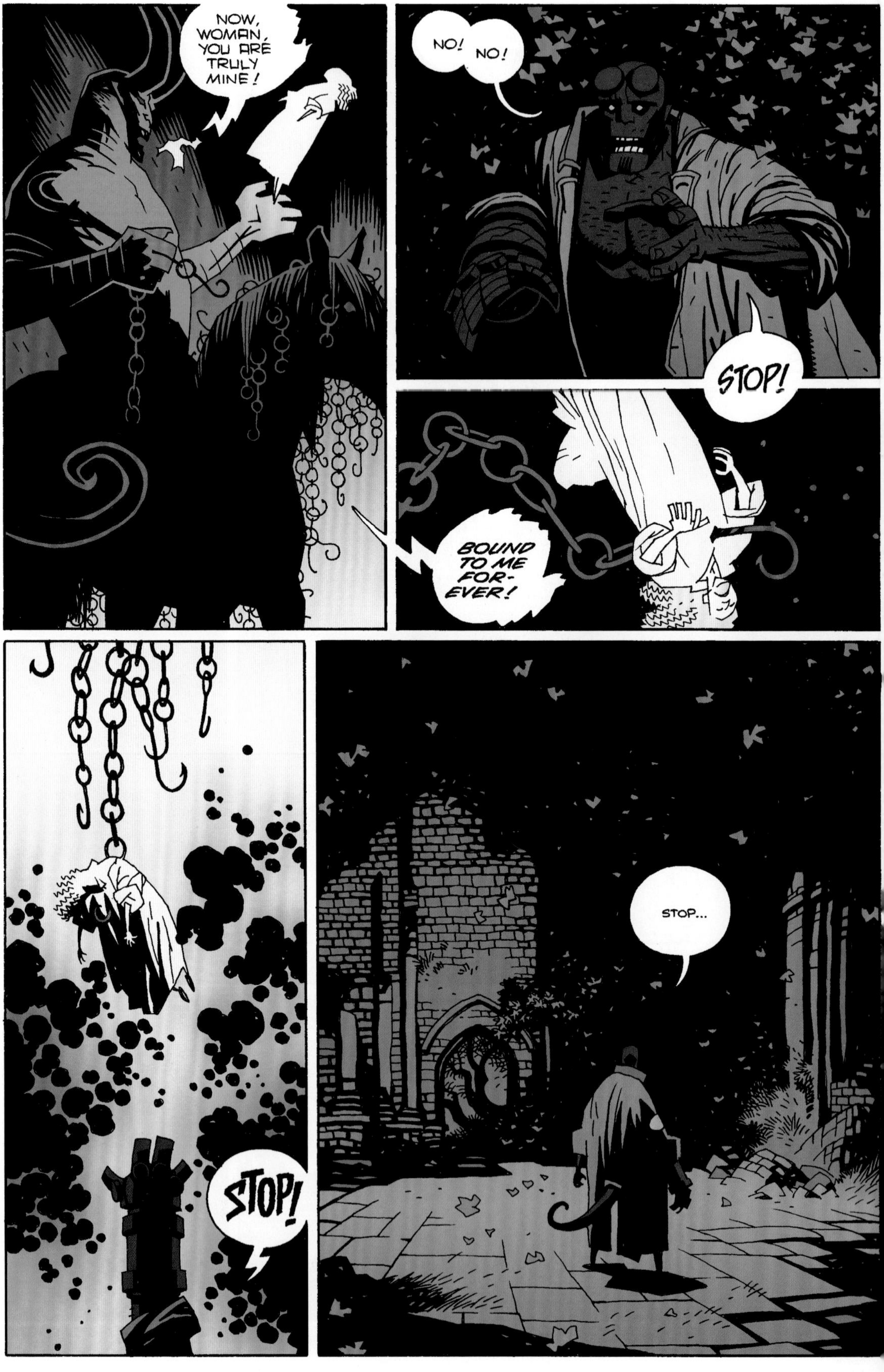
NOW, WOMAN, YOU ARE TRULY MINE!
NO!
NO!
STOP!
BOUND TO ME FOR-EVER!
STOP!
STOP...

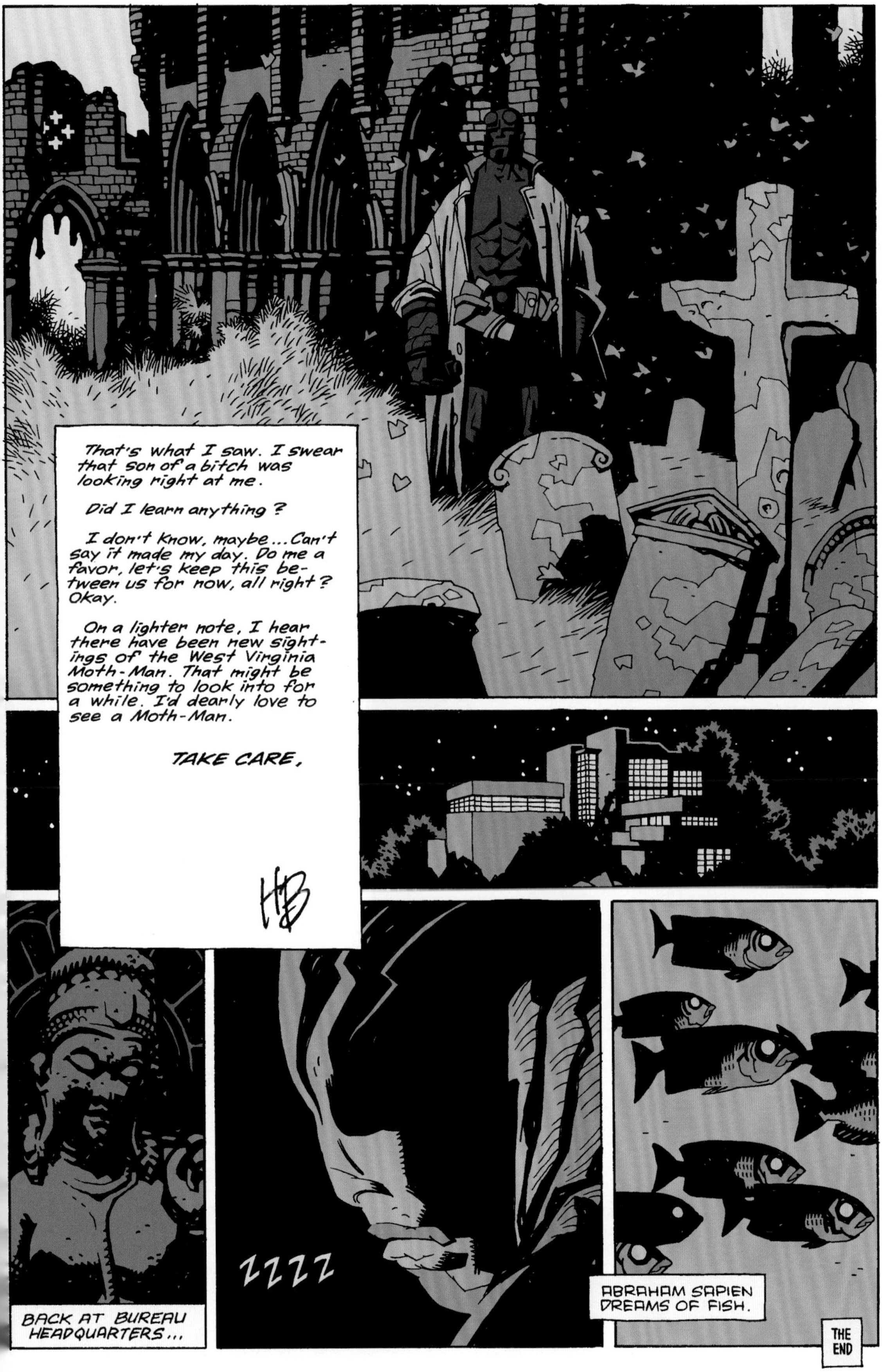
That's what I saw. I swear that son of a bitch was looking right at me.
Did I learn anything?
I don't know, maybe... Can't say it made my day. Do me a favor, let's keep this between us for now, all right? Okay.
On a lighter note, I hear there have been new sightings of the West Virginia Moth-Man. That might be something to look into for a while. I'd dearly love to see a Moth-Man.
TAKE CARE,
HB
BACK AT BUREAU HEADQUARTERS...
ZZZZ
ABRAHAM SAPIEN DREAMS OF FISH.
THE END

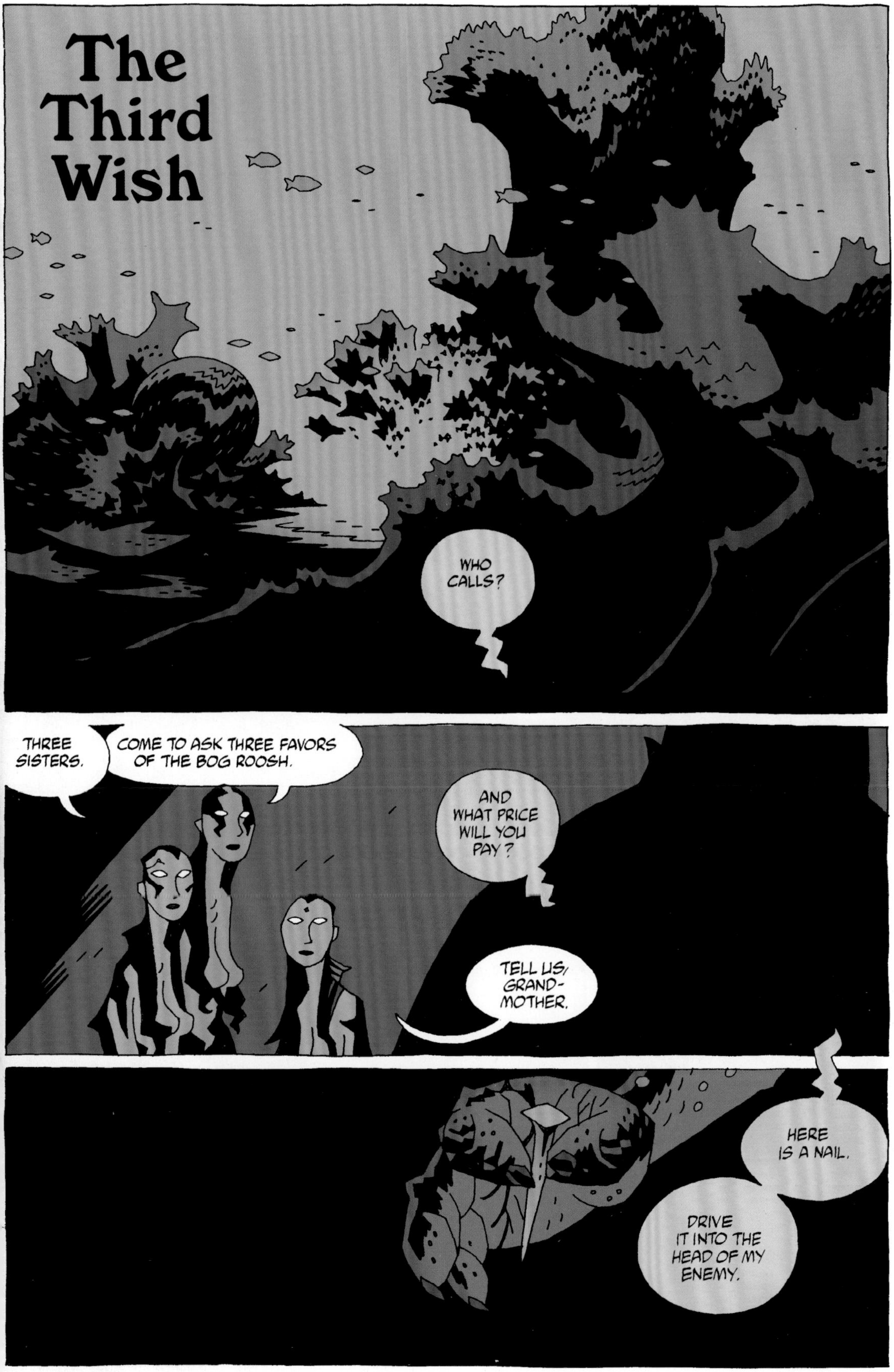
The Third Wish
WHO CALLS?
THREE SISTERS.
COME TO ASK THREE FAVORS OF THE BOG ROOSH.
AND WHAT PRICE WILL YOU PAY?
TELL US, GRANDMOTHER.
HERE IS A NAIL.
DRIVE IT INTO THE HEAD OF MY ENEMY.

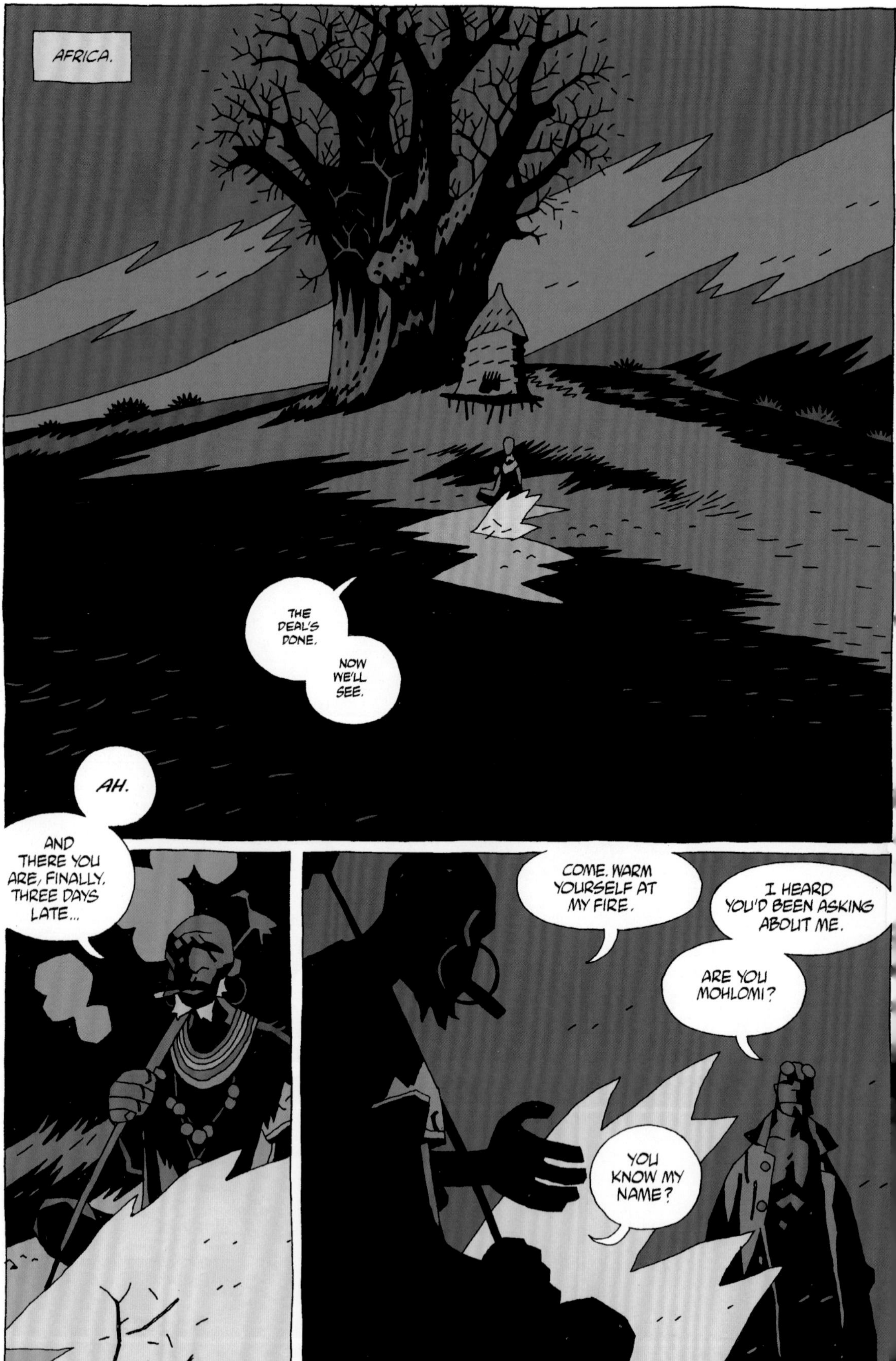
AFRICA.
THE DEAL'S DONE.
NOW WE'LL SEE.
AH.
AND THERE YOU ARE, FINALLY. THREE DAYS LATE...
COME. WARM YOURSELF AT MY FIRE.
I HEARD YOU'D BEEN ASKING ABOUT ME.
ARE YOU MOHLOMI?
YOU KNOW MY NAME?

AM I FAMOUS?

MAYBE.

IN THE VILLAGES AROUND HERE EVERYBODY SEEMS TO KNOW YOU. THEY TELL STORIES ABOUT YOU...

YES.

THING IS, THEY ALSO SAY THAT THE GREAT WITCH-DOCTOR MOHLOMI *DIED* TWO HUNDRED YEARS AGO.

SO LONG?

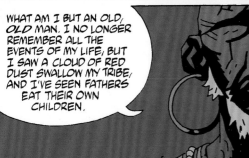

WHAT AM I BUT AN OLD, *OLD* MAN. I NO LONGER REMEMBER ALL THE EVENTS OF MY LIFE, BUT I SAW A CLOUD OF RED DUST SWALLOW MY TRIBE, AND I'VE SEEN FATHERS EAT THEIR OWN CHILDREN.

YEAH...

HOW'D YOU KNOW I WAS COMING?

KWAKU ANANSE THE SPIDER...

"ONCE HE TRAPPED A PYTHON, A FAIRY, A LEOPARD, AND A HORNET, AND TRADED THEM TO THE SKY GOD FOR ALL HIS STORIES..."

"AND WHEN I WAS YOUNG THE SPIDER USED TO SPIN HIS WEB IN MY EAR AND TELL THE STORIES TO ME. AND ONE OF THE STORIES WAS YOURS..."

HELLBOY

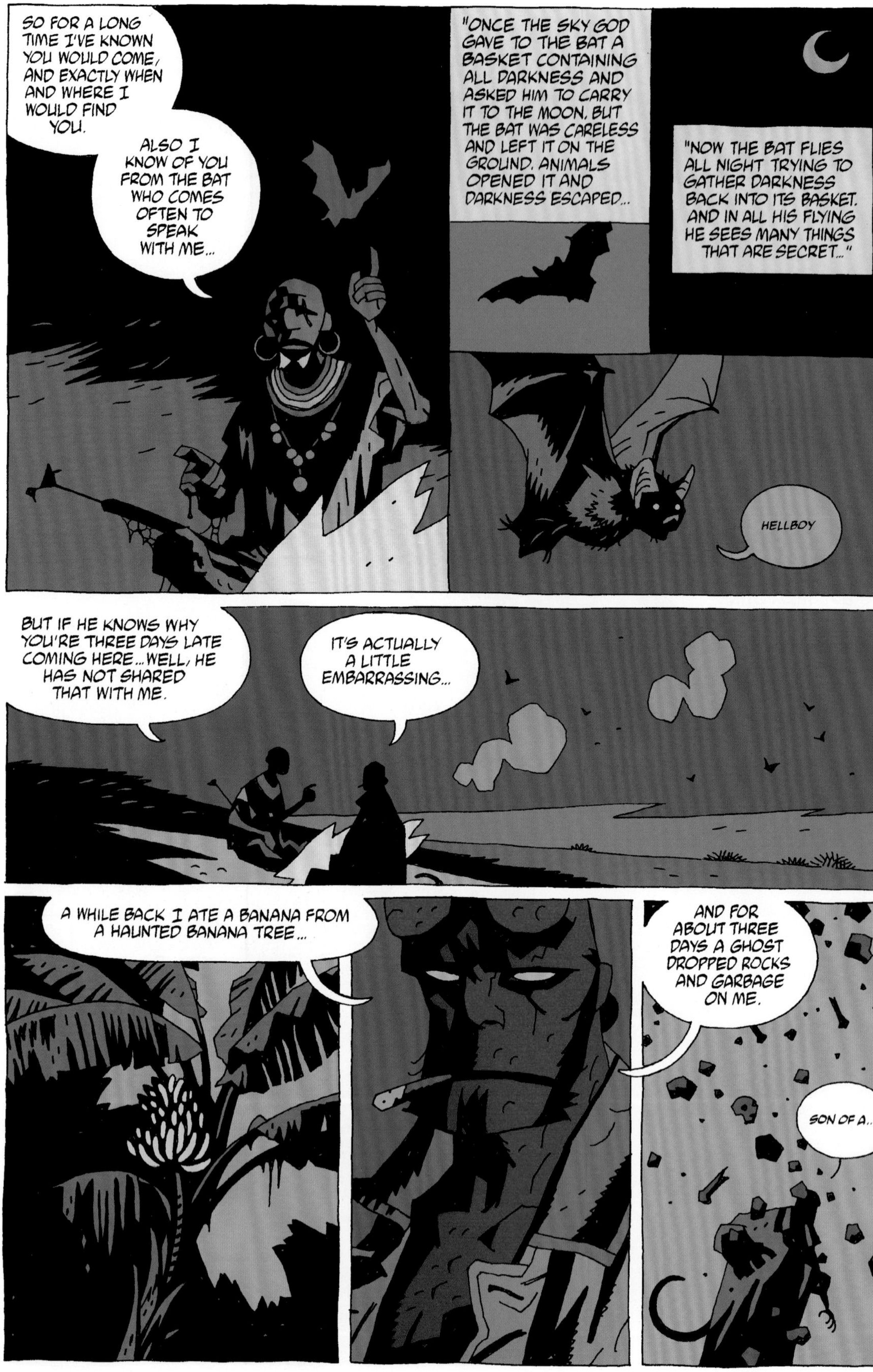
SO FOR A LONG TIME I'VE KNOWN YOU WOULD COME, AND EXACTLY WHEN AND WHERE I WOULD FIND YOU.
ALSO I KNOW OF YOU FROM THE BAT WHO COMES OFTEN TO SPEAK WITH ME...
"ONCE THE SKY GOD GAVE TO THE BAT A BASKET CONTAINING ALL DARKNESS AND ASKED HIM TO CARRY IT TO THE MOON. BUT THE BAT WAS CARELESS AND LEFT IT ON THE GROUND. ANIMALS OPENED IT AND DARKNESS ESCAPED...
"NOW THE BAT FLIES ALL NIGHT TRYING TO GATHER DARKNESS BACK INTO ITS BASKET. AND IN ALL HIS FLYING HE SEES MANY THINGS THAT ARE SECRET..."
HELLBOY
BUT IF HE KNOWS WHY YOU'RE THREE DAYS LATE COMING HERE...WELL, HE HAS NOT SHARED THAT WITH ME.
IT'S ACTUALLY A LITTLE EMBARRASSING...
A WHILE BACK I ATE A BANANA FROM A HAUNTED BANANA TREE...
AND FOR ABOUT THREE DAYS A GHOST DROPPED ROCKS AND GARBAGE ON ME.
SON OF A...

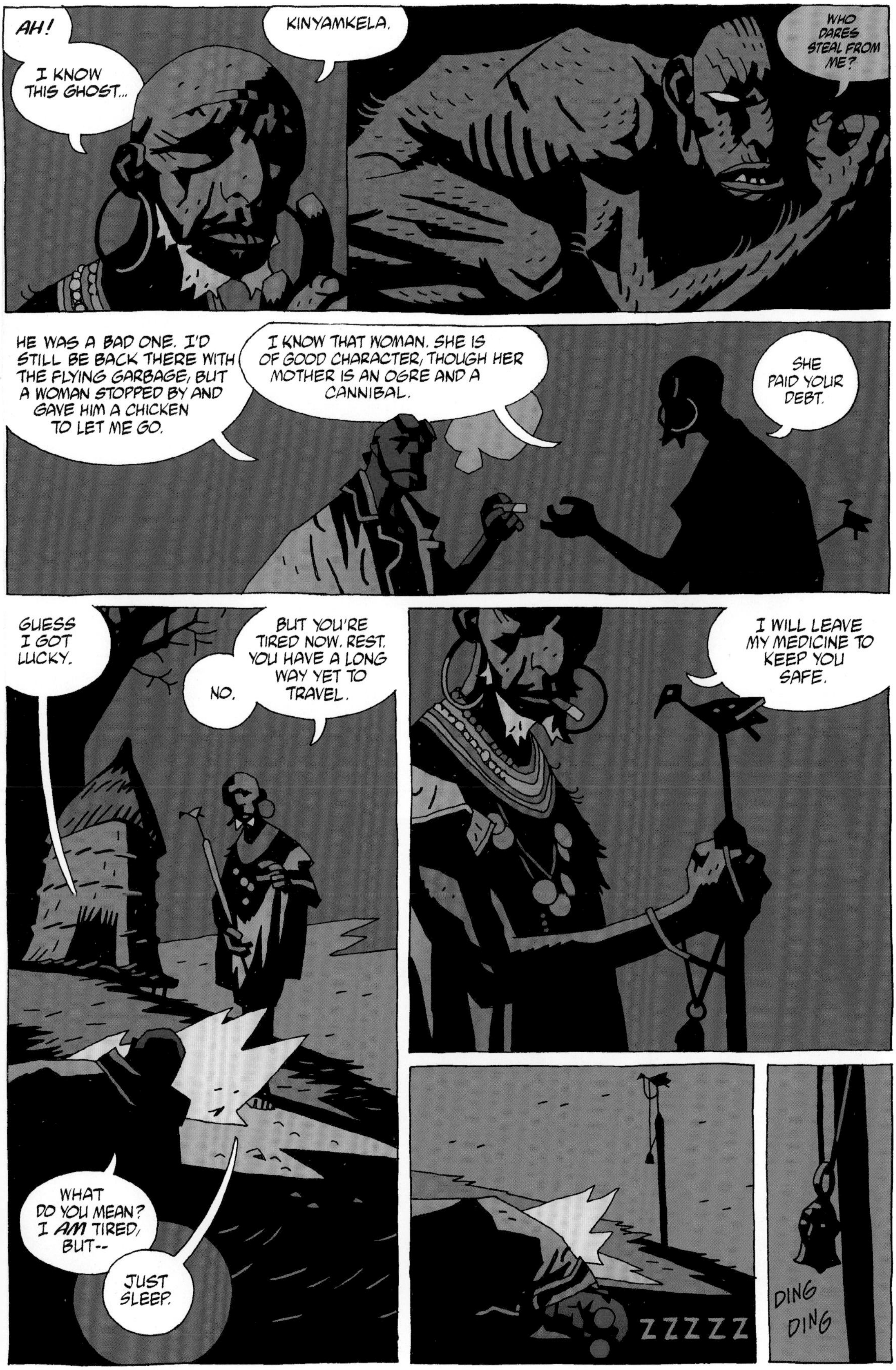
AH!
I KNOW THIS GHOST...
KINYAMKELA.
WHO DARES STEAL FROM ME?
HE WAS A BAD ONE. I'D STILL BE BACK THERE WITH THE FLYING GARBAGE, BUT A WOMAN STOPPED BY AND GAVE HIM A CHICKEN TO LET ME GO.
I KNOW THAT WOMAN. SHE IS OF GOOD CHARACTER, THOUGH HER MOTHER IS AN OGRE AND A CANNIBAL.
SHE PAID YOUR DEBT.
GUESS I GOT LUCKY.
NO.
BUT YOU'RE TIRED NOW. REST. YOU HAVE A LONG WAY YET TO TRAVEL.
WHAT DO YOU MEAN? I *AM* TIRED, BUT--
JUST SLEEP.
I WILL LEAVE MY MEDICINE TO KEEP YOU SAFE.
ZZZZZ
DING
DING

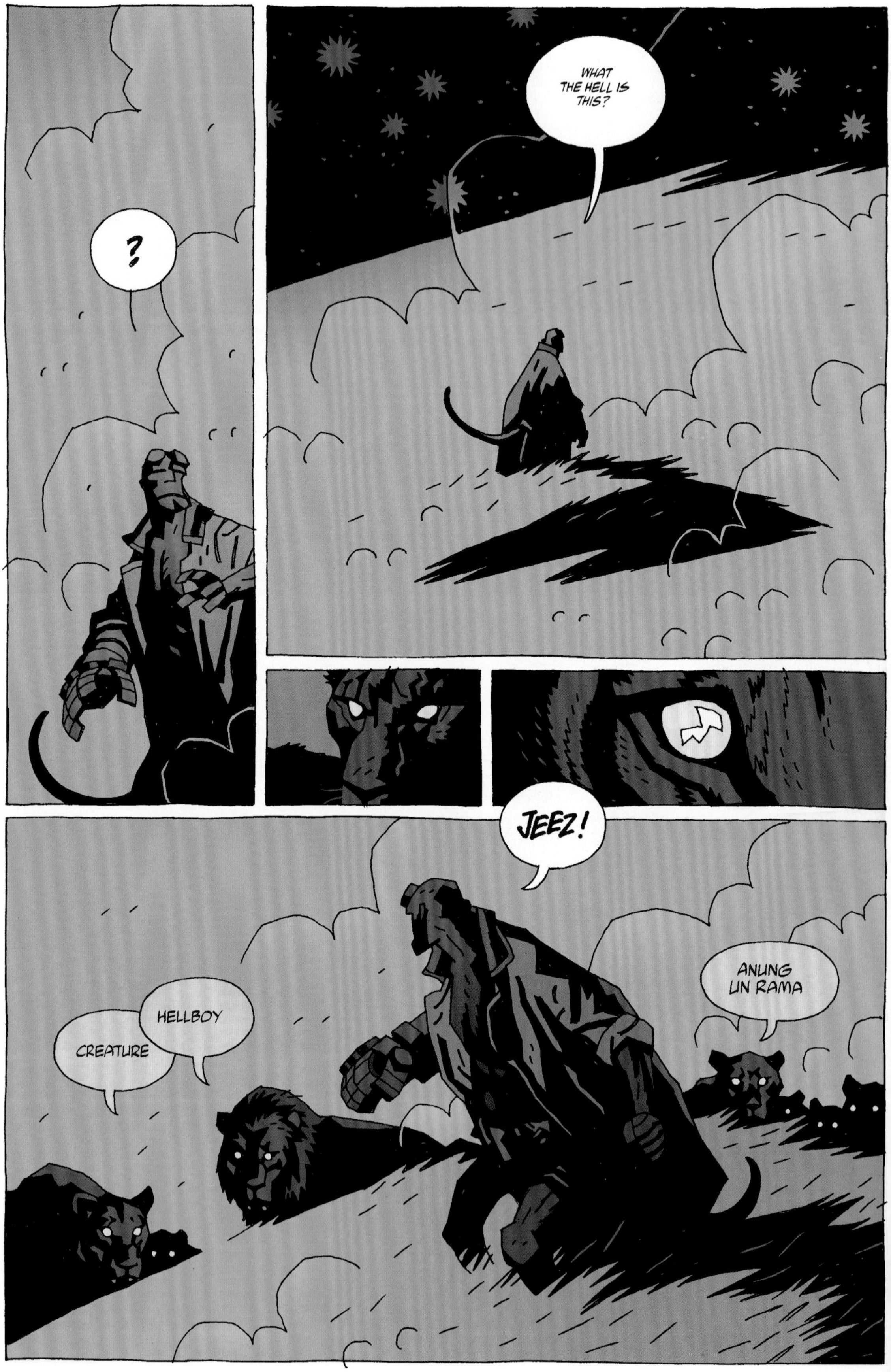
?
WHAT THE HELL IS THIS?
JEEZ!
CREATURE
HELLBOY
ANUNG UN RAMA

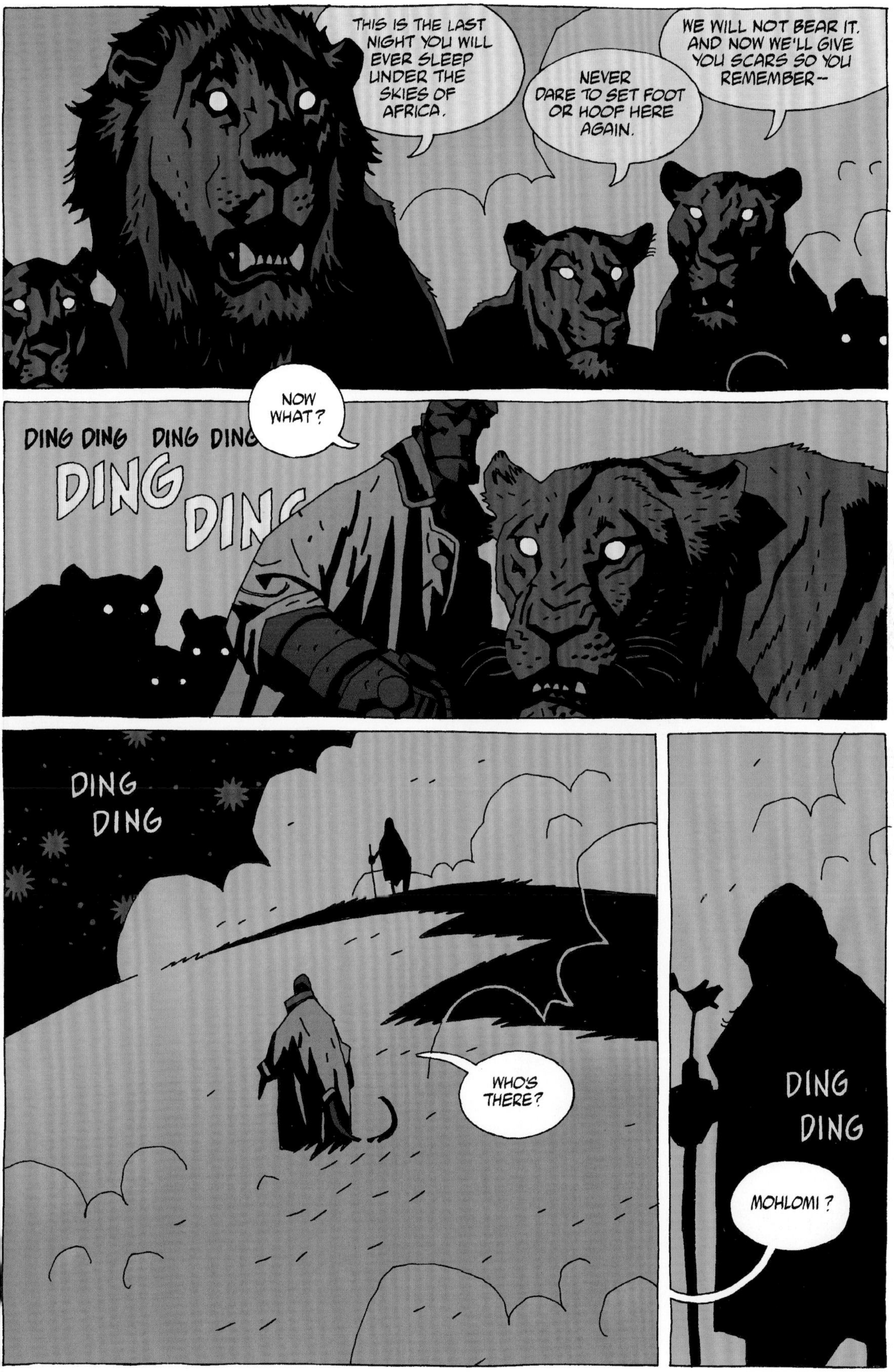

THIS IS THE LAST NIGHT YOU WILL EVER SLEEP UNDER THE SKIES OF AFRICA.
NEVER DARE TO SET FOOT OR HOOF HERE AGAIN.
WE WILL NOT BEAR IT. AND NOW WE'LL GIVE YOU SCARS SO YOU REMEMBER--
NOW WHAT?
DING DING DING DING
DING
DING
DING DING
WHO'S THERE?
DING DING
MOHLOMI?

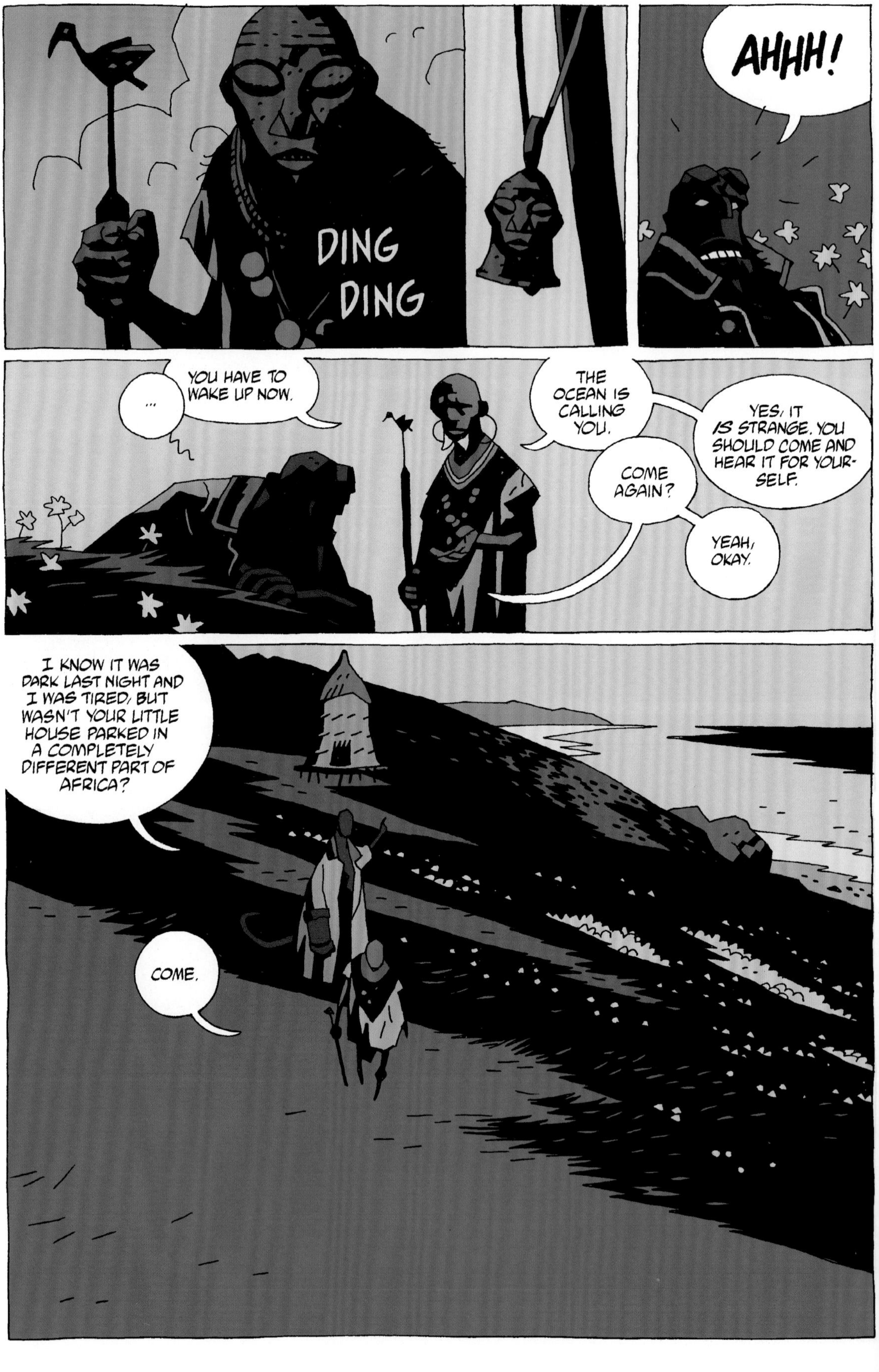
DING
DING
AHHH!
...
YOU HAVE TO WAKE UP NOW.
THE OCEAN IS CALLING YOU.
COME AGAIN?
YES, IT IS STRANGE. YOU SHOULD COME AND HEAR IT FOR YOURSELF.
YEAH, OKAY.
I KNOW IT WAS DARK LAST NIGHT AND I WAS TIRED, BUT WASN'T YOUR LITTLE HOUSE PARKED IN A COMPLETELY DIFFERENT PART OF AFRICA?
COME.

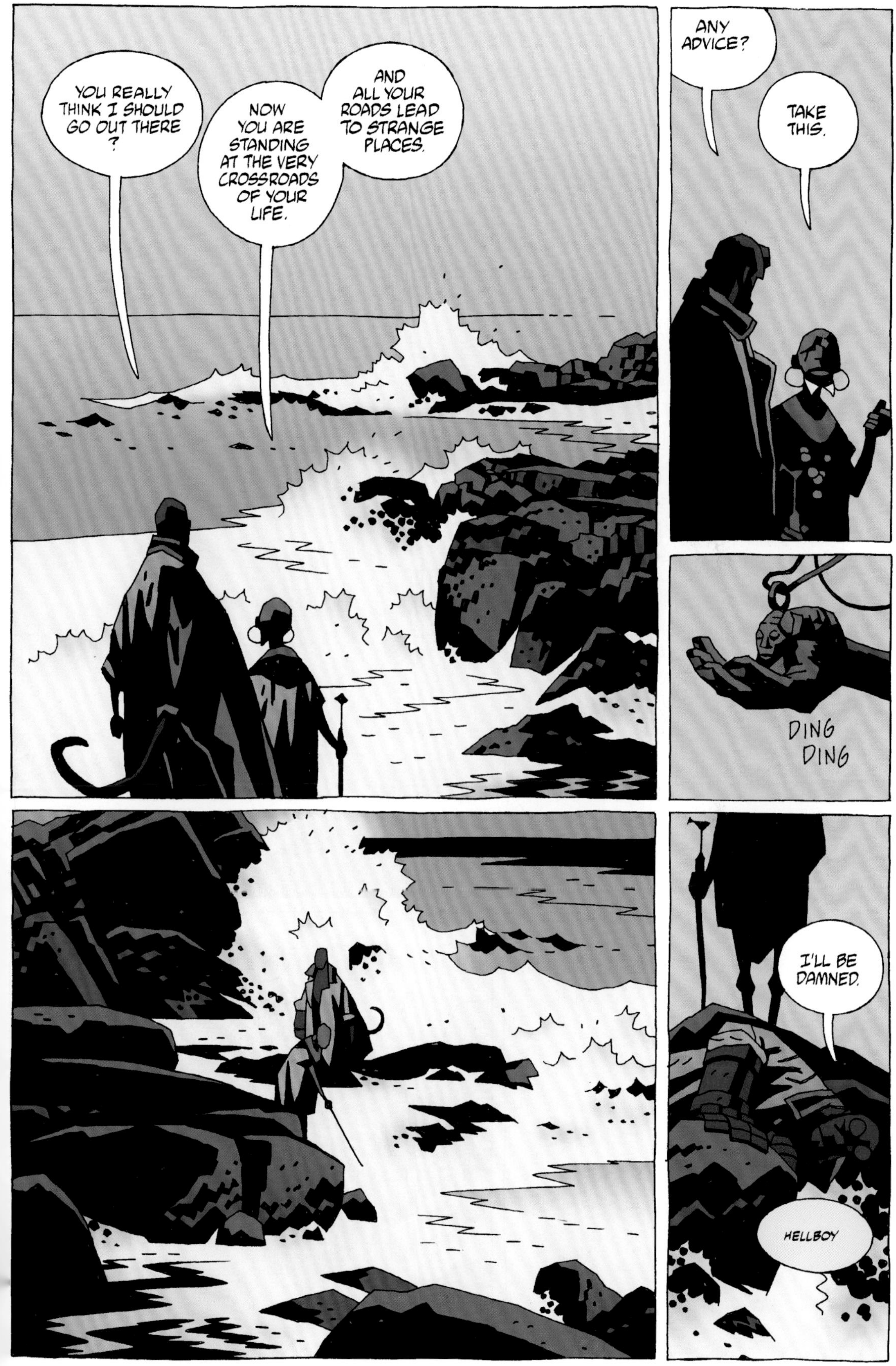
YOU REALLY THINK I SHOULD GO OUT THERE ?
NOW YOU ARE STANDING AT THE VERY CROSSROADS OF YOUR LIFE.
AND ALL YOUR ROADS LEAD TO STRANGE PLACES.
ANY ADVICE?
TAKE THIS.
DING DING
I'LL BE DAMNED.
HELLBOY

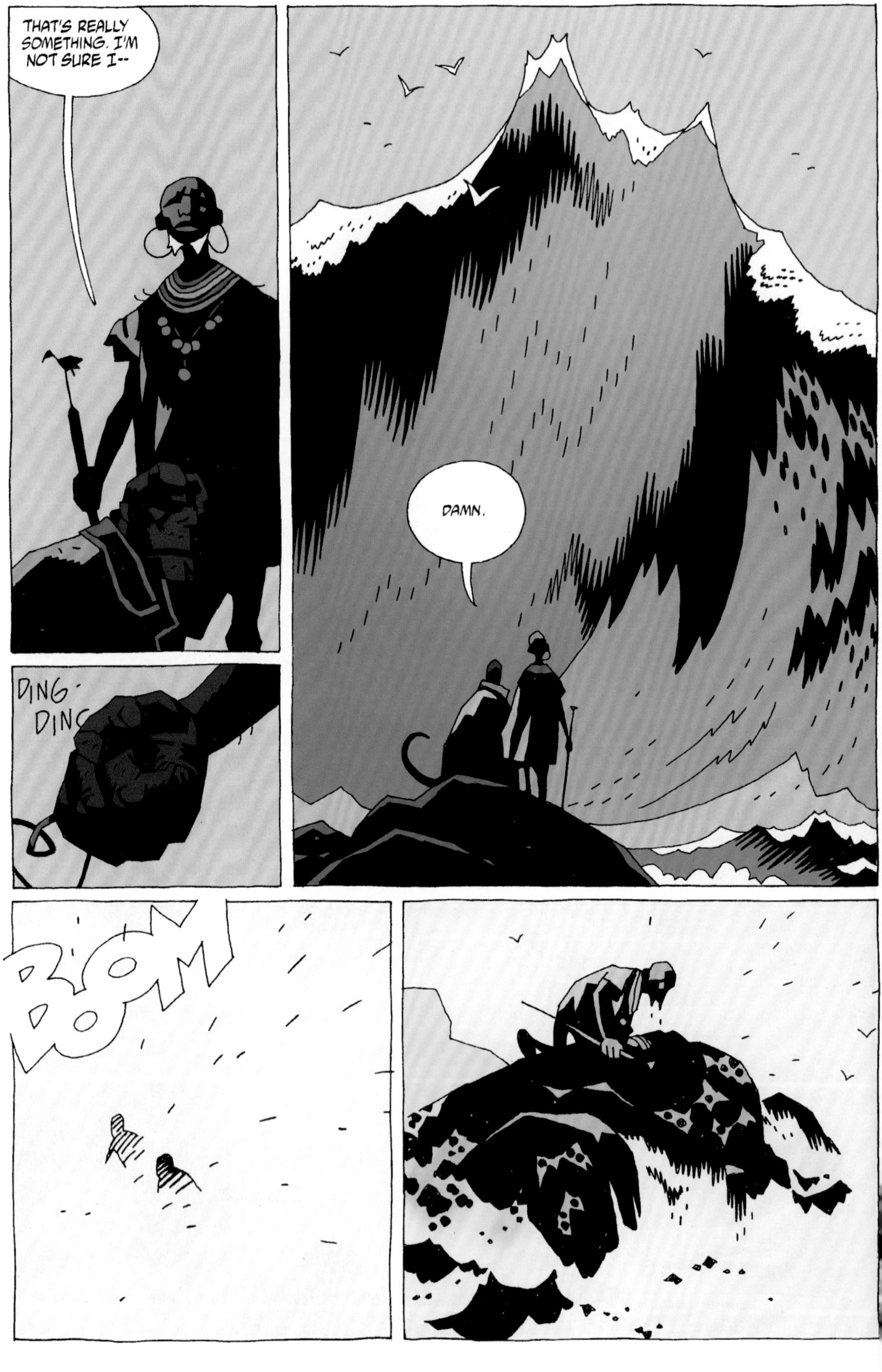
THAT'S REALLY SOMETHING. I'M NOT SURE I--
DAMN.
DING-DING
BOOM

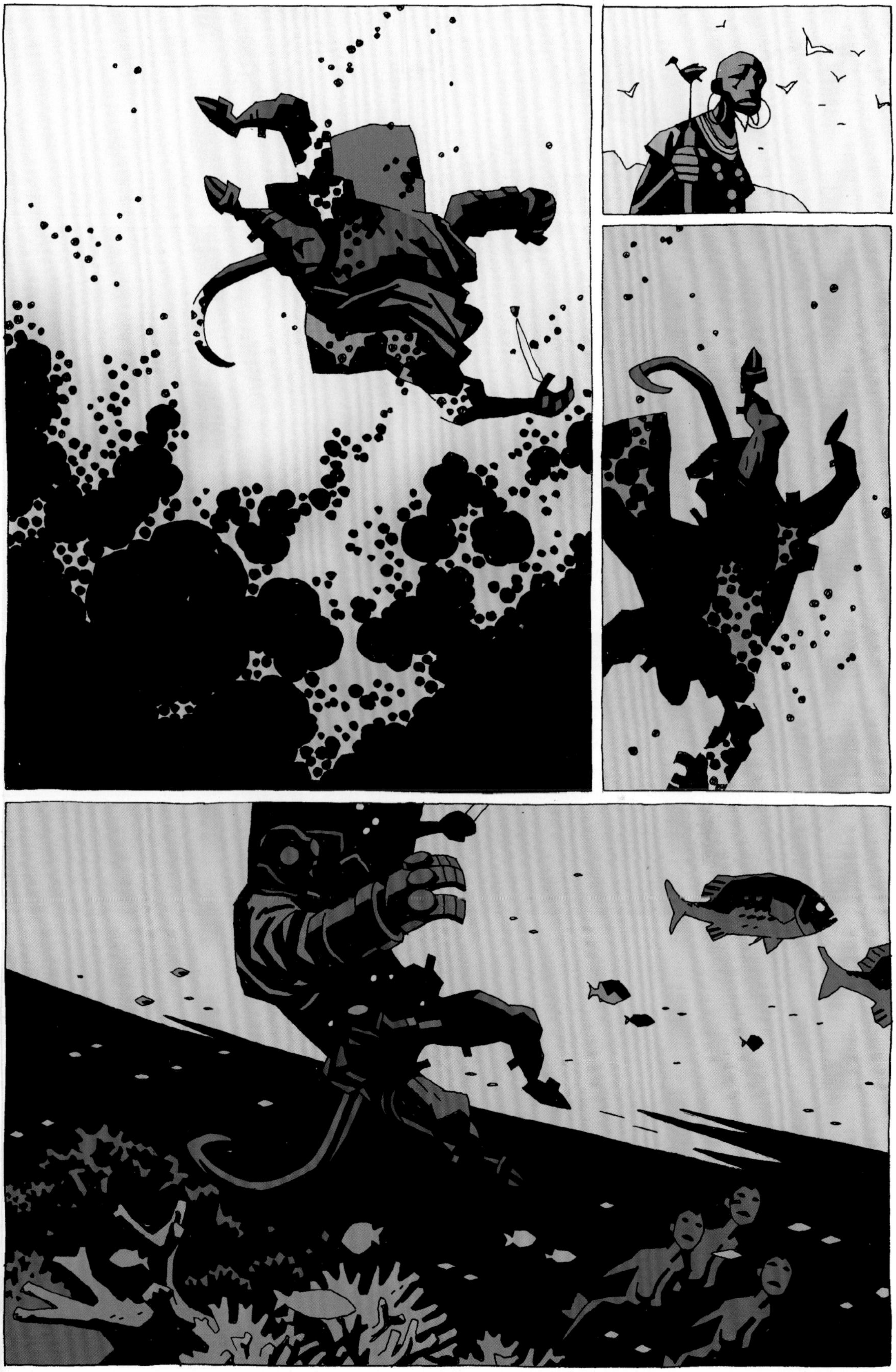

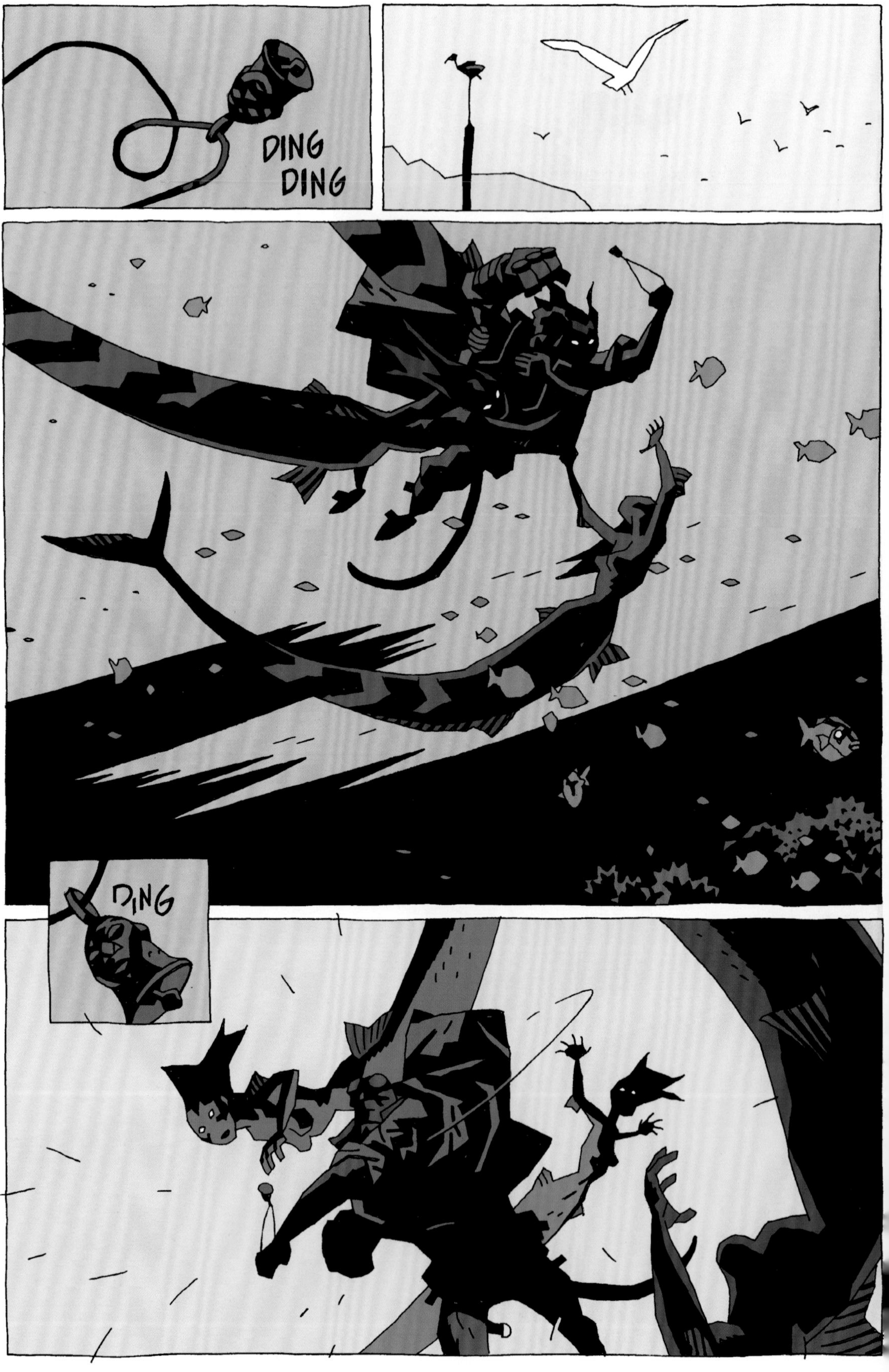
DING
DING
DING

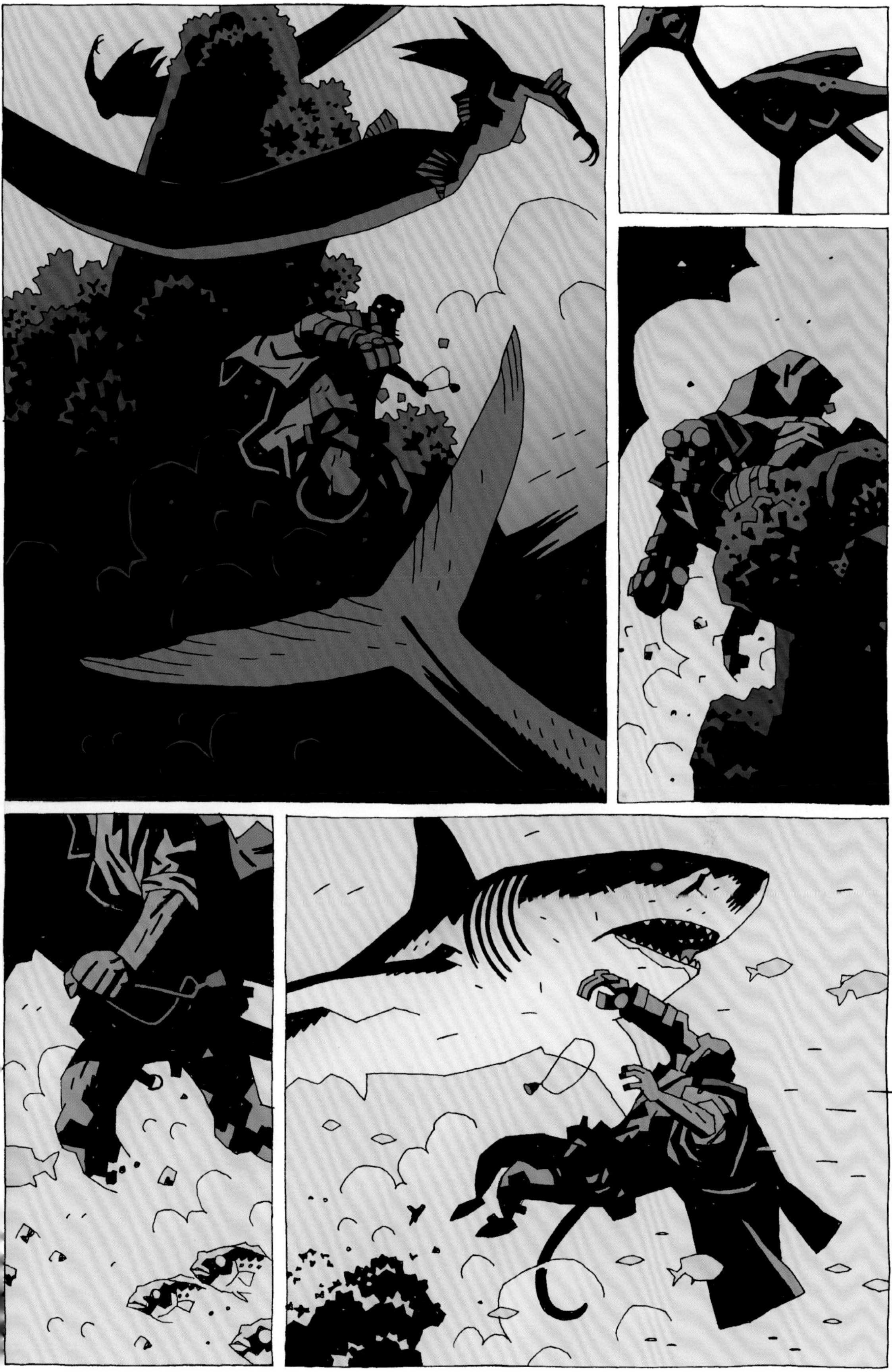

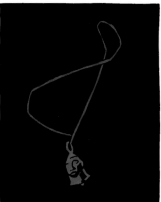

DING DING

DING DING

116

BRANG

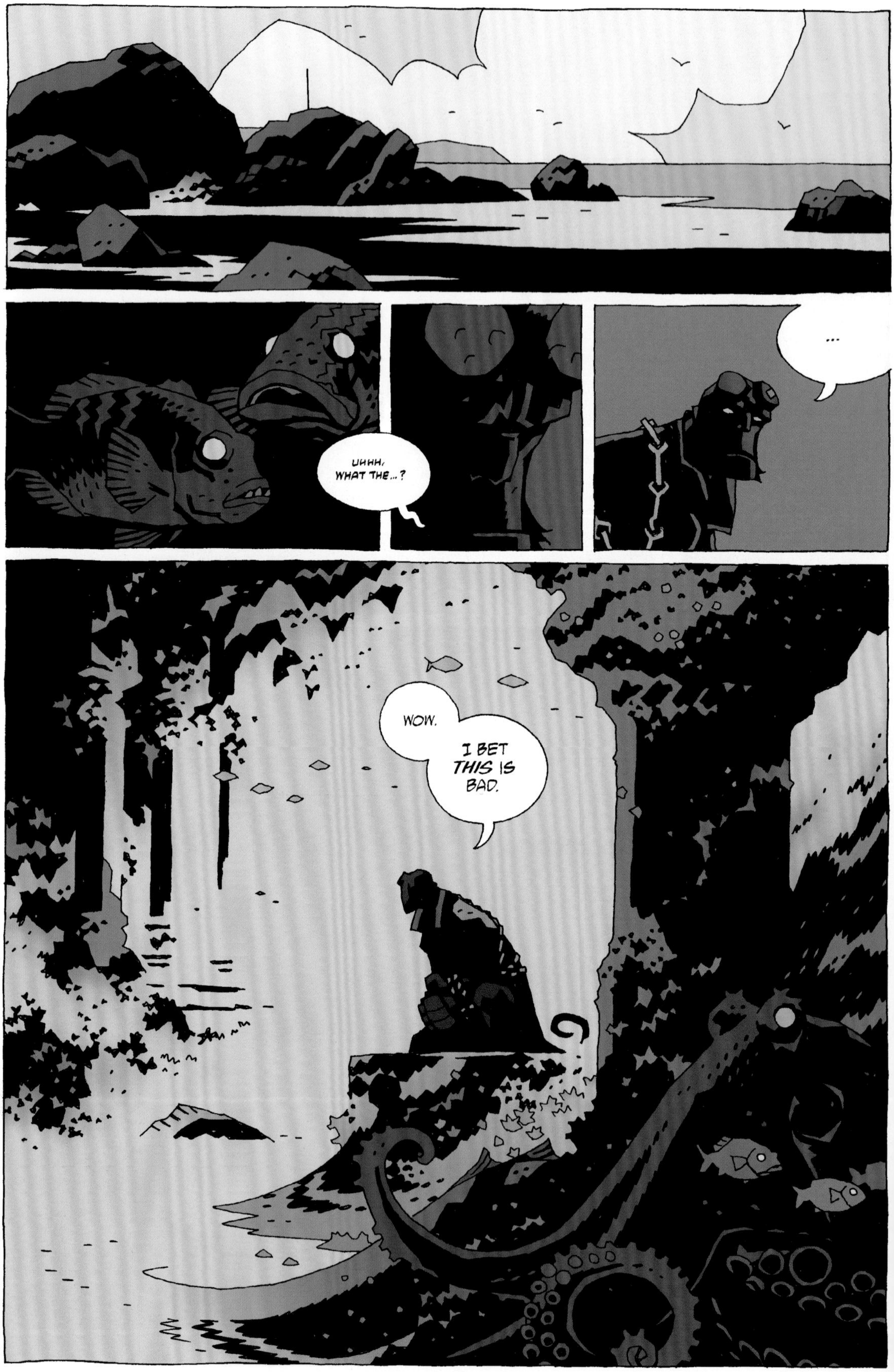
UHHH, WHAT THE...?
...
WOW.
I BET THIS IS BAD.

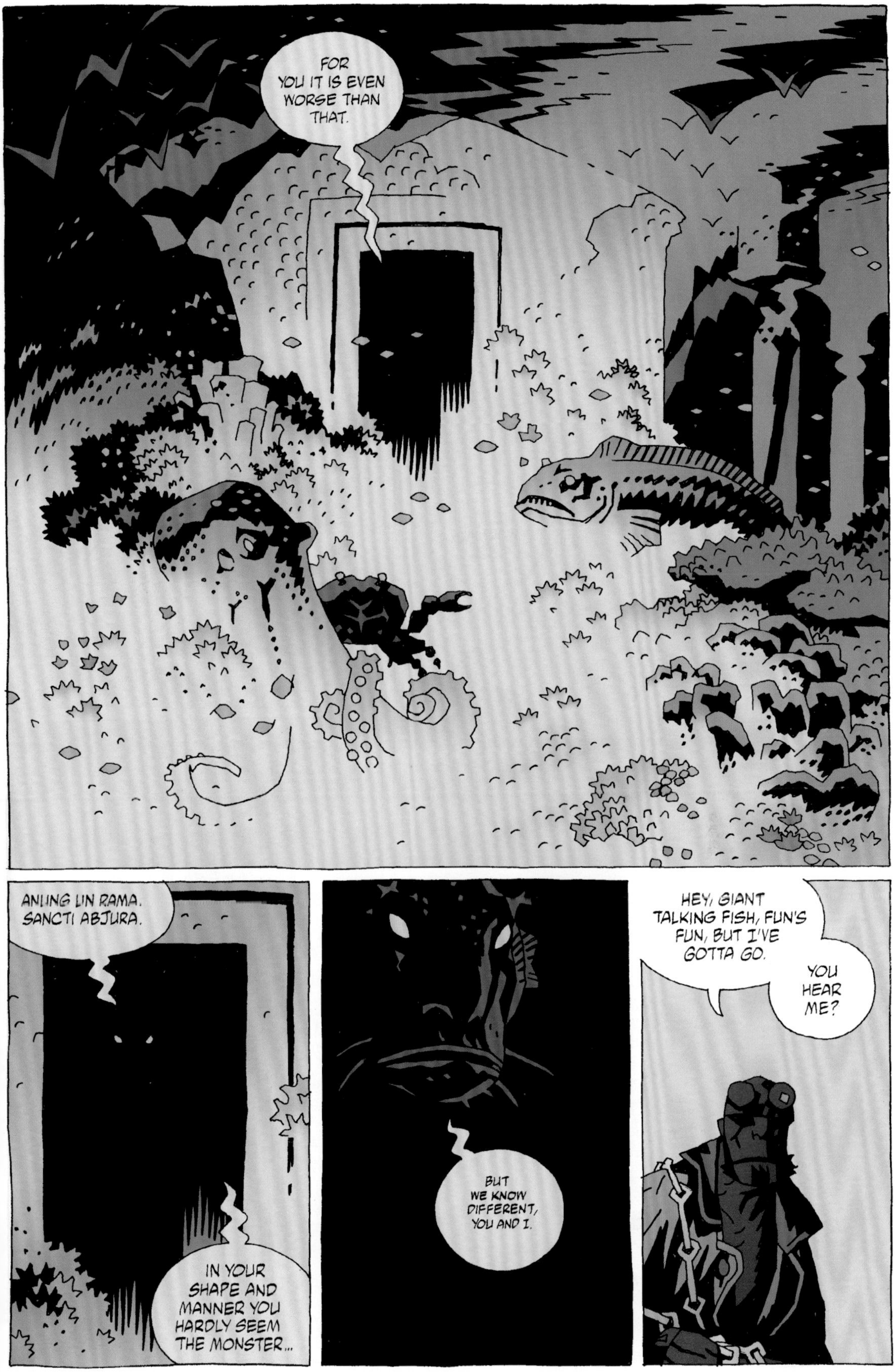
FOR YOU IT IS EVEN WORSE THAN THAT.
ANUNG UN RAMA. SANCTI ABJURA.
IN YOUR SHAPE AND MANNER YOU HARDLY SEEM THE MONSTER...
BUT WE KNOW DIFFERENT, YOU AND I.
HEY, GIANT TALKING FISH, FUN'S FUN, BUT I'VE GOTTA GO.
YOU HEAR ME?

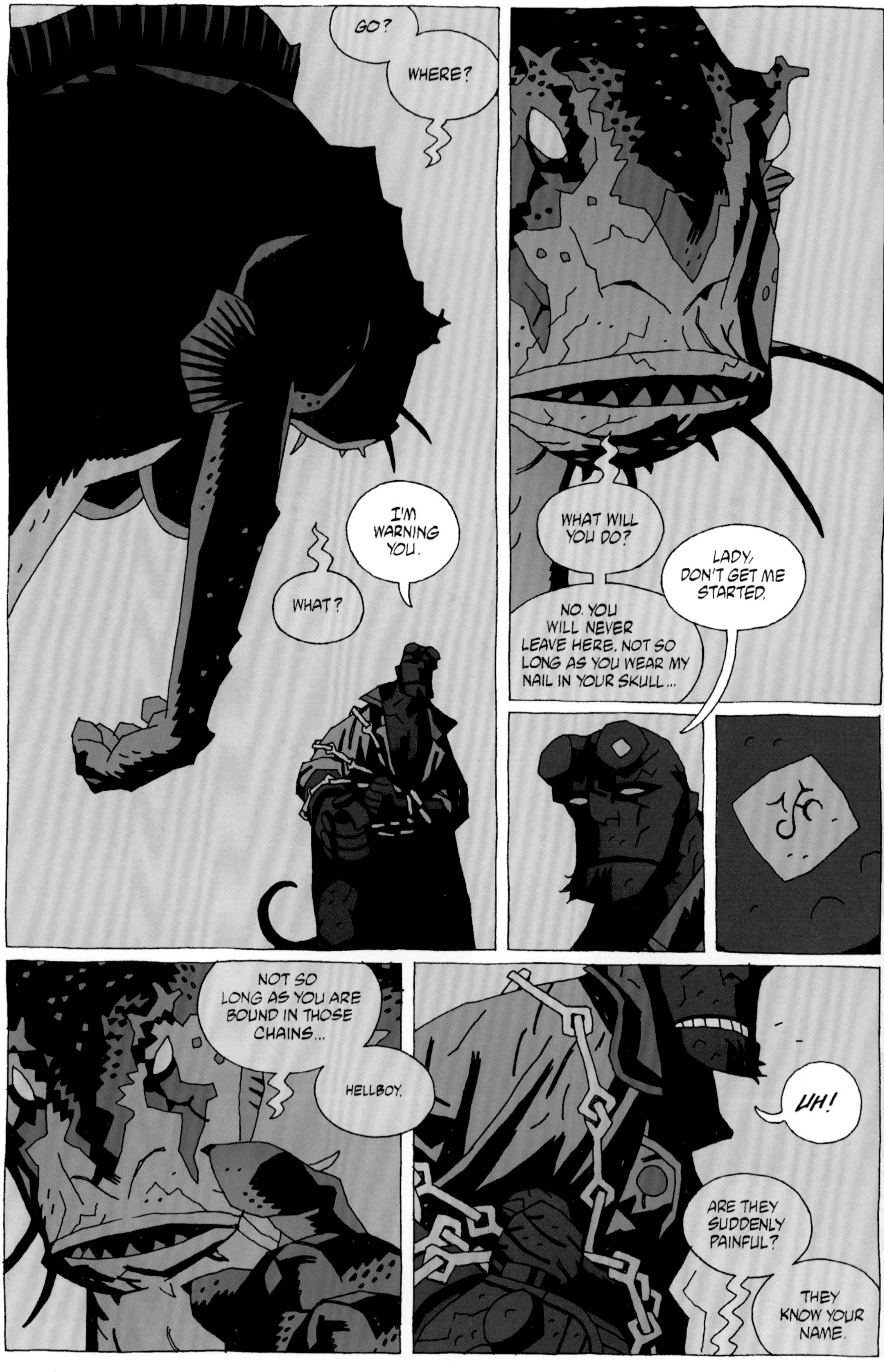
GO?
WHERE?
I'M WARNING YOU.
WHAT?
WHAT WILL YOU DO?
NO. YOU WILL NEVER LEAVE HERE. NOT SO LONG AS YOU WEAR MY NAIL IN YOUR SKULL...
LADY, DON'T GET ME STARTED.
NOT SO LONG AS YOU ARE BOUND IN THOSE CHAINS...
HELLBOY.
UH!
ARE THEY SUDDENLY PAINFUL?
THEY KNOW YOUR NAME.

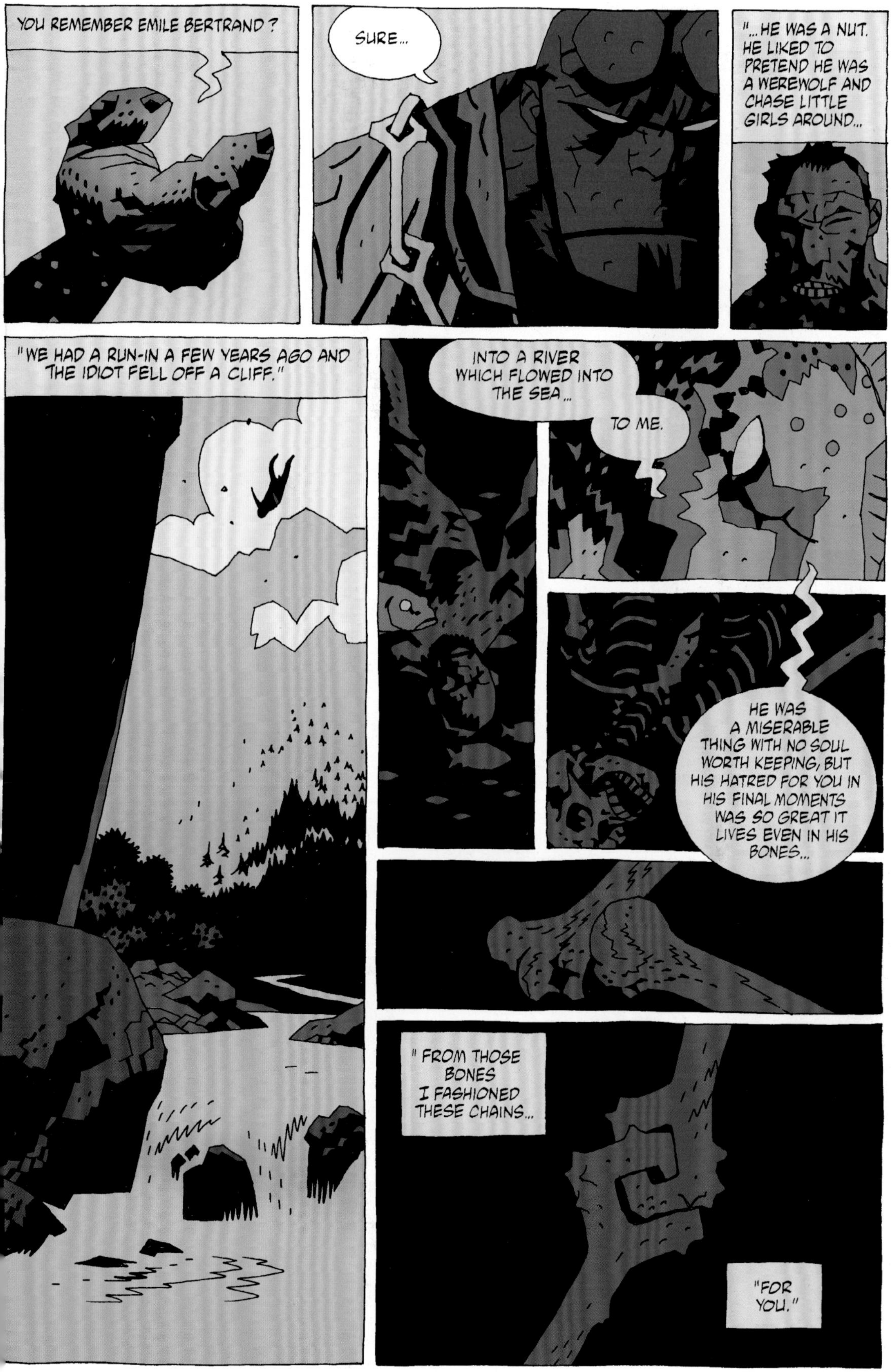
YOU REMEMBER EMILE BERTRAND?
SURE...
"...HE WAS A NUT. HE LIKED TO PRETEND HE WAS A WEREWOLF AND CHASE LITTLE GIRLS AROUND...
"WE HAD A RUN-IN A FEW YEARS AGO AND THE IDIOT FELL OFF A CLIFF."
INTO A RIVER WHICH FLOWED INTO THE SEA...
TO ME.
HE WAS A MISERABLE THING WITH NO SOUL WORTH KEEPING, BUT HIS HATRED FOR YOU IN HIS FINAL MOMENTS WAS SO GREAT IT LIVES EVEN IN HIS BONES...
"FROM THOSE BONES I FASHIONED THESE CHAINS...
"FOR YOU."

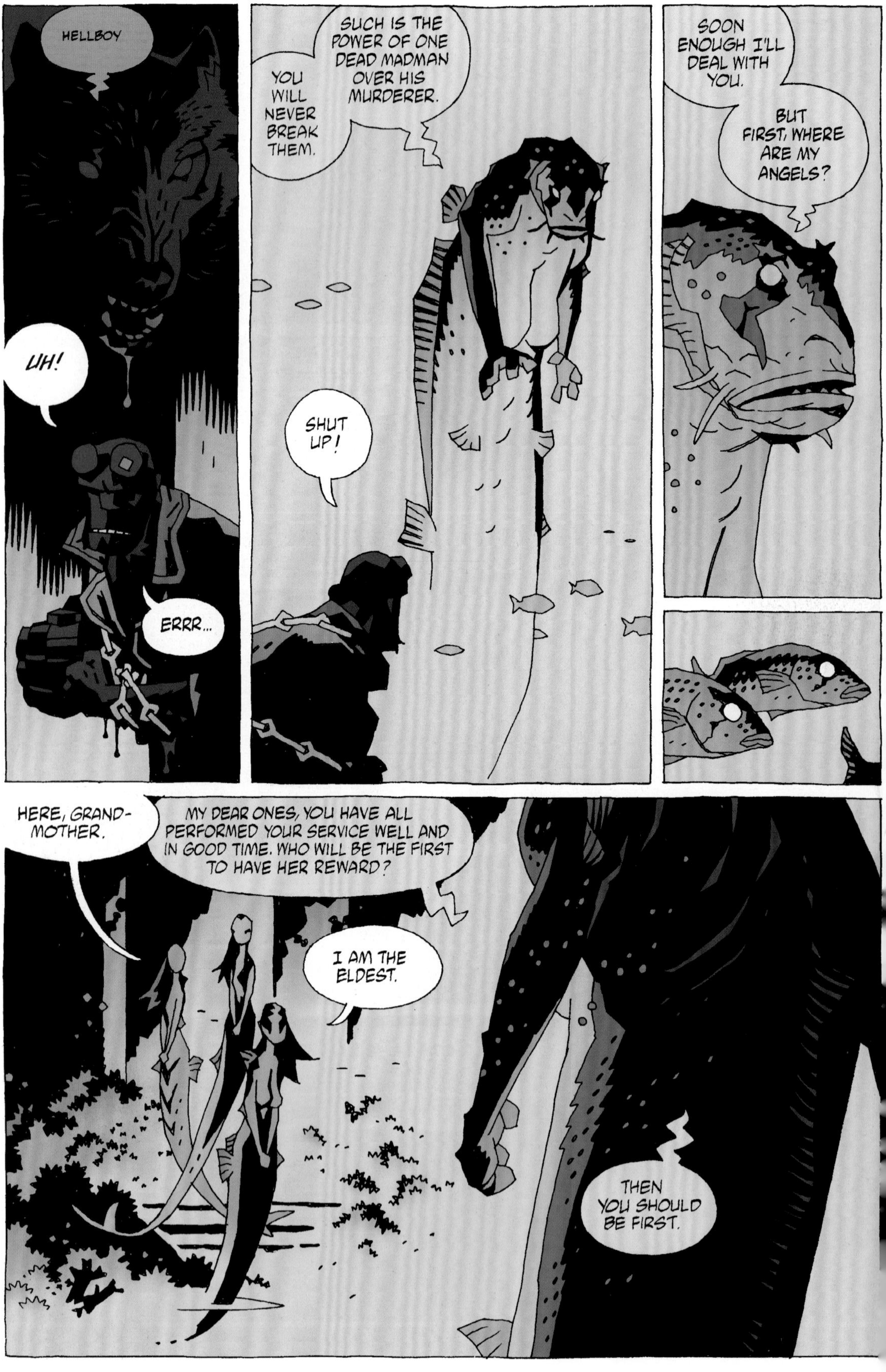
HELLBOY
UH!
ERRR...
YOU WILL NEVER BREAK THEM.
SUCH IS THE POWER OF ONE DEAD MADMAN OVER HIS MURDERER.
SHUT UP!
SOON ENOUGH I'LL DEAL WITH YOU.
BUT FIRST, WHERE ARE MY ANGELS?
HERE, GRAND-MOTHER.
MY DEAR ONES, YOU HAVE ALL PERFORMED YOUR SERVICE WELL AND IN GOOD TIME. WHO WILL BE THE FIRST TO HAVE HER REWARD?
I AM THE ELDEST.
THEN YOU SHOULD BE FIRST.

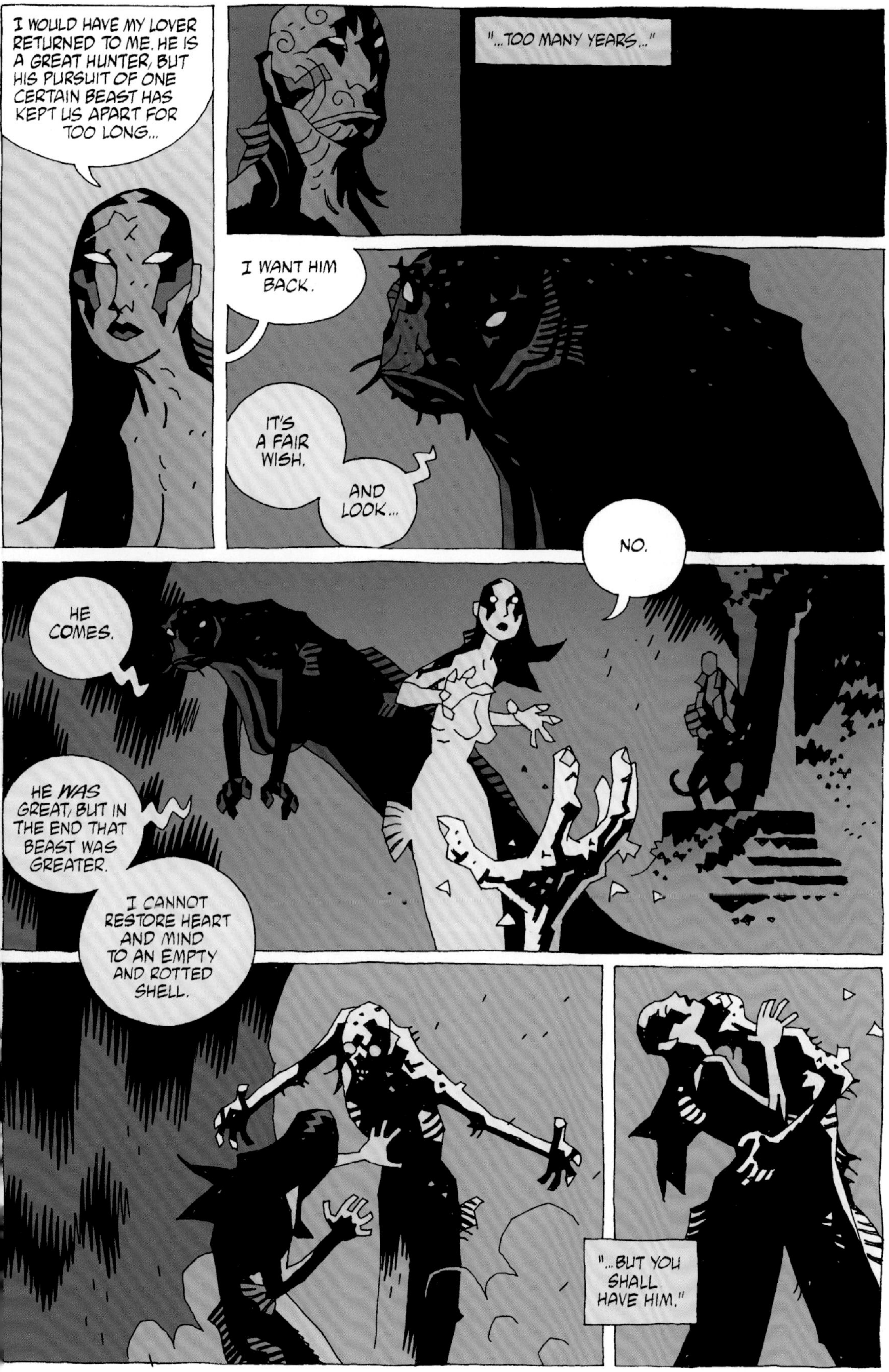
I WOULD HAVE MY LOVER RETURNED TO ME. HE IS A GREAT HUNTER, BUT HIS PURSUIT OF ONE CERTAIN BEAST HAS KEPT US APART FOR TOO LONG...
"...TOO MANY YEARS..."
I WANT HIM BACK.
IT'S A FAIR WISH.
AND LOOK...
NO.
HE COMES.
HE WAS GREAT, BUT IN THE END THAT BEAST WAS GREATER.
I CANNOT RESTORE HEART AND MIND TO AN EMPTY AND ROTTED SHELL.
"...BUT YOU SHALL HAVE HIM."

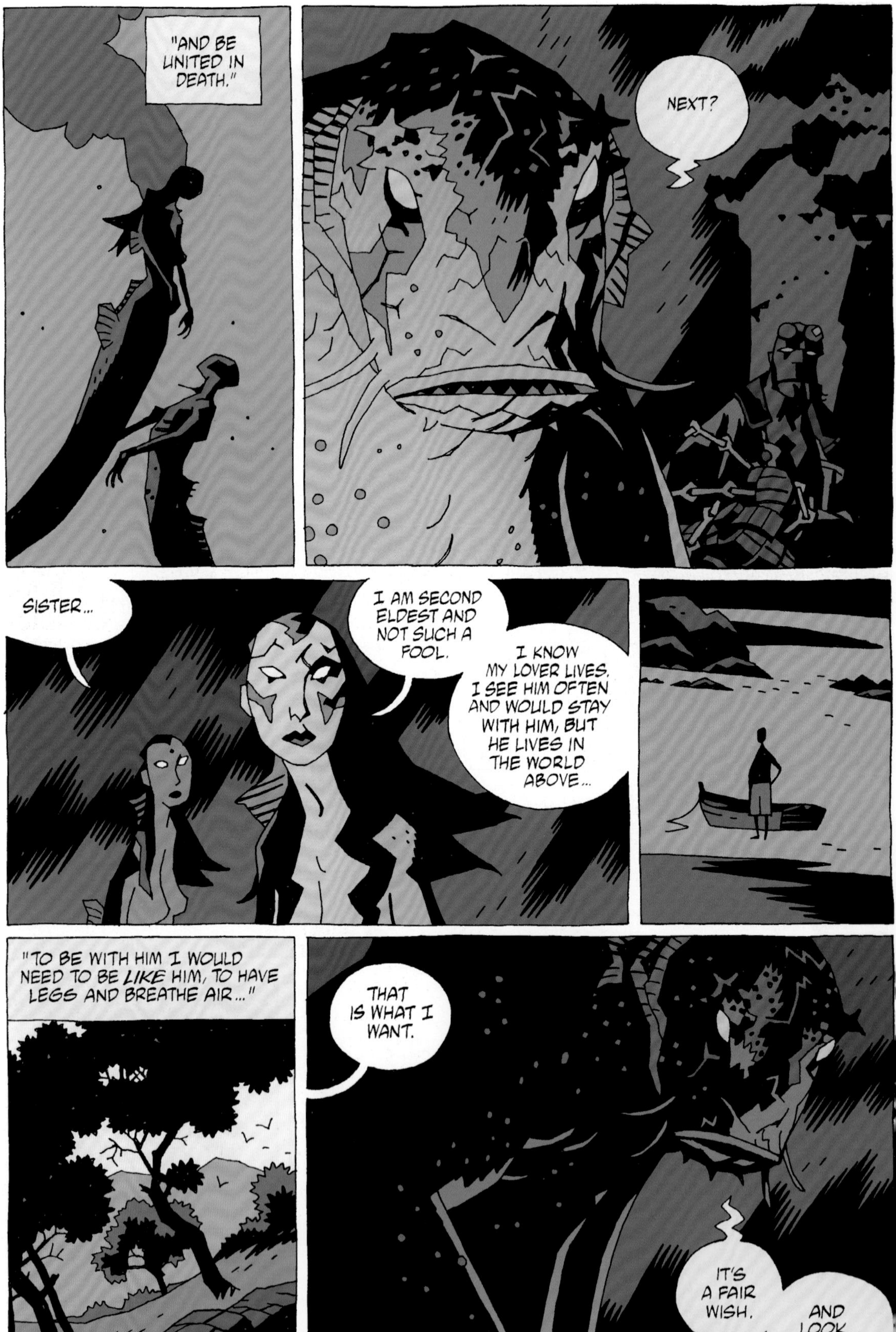
"AND BE UNITED IN DEATH."
NEXT?
SISTER...
I AM SECOND ELDEST AND NOT SUCH A FOOL.
I KNOW MY LOVER LIVES. I SEE HIM OFTEN AND WOULD STAY WITH HIM, BUT HE LIVES IN THE WORLD ABOVE...
"TO BE WITH HIM I WOULD NEED TO BE *LIKE* HIM, TO HAVE LEGS AND BREATHE AIR..."
THAT IS WHAT I WANT.
IT'S A FAIR WISH.
AND LOOK...

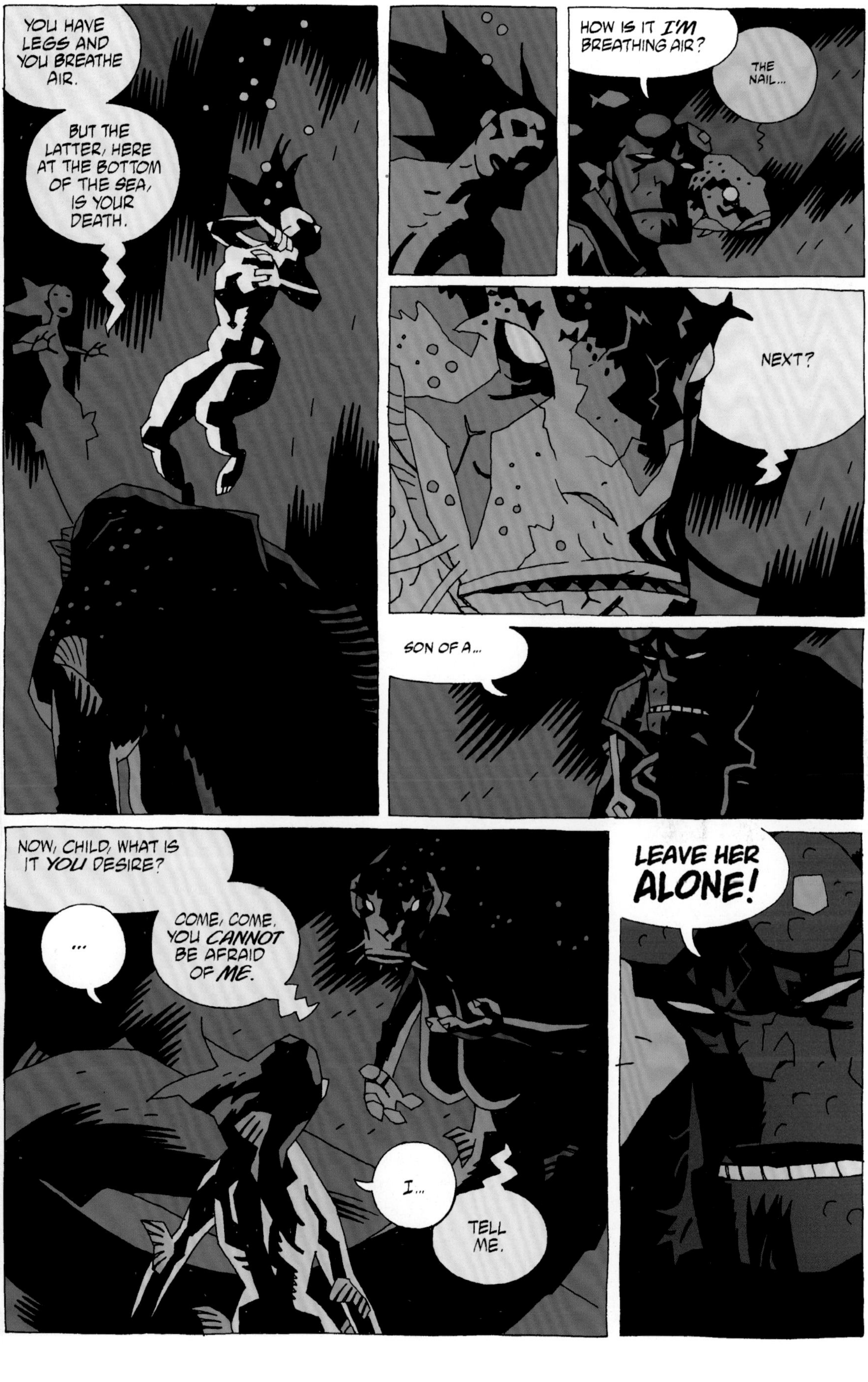
YOU HAVE LEGS AND YOU BREATHE AIR.
BUT THE LATTER, HERE AT THE BOTTOM OF THE SEA, IS YOUR DEATH.
HOW IS IT I'M BREATHING AIR?
THE NAIL...
NEXT?
SON OF A...
NOW, CHILD, WHAT IS IT YOU DESIRE?
...
COME, COME. YOU CANNOT BE AFRAID OF ME.
I...
TELL ME.
LEAVE HER ALONE!

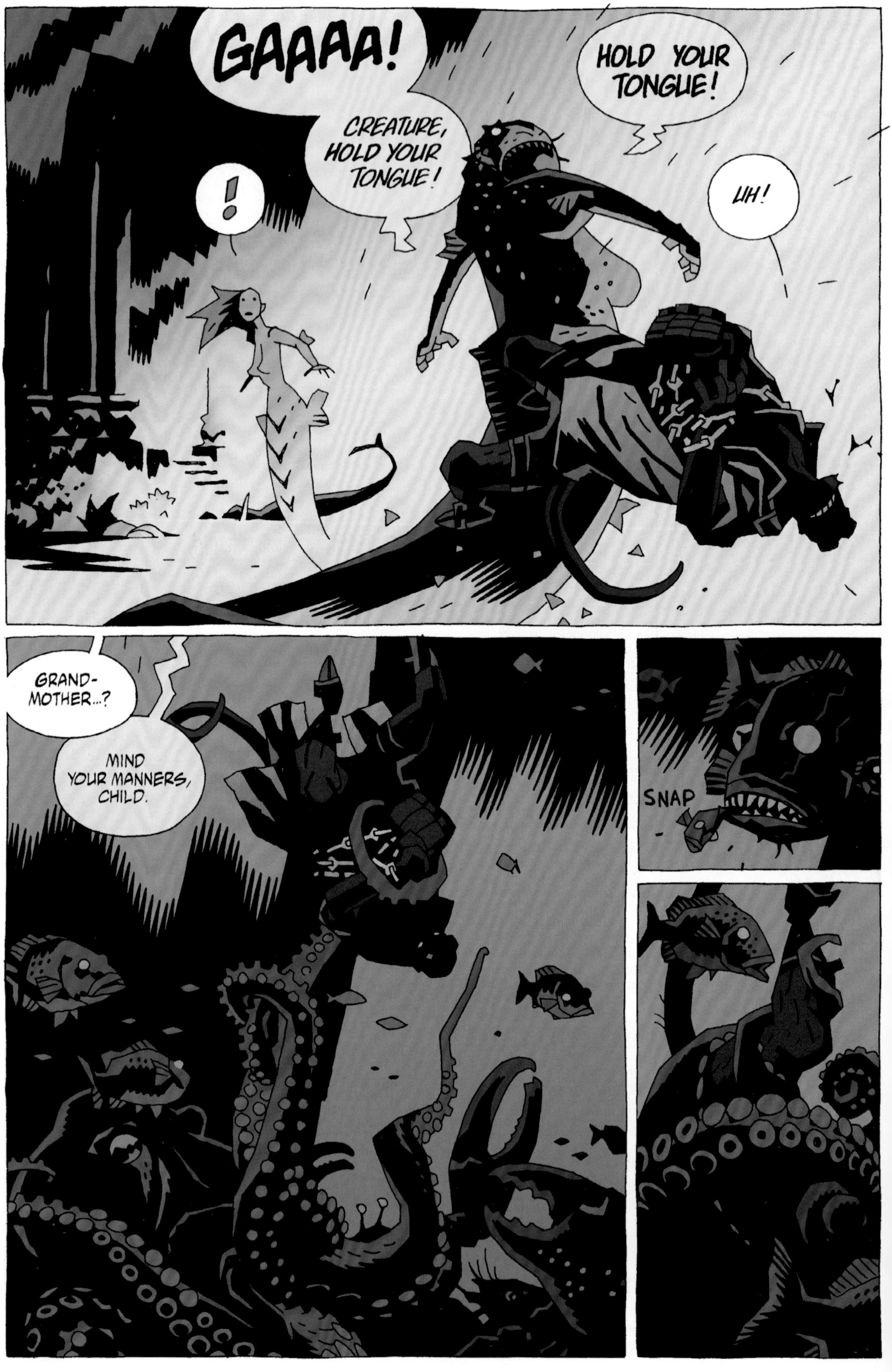
GAAAA!
CREATURE, HOLD YOUR TONGUE!
!
HOLD YOUR TONGUE!
UH!
GRAND-MOTHER...?
MIND YOUR MANNERS, CHILD.
SNAP

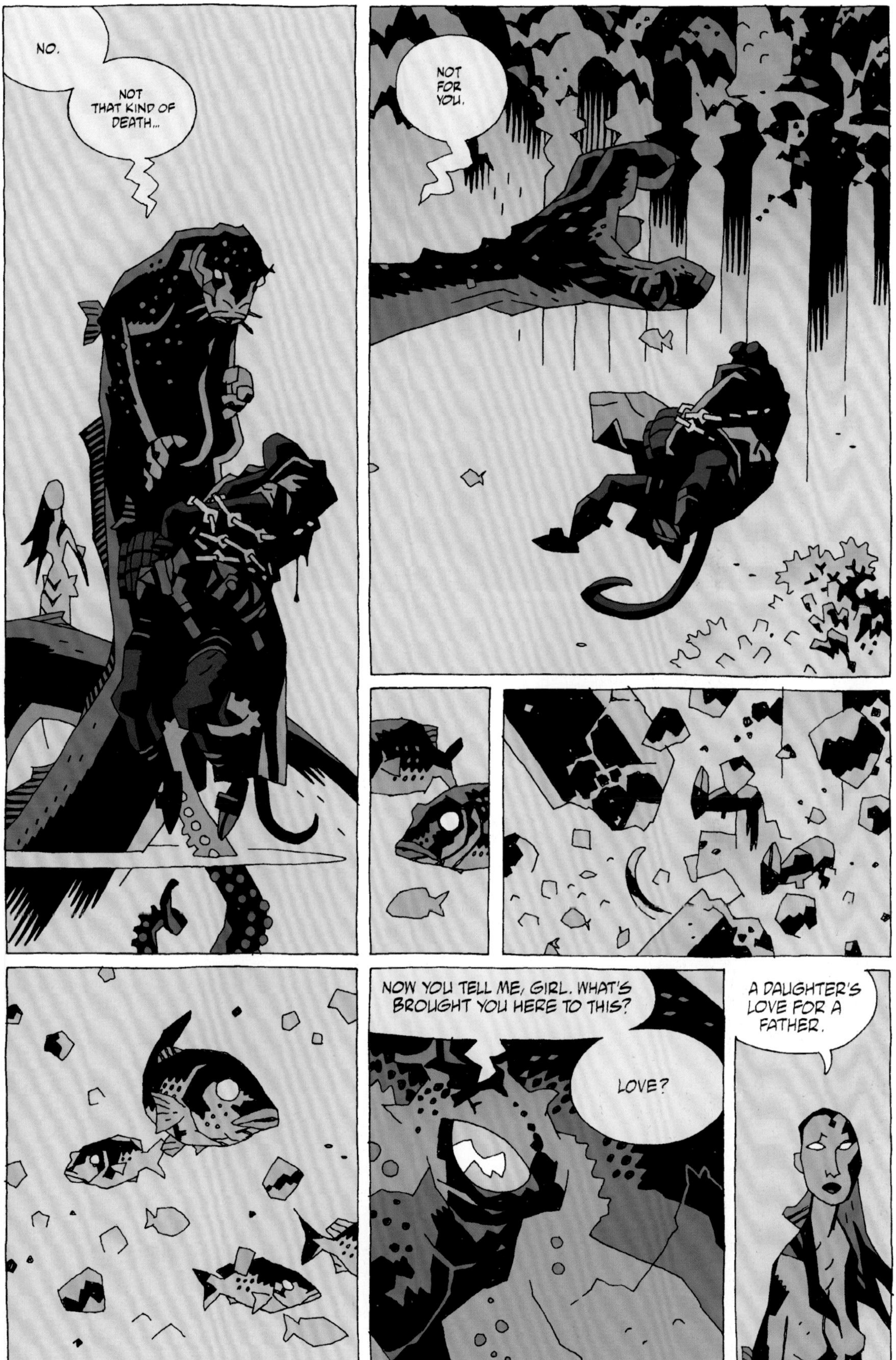
NO.
NOT THAT KIND OF DEATH...
NOT FOR YOU.
NOW YOU TELL ME, GIRL. WHAT'S BROUGHT YOU HERE TO THIS?
LOVE?
A DAUGHTER'S LOVE FOR A FATHER.

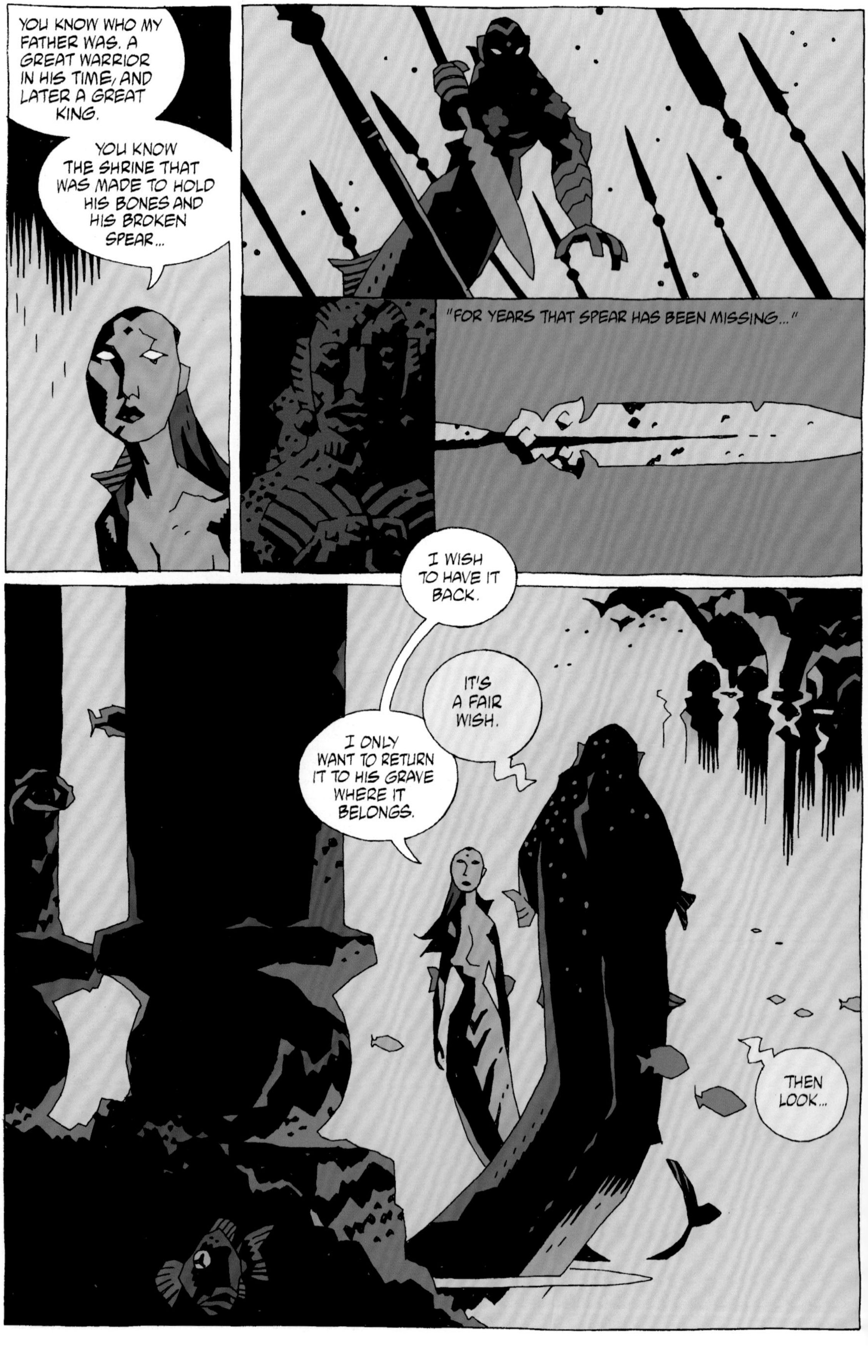
YOU KNOW WHO MY FATHER WAS. A GREAT WARRIOR IN HIS TIME, AND LATER A GREAT KING.
YOU KNOW THE SHRINE THAT WAS MADE TO HOLD HIS BONES AND HIS BROKEN SPEAR...
"FOR YEARS THAT SPEAR HAS BEEN MISSING..."
I WISH TO HAVE IT BACK.
I ONLY WANT TO RETURN IT TO HIS GRAVE WHERE IT BELONGS.
IT'S A FAIR WISH.
THEN LOOK...

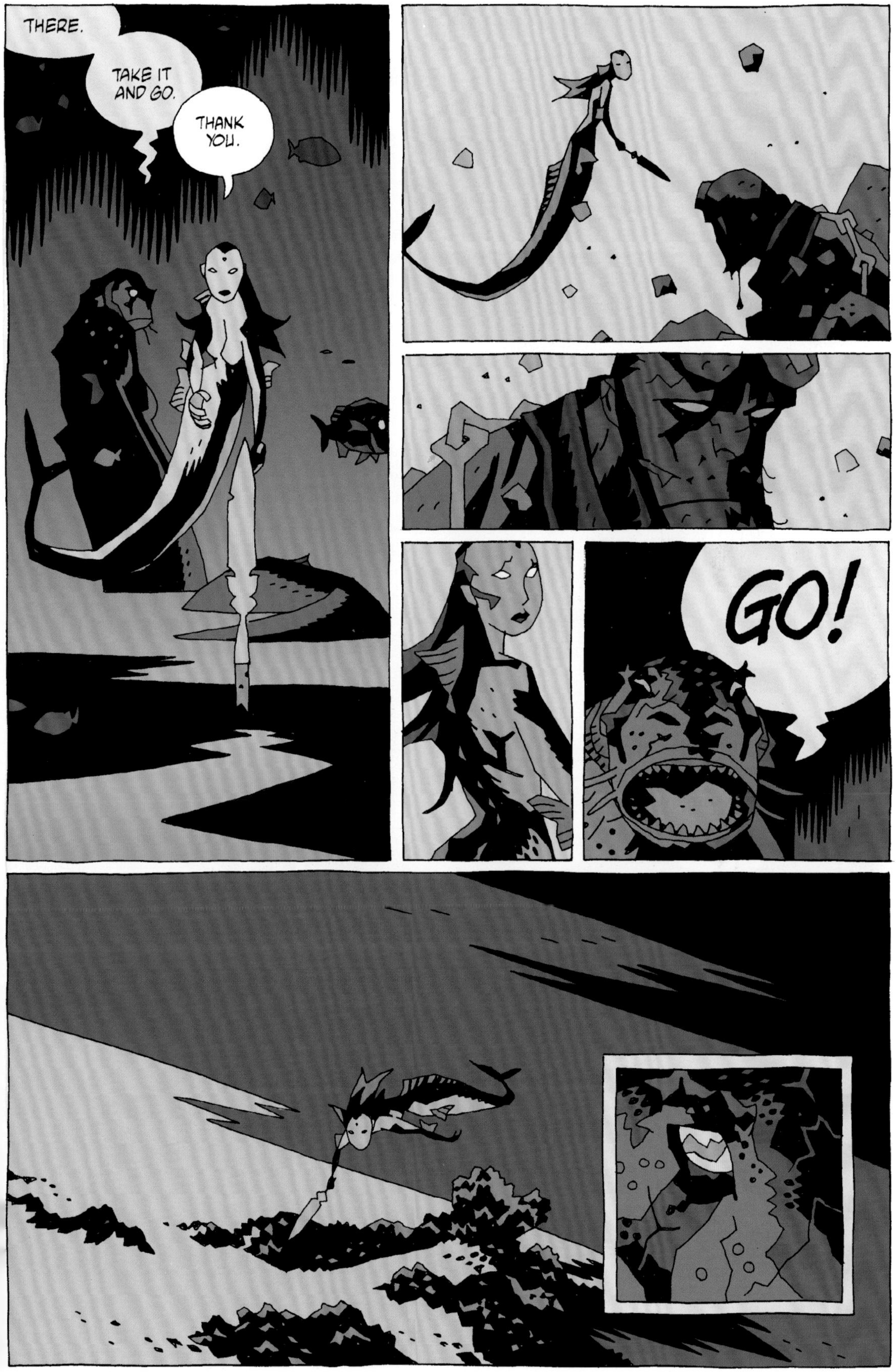
THERE.
TAKE IT AND GO.
THANK YOU.
GO!

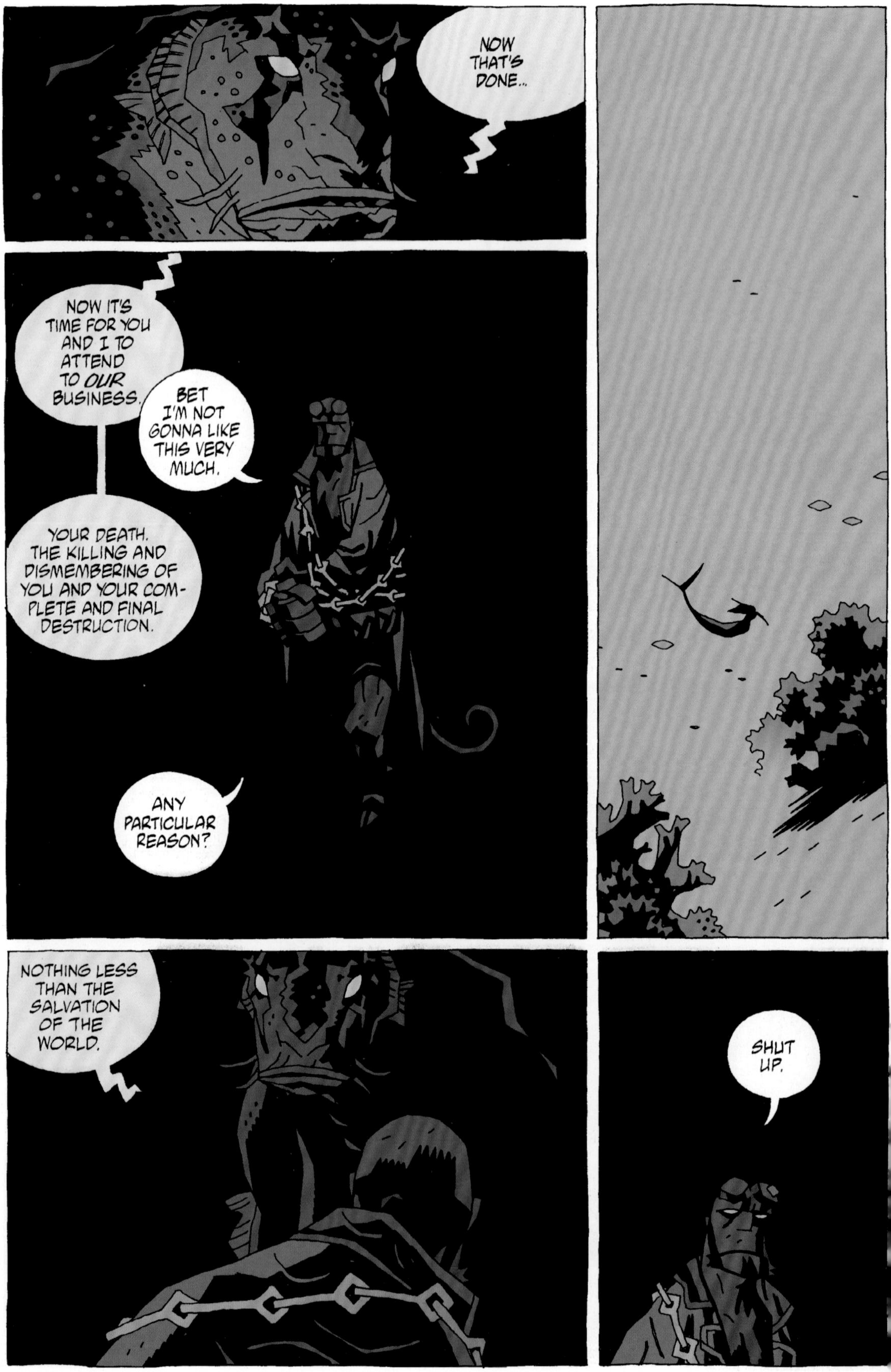
NOW THAT'S DONE...
NOW IT'S TIME FOR YOU AND I TO ATTEND TO *OUR* BUSINESS.
BET I'M NOT GONNA LIKE THIS VERY MUCH.
YOUR DEATH. THE KILLING AND DISMEMBERING OF YOU AND YOUR COMPLETE AND FINAL DESTRUCTION.
ANY PARTICULAR REASON?
NOTHING LESS THAN THE SALVATION OF THE WORLD.
SHUT UP.

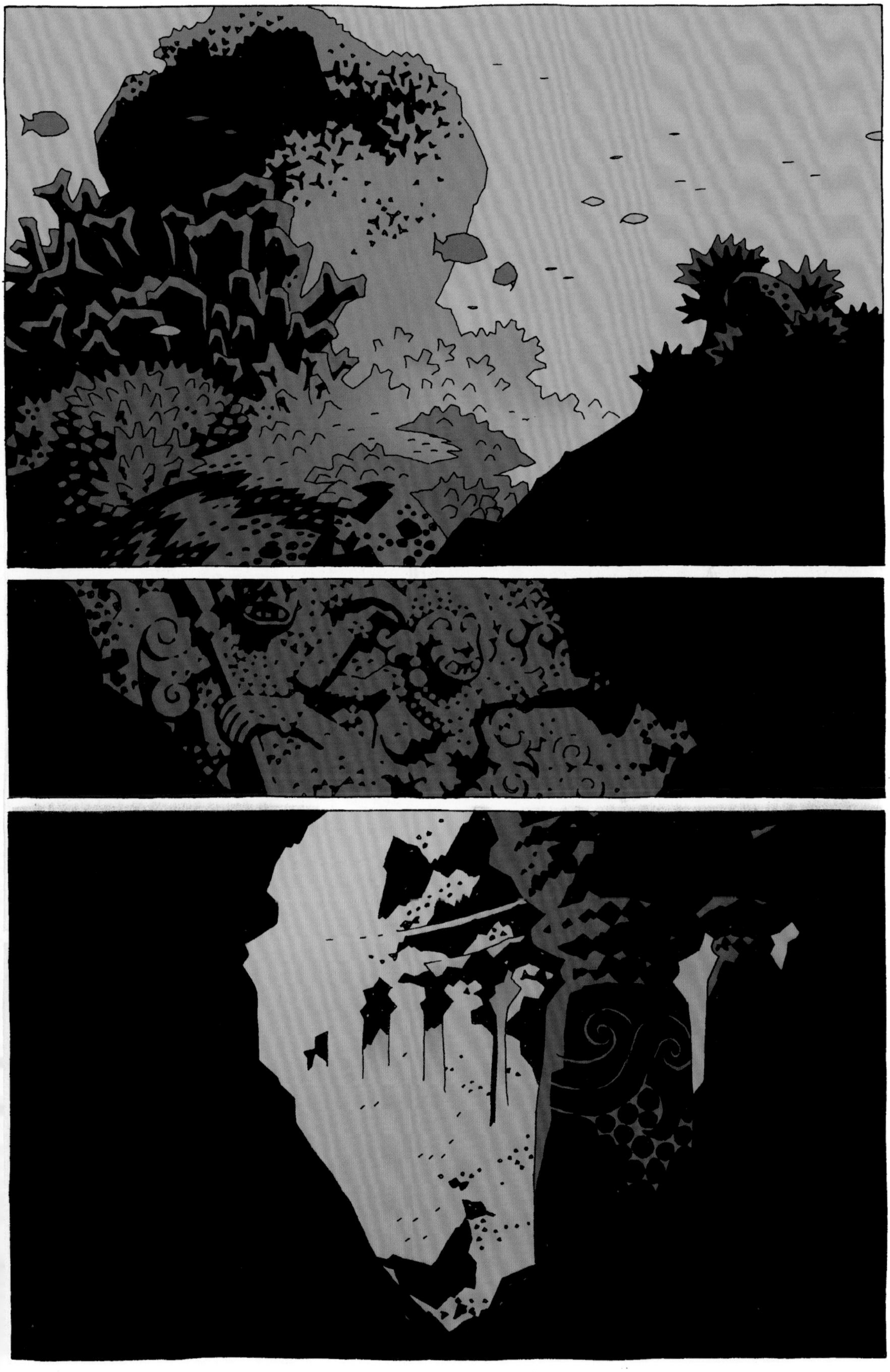

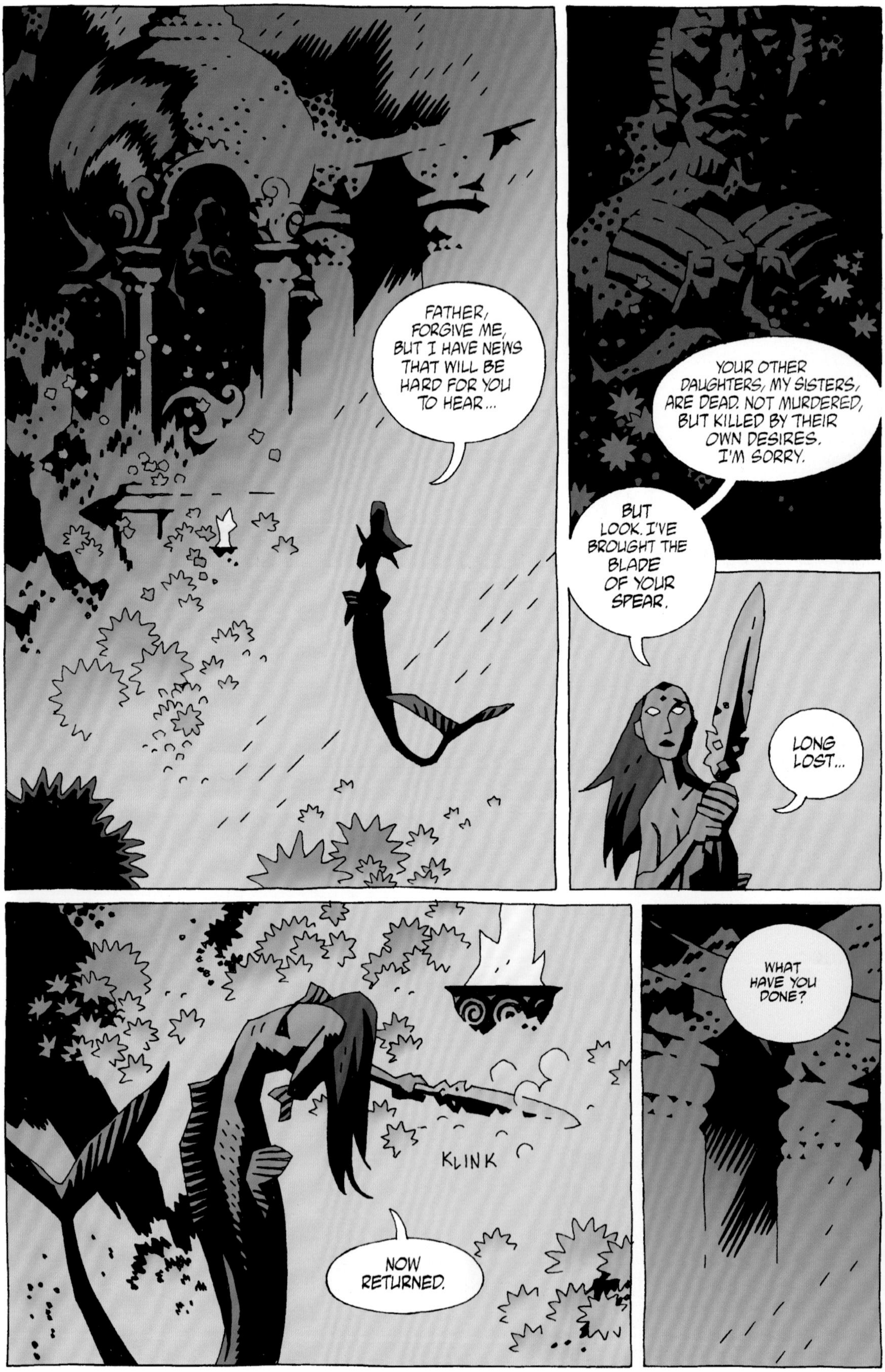
FATHER, FORGIVE ME, BUT I HAVE NEWS THAT WILL BE HARD FOR YOU TO HEAR...
YOUR OTHER DAUGHTERS, MY SISTERS, ARE DEAD. NOT MURDERED, BUT KILLED BY THEIR OWN DESIRES. I'M SORRY.
BUT LOOK. I'VE BROUGHT THE BLADE OF YOUR SPEAR.
LONG LOST...
KLINK
NOW RETURNED.
WHAT HAVE YOU DONE?

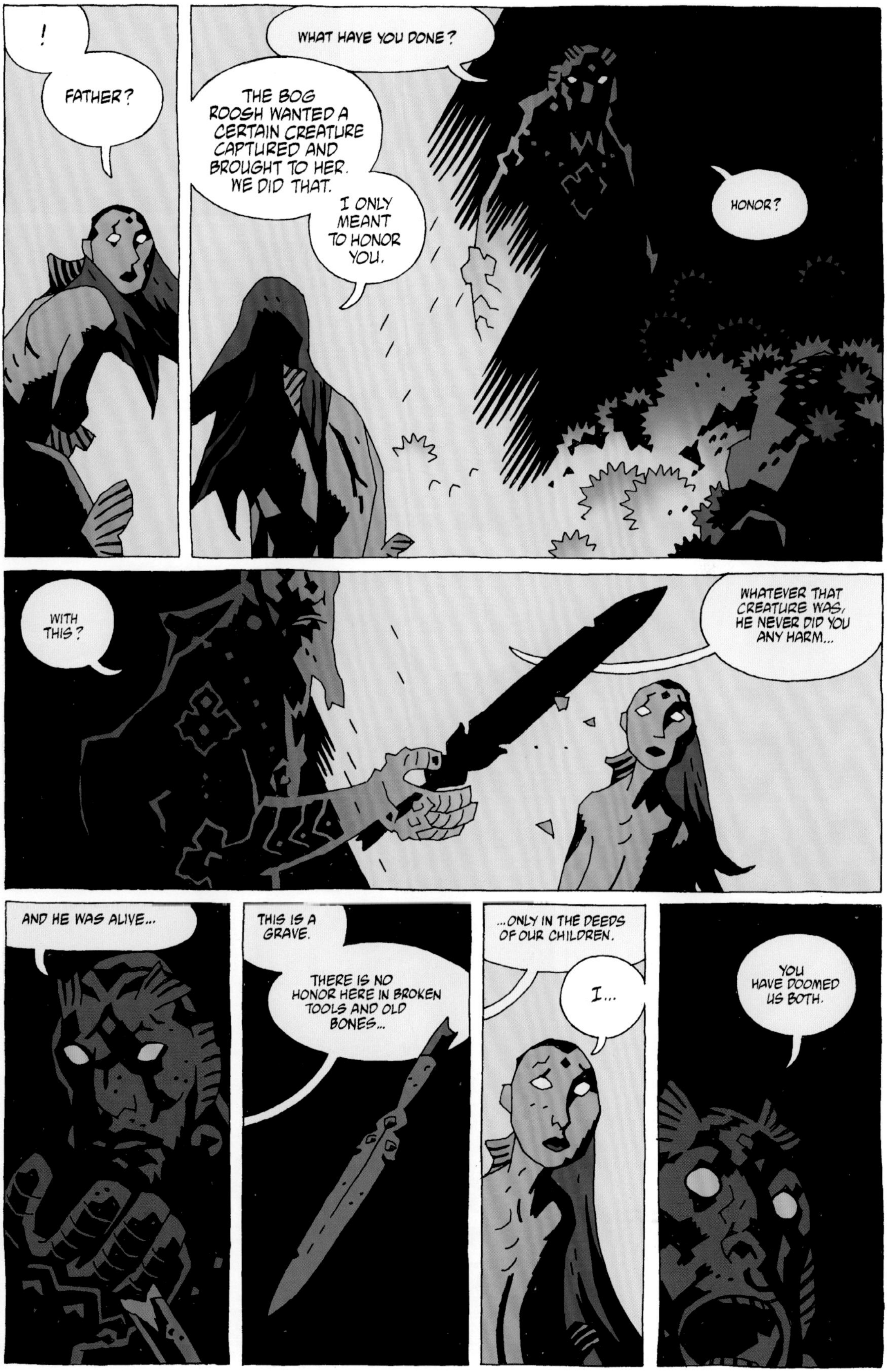
!
FATHER?
WHAT HAVE YOU DONE?
THE BOG ROOSH WANTED A CERTAIN CREATURE CAPTURED AND BROUGHT TO HER. WE DID THAT.
I ONLY MEANT TO HONOR YOU.
HONOR?
WITH THIS?
WHATEVER THAT CREATURE WAS, HE NEVER DID YOU ANY HARM...
AND HE WAS ALIVE...
THIS IS A GRAVE.
THERE IS NO HONOR HERE IN BROKEN TOOLS AND OLD BONES...
...ONLY IN THE DEEDS OF OUR CHILDREN.
I...
YOU HAVE DOOMED US BOTH.

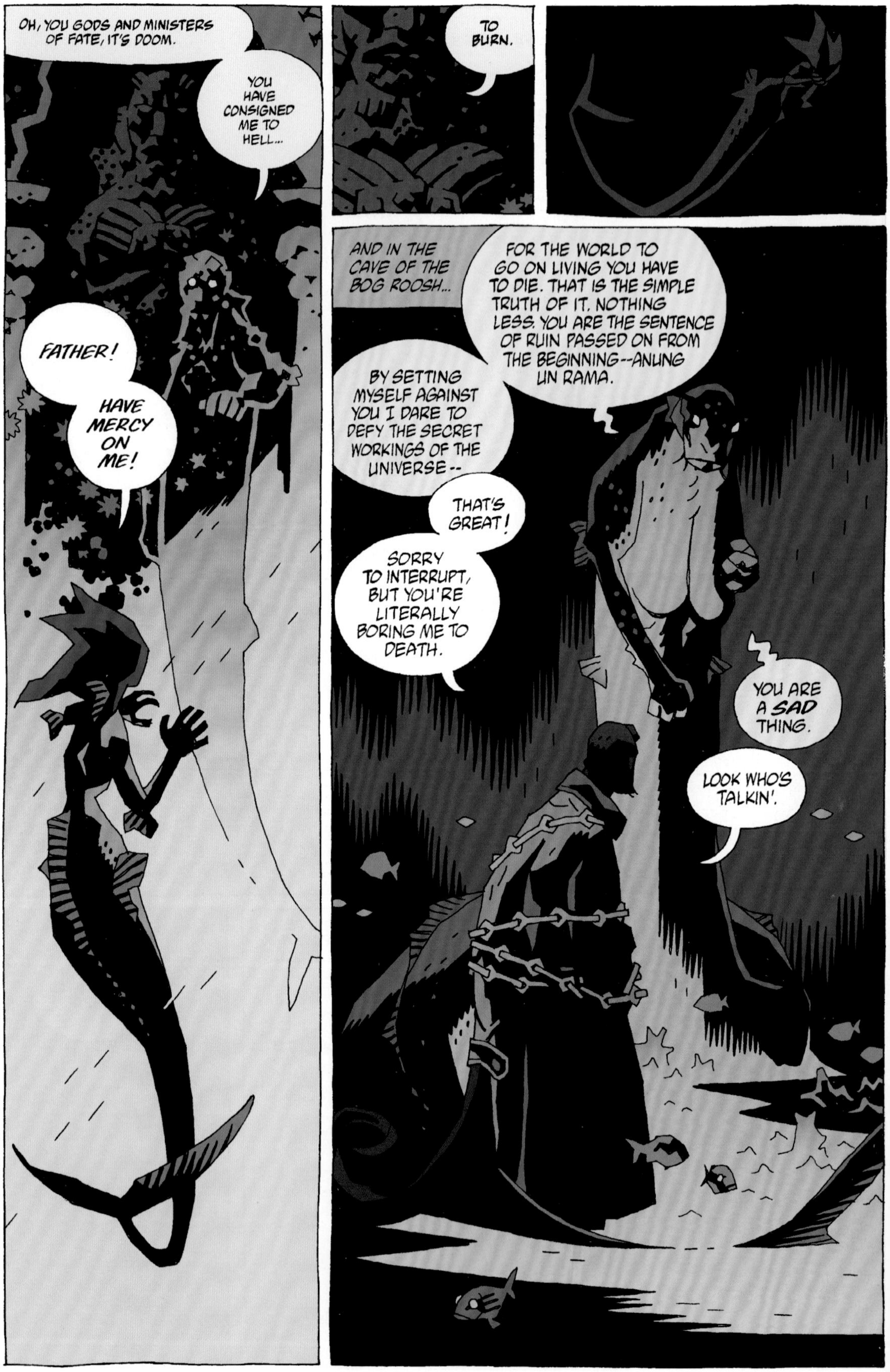
OH, YOU GODS AND MINISTERS OF FATE, IT'S DOOM.
YOU HAVE CONSIGNED ME TO HELL...
FATHER!
HAVE MERCY ON ME!
TO BURN.
AND IN THE CAVE OF THE BOG ROOSH...
FOR THE WORLD TO GO ON LIVING YOU HAVE TO DIE. THAT IS THE SIMPLE TRUTH OF IT. NOTHING LESS. YOU ARE THE SENTENCE OF RUIN PASSED ON FROM THE BEGINNING--ANUNG UN RAMA.
BY SETTING MYSELF AGAINST YOU I DARE TO DEFY THE SECRET WORKINGS OF THE UNIVERSE--
THAT'S GREAT!
SORRY TO INTERRUPT, BUT YOU'RE LITERALLY BORING ME TO DEATH.
YOU ARE A SAD THING.
LOOK WHO'S TALKIN'.

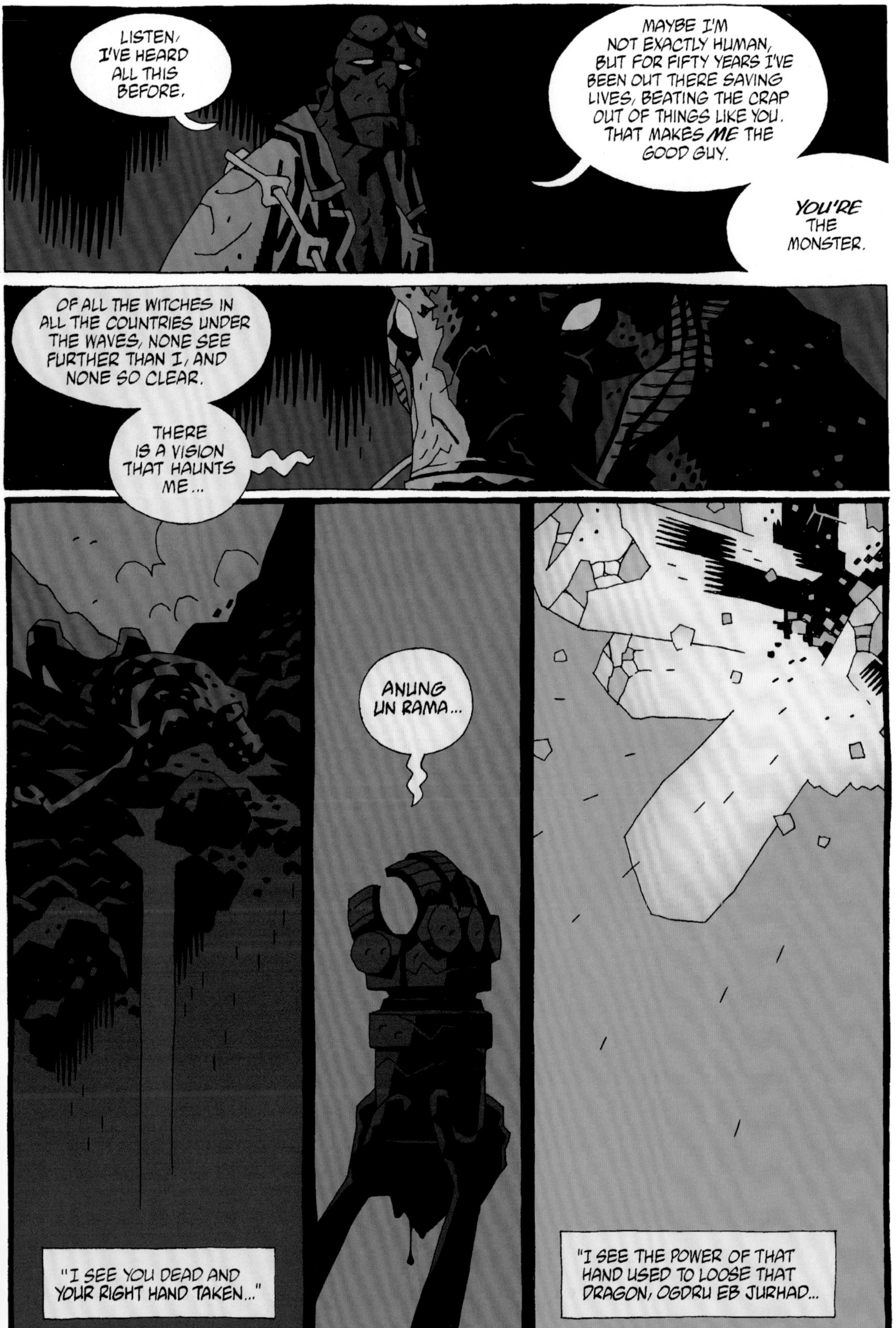

LISTEN, I'VE HEARD ALL THIS BEFORE.
MAYBE I'M NOT EXACTLY HUMAN, BUT FOR FIFTY YEARS I'VE BEEN OUT THERE SAVING LIVES, BEATING THE CRAP OUT OF THINGS LIKE YOU. THAT MAKES ME THE GOOD GUY.
YOU'RE THE MONSTER.
OF ALL THE WITCHES IN ALL THE COUNTRIES UNDER THE WAVES, NONE SEE FURTHER THAN I, AND NONE SO CLEAR.
THERE IS A VISION THAT HAUNTS ME...
"I SEE YOU DEAD AND YOUR RIGHT HAND TAKEN..."
ANUNG UN RAMA...
"I SEE THE POWER OF THAT HAND USED TO LOOSE THAT DRAGON, OGDRU EB JURHAD...

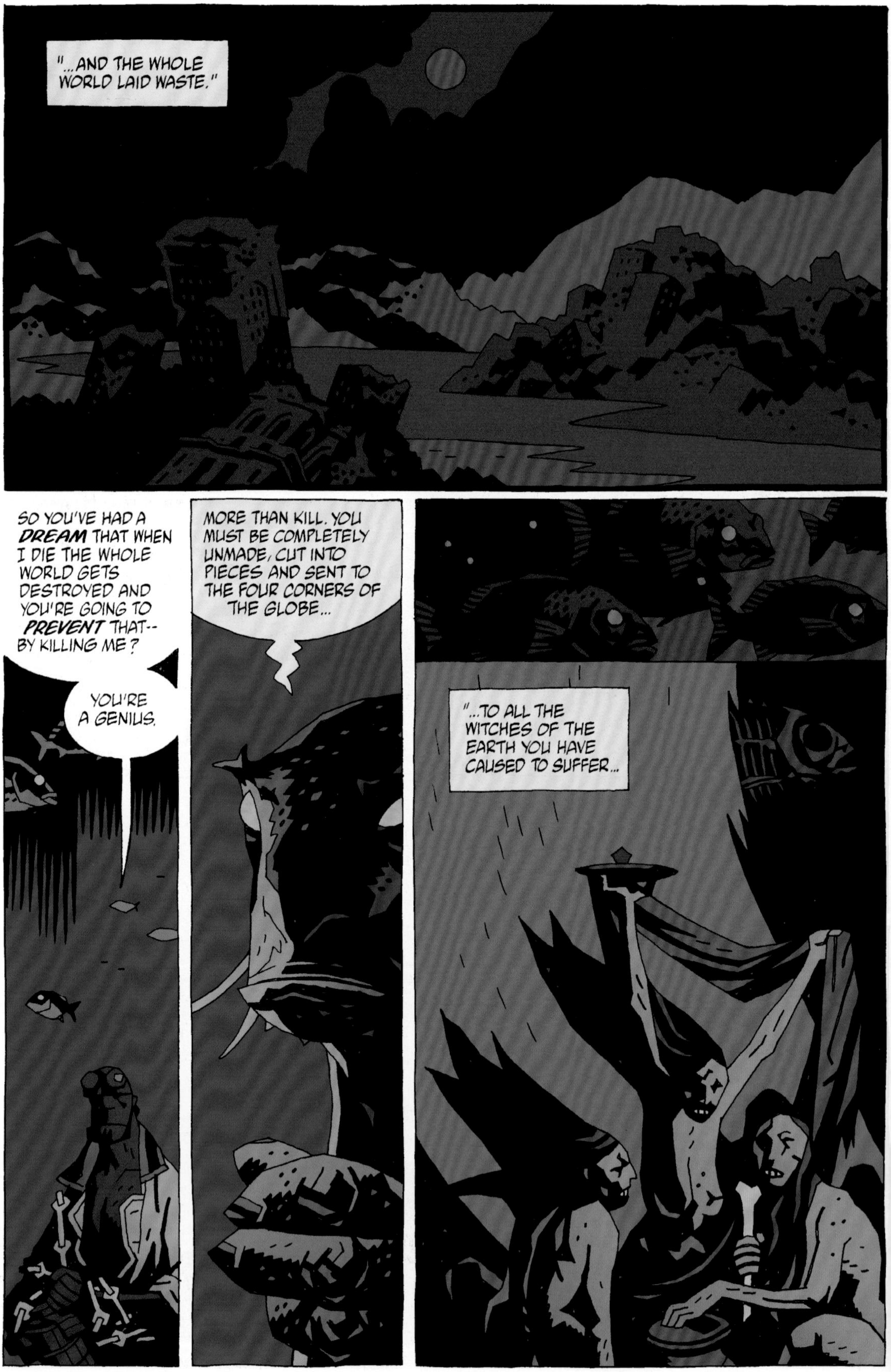
"...AND THE WHOLE WORLD LAID WASTE."
SO YOU'VE HAD A DREAM THAT WHEN I DIE THE WHOLE WORLD GETS DESTROYED AND YOU'RE GOING TO PREVENT THAT-- BY KILLING ME?
YOU'RE A GENIUS.
MORE THAN KILL. YOU MUST BE COMPLETELY UNMADE, CUT INTO PIECES AND SENT TO THE FOUR CORNERS OF THE GLOBE...
"...TO ALL THE WITCHES OF THE EARTH YOU HAVE CAUSED TO SUFFER...

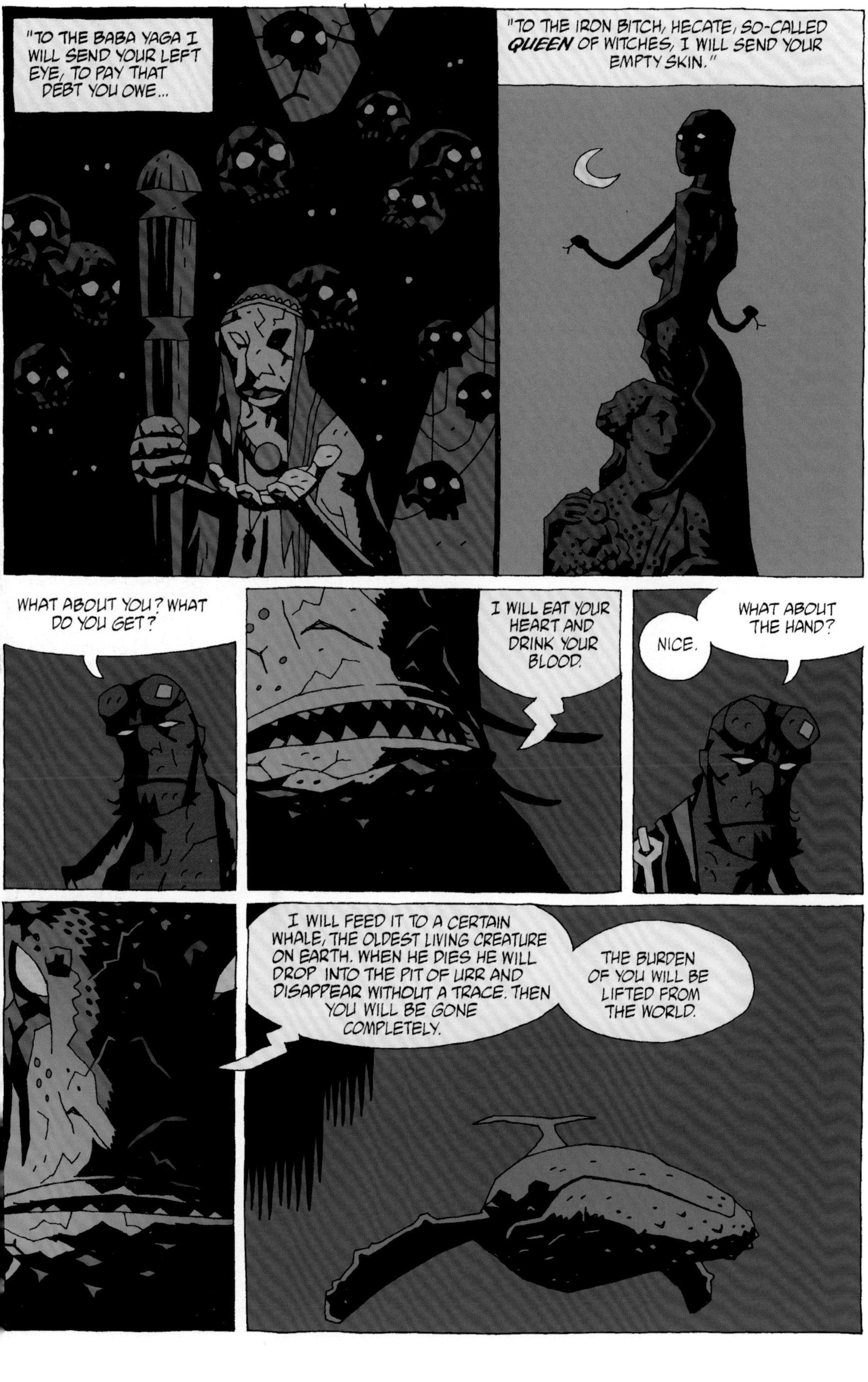
"TO THE BABA YAGA I WILL SEND YOUR LEFT EYE, TO PAY THAT DEBT YOU OWE...
"TO THE IRON BITCH, HECATE, SO-CALLED QUEEN OF WITCHES, I WILL SEND YOUR EMPTY SKIN."
WHAT ABOUT YOU? WHAT DO YOU GET?
I WILL EAT YOUR HEART AND DRINK YOUR BLOOD.
NICE.
WHAT ABOUT THE HAND?
I WILL FEED IT TO A CERTAIN WHALE, THE OLDEST LIVING CREATURE ON EARTH. WHEN HE DIES HE WILL DROP INTO THE PIT OF URR AND DISAPPEAR WITHOUT A TRACE. THEN YOU WILL BE GONE COMPLETELY.
THE BURDEN OF YOU WILL BE LIFTED FROM THE WORLD.

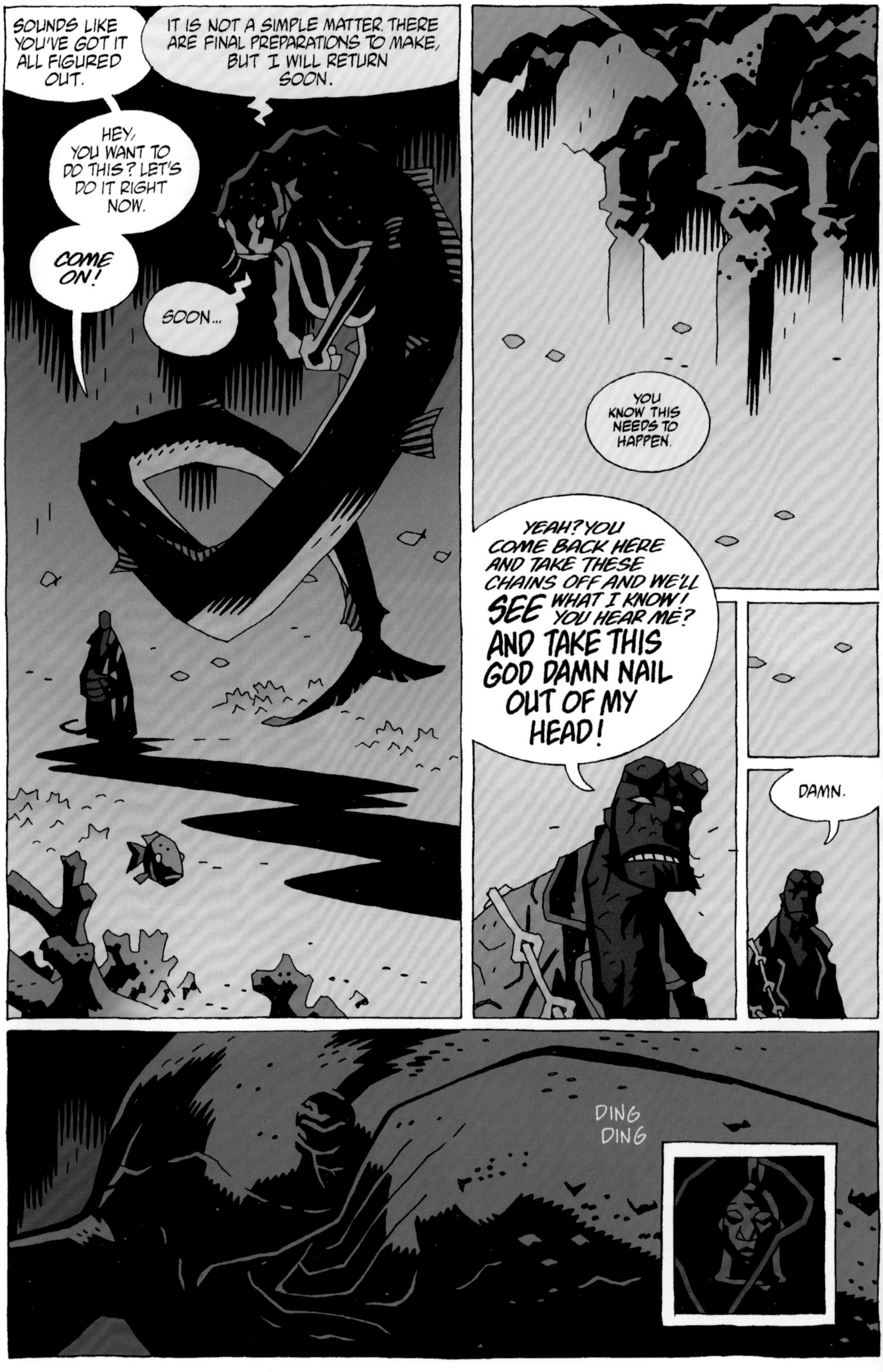

SOUNDS LIKE YOU'VE GOT IT ALL FIGURED OUT.
IT IS NOT A SIMPLE MATTER. THERE ARE FINAL PREPARATIONS TO MAKE, BUT I WILL RETURN SOON.
HEY, YOU WANT TO DO THIS? LET'S DO IT RIGHT NOW.
COME ON!
SOON...
YOU KNOW THIS NEEDS TO HAPPEN.
YEAH? YOU COME BACK HERE AND TAKE THESE CHAINS OFF AND WE'LL SEE WHAT I KNOW! YOU HEAR ME? AND TAKE THIS GOD DAMN NAIL OUT OF MY HEAD!
DAMN.
DING DING

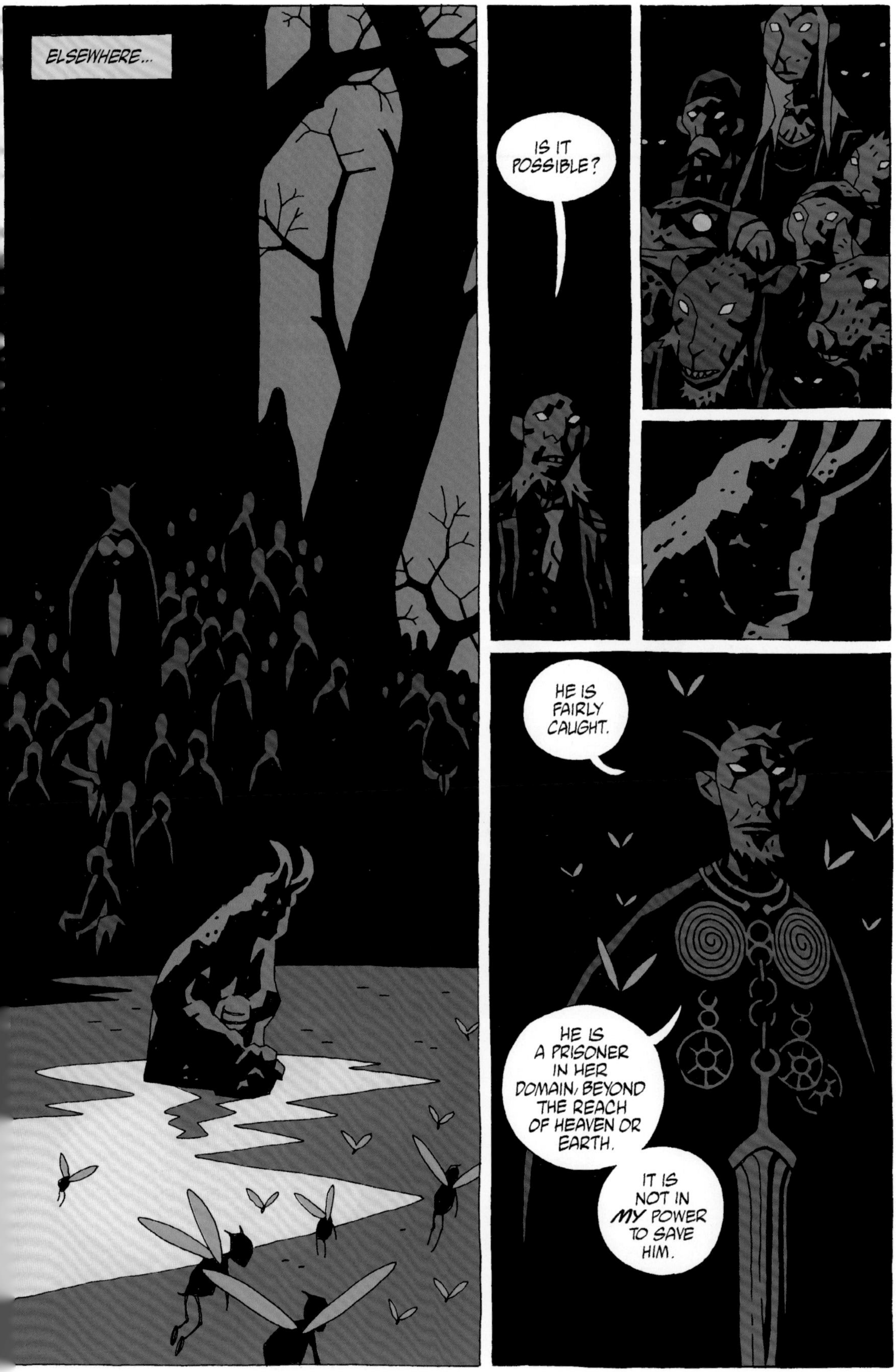
ELSEWHERE...
IS IT POSSIBLE?
HE IS FAIRLY CAUGHT.
HE IS A PRISONER IN HER DOMAIN, BEYOND THE REACH OF HEAVEN OR EARTH.
IT IS NOT IN MY POWER TO SAVE HIM.

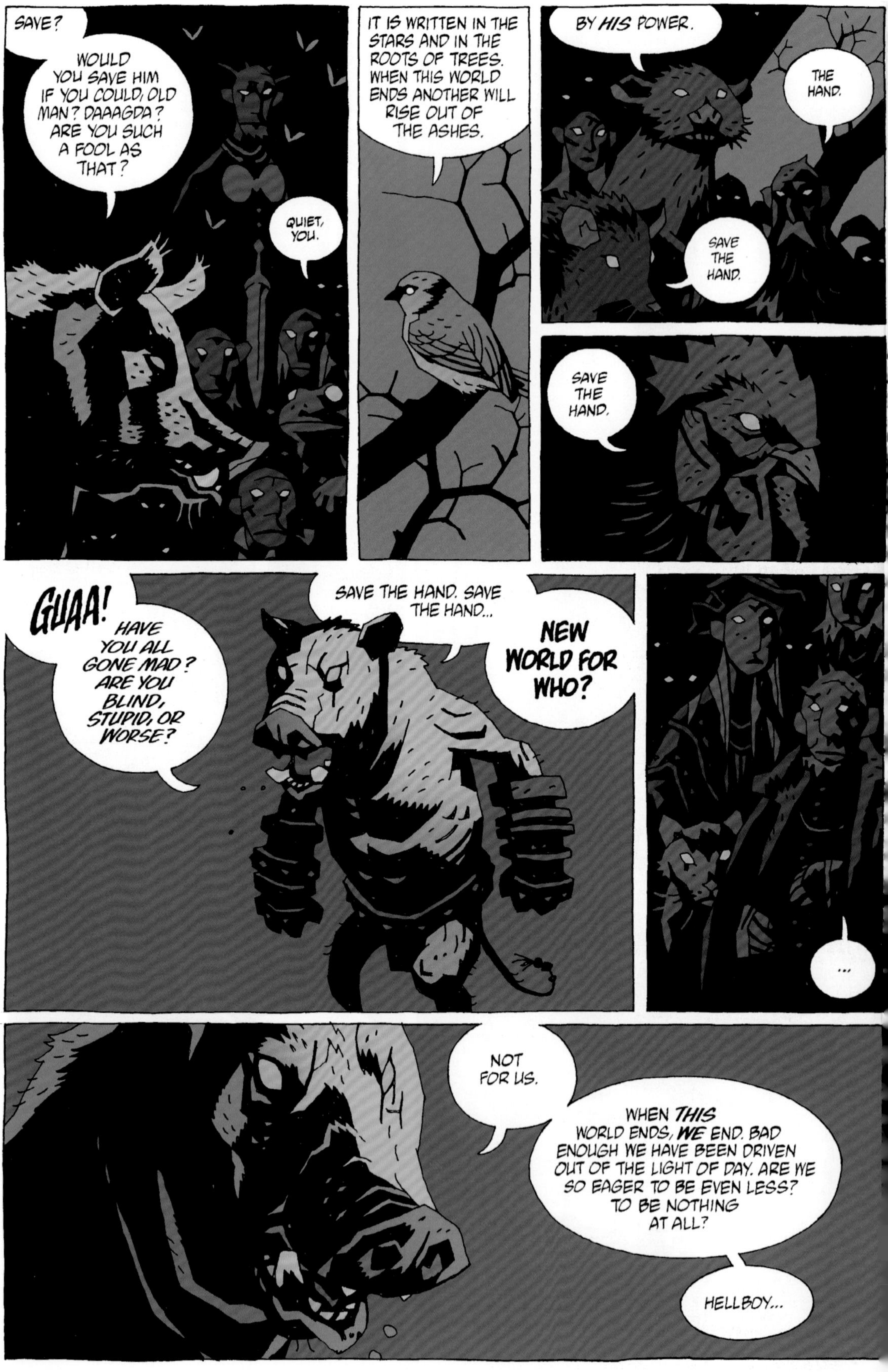
SAVE?
WOULD YOU SAVE HIM IF YOU COULD, OLD MAN? DAAAGDA? ARE YOU SUCH A FOOL AS THAT?
QUIET, YOU.
IT IS WRITTEN IN THE STARS AND IN THE ROOTS OF TREES. WHEN THIS WORLD ENDS ANOTHER WILL RISE OUT OF THE ASHES.
BY HIS POWER.
THE HAND.
SAVE THE HAND.
SAVE THE HAND.
GUAA!
HAVE YOU ALL GONE MAD? ARE YOU BLIND, STUPID, OR WORSE?
SAVE THE HAND. SAVE THE HAND...
NEW WORLD FOR WHO?
...
NOT FOR US.
WHEN THIS WORLD ENDS, WE END. BAD ENOUGH WE HAVE BEEN DRIVEN OUT OF THE LIGHT OF DAY. ARE WE SO EAGER TO BE EVEN LESS? TO BE NOTHING AT ALL?
HELLBOY...

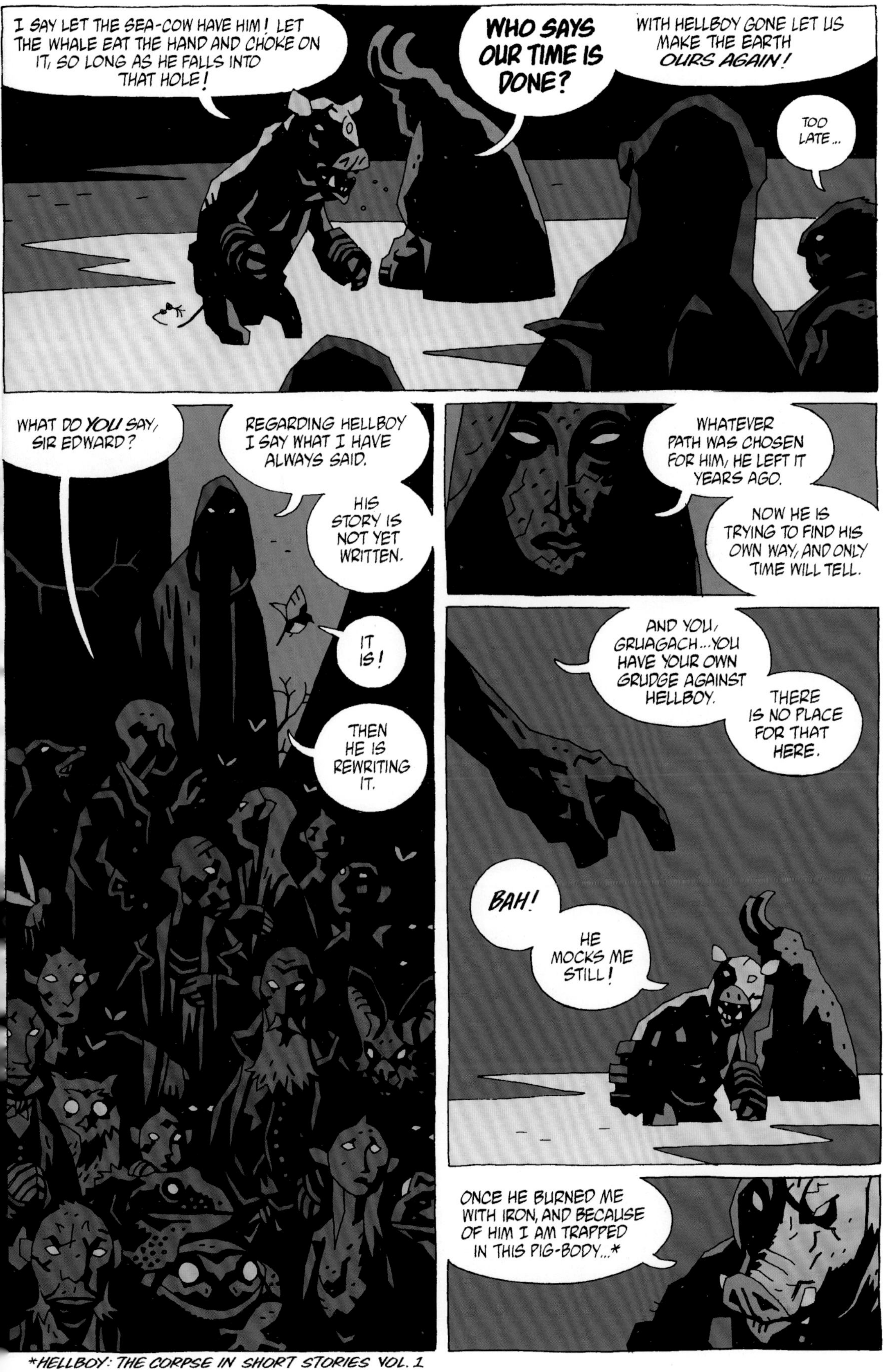
I SAY LET THE SEA-COW HAVE HIM! LET THE WHALE EAT THE HAND AND CHOKE ON IT, SO LONG AS HE FALLS INTO THAT HOLE!
WHO SAYS OUR TIME IS DONE?
WITH HELLBOY GONE LET US MAKE THE EARTH OURS AGAIN!
TOO LATE...
WHAT DO YOU SAY, SIR EDWARD?
REGARDING HELLBOY I SAY WHAT I HAVE ALWAYS SAID.
HIS STORY IS NOT YET WRITTEN.
IT IS!
THEN HE IS REWRITING IT.
WHATEVER PATH WAS CHOSEN FOR HIM, HE LEFT IT YEARS AGO.
NOW HE IS TRYING TO FIND HIS OWN WAY, AND ONLY TIME WILL TELL.
AND YOU, GRUAGACH...YOU HAVE YOUR OWN GRUDGE AGAINST HELLBOY.
THERE IS NO PLACE FOR THAT HERE.
BAH!
HE MOCKS ME STILL!
ONCE HE BURNED ME WITH IRON, AND BECAUSE OF HIM I AM TRAPPED IN THIS PIG-BODY...*

*HELLBOY: THE CORPSE IN SHORT STORIES VOL. 1

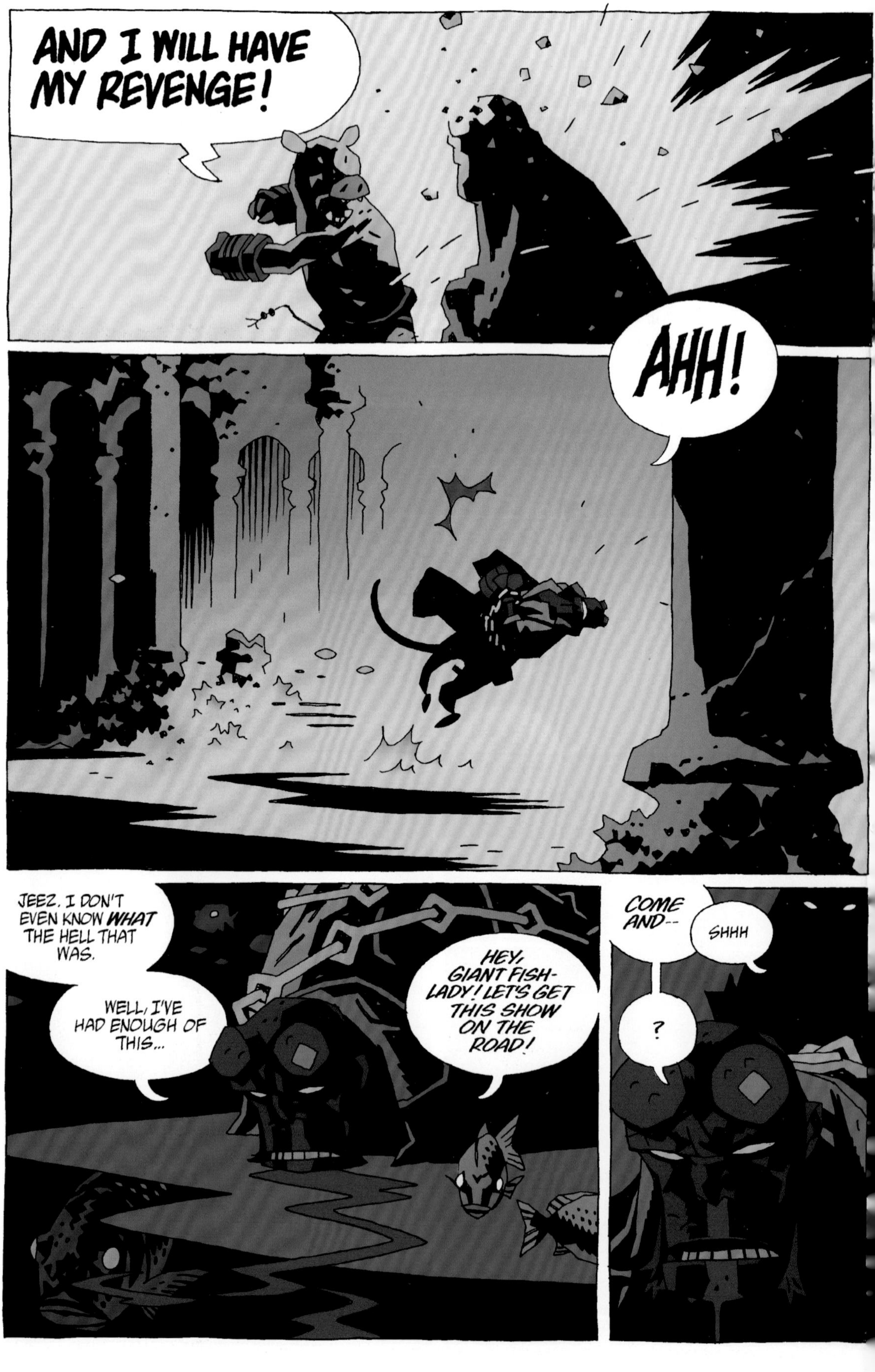
AND I WILL HAVE MY REVENGE!
AHH!
JEEZ. I DON'T EVEN KNOW WHAT THE HELL THAT WAS.
WELL, I'VE HAD ENOUGH OF THIS...
HEY, GIANT FISH-LADY! LET'S GET THIS SHOW ON THE ROAD!
COME AND--
SHHH
?

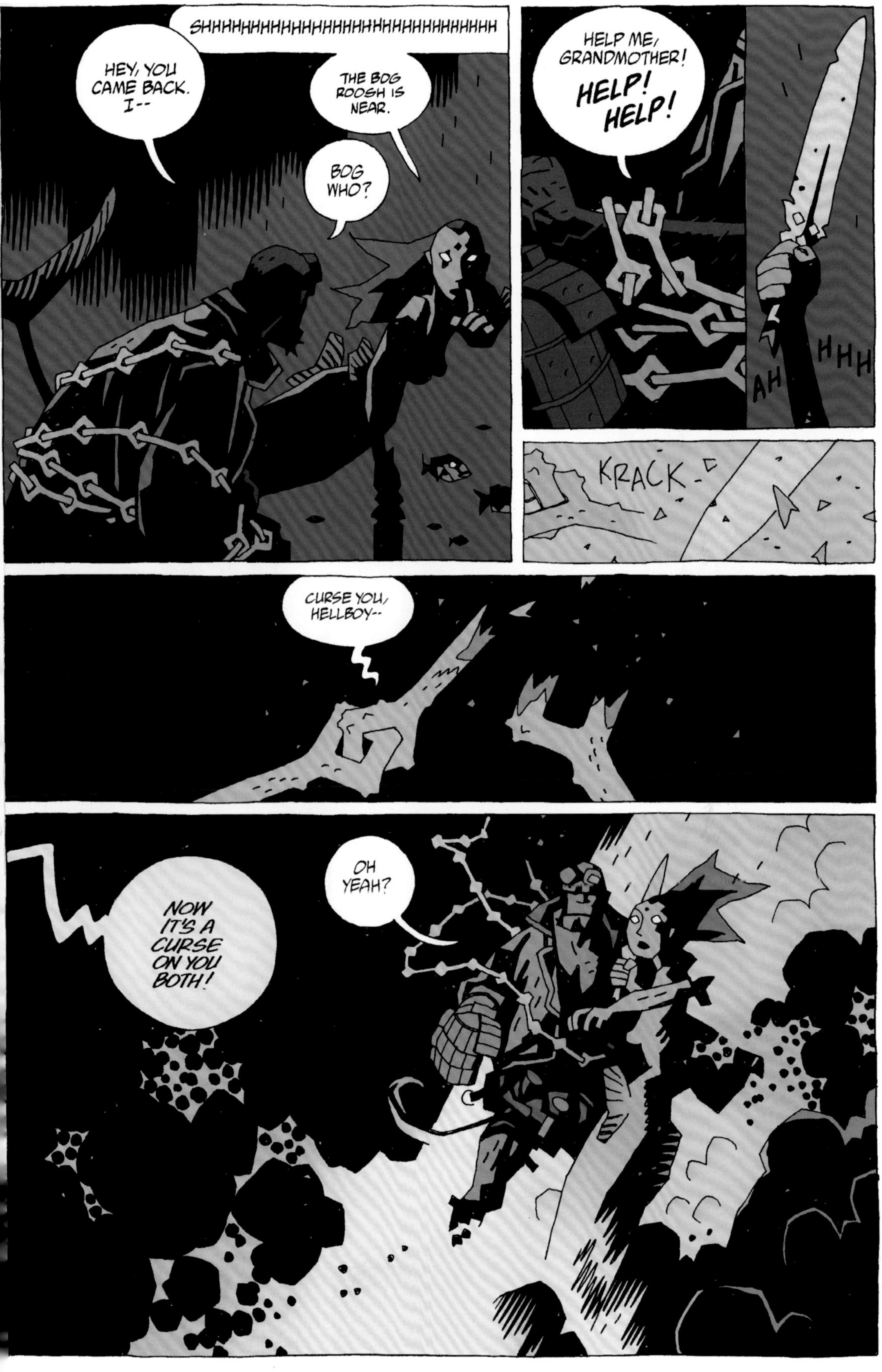
SHHHHHHHHHHHHHHHHHHHHHHHHHHHHHHHH
HEY, YOU CAME BACK. I--
THE BOG ROOSH IS NEAR.
BOG WHO?
HELP ME, GRANDMOTHER! HELP! HELP!
AHHHH
KRACK
CURSE YOU, HELLBOY--
OH YEAH?
NOW IT'S A CURSE ON YOU BOTH!

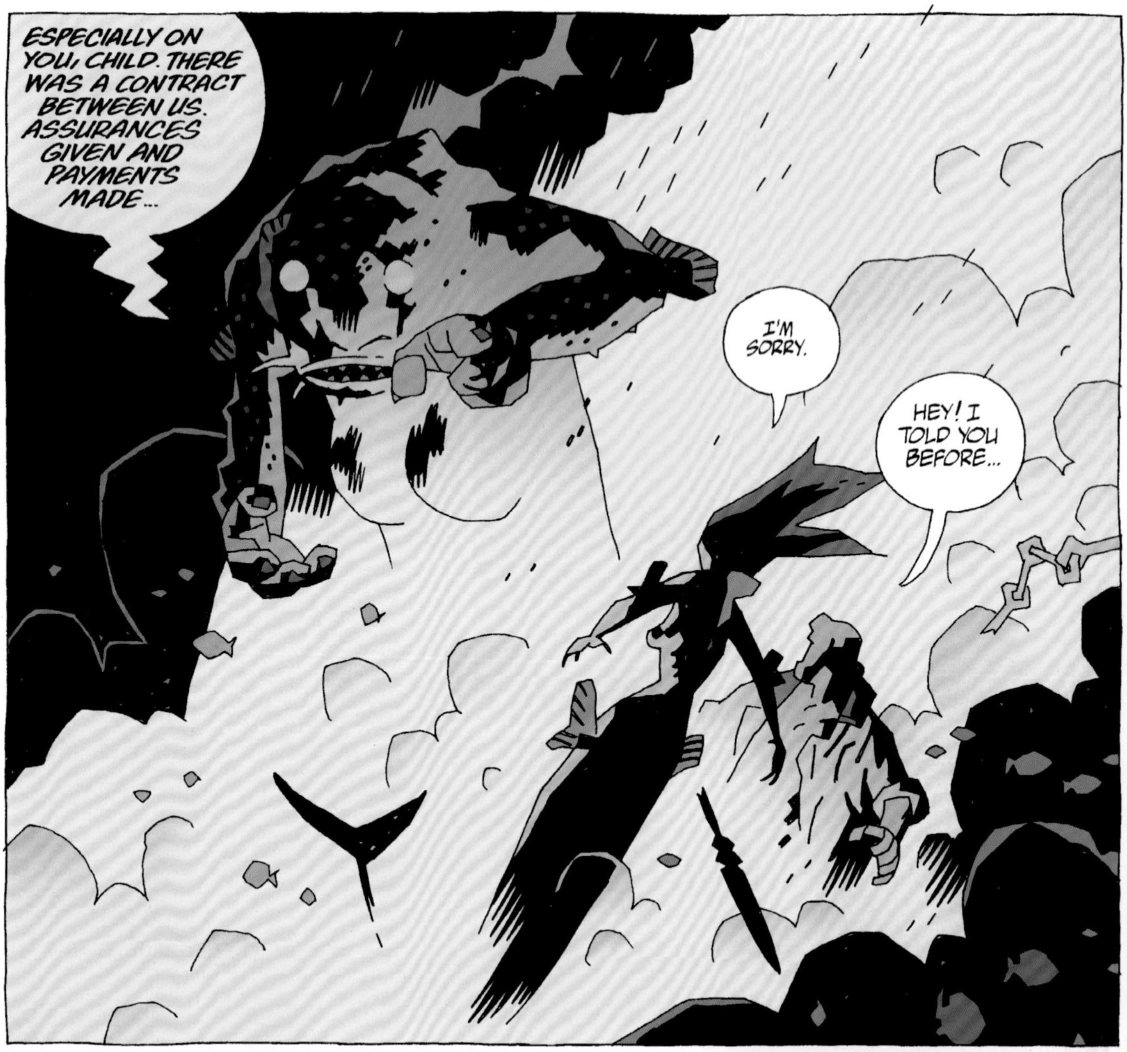
ESPECIALLY ON YOU, CHILD. THERE WAS A CONTRACT BETWEEN US. ASSURANCES GIVEN AND PAYMENTS MADE...
I'M SORRY.
HEY! I TOLD YOU BEFORE...

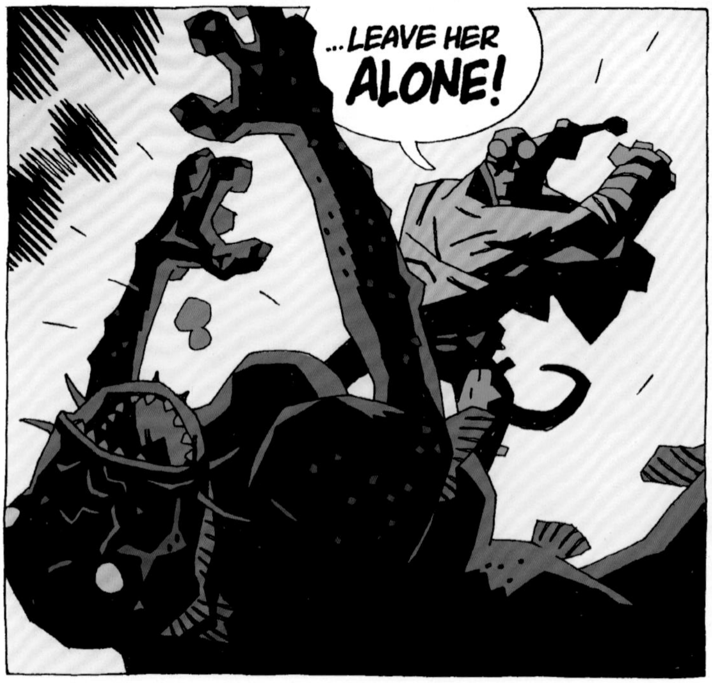
...LEAVE HER ALONE!

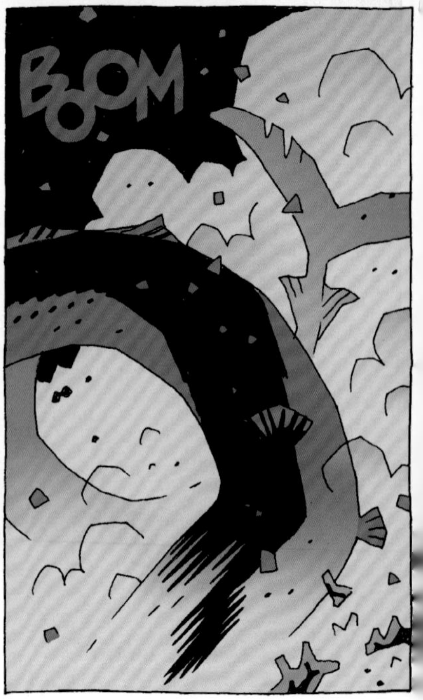
BOOM

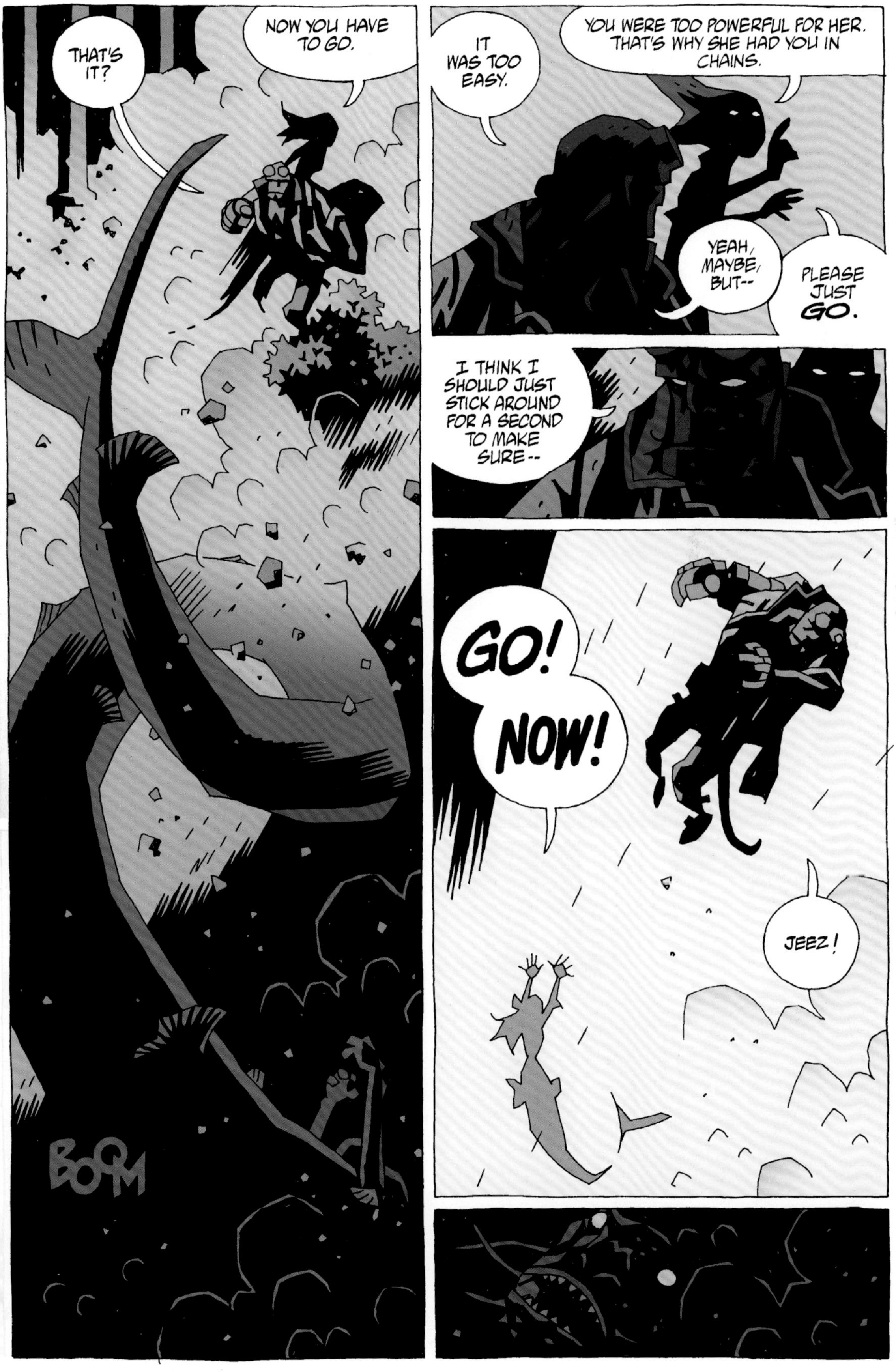
THAT'S IT?
NOW YOU HAVE TO GO.
BOOM
IT WAS TOO EASY.
YOU WERE TOO POWERFUL FOR HER. THAT'S WHY SHE HAD YOU IN CHAINS.
YEAH, MAYBE, BUT--
PLEASE JUST GO.
I THINK I SHOULD JUST STICK AROUND FOR A SECOND TO MAKE SURE--
GO!
NOW!
JEEZ!

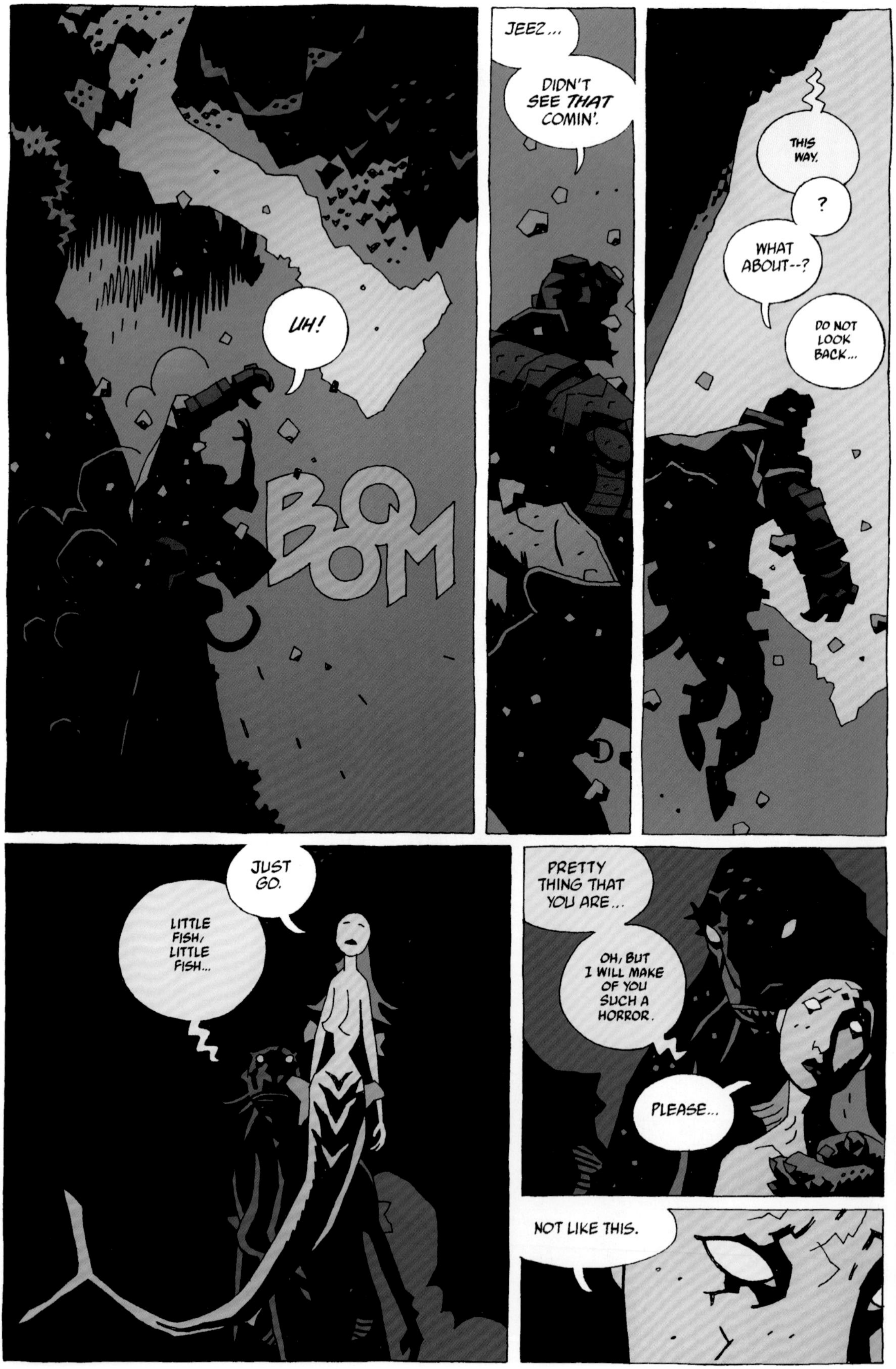
UH!
BOOM
JEEZ...
DIDN'T SEE THAT COMIN'.
THIS WAY.
?
WHAT ABOUT--?
DO NOT LOOK BACK...
JUST GO.
LITTLE FISH, LITTLE FISH...
PRETTY THING THAT YOU ARE...
OH, BUT I WILL MAKE OF YOU SUCH A HORROR.
PLEASE...
NOT LIKE THIS.

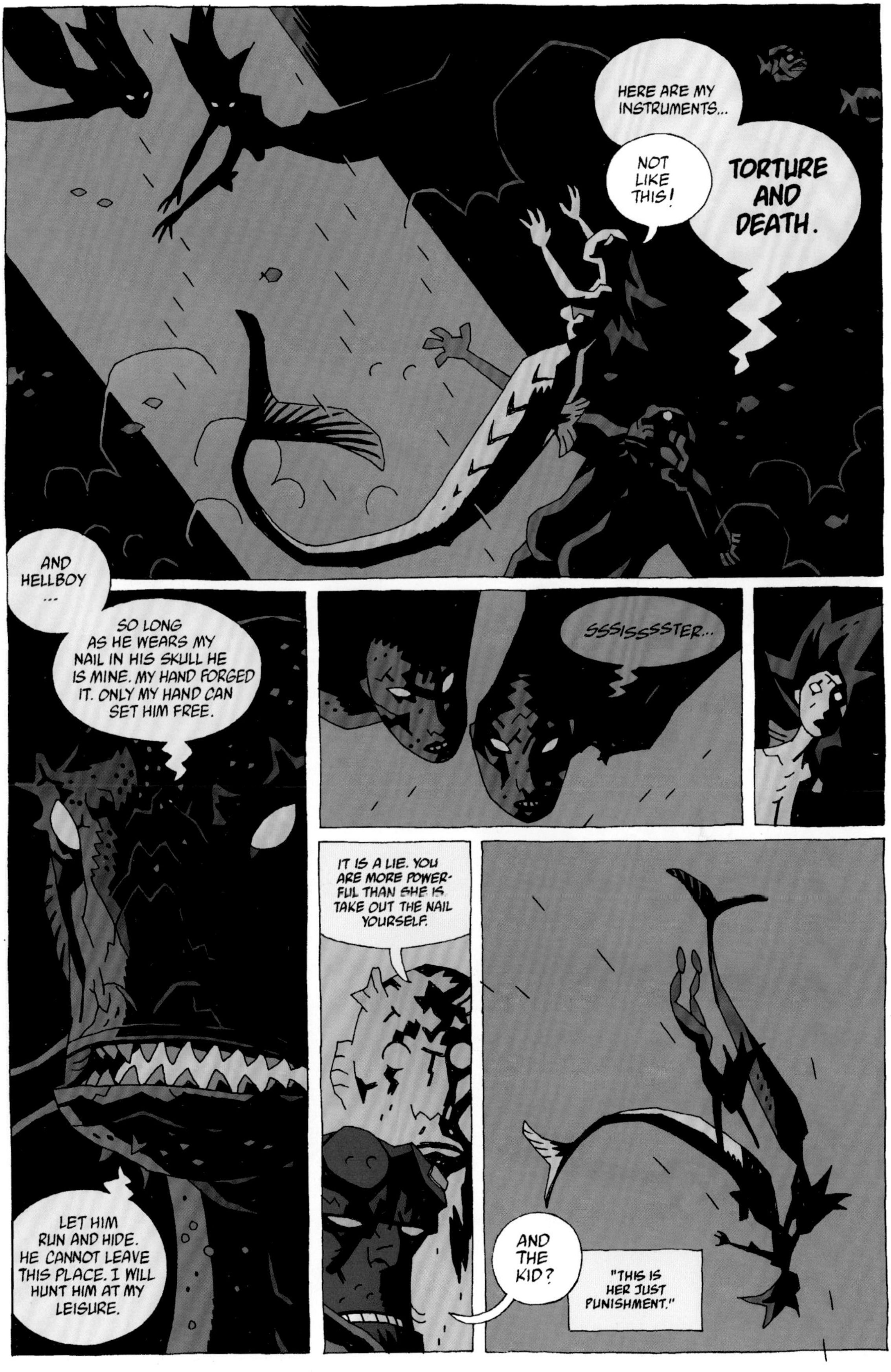
HERE ARE MY INSTRUMENTS...
NOT LIKE THIS!
TORTURE AND DEATH.
AND HELLBOY ...
SO LONG AS HE WEARS MY NAIL IN HIS SKULL HE IS MINE. MY HAND FORGED IT. ONLY MY HAND CAN SET HIM FREE.
LET HIM RUN AND HIDE. HE CANNOT LEAVE THIS PLACE. I WILL HUNT HIM AT MY LEISURE.
SSSISSSSTER...
IT IS A LIE. YOU ARE MORE POWERFUL THAN SHE IS. TAKE OUT THE NAIL YOURSELF.
AND THE KID?
"THIS IS HER JUST PUNISHMENT."

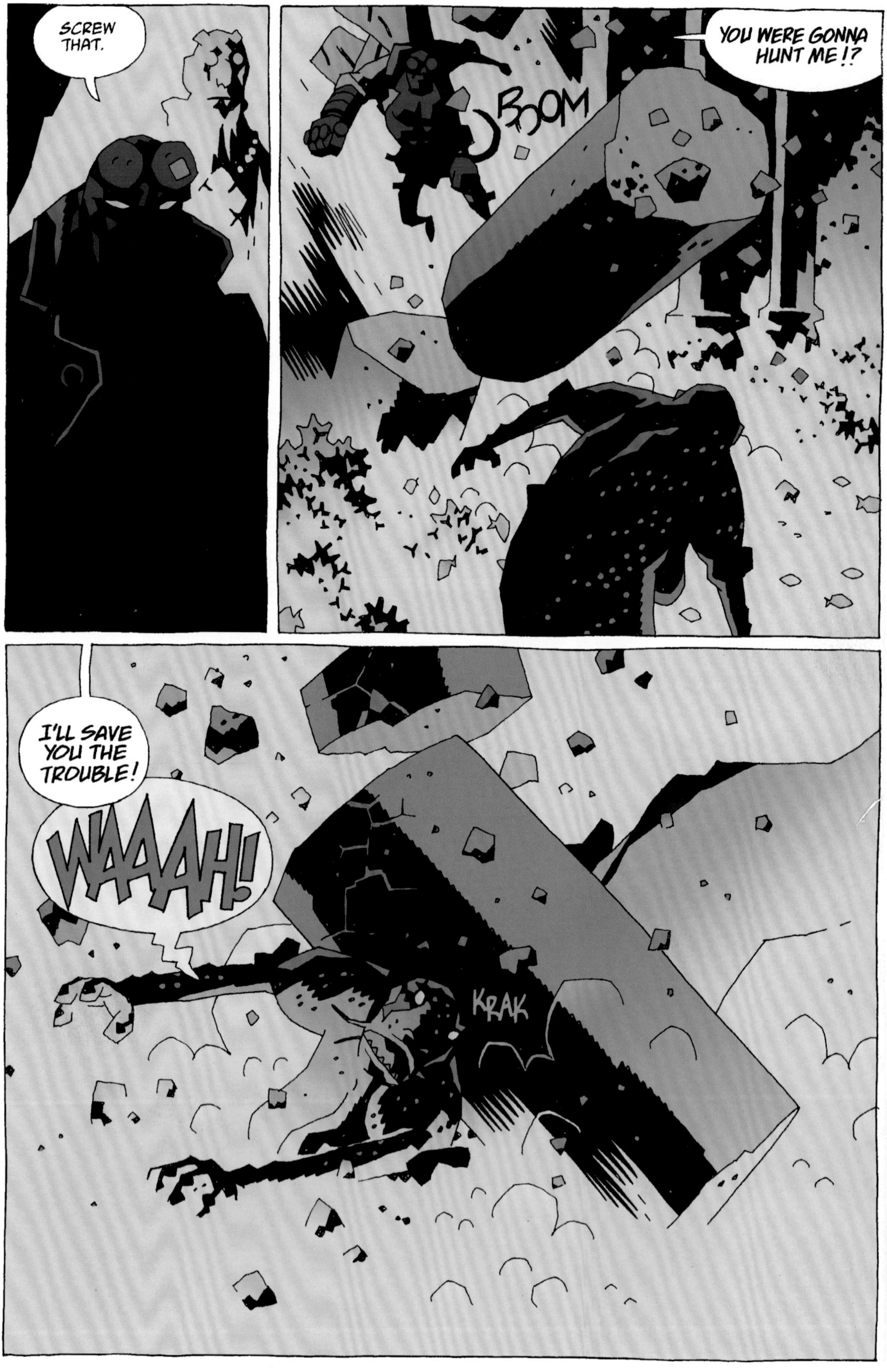
SCREW THAT.
YOU WERE GONNA HUNT ME!?
BOOM
I'LL SAVE YOU THE TROUBLE!
WAAAH!
KRAK

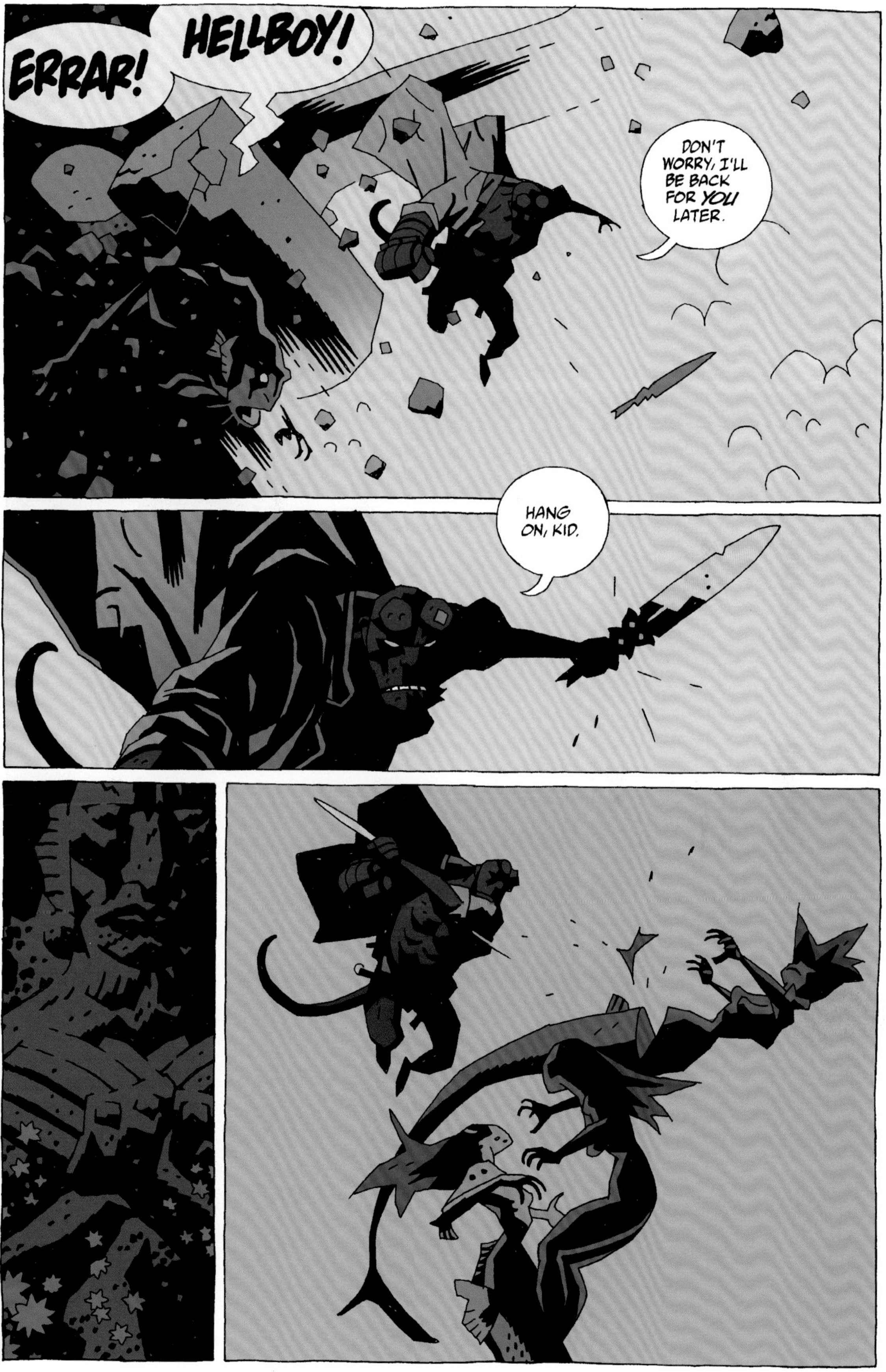
ERRAR!
HELLBOY!
DON'T WORRY, I'LL BE BACK FOR YOU LATER.
HANG ON, KID.

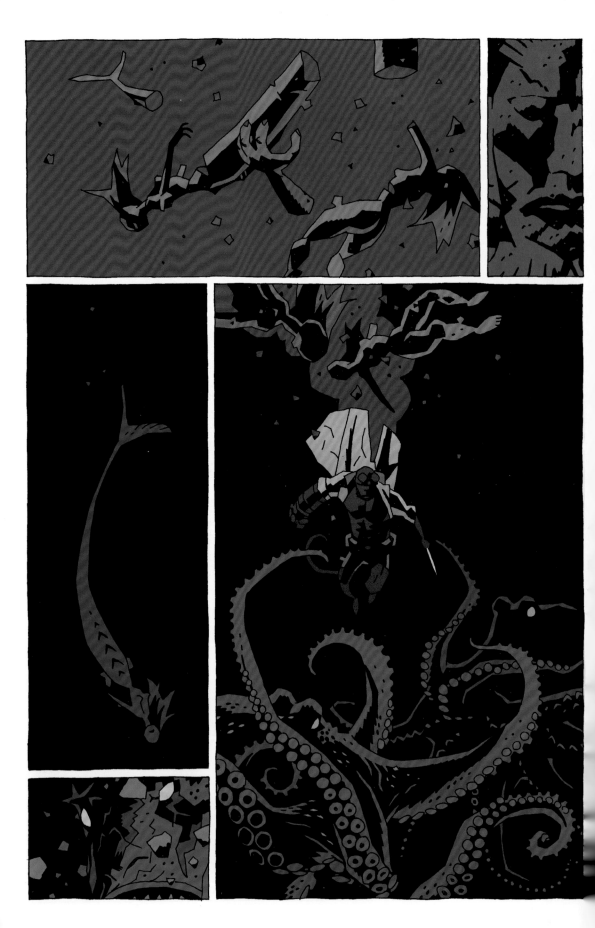

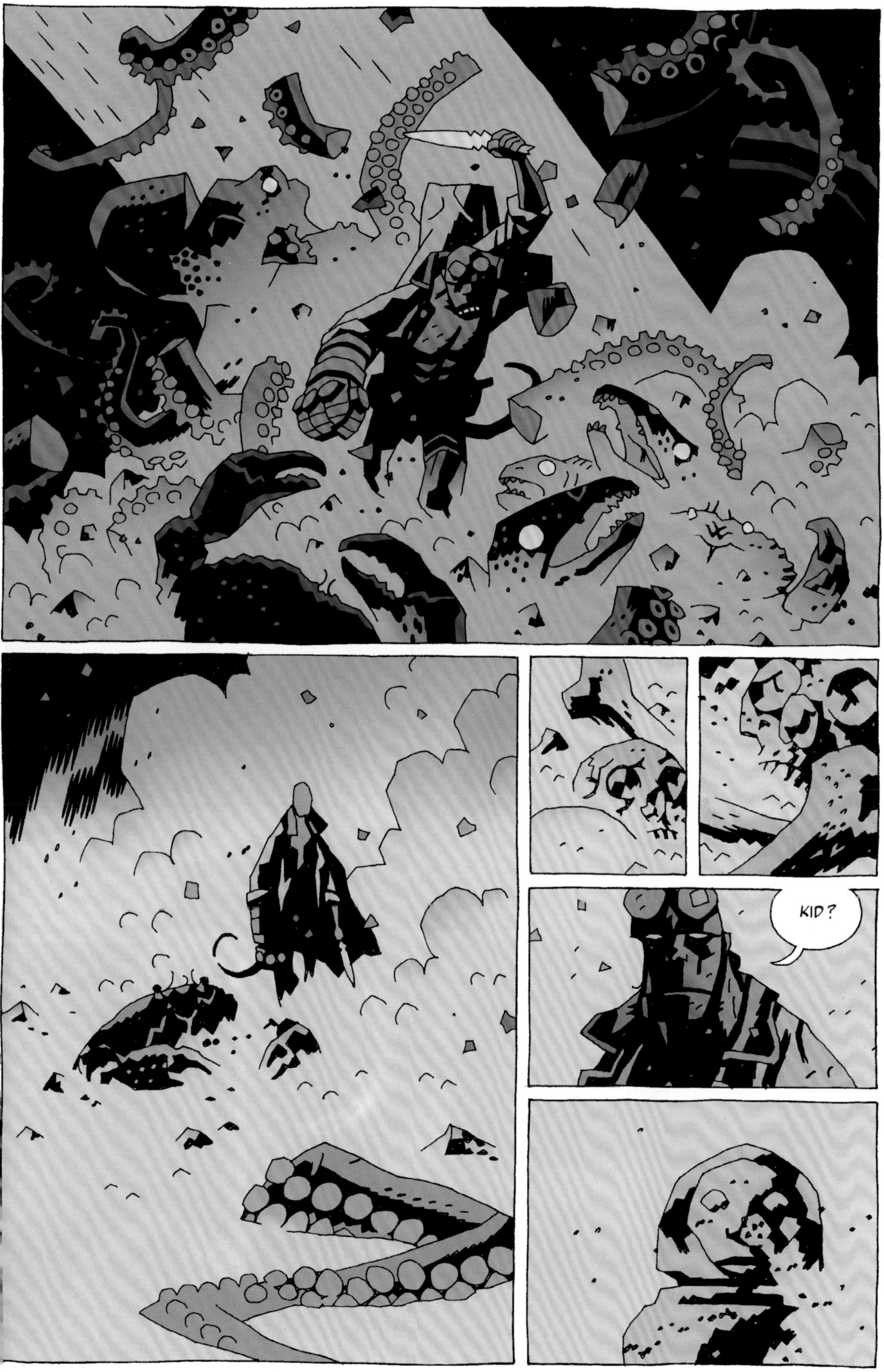
KID?

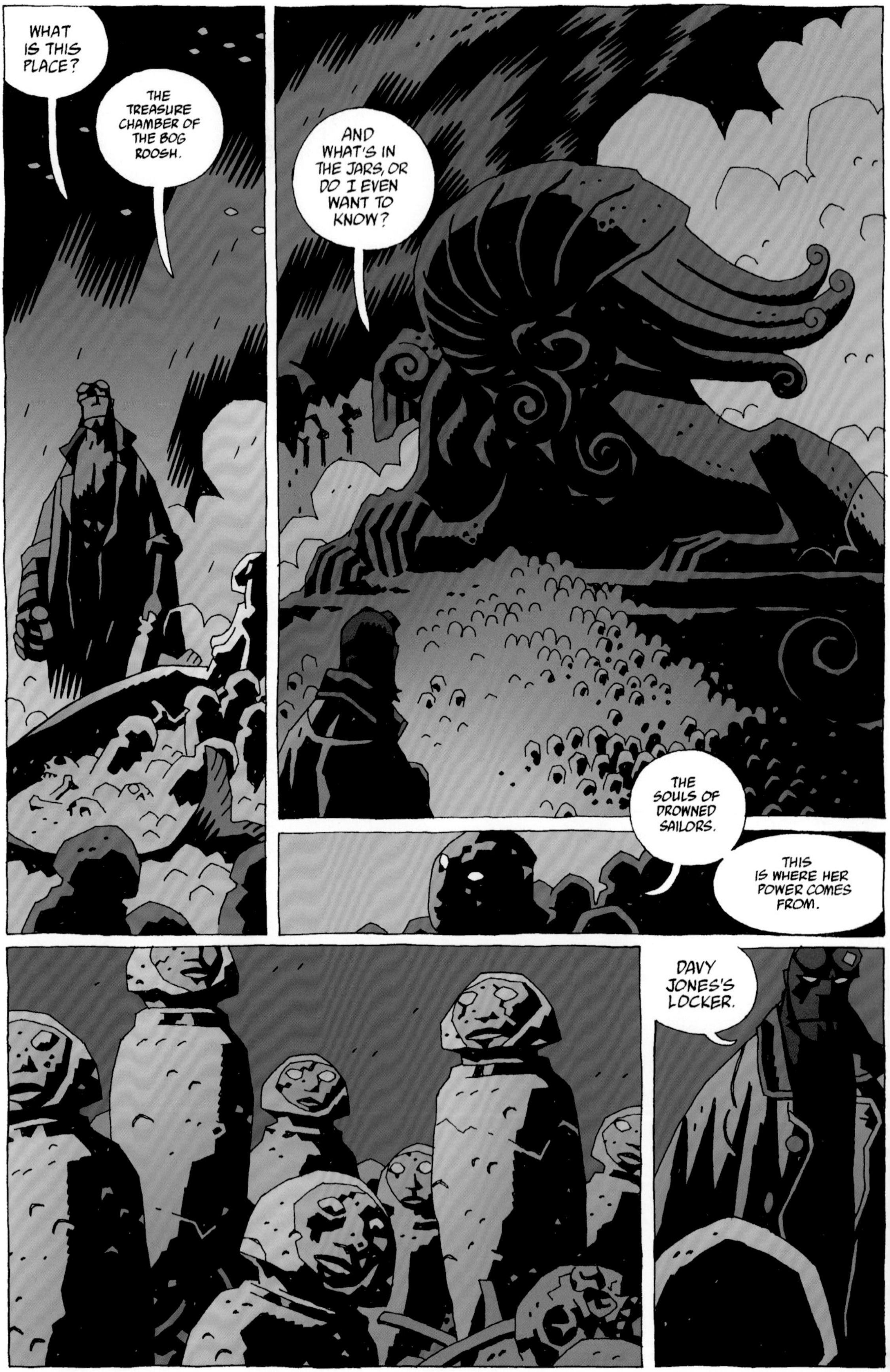
WHAT IS THIS PLACE?
THE TREASURE CHAMBER OF THE BOG ROOSH.
AND WHAT'S IN THE JARS, OR DO I EVEN WANT TO KNOW?
THE SOULS OF DROWNED SAILORS.
THIS IS WHERE HER POWER COMES FROM.
DAVY JONES'S LOCKER.

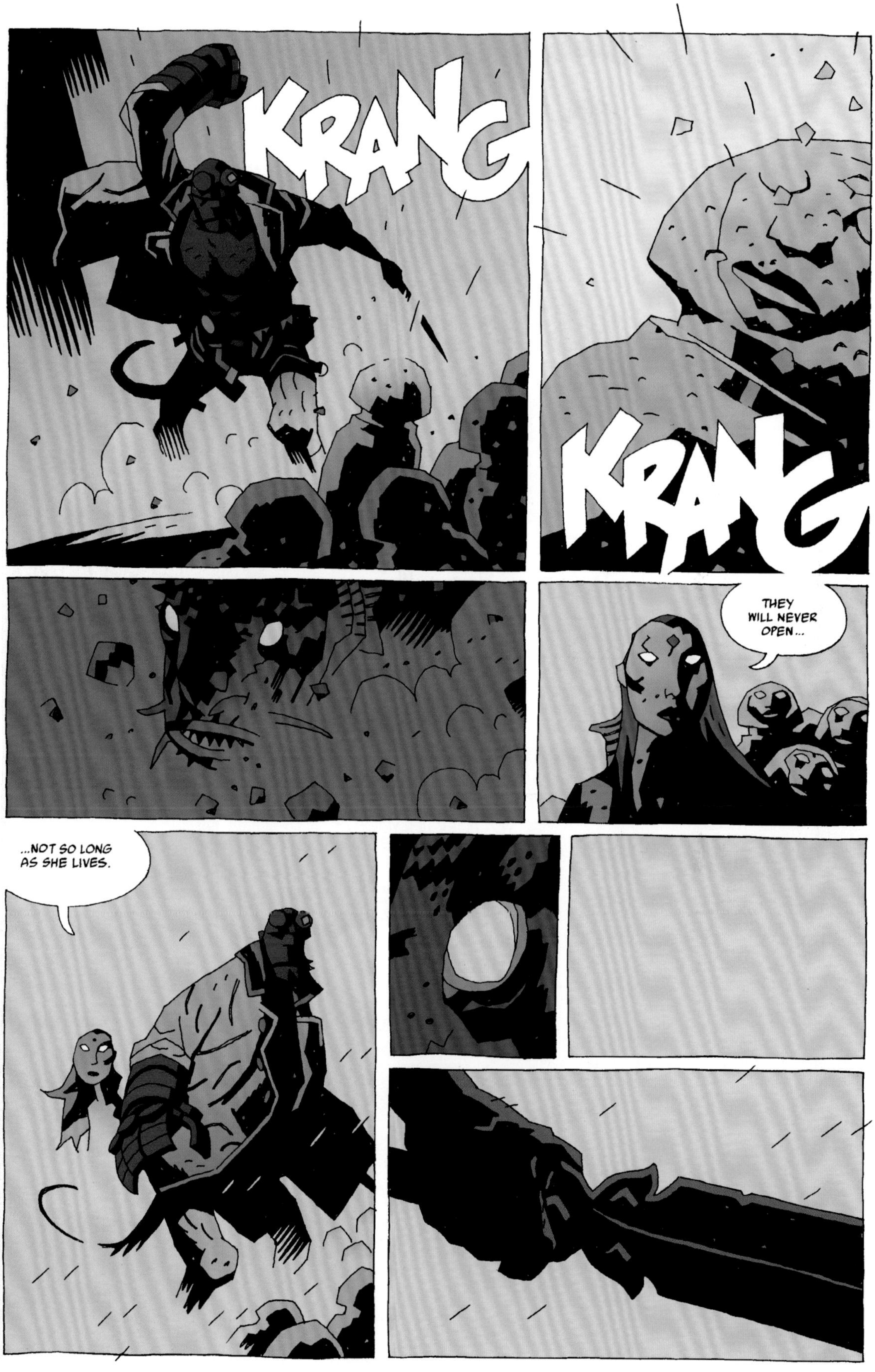
KRANG
KRANG
THEY WILL NEVER OPEN...
...NOT SO LONG AS SHE LIVES.

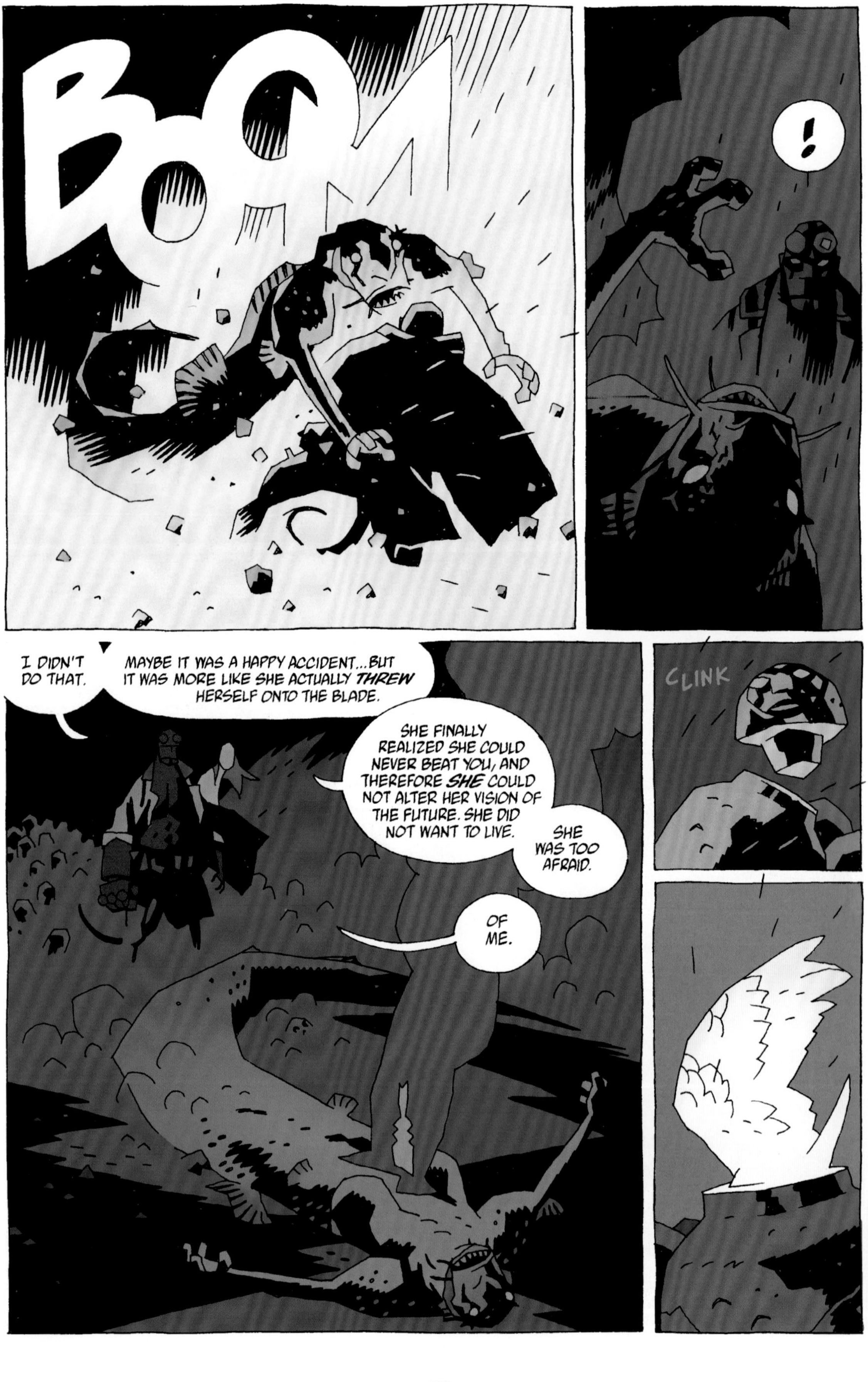
BOOM
!
I DIDN'T DO THAT.
MAYBE IT WAS A HAPPY ACCIDENT...BUT IT WAS MORE LIKE SHE ACTUALLY THREW HERSELF ONTO THE BLADE.
SHE FINALLY REALIZED SHE COULD NEVER BEAT YOU, AND THEREFORE SHE COULD NOT ALTER HER VISION OF THE FUTURE. SHE DID NOT WANT TO LIVE.
SHE WAS TOO AFRAID.
OF ME.
CLINK

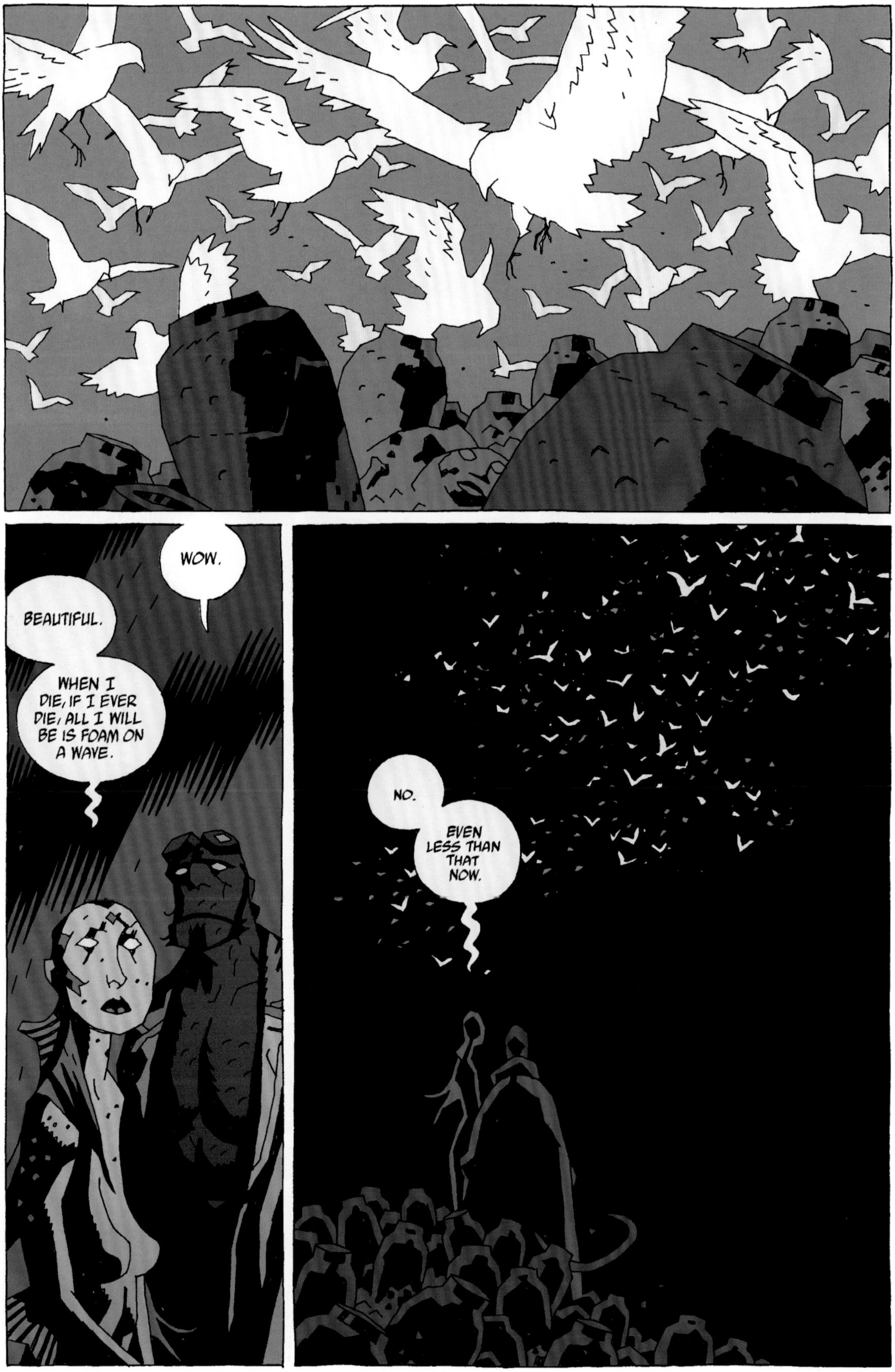
WOW.
BEAUTIFUL.
WHEN I DIE, IF I EVER DIE, ALL I WILL BE IS FOAM ON A WAVE.
NO.
EVEN LESS THAN THAT NOW.

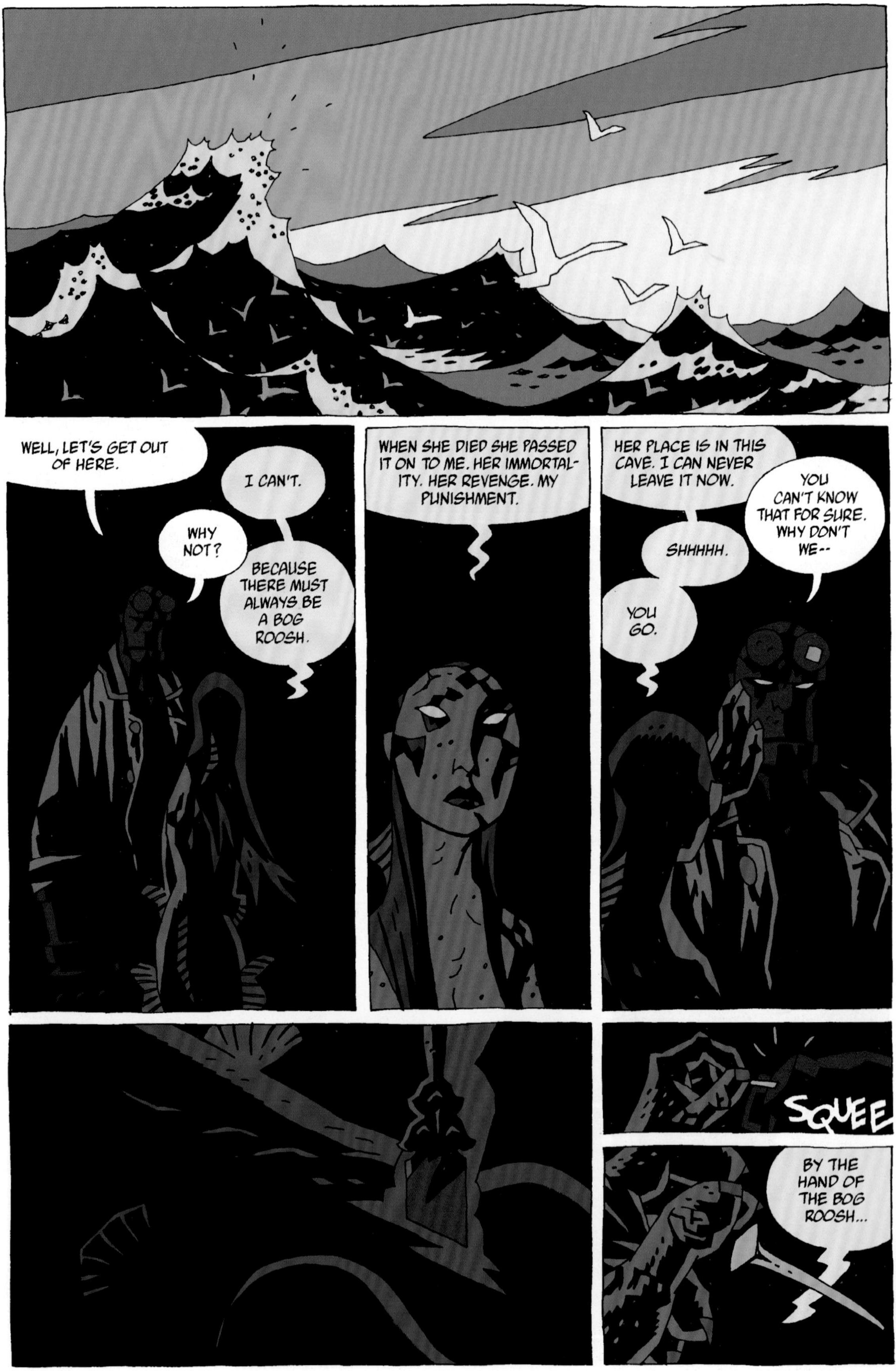
WELL, LET'S GET OUT OF HERE.
I CAN'T.
WHY NOT?
BECAUSE THERE MUST ALWAYS BE A BOG ROOSH.
WHEN SHE DIED SHE PASSED IT ON TO ME. HER IMMORTALITY. HER REVENGE. MY PUNISHMENT.
HER PLACE IS IN THIS CAVE. I CAN NEVER LEAVE IT NOW.
YOU CAN'T KNOW THAT FOR SURE. WHY DON'T WE--
SHHHHH.
YOU GO.
SQUEE
BY THE HAND OF THE BOG ROOSH...

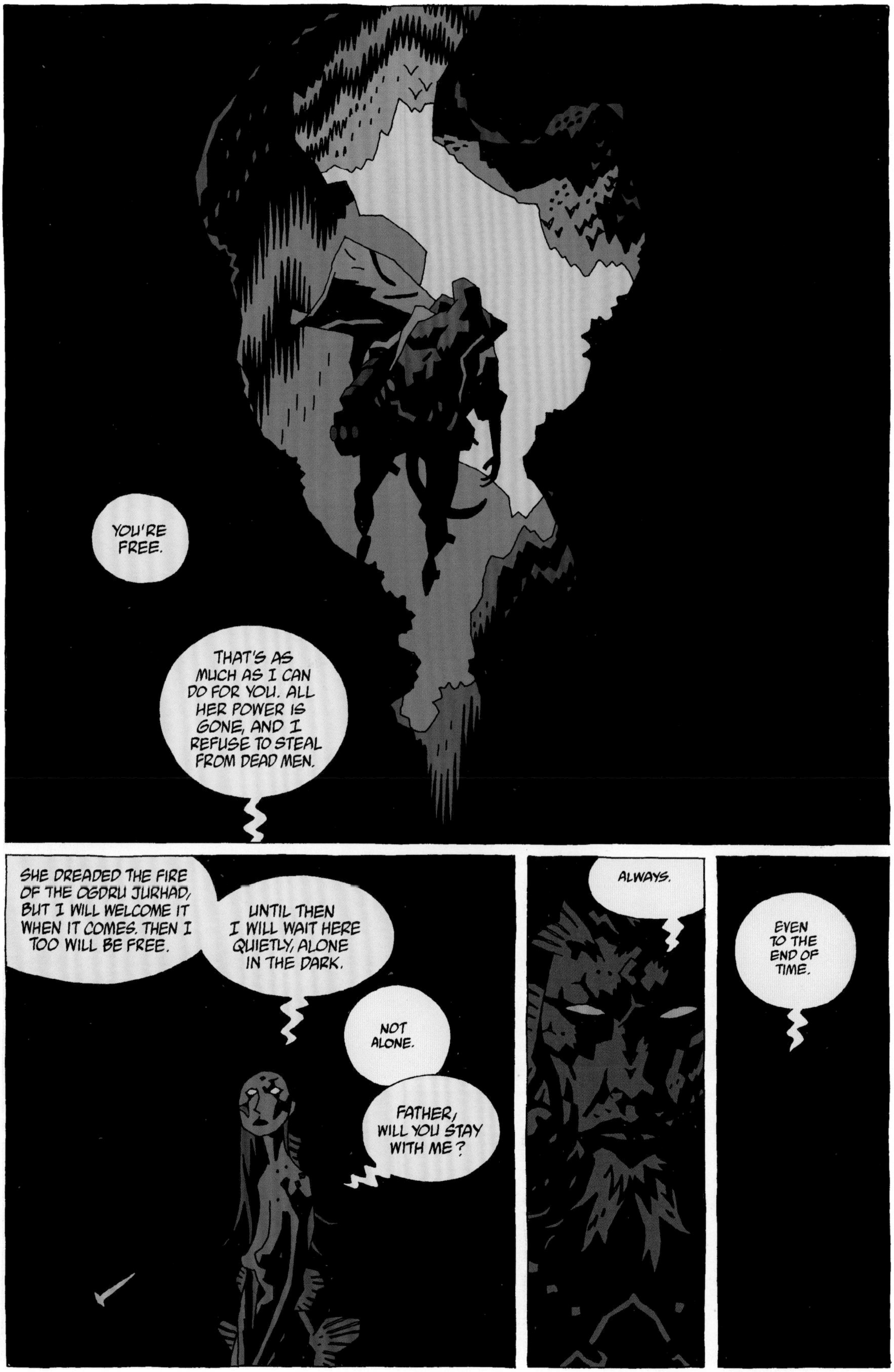
YOU'RE FREE.
THAT'S AS MUCH AS I CAN DO FOR YOU. ALL HER POWER IS GONE, AND I REFUSE TO STEAL FROM DEAD MEN.
SHE DREADED THE FIRE OF THE OGDRU JURHAD, BUT I WILL WELCOME IT WHEN IT COMES. THEN I TOO WILL BE FREE.
UNTIL THEN I WILL WAIT HERE QUIETLY, ALONE IN THE DARK.
NOT ALONE.
FATHER, WILL YOU STAY WITH ME?
ALWAYS.
EVEN TO THE END OF TIME.

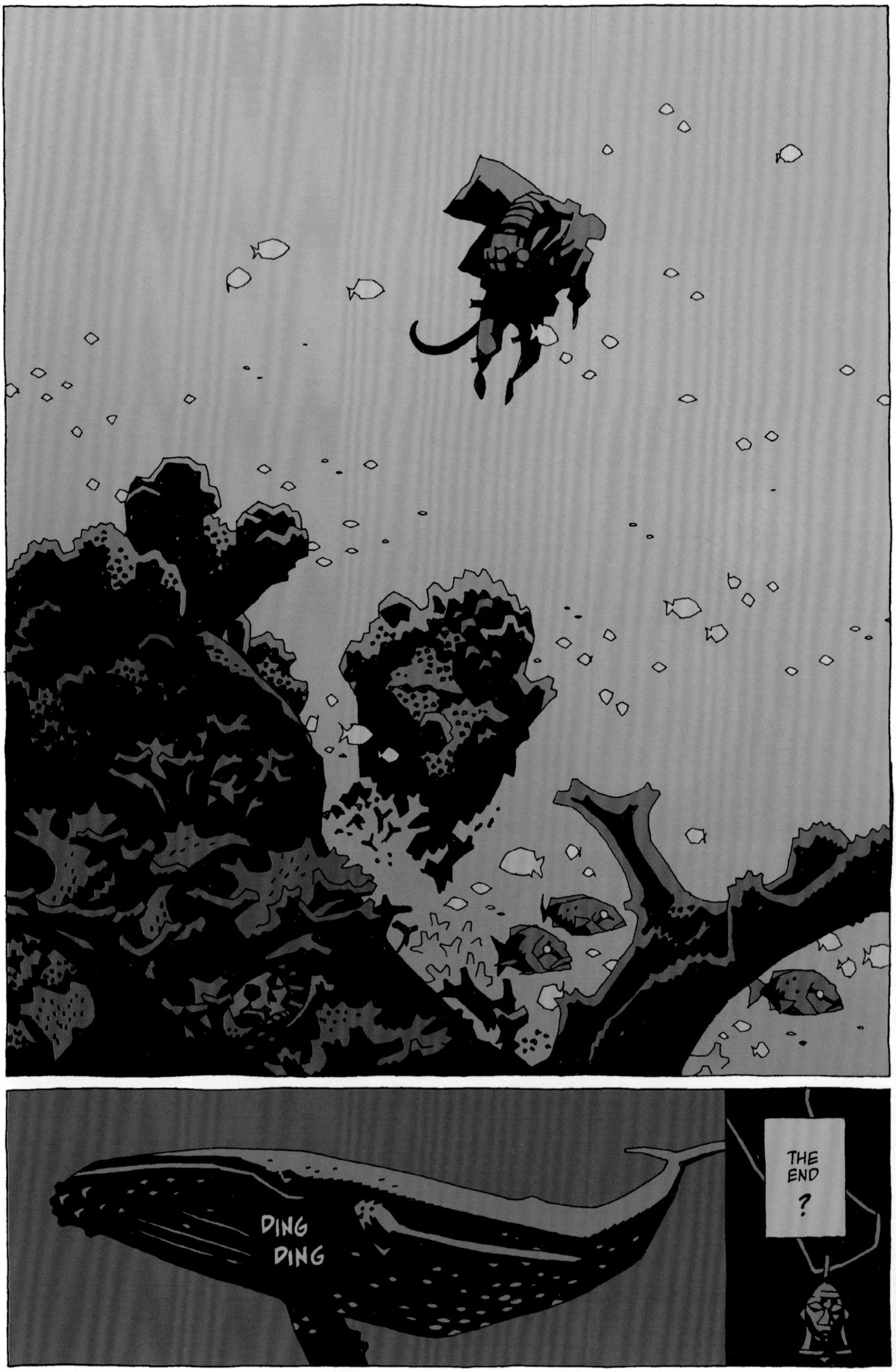
DING
DING
THE
END
?

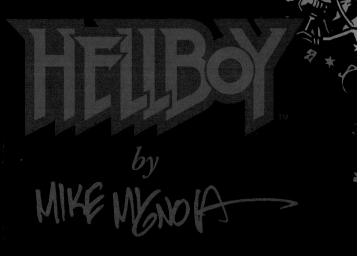

# HELLBOY™

by MIKE MIGNOLA

## HELLBOY LIBRARY EDITION

**VOLUME 1: Seed of Destruction and Wake the Devil**
ISBN 978-1-59307-910-9 | $49.99

**VOLUME 2: The Chained Coffin and The Right Hand of Doom**
ISBN 978-1-59307-989-5 | $49.99

**VOLUME 3: Conqueror Worm and Strange Places**
ISBN 978-1-59582-352-6 | $49.99

**VOLUME 4: The Crooked Man and The Troll Witch**
with Richard Corben and others
ISBN 978-1-59582-658-9 | $49.99

**VOLUME 5: Darkness Calls and The Wild Hunt**
with Duncan Fegredo
ISBN 978-1-59582-886-6 | $49.99

**VOLUME 6: The Storm and the Fury and The Bride of Hell**
with Duncan Fegredo, Richard Corben, Kevin Nowlan, and Scott Hampton
ISBN 978-1-61655-133-9 | $49.99

**HELLBOY IN HELL**
ISBN 978-1-50670-363-3 | $49.99

## HELLBOY OMNIBUS

**VOLUME 1: Seed of Destruction**
with John Byrne
ISBN 978-1-50670-666-5 | $24.99

**VOLUME 2: Strange Places**
with John Byrne
ISBN 978-1-50670-667-2 | $24.99

**VOLUME 3: The Wild Hunt**
with Duncan Fegredo
ISBN 978-1-50670-668-9 | $24.99

**VOLUME 4: Hellboy In Hell**
with Richard Corben and Gary Gianni
ISBN 978-1-50670-749-5 | $24.99

## HELLBOY: THE COMPLETE SHORT STORIES

**VOLUME 1**
with John Byrne, Corben, Fegredo, and others
ISBN 978-1-50670-664-1 | $24.99

**VOLUME 2**
with Jason Shawn Alexander, P. Craig Russell, Corben, and others
ISBN 978-1-50670-665-8 | $24.99

**HELLBOY UNIVERSE: THE SECRET HISTORIES**
with Arcudi, Mitten, Golden, Roberson, and Campbell
ISBN 978-1-50671-130-0 | $39.99

**HELLBOY: 25 YEARS OF COVERS**
ISBN 978-1-50671-455-4 | $34.99

**INTO THE SILENT SEA**
with Gary Gianni
ISBN 978-1-50670-143-1 | $14.99

**HELLBOY IN MEXICO**
with Richard Corben, Fábio Moon, Gabriel Bá, and others
ISBN 978-1-61655-897-0 | $19.99

**HELLBOY: THE FIRST 20 YEARS**
ISBN 978-1-61655-353-1 | $19.99

**GARY GIANNI'S MONSTERMEN AND OTHER SCARY STORIES**
by Gary Gianni
ISBN 978-1-59582-829-3 | $24.99

**HELLBOY: WEIRD TALES**
ISBN 978-1-61655-510-8 | $24.99

**HELLBOY: MASKS AND MONSTERS**
with James Robinson and Scott Benefiel
ISBN 978-1-59582-567-4 | $17.99

**HELLBOY: AN ASSORTMENT OF HORRORS**
ISBN 978-1-50670-343-5 | $14.99

**HELLBOY AND THE B.P.R.D.: 1952**
with John Arcudi and Alex Maleev
ISBN 978-1-61655-660-0 | $19.99

**HELLBOY AND THE B.P.R.D.: 1953**
with Chris Roberson, Ben Stenbeck, Paolo Rivera, and Joe Rivera
ISBN 978-1-61655-967-0 | $19.99

**HELLBOY AND THE B.P.R.D.: 1954**
with Roberson, Corben, Churilla, and others
ISBN 978-1-50670-207-0 | $19.99

**HELLBOY AND THE B.P.R.D.: 1955**
with Roberson, Churilla, Rivera, and Shawn Martinbrough
ISBN 978-1-50670-531-6 | $19.99

**HELLBOY AND THE B.P.R.D.: 1956**
with Roberson, Mike Norton, Yishan Li, Michael Avon Oeming, and Paul Grist
ISBN 978-1-50671-105-8 | $19.99

**HELLBOY AND THE B.P.R.D.: THE BEAST OF VARGU AND OTHERS**
with Fegredo, Stenbeck, Christopher Mitten, and Adam Hughes
ISBN 978-1-50671-130-0 | $19.99

**THE HELLBOY 100 PROJECT**
TPB: ISBN 978-1-61655-932-8 | $12.99
HC: ISBN 978-1-61655-933-5 | $24.99

## NOVELS

**HELLBOY: EMERALD HELL**
by Tom Piccirilli
ISBN 978-1-59582-141-6 | $12.99

**HELLBOY: THE ALL-SEEING EYE**
by Mark Morris
ISBN 978-1-59582-142-3 | $12.99

**HELLBOY: THE FIRE WOLVES**
by Tim Lebbon
ISBN 978-1-59582-204-8 | $12.99

**HELLBOY: THE ICE WOLVES**
by Mark Chadbourn
ISBN 978-1-59582-205-5 | $12.99

DARK HORSE BOOKS
DarkHorse.com

AVAILABLE AT YOUR LOCAL COMICS SHOP OR BOOKSTORE! • To find a comics shop in your area, visit comicshoplocator.com.
For more information or to order direct, visit DarkHorse.com. Prices and availability subject to change without notice.

# Also by MIKE MIGNOLA

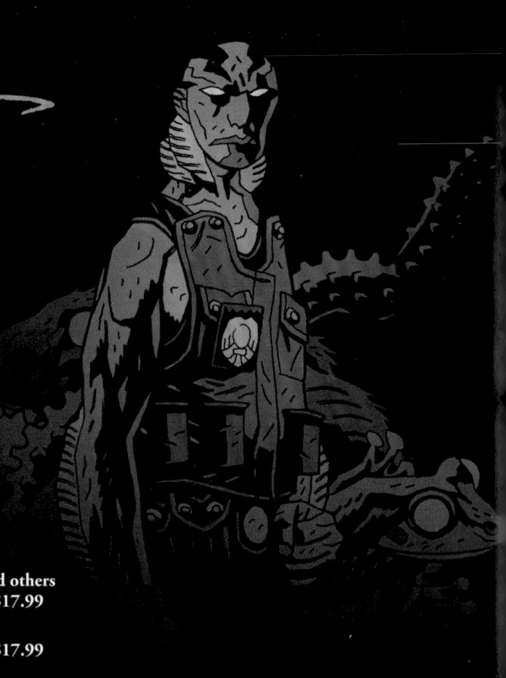

## B.P.R.D. PLAGUE OF FROGS

VOLUME 1
with John Arcudi, Guy Davis, and others
TPB: ISBN 978-1-59582-675-6 | $19.99

VOLUME 2
ISBN 978-1-59582-676-3 | $24.99

VOLUME 3
ISBN 978-1-61655-622-8 | $24.99

VOLUME 4
ISBN 978-1-61655-641-9 | $24.99

1946–1948
with Joshua Dysart, Paul Azaceta, Fábio Moon, Gabriel Bá, Max Fiumara, and Arcudi
ISBN 978-1-50671-433-2 | $24.99

BEING HUMAN
with Scott Allie, Arcudi, Davis, and others
ISBN 978-1-59582-756-2 | $17.99

BPRD: VAMPIRE Second Edition
with Moon and Bá
ISBN 978-1-50671-189-8 | $19.99

## B.P.R.D. HELL ON EARTH

VOLUME 1
with Allie, Arcudi, Davis, Tyler Crook, and others
HC: ISBN 978-1-50670-360-2 | $34.99
TPB: ISBN 978-1-50671-970-2 | $29.99

VOLUME 2
ISBN 978-1-50670-388-6 | $34.99

VOLUME 3
ISBN 978-1-50670-490-6 | $34.99

VOLUME 4
ISBN 978-1-50670-654-2 | $34.99

VOLUME 5
ISBN 978-1-50670-815-7 | $34.99

## B.P.R.D. THE DEVIL YOU KNOW

with Laurence Campbell, Chris Mitten, and Sebastián Fiumara
OMNIBUS
ISBN 978-1-50671-971-9 | $24.99

VOLUME 1: MESSIAH
ISBN 978-1-50670-196-7 | $19.99

VOLUME 2: PANDEMONIUM
ISBN 978-1-50670-653-5 | $19.99

VOLUME 3: RAGNA ROK
ISBN 978-1-50670-814-0 | $19.99

## MIKE MIGNOLA: THE QUARANTINE SKETCHBOOK

ISBN 978-1-50672-427-0 | $39.99

## ABE SAPIEN

DARK AND TERRIBLE
VOLUME 1
with Allie, S. Fiumara, and M. Fiumara
ISBN 978-1-50670-538-5 | $34.99

VOLUME 2
ISBN 978-1-50670-385-5 | $34.99

LOST LIVES
AND OTHER STORIES
with Allie, Arcudi, Michael Avon Oeming, and others
ISBN 978-1-50670-220-9 | $19.99

## LOBSTER JOHNSON

THE IRON PROMETHEUS
with Arcudi, Tonci Zonjic, and others
ISBN 978-1-59307-975-8 | $17.99

THE BURNING HAND
ISBN 978-1-61655-031-8 | $17.99

SATAN SMELLS A RAT
ISBN 978-1-61655-203-9 | $18.99

GET THE LOBSTER
ISBN 978-1-61655-505-4 | $19.99

THE PIRATE'S GHOST AND METAL MONSTERS OF MIDTOWN
ISBN 978-1-50670-206-3 | $19.99

A CHAIN FORGED IN LIFE
ISBN 978-1-50670-178-3 | $19.99

## WITCHFINDER

OMNIBUS VOLUME 1
With Ben Stenbeck, John Arcudi, Tyler Crook, and others
ISBN 978-1-50671-442-4 | $34.99

CITY OF THE DEAD
with Roberson and Stenbeck
ISBN 978-1-50670-166-0 | $19.99

THE GATES OF HEAVEN
with Roberson, D'Israeli, and Clem Robins
ISBN 978-1-50670-683-2 | $19.99

THE REIGN OF DARKNESS
with Christopher Mitten and Chris Roberson
ISBN 978-1-50671-406-6 | $19.99

## RISE OF THE BLACK FLAME

with Roberson and Christopher Mitten
ISBN 978-1-50670-155-4 | $19.99

## THE VISITOR: HOW AND WHY HE STAYED

with Roberson, Paul Grist, and Bill Crabtree
ISBN 978-1-50670-345-9 | $19.99

## FRANKENSTEIN UNDERGROUND

with Stenbeck
ISBN 978-1-61655-782-9 | $19.99

## RASPUTIN: THE VOICE OF THE DRAGON

with Roberson and Mitten
ISBN 978-1-50670-498-2 | $19.99

## KOSHCHEI THE DEATHLESS

with Ben Stenbeck
ISBN 978-1-50670-672-6 | $19.99

## CRIMSON LOTUS

John Arcudi and Mindy Lee
ISBN 978-1-50670-822-5 | $19.99

## JOE GOLEM: OCCULT DETECTIVE—

THE RAT CATCHER & THE SUNKEN DEAD
with Christopher Golden and Patric Reynolds
ISBN 978-1-61655-964-9 | $24.99

THE OUTER DARK
with Golden and Reynolds
ISBN 978-1-50670-395-4 | $24.99

THE DROWNING CITY
with Golden and Bergting
ISBN 978-1-50670-945-1 | $24.99

THE CONJURORS
With Golden and Bergting
ISBN 978-1-50671-413-4 | $24.99

## BALTIMORE

OMNIBUS VOLUME 1
With Golden, Stenbeck, and Peter Bergting
ISBN 978-1-50671-246-8 | $34.99

OMNIBUS VOLUME 2
ISBN 978-1-50671-247-5 | $34.99

## NOVELS

LOBSTER JOHNSON: THE SATAN FACTORY
with Thomas E. Sniegoski
ISBN 978-1-59582-203-1 | $12.95

JOE GOLEM AND THE DROWNING CITY
with Golden
ISBN 978-1-59582-971-9 | $99.99

BALTIMORE; OR, THE STEADFAST TIN SOLDIER & THE VAMPIRE
with Golden
ISBN 978-1-61655-803-1 | $12.99